arihant
SUCCESS AND NOTHING LESS

AF819952

Be a TOP SCORER
in ISC Exams 2025

# i Succeed 15 Sample Question Papers

**with Quick Study Notes**

# Accounts 12th

**AUTHOR**
Swati Mittal

**Arihant Prakashan**
(School Division Series)


**Administrative & Production Offices**

**Regd. Office**
'Ramchhaya' 4577/15, Agarwal Road, Darya Ganj, New Delhi -110002
Tele: 011- 47630600, 43518550

**Head Office**
Kalindi, TP Nagar, Meerut (UP) - 250002
Tel: 0121-7156203, 7156204

**Sales & Support Offices**
Agra, Ahmedabad, Bengaluru, Bareilly, Chennai, Delhi, Guwahati, Hyderabad, Jaipur, Jhansi, Kolkata, Lucknow, Nagpur & Pune.

**PRICE** ₹350.00

**PO No :** TXT-XX-XXXXXXX-X-XX

Published by Arihant Publications (India) Ltd.

For further information about the books published by Arihant, log on to www.arihantbooks.com or e-mail at info@arihantbooks.com

Follow us on

*i Succeed*

# SAMPLE QUESTION PAPERS

THE **BEST CHOICE** OF TEACHERS & STUDENTS, Why?

## 01 Exact Exam Pattern

All Sample Papers have been designed on the actual exam format of ISC

## 02 Complete Syllabus

Complete coverage of syllabus through different types of questions across all the sample papers

## 03 Latest Specimen Question Paper

Latest Specimen Question Paper with detailed solutions.

## 04 Detailed Solutions

Step-by-step solutions to help you understand concepts and improve problem-solving skills.

## 05 Quick Study Notes

Focused revision of the whole syllabus through Quick Study Notes.

## 06 All Types of Questions

Coverage of all types of exam pattern questions, analysis, application, etc.

With Free
DOUBT SOLVING APP

**Free Doubt Solving APP**

To help you sort out your doubts at any time any place.

*i* *Succeed*

# Accounts Class 12

# Course Structure
## 2024-25

**PAPER - I** (Theory) **80 Marks**

| S. No. | UNIT | TOTAL WEIGHTAGE |
|---|---|---|
| | **SECTION A** | **60 Marks** |
| **1.** | **Partnership Accounts** | |
| | A. Fundamentals of Partnership | 11 Marks |
| | B. Goodwill | |
| | C. Reconstitution of Partnership | 15 Marks |
| | I. Admission | |
| | II. Retirement and Death of a Partner | |
| | III. Dissolution of a Partnership Firm | 8 Marks |
| **2.** | **Joint Stock Company Accounts** | |
| | A. Issue of Shares | 11 Marks |
| | B. Issue of Debentures | 8 Marks |
| | C. Redemption of Debentures | |
| | D. Final Accounts of Companies | 7 Marks |
| | **SECTION B (MANAGEMENT ACCOUNTING)** | **20 Marks** |
| **3.** | **Financial Statement Analysis** | 4 Marks |
| **4.** | **Cash Flow Statement** | 8 Marks |
| **5.** | **Ratio Analysis** | 8 Marks |
| | **OR**<br>**SECTION C (COMPUTERISED ACCOUNTING)** | **20 Marks** |
| **6.** | Accounting Application of Electronic Spread Sheet | 10 Marks |
| **7.** | Database Management System (DBMS) | 10 Marks |
| | **TOTAL** | **80 Marks** |

# SECTION A

## 1. Partnership Accounts

### A. Fundamentals of Partnership

(i) Definition, meaning and features of a partnership.

(ii) Provisions of the Indian Partnership Act, 1932, with respect to books of accounts.

(iii) Preparation of profit and loss appropriation account and partners' capital and current accounts.

### B. Goodwill

Concept of goodwill and mode of valuation.

### C. Reconstitution of Partnership

**I. Admission**

(i) Calculation of new profit sharing ratio, sacrificing ratio and gaining ratio.

(ii) Accounting treatment of goodwill on admission of a partner.

(iii) Preparation of revaluation account.

(iv) Accounting treatment of accumulated profits and losses.

(v) Adjustment of capitals.

(vi) Change in profit sharing ratio

**II. Retirement and Death of a Partner**

(i) Calculation of new profit sharing ratio, gaining ratio and sacrificing ratio.

(ii) Adjustment with regard to goodwill including hidden goodwill.

(iii) Adjustment with regard to undistributed profits and losses.

(iv) Adjustment with regard to share of profits of the retiring or deceased partner from the date of the last balance sheet to the date of retirement or death (on the basis of time or turnover).

(v) Preparation of revaluation account on retirement or death of a partner.

(vi) Adjustment of capitals.

(vii) Calculation and payment of amount due to retiring partner.

(viii) Preparation of retiring partner's loan account and deceased partner's executor's loan accounts (with interest on loan accrued and due and interest on loan accrued but not due).

(ix) Change in profit sharing ratio.

**III. Dissolution of a Partnership Firm**

(i) Meaning of dissolution and settlement of accounts under Section 48 of the Indian Partnership Act, 1932.

(ii) Preparation of memorandum balance sheet, realisation account, partner's loan account, partner's capital account and cash/bank account.

## 2. Joint Stock Company Accounts

### A. Issue of Shares

Problems on issue of shares.

(i) Issue of shares at par and premium under Companies Act, 2013.

(ii) Issue of shares for considerations other than cash:

  (a) To promoters (can be considered either through goodwill account or incorporation costs account).

  (b) To underwriters.

  (c) To vendors.

(iii) Calls-in-arrears, calls-in-advance and interest thereon

(iv) Over and undersubscription (including prorata allotment).

(v) Preparation of journal, cash book and journal proper, ledger accounts

(vi) Forfeiture and reissue of shares at par, premium or discount.

(vii) Disclosure of share capital in company's balance sheet.

### B. Issue of Debentures

Problems on issue of debentures (at par, at premium and at discount).

### C. Redemption of Debentures

### D. Final Accounts of Companies

Preparation of the balance sheet of a company (alongwith notes to accounts) as per Schedule III Part I of Companies Act, 2013.

# SECTION B (MANAGEMENT ACCOUNTING)

## 3. Financial Statement Analysis

Comparative Statements and Common Size Statements.

## 4. Cash Flow Statement (Only for Manufacturing Companies)

(i) Meaning, importance and preparation of a cash flow statement.

(ii) Calculation of net cash flows from operating activities based on indirect method only.

(iii) Preparation of cash flow statement on basis of operating, investing and financing activities.

## 5. Ratio Analysis

# Preparation Assessment Zone

## Welcome to the Preparation Assessment Zone !

In this section, you'll find **ISC Specimen Paper** and **Board Exam Paper 2024** to help you assess your readiness. Attempt these papers to familiarise yourself with the exam format and identify areas that need improvement.

Progress Tracker Tick the papers as you complete them.

☐ ISC Specimen Paper

☐ Board Exam Paper 2024

# ISC Specimen Paper 2025

## Accounts (Code 858)

### Class 12

**General Instructions**

1. Candidates are allowed additional 15 minutes for only reading the paper. They must not start writing during this time.
2. Section-A is compulsory for all candidates and has ten questions.
3. Candidates have to attempt all questions from either Section-B or Section-C*.
4. Internal choices have been provided in five questions in Section-A and one question in Section-B.
5. The intended marks for questions or parts of questions are given in the brackets [ ].
6. All calculations should be shown clearly.
7. All workings, including rough work, should be done on the same page as, and adjacent to, the rest of the answer.

*Section-C has not been covered.

- No. of Questions : 14
- No. of Sections : 2
- Time Alloted : 3 Hrs.
- Max. Marks : 80

## Section A Answer All Questions [60 Marks]

1. In subparts (i) to (iv) choose the correct options and in subparts (v) to (x) answer the questions as instructed.

(i) The commission due to a partner is closed by (Understanding) [1]

(a) debiting it to partner's capital account
(b) crediting it to partner's capital account
(c) debiting it to profit and loss appropriation account
(d) crediting it to profit and loss appropriation account

(ii) On the admission of Adil as a partner, the capitals of Rohan and Pavan, after all adjustments were ₹ 50,000 and ₹ 40,000. Their capitals before Adil's admission were ₹ 45,000 and ₹ 48,000.

The capital account of the partner having surplus capital was adjusted through his current account by passing the journal entry. (Application) [1]

(a) Debit Rohan's Capital A/c ₹ 5,000; Credit Rohan's Current A/c ₹ 5,000
(b) Debit Pavan's Capital A/c ₹ 8,000; Credit Pavan's Current A/c ₹ 8,000
(c) Debit Rohan's Current A/c ₹ 5,000; Credit Rohan's Capital A/c ₹ 5,000
(d) Debit Pavan's Current A/c ₹ 8,000; Credit Pavan's Capital A/c ₹ 8,000

(iii) Choose the components required to calculate goodwill of a firm by capitalisation of average profits method. (Recall) [1]

P – The normal profits of a similar firm in the industry.
Q – The average profits of the firm.
R – The number of years' purchase.
S – The actual capital employed in the business.

**Codes**

(a) P, Q, R
(b) Q, R, S
(c) P, Q, S
(d) P, R, S

(iv) Given below is a fictitious scenario. Read the information and answer the question that follows

Bhim International Ltd. in order to raise additional funds for expansion purpose, took a loan of ₹ 10,00,000 at a rate of 12% per annum from NZ Bank on 1st July, 2023, against which it offered ₹ 15,00,000, 8% debentures of ₹ 100 each as a collateral security.

Calculate the finance cost to the company for the year 2023-24. (Application) [1]

(a) ₹ 1,20,000 (b) ₹ 2,40,000
(c) ₹ 90,000 (d) ₹ 1,80,000

(v) Ira (a partner in a firm) was allowed to retain the whole of the stock as her remuneration for services rendered by her in the course of dissolution of the firm. The value of stock was ₹ 10,000 which had been transferred to the realisation account.

Complying with the accounting principle of full disclosure, record the above transaction in the books of the partnership firm at the time of its dissolution. (Application) [1]

(vi) Aman and Vinod are partners in a firm. Their balance sheet showed

Gross debtors ₹ 1,52,000

Provision for doubtful debts ₹ 1,000

On Milin's admission as a new partner, the assets and liabilities are to be revalued as

(a) Unaccounted accrued income of ₹ 10,000 to be provided for.

(b) Bills payable of ₹ 10,000 which were recorded, to be discharged at a rebate of 10%.

(c) Debtors of ₹ 2,000 to be irrecoverable.

(d) Provision for doubtful debts to be provided @ 2% of the debtors.

What is the net effect of revaluation of assets and liabilities? (Application) [1]

(vii) **Assertion** (A) A company can re-issue a forfeited share at an amount which is less than the amount not received on it.

**Reason** (R) A company can write-off the net loss made on the re-issue of a forfeited share from its capital reserve. (Evaluate) [1]

**Alternatives**

(a) Both Assertion (A) and Reason (R) are true and Reason (R) is the correct explanation of Assertion (A)

(b) Both Assertion (A) and Reason (R) are true, but Reason (R) is not the correct explanation of Assertion (A)

(c) Assertion (A) is false, but Reason (R) is true

(d) Both Assertion (A) and Reason (R) are false

(viii) Mention the liability of a partnership firm which is not shown in its balance sheet, but is paid-off at the time of the dissolution of the firm. (Understanding) [1]

(ix) The Adani family has raised their stake in Ambuja Cements by the conversion of 21.20 crore warrants into shares in a transaction that will see them infusing nearly ₹ 6,661 crore.

**Source** *The Telegraph, Kolkata, 29th March, 2024*

(a) What is a share warrant?

(b) Mention the head under which money received against share warrants is shown in the balance sheet of a company prepared as per Schedule III of the Companies Act, 2013. (Recall) [1]

(x) On 1st April, 2023, Zara Ltd. issued ₹ 10,000, 6% debentures of ₹ 100 each at a discount of 5%. On 31st March, 2024, the company had ₹ 40,000 in its capital reserve account and ₹ 30,000 as balance of securities premium.

Give the journal entry to write-off the discount on issue of debentures on 31st March, 2024. (Application) [1]

**2.** Mita, Sita and Rita are partners in a firm. Rita retires from the firm on 31st March, 2024. Her claim, including her capital and her share of goodwill, is determined at ₹ 2,50,000.

On this date the firm's books showed

(i) An unrecorded investment valued at ₹ 60,000 which was given to an unrecorded creditor of ₹ 1,16,000 in settlement of his claim of ₹ 70,000.

(ii) An unrecorded vehicle which was given to Rita at the market value of ₹ 46,000 in part settlement of her claim. The balance of Rita's claim was discharged by cheque.

You are required to pass journal entries to record the above transactions in the books of the firm on 31st March, 2024. (Application) [3]

*Or* Akshat, Javed and Gaurav are partners in a firm sharing profits in the ratio of 5 : 3 : 7. Akshat died on 31st March, 2024.

Javed and Gaurav decided to share the profits in reconstituted firm in the ratio 2 : 3. The capital accounts of the partners on 31st March, 2024, before considering the firm's goodwill were

Akshat ₹ 1,66,000
Javed ₹ 66,000
Gaurav ₹ 1,41,000

After considering the adjustment for goodwill, Akshat's share was determined to be ₹ 1,81,000.

It was decided that this amount would be paid to Akshat's executor immediately by the firm through a cheque, the amount being contributed by Javed and Gaurav in such a manner that their capitals would become proportionate to their new profit sharing ratio.

You are required to pass journal entries to record

(i) The adjustment for self-generated goodwill of the firm.
(ii) Cash brought in by Javed and Gaurav to pay-off Akshat's executor.
(iii) Payment made to Akshat's executor.

(Application)

3. On 1st April, 2023, Ruth Ltd. purchased plant and machinery for ₹ 11,00,000 from Pablo Ltd. payable as to ₹ 1,00,000 by accepting a promissory note and the balance by an issue of 11% debentures of ₹ 100 each at a premium of 10% to be redeemed at a premium of 2% after six years.

You are required to pass journal entries in the books of Ruth Ltd. only to record the payment made to Pablo Ltd. (Application) [3]

*Or* A limited company made an issue, which was fully subscribed of 2,000, 5% debentures of ₹ 100 each at ₹ 96, to be redeemed at par after five years. The debentures were allotted on 31st May, 2023, subscriptions being payable

15% on application
30% on allotment
30% on 30th June, 2023
Balance on 30th September, 2023

One debentureholder holding 100 debentures paid the allotment with the first call along with interest on calls-in-arrears @ 10% per annum.

You are required to

(i) Give the amounts in rupees payable with
 (a) Allotment
 (b) Second and final call [2]
(ii) Prepare the interest on calls-in-arrears account (Application) [1]

4. Ronny Ltd. (an unlisted construction company) redeems its 7,000, 10% debentures of ₹ 100 each at a premium of 5% in instalments, as follows

| Date of Redemption | Debentures to be Redeemed |
|---|---|
| 31st March, 2022 | 2,000 |
| 31st March, 2023 | 3,000 |
| 31st March, 2024 | 2,000 |

You are required to prepare for the year 2023-24

(i) General reserve account.
(ii) Debentureholders' account. (Ignore interest on debentures) (Application) [3]

5. Kriti and Atif are partners sharing profits and losses equally. On 31st March, 2024, they admitted David as a third partner for 1/5 share in the profits.

It is decided that on David's admission

- Atif would retain his original share.
- Goodwill would be valued by the super profit method on the basis of the following information

(i) **Balance Sheet of Kriti and Atif** (An extract) as at 31st March, 2024

| Liabilities | | Amt (₹) | Assets | Amt (₹) |
|---|---|---|---|---|
| General Reserve | | 25,000 | Current A/c | |
| Captial A/cs | | | Atif | 10,000 |
| Kriti | 2,50,000 | | | |
| Atif | 1,75,000 | 4,25,000 | | |
| Current A/c | | | | |
| Kriti | | 40,000 | | |

(ii) The normal rate of return is 12% per annum.
(iii) Average profits of the firm for last four years are ₹ 74,000.

You are required to calculate

(a) The sacrificing ratio of the partners.
(b) The value of goodwill of the firm at four years' purchase of the super profit.

(Application) [3]

6. The following balances have been extracted from the books of Nirvana Ltd. as at 31st March, 2024

| Particulars | Amt (₹) | Particulars | Amt (₹) |
|---|---|---|---|
| Security Deposit for Electricity for Ten Years | 30,000 | Uncalled Amount on Partly Paid-up Shares | 8,00,000 |
| Underwriting Commission | 20,000 | 10% Debentures | 5,00,000 |
| General Reserve | 70,000 | Statement of Profit and Loss (Dr) | 10,000 |
| Fixed Deposits | 2,00,000 | Calls-in-arrears @ ₹ 1 per Share | 40,000 |
| Premium on Redemption of Debentures | 20,000 | Securities Premium | 2,00,000 |
| Equity Share Capital (1,00,000 shares of ₹ 10 each) | 10,00,000 | | |

You are required to show the above items in notes to accounts accompanying the balance sheet of Nirvana Ltd. prepared as per Schedule III of the Companies Act, 2013 as at 31st March, 2024.

(Application) [6]

7. Anita and Anil are partners in a firm. On 1st April, 2024, they admitted Jia as a third partner. The capital accounts of the partners after considering the following adjustments on Jia's admission are given below

(i) Loss on revaluation due to depreciation on machinery @ 20% per annum.

(ii) The general reserve maintained in the old firm was not to be disturbed in the reconstituted firm.

Dr **Partners' Capital Account** Cr

| Particulars | Anita (₹) | Anil (₹) | Jia (₹) | Particulars | Anita (₹) | Anil (₹) | Jia (₹) |
|---|---|---|---|---|---|---|---|
| To Goodwill A/c | 10,000 | 10,000 | — | By Balance b/d | 90,000 | 80,000 | — |
| To Profit and Loss A/c | 5,000 | 5,000 | — | By Bank A/c | — | — | 75,000 |
| To Revaluation A/c | 7,500 | 7,500 | — | By Premium for Goodwill A/c | 25,000 | 25,000 | — |
| To Balance c/d | 1,17,500 | 1,07,500 | 75,000 | By Jia's Current A/c | 25,000 | 25,000 | — |
| | 1,40,000 | 1,30,000 | 75,000 | | 1,40,000 | 1,30,000 | 75,000 |

**Additional Information**

On 31st March, 2024, the firm of Anita and Anil, apart from plant and machinery and a bank balance of ₹ 15,000, had no other asset.

You are required to prepare the balance sheet of the reconstituted firm on the date of Jia's admission after considering the information given above. (Show your workings clearly)

(Application) [6]

*Or* Alfa and Beta are partners in a firm. Their balance sheet as at 31st March, 2024, is given below

**Balance Sheet of Alfa and Beta**
as at 31st March, 2024

| Liabilities | | Amt (₹) | Assets | Amt (₹) |
|---|---|---|---|---|
| Sundry Creditors | | 1,16,000 | Cash at Bank | 93,600 |
| Workmen's Compensation Reserve | | 24,000 | Sundry Debtors | 76,400 |
| Capital A/cs | | | Stock | 1,10,000 |
| Alfa | 1,00,000 | | Investment | 20,000 |
| Beta | 80,000 | 1,80,000 | Goodwill | 20,000 |
| | | 3,20,000 | | 3,20,000 |

On 1st April, 2024, they admit Beta's son Gama, as a partner on the following terms

(i) Gama to have 1/4 share of profits, half of which is to be gifted to him by his father and the remaining half to be purchased from Alfa.

(ii) Gama to bring in ₹ 60,000 as his capital but would be unable to bring in cash his share of goodwill.

(iii) Goodwill of the firm to be valued at ₹ 40,000.

(iv) 50% of the investment to be taken over by Alfa and Beta in their profit sharing ratio.

(v) The liability on account of workmen's compensation claim to be ₹ 30,000.

You are required to

(a) Calculate the new profit sharing ratio of all the partners. [1]

(b) Prepare the partners' capital account. (Application) [5]

8. Atul and Peter were partners in a firm sharing profits and losses in the ratio of 3 : 5. They dissolved their firm on 31st March, 2024, when their balance sheet showed the following balances.

| Particulars | Amt (₹) |
|---|---|
| Atul's Capital | 40,000 |
| Peter's Capital | 35,000 |
| Atul's Current Account | 3,000 (Dr) |
| General Reserve | 22,000 |
| Loan from Atul | 12,000 |

On the date of dissolution of the firm

(i) Peter paid the realisation expenses of ₹ 2,000 on behalf of the firm.

(ii) Atul discharged his wife's loan of ₹ 5,000 which she had given to the firm.

(iii) The dissolution resulted in a profit of ₹ 24,000 from the realisation of assets and settlement of liabilities.

You are required to pass journal entries to close the books of the firm (including the entries to show the final settlement of the amount due from the partners/due to the partners by the firm). (Application) [6]

9. (i) Deb, Riza and Ved entered into a partnership on 1st July, 2023, without any agreement as to profit sharing, except that Deb guaranteed that Ved's share of profit, after considering interest into account, would not be less than ₹ 8,500 per annum.

The initial capital provided by the partners was as follows

Deb ₹ 60,000

Riza ₹ 20,000

Ved ₹ 12,000 (increased on the following 1st January, 2024, to ₹ 16,000)

In addition to the above capital, Deb and Riza gave temporary loans to the partnership firm as follows

- Deb advanced ₹ 18,000 on 1st October, 2023 and was repaid on 1st April following.
- Riza advanced ₹ 40,000 on 1st September, 2023 and was repaid along with interest, on 1st December, 2023.

The profit of the firm for the year ended 31st March, 2024, before providing for any interest was ₹ 21,000.

You are required to prepare for the year 2023-24

(a) Profit and loss appropriation account [4½]

(b) Riza's loan account [1½]

(c) Ved's capital account (Application) [2]

(ii) Krish and Tarun are partners in a firm with capitals of ₹ 40,000 and ₹ 60,000. As per their partnership deed

(a) Interest on capital is to be allowed to them @ 5% per annum.

(b) Profits are to be shared in the ratio of 3 : 2.

The trading profits for the year 2023-24 was ₹ 3,600.

You are required to calculate the interest on capital allowed to the partners in the year 2023-24. (Application) [2]

*Or* Deepa, Ridhi and Adit are partners in a firm. Following are the particulars of their capital and drawings accounts for the year 2023-24

| Particulars | Deepa (₹) | Ridhi (₹) | Adit (₹) |
|---|---|---|---|
| Capital as on 1st April, 2023 | 1,00,000 | 80,000 | 20,000 (Dr) |
| Drawings (in two instalments of ₹ 7,500 each made at the end of every half year) | — | 15,000 | — |
| Interest free Loan from the Firm | — | — | 5,000 |

According to their partnership deed

- Profits were to be shared in the ratio of 2 : 2 : 1.
- Interest on capital to be allowed @ 5% per annum.
- Interest on drawings to be charged @ 8% per annum.

The trading profits of the firm for the financial year 2023-24 were ₹ 50,000, before considering the discrepancy of having recorded the inventory at ₹ 10,000 when its realisable value was ₹ 4,000.

(i) You are required to give

(a) The adjusting entry and closing entry for drawings made by Ridhi. (Recall) [2]

(b) The adjusting entry and closing entry for interest on drawings. (Application) [2]

(c) The adjusting entry and closing entry for interest on capital. (Application) [2]

(d) The entry to close the Adit's loan account. (Application) [2]

(ii) The accountant of the firm distributed the divisible profit among the partners in the ratio 2:1:2 instead of in the ratio mentioned in the deed.

You are required to rectify the lapse in accounting by passing a single adjusting entry. (Application) [2]

**10.** Hero Ltd. was registered with a capital of ₹ 5,00,000 divided into 20,000 shares of ₹ 25 each, payable as

| | |
|---|---|
| On Application | ₹ 5 per share |
| On Allotment | ₹ 10 per share |
| On Call | ₹ The balance |

The company offered to the public for subscription 10,000 shares. It received applications for 11,100 shares.

From amongst the applicants

(i) Vimal, who had applied for 1,200 shares, paid ₹ 6,000 on application, but was allotted only 600 shares.

(ii) Mohan applied for 1,000 shares, paid the full amount of ₹ 25,000 with his application but was allotted only 500 shares.

(iii) Vineet, who had applied for 1,500 shares, paid his application and allotment money in order but did not pay the call money.

(iv) The remaining applicants paid as and when due.

The surplus money paid by both Vimal and Mohan was used towards allotment and call and any surplus beyond the call was refunded.

The company forfeited Vineet's shares and later re-issued 500 of the forfeited shares @ ₹ 20 per share fully paid-up.

You are required to pass journal entries in the books of Hero Ltd. (Application) [10]

*Or*

Stem Ltd. came up with an IPO inviting the public to subscribe to its equity shares of ₹ 10 each. The issue was oversubscribed. The company allotted 80,000 shares to all the applicants making a pro-rata allotment in the ratio of 3 : 2.

The face value of the share was payable in three instalments.

Based on the information given above and the following extract of ledger accounts and cash book (bank column), answer the questions that follow

Dr **Cash Book** (Bank column) (Extract) Cr

| Particulars | Amt (₹) | Particulars | Amt (₹) |
|---|---|---|---|
| To Share Application A/c | 4,80,000 | By Balance c/d | ...... |
| To Share Allotment A/c | ...... | | |

Dr **Share Capital Account** (Extract) Cr

| Particulars | Amt (₹) | Particulars | Amt (₹) |
|---|---|---|---|
| To Share Forfeiture A/c | ...... | By Share Allotment A/c | ...... |
| To Calls-in-arrears A/c | ...... | By Share Allotment A/c | 4,00,000 |
| | | By Share Final Call A/c | ...... |

Dr **Calls-in-arrears Account** (Extract) Cr

| Particulars | Amt (₹) | Particulars | Amt (₹) |
|---|---|---|---|
| To Share Allotment A/c | 6,000 | | |

(i) What are the number of shares applied for by the public? [1]

(ii) What is the amount payable per share with application? [1]

(iii) What is the amount payable per share with first and final call? [1]

(iv) Stem Ltd. did not receive the allotment money and call money due from the shareholder Rehan, who had applied for 3,000 shares.

What is the amount received by Stem Ltd. with allotment? [2]

(v) Stem Ltd. forfeited Rehan's shares after the final call. It re-issued 1,500 forfeited shares fully called-up @ ₹ 13 per share.

Give the journal entries passed by the company for

(a) Forfeiture of these shares. [2]

(b) Re-issue of the forfeited shares. (Application) [3]

## Section B

[20 Marks]

11. In subparts (i) and (ii) choose the correct options and in subparts (iii) to (v) answer the questions as instructed.

(i) According to the ratings agency Chrisil, healthy demand for grocery items and expansion into tier II and III cities will help organised brick-and-mortar Food and Grocery (F&G) retailers log a revenue of 14-15% in FY25. The agency further said the debt raising will be capped to ensure healthy key debt protection metrics.

**Source** *(Edited) Financial Express, 23rd December, 2023*

From the following ratios

- Choose the formula of the ratio to be used by the F&G retailers as a debt protection metrics. (Analysis)

(a) $\frac{\text{Revenue Operations}}{\text{Working Capital}}$

(b) $\frac{\text{Cost of Revenue from Operations + Operating Expenses}}{\text{Revenue from Operations}} \times 100$

(c) $\frac{\text{Net Profit before Interest and Taxes}}{\text{Fixed Interest Charges}}$

(d) $\frac{\text{Net Profit after Tax and Preference Dividend}}{\text{Number of Equity Shares}}$

- Mention the name of the ratio so chosen. (Recall) [1]

(ii) Read the following news item of ITC Ltd. and answer the question that follows

The company's board declared an interim dividend of ₹ 6.25 per share for the financial year ending March, 2024. The dividend will be paid between 26-28th February, 2024, to the eligible shareholders.

**Source** *The Hindu, Financial Express, 30th January, 2024*

Which of the following are the attributes of interim dividend? (Understanding) [1]

P – It is a charge against profits.

Q – It is an appropriation of profits.

R – Its declaration and payment will decrease the company's current ratio.

S – Its declaration and payment will increase the company's debt equity ratio.

**Codes**

(a) Only P (b) Only Q

(c) P, R and S (d) Q, R and S

(iii) Bajaj Hindustan Sugar, one of the largest sugar and ethanol producers, in order to revive the company, has offered to invest ₹ 2,500 crore as fresh equity of which ₹ 1,000 crore has already been infused.

**Source** *(Edited) Economic Times, Mumbai Edition 8th August, 2023*

What will be the effect of this decision of Bajaj Hindustan Sugar on its debt equity ratio? (Analysis) [1]

(iv) Jubilant Food Works Ltd. the company that operates Domino's restaurants in India, reported a net profit of ₹ 65.7 crore for the three months ending, 31st December, 2023, against ₹ 80 crore for the three months ending, 31st December, 2022.

**Source** *(Edited) Mint, 1st February, 2024*

You are required to give, for the three months ending, 31st December, 2023, as compared to the same period ending, 31st December, 2022

(a) The formula to calculate the percentage change in net profit of the company.

(b) The percentage change in the net profit of Jubilant Food Works Ltd. of the three months ending 31st December, 2023 *vis-a-vis* the three months ending, 31st December, 2022, mentioning the increase/decrease. (Analysis) [1]

(v) Read the news item given below and answer the questions which follow

Tata Consultancy Services ₹ 17,000 crore share buy-back programme will open on 1st December and close on 7th December, India's largest software exporter said on Tuesday.

"The company believes that the buy-back is not likely to cause any material impact on the profitability or earnings of the company except to the extent of reduction in the amount available for investment, which the company could have otherwise deployed towards generating investment income", TCS said in a regulatory filing.

**Source** *Economic Times, 29th December, 2023*

How would the cash flow from investing activities of TCS be affected, if instead of buying-back its shares, the company had proceeded with its investing programme? **(Application) [1]**

**12.** From the following information, you are required to prepare a common size balance sheet of Super Ltd. as at 31st March, 2024. **(Application) [3]**

| Particulars | Amt |
|---|---|
| Non-current Liabilities | ₹ 2,00,000 |
| Shareholders' Funds | 2.5 times more than the non-current liabilities |
| Current Liabilities | ₹ 1,00,000 |
| Current Assets | ₹ 3,00,000 |
| Non-current Assets | 70% of the equity and liabilities |

**13.** Anand Ltd. reported a loss of ₹ 80,000 for the year ended 31st March, 2024, after considering the depreciation charged on plant and machinery represented by '??' and the following items.

| S. No. | Particulars | Amt (₹) |
|---|---|---|
| (a) | Tax provided during the Year | 84,000 |
| (b) | Loss on Sale of Plant and Machinery | 15,000 |
| (c) | Interest on Short-term Loans and Advances | 2,000 |
| (d) | Depreciation on Plant and Machinery | ?? |

**Additional Information**

1. During the year 2023-24
   - A machine having a book value ₹ 40,000, was disposed-off for ₹ 25,000 and a machine costing ₹ 2,20,000 was purchased.
   - Credit sales were ₹ 1,00,000.
2. An extract of the balance sheet of the company as at 31st March, 2023, and as at 31st March, 2024

| Particulars | 31st March, 2024 (₹) | 31st March, 2023 (₹) |
|---|---|---|
| Trade Receivables | 20,000 | 15,000 |
| Cash at Bank | 8,000 | 10,000 |
| Short-term Loans and Advances | 49,000 | 11,000 |
| Trade Payables | 5,000 | 2,000 |
| Plant and Machinery (At net value) | 6,00,000 | 4,90,000 |
| Provision for Depreciation | 1,50,000 | 1,10,000 |

(i) You are required to calculate for the year 2023-24. (Show the workings clearly)
  (a) The net operating profit of the company before working capital changes. [2]
  (b) Cash from investing activity. [2]

(ii) Taking the information of credit sales into consideration, state with reason, whether the increase in trade receivables in the year 2023-24 over the year 2022-23 will cause the cash from operating activities before tax paid to be more or less then the net operating profit of the company before its working capital changes. **(Evaluate) [2]**

*Or* From the following balance sheets of Ronald Ltd. you are required to prepare a cash flow statement (as per AS-3) for the year 2023-24.

**Balance Sheets of Ronald Ltd.**
as at 31st March, 2024 and 31st March, 2023

| Particulars | Note No. | 31st March, 20024 (₹) | 31st March, 2023 (₹) |
|---|---|---|---|
| I. **EQUITY AND LIABILITIES** | | | |
| 1. **Shareholders' Funds** | | | |
| (i) Share Capital | | 6,00,000 | 6,00,000 |
| (ii) Reserves and Surplus (Statement of profit and loss) | | 80,000 | (60,000) |
| 2. **Non-current Liabilities** | | | |
| Long-term Borrowings | | 1,00,000 | 1,50,000 |
| 3. **Current Liabilities** | | | |
| (i) Short-term Borrowings (Bank overdraft) | | 1,75,000 | 22,000 |
| (ii) Short-term Provisions (Provision for tax) | | 15,000 | 28,000 |
| **Total** | | 9,70,000 | 7,40,000 |
| II. **ASSETS** | | | |
| 1. **Non-current Assets** | | | |
| (i) Property, Plant & Equipment and Intangible Assets | | | |
| (i) Property, Plant and Equipment (Plant and machinery ) | | 5,50,000 | 6,40,000 |
| (ii) Non-current Investments (7% debentures of Violet Ltd.) | | 1,40,000 | 50,000 |
| 2. **Current Assets** | | | |
| Cash and Bank Balance (Bank) | | 2,80,000 | 50,000 |
| **Total** | | 9,70,000 | 7,40,000 |

**Additional Information**

(i) The debentures of Violet Ltd. were purchased on 31st March, 2024.

(ii) During the year 2023-24

(a) Tax of ₹ 20,000 was paid.

(b) Interest on all borrowings due and paid was ₹ 25,000. (Application) [6]

14. Answer any three of the following questions. (Application) [6]

(i) Calculate interest coverage ratio of Criss Cross Ltd. (upto two decimal places) from the following information.

| Particulars | Amt (₹) |
|---|---|
| Net Profit after Interest and Tax | 80,000 |
| Tax Rate | 50 % |
| 12% Debentures | 3,00,000 |
| 9% Bank Loan | 1,00,000 |

(ii) Calculate the operating ratio of Zen Ltd. (upto two decimal places) from the following information.

Revenue from Operations – ₹ 9,00,000; Gross Profit – 20 % of cost

Operating Expenses – ₹ 60,000

(iii) A company had current assets of ₹ 3,00,000 and current liabilities of ₹ 1,50,000, having a current ratio of 2:1. What will be its revised current ratio after it endorses a bills receivable of ₹ 40,000 to one of its creditors?

(iv) From the following particulars of NB Ltd. calculate its cost of revenue from operations for the year 2023-24.

Current Assets – ₹ 6,80,000 ; Current Liabilities – ₹ 3,40,000

Quick Ratio – 1·5 : 1 ; Inventory Turnover Ratio – 4 times

# **Solutions** *in Topper's Style*

1. (i) (*c*) debiting it to profit and loss appropriation account

(ii) (*b*) Debit Pavan's Capital A/c account ₹ 8,000; Credit Pavan's Current A/c ₹ 8,000

(iii) (*c*) P, Q, S

(iv) (*c*) $10,00,000 \times 12\% \times 9/12 =$ ₹ 90,000

(v)

| | | | |
|---|---|---|---|
| Ira's Capital A/c | Dr | 10,000 | |
| To Realisation A/c | | | 10,000 |
| Realisation A/c | Dr | 10,000 | |
| To Ira's Capital A/c | | | 10,000 |

(vi) Net gain of ₹ 7,000

**Working Note**

Dr **Revaluation Account** Cr

| Particulars | Amt (₹) | Particulars | Amt (₹) |
|---|---|---|---|
| To Provision of Doubtful Debts | 4,000 | By Unrecorded Income | 10,000 |
| To Gain on Revaluation | 7,000 | By Discount on Bills Payable | 1,000 |
| | 11,000 | | 11,000 |

(vii) (*d*) Both Assertion (A) and Reason (R) are false

(viii) Unrecorded liability *or* contingent liability which becomes a definite liability

(ix) (a) A share warrant is a financial instrument which gives the holder the right to acquire equity shares specified therein at a specified date at a pre-determined price.

(b) Shareholder's funds.

(x)

| | | | |
|---|---|---|---|
| Securities Premium A/c | Dr | 30,000 | |
| Statement of profit and loss | Dr | 20,000 | |
| To Discount on Issue of Debentures A/c | | | 50,000 |

2. **JOURNAL**

| Date | Particulars | | LF | Amt (Dr) | Amt (Cr) |
|---|---|---|---|---|---|
| | Revaluation A/c | Dr | | 46,000 | |
| | To Creditors A/c | | | | 46,000 |
| | (Being creditors revalued and settled) | | | | |
| | Vehicle A/c | Dr | | 46,000 | |
| | To Revaluation A/c | | | | 46,000 |
| | (Being vehicle revalued) | | | | |
| | Rita's Capital A/c | Dr | | 2,50,000 | |
| | To Vehicle A/c | | | | 46,000 |
| | To Bank A/c | | | | 2,04,000 |
| | (Being Rita's claim settled) | | | | |

*Or*

**JOURNAL**

| Date | Particulars | | LF | Amt (Dr) | Amt (Cr) |
|---|---|---|---|---|---|
| | Javed's Capital A/c | Dr | | 9,000 | |
| | Gaurav's Capital A/c | Dr | | 6,000 | |
| | To Akshat's Capital A/c | | | | 15,000 |
| | (Being Akshat compensated for his share of goodwill) | | | | |

| Date | Particulars | | LF | Amt (Dr) | Amt (Cr) |
|---|---|---|---|---|---|
| | Bank A/c | Dr | | 1,81,000 | |
| | To Javed's Capital A/c | Dr | | | 89,200 |
| | To Gaurav's Capital A/c | Dr | | | 91,800 |
| | (Being cash brought in by Javad and Gaurav to pay-off Akshat's executor) | | | | |
| | Akshat's Executor's A/c | Dr | | 1,81,000 | |
| | To Bank A/c | | | | 1,81,000 |
| | (Being Akshat's executor paid-off) | | | | |

3. **In the Books of Ruth Ltd.**

**JOURNAL**

| Date | Particulars | | LF | Amt (Dr) | Amt (Cr) |
|---|---|---|---|---|---|
| | Pablo Ltd. A/c | Dr | | 1,00,000 | |
| | To Bills Payable A/c | | | | 1,00,000 |
| | (Being part payment made by accepting a bill of exchange) | | | | |
| | Pablo Ltd. A/c | Dr | | 10,00,000 | |
| | Loss on Issue of Debentures A/c | Dr | | 18,180 | |
| | To 11% Debentures A/c | | | | 9,09,000 |
| | To Securities Premium A/c | | | | 90,900 |
| | To Premium on Redemption of Debentures A/c | | | | 18,180 |
| | To Bank A/c | | | | 100 |
| | (Being 9,090, 11% debentures issued at a premium of 10%) | | | | |

**Working Notes**

Number of Debentures $= \frac{10,00,000}{110} = 9,090$ Debentures

*Or* (i) (a) ₹ 30

(b) ₹ 21 (100 – 4 – 15 – 30 – 30)

(ii) Dr **Interest on Calls-in-arrears Account** Cr

| Date | Particulars | Amt (₹) | Date | Particulars | Amt (₹) |
|---|---|---|---|---|---|
| 2024 | | | 2023 | | |
| Mar 31 | To Statement of Profit and Loss | 25 | Jun 31 | By Debentureholders' A/c | 25 |
| | | 25 | | | 25 |

**Working Note**

Amount to be paid by holder of 100 debentures on allotment $(100 \times 30) = 3,000$

Interest on calls-in-arrears $= 3,000 \times \frac{10}{100} \times \frac{1}{12} =$ ₹ 25

4. Dr **General Reserve Account** Cr

| Date | Particulars | Amt (₹) | Date | Particulars | Amt (₹) |
|---|---|---|---|---|---|
| 2024 | | | 2024 | | |
| Mar 31 | To Balance c/d | 70,000 | Apr 1 | By Balance b/d | 50,000 |
| | | | 2024 | | |
| | | | Mar 31 | By DRR | 20,000 |
| | | 70,000 | | | 70,000 |

Dr **Debentureholders' Account** Cr

| Date | Particulars | Amt (₹) | Date | Particulars | Amt (₹) |
|---|---|---|---|---|---|
| 2024 | | | 2024 | | |
| Mar 31 | To Bank A/c | 2,20,000 | Mar 31 | By 10% Debentures A/c | 2,00,000 |
| | | | | To Premium on Redemption of Debentures A/c | 20,000 |
| | | 2,20,000 | | | 2,20,000 |

**5.** (a) Sacrificing Ratio $= \frac{1}{5} : 0$

(b) Normal Profit = Capital Employed $\times \frac{\text{Normal Rate of Return}}{100} = 4{,}80{,}000^* \times \frac{12}{100} =$ ₹ 57,600

*Capital employed = ₹ 4,80,000

Now, Super Profit = Average Profit – Normal Profit

= 74,000 – 57,600 = ₹ 16,400

Goodwill = 16,400 × 4 = ₹ 65,600

**6.** **Notes to Accounts**

| Particulars | | Amt (₹) |
|---|---|---|
| 1. **Share Capital** | | |
| **Authorised Capital** | | |
| ......... Equity Shares @ ₹ 10 each | | ............ |
| **Issued Capital** | | |
| .......... Equity Shares @ ₹ 10 each | | ............ |
| **Subscribed Capital** | | |
| Subscribed and Fully Paid | | |
| 60,000 Equity Shares @ ₹ 10 each | | 6,00,000 |
| Subscribed, but not Fully Paid | | |
| 40,000 Equity Shares @ ₹ 10 each | 4,00,000 | |
| (–) Calls-in-arrears | (40,000) | 3,60,000 |
| | | 9,60,000 |
| 2. **Reserves and Surplus** | | |
| Securities Premium | 2,00,000 | |
| (–) Underwriting Commission | (20,000) | |
| General Reserve | 70,000 | |
| Statement fo Profit and Loss (Dr) | (10,000) | 2,40,000 |
| 3. **Long-term Borrowings** | | |
| 10% Debentures | 5,00,000 | |
| Premium on Redemption of Debentures | 20,000 | |
| Fixed Deposits | 2,00,000 | 7,20,000 |
| 4. **Long-term Loans and Advances** | | |
| Security Deposit for Electricity for Ten Years | | 30,000 |
| 5. **Contingent Liabilities and Capital Commitments** | | |
| Capital Commitments | | |
| Uncalled Amount on Partly Paid-up Shares | | 8,00,000 |

7.

**Balance Sheet of Anita, Anil and Jia**
as at 1st April, 2024

| Liabilities | | Amt (₹) | Assets | Amt (₹) |
|---|---|---|---|---|
| Capital A/cs | | | Cash at Bank | 3,40,000 |
| Anita | 1,17,500 | | Plant and Machinery | 60,000 |
| Anil | 1,07,500 | | Jia's Current A/c | 50,000 |
| Jia | 75,000 | 3,00,000 | | |
| General Reserve | | 1,50,000 | | |
| | | 4,50,000 | | 4,50,000 |

**Working Notes**

Value of Machinery $= 15,000 \times \frac{100}{20} =$ ₹ 75,000

Amount of General Reserve $= 50,000 \times 3 =$ ₹ 1,50,000

*Or* (a) New Ratio = 7 : 7 : 2

**Working Note**

Gifted by Beta $= \frac{1}{2}$ of $\frac{1}{4} = \frac{1}{8}$ Purchased from Alfa $= \frac{1}{8}$

New Ratio Alfa $= 1 - \frac{1}{8} = \frac{7}{8}$; Beta $= 1 - \frac{1}{8} = \frac{7}{8}$; Gama $= \frac{1}{4}$

New Ratio = 7 : 7 : 2

(b) Dr **Partners' Capital Account** Cr

| Particulars | Alpha (₹) | Beta (₹) | Gama (₹) | Particulars | Alpha (₹) | Beta (₹) | Gama (₹) |
|---|---|---|---|---|---|---|---|
| To Goodwill | 10,000 | 10,000 | | By Balance b/d | 1,00,000 | 80,000 | |
| To Investment | 5,000 | 5,000 | | By Cash/Bank | — | — | 60,000 |
| To Revaluation | 3,000 | 3,000 | | By Gama's Current A/c | 5,000 | — | — |
| To Balance c/d | 87,000 | 62,000 | 60,000 | | | | |
| | 1,05,000 | 80,000 | 60,000 | | 1,05,000 | 80,000 | 60,000 |

**Working Note**

Sacrificing Ratio $= 0 : \frac{1}{8}$

Gama's Share of Goodwill $= \frac{1}{8}$ of 40,000 = ₹ 5,000

8.

**JOURNAL**

| Date | Particulars | | LF | Amt (Dr) | Amt (Cr) |
|---|---|---|---|---|---|
| | Atul's Capital A/c | Dr | | 3,000 | |
| | To Atul's Current A/c | | | | 3,000 |
| | (Being Atul's current account closed) | | | | |
| | Atul's Loan A/c | Dr | | 12,000 | |
| | To Bank A/c | | | | 12,000 |
| | (Being workmen compensation claim met out of the reserve) | | | | |
| | General Reserve A/c | Dr | | 22,000 | |
| | To Atul's Capital A/c | | | | 8,250 |
| | To Peter's Capital A/c | | | | 13,750 |
| | (Being balance of general reserve transferred to partners' capital account) | | | | |
| | Realisation A/c | Dr | | 2,000 | |
| | To Peter's Capital A/c | | | | 2,000 |
| | (Being realisation expenses paid by Peter) | | | | |

| Date | Particulars | | LF | Amt (Dr) | Amt (Cr) |
|---|---|---|---|---|---|
| | Realisation A/c | Dr | | 5,000 | |
| | To Atul's Capital A/c | | | | 5,000 |
| | (Being Atul's wife's loan discharged by Atul) | | | | |
| | Reaslisation A/c | Dr | | 24,000 | |
| | To Atul's Capital A/c | | | | 9,000 |
| | To Peter's Capital A/c | | | | 15,000 |
| | (Being profit on realisation transferred to partners' capital account) | | | | |
| | Atul's Capital A/c | Dr | | 59,250 | |
| | Peter's Capital A/c | Dr | | 65,750 | |
| | To Bank A/c | | | | 1,25,000 |
| | (Being partner's capital account settled) | | | | |

**9.** (i) (a)

**Profit and Loss Appropriation Account**
**for ending 31st March, 2024**

Dr | Cr

| Particulars | | Amt (₹) | Particulars | | Amt (₹) |
|---|---|---|---|---|---|
| To Deb's Capital A/c | 6,620 | | By Profit and Loss A/c | | 21,000 |
| | (1,880) | 4,740 | (−) Interest on Loan | | |
| To Riza's Capital A/c | | 6,620 | Deb | 540 | |
| To Ved's Capital A/c | 6,620 | | Riza | 600 | (1,140) |
| | 1,880 | 8,500 | | | |
| | | 19,860 | | | 19,860 |

**Working Notes**

**Interest on Loan**

$$\text{Deb} = 18{,}000 \times \frac{6}{100} \times \frac{6}{12} = ₹\,540 \qquad \text{Riza} = 40{,}000 \times \frac{6}{100} \times \frac{3}{12} = ₹\,600$$

(b) Dr **Riza's Loan Account** Cr

| Date | Particulars | Amt (₹) | Date | Particulars | Amt (₹) |
|---|---|---|---|---|---|
| 2023 | | | 2023 | | |
| Dec 1 | To Bank | 40,600 | Sep 1 | By Bank A/c | 40,000 |
| | | | Dec 1 | By Interest on Loan | 600 |
| | | 40,600 | | | 40,600 |

(c) Dr **Ved's Capital Account** Cr

| Date | Particulars | Amt (₹) | Date | Particulars | Amt (₹) |
|---|---|---|---|---|---|
| 2023 | | | 2023 | | |
| Mar 31 | To Balance c/d | 24,500 | Jul 1 | By Bank A/c | 12,000 |
| | | | Apr 1 | By Bank A/c | 4,000 |
| | | | Mar 31 | By Profit and Loss Appropriation A/c | 6,620 |
| | | | | By Deb's Capital | 1,880 |
| | | 24,500 | | | 24,500 |

(ii) Interest on Capital

Krish = 40,000 × 5% = ₹ 2,000

Tarun = 60,000 × 5% = ₹ 3,000

Since, total profit is less than interest on capital, therefore profit will be distributed in the ratio of interest on capital.

∴ Interest on Capital (Available profit only)

$$\text{Krish} = 3{,}600 \times \frac{2}{5} = ₹\,1{,}440; \qquad \text{Tarun} = 3{,}600 \times \frac{3}{5} = ₹\,2{,}160$$

*Or* (i) (a) **JOURNAL**

| Date | Particulars | | LF | Amt (Dr) | Amt (Cr) |
|---|---|---|---|---|---|
| 2023 Sep 30 | Ridhi's Capital A/c | Dr | | 7,500 | |
| | To Cash/ Bank A/c | | | | 7,500 |
| | (Being drawings made by Ridhi) | | | | |
| 2024 Mar 31 | Ridhi's Capital A/c | Dr | | 7,500 | |
| | To Cash/ Bank A/c | | | | 7,500 |
| | (Being drawings made by Ridhi) | | | | |
| 2024 Mar 31 | Ridhi's Capital A/c | Dr | | 15,000 | |
| | To Ridhi's Drawing A/c | | | | 15,000 |
| | (Being drawings account closed by transferring to capital account) | | | | |

(b) **JOURNAL**

| Date | Particulars | | LF | Amt (Dr) | Amt (Cr) |
|---|---|---|---|---|---|
| 2024 Mar 31 | Ridhi' Capital A/c | Dr | | 300 | |
| | To Interest on Drawings A/c | | | | 300 |
| | (Being interest on drawings charged) | | | | |
| 2024 Mar 31 | Interest on Drawings A/c | Dr | | 300 | |
| | To Profit and Loss Appropriation A/c | | | | 300 |
| | (Being interest on drawings account closed) | | | | |

(c) **JOURNAL**

| Date | Particulars | | LF | Amt (Dr) | Amt (Cr) |
|---|---|---|---|---|---|
| 2024 Mar 31 | Interest on Capital A/c | Dr | | 9,000 | |
| | To Deepa's Capital A/c | | | | 5,000 |
| | To Rishi's Capital A/c | | | | 4,000 |
| | (Being interest on capital allowed) | | | | |
| 2024 Mar 31 | Profit and Loss Appropriation A/c | Dr | | 9,000 | |
| | To Interest on Capital A/c | | | | 9,000 |
| | (Being interest on capital account closed) | | | | |

(d) **JOURNAL**

| Date | Particulars | | LF | Amt (Dr) | Amt (Cr) |
|---|---|---|---|---|---|
| 2024 Mar 31 | Adit's Capital A/c | Dr | | 5,000 | |
| | To Loan to Adit A/c | | | | |
| | (Being Adit's loan account closed) | | | | 5,000 |

(ii) **Adjusting Journal Entry**

| Date | Particulars | | LF | Amt (Dr) | Amt (Cr) |
|---|---|---|---|---|---|
| 2024 Mar 31 | Adit's Capital A/c | Dr | | 7,060 | |
| | To Ridhi's Capital A/c | | | | 7,060 |
| | (Being error of profits distributed in incorrect ratio rectified) | | | | |

**Working Notes**

**Table Showing Adjustments**

| Partners | Amount which has been credited in the ratio 2 :1 : 2<br>44,000 + 300 – 9,000 = 35,300 | Amount which should have been credited in the ratio 2: 2 :1<br>44,000 + 300 – 9,000 = 35,300 | Difference (Dr or Cr) |
|---|---|---|---|
| Deepa | 14,120 | 14,120 | – |
| Ridhi | 7,060 | 14,120 | 7,060 (Cr) |
| Adit | 14,120 | 7,060 | 7,060 (Dr) |

10.

**In the Books of Hero Ltd.**

**JOURNAL**

| Date | Particulars | | LF | Amt (Dr) | Amt (Cr) |
|---|---|---|---|---|---|
| | Bank A/c | Dr | | 75, 500 | |
| | To Share Application A/c | | | | 75, 500 |
| | (Being share application received) | | | | |
| | Share Application A/c | Dr | | 75,500 | |
| | To Share Capital A/c | | | | 50,000 |
| | To Share Allotment A/c | | | | 8,000 |
| | To Calls-in-Advance A/c | | | | 5,000 |
| | To Bank A/c | | | | 12,500 |
| | (Being share application transferred to share capital and subsequent instalments) | | | | |
| | Share Allotment A/c | Dr | | 1,00,000 | |
| | To Share Capital A/c | | | | 1,00,000 |
| | (Being share allotment due) | | | | |
| | Bank A/c | Dr | | 92,000 | |
| | To Share Allotment A/c | | | | 92,000 |
| | (Being share allotment received) | | | | |
| | Share First and Final Call A/c | Dr | | 1,00,000 | |
| | To Share Capital A/c | | | | 1,00,000 |
| | (Being share capital due) | | | | |
| | Bank A/c | Dr | | 80,000 | |
| | Calls-in-advance A/c | Dr | | 5,000 | |
| | Calls-in-arrear A/c | Dr | | 15,000 | |
| | To Share First and Final Call A/c | | | | 1,00,000 |
| | (Being share final call received) | | | | |
| | Share Capital A/c | Dr | | 37,500 | |
| | To Share Forfeiture A/c | | | | 22,500 |
| | To Calls-in-arrear A/c | | | | 15,000 |
| | (Being 1,500 shares forfeited) | | | | |
| | Bank A/c | Dr | | 10,000 | |
| | Shares Forfeiture A/c | Dr | | 2,500 | |
| | To Share Capital A/c | | | | 12,500 |
| | (Being 1,500 shares re-issued) | | | | |
| | Share Forfeiture A/c | Dr | | 5,000 | |
| | To Capital Reserve A/c | | | | 5,000 |
| | (Bing net gain on re-issued shares trnansferred to capital reserve) | | | | |

*Or* (i) Share applied = $80,000 \times \frac{3}{2} = 1,20,000$ shares

(ii) ₹ 4

**Working Note**

Amount Payable per Share with Application = $\frac{\text{Total Amount paid on Application}}{\text{Number of Shares Applied}} = \frac{4,80,000}{1,20,000}$ = ₹ 4

(iii) ₹ 1 (10 – 4 – 5)

(iv) ₹ 2,34,000

| **Working Note** | | **Amt (₹)** |
|---|---|---|
| Amount to be received on Allotment | = | 4,00,000 |
| (–) Amount to received on Application adjusted in Allotment (40,000 × 4) | = | (1,60,000) |
| (–) Amount not received from Rehan a shareholder of $3,000 \times \frac{2}{3}$ = 2,000 shares [(2,000 × 5) – (1,000 × 4)] | = | 6,000 |
| | = | 2,34,000 |

(v) (a)

**JOURNAL**

| Date | Particulars | | LF | Amt (Dr) | Amt (Cr) |
|---|---|---|---|---|---|
| | Share Capital A/c | Dr | | 20,000 | |
| | To Share Forfeiture A/c | | | | 12,000 |
| | To Calls-in-arrear A/c | | | | 8,000 |
| | (Being 2,000 shares forfeited) | | | | |

(b)

**JOURNAL**

| Date | Particulars | | LF | Amt (Dr) | Amt (Cr) |
|---|---|---|---|---|---|
| | Bank A/c | Dr | | 19,500 | |
| | To Share Capital A/c | | | | 15,000 |
| | To Securities Premium | | | | 4,500 |
| | (Being 1,500 shares re-issued ) | | | | |
| | Share Forfeiture A/c | Dr | | 9,000 | |
| | To Capital Reserve A/c | | | | 9,000 |
| | (Being net gain on re-issued shares transferred to capital reserve ) | | | | |

11. (i) • (*c*) $\frac{\text{Net Profit before Interest and Taxes}}{\text{Fixed Interest Charges}}$ • Interest coverage ratio

(ii) (*d*) Q, R and S

(iii) The ratio will reduced/decline

(iv) (a) $\frac{\text{Absolute Change in Net Profit}}{\text{Base Year (Previous Year) Profit}} \times 100$ (b) Decrease of 21.77 %

(v) Outflow of cash to the extent of investment made.

Inflow of cash – Interest income from the investments.

12. **Common Size Balance Sheet of Super Ltd.**

as at 31st March, 2024

| Particulars | Note. No. | 31st March, 2024 (₹) | % to Balance Sheet Total |
|---|---|---|---|
| **I. EQUITY AND LIABILITIES** | | | |
| 1. Shareholders' Fund | | 7,00,000 | 70 |
| 2. Non-current Liabilities | | 2,00,000 | 20 |
| 3. Current Liabilities | | 1,00,000 | 10 |
| **Total** | | 10,00,000 | 100 |
| **II. ASSETS** | | | |
| 1. Non-current Assets | | 7,00,000 | 70 |
| 2. Current Assets | | 3,00,000 | 30 |
| **Total** | | 10,00,000 | 100 |

**13.** (i) (a)

| Particulars | Amt (₹) |
|---|---|
| Net Profit for the Year | (80,000) |
| Provision for Tax | 84,000 |
| Net Profit before Tax | 4,000 |
| (+) Depreciation on Plant and Machinery (WN1) | 70,000 |
| (+) Loss on Sale of Machine (WN2) | 15,000 |
| (−) Interest on Short-term Loans and Advances | (2,000) |
| Net Operating Profit before Working Capital changes | 87,000 |

**Working Notes**

1. Dr **Provision for Depreciation Account** Cr

| Particulars | Amt (₹) | Particulars | Amt (₹) |
|---|---|---|---|
| To Plant and Machinery A/c | 30,000 | By Balance b/d | 1,10,000 |
| To Balance c/d | 1,50,000 | By Depreciation A/c | 70,000 |
| | 1,80,000 | | 1,80,000 |

2. Dr **Plant and Machinery Account** Cr

| Particulars | Amt (₹) | Particulars | Amt (₹) |
|---|---|---|---|
| To Balance b/d | 6,00,000 | By Provision for Depreciation A/c | 30,000 |
| To Bank A/c | 2,20,000 | By Bank A/c | 25,000 |
| | | By Loss on Sale A/c | 15,000 |
| | | By Balance c/d | 7,50,000 |
| | 8,20,000 | | 8,20,000 |

(b)

| Particulars | Amt (₹) |
|---|---|
| Purchase of Plant and Machinery | (2,20,000) |
| Sale of Plant and Machinery | 25,000 |
| Short-term Loans and Advances | (38,000) |
| Interest on Short-term Loans and Advances | 2,000 |
| Cash used in Investing Activities | (2,31,000) |

(ii) **Less** Although the operating profit increased by ₹ 1,000,000 because of the credit sales, the increase in cash was only ₹ 95,000 (1,00,000 + 15,000– 20,000).

*Or*

**Cash Flow Statement of Rohald Ltd.**
for the year ending 31st March, 2024

| Particulars | | Amt (₹) |
|---|---|---|
| I. **Cash Flow from Operating Activities** | | |
| Net Profit before Tax (WN 3) | 1,47,000 | |
| (+) Non operating/Non-cash Expenses | | |
| Depreciation on Plant and Machinery | 90,000 | |
| Interest on Borrowings | 25,000 | |
| (−) Interest on Investment Received | (3,500) | |
| Net Operating Profit before Working Capital Changes /Cash from Operating Activities before Tax Paid | 2,58,500 | |
| (−) Tax Paid | (20,000) | |
| Cash Flow from Operating Activities | | 2,38,500 |
| II. **Cash Flow from Investing Activities** | | |
| Purchase of Investments | (90,000) | |
| Interest on Investments Received | 3,500 | |
| Cash used in Investing Activities | | (86,500) |

| Particulars | | Amt (₹) |
|---|---|---|
| III. **Cash Flow from Financing Activities** | | |
| Repayment of Long-term Borrowings | (50,000) | |
| Interest on Borrwings Paid | (25,000) | |
| Bank Overdraft taken | 1,53,000 | |
| Cash Flow from Financing Activities | | 78,000 |
| Net Increase in Cash as per I, II and III | | 2,30,000 |
| (+) Opening Cash and Cash Equivalents | | |
| Bank | | 50,000 |
| Closing Cash and Cash Equivalents | | |
| Bank | | |
| | | 2,80,000 |

**Working Notes**

1. Dr **Provision for Tax Account** Cr

| Particulars | Amt (₹) | Particulars | Amt (₹) |
|---|---|---|---|
| To Bank A/c | 20,000 | By Balance b/d | 28,000 |
| To Balance c/d | 15,000 | By Statement of Profit and loss | 7,000 |
| | 35,000 | | 35,000 |

2.

| Particulars | Amt (₹) |
|---|---|
| Statement of Profit and Loss | 1,40,000 |
| Provision for Tax | 7,000 |
| Net Profit before Tax | 1,47,000 |

**14.** (i) Interest Coverage Ratio $= \frac{\text{Net Profit before Interest and Taxes}}{\text{Fixed Interest Charges}} = \frac{2,05,000}{45,000} = 4.56$ times

(ii) Operating Ratio $= \frac{\text{Cost of Revenue from Operations + Operating Expenses}}{\text{Revenue from Operations}} \times 100$

*Or* $= \frac{\text{Cost of Revenue from Operations + Operating Expenses − Operating Income}}{\text{Revenue from Operations}} \times 100 = \frac{8,10,000}{9,00,000} \times 100 = 90\%$

(iii) Current Ratio $= \frac{\text{Current Assets}}{\text{Current Liabilities}} = \frac{2,60,000}{1,10,000} = 2.36:1$

(iv) Quick Ratio $= \frac{\text{All Current Assets − Inventories (Excluding Loose Tools and Spare Parts) − Prepaid Expenses}}{\text{Current Liabilities}}$

$$\frac{1.5}{1} = \frac{6,80,000 - \text{Inventory}}{3,4,000}$$

∴ Inventory = ₹ 1,70,000

Now, Inventory Turnover Ratio $= \frac{\text{Cost of Revenue from Operations}}{\text{Average Inventory}}$

$$4 = \frac{\text{Cost of Revenue Operations}}{1,70,000}$$

∴ Cost of Revenue from Operations = ₹ 6,80,000

Write your Roll No.

| | | | | | | | | |
|---|---|---|---|---|---|---|---|---|
| | | | | | | | | |

# Board Exam Paper 2024

## Accounts 12th (Code 858)

**No. of Ques :** 14 **No. of Sections :** 2 **Time :** 3 Hrs. **Max. Marks :** 80

### General Instructions

1. Candidates are allowed additional 15 minutes for only reading the paper. They must not start writing during this time.
2. Section-A is compulsory for all candidates.
3. Candidates have to attempt all questions from either Section-B or Section-C*.
4. There are internal choices provided in each section.
5. The intended marks for questions or parts of questions are given in the brackets [ ].
6. All calculations should be shown clearly.
7. All working, including rough work, should be done on the same page as and adjacent to, the rest of the answer.

* Section-C has not been covered.

## Section A Answer All Questions

[60 Marks]

1. In sub-parts (i) to (iv), choose the correct option and in sub-parts (v) to (x) answer the questions as instructed.

(i) On the date of admission of Ajay as a partner, the balance sheet of the firm of Nita and Rita showed a balance of ₹ 80,000 in the workmen compensation reserve.

Choose the correct option to record the effect of a workmen compensation claim of ₹ 90,000 on the accounts of the partnership firm. [1]

(a) The revaluation account to be credited with ₹ 10,000

(b) The revaluation account to be debited with ₹ 10,000

(c) The capital accounts of Nita and Rita to be debited with ₹ 90,000

(d) The capital accounts of Nita and Rita to be credited with ₹ 90,000

(ii) CreditAccess Grameen Ltd. a listed NBFC-MFI (Micro Finance Institution), is all set to enter the bond market next week to raise up to ₹ 1,000 crore in non-convertible debentures, as it looks to diversify its liability profile.

**Source** *Economic Times, 20th August, 2023*

According to the provisions of the Companies Act, 2013, what is the maximum amount of these non-convertible debentures which CreditAccess Grameen Ltd. will redeem out of its capital? [1]

(a) ₹ 100 crore (b) ₹ 150 crore
(c) ₹ 900 crore (d) ₹ 1,000 crore

(iii) Choose the correct order in which a partnership firm at the time of its dissolution, will apply the amount realised from the sale of its assets, including any amount contributed by the partners, towards the payment of [1]

P – Partners' loan

Q – Firm's debts

R – Balance of partners' capital

S – Surplus divided amongst the partners in their profit sharing ratio

**Codes**

(a) P, Q, R, S (b) Q, P, S, R
(c) S, P, Q, R (d) Q, P, R, S

(iv) Tulip Ltd. allotted 45,000 equity shares of ₹ 10 each to the public. The first and final call of ₹ 2 per share was not received on 1,000 shares, which were forfeited by the company. Later, 600 of the forfeited shares were re-issued at ₹ 7 fully paid-up.

What is the subscribed capital of the company? [1]

(a) ₹ 4,49,200 (b) ₹ 4,50,000
(c) ₹ 4,40,000 (d) ₹ 4,46,000

(v) **Assertion** (A) A revaluation account is prepared at the time of dissolution of a partnership.

**Reason** (R) A revaluation account is prepared to determine the net gain/loss on realisation of assets and settlement of liabilities. [1]

**Alternatives**

(a) Both Assertion (A) and Reason (R) are true and Reason (R) is the correct explanation of Assertion (A)
(b) Both Assertion (A) and Reason (R) are true, but Reason (R) is not the correct explanation of Assertion (A)
(c) Both Assertion (A) and Reason (R) are false
(d) Assertion (A) is true, but Reason (R) is false

(vi) A firm having a debtor of ₹ 30,000 from whom the amount was due on 30th June, 2023, gets dissolved on 31st March, 2023. The debtor cleared his dues on the date of dissolution of the firm at a discount of 4% per annum.

Give the journal entry passed by the firm to realise the payment from the debtor. [1]

(vii) Xylo Ltd. issued 9,000, 7% debentures of ₹ 100 each at a certain rate of discount. After writing-off the discount on the issue of debentures, the company was left with a balance of ₹ 35,000 in its securities premium out of the original amount of ₹ 71,000.

At what rate of discount did the company issue these debentures? [1]

(viii) The Annual Report of ITC Ltd. for the financial year 2021-22, showed claims against the company not acknowledged as debts of ₹ 880.58 crores including third party claims arising from disputes relating to contracts aggregating ₹ 29.22 crores.

**Source** *Annual Report of ITC Ltd. 2021-22*

Mention the heading and the sub-heading under which this item would have been shown in the notes to accounts accompanying the balance sheet of ITC Ltd. as at 31st March, 2022. [1]

(ix) Deepa and Pia are in partnership sharing profits and losses in the ratio of 3 : 2. They admit Charu as a partner for 1/5 share in the profits. The capitals of Deepa and Pia, before adjusting the loss of ₹ 5,000 on revaluation of assets and liabilities are ₹ 30,000 and ₹ 20,000 respectively.

It is decided that Charu will contribute 25% of the combined capitals of Deepa and Pia.

What is Charu's capital contribution? [1]

(x) The balance sheet of Anjum Ltd. as at 31st March, 2022, had outstanding 1,000, 8% debentures of ₹ 100 each. These debentures were to be redeemed by the company on 31st March, 2023.

Give the journal entry for the amount due to the debentureholders on 31st March, 2023, including the interest on debentures due to them. [1]

**2.** The balance sheet of Hari, Jacob and James as at 31st March, 2023, stood as follows

**Balance Sheet of Hari, Jacob and James**
as at 31st March, 2023

| Liabilities | | Amt (₹) | Assets | Amt (₹) |
|---|---|---|---|---|
| Capital A/cs | | | Fixed Assets | 3,50,000 |
| Hari | 3,40,000 | | Debtors | 2,50,000 |
| Jacob | 1,90,000 | | Bank | 1,50,000 |
| James | 2,20,000 | 7,50,000 | | |
| | | 7,50,000 | | 7,50,000 |

Jacob died on 30th June, 2023.

His drawings from 1st April, 2023, up to the date of his death amounted to ₹ 1,00,000.

According to the partnership deed, Jacob was

(i) To be charged with interest on drawings @ 4% per annum.

(ii) Entitled to his share of interim profits for which his capital account was credited with ₹ 1,10,000.

(iii) Entitled to his share in the non-purchased goodwill of the firm.

The firm's non-purchased goodwill on the date of Jacob's death had no value.
The final amount due to Jacob by the firm was transferred to his executor's loan account.

You are required to prepare the interim balance sheet of the reconstituted firm as at 30th June, 2023. [3]

*Or*

Kamal, Ali and John are partners in a firm. On Kamal's retirement from the firm on 30th June, 2023, his capital account stood at ₹ 40,000 after all adjustments.

The partners decided that Kamal be paid 50% of the amount due to him immediately and the balance, along with interest @ 6% per annum, be paid on 30th June, 2024.

The firm closes its books on 31st March every year.

You are required to prepare Kamal's loan account till it is finally closed.

**3.** On 1st April, 2022, Harbour Ltd. issued 50,000, 6% debentures of ₹ 100 each to the public at a discount of 5% to be redeemed after three years at a premium of 7%.

On this date, the company also issued 1,00,000 equity shares of ₹ 10 each at a premium of ₹ 2 per share.
Both the issues were fully subscribed.
You are required to prepare the following accounts for the year 2022-23 in the books of Harbour Ltd.

(i) 6% Debentures account

(ii) Loss on issue of debentures account [3]

**4.** On 1st April, 2022, the following balances appeared in the books of Alpha Pvt. Ltd.

9% Debentures (redeemable on 31st March, 2023, at a premium of 2%) ₹ 50,00,000

Debenture Redemption Reserve ₹ 5,00,000

The debenture redemption investment, which was purchased by the company on 1st April, 2022, was realised at 101% on the date of redemption and the debentures were redeemed on the due date.

You are required to prepare the following accounts for the year 2022-23 in the books of Alpha Pvt. Ltd.

(i) Debentureholders' account.

(ii) Debenture redemption investment account. [3]

*Or* On 1st April, 2022, Resorts Ltd. (a listed construction company) had 60,000, 5% debentures of ₹ 100 each due for redemption at par on 31st March, 2023.
As per the law, investment was made in a fixed deposit of a bank on 30th April, 2022, earning interest @ 5% per annum.
Tax @ 10% was deducted by the bank on the interest.
You are required to pass necessary journal entries in the year of redemption of debentures, including entries for interest on debenture redemption investment. (Ignore the interest on debentures).

5. On 1st April, 2020, Anish started a business with a capital of ₹ 3,00,000.

During the three years ending 31st March, 2023, the results of his business were

| Year | | Amt (₹) |
|---|---|---|
| 2020-21 | Loss | 20,000 |
| 2021-22 | Profit | 34,000 |
| 2022-23 | Profit | 46,000 |

From the year 2020-21 to the year 2022-23, Anish withdrew ₹ 30,000 from the firm for his personal use.

On 1st April, 2023, he admitted Danish into partnership on the following terms

(i) Goodwill of the firm to be valued at two years' purchase of the average profits of the last three years.

(ii) Danish to have 1/4 share in the future profits.

(iii) Danish's capital to be equal to 1/4 of Anish's capital determined on 1st April, 2023, after the goodwill compensation has been taken into account.

You are required to give

(a) The formula to calculate goodwill by the average profit method.

(b) The value of self-generated goodwill of the firm.

(c) Danish's capital contribution. [3]

6. The following balances have been extracted from the books of Meadow Ltd. as at 31st March, 2023.

| Particulars | Amt (₹) | Particulars | Amt (₹) |
|---|---|---|---|
| Capital Reserve | 1,20,000 | Bank Overdraft | 40,000 |
| Plant and Machinery (At cost) | 6,00,000 | Bills Receivables | 20,000 |
| | | Patents | 80,000 |
| Land and Building | 6,80,000 | Sundry Debtors | 90,000 |
| Statement of Profit and Loss (Dr) | 1,70,000 | Provision for Doubtful Debts | 10,000 |
| | | Inventories | 30,000 |
| Short-term Loans and Advances | 50,000 | Share Capital | 12,20,000 |
| Cash and Bank Balances | 1,60,000 | 5% Debentures (1/5 of the debentures to be redeemed on 31st March, 2024) | 3,00,000 |
| Trade Payables | 90,000 | | |
| Accumulated Depreciation on Plant and Machinery | 1,00,000 | | |

**Additional Information**

- The company had issued 1,25,000 equity shares of ₹ 10 each which were all applied for and allotted to the public. These shares were fully called-up by the company.
- There were calls-in-arrears @ ₹ 2 per share on 15,000 shares out of which 5,000 shares were forfeited by the company.

You are required to

(i) Show the share capital in the notes to accounts.

(ii) Give the amount for each of the following

(a) Short-term borrowings

(b) Current assets

(c) Property, plant & equipment and intangible assets

- Property, plant and equipment [6]

7. Amay and Sujoy are partners sharing profits and losses in the ratio of 3 : 1. Their balance sheet as at 31st March, 2023, is given below

**Balance Sheet of Amay and Sujoy**
as at 31st March, 2023

| Liabilities | | Amt (₹) | Assets | | Amt (₹) |
|---|---|---|---|---|---|
| Bills Payable | | 70,000 | Land and Building | | 1,65,000 |
| Capital A/cs | | | Stock | | 60,000 |
| Amay | 1,30,000 | | Sundry Debtors | 70,000 | |
| Sujoy | 1,25,000 | 2,55,000 | (−) Provision for Doubtful Debts | (10,000) | 60,000 |
| | | | Cash in Hand | | 40,000 |
| | | 3,25,000 | | | 3,25,000 |

On 1st April, 2023, they admit Malay as a new partner for 1/4 share in the profits on the following terms

(i) Malay to bring his share of capital of ₹ 1,20,000 and to pay ₹ 10,000 in cash for his share of goodwill.

(ii) Stock worth ₹ 45,000 to be taken over by Amay at ₹ 25,000.

(iii) Bills payable of ₹ 20,000 to be honoured by Sujoy, for which he is not to be reimbursed.

(iv) The capitals of Amay and Sujoy to be adjusted on the basis of Malay's capital and his share in the profits, any surplus to be readjusted through current account and deficiency through cash.

You are required to prepare the partners' capital account. [6]

*Or* Mitu and Ritu are partners sharing profits and losses in the ratio of 2 : 3. An extract of their balance sheet as at 31st March, 2023, is given below

**Balance Sheet of Mitu and Ritu** (An extract)
as at 31st March, 2023

| Liabilities | Amt (₹) | Assets | Amt (₹) |
|---|---|---|---|
| Workmen Compensation Reserve | 30,000 | Investments (Market value ₹ 76,000) | 80,000 |
| General Reserve | 40,000 | Sundry Debtors | 1,00,000 |
| Investment Fluctuation Reserve | 10,000 | Profit and Loss Account | 55,000 |

On 1st April, 2023, they admit Nitu as a new partner for 1/5 share in the profits on the following terms regarding the treatment of the reserves and the accumulated losses.

(i) Accumulated losses, if any, to be written-off.
(ii) A workmen compensation claim of ₹ 10,000 to be adjusted against the workmen compensation reserve. The balance of the reserve is not to be distributed.
(iii) Any loss in the value of investments to be adjusted against the investment fluctuation reserve. The balance of the investment fluctuation reserve is to be distributed.
(iv) Provision for doubtful debts to be created to the extent of 10% of the debtors from the general reserve. The remaining amount in the general reserve is to be distributed.

You are required to pass necessary journal entries to record the above adjustments at the time of Nitu's admission.

**8.** Adit and Shiv were partners sharing profits and losses in the ratio of 5:4. They dissolved their partnership firm on 31st March, 2023, when their balance sheet showed the following balances

| Particulars | Amt (₹) |
|---|---|
| Adit's Capital | 40,000 |
| Shiv's Capital | 30,000 |
| Adit's Current A/c (Cr) | 3,000 |
| Shiv's Current A/c (Dr) | 6,000 |
| Loan by the Firm to Shiv | 22,000 |
| Profit and Loss Account (Dr) | 4,500 |

On the date of dissolution of the firm

(i) The firm suffered a loss of ₹18,000 upon realisation of assets and settlement of liabilities.
(ii) The expenses of dissolution of ₹ 3,000, to be borne by Shiv, were paid by the firm on his behalf.
(iii) The firm had furniture of ₹ 15,000. Adit took over some pieces of the furniture at ₹ 9,000 (being 10% less than the book value). Shiv took over the remaining furniture at 80% of its book value.

You are required to prepare the partners' capital account. [6]

**9.** Tanuj and Ravi are partners in a business with capital balances of ₹ 1,50,000 and ₹ 1,00,000 respectively on 1st April, 2022.

Their partnership deed contains the following clauses

(i) Interest on capital to be allowed @ 10% per annum.
(ii) Interest on drawings to be charged @ 4% per annum.
(iii) Tanuj to be allowed a commission @ 5% of the trading profit after charging his commission.
(iv) Ravi to be allowed an annual commission of ₹ 10,000.

**Additional Information**

During the year 2022-23

- Tanuj withdrew ₹ 6,000 at the end of every quarter.
- The trading profit of the firm was ₹ 84,000.
- The firm's divisible profit was ₹ 46,360.
- On 1st October, 2022, Ravi permanently withdrew ₹ 20,000 from his capital.

You are required to do the following

(a) Pass the journal entries to record [6]
  (i) The permanent withdrawal made by Ravi.
  (ii) The distribution of the divisible profits between the partners.
  (iii) The adjusting entry for commission due to Ravi.

(b) Calculate the interest on capital allowed to [2]

(i) Tanuj (ii) Ravi

(c) Calculate the commission allowed to Tanuj. [1]

(d) Calculate the interest on drawings charged from Tanuj. [1]

*Or*

Amit and Iqbal are partners in a business. Their partnership deed contained the following clauses

(i) Interest on drawings to be charged @ 6% per annum.

(ii) Amit to get a salary of ₹ 1,000 per month.

(iii) Iqbal to get an annual commission of ₹ 10,000.

(iv) Any partner taking a loan from the firm to be charged interest on it @ 8% per annum.

**Additional Information**

| Particulars | Amit (₹) | Iqbal (₹) |
|---|---|---|
| Drawings made on 1st May, 2022 | — | 30,000 |
| Borrowed from the Firm on 1st July, 2022 | 10,000 | — |
| Capital Balances on 31st March, 2023 | 75,000 | 10,000 (Dr) |
| Divisible Profits for the Year 2022-23 Credited to the Partners' Capital Account | 9,000 | 9,000 |

You are required to

(a) Give the closing journal entry for interest on loan due from Amit. [1]

(b) Find the opening capital balance of the partners on 1st April, 2022 by preparing the partners' capital account for the year 2022-23. [9]

10. Gama Ltd. issued 20,000 equity shares of ₹ 10 each to the public, payable as follows

₹ 2 on Application

₹ 3 on Allotment (on 1st November, 2022)

₹ 5 on First and Final Call (on 1st March, 2023)

Applications were received for 25,000 shares. The directors of the company accepted applications for 20,000 shares and refunded the application money on the remaining shares.

One shareholder who was allotted 30 shares paid the first and final call with allotment.

Another shareholder did not pay his allotment on 20 shares when due but paid it with the first and final call along with interest on calls-in-arrears.

The directors of the company charged interest on calls-in-arrears at the rate provided in Table F of the Companies Act, 2013. No interest was allowed on calls-in-advance.

You are required to pass journal entries to record the above transactions in the books of Gama Ltd. [10]

*Or* (i) Roxy Ltd. issued equity shares of ₹ 10 each payable as ₹ 4 on application and allotment; ₹ 2 on first call; ₹ 4 on second and final call. Following is an extract of the journal of Roxy Ltd.

**Journal of Roxy Ltd.** (An extract)

| Date | Particulars | | LF | Amt (Dr) | Amt (Cr) |
|---|---|---|---|---|---|
| | Share First Call A/c | Dr | | 28,000 | |
| | To Share Capital A/c | | | | 28,000 |
| | (Being first call due on ......... shares @ ₹ 2 each) | | | | |
| | Bank A/c | Dr | | ... | |
| | Calls-in-arrears A/c | Dr | | 2,000 | |
| | To Share First Call A/c | | | | 28,000 |
| | (Being first call received on ...... shares) | | | | |
| | Share Capital A/c | Dr | | ... | |
| | To Shares Forfeited A/c | | | | 4,000 |
| | To Calls-in-arrears A/c | | | | ... |
| | (Being...shares of ₹ 10 each forfeited for non-payment of first call) | | | | |

| Date | Particulars | | LF | Amt (Dr) | Amt (Cr) |
|---|---|---|---|---|---|
| | Share Second and Final Call A/c | Dr | | 52,000 | |
| | To Share Capital A/c | | | | 52,000 |
| | (Being second and final call due on ...... shares @ ₹ 4 each) | | | | |
| | Bank A/c | Dr | | ... | |
| | Calls-in-arrears A/c | Dr | | 10,000 | |
| | To Share Second and Final Call A/c | | | | 52,000 |
| | (Being second call received on ...... shares) | | | | |
| | Share Capital A/c | Dr | | ... | |
| | To Shares Forfeited A/c | | | | ... |
| | To Calls-in-arrears A/c | | | | 10,000 |
| | (Being ... shares of ₹ 10 each forfeited for non-payment of final call) | | | | |
| | Bank A/c | Dr | | ... | |
| | Shares Forfeited A/c | Dr | | ... | |
| | To Share Capital A/c | | | | ... |
| | (Being 1,500 forfeited shares, including those on which the first call was not received, re-issued @ ₹ 6 per share fully called-up) | | | | |
| | Share Forfeiture A/c | Dr | | ... | |
| | To Capital Reserve A/c | | | | ... |
| | (Being ...........) | | | | |

You are required to complete the journal entries by filling up the missing information represented by '...', including the number of shares and narration, if any. [9]

(ii) Savi Ltd. forfeited 50 shares of ₹ 100 each issued at a premium of 10%, on which allotment money of ₹ 30 per share (including premium) and first and final call of ₹ 40 per share were not received. What is the minimum amount per share at which the company can re-issue these shares? [1]

## Section B Answer All Questions [20 Marks]

**11.** In sub-parts (i) and (ii) choose the correct option and in sub-parts (iii) to (v) answer the questions as instructed.

(i) What is the difference between total assets and current liabilities? [1]

(a) Total liabilities (b) Shareholders' funds
(c) Total debt (d) Capital employed

(ii) While preparing its cash flow statement, which of the following will be classified by a company as its cash outflow from investing activities? [1]

P– Investment in government securities.

Q– Investment in bank deposits (having maturity of six months).

R– Proceeds from redemption of liquid mutual fund units.

S– Proceeds from bank deposits with original maturity of less than three months.

**Codes**

(a) P and Q
(b) R and S
(c) Only P (d) Only R

(iii) A company has a quick ratio of 1.8 : 1. Mention whether this ratio will improve/ reduce / not change after it sells a machine worth ₹ 1,20,000 at a loss of ₹ 30,000. [1]

(iv) State whether creditors would prefer lending to a company with a high debt-equity ratio or a low debt-equity ratio. Give a reason. [1]

(v) An extract of the balance sheet of Nova Ltd. shows

| Particulars | 31st March, 2023 (₹) | 31st March 2022 (₹) |
|---|---|---|
| Share Capital (Equity shares @ ₹ 10 each) | 8,00,000 | 5,00,000 |
| Securities Premium | 70,000 | 1,70,000 |

During the year 2022-23, the company raised its share capital by issuing bonus shares to the shareholders at the beginning of the year in the ratio of 1 : 5 (one bonus share was issued for every five equity shares). The balance shares were issued for cash to the public.

How many shares were issued for cash by the company? [1]

12. Following is the comparative income statement of Violet Ltd. for the years ending 31st March, 2023 and 31st March, 2022.

You are required to present the comparative income statement in its complete form after calculating the missing information represented by "...". [3]

**Comparative Income Statement of Violet Ltd.**
for the years ending 31st March, 2023 and 31st March, 2022

| Particulars | 31st March, 2023 (₹) | 31st March, 2022 (₹) | Absolute Change | % Change |
|---|---|---|---|---|
| Revenue from Operations | ... | 7,098 | 364 | ... |
| Expenses | 8,998 | 7,931 | ... | ... |
| Net Profit | ... | (833) | (703) | ... |

13. Based on the following information of Neon Ltd, answer the questions given below in relation to the cash flow statement of the company for the year 2022-23.

| Particulars | 31st March, 2023 (₹) | 31st March, 2022 (₹) |
|---|---|---|
| Provision for Tax | 80,000 | 50,000 |
| 7% Debentures | 8,00,000 | 3,00,000 |
| Unclaimed Dividend | 6,000 | — |
| Plant and Machinery (At book value) | 1,00,000 | 1,00,000 |
| Land | 4,50,000 | 6,00,000 |

**Note** Dividend proposed in the years 2021-22 and 2022-23 were ₹ 30,000 and 40,000 respectively.

**Additional Information**

During the year 2022-23, the company

(i) Provided ₹ 75,000 for tax.

(ii) Issued 7% debentures at a discount of 5%.

(iii) Purchased plant and machinery for ₹ 40,000.

(a) What is the amount of tax paid by the company? [1]

(b) Give the reason for the opening book value and closing book value of plant and machinery remaining the same, despite the purchase of a machine during the year. [1]

(c) What is the inflow of cash from the issue of 7% debentures? [1]

(d) Give the company's outflow of cash for dividend paid to the shareholders. [1]

(e) State with reason whether Neon Ltd. will consider the decrease in the amount of land as an operating activity or as an investing activity, while preparing its cash flow statement. [2]

*Or* From the following balance sheets of Halogen Ltd. you are required to prepare a cash flow statement (as per AS-3) for the year 2022-23.

**Balance Sheet of Halogen Ltd.**
as at 31st March, 2023 and 31st March, 2022

| Particulars | Note No. | 31st March, 2023 (₹) | 31st March, 2022 (₹) |
|---|---|---|---|
| I. EQUITY AND LIABILITIES | | | |
| 1. **Shareholders' Funds** | | | |
| (i) Share Capital (Equity shares @ ₹ 10 each) | | 4,50,000 | 4,00,000 |
| (ii) Reserves and Surplus (Statement of P and L) | | 1,06,000 | (20,000) |
| 2. **Non-current Liabilities** | | | |
| Long-term Borrowings (15% debentures) | | 6,00,000 | 4,00,000 |
| 3. **Current Liabilities** | | | |
| Short-term Provisions (Provision for tax) | | 50,000 | 70,000 |
| **Total** | | 12,06,000 | 8,50,000 |
| II. ASSETS | | | |
| 1. **Non-current Assets** | | | |
| (i) Property, Plant & Equipment and Intangible Assets | | | |
| (a) Property, Plant and Equipment | 1 | 4,80,000 | 7,00,000 |
| 2. **Current Assets** | | | |
| (i) Current Investments | | 2,56,000 | 10,000 |
| (ii) Cash and Bank Balances | | 4,70,000 | 1,40,000 |
| **Total** | | 12,06,000 | 8,50,000 |

**Notes to Accounts**

| Particulars | 31st March, 2023 (₹) | 31st March, 2022 (₹) |
|---|---|---|
| 1. **Property, Plant and Equipment** | | |
| Plant and Machinery | 7,42,000 | 9,00,000 |
| (−) Accumulated Depreciation | (2,62,000) | (2,00,000) |

**Additional Information**

During the year 2022-23, the company

(i) Issued additional debentures on 1st October, 2022.

(ii) Sold plant and machinery, the book value of which was ₹ 1,20,000 (accumulated depreciation ₹ 38,000) for ₹ 50,000. [6]

**14.** Answer any three of the following questions. [6]

(i) From the following particulars of Hind Ltd. calculate the preference dividend paid by the company.

| Particulars | Amt (₹) |
|---|---|
| Net Profit before Tax | 20,00,000 |
| Equity Shares of ₹ 10 each (Market value ₹ 15) | 40,00,000 |
| Tax Rate | 30% |
| Earning Per Share | 2.75 |

(ii) Calculate the current ratio (upto two decimal places) of Windlas Biotech Ltd. from the following extract of its annual report of 2021-22.

| Particulars | Amt (₹) (in millions) |
|---|---|
| Opening Inventory of Consumables (Raw materials) | 264.79 |
| Closing Inventory of Consumables (Raw materials) | 389.85 |
| Opening Inventory of Finished Goods and Work-in-progress | 149.82 |
| Closing Inventory of Finished Goods and Work-in-progress | 197.24 |
| Current Assets (Other than inventory of consumables and of finished goods and work-in-progress) | 3,229.23 |
| Current Liabilities | 936.52 |

**Source** *Annual Report 2021-22 of Windlas Biotech Ltd.*

(iii) For the year 2022-23, the return on investment of Yolo Ltd. was 20%; its capital employed being ₹ 50,00,000.

(a) You are required to give the formula used by Yolo Ltd. to calculate the return on investment.

(b) You have been provided with two components for calculating return on investment. Calculate the missing third component.

(iv) Calculate the working capital turnover ratio of Moonlight Ltd., (upto two decimal places) from the following particulars

| Particulars | Amt (₹) |
|---|---|
| Cash | 10,00,000 |
| Short-term Loans and Advances | 3,00,000 |
| Inventory | 2,00,000 |
| Trade Payables | 5,00,000 |
| Cost of Revenue from Operations | 12,00,000 |
| Gross Profit on Cost of Revenue from Operations | 25% |

# Solutions *in Topper's Style*

My Commitment *I affirm that I am reviewing these solutions only after I have solved the Board Exam Paper 2024 on my own. My purpose of looking the solutions is solely to verify whether my answers/solutions were correct or not and to identify my mistakes in case my solutions were wrong or I could not solve that.*

1. (i) (*b*) The excess claim i.e. 90,000 – 80,000 = ₹ 10,000 will be debited to revaluation account as increase in liability.

(ii) (*d*) CreditAccess is a listed NBFC, so they are exempted from creating DRR.

(iii) (*d*) The assets of the firm, including amount contributed by the partners to make up deficiency of capital, is applied in the following order

- Payment to outsiders/creditors.
- Payment of loans and advances of partners.
- Payment of capital of partners.
- The remaining amount shall be divided among the partners in their profit sharing ratio.

(iv) (*a*)

| **Subscribed Share Capital** | **Amt (₹)** |
|---|---|
| Subscribed and Fully Paid-up (44,600 × 10) | 4,46,000 |
| (+) Share Forfeiture Account (400 × 8) | 3,200 |
| | 4,49,200 |

(v) (*d*) A dissolution of partnership implies change in relationship of partners of the firm and the firm continues its business i.e. dissolution of partnership happens whenever a partnership is reconstituted-admission, reltirement, death, etc.

(vi)

**JOURNAL**

| Date | Particulars | LF | Amt (Dr) | Amt (Cr) |
|---|---|---|---|---|
| | Cash A/c Dr | | 29,700 | |
| | To Realisation A/c | | | 29,700 |
| | (Being cash received from debtors) | | | |

**Working Note**

Discount to Debtors $= 30{,}000 \times \frac{4}{100} \times \frac{3}{12} =$ ₹ 300

(vii) Discount written-off from Securities Premium = 71,000 – 35,000 = ₹ 36,000

Percentage of Discount $= \frac{\text{Discount}}{\text{Face Value}} \times 100 = \frac{36{,}000}{9{,}00{,}000} \times 100 = 4\%$

(viii) The amount will be shown as contingent liability because it is not acknowledged as debts.

(ix)

| | |
|---|---|
| Deepa's Capital after Adjustment of Loss (30,000 – 3,000) | ₹ 27,000 |
| Pia's Capital after Adjustment of Loss (20,000 – 2,000) | ₹ 18,000 |
| Total Capital | ₹ 45,000 |

Charu's Capital = 45,000 × 25/100 = ₹ 11,250

(x)

**JOURNAL**

| Date | Particulars | LF | Amt (Dr) | Amt (Cr) |
|---|---|---|---|---|
| | 8% Debentures A/c Dr | | 1,00,000 | |
| | Debentures Interest A/c Dr | | 8,000 | |
| | To Debentureholders' A/c | | | 1,08,000 |
| | (Being 8% debentures due for redemption) | | | |

2.

**Balance Sheet**
as at 30th June, 2023

| Liabilities | | Amt (₹) | Assets | Amt (₹) |
|---|---|---|---|---|
| Capital A/cs | | | Fixed Assets | 3,50,000 |
| Hari | 3,40,000 | | Debtors | 2,50,000 |
| James | 2,20,000 | 5,60,000 | Bank (1,50,000 – 1,00,000) | 50,000 |
| Jacob's Executor A/c | | 1,99,500 | Profit and Loss Suspense A/c | 1,09,500 |
| | | 7,59,500 | | 7,59,500 |

**Working Notes**

1. Dr **Jacob's Capital Account** Cr

| Particulars | Amt (₹) | Particulars | Amt (₹) |
|---|---|---|---|
| To Bank A/c (Drawings) | 1,00,000 | By Balance b/d | 1,90,000 |
| To Profit and Loss Suspense A/c (Interest on drawings) | 500 | By Profit and Loss Suspense A/c (Share of Profit) | 1,10,000 |
| To Jacob's Executor A/c | 1,99,500 | | |
| | 3,00,000 | | 3,00,000 |

2. Interest on Jacob's Drawings = $1,00,000 \times \frac{4}{100} \times \frac{1.5}{12} =$ ₹ 500

3. Profit and Loss Suspense Account = 1,10,000 – 500 = ₹ 1,09,500

*Or* Dr **Kamal's Loan Account** Cr

| Date | Particulars | Amt (₹) | Date | Particulars | Amt (₹) |
|---|---|---|---|---|---|
| 2024 Mar 31 | To Balance c/d | 20,900 | 2023 Jun 30 | By Kamal's Capital A/c | 20,000 |
| | | | 2024 Mar 31 | By Interest A/c $\left(20,000 \times \frac{6}{100} \times \frac{9}{12}\right)$ | 900 |
| | | 20,900 | | | 20,900 |
| 2024 Jun 30 | To Bank A/c (20,000 + 900 + 300) | 21,200 | 2024 Apr 1 | By Balance b/d | 20,900 |
| | | | Jun 30 | By Interest A/c $\left(20,000 \times \frac{6}{100} \times \frac{3}{12}\right)$ | 300 |
| | | 21,200 | | | 21,200 |

**3.** (i) Dr **6% Debentures Account** Cr

| Particulars | Amt (₹) | Particulars | Amt (₹) |
|---|---|---|---|
| To Balance c/d | 50,00,000 | By Debentures Application and Allotment A/c | 47,50,000 |
| | | By Discount on Issue of Debentures A/c | 2,50,000 |
| | 50,00,000 | | 50,00,000 |

(ii) Dr **Loss on Issue of Debentures Account** Cr

| Particulars | Amt (₹) | Particulars | Amt (₹) |
|---|---|---|---|
| To 6% Debentures A/c | 2,50,000 | By Securities Premium A/c | 2,00,000 |
| To Premium on Redemption of Debentures A/c | 3,50,000 | By Statement of Profit and Loss (Balancing Figure) | 4,00,000 |
| | 6,00,000 | | 6,00,000 |

**Important Note** Discount on issue of debentures is also a loss on issue of debentures. Thus, it can be further combined into one account.

**4.** (i) Dr **Debentureholders' Account** Cr

| Date | Particulars | Amt (₹) | Date | Particulars | Amt (₹) |
|---|---|---|---|---|---|
| 2023 Mar 31 | To Bank A/c | 51,00,000 | 2023 Mar 31 | By 9% Debentures A/c | 50,00,000 |
| | | | Mar 31 | By Premium on Redemption of Debentures A/c $\left(50,00,000 \times \frac{2}{100}\right)$ | 1,00,000 |
| | | 51,00,000 | | | 51,00,000 |

(ii) Dr **Debenture Redemption Investment Account** Cr

| Date | Particulars | Amt (₹) | Date | Particulars | Amt (₹) |
|---|---|---|---|---|---|
| 2022 Apr 1 | To Bank A/c $\left(50,00,000 \times \frac{15}{100}\right)$ | 7,50,000 | 2023 Mar 31 | By Bank A/c | 7,57,500 |
| 2023 Mar 31 | To Profit on Sale of Investment $\left(7,50,000 \times \frac{1}{100}\right)$ | 7,500 | | | |
| | | 7,57,500 | | | 7,57,500 |

*Or*

**JOURNAL**

| Date | Particulars | | LF | Amt (Dr) | Amt (Cr) |
|---|---|---|---|---|---|
| 2022 Apr 30 | Debenture Redemption Investment A/c | Dr | | 9,00,000 | |
| | To Bank A/c (60,00,000 × 15%) | | | | 9,00,000 |
| | (Being 15% of the face value is invested) | | | | |
| 2023 Mar 31 | Bank A/c | Dr | | 9,37,125 | |
| | TDS Deposited A/c | Dr | | 4,125 | |
| | To Debenture Redemption Investment A/c | | | | 9,00,000 |
| | To Interest on Investment A/c $\left(9,00,000 \times \frac{5}{100} \times \frac{11}{12}\right)$ | | | | 41,250 |
| | (Being investment bearing 5% p.a. interest encashed) | | | | |
| Mar 31 | 5% Debentures A/c | Dr | | 60,00,000 | |
| | To Debentureholders' A/c | | | | 60,00,000 |
| | (Being amount due to debentures) | | | | |
| Mar 31 | Debentureholders' A/c | Dr | | 60,00,000 | |
| | To Bank A/c | | | | 60,00,000 |
| | (Being amount paid on redemption) | | | | |
| Mar 31 | Interest on Investment A/c | Dr | | 41,250 | |
| | To Statement of Profit and Loss | | | | 41,250 |
| | (Being interest on investment transferred to statement of profit and loss) | | | | |

5. (a) **Simple Average Profit Method**

Value of Goodwill = Average Profit* × Number of Years' Purchase

$$\text{*Average Profit} = \frac{\text{Total Actual Profits of Given Number of Years Before Abnormal and Non-business Items}}{\text{Given Number of Years}}$$

(b) $\text{Average Profit} = \frac{(20,000) + 34,000 + 46,000}{3} = \frac{60,000}{3} = ₹\,20,000$

Goodwill = 20,000 × 2 = ₹ 40,000

(c) Danish's share of goodwill $= 40,000 \times \frac{1}{4} = ₹\,10,000$

| **Anish's Capital on 1st April, 2023** | **Amt (₹)** |
|---|---|
| Opening Capital of Anish | 3,00,000 |
| (+) Profit/Loss of Last 3 Years | (20,000) |
| | 34,000 |
| | 46,000 |
| (−) Drawings | (30,000) |
| (+) Premium for Goodwill | 10,000 |
| Anish's Capital | 3,40,000 |

Danish's Capital = 3,40,000 × 1/4 = ₹ 85,000

**6.** (i) **Notes to Accounts**

| Particulars | | Amt (₹) |
|---|---|---|
| **Share Capital** | | |
| **Authorised Capital** | | |
| ........Equity Shares of ₹ 10 each | | — |
| **Issued Capital** | | |
| 1,25,000 Equity Shares of ₹ 10 each | | 12,50,000 |
| **Subscribed Capital** | | |
| Subscribed and Fully Paid-up | | |
| 1,10,000 Equity Shares of ₹ 10 each | | 11,00,000 |
| Subscribed but not Fully Paid-up | | |
| 10,000 Equity Share of ₹ 10 each | 1,00,000 | |
| (−) Calls-in-arrears (10,000 × 2) | (20,000) | 80,000 |
| (+) **Share Forfeiture Account** (5,000 × 8) | | 40,000 |
| | | 12,20,000 |

(ii) (a) **Short-term Borrowings**

| | Amt (₹) |
|---|---|
| Bank Overdraft | 40,000 |
| (+) Matured Debentures (1/5 × 3,00,000) | 60,000 |
| | 1,00,000 |

(b) **Current Assets**

| | | Amt (₹) |
|---|---|---|
| Short-term Loans and Advances | | 50,000 |
| Cash and Bank Balances | | 1,60,000 |
| Inventories | | 30,000 |
| Bills Receivables | | 20,000 |
| Debtors | 90,000 | |
| (−) Provision | (10,000) | 80,000 |
| | | 3,40,000 |

(c) **Property, Plant and Equipment**

| | | Amt (₹) |
|---|---|---|
| Plant and Machinery | 6,00,000 | |
| (−) Accumulated Depreciation | (1,00,000) | 5,00,000 |
| Land and Building | | 6,80,000 |
| | | 11,80,000 |

**7.** Dr **Partners' Capital Account** Cr

| Particulars | Amay (₹) | Sujoy (₹) | Malay (₹) | Particulars | Amay (₹) | Sujoy (₹) | Malay (₹) |
|---|---|---|---|---|---|---|---|
| To Stock | 25,000 | — | — | By Balance b/d | 1,30,000 | 1,25,000 | — |
| To Sujoy's Current A/c | — | 37,500 | — | By Cash A/c | — | — | 1,20,000 |
| To Balance c/d | 2,70,000 | 90,000 | 1,20,000 | By Premium for Goodwill A/c | 7,500 | 2,500 | — |
| | | | | By Cash A/c (Cash bought in) | 1,57,500 | — | — |
| | 2,95,000 | 1,27,500 | 1,20,000 | | 2,95,000 | 1,27,500 | 1,20,000 |

**Working Notes**

1. **JOURNAL**

| Date | Particulars | | LF | Amt (Dr) | Amt (Cr) |
|---|---|---|---|---|---|
| | Cash A/c | Dr | | 1,30,000 | |
| | To Malay's Capital A/c | | | | 1,20,000 |
| | To Premium for Goodwill A/c | | | | 10,000 |
| | (Being goodwill and capital brought in by new partner) | | | | |

| Date | Particulars | | LF | Amt (Dr) | Amt (Cr) |
|---|---|---|---|---|---|
| | Premium for Goodwill A/c | Dr | | 10,000 | |
| | To Amay's Capital A/c | | | | 7,500 |
| | To Sujoy's Capital A/c | | | | 2,500 |
| | (Being goodwill distributed between sacrificing partner) | | | | |

2. Dr **Revaluation Account** Cr

| Particulars | Amt (₹) | Particulars | Amt (₹) |
|---|---|---|---|
| To Stock A/c | 20,000 | By Bills Payable A/c | 20,000 |
| | 20,000 | | 20,000 |

3. **Adjustment of Capital**

New Firm's Capital $= 1{,}20{,}000 \times \frac{4}{1} =$ ₹ 4,80,000

New Profit Sharing Ratio

Let profit be ₹ 1

Remaining Share $= 1 - \frac{1}{4} = \frac{3}{4}$;

Amay's New Share $= \frac{3}{4} \times \frac{3}{4} = \frac{9}{16}$

Sujoy's New Share $= \frac{1}{4} \times \frac{3}{4} = \frac{3}{16}$;

Malay's Share $= \frac{1}{4} \times \frac{4}{4} = \frac{4}{16}$

New Ratio = 9 : 3 : 4

Amay's New Capital $= 4{,}80{,}000 \times \frac{9}{16} =$ ₹ 2,70,000 ; Sujoy's New Capital $= 4{,}80{,}000 \times \frac{3}{16} =$ ₹ 90,000

*Or*

**JOURNAL**

| Date | Particulars | | LF | Amt (Dr) | Amt (Cr) |
|---|---|---|---|---|---|
| (i) | Mitu's Capital A/c | Dr | | 22,000 | |
| | Ritu's Capital A/c | Dr | | 33,000 | |
| | To Profit and Loss A/c | | | | 55,000 |
| | (Being balance of profit and loss account adjusted) | | | | |
| (ii) (a) | Workmen Compensation Reserve A/c | Dr | | 10,000 | |
| | To Outstanding Workmen Claim A/c | | | | 10,000 |
| | (Being workmen claim adjusted) | | | | |
| (b) | Nitu's Capital A/c | Dr | | 4,000 | |
| | To Mitu's Capital A/c | | | | 1,600 |
| | To Ritu's Capital A/c | | | | 2,400 |
| | (Being adjustment of workmen compensation reserve) | | | | |
| (iii) | Investment Fluctuation Reserve A/c | Dr | | 10,000 | |
| | To Investment A/c | | | | 4,000 |
| | To Mitu's Capital A/c | | | | 2,400 |
| | To Ritu's Capital A/c | | | | 3,600 |
| | (Being transfer of excess investment fluctuation reserve to partners' capital account) | | | | |
| (iv) | General Reserve A/c | Dr | | 40,000 | |
| | To Provision for Doubtful Debts | | | | 10,000 |
| | To Mitu's Capital A/c | | | | 12,000 |
| | To Ritu's Capital A/c | | | | 18,000 |
| | (Being transfer of excess general reserve to partners' capital account) | | | | |

8. Dr **Partners' Capital Account** Cr

| Particulars | Adit (₹) | Shiv (₹) | Particulars | Adit (₹) | Shiv (₹) |
|---|---|---|---|---|---|
| To Shiv's Current A/c | — | 6,000 | By Balance b/d | 40,000 | 30,000 |
| To Profit and Loss (Debit Balance) | 2,500 | 2,000 | By Adit's Current A/c | 3,000 | — |
| To Loan to Shiv | — | 22,000 | By Cash A/c | — | 15,000 |

| Particulars | Adit (₹) | Shiv (₹) | Particulars | Adit (₹) | Shiv (₹) |
|---|---|---|---|---|---|
| To Realisation Loss | 10,000 | 8,000 | | | |
| To Cash A/c (Dissolution Expenses) | — | 3,000 | | | |
| To Realisation A/c (Furniture) | 9,000 | 4,000 | | | |
| To Cash A/c | 21,500 | — | | | |
| | 43,000 | 45,000 | | 43,000 | 45,000 |

**Working Note**

Let the book value of furniture taken over by Adit be $x$

$$9,000 = x - 10\% \text{ of } x \Rightarrow 9,000 = 0.9x \Rightarrow x = \frac{9,000}{0.9} = ₹\,10,000$$

Total value of furniture = ₹ 15,000 ; Remaining furniture = 15,000 – 10,000 = ₹ 5,000

Furniture taken over by Shiv = $5,000 \times \frac{80}{100} = ₹\,4,000$

**9.** (a)

**JOURNAL**

| Date | Particulars | | LF | Amt (Dr) | Amt (Cr) |
|---|---|---|---|---|---|
| 2022 (i) Oct 1 | Ravi's Capital A/c | Dr | | 20,000 | |
| | To Cash A/c | | | | 20,000 |
| | (Being permanent withdrawal of capital by Ravi) | | | | |
| 2023 (ii) Mar 31 | Profit and Loss Appropriation A/c | Dr | | 46,360 | |
| | To Tanuj's Capital A/c | | | | 23,180 |
| | To Ravi's Capital A/c | | | | 23,180 |
| | (Being divisible profit distributed) | | | | |
| (iii) Mar 31 | Ravi's Commission A/c | Dr | | 10,000 | |
| | To Ravi's Capital A/c | | | | 10,000 |
| | (Being commission due to Ravi) | | | | |

(b) (i) Interest on Tanuj's Capital = 1,50,000 × 10/100 = ₹ 15,000

(ii) Interest on Ravi's Capital = $\left[\left(1,00,000 \times \frac{10}{100} \times \frac{6}{12}\right) + \left(80,000 \times \frac{10}{100} \times \frac{6}{12}\right)\right] = 5,000 + 4,000 = ₹\,9,000$

(c) Tanuj's Commission = $\frac{\text{Trading Profit} \times \text{Rate}}{100 + \text{Rate}} = 84,000 \times \frac{5}{105} = ₹\,4,000$

(d) Interest on Tanuj's Drawings = $\text{Drawings} \times \frac{\text{Rate}}{100} \times \frac{\text{Average Period}}{12} = 24,000 \times \frac{4}{100} \times \frac{4.5}{12} = ₹\,360$

*Or* (a)

**JOURNAL**

| Date | Particulars | | LF | Amt (Dr) | Amt (Cr) |
|---|---|---|---|---|---|
| | Interest on Amit's Loan A/c (10,000 × 8/100 × 9/12) | Dr | | 600 | |
| | To Profit and Loss A/c | | | | 600 |
| | (Being interest on loan transferred to profit and loss account) | | | | |

(b) Dr **Partners' Capital Account** Cr

| Particulars | Amit (₹) | Iqbal (₹) | Particulars | Amit (₹) | Iqbal (₹) |
|---|---|---|---|---|---|
| To Drawings A/c | — | 30,000 | By Balance b/d (Bal. Fig.) | 54,000 | 2,650 |
| To Interest on Drawings $\left(30,000 \times \frac{6}{100} \times \frac{11}{12}\right)$ | — | 1,650 | By Partner's Salary A/c | 12,000 | — |
| | | | By Divisible Profits A/c | 9,000 | 9,000 |
| To Balance c/d | 75,000 | — | By Partners' Commission A/c | — | 10,000 |
| | | | By Balance c/d | — | 10,000 |
| | 75,000 | 31,650 | | 75,000 | 31,650 |

10. **JOURNAL**

| Date | Particulars | | LF | Amt (Dr) | Amt (Cr) |
|---|---|---|---|---|---|
| | Bank A/c | Dr | | 50,000 | |
| | To Equity Share Application A/c | | | | 50,000 |
| | (Being application money received on 25,000 shares @ ₹ 2 each) | | | | |
| | Equity Share Application A/c | Dr | | 50,000 | |
| | To Equity Share Capital A/c | | | | 40,000 |
| | To Bank A/c | | | | 10,000 |
| | (Being 20,000 equity shares allotted and excess application money on 5,000 shares refunded) | | | | |
| | Equity Share Allotment A/c | Dr | | 60,000 | |
| | To Equity Share Capital A/c | | | | 60,000 |
| | (Being allotment money made due to 20,000 equity shares @ ₹ 3 per share) | | | | |
| | Bank A/c | Dr | | 60,090 | |
| | Calls-in-arrear A/c (20 × 3) | Dr | | 60 | |
| | To Equity Share Allotment A/c | | | | 60,000 |
| | To Calls-in-advance A/c (30 × 5) | | | | 150 |
| | (Being allotment money received except for 20 shares, along with first and final call money on 30 shares) | | | | |
| | Equity Share First and Final Call A/c | Dr | | 1,00,000 | |
| | To Equity Share Capital A/c | | | | 1,00,000 |
| | (Being first and final call money made due on 20,000 equity shares @ ₹ 5 each) | | | | |
| | Bank A/c | Dr | | 99,910 | |
| | Calls-in-advance A/c | Dr | | 150 | |
| | To Equity Share First and Final Call A/c | | | | 1,00,000 |
| | To Calls-in-arrears A/c | | | | 60 |
| | (Being first and final call money received on 20,000 equity shares along with allotment money on 20 shares and calls-in-advance on 30 shares adjusted) | | | | |
| | Sundry Members A/c | Dr | | 2 | |
| | To Interest on Calls-in-arrears A/c (60 × 10 / 100 × 4 × 12) | | | | 2 |
| | (Being interest on calls-in-arrears due) | | | | |
| | Bank A/c | Dr | | 2 | |
| | To Sundry Members A/c | | | | 2 |
| | (Being interest on calls-in-arrears paid) | | | | |
| | Interest on Calls-in-arrears A/c | Dr | | 2 | |
| | To Statement of Profit and Loss | | | | 2 |
| | (Being interest on calls-in-arrears transferred to statement of profit and loss) | | | | |

*Or* (i) **JOURNAL of Roxy Ltd.** (An extract)

| Date | Particulars | | LF | Amt (Dr) | Amt (Cr) |
|---|---|---|---|---|---|
| | Share First Call A/c | Dr | | 28,000 | |
| | To Share Capital A/c | | | | 28,000 |
| | (Being first call due on **14,000** shares @ ₹ 2 each) | | | | |
| | Bank A/c (13,000 × 2) | Dr | | **26,000** | |
| | Calls-in-arrears A/c (1,000 × 2) | Dr | | 2,000 | |
| | To Share First Call A/c | | | | 28,000 |
| | (Being first call received on **13,000** shares) | | | | |
| | Share Capital A/c (1,000 ×6) | Dr | | **6,000** | |
| | To Shares Forfeited A/c (1,000 × 4) | | | | 4,000 |
| | To Calls-in-arrears A/c (1,000 × 2) | | | | **2,000** |
| | (Being **1,000** shares of ₹ 10 each forfeited for non-payment of first call) | | | | |
| | Share Second and Final Call A/c | Dr | | 52,000 | |
| | To Share Capital A/c | | | | 52,000 |
| | (Being second and final call due on **13,000** shares @ ₹ 4 each) | | | | |

| Date | Particulars | LF | Amt (Dr) | Amt (Cr) |
|---|---|---|---|---|
| | Bank A/c (10,500 × 4) Dr | | **42,000** | |
| | Calls-in-arrears A/c (2,500 × 4) Dr | | 10,000 | |
| | To Share Second and Final Call A/c | | | 52,000 |
| | (Being second call received on **10,500** shares) | | | |
| | Share Capital A/c (2,500 × 10) Dr | | **25,000** | |
| | To Shares Forfeited A/c (2,500 × 6) | | | **15,000** |
| | To Calls-in-arrears A/c (2,500 × 4) | | | 10,000 |
| | (Being **2,500** shares of ₹ 10 each forfeited for non-payment of final call) | | | |
| | Bank A/c (1,500 × 6) Dr | | **9,000** | |
| | Shares Forfeited A/c (1,500 × 4) Dr | | **6,000** | |
| | To Share Capital A/c (1,500 × 10) | | | **15,000** |
| | (Being 1,500 forfeited shares, including those on which the first call was not received , re-issued @ ₹ 6 per share fully called-up) | | | |
| | Share Forfeiture A/c Dr | | **1,000** | |
| | To Capital Reserve A/c (WN) | | | **1,000** |
| | (Being **profit on 1,500 forfeited shares transferred to capital reserve)** | | | |

**Working Note**

$$\text{Amount of Capital Reserve} = \left[\text{Profit on Forfeiture} + \left(\frac{\text{Profit on Forfeiture}}{\text{Forfeited Shares}} \times \text{Re-issued Shares}\right)\right] - \text{Loss on Re-issue}$$

$$= \left[4{,}000 + \left(\frac{15{,}000}{2{,}500} \times 500\right)\right] - 6{,}000 = 7{,}000 - 6{,}000 = ₹\ 1{,}000$$

(ii) Amount (per share) received on forfeited shares = ₹ 40

The maximum amount of discount the company can allow is ₹ 40. Therefore, the minimum amount at which the company can re-issue these shares is ₹ 60.

**11.** (i) (*d*) Capital Employed = Total Assets – Current Liabilities

(ii) (*c*) Only P

(iii) Sale of machinery will increase bank (current asset) and will not put any impact on current liabilities. The ratio will improve.

(iv) Creditors would prefer to lend a low debt–equity ratio, because low debt-equity ratio means the company's debt burden is low and the company is in better position to pay back its debts.

(v) Total shares issued by the company (8,00,000 – 5,00,000) = ₹ 3,00,000

(–) Total securities premium used to issue bonus shares = ₹ (1,00,000)

Total amount received in cash = ₹ 2,00,000

Face value of share = ₹ 10

Number of shares $\left(\frac{2{,}00{,}000}{10}\right) = 20{,}000$

**12.**

**Comparative Income Statement of Violet Ltd.**

for the years ending 31st March, 2023 and 31st March, 2022

| Particulars | 31st March, 2022 (₹) | 31st March, 2023 (₹) | Absolute Change | % Change |
|---|---|---|---|---|
| Revenue from Operations | 7,098 | **7,462** | 364 | **5.13** |
| Expenses | 7,931 | 8,998 | **1,067** | **13.45** |
| Net Profit | (833) | **(1,536)** | (703) | **84.39** |

**Working Note**

Absolute Change = Current Year's Figures – Previous Year's Figures

$$\% \text{ Change} = \frac{\text{Absolute Change}}{\text{Previous Year}} \times 100$$

13. (a) Dr **Provision for Tax Account** Cr

| Particulars | Amt (₹) | Particulars | Amt (₹) |
|---|---|---|---|
| To Bank A/c (Paid) (Balancing Figure) | 45,000 | By Balance b/d | 50,000 |
| To Balance c/d | 80,000 | By Statement of Profit and Loss (Made) | 75,000 |
| | 1,25,000 | | 1,25,000 |

Tax paid by the company = ₹ 45,000

(b) The opening value and closing value of plant and machinery is same despite the purchase of machinery due to "depreciation" provided on the fixed asset.

(c) Cash Inflow from Issue of 7% Debentures = Face Value of Debentures – Discount on Debentures
= 5,00,000 – 25,000 = ₹ 4,75,000

(d) Cash Outflow for Dividend Paid = Dividend of Previous Year – Unclaimed Dividend
= 30,000 – 6,000 = ₹ 24,000

(e) The value of land appreciates over time. So, decrease in the value of land is "sale of land" and will be shown under investing activities.

*Or* **Cash Flow Statement**

| Particulars | | Amt (₹) |
|---|---|---|
| A. **Cash Flow from Operating Activities** | | |
| Net Profit before Appropriation and Tax | | 1,76,000 |
| Adjustments for Non-cash and Non-operating Items | | |
| (+) Interest on Debentures | 75,000 | |
| Depreciation | 1,00,000 | |
| Loss on Sale of Plant and Machinery | 70,000 | 2,45,000 |
| Operating Profit before Working Capital Changes | | 4,21,000 |
| (–) Increase in Current Assets and Decrease in Current Liabilities | | |
| Current Investments | (2,46,000) | (2,46,000) |
| Cash Generated from Operations | | 1,75,000 |
| (–) Tax Paid During the Year | | (70,000) |
| Cash Flow from Operating Activities | | 1,05,000 |
| B. **Cash Flow from Investing Activities** | | |
| Sale of Plant and Machinery | 50,000 | |
| Cash Flow from Investing Activities | | 50,000 |
| C. **Cash Flow from Financing Activities** | | |
| Issue of Share Capital | | 50,000 |
| Issue of 15% Debentures | | 2,00,000 |
| Interest on Debentures | | (75,000) |
| Cash flow from Financing Activities | | 1,75,000 |
| Net Increase in Cash and Cash Equivalents (A + B + C) | | 3,30,000 |
| (+) Cash and Cash Equivalents in the Beginning of the Year | | 1,40,000 |
| Cash and Cash Equivalents in the End of the Year | | 4,70,000 |

**Working Notes**

1. Calculation of Net Profit before Tax

| | |
|---|---|
| Net Profit after Appropriation and Tax [1,06,000 – (– 20,000)] | = 1,26,000 |
| (+) Provision for Tax | = 50,000 |
| Net Profit before Appropriation and Tax | 1,76,000 |

2. Interest on Debentures $= \left[\left(4{,}00{,}000 \times \frac{15}{100} \times \frac{6}{12}\right) + \left(6{,}00{,}000 \times \frac{15}{100} \times \frac{6}{12}\right)\right] = 30{,}000 + 45{,}000 =$ ₹ 75,000

3. Dr **Plant and Machinery Account** Cr

| Particulars | Amt (₹) | Particulars | Amt (₹) |
|---|---|---|---|
| To Balance b/d | 9,00,000 | By Accumulated Depreciation A/c | 38,000 |
| | | By Bank A/c | 50,000 |
| | | By Statement of Profit and Loss | 70,000 |
| | | By Balance c/d | 7,42,000 |
| | 9,00,000 | | 9,00,000 |

4. Dr **Accumulated Depreciation Account** Cr

| Particulars | Amt (₹) | Particulars | Amt (₹) |
|---|---|---|---|
| To Plant and Machinery A/c | 38,000 | By Balance b/d | 2,00,000 |
| To Balance c/d | 2,62,000 | By Depreciation A/c | 1,00,000 |
| | 3,00,000 | | 3,00,000 |

**14.** (i) Net Profit after Tax but before Preference Dividend = Net Profit before Tax – Tax

$= 20,00,000 - (30\% \times 20,00,000)$

$= 20,00,000 - 6,00,000$

$=$ ₹ 14,00,000

$$\text{Earning Per Share} = \frac{\text{Net Profit after Tax and Preference Dividend}}{\text{Number of Equity shares}}$$

Net Profit after Tax and Preference Dividend = EPS × Number of Equity Shares

$= 2.75 \times 4,00,000$

$=$ ₹ 11,00,000

Now, Preference Dividend = 14,00,000 – 11,00,000 = ₹ 3,00,000

(ii) **Total Current Assets**

| | Amt (₹) |
|---|---|
| Current Assets (Other than inventory of consumables, finished goods and WIP) | 3,229.23 |
| (+) Closing Inventory of Consumables (Raw materials) | 389.85 |
| Closing Inventory of Finished Goods and working-in-progress | 197.24 |
| Total Current Assets | 3,816.32 |

$$\text{Current Ratio} = \frac{\text{Current Assets}}{\text{Current Liabilities}} = \frac{3,816.32}{936.52} = 4.08:1$$

(iii) (a) $\text{Return on Investment} = \dfrac{\text{Net Profit before Interest and Tax}}{\text{Capital Employed}} \times 100$

(b) $20\% = \dfrac{\text{Net Profit before Interest and Tax}}{50,00,000}$

Net Profit before Interest and Tax $= 50,00,000 \times \dfrac{20}{100} =$ ₹ 10,00,000

(iv) Working Capital = Current Assets* – Current Liabilities** = 15,00,000 – 5,00,000 = ₹ 10,00,000

*Current Assets = 10,00,000 + 3,00,000 + 2,00,000 = ₹ 15,00,000

**Current Liabilities = ₹ 5,00,000

$$\text{Working Capital Turnover Ratio} = \frac{\text{Revenue from Operations ***}}{\text{Working Capital}} = \frac{15,00,000}{10,00,000} = 1.5 \text{ times}$$

***Revenue from Operations = Cost of Revenue from Operations + Gross Profit#

= 12,00,000 + 3,00,000 = ₹ 15,00,000

#Gross Profit $= 12,00,000 \times \dfrac{25}{100} =$ ₹ 3,00,000

# Proficiency Building Zone

## Welcome to the Proficiency Building Zone !

This section contains **15 Sample Question Papers** designed to enhance your problem-solving skills and proficiency. Use these papers to practice regularly and track your progress. Remember, consistent practice is key to mastering Accounts.

**Progress Tracker** Tick the papers as you complete them.

- ☐ Sample Paper 1 _____ (Fill your score)
- ☐ Sample Paper 2 _____ (Fill your score)
- ☐ Sample Paper 3 _____ (Fill your score)
- ☐ Sample Paper 4 _____ (Fill your score)
- ☐ Sample Paper 5 _____ (Fill your score)
- ☐ Sample Paper 6 _____ (Fill your score)
- ☐ Sample Paper 7 _____ (Fill your score)
- ☐ Sample Paper 8 _____ (Fill your score)
- ☐ Sample Paper 9 _____ (Fill your score)
- ☐ Sample Paper 10 _____ (Fill your score)
- ☐ Sample Paper 11 _____ (Fill your score)
- ☐ Sample Paper 12 _____ (Fill your score)
- ☐ Sample Paper 13 _____ (Fill your score)
- ☐ Sample Paper 14 _____ (Fill your score)
- ☐ Sample Paper 15 _____ (Fill your score)

SQP Code : **PB-1/15** Series ***i*-Succeed 1-25/15** Roll No. | | | | | | | | |

# Sample Question Paper 01

## Accounts 12th (Code 858)

### General Instructions

1. Candidates are allowed additional 15 minutes for only reading the paper. They must not start writing during this time.
2. Section-A is compulsory for all candidates and has ten questions.
3. Candidates have to attempt all questions from either Section-B or Section-C*.
4. Internal choices have been provided in five questions in Section-A and one question in Section-B.
5. The intended marks for questions or parts of questions are given in the brackets [ ].
6. All calculations should be shown clearly.
7. All workings, including rough work, should be done on the same page as, and adjacent to, the rest of the answer.

*Section-C has not been covered.

**Time :** 3 Hrs.

**Max. Marks :** 80

## Section A Answer All Questions [60 Marks]

**Que 1.**

In sub-parts (i) to (iv), choose the correct option and in sub-parts (v) to (x) answer the questions as instructed.

(i) Choose the correct sequence of the following in relation to the division of profit. (Recall) [1]

A – Transfer to reserve.
B – Transfer of net profit to profit and loss appropriation account.
C – Interest on loan by partner.
D – Distribution of profit among the partners.

**Codes**

(a) A, B, C, D (b) C, A, B, D
(c) D, B, A, C (d) C, B, A, D

(ii) X, Y, Z are partners sharing profits and losses in the ratio of 2:2:1. 'Z' retires on 31st December, 2023.

The following is the extract of the balance sheet of the firm at as 31 December, 2023.

| Liabilities | Amt (₹) | Assets | Amt (₹) |
|---|---|---|---|
| | | Land and Building | 20,00,000 |

How will you show that effect of change in value of land and building in revaluation account if land and building is revalued at ₹ 24,00,000? (Application) [1]

(a) Land and Building A/c ₹ 4,00,000 (Cr)
(b) Land and Building A/c ₹ 4,00,000 (Dr)
(c) Land and Building A/c ₹ 24,00,000 (Cr)
(d) Land and Building A/c ₹ 24,00,000 (Dr)

(iii) Sita and Gita are partners in a firm. Sita had given a loan of ₹ 20,000 to the firm. How will Sita's loan be closed in event of dissolution of the firm? (Understanding) [1]

(a) Sita's Loan A/c Dr 20,000
To Sita's Capital A/c 20,000

(b) Sita's Loan A/c Dr 20,000
To Realisation A/c 20,000

(c) Sita's Capital A/c Dr 20,000
To Sita's Loan A/c 20,000

(d) Sita's Loan A/c Dr 20,000
To Cash A/c 20,000

(iv) Godrej Limited which is listed on stock exchange has 8,000, 9% debentures of ₹ 100 each due for redemption at 5% premium in three annual instalments starting from 31st March, 2023.

Identify the amount to be transferred to debenture redemption reserve account on 31st March, 2022. **(Application) [1]**

(a) ₹ 80,000 (b) ₹ 2,00,000
(c) ₹ 20,000 (d) Nil

(v) Retirement of one partner amounts to dissolution of partnership firm.

**Source** *Livelaw.in.*

State under what circumstances this situation is possible? **(Understanding) [1]**

(vi) **Assertion** (A) Companies may use a combined account for share application and allotment called 'share application and allotment account'.

**Reason** (R) Allotment without application is impossible while application without allotment is meaningless. **(Evaluate) [1]**

**Alternatives**

(a) Both Assertion (A) and Reason (R) are true and Reason (R) is the correct explanation of Assertion (A)
(b) Both Assertion (A) and Reason (R) are true, but Reason (R) is not the correct explanation of Assertion (A)
(c) Assertion (A) is true, but Reason (R) is false
(d) Assertion (A) is false, but Reason (R) is true

SP-01

(vii) The profit of PQR & Co. for the year ended 31st March, 2023 is ₹ 60,000 before considering rent of ₹ 4,000 to a partner. Ascertain the net profit transferred to the profit and loss appropriation account. **(Application) [1]**

(viii) You are required to pass journal entries for the issue of debentures if Supertech Cements Ltd. issued ₹ 2,00,000, 12% debentures of ₹ 100 each at a discount of 2% redeemable at a premium of 5% after 10 years. **(Application) [1]**

(ix) Lavanya and Priyanka were partners sharing profits in the ratio of 3 : 1. They decided to dissolve their firm.

At the time of dissolution, workmen compensation reserve stood at ₹ 2,00,000 in the balance sheet while liability in respect of it was ascertained at ₹ 2,50,000. You are required to pass the necessary journal entry at the time of dissolution. **(Application) [1]**

(x) The notes to accounts should also contain information about items that do not qualify for recognition in financial statements. These disclosures normally refer to items such as contingent liabilities.

**Source** *Guidance note on Schedule III Companies Act, 2013*

(a) What are contingent liabilities?
(b) Based on the above information, how are the contingent liabilities shown in the balance sheet of a company? **(Recall) [1]**

**Que 2.**

X, Y and Z are partners in a firm sharing profits and losses in the ratio of 2 : 2 : 1. Z dies on 1st April, 2021.

On the date of his death, it was decided to value goodwill on the basis of two year's purchases of weighted average profit of the firm for the last three years. The profit of the last three years and weights assigned were

| Year | Profit (₹) | Weights Assigned |
|---|---|---|
| 2019 | 69,000 | 1 |
| 2020 | 1,84,000 | 2 |
| 2021 | 2,30,000 | 3 |

Gain from speculation ₹ 23,000 is included in 2019 profit. You are required to

(i) Calculate the firm's goodwill on the date of Z's death.
(ii) Calculate the amount to be credited to Z's capital account with his share of goodwill. **(Application) [3]**

*Or*

R, K and N are partners sharing profits and losses in the ratio of 5 : 3 : 2. Their balance sheet as at 1st April, 2021 was as follows

**Balance Sheet**
as at 1st April, 2021

| Liabilities | | Amt (₹) | Assets | Amt (₹) |
|---|---|---|---|---|
| Capital A/cs | | | Bank | 45,000 |
| R | 54,000 | | Building | 45,000 |
| K | 36,000 | | Plant and Machinery | 27,000 |
| N | 36,000 | 1,26,000 | Investments | 18,000 |
| General Reserve | | 18,000 | Debtors | 18,000 |
| Creditors | | 12,600 | Stock | 9,000 |
| Bills Payable | | 5,400 | | |
| | | 1,62,000 | | 1,62,000 |

K decided to retire on the following terms

(i) He sells his share of goodwill to R for ₹ 14,400 and to N for ₹ 7,200.

(ii) Stock to be appreciated by 20% and building by ₹ 9,000.

(iii) Investments were sold for ₹ 39,600.

(iv) K is paid-off in cash.

If the profit on account of revaluation of assets and reassessment of liabilities is ₹ 32,400,

(a) Prepare partners' capital account

(b) Bank account (Application)

**Que. 3.**

Nath Ltd. issued ₹ 40,00,000, 9% debentures @ ₹ 100/debenture on 1st April, 2019 at a premium of 6%, redeemable at a premium of 10% on 31st March, 2023.

Assume that required investment was made in 10% government securities on 30th April of the financial year in which redemption is due. Debentures were redeemed on the due date. Pass journal entries at the time of redemption of debentures. (Application) [3]

**Que. 4.**

Sarika and Sagarika were partners in a firm with fixed capitals of ₹ 10,00,000 and 8,00,000 respectively.

It was discovered that interest on capital @ 6% p.a. was credited to the partners for the two years ending 31st March, 2022 and 31st March, 2023 while there was no such provision in the partnership deed.

Their profit sharing ratio during the last two years was 2021-2022 – 4 : 5, 2022-2023 – 5 : 1.

(i) Calculate the profit to be credited in 2022.

(ii) Calculate the amount to be adjusted.

(iii) Pass the necessary adjustment entry to rectify the error. (Application) [3]

**Que 5.**

Aakash Ltd. issued 10,000, 8% debentures of ₹ 100 each at a premium of 10% on 1st April, 2022. It purchased fixed assets of the value of ₹ 2,50,000 and took over current liabilities of ₹ 40,000 and issued 8% debentures at a premium of 5% to the vendor. On the same date, it took loan from the bank for ₹ 1,00,000 and issued 8% debentures as collateral security.

(i) You are required to give the amounts payable to

(a) Vendors (b) Debenture suspense [2]

(ii) Prepare securities premium account. (Application) [1]

*Or*

Sangam Ltd. issued 7,000, 10% debentures of ₹ 500 each at a premium of ₹ 50 per debenture redeemable at a premium of 10% after 5 years. According to the terms of issue, 200 was payable on application and balance on allotment. Record necessary journal entries at the time of issue of 10% debentures. (Application) [3]

**Que 6.**

Ram, Vijay and Jayant were partners in a firm sharing profits and losses in the ratio of 2 : 1 : 2.

Their firm was incurring huge losses thus it had to be closed. After transferring assets (other than cash in hand and cash at bank) and third party liabilities to realisation account, the following transactions took place

(i) Ram took away 50% of the stock at book value less 10% for ₹ 45,000 and the remaining stock was sold for ₹ 20,000.

(ii) Creditors of ₹ 78,000 took over machinery of ₹ 80,000 in full settlement of their claim.

(iii) Mrs. Jayant's loan of ₹ 36,000 was paid by the firm.

(iv) ₹ 2,500 debtors previously written-off were now recovered.

(v) Loss on dissolution was ₹ 40,000.

Pass necessary journal entries for the above transactions in the books of Ram, Vijay and Jayant. (Application) [6]

**Que 7.**

Under which head and sub-head will the following items appear in the balance sheet of the company as per Schedule III of the Companies Act, 2013.

(i) Debentures
(ii) Securities premium
(iii) Forfeited shares account
(iv) Bills payable
(v) Unclaimed dividend
(vi) Calls-in-arrears (Application) [6]

SP-01

**Que 8.**

Tom, Jack and Romy were partners in a firm having capitals of ₹ 60,000, ₹ 60,000 and ₹ 80,000 respectively. Their current account balances were Tom ₹ 10,000, Jack ₹ 5,000 and Romy ₹ 2,000 (Dr).

According to the partnership deed, the partners were entitled to an interest on capital @ 5% per annum.

Romy being the working partner was also entitled to a salary of ₹ 6,000 per annum. The profits were to be divided as follows

(i) The first ₹ 20,000 in proportion to their capitals.

(ii) Next ₹ 30,000 in the ratio of 3 : 5 : 2.

(iii) Remaining profits to be shared equally.

During the year, the firm made a profit of ₹ 1,56,000 before charging any of the above items.

Prepare the profit and loss appropriation account. (Application) [6]

*Or*

Sameer and Yasmin are partners with capitals of ₹ 15,00,000 and ₹ 10,00,000 respectively. They agree to share profits in the ratio of 3:2. Show how the following transactions will be recorded in the capital accounts of the partners in case

(i) The capitals are fixed. [5]

(ii) The capitals are fluctuating. (Application) [1]

The books are closed on 31st December every year.

| Particulars | Sameer (₹) | Yasmin (₹) |
|---|---|---|
| Additional Capital Contributed on 1st July, 2022 | 3,00,000 | 2,00,000 |
| Interest on Capital | 5% | 5% |
| Drawings (During 2022) | 30,000 | 20,000 |
| Interest on Drawings | 1,800 | 1,200 |
| Salary | 20,000 | 7,000 |
| Commission | 10,000 | — |
| Share in Loss for the Year 2022 | 60,000 | 40,000 |

**Que 9.**

Premium Ltd. issued 80,000 equity shares of ₹ 10 each at a premium of ₹ 2.50 per share. The amount was payable as follows

| | |
|---|---|
| On application | ₹ 2 per share |
| On allotment | ₹ 4.50 per share (including premium) |
| On call | Balance ₹ 6 per share |

Owing to heavy subscription, the allotment was made on pro-rata basis as follows

(i) Applications for 40,000 shares were allotted 20,000 shares.

(ii) Applications for 1,12,000 shares were allotted 28,000 shares.

(iii) Applications for 96,000 shares were allotted 32,000 shares.

It was decided that excess amount received on applications would be utilised on allotment and the surplus would be refunded.

Golu, to whom 2,000 shares were allotted, who belongs to category (i), failed to pay allotment money. His shares were forfeited after the call.

Pass necessary journal entries in the books of Premium Ltd. for the above transactions.
(Application) [10]

*Or*

Following information is provided to you.

A company issued shares for ₹ 1,10,000 and the amount payable was as follows

₹ 4 per share on application

₹ 4 per share (including ₹ 1 premium) on allotment

Balance ₹ 2 on final call

(i) What are the number of shares applied for? [1]

(ii) What is total amount payable on allotment? [1]

(iii) The company did not receive the allotment money and call money on the 3,000 shares from Amit. What is the amount received by the company on allotment? [1]

(iv) What is amount transferred to calls-in-arrears account? [2]

(v) The company forfeited Amit's 3,000 shares and re-issued 2,000 @ ₹ 9 per share. You are required to give journal entries for

(a) Forfeiture of Amit's shares [2]

(b) Re-issue of the forfeited shares (Application) [3]

**Que 10.**

Anand and Bheem share profits and losses in the ratio of 3 : 2. Their balance sheet as at 31st March, 2021 was as follows

**Balance Sheet**
as at 31st March, 2021

| Liabilities | | Amt (₹) | Assets | Amt (₹) |
|---|---|---|---|---|
| Provision for Doubtful Debts | | 2,000 | Cash at Bank | 15,000 |
| Bank Overdraft | | 60,000 | Sundry Debtors | 50,000 |
| Sundry Creditors | | 63,000 | Stock | 1,00,000 |
| Capital A/cs | | | Building | 1,65,000 |
| Anand | 1,50,000 | | Profit and Loss A/c | 45,000 |
| Bheem | 1,00,000 | 2,50,000 | | |
| | | 3,75,000 | | 3,75,000 |

Naveen is admitted into partnership on the following terms

(i) The provision for doubtful debts is to be raised to ₹ 5,000.

(ii) Stock be depreciated by ₹ 12,500.

(iii) Provision be made for outstanding expenses amounting to ₹ 7,000.

(iv) New profit sharing ratio will be 3 : 2 : 4 and Naveen will pay ₹ 1,00,000 as his capital.

(v) Goodwill of the firm is valued at ₹ 1,12,500 but Naveen is unable to bring any amount for goodwill.

(vi) Capitals of old partners be adjusted on the basis of new partner's capital. Any excess or deficiency be adjusted by payment or receipt of amount.

(a) Calculate the gaining/sacrificing ratio of old partners. (Application) [2]

(b) Pass journal entries related to Naveen's capital and his share of goodwill. (Recall) [2]

(c) Pass the journal entry for the profit/loss on revaluation transferred to partners' capital account. (Application) [2]

(d) Prepare partners' capital account. (Application) [2]

(e) Pass the necessary entry for the excess or deficiency transferred to the bank. (Application) [2]

SP-01

*Or*

(A) A and B are partners in a firm sharing profits in the ratio of 3 : 2. Their balance sheet as at 31st December, 2021 stood as under

**Balance Sheet**
as at 31st December, 2021

| Liabilities | | Amt (₹) | Assets | | Amt (₹) |
|---|---|---|---|---|---|
| Capital A/cs | | | Machinery | | 33,000 |
| A | 35,000 | | Furniture | | 15,000 |
| B | 30,000 | 65,000 | Investments | | 20,000 |
| General Reserve | | 10,000 | Stock | | 23,000 |
| Bank Loan | | 9,000 | Debtors | 19,000 | |
| Sundry Creditors | | 36,000 | (–) Provision for Doubtful Debts | (2,000) | 17,000 |
| | | | Cash | | 12,000 |
| | | 1,20,000 | | | 1,20,000 |

On that date, they admitted C into partnership for 1/4th share in the profit on the following terms

(i) C brings capital proportionate to his share. He brings ₹ 7,000 in cash as his share of goodwill.
(ii) Debtors are all good.
(iii) Depreciate stock by 5% and furniture by 10%. Market value of machinery was ₹ 45,000.
(iv) An outstanding bill for repair ₹ 1,000 will be brought in books.
(v) Half of the investments were to be taken over by A and B in their profit sharing ratio at book value.
(vi) Bank loan is paid-off.
(vii) Partners agreed to share future profits in ratio 3 : 3 : 2.
(viii) Capital of the firm is fixed at ₹ 1,60,000. Excees or shortfall, if any, to be transferred to current accounts.

(a) Calculate gain/sacrifice of the old partners and prepare revaluation account. [1½]
(b) Prepare partners' capital account. [4½]
(c) Prepare cash account. [2]

(B) Sonu and Monu are partners sharing profits and losses in the ratio of 3 : 2. Tanu is admitted for $\frac{1}{5}$th share of profits. After a while Deenu also enters for $\frac{1}{4}$th share. Calculate the new ratio of Sonu, Monu, Tanu and Deenu. (Application) [2]

SP-01

## Section B

**[20 Marks]**

**Que 11.**

(i) Tata Power looks to fund its capital expenditure (capex) through debt and cash flow generated from its multiple businesses, said company chairman N Chandrasekaran. The chairman was addressing the company's shareholders at its annual general meeting.

**Source** *business standards*

Keeping in view the various inflows and outflows of cash, suggest if a mutual fund company receives a dividend of ₹ 5,00,000 on its investments in PQR Ltd. company's shares

- Whether it will be a inflow or outflow of cash? (Recall)
- Where will it appear in a cash flow statement? (Analysis) [1]

(a) Cash flow from operating activities (b) Cash flow from investing activities
(c) Cash flow from financing activities (d) No cash flow

(ii) It is important to judge the scope of a stock and its growth potential by checking the key financial ratios of the company and comparing them with the industry standards. Every ratio helps in ascertaining various decisions for the company. But despite of its importance, it has a few limitations as well.

**Source** *Livemint (edited)*

Which of the following are limitations of ratio analysis? (Analysis) [1]

A. Ratio analysis may result in false results if variations in price levels are not considered.

B. Ratio analysis ignores qualitative factors.

C. Ratio analysis ignores quantitative factors.

D. Ratio analysis is historical analysis.

**Codes**

(a) A, B and D
(b) A, C and D
(c) A, B and C
(d) A, B , C, D

(iii) "A solid debt to income ratio is an important indicator for overall financial well-being," says Ohan Kayikchyan, a certified financial planner and economist.

**Source** *US news*

The debt equity ratio of a company is 1 : 2. What will be the effect of issue of debentures for cash? (Analysis) [1]

(iv) Each time Apple Inc. (ticker: AAPL) sells an iPhone, the company's cash flow from operating activities increases. iPhones are one of the components of Apple's operating business and more sales equate to a higher cash flow from operating activities.

**Source** *Business news(edited)*

Based on this news, what feature of cash flow statement can be depicted? (Analysis) [1]

(v) Tata Motors operating income during the year fell 4.3% on a Year-on-Year (YoY) basis. The company's operating profit increased by 3.8% YoY during the fiscal. Operating profit margins witnessed a fall and down at 6.2% in FY21 as against 5.7% in FY20. Depreciation charges increased by 9.9% and finance costs increased by 11.8% YoY, respectively. Other income grew by 77.1% YoY.

**Source** *Equity master.com(edited)*

(a) Trade receivables are ₹ 43,000 and total of asset side of balance sheet is ₹ 4,39,000. What will be the percentage of trade receivables as per common size statement of balance sheet?

(b) If opening inventory is ₹ 1,50,000 crore and closing inventory ₹ 60,000 crore, what amount will be shown in the statement of profit and loss as changes in inventory? (Application) [1]

SP-01

**Que 12.**

From the following information,prepare a comparative statement of profit and loss of V Ltd. for the year ended 31st March, 2024. (Application) [3]

| Particulars | 31st March, 2024 | 31st March, 2023 |
|---|---|---|
| Revenue from Operations | ₹ 10,00,000 | ₹ 5,00,000 |
| Cost of Material Consumed | ₹ 7,50,000 | ₹ 3,00,000 |
| Tax Rate | 40% | 30% |

**Que 13.**

Answer any three of the following questions (Application) [6]

(i) Calculate trade receivables turnover ratio from the following information

| | |
|---|---|
| Trade receivables in the beginning of the year | ₹ 1,66,000 |
| Trade receivables at the end of the year | ₹ 2,34,000 |
| Gross revenue from operations | ₹ 18,00,000 |
| Revenue from operations returns | ₹ 2,00,000 |

(ii) Calculate debt to total asset ratio from the following information

| | |
|---|---|
| Equity share capital | ₹ 10,00,000 |
| 9% preference share capital | ₹ 8,00,000 |
| Property, plant and equipment | ₹ 24,00,000 |
| Non-current investments | ₹ 3,00,000 |
| Reserves and surplus | ₹ 4,80,000 |
| Current assets | ₹ 3,80,000 |
| Current liabilities | ₹ 2,00,000 |

(iii) From the following information, calculate proprietary ratio

| | |
|---|---|
| 9% debentures | ₹ 3,00,000 |
| Long-term provision | ₹ 1,50,000 |
| Current liabilities | ₹ 75,000 |
| Property, plant and equipment and intangible assets | ₹ 5,40,000 |
| Current assets | ₹ 1,35,000 |

(iv) Following figures are extracted from the books of ABC Ltd.

| Particulars | Amt (₹) |
|---|---|
| Cost of Revenue from Operation | 1,90,000 |
| Revenue from Operations | 25,00,000 |
| Number of Units Sold | 10,000 |

Find out the gross profit ratio.

**Que 14.**

Following are the Balance Sheets of Amol Ltd. Prepare cash flow from operating activities and investing activities. (Application) [6]

| Particulars | Note No. | 31st March, 2023 (₹) | 31st March, 2022 (₹) |
|---|---|---|---|
| I. **EQUITY AND LIABILITIES** | | | |
| 1. **Shareholders' Funds** | | | |
| (i) Share Capital | | 4,00,000 | 3,00,000 |
| (ii) Reserves and Surplus | 1 | 58,000 | 50,000 |
| 2. **Non-current Liabilities** | | | |
| Long-term Borrowings (Mortgage loan) | | 1,40,000 | 1,70,000 |
| 3. **Current Liabilities** | | | |
| Trade Payables | | 1,48,000 | 1,25,000 |
| **Total** | | 7,46,000 | 6,45,000 |
| II. **ASSETS** | | | |
| 1. **Non-current Assets** | | | |
| Property, Plant & Equipment and Intangible Assets | 2 | 3,41,000 | 2,32,000 |

SP-01

| Particulars | Note No. | 31st March, 2023 (₹) | 31st March, 2022 (₹) |
|---|---|---|---|
| 2. **Current Assets** | | | |
| (i) Inventories | | 2,80,000 | 2,00,000 |
| (ii) Trade Receivables | | 1,07,000 | 1,30,000 |
| (iii) Other Current Assets (Share issue expenses) | | — | 3,000 |
| (iv) Cash and Cash Equivalents | 3 | 18,000 | 80,000 |
| **Total** | | 7,46,000 | 6,45,000 |

**Notes to Accounts**

| Particulars | 31st March, 2023 (₹) | 31st March, 2022 (₹) |
|---|---|---|
| 1. **Reserves and Surplus** | | |
| Surplus, i.e. Balance in Statement of Profit and Loss | 58,000 | 50,000 |
| 2. **Property, Plant and Equipment and Intangible Assets** | | |
| Plant | 2,96,000 | 1,72,000 |
| Goodwill | 45,000 | 60,000 |
| | 3,41,000 | 2,32,000 |
| 3. **Cash and Cash Equivalents** | | |
| Cash in Hand | 16,000 | 50,000 |
| Cash at Bank | 2,000 | 30,000 |
| | 18,000 | 80,000 |

*Or* Following are the Balance Sheets of Mittal Ltd. as at 31st March, 2022 and 2023

| Particulars | Note No. | 2022-23 (₹) | 2021-22 (₹) |
|---|---|---|---|
| I. **EQUITY AND LIABILITIES** | | | |
| 1. **Shareholders' Funds** | | | |
| (i) Share Capital | | 14,00,000 | 10,00,000 |
| (ii) Reserves and Surplus | 1 | 5,00,000 | 4,00,000 |
| 2. **Non-current Liabilities** | | | |
| Long-term Borrowings | 2 | 6,00,000 | 2,00,000 |
| 3. **Current Liabilities** | | | |
| Short-term Provisions | 3 | 80,000 | 60,000 |
| **Total** | | 25,80,000 | 16,60,000 |
| II. **ASSETS** | | | |
| 1. **Non-current Assets** | | | |
| (i) Property, Plant & Equipment and Intangible Assets | | | |
| (a) Property, Plant and Equipment | 4 | 16,00,000 | 9,00,000 |
| (b) Intangible Assets | 5 | 1,40,000 | 2,00,000 |
| 2. **Current Assets** | | | |
| (i) Inventories | | 2,50,000 | 2,00,000 |
| (ii) Trade Receivables | | 5,00,000 | 3,00,000 |
| (iii) Cash and Cash Equivalents | | 90,000 | 60,000 |
| **Total** | | 25,80,000 | 16,60,000 |

**Notes to Accounts**

| Particulars | 31st March, 2022-23 (₹) | 31st March, 2021-22 (₹) |
|---|---|---|
| 1. **Reserves and Surplus** | | |
| Surplus (Balance in statement of profit and loss) | 5,00,000 | 4,00,000 |
| 2. **Long-term Borrowings** | | |
| 9% Deposits | 6,00,000 | 2,00,000 |
| 3. **Short-term Provisions** | | |
| Provision for Tax | 80,000 | 60,000 |
| 4. **Property, Plant and Equipment** | | |
| Machinery | 16,00,000 | 9,00,000 |
| 5. **Intangible Assets** | | |
| Goodwill | 1,40,000 | 2,00,000 |

Prepare a cash flow statement after taking into account the following adjustments

(i) The company paid interest ₹ 45,000 on its deposits.

(ii) Depreciation provided on machinery during the year ₹ 2,00,000.

(iii) Tax paid during the year ₹ 30,000.

(a) Find out the value of net profit before tax. [2]

(b) After reviewing the given information, state how much will be the cash generated from operating activities. [2]

(c) Calculate cash flow from financing activity. (Evaluate) [2]

# Solutions *in Topper's Style*

My Commitment *I affirm that I am reviewing these solutions only after I have solved the Sample Question Paper 1 on my own. My purpose of looking the solutions is solely to verify whether my answers/solutions were correct or not and to identify my mistakes in case my solutions were wrong or I could not solve that.*

1. (i) (*d*) C, B, A, D

(ii) (*a*) Profit on revaluation = 24,00,000 – 20,00,000 = ₹ 4,00,000

(iii) (*d*) Loan taken from a partner will be passed through cash or bank account even if the partner's capital has a debit balance.

| | | | |
|---|---|---|---|
| Sita's Loan A/c | Dr | 20,000 | |
| To Cash A/c | | | 20,000 |

(iv) (*d*) Since Godrej Limited is listed on stock exchange, it does not require to transfer its profit to DRR.

(v) When firm consists of only two partners.

(vi) (*a*) Both Assertion (A) and Reason (R) are true and Reason (R) is the correct explanation of Assertion (A)

(vii) Net Profit = 60,000 – 4,000 = ₹ 56,000

(viii) **JOURNAL**

| Date | Particulars | | LF | Amt (Dr) | Amt (Cr) |
|---|---|---|---|---|---|
| | Bank A/c | Dr | | 1,96,000 | |
| | To Debenture Application and Allotment A/c | | | | 1,96,000 |
| | (Being the application money received) | | | | |
| | Debenture Application and Allotment A/c | Dr | | 1,96,000 | |
| | Loss on Issue of Debentures A/c (4,000 + 10,000) | Dr | | 14,000 | |
| | To 12% Debentures A/c | | | | 2,00,000 |
| | To Premium on Redemption of Debentures A/c | | | | 10,000 |
| | (Being the debentures issued at discount, redeemable at premium) | | | | |

(ix) **JOURNAL**

| Date | Particulars | | LF | Amt (Dr) | Amt (Cr) |
|---|---|---|---|---|---|
| | Workmen Compensation Reserve A/c | Dr | | 2,00,000 | |
| | To Realisation A/c | | | | 2,00,000 |
| | (Being the workmen compensation reserve transferred to realisation account) | | | | |
| | Realisation A/c | Dr | | 2,50,000 | |
| | To Bank A/c | | | | 2,50,000 |
| | (Being the payment made of liability on account of workmen compensation) | | | | |

(x) (a) Contingent liabilities are those liabilities which may or may not arise as they are dependent on the happening of an event in future.

(b) Contingent liabilities are shown as a footnote to the balance sheet of a company.

2. (i) **Calculation of Weighted Average Profit**

| Year | Actual Profit (X) | Weight (W) | Product (WX) |
|---|---|---|---|
| 2019 | 69,000 – 23,000 = 46,000 | 1 | 46,000 |
| 2020 | 1,84,000 | 2 | 3,68,000 |
| 2021 | 2,30,000 | 3 | 6,90,000 |
| **Total** | | 6 | 11,04,000 |

$$\text{Weighted Average Profit} = \frac{\text{Total of Product}}{\text{Total of Weight}} = \frac{11,04,000}{6} = ₹\ 1,84,000$$

Goodwill = Weighted Average Profit × Number of Years' Purchase

= 1,84,000 × 2 = ₹ 3,68,000

(ii) Z's share of goodwill = 3,68,000 × $\frac{1}{5}$ = ₹ 73,600

To be distributed among X and Y in gaining ratio, i.e. 2 : 2 *or* 1 : 1.

*Or* (a) Dr **Partners' Capital Account** Cr

| Particulars | R (₹) | K (₹) | N (₹) | Particulars | R (₹) | K (₹) | N (₹) |
|---|---|---|---|---|---|---|---|
| To K's Capital A/c | 14,400 | — | 7,200 | By Balance b/d | 54,000 | 36,000 | 36,000 |
| To Bank A/c | — | 72,720 | — | By General Reserve A/c | 9,000 | 5,400 | 3,600 |
| To Balance c/d | 64,800 | — | 38,880 | By Revaluation (Profit) | 16,200 | 9,720 | 6,480 |
| | | | | By R's Capital A/c | — | 14,400 | — |
| | | | | By N's Capital A/c | — | 7,200 | — |
| | 79,200 | 72,720 | 46,080 | | 79,200 | 72,720 | 46,080 |

(b) Dr **Bank Account** Cr

| Particulars | Amt (₹) | Particulars | Amt (₹) |
|---|---|---|---|
| To Balance b/d | 45,000 | By K's Capital A/c | 72,720 |
| To Investment | 39,600 | By Balance c/d | 11,880 |
| | 84,600 | | 84,600 |

**Value Point**

- Since individual share of goodwill is given, sacrificing ratio will be computed using that share.

3. **In the Books of Nath Ltd.**

**JOURNAL**

| Date | Particulars | | LF | Amt (Dr) | Amt (Cr) |
|---|---|---|---|---|---|
| 2022 | | | | | |
| Mar 31 | Surplus in Statement of Profit and Loss | Dr | | 4,00,000 | |
| | To Debenture Redemption Reserve A/c | | | | 4,00,000 |
| | (Being the transfer of profits equal to 10% of the nominal value of debentures outstanding) | | | | |
| Apr 30 | Debenture Redemption Investment A/c | Dr | | 6,00,000 | |
| | To Bank A/c | | | | 6,00,000 |
| | (Being the investment made @ 15% of the face value of debentures to be redeemed) | | | | |
| 2023 | | | | | |
| Mar 31 | Bank A/c | Dr | | 6,55,000 | |
| | To Debenture Redemption Investment A/c | | | | 6,00,000 |
| | To Interest Received A/c | | | | 55,000 |
| | (Being the investment bearing 10% p.a. interest encashed) | | | | |
| Mar 31 | 9% Debentures A/c | Dr | | 40,00,000 | |
| | Premium on Redemption of Debentures A/c | Dr | | 4,00,000 | |
| | To Debentureholders' A/c | | | | 44,00,000 |
| | (Being the amount due on redemption) | | | | |
| Mar 31 | Debentureholders' A/c | Dr | | 44,00,000 | |
| | To Bank A/c | | | | 44,00,000 |
| | (Being the payment of amount due to debentureholders) | | | | |

| Date | Particulars | | LF | Amt (Dr) | Amt (Cr) |
|---|---|---|---|---|---|
| Mar 31 | Debenture Redemption Reserve A/c | Dr | | 4,00,000 | |
| | To General Reserve A/c | | | | 4,00,000 |
| | (Being the transfer of debenture redemption reserve account to general reserve account on redemption) | | | | |
| Mar 31 | Interest Received A/c | Dr | | 55,000 | |
| | To Statement of Profit and Loss | | | | 55,000 |
| | (Being the transfer of interest on investments) | | | | |

**Common Mistake** Students normally calculate interest on government securities for the whole year. Since the investment is done on 30th April, interest will be calculated for 11 months only.

4. (i) Calculation of profit to be credited to partners in the year 2022

Total Profit (4 : 5) = Interest on capital of Sarika and Sagarika which was wrongly debited

= 60,000 + 48,000 = ₹ 1,08,000

Sarika's share = $1,08,000 \times \frac{4}{9}$ = ₹ 48,000 ; Sagarika's share = $1,08,000 \times \frac{5}{9}$ = ₹ 60,000

(ii) **Calculation of Amount to be Adjusted**

| Particulars | Sarika (₹) | Sagar (₹) | Total (₹) |
|---|---|---|---|
| Interest on Capital to Debited (2 years) | 1,20,000 | 96,000 | 2,16,000 |
| Profit to be Credited | | | |
| 2022 : 1,08,000 (4 : 5) | 48,000 | 60,000 | 1,08,000 |
| 2023 : 1,08,000 (5 : 1) | 90,000 | 18,000 | 1,08,000 |
| | 1,38,000 | 78,000 | 2,16,000 |
| Amount to be Adjusted | 18,000 (Cr) | 18,000 (Dr) | – |

(iii) **JOURNAL**

| Date | Particulars | | LF | Amt (Dr) | Amt (Cr) |
|---|---|---|---|---|---|
| | Sagar's Current A/c | Dr | | 18,000 | |
| | To Sarika's Current A/c | | | | 18,000 |
| | (Being adjustment entry passed) | | | | |

5. (i) (a) Amount payable to Vendors = Fixed Assets – Current Liabilities

= 2,50,000 – 40,000 = ₹ 2,10,000

(b) Amount to be adjusted in debenture suspense account will be the amount of debentures issued as collateral security

∴ = ₹ 1,00,000

(ii) Dr **Securities Premium Account** Cr

| Date | Particulars | Amt (₹) | Date | Particulars | Amt (₹) |
|---|---|---|---|---|---|
| 2022 | | | 2022 | | |
| Mar 31 | To Balance c/d | 1,10,000 | Apr 1 | By Debenture Application and Allotment A/c | 1,00,000 |
| | | | Apr 1 | By Vendor's | 10,000 |
| | | 1,10,000 | | | 1,10,000 |

*Or*

**JOURNAL**

| Date | Particulars | | LF | Amt (Dr) | Amt (Cr) |
|---|---|---|---|---|---|
| | Bank A/c (7,000 × 200) | Dr | | 14,00,000 | |
| | To Debenture Application A/c | | | | 14,00,000 |
| | (Being the receipt of debenture application money) | | | | |
| | Debenture Application A/c (7,000 × 200) | Dr | | 14,00,000 | |
| | To 10% Debentures A/c | | | | 14,00,000 |
| | (Being application money transferred) | | | | |
| | Debenture Allotment A/c (7,000 × 350) | Dr | | 24,50,000 | |
| | Loss on Issue of Debentures A/c (7,000 × 50) | Dr | | 3,50,000 | |
| | To 10% Debentures A/c (7,000 × 300) | | | | 21,00,000 |
| | To Securities Premium Reserve (7,000 × 50) | | | | 3,50,000 |
| | To Premium on Redemption of Debentures A/c (7,000 × 50) | | | | 3,50,000 |
| | (Being issue of debentures at premium redeemable at premium, recorded) | | | | |
| | Bank A/c (7,000 × 350) | Dr | | 24,50,000 | |
| | To Debenture Allotment A/c | | | | 24,50,000 |
| | (Being the receipt of debenture allotment money) | | | | |

**6.**

**JOURNAL**

| Date | Particulars | | LF | Amt (Dr) | Amt (Cr) |
|---|---|---|---|---|---|
| (i) | Ram's Capital A/c | Dr | | 45,000 | |
| | To Realisation A/c | | | | 45,000 |
| | (Being 50% stock taken over by Ram) | | | | |
| | Cash A/c | Dr | | 20,000 | |
| | To Realisation A/c | | | | 20,000 |
| | (Being remaining stock sold for cash) | | | | |
| (ii) | No entry will be passed | | | | |
| (iii) | Realisation A/c | Dr | | 36,000 | |
| | To Cash A/c | | | | 36,000 |
| | (Being Mrs. Jayant paid by firm) | | | | |
| (iv) | Cash A/c | Dr | | 2,500 | |
| | To Realisation A/c | | | | 2,500 |
| | (Being debtors previously written-off recovered) | | | | |
| (v) | Ram's Capital A/c | Dr | | 16,000 | |
| | Vijay's Capital A/c | Dr | | 8,000 | |
| | Jayant's Capital A/c | Dr | | 16,000 | |
| | To Realisation A/c | | | | 40,000 |
| | (Being loss on realisation transferred to partner's capital) | | | | |

**7.**

| S.No. | Heads | Major Heads | Sub-heads |
|---|---|---|---|
| (i) | Debentures | Non-current Liabilities | Long-term Borrowings |
| (ii) | Securities Premium | Shareholders' Funds | Reserves and Surplus |
| (iii) | Forfeited Shares Account | Shareholders' Funds | Subscribed Capital Subscribed but not Fully Paid-up (Shown by way of addition) |
| (iv) | Bills Payable | Current Liabilities | Trade Payables |
| (v) | Unclaimed Dividend | Current Liabilities | Other Current Liabilities |
| (vi) | Calls-in-arrears | Shareholders' Funds | Subscribed Capital Subscribed but not Fully Paid-up (Shown by way of deduction) |

8.

**Profit and Loss Appropriation Account**
**for the year ended......**

| Dr Particulars | | Amt (₹) | Particulars | Cr Amt (₹) |
|---|---|---|---|---|
| To Interest on Capital A/cs | | | By Net Profit as per Profit and Loss A/c | 1,56,000 |
| Tom (60,000 × 5%) | 3,000 | | | |
| Jack (60,000 × 5%) | 3,000 | | | |
| Romy (80,000 × 5%) | 4,000 | 10,000 | | |
| To Salary – Romy | | 6,000 | | |
| To Net Profit transferred to | | | | |
| Tom's Capital A/c | 45,000 | | | |
| Jack's Capital A/c | 51,000 | | | |
| Romy's Capital A/c | 44,000 | 1,40,000 | | |
| | | 1,56,000 | | 1,56,000 |

**Working Notes**

**Calculation of Profits**

Divisible profits = ₹ 1,40,000

1. First ₹ 20,000 in capital ratio, i.e. 6 : 6 : 8 or 3 : 3 : 4

   Tom's share = $20,000 \times \frac{3}{10}$ = ₹ 6,000 ; Jack's share = $20,000 \times \frac{3}{10}$ = ₹ 6,000; Romy's share = $20,000 \times \frac{4}{10}$ = ₹ 8,000

2. Next ₹ 30,000 in 3 : 5 : 2.

   Tom's share = $30,000 \times \frac{3}{10}$ = ₹ 9,000 ; Jack's share = $30,000 \times \frac{5}{10}$ = ₹ 15,000

   Romy's share = $30,000 \times \frac{2}{10}$ = ₹ 6,000

3. Remaining profits in 1 : 1 : 1 (i.e. 1,40,000 – 20,000 – 30,000 = ₹ 90,000)

   Tom's share = $90,000 \times \frac{1}{3}$ = ₹ 30,000 ; Jack's share = $90,000 \times \frac{1}{3}$ = ₹ 30,000

   Romy's share = $90,000 \times \frac{1}{3}$ = ₹ 30,000

   Total Share of Tom = (6,000 + 9,000 + 30,000) = ₹ 45,000

   Total Share of Jack = (6,000 + 15,000 + 30,000) = ₹ 51,000

   Total Share of Romy = (8,000 + 6,000 + 30,000) = ₹ 44,000

*Or* (i) **Fixed Capital Method**

**Partners' Capital Account**

| Dr Date | Particulars | LF | Sameer (₹) | Yasmin (₹) | Date | Particulars | LF | Sameer (₹) | Cr Yasmin (₹) |
|---|---|---|---|---|---|---|---|---|---|
| | To Balance c/d | | 18,00,000 | 12,00,000 | | By Balance b/d | | 15,00,000 | 10,00,000 |
| | | | | | | By Bank A/c (Additional capital) | | 3,00,000 | 2,00,000 |
| | | | 18,00,000 | 12,00,000 | | | | 18,00,000 | 12,00,000 |

**Partners' Current Account**

| Dr Date | Particulars | LF | Sameer (₹) | Yasmin (₹) | Date | Particulars | LF | Sameer (₹) | Cr Yasmin (₹) |
|---|---|---|---|---|---|---|---|---|---|
| | To Drawings A/c | | 30,000 | 20,000 | | By Interest on Capital A/c | | 82,500 | 55,000 |
| | To Interest on Drawings A/c | | 1,800 | 1,200 | | By Partners' Salary A/c | | 20,000 | 7,000 |
| | To Profit and Loss Appropriation A/c (Loss) | | 60,000 | 40,000 | | By Commission A/c | | 10,000 | — |
| | To Balance c/d | | 20,700 | 800 | | | | | |
| | | | 1,12,500 | 62,000 | | | | 1,12,500 | 62,000 |

**Working Note**

**Calculation of Interest on Capital** Amt (₹)

**Sameer** 5% on ₹ 15,00,000 for 1 year = $15,00,000 \times 5/100$ = 75,000

5% on ₹ 3,00,000 for 6 months = $3,00,000 \times \frac{6}{12} \times \frac{5}{100}$ = 7,500

82,500

**Yasmin** 5% on ₹ 10,00,000 for 1 year = $10,00,000 \times \frac{5}{100}$ = 50,000

5% on ₹ 2,00,000 for 6 months = $2,00,000 \times \frac{6}{12} \times \frac{5}{100}$ = 5,000

55,000

(ii) **Fluctuating Capital Method**

Dr **Partners' Capital Account** Cr

| Date | Particulars | LF | Sameer (₹) | Yasmin (₹) | Date | Particulars | LF | Sameer (₹) | Yasmin (₹) |
|---|---|---|---|---|---|---|---|---|---|
| | To Drawings A/c | | 30,000 | 20,000 | | By Balance b/d | | 15,00,000 | 10,00,000 |
| | To Interest on Drawings A/c | | 1,800 | 1,200 | | By Bank A/c (Additional capital) | | 3,00,000 | 2,00,000 |
| | To Profit and Loss A/c | | 60,000 | 40,000 | | By Interest on Capital A/c | | 82,500 | 55,000 |
| | To Balance c/d | | 18,20,700 | 12,00,800 | | By Salary A/c | | 20,000 | 7,000 |
| | | | | | | By Commission A/c | | 10,000 | – |
| | | | 19,12,500 | 12,62,000 | | | | 19,12,500 | 12,62,000 |

9. **JOURNAL**

| Date | Particulars | | LF | Amt (Dr) | Amt (Cr) |
|---|---|---|---|---|---|
| (i) | Bank A/c ( 2,48,000 × 2) | Dr | | 4,96,000 | |
| | To Equity Share Application A/c | | | | 4,96,000 |
| | (Being share application money received on 2,48,000 equity shares @ ₹ 2 per share) | | | | |
| (ii) | Equity Share Application A/c | Dr | | 4,96,000 | |
| | To Equity Share Capital A/c (WN 1) | | | | 1,60,000 |
| | To Equity Share Allotment A/c (WN 2) | | | | 2,94,000 |
| | To Bank A/c (WN 3) | | | | 42,000 |
| | (Being share application money adjusted) | | | | |
| (iii) | Equity Share Allotment A/c | Dr | | 3,60,000 | |
| | To Equity Share Capital A/c (80,000 × 2) | | | | 1,60,000 |
| | To Securities Premium A/c (80,000 × 2.5) | | | | 2,00,000 |
| | (Being allotment money due on 80,000 equity shares @ ₹ 4.50 per share including premium of ₹ 2.50 each) | | | | |
| (iv) | Bank A/c | Dr | | 61,000 | |
| | To Equity Share Allotment A/c (WN 4) | | | | 61,000 |
| | (Being allotment money received and excess on application adjusted) | | | | |
| (v) | Equity Share First and Final Call A/c (80,000 × 6) | Dr | | 4,80,000 | |
| | To Equity Share Capital A/c | | | | 4,80,000 |
| | (Being first and final call money due on 80,000 equity shares @ ₹ 6 per share) | | | | |
| (vi) | Bank A/c | Dr | | 4,68,000 | |
| | To Equity Share First and Final Call A/c | | | | 4,68,000 |
| | (Being share first and final call money received on 78,000 equity shares @ ₹ 6) | | | | |
| (vii) | Equity Share Capital A/c (2,000 × 10) | Dr | | 20,000 | |
| | Securities Premium A/c (2,000 × 2.5) | Dr | | 5,000 | |
| | To Forfeited Shares A/c | | | | 8,000 |
| | To Equity Share Allotment A/c | | | | 5,000 |
| | To Equity Share First and Final Call A/c ( 2,000 × 6) | | | | 12,000 |
| | (Being 2,000 shares forfeited) | | | | |

**Working Notes**

1.

| Shares Applied | Shares Allotted | Application Money Received @ ₹ 2 | Application Money Transferred | Excess Money on Application | Allotment Due @ ₹ 4.50 | Excess Application Money Adjusted | Allotment Money Required | Refunded Money |
|---|---|---|---|---|---|---|---|---|
| 40,000 | 20,000 | 80,000 | 40,000 | 40,000 | 90,000 | 40,000 | 50,000 | — |
| 1,12,000 | 28,000 | 2,24,000 | 56,000 | 1,68,000 | 1,26,000 | 1,26,000 | — | 42,000 |
| 96,000 | 32,000 | 1,92,000 | 64,000 | 1,28,000 | 1,44,000 | 1,28,000 | 16,000 | — |
| 2,48,000 | 80,000 | 4,96,000 | 1,60,000 | 3,36,000 | 3,60,000 | 2,94,000 | 66,000 | 42,000 |

Number of shares applied by Golu $= 2{,}000 \times \frac{40{,}000}{20{,}000} = 4{,}000$ shares

2. **Surplus towards Allotment on Golu's shares**

| | | Amt (₹) |
|---|---|---|
| Application money received (4,000 × 2) | | 8,000 |
| (–) Application money required ( 2,000 × 2) | | (4,000) |
| Surplus towards allotment | | 4,000 |

3. **Calculation of Amount received on Allotment**

| | | |
|---|---|---|
| Allotment money due (80,000 × 4.50) | | 3,60,000 |
| (–) Excess received with application | | (2,94,000) |
| | | 66,000 |
| (–) Calls-in-arrears (Golu) | | |
| Due (2,000 × 4.50) | 9,000 | |
| (–) Surplus | (4,000) | (5,000) |
| Amount received with allotment | | 61,000 |

*Or* (i) Number of shares applied $= \frac{1{,}10{,}000}{11} = 10{,}000$

(ii) Amount payable on allotment $= 10{,}000 \times 4 =$ ₹ 40,000

| | | |
|---|---|---|
| (iii) The amount to be received on allotment | = ₹ | 40,000 |
| (–) Allotment money not received (3,000 × 4) | = ₹ | (12,000) |
| | ₹ | 28,000 |

| (iv) **Amount transferred to Calls-in-arrears Account** | | **Amt (₹)** |
|---|---|---|
| Amount not received on allotment (3,000 × 4) | = | 12,000 |
| (+) Amount not received on final call (3,000 × 3) | = | 9,000 |
| Calls-in-arrears | = | 21,000 |

(v) **JOURNAL**

| Date | Particulars | | LF | Amt (Dr) | Amt (Cr) |
|---|---|---|---|---|---|
| (a) | Share Capital A/c (3,000 × 10) | Dr | | 30,000 | |
| | Securities Premium A/c (3,000 × 1) | Dr | | 3,000 | |
| | To Forfeited Shares A/c | | | | 12,000 |
| | To Share Allotment A/c (3,000 × 4) | | | | 12,000 |
| | To Share Final Call A/c (3,000 × 3) | | | | 9,000 |
| | (Being 3,000 shares forfeited for non-payment of allotment and call money) | | | | |
| (b) | Bank A/c (2,000 × 9) | Dr | | 18,000 | |
| | Forfeited Shares A/c | Dr | | 2,000 | |
| | To Share Capital A/c (2,000 × 10) | | | | 20,000 |
| | (Being 2,000 shares re-issued @ ₹ 6 per share as ₹ 7 called-up) | | | | |
| | Forfeited Shares A/c | Dr | | 6,000 | |
| | To Capital Reserve A/c (WN) | | | | 6,000 |
| | (Being the transfer of giain (profit) on re-issue) | | | | |

**Working Note**

$$\text{Capital Reserve} = \left[\left(\frac{\text{Profit on Forfeiture}}{\text{Forfeited Shares}} \times \text{Re-issued Shares}\right) - \text{Loss on Re-issue}\right]$$

$$= \left[\left(\frac{12{,}000}{3{,}000} \times 2{,}000\right) - 2{,}000\right] = 8{,}000 - 2{,}000 = ₹\ 6{,}000$$

**10.** (a) Calculation of sacrificing ratio

$$\text{Anand's sacrifice (Old share} - \text{New share)} = \frac{3}{5} - \frac{3}{9} = \frac{27-15}{45} = \frac{12}{45}$$

$$\text{Bheem's sacrifice (Old share} - \text{New share)} = \frac{2}{5} - \frac{2}{9} = \frac{18-10}{45} = \frac{8}{45}$$

Hence, sacrificing ratio = 12 : 8 or 3 : 2

(b) **JOURNAL**

| Date | Particulars | | LF | Amt (Dr) | Amt (Cr) |
|---|---|---|---|---|---|
| | Bank A/c | Dr | | 1,00,000 | |
| | To Naveen's Capital A/c | | | | 1,00,000 |
| | (Being the amount of capital brought in by Naveen) | | | | |
| | Naveen's Current A/c (1, 12,500 × 4/9) | Dr | | 50,000 | |
| | To Anand's Capital A/c | | | | 30,000 |
| | To Bheem's Capital A/c | | | | 20,000 |
| | (Being the capital accounts of Anand and Bheem credited in their sacrificing ratio, i.e. 3:2 for Naveen's share of goodwill on his admission) | | | | |

(c) **JOURNAL**

| Date | Particulars | | LF | Amt (Dr) | Amt (Cr) |
|---|---|---|---|---|---|
| | Anand's Capital A/c | Dr | | 13,500 | |
| | To Bheem's Capital A/c | | | 9,000 | |
| | To Revaluation A/c | | | | 22,500 |
| | (Being loss on revaluation account transferred to partners' capital account) | | | | |

**Working Note**

Dr **Revaluation Account** Cr

| Particulars | Amt (₹) | Particulars | | Amt (₹) |
|---|---|---|---|---|
| To Provision for Doubtful Debts A/c | 3,000 | By Loss transferred to | | |
| To Stock A/c | 12,500 | Anand's Capital A/c | 13,500 | |
| To Outstanding Expenses A/c | 7,000 | Bheem's Capital A/c | 9,000 | 22,500 |
| | 22,500 | | | 22,500 |

(d) Dr **Partners' Capital Account** Cr

| Particulars | Anand (₹) | Bheem (₹) | Naveen (₹) | Particulars | Anand (₹) | Bheem (₹) | Naveen (₹) |
|---|---|---|---|---|---|---|---|
| To Profit and Loss A/c | 27,000 | 18,000 | – | By Balance b/d | 1,50,000 | 1,00,000 | – |
| To Revaluation A/c (Loss) | 13,500 | 9,000 | – | By Bank A/c | – | – | 1,00,000 |
| To Bank A/c (Balancing fig.) | 64,500 | 43,000 | – | By Naveen's Current A/c (Premium for goodwill) | 30,000 | 20,000 | – |
| To Balance c/d | 75,000 | 50,000 | 1,00,000 | | | | |
| | 1,80,000 | 1,20,000 | 1,00,000 | | 1,80,000 | 1,20,000 | 1,00,000 |

**Working Note**

Calculation of adjusted capitals of old partners

$$\text{Total Capital of New Firm} = \frac{\text{Naveen's Capital}}{\text{Naveen's Profit Share}} = \frac{1{,}00{,}000}{4/9} = ₹\ 2{,}25{,}000$$

Anand's new capital = 2,25,000 × 3/9 = ₹ 75,000

Bheem's new capital = 2,25,000 × 2/9 = ₹ 50,000

Naveen's new capital = 2,25,000 × 4/9 = ₹ 1,00,000

(e)

**JOURNAL**

| Date | Particulars | | LF | Amt (Dr) | Amt (Cr) |
|---|---|---|---|---|---|
| | Anand's Capital A/c | Dr | | 64,500 | |
| | Bheem's Capital A/c | Dr | | 43,000 | |
| | To Bank A/c | | | | 1,07,500 |
| | (Being excess amount adjusted from the capital account of partners) | | | | |

*Or* (A) (a) Calculation of sacrificing ratio

A's sacrificing ratio $= \frac{3}{5} - \frac{3}{8} = \frac{24-15}{40} = \frac{9}{40}$; B's sacrificing ratio $= \frac{2}{5} - \frac{3}{8} = \frac{16-15}{40} = \frac{1}{40}$

Sacrificing ratio = 9 : 1

Dr **Revaluation Account** Cr

| Particulars | Amt (₹) | Particulars | | Amt (₹) |
|---|---|---|---|---|
| To Stock A/c | 1,150 | By Provision on Debtors A/c | | 2,000 |
| To Furniture A/c | 1,500 | By Loss transferred to | | |
| To Outstanding Bill A/c | 1,000 | A | 990 | |
| | | B | 660 | 1,650 |
| | 3,650 | | | 3,650 |

(b) Dr **Partners' Capital Account** Cr

| Particulars | A (₹) | B (₹) | C (₹) | Particulars | A (₹) | B (₹) | C (₹) |
|---|---|---|---|---|---|---|---|
| To Revaluation A/c | 990 | 660 | — | By Balance b/d | 35,000 | 30,000 | — |
| To Investment A/c | 6,000 | 4,000 | — | By Cash A/c | — | — | 40,000 |
| To Balance c/d | 40,310 | 30,040 | 40,000 | By General Reserve A/c | 6,000 | 4,000 | — |
| | | | | By Premium for Goodwill A/c | 6,300 | 700 | — |
| | 47,300 | 34,700 | 40,000 | | 47,300 | 34,700 | 40,000 |
| To Balance c/d | 60,000 | 60,000 | 40,000 | By Balance b/d | 40,310 | 30,040 | 40,000 |
| | | | | By Current A/c | 19,690 | 29,960 | — |
| | 60,000 | 60,000 | 40,000 | | 60,000 | 60,000 | 40,000 |

**Working Note**

Total capital of the firm = ₹ 1,60,000 (Given)

A's new capital = 1,60,000 × 3/8 = ₹ 60,000; B's new capital = 1,60,000 × 3/8 = ₹ 60,000

C will bring cash for his capital $= 1{,}60{,}000 \times \frac{2}{8} =$ ₹ 40,000

**Cash Account**
as at...

(c) Dr Cr

| Particulars | Amt (₹) | Particulars | Amt (₹) |
|---|---|---|---|
| To Balance b/d | 12,000 | By Bank Loan A/c | 9,000 |
| To C's Capital A/c | 40,000 | By Balance c/d | 50,000 |
| To Premium for Goodwill A/c | 7,000 | | |
| | 59,000 | | 59,000 |

**Note**
- Market value of machinery is ignored because all fixed tangible assets are recorded at their cost price.
- Some assets like closing stock and inventories are valued at their cost price or market price whichever is less.

(B) Old ratio of Sonu : Monu = 3 : 2

Tanu's share $\frac{1}{5}$; Remaining share $= 1 - \frac{1}{5} = \frac{4}{5}$

Sonu's new share $= \frac{3}{5} \times \frac{4}{5} = \frac{12}{25}$; Monu's new share $= \frac{2}{5} \times \frac{4}{5} = \frac{8}{25}$; Tonu's new share $= \frac{1}{5} \times \frac{5}{5} = \frac{5}{25}$

New profit sharing ratio of Sonu, Monu and Tanu = 12 : 8 : 5

Now D's share = $\frac{1}{4}$

Remaining share = $1 - \frac{1}{4} = \frac{3}{4}$

Sonu's new share $= \frac{12}{25} \times \frac{3}{4} = \frac{36}{100}$; Monu's new share $= \frac{8}{25} \times \frac{3}{4} = \frac{24}{100}$

Tanu's new share $= \frac{5}{25} \times \frac{3}{4} = \frac{15}{100}$; Deenu's new share $= \frac{1}{4} \times \frac{25}{25} = \frac{25}{100}$

New profit sharing ratio = 36 : 24 : 15 : 25

**11.** (i) • Inflow of cash • (a) Cash flow from operating activities

(ii) (*a*) A, B and D

(iii) It will increase the ratio

(iv) It helps in checking the accuracy of past assessments of future cash flows and in examining the relationship between profitability and net cash flow and impact of changing prices.

(v) (a) % of Trade Receivables $= \frac{43,000}{4,39,000} \times 100 = 9.80\%$

(b) Amount to be shown = (1,50,000 – 60,000) crore = ₹ 90,000 crore

**12.**

**Comparative Statement of Profit and Loss**

for the years ended 31st March, 2023 and 2024

| Particulars | 31st March, 2023 (₹) | 31st March, 2024 (₹) | Absolute Change (₹) | Percentage Change (%) |
|---|---|---|---|---|
| I. Revenue from Operations | 5,00,000 | 10,00,000 | 5,00,000 | 100 |
| II. **Expenses** | | | | |
| Cost of Material Consumed | 3,00,000 | 7,50,000 | 4,50,000 | 150 |
| III. Profit before Tax (I – II) | 2,00,000 | 2,50,000 | 50,000 | 25 |
| (–) Tax | (60,000) | (1,00,000) | (40,000) | (66.67) |
| IV. Profit after Tax | 1,40,000 | 1,50,000 | 10,000 | 7.142 |

**13.** (i) Trade Receivable Turnover Ratio $= \frac{\text{Net Credit Revenue from Operations}}{\text{Average Trade Receivables}} = \frac{18,00,000 - 2,00,000}{2,00,000} = \frac{16,00,000}{2,00,000} = 8$ times

where, Average Trade Receivable $= \frac{1,66,000 + 2,34,000}{2} = \frac{4,00,000}{2} = ₹\ 2,00,000$

(ii) Total Assets = Property, Plant and Equipment + Non-current Investments + Current Assets

= 24,00,000 + 3,00,000 + 3,80,000 = ₹ 30,80,000

Total Assets = Total of Liabilities Side

Total of Liabilities Side = Equity Share Capital + 9% Preference Share Capital + Reserves and Surplus + Non-current Liabilities (Debt) + Current Liabilities

30,80,000 = 10,00,000 + 8,00,000 + 4,80,000 + Debts + 2,00,000

⇒ Debts = 30,80,000 – (10,00,000 + 8,00,000 + 4,80,000 + 2,00,000) = 30,80,000 – 24,80,000 = ₹ 6,00,000

Now, Debt to total Assets Ratio $= \frac{\text{Debt}}{\text{Total Assets}} = \frac{6,00,000}{30,80,000} = 0.19 : 1$

(iii) Proprietory Ratio $= \frac{\text{Shareholders' Funds}}{\text{Total Assets}} = \frac{1,50,000\ (5,40,000 + 1,35,000 - 75,000 - 3,00,000 - 1,50,000)}{6,75,000\ (1,35,000 + 5,40,000)} = 0.22 : 1$

(iv) Gross Profit Ratio $= \frac{\text{Gross Profit}}{\text{Revenue from Operations}} \times 100 = \frac{6,00,000}{25,00,000} \times 100 = 24\%$

where, Gross Profit = Revenue from Operations – Cost of Revenue from Operation

= 25,00,000 – 19,00,000 = ₹ 6,00,000

14.

**Cash Flow Statement**
for the year ended 31st March, 2023

| Particulars | | Amt (₹) |
|---|---|---|
| I. **Cash Flow from Operating Activities** | | |
| Net Profit before Tax | | 8,000 |
| (+) Non-cash Expenses | | |
| Goodwill Written-off | | 15,000 |
| Share Issue Expenses Written-off | | 3,000 |
| Operating Profit before Working Capital Changes | | 26,000 |
| (+) Increase in Current Liabilities and Decrease in Current Assets | | |
| Trade Payables | 23,000 | |
| Trade Receivables | 23,000 | 46,000 |
| (–) Increase in Current Assets and Decrease in Current Liabilities (Stock) | (80,000) | |
| Cash Used in Operating Activities | | (8,000) |
| II. **Cash Flow from Investing Activities** | | |
| Plant Purchased | (1,24,000) | |
| Net Cash used in Investing Activities | | (1,24,000) |

*Or* (a) Net profit before tax **Amt (₹)**

Net profit (5,00,000 – 4,00,000) = 1,00,000

(+) Tax provided (WN) = 50,000

= 1,50,000

**Working Note**

Dr **Provision for Tax Account** Cr

| Particulars | Amt (₹) | Particulars | Amt (₹) |
|---|---|---|---|
| To Bank A/c (Tax paid) | 30,000 | By Balance b/d | 60,000 |
| To Balance c/d | 80,000 | By Statement of Profit and Loss (Tax provided) | 50,000 |
| | 1,10,000 | | 1,10,000 |

(b)

| Particulars | | Amt (₹) |
|---|---|---|
| **Cash Flow from Operating Activities** | | |
| Net Profit before Tax | | 1,50,000 |
| **Adjustments for** | | |
| (+) Depreciation on Machinery | 2,00,000 | |
| Interest on Deposits | 45,000 | |
| Goodwill Written-off | 60,000 | 3,05,000 |
| Operating Profit before Working Capital Changes | | 4,55,000 |
| (–) Increase in Current Assets and Decrease in Current Liabilities | | |
| Increase in Inventories | (50,000) | |
| Increase in Trade Receivables | (2,00,000) | (2,50,000) |
| Cash Generated from Operations | | 2,05,000 |

(c)

| Particulars | | Amt (₹) |
|---|---|---|
| **Cash Flow from Financing Activities** | | |
| Issue of Shares | 4,00,000 | |
| 9% Deposits Raised | 4,00,000 | |
| Interest Paid | (45,000) | |
| Net Cash from Financing Activities | | 7,55,000 |

SQP Code : **PB-2/15** Series ***i*-Succeed 2-25/15** Roll No.

# Sample Question Paper 02

## Accounts 12th (Code 858)

### General Instructions

1. Candidates are allowed additional 15 minutes for only reading the paper. They must not start writing during this time.
2. Section-A is compulsory for all candidates and has ten questions.
3. Candidates have to attempt all questions from either Section-B or Section-C*.
4. Internal choices have been provided in five questions in Section-A and one question in Section-B.
5. The intended marks for questions or parts of questions are given in the brackets [ ].
6. All calculations should be shown clearly.
7. All workings, including rough work, should be done on the same page as, and adjacent to, the rest of the answer.

*Section-C has not been covered.

**Time : 3 Hrs.**

**Max. Marks : 80**

## Section A Answer All Questions [60 Marks]

**Que 1.**

In sub-parts (i) to (iv), choose the correct option and in sub-parts (v) to (x) answer the questions as instructed.

(i) PMC Ltd. took a loan of ₹ 1,20,000 from HFC Global Bank and issued 1,200, 13% debentures as collateral security. Journal entry passed by PMC for loan will be (Application) [1]

(a) Debit Debenture Suspense A/c and Credit 13% Debentures A/c by ₹ 1,20,000

(b) Debit 13% Debentures A/c and Credit Debenture Suspense A/c by ₹ 1,20,000

(c) Debit Bank A/c and Credit HFC Global Bank by ₹ 1,20,000

(d) Debit HFC Global Bank and Credit Bank A/c by ₹ 1,20,000

(ii) A and B are partners in a firm. Realisation expenses of ₹ 18,000 are paid by the firm on behalf of A. Such expenses are (Understanding) [1]

(a) debited to realisation account

(b) debited to A's capital account

(c) credited to A's loan account

(d) debited to A's loan account

(iii) Priyank Ltd. issued 30,000, 9% debentures of ₹ 100 each at a discount of 5%, redeemable at a premium of 6% after 3 years.

Priyank Ltd. has a balance of ₹ 90,000 in securities premium and ₹ 2,00,000 in general reserve. Company decided to write-off the entire loss on issue of debentures in the first year itself.

Identify the amount of loss on issue of debentures written-off from statement of profit and loss. (Application) [1]

(a) ₹ 40,000 (b) ₹ 1,80,000

(c) ₹ 1,50,000 (d) ₹ 3,30,000

(iv) Choose the correct sequence of the following transactions in relation to the admission of a partner in the partnership firm. (Recall) [1]

A – Adjustment of capital.

B – Calculation of self-generated goodwill.

C – Preparation of profit and loss adjustment account.

D – Adjustment of accumulated profit and reserves.

**Codes**
(a) A, D, B, C
(b) B, C, D, A
(c) B, C, A, D
(d) D, B, A, C

(v) "35 senior partners to take early retirement from Deloitte India."

**Source** *money control*

(a) What happens to the firm at the time of retirement of a partner?
(b) Name a circumstance, under which a partner may retire from the firm.
(Recall) [1]

(vi) Amit, Bhramit and Chetan are partners in a firm sharing profits and losses in 3 : 2 : 1 ratio. They decided to share future profits in the ratio of 5 : 3 : 2. For this purpose, the goodwill of the firm was valued at ₹ 1,20,000. Show how this will be recorded.
(Application) [1]

(vii) **Assertion** (A) Forfeited shares can be re-issued at discount, provided the amount of discount cannot exceed the profit earned on forfeiture of shares.

**Reason** (R) Forfeited shares can be re-issued at discount, provided these shares are issued as ESOPs. (Evaluate) [1]

**Alternatives**
(a) Both Assertion (A) and Reason (R) are true and Reason (R) is the correct explanation of Assertion (A)
(b) Both Assertion (A) and Reason (R) are true, but Reason (R) is not the correct explanation of Assertion (A)
(c) Assertion (A) is true, but Reason (R) is false
(d) Assertion (A) is false, but Reason (R) is true

(viii) On dissolution, C's capital account has a credit balance of ₹ 21,000. He paid realisation expenses of ₹ 1,500 and his share of realisation profit is ₹ 4,500. Calculate the amount to be paid to C.
(Application) [1]

(ix) Raj and Simran were partners in a firm sharing profits and losses in the ratio of 5 : 3. During the year ended 31st March, 2022, Raj had withdrawn ₹ 80,000. Interest on his drawings amounted to ₹ 4,000. What will be journal entry for charging interest on drawings?
(Application) [1]

(x) Where will the short-term provision come in the balance sheet of the company for the year ended 31st March, 2023?
(Understanding) [1]

## Que 2.

You are required to pass journal entries for the issue of debentures in the following condition.

Hamdard India Ltd. issued 6,000, 12% debentures of ₹ 100 each at a premium of 5%, redeemable at a premium of 10% after 6 years.
(Application) [3]

*Or*

Sandhya Ltd. issued 15,000, 10% debentures of ₹ 100 each issued at 10% premium, repayable at par.

You are required to calculate

(i) (a) The amount to be transferred to debenture redemption reserve.
(b) The amount to be transferred to debenture redemption investment account. [2]

(ii) Pass the necessary entries at the time of issue of debentures. (Application) [1]

## Que 3.

A, B and C are partners in a firm sharing profits and losses in the ratio of 4 : 3 : 1. As per the terms of partnership deed, on death of any partner, goodwill is to be valued at 50% of the net profit credited to the partner's capital account during the last three completed years before his death. 'A' died on 28th February, 2022.

The profit for the last five years ended 31st March were

| | |
|---|---|
| 2017 – ₹ 60,000 | 2018 – ₹ 97,000 |
| 2019 – ₹ 1,05,000 | 2020 – ₹ 30,000 |
| 2021 – ₹ 84,000 | |

On the date of A's death, building was found undervalued by ₹ 80,000 which was to be considered.

You are required to

(i) Calculate the gaining/sacrificing ratio of the partners.
(ii) Calculate the amount of A's share of goodwill in the firm and the contribution to be made by remaining partners.

The new profit sharing ratio between B and C will be equal. (Application) [3]

**Que 4.**

N, S and B are partners in a firm, sharing profits and losses in ratio of 3 : 1 : 2. The balance sheet as at 31st March, 2022 was as follows

**Balance Sheet**
as at 31st March, 2022

| Liabilities | Amt (₹) | Assets | Amt (₹) |
|---|---|---|---|
| Bills Payable | 12,000 | Freehold Premises | 40,000 |
| Sundry Creditors | 18,000 | Machinery | 30,000 |
| Reserves | 12,000 | Furniture | 12,000 |
| Capital A/cs | | Stock | 22,000 |
| N 30,000 | | Sundry Deb. 20,000 | |
| S 30,000 | | (–) Provision for | |
| B 28,000 | 88,000 | Doubtful Deb. (1,000) | 19,000 |
| | | Cash | 7,000 |
| | 1,30,000 | | 1,30,000 |

B retires from the business and the partners agree to the following

(i) The firm upon revaluation of assets and the reassessment of liabilities made a profit of ₹ 6,960.

(ii) Goodwill is valued at ₹ 21,000 on B's retirement.

(iii) The continuing partners have decided to adjust their capitals in their new profit sharing ratio after retirement of B. Surplus/Deficit, if any, in their capital accounts will be adjusted through current accounts.

Prepare partners' capital account. **(Application) [3]**

*Or*

Aruna and Karuna are partners. Their profit sharing ratio is 3 : 2. Neena joins the partnership for 1/4th share in profits (of which he acquires 2/3 from Aruna and 1/3 from Karuna).

Neena brings in ₹ 2,40,000 for capital and ₹ 96,000 for goodwill. 1/4th of the amount of goodwill is withdrawn by old partners. Pass necessary journal entries and find out new profit sharing ratio. **(Application)**

**Que 5.**

On 1st January, 2023, Megha Ltd. issued 2,000, 11% debentures of ₹ 100 each at a discount of 5%, repayable as follows

On 31st December, 2025 – ₹ 40,000
On 31st December, 2026 – ₹ 1,20,000
On 31st December, 2027 – Balance amount

The company pays interest on debentures annually. You are required to pass the journal entries (including interest) for the year beginning lst January, 2023 to 31st December, 2023. **(Application) [3]**

**Que 6.**

Ashu, Pashu and Tashu are partners in a firm, sharing profits and losses in the ratio of 3 : 2 : 1. On 31st March, 2023, their balance sheet was as under

**SP-02**

**Balance Sheet**
as at 31st March, 2023

| Liabilities | | Amt (₹) | Assets | | Amt (₹) |
|---|---|---|---|---|---|
| Sundry Creditors | | 45,000 | Cash at Bank | | 48,000 |
| General Reserve | | 27,000 | Sundry Debtors | 75,000 | |
| Capital A/cs | | | (–) Provision for Doubtful Debts | (3,900) | 71,100 |
| Ashu | 2,37,000 | | Stock | | 42,900 |
| Pashu | 2,10,000 | | Plant and Machinery | | 1,80,000 |
| Tashu | 1,83,000 | 6,30,000 | Land and Building | | 3,60,000 |
| | | 7,02,000 | | | 7,02,000 |

Tashu retires on 1st April, 2023, subject to the following adjustments

(i) Land and building to be reduced by 10%.

(ii) Goodwill to be valued at ₹ 1,62,000.

(iii) Provision for doubtful debts to be raised to 10% of the debtors, the excess provision being created from general reserve. The balance of the general reserve to be distributed amongst the partners.

(iv) Creditors of ₹ 9,000 were paid by Ashu for which she is not to be reimbursed.

(v) The continuing partners to share profits and losses in future in the ratio of 5 : 4.

(vi) Tashu to be paid ₹ 89,400 on retirement and the remaining amount which is to be transferred to her loan account.

You are required to prepare revaluation account and partners' capital account. (Application) [6]

*Or*

Bimal and Chetan were partners, sharing profits in the ratio of 3 : 2. Their balance sheet as at 31st March, 2021 was as follows

**Balance Sheet**
as at 31st March, 2021

| Liabilities | | Amt (₹) | Assets | Amt (₹) |
|---|---|---|---|---|
| Capital A/cs | | | Land & Buildings | 40,000 |
| Bimal | 30,000 | | Machinery | 10,000 |
| Chetan | 20,000 | 50,000 | Furniture | 5,000 |
| Provision for Doubtful Debts | | 500 | Debtors | 12,500 |
| | | | Cash | 8,000 |
| Creditors | | 30,000 | Profit and Loss A/c | 5,000 |
| | | 80,500 | | 80,500 |

Dinesh was admitted for 1/5th share on following terms

(i) The new profit sharing ratio was decided as 2 : 2 : 1.

(ii) Dinesh will bring ₹ 15,000 as his capital and ₹ 7,500 for his share of goodwill.

(iii) Half of the goodwill amount was withdrawn by the partner who sacrificed his share of profit in favour of Dinesh.

(iv) A provision of 5% for doubtful debts was to be maintained.

(v) An item of ₹ 250 included in sundry creditors was not likely to be paid.

(vi) A provision of ₹ 400 was to be made for claims for damages against the firm.

(vii) The capital accounts of Bimal and Chetan were to be adjusted on the basis of Dinesh's capital.

The necessary adjustment of surplus/deficiency if any, made in cash.

You are required to

(a) Calculate gaining/sacrificing ratio. [1]

(b) Prepare partners' capital account. (Application) [5]

**Que 7.**

Prepare the balance sheet for Gopal Ltd. as on 31st March, 2023 from the following information as per provisions of Schedule III, Part I of the Companies Act, 2013. (Application) [6]

| Particulars | Amt (₹) |
|---|---|
| General Reserve | 3,00,000 |
| 8% Debentures | 3,00,000 |
| Balance of Statement of Profit and Loss (Credit) | 1,20,000 |
| Depreciation of Property, Plant and Equipment | 70,000 |
| Property, Plant and Equipment (Cost) | 9,00,000 |
| Trade Payables | 2,50,000 |
| Preference Share Capital | 5,00,000 |
| Inventories | 64,000 |
| Trade Receivables | 2,56,000 |
| Cash and Cash Equivalents | 3,20,000 |

**Que 8.**

P, Q and R are partners sharing profits in the ratio of 3 : 1 : 1. On 31st March, 2023, they decided to dissolve their firm. On that date the balance sheet was as follows

**Balance Sheet**
as at 31st March, 2023

| Liabilities | | Amt (₹) | Assets | | Amt (₹) |
|---|---|---|---|---|---|
| Capital A/cs | | | Sundry Assets | | 15,200 |
| P | 22,000 | | Furniture | | 800 |
| Q | 8,000 | | Stock | | 6,240 |
| R | 5,600 | 35,600 | Debtors | 19,360 | |
| Creditors | | 6,400 | (–) Provision for Doubtful Debts | (960) | 18,400 |
| Loan A/c | | 1,200 | Cash | | 2,560 |
| | | 43,200 | | | 43,200 |

It is agreed that

(i) P is to take over the furniture at ₹ 640 and debtors amounting to ₹ 16,000 at ₹ 13,760 and also he agreed to pay the creditors of ₹ 6,400.

(ii) Q is to take over the stock at ₹ 5,600 and part of sundry assets at ₹ 5,760 which is 10% less than the book value.

(iii) R is to take over the remaining sundry assets at 90% of the book value, less ₹ 80 as discount and also agreed to pay the loan alongwith accrued interest of ₹ 24 which has not been recorded in the books.

(iv) The dissolution expenses were ₹ 216.

(v) The remaining debtors were sold to a debt collecting agency for 50% of the book value.

Prepare necessary ledger accounts showing your working clearly. **(Application) [6]**

**Que 9.**

Tagmark India Ltd. invited applications for 15,000 shares of ₹ 100 each at a premium of ₹ 20 per share payable as follows

On application ₹ 40 (including ₹ 10 Premium)
On allotment ₹ 30 (including ₹ 10 premium)
On first call ₹ 30
On second and final call ₹ 20

Applications were received for 20,000 shares and pro-rata allotment was made on the application for 17,500 shares. Excess application money is to be utilised towards allotment.

SP-02

Rohan to whom 300 shares allotted failed to pay the allotment money and his shares were forfeited after allotment.

Aman who applied for 525 shares failed to pay first call and his share were forfeited after first call.

Second and final call was made. All the money due on second call has been received.

Of the shares forfeited, 500 shares were re-issued as fully paid-up for ₹ 80 per share, which included the whole of Aman's shares.

You are required of pass journal entries in the books of Tagmark India Ltd. also show working notes clearly. **(Application) [10]**

*Or*

Following is the information of Gaurav Ltd. You are required to answer the question following the information.

Ram, whose shares were forfeited (for non-payment of allotment and call money) applied 360 shares. The amount payable on various calls was as follows

₹ 2 on application, ₹ 5 on allotment (including premium) and ₹ 5 on final call.

Shares were allotted on a pro-rata basis in the ratio of 6 : 5.

(i) How many shares were allotted to Ram? [1]

(ii) What is the amount transferred to securities premium account? [1]

(iii) What is the amount forfeited on Ram's shares? [1]

(iv) Calculate the amount due but not paid on allotment. [2]

(v) Ram's 100 shares were re-issued @ ₹ 9 per share fully paid up.
Give the journal entries passed by the Gaurav Ltd. for
(a) Forfeiture of Ram's shares [2]
(b) Re-issue of Ram's shares **(Application) [3]**

**Que 10.**

(A) Devakshi and Ragini are partners with capitals of ₹ 60,000 and ₹ 40,000 respectively. The profit and loss account of the firm showed a net profit of ₹ 42,680 for the year.

Following information is provided to you

(i) Interest on Devakshi's loan of ₹ 20,000 to the firm.

(ii) Interest on capital to be allowed @ 6% per annum.

(iii) Interest on drawings @ 8% per annum and drawings were Devakshi ₹ 8,000 and Ragini ₹ 10,000.

(iv) 10% of the divisible profits is to be kept in a reserve account.

You are required to

(a) Calculate interest on drawings to be charged from Devakshi and Ragini. **(Application) [2]**

(b) Pass journal entries related to providing interest on loan and closing it. **(Application) [2]**

(c) Give the journal entry with the amount to be transferred to reserve account. **(Recall) [2]**

(d) Give the journal entry for interest on capital account. **(Application) [2]**

(B) Apart from above adjustments, Ragini is to be allowed a commission on sales @ 4%. Sales for the year was ₹ 1,00,000.

You are required to pass the entry for the transfer of the profit or loss to the partner's capital account.

(Application) [2]

*Or*

(A) The partnership agreement of R, A and S provides that

(i) Profits will be shared by them in the ratio of 2 : 2 : 1.

(ii) Interest on capital to be allowed at the rate of 6% per annum.

(iii) Interest on drawings to be charged at the rate of 3% per annum.

(iv) A to be given a salary of ₹ 1,500 per month.

A gave guarantee to the firm that the firm would earn a net profit of at least ₹ 8,00,000 per annum and any shortfall in these profits would be personally met by him.

The capitals of the partners on 1st April, 2021 were

R = ₹ 12,00,000 ; A = ₹ 10,00,000
S = ₹ 10,00,000

During the financial year 2021-22, all the three partners withdrew ₹ 10,000 each at the beginning of every month. The net profit of the firm for the year 2021-22 was ₹ 7,00,000.

You are required to

(a) Calculate total interest on drawings to be charged from the partner. [2]

(b) Prepare profit and loss appropriation account [4½]

(c) Prepare A's capital account. (Application) [1½]

(B) Somil and Vomil are partners sharing profits and losses in the ratio of 5 : 3. On 1st April, 2023 then capital account showed a balance of ₹ 6,00,000 and ₹ 4,00,000 respectively. Calculate the amount of profit to be distributed between the partners, if the partnership deed provides for interest on capital @ 10% p.a. and the firm earned a profit of ₹ 90,000 for the year ended 31st March, 2024. (Application) [2]

## Section B

[20 Marks]

**Que 11.**

(i) ABC Systems sells an operating system to a company that makes smart toasters for ₹ 1,50,000 and gives it 60 days to pay, the ₹ 1,50,000 would be entered into trade receivable, not trade payable.

**Source** *US.news*

- Mention the ratio that will have effect of both the trade payables and trade receivables.
- What will be the impact of cash paid to trade payables on a current ratio of 2 : 1? (Analysis) [1]

(a) Current ratio will improve
(b) Current ratio will reduce
(c) Either (a) or (b)
(d) No change on current ratio

(ii) Earnings Per Share (EPS) indicates how much money a firm earns for each share of its stock and is a widely-used metric to estimate corporate value.

**Source** *Economic Times*

Based on the above statement, which of the following statements is correct for earnings per share? (Understanding) [1]

(a) High EPS indicates better liquidity position
(b) High EPS indicates good long-term solvency of the company
(c) High EPS indicates more profitability
(d) None of the above

(iii) Adani group saw a profit surge in the fiscal year ended March 2024 as the apples-to-airport conglomerate is back on an expansion spree and eyeing a $90 billion capex over the next decade.

Emerging from a damning report of a US short seller, which hit market value of its listed companies, Adani group in 2023-24 (April 2023 to March 2024) fiscal focused on containing debt, reducing founder share pledge and consolidating business in core competencies.

This helped net profit surge to ₹ 30,767 crore for the group's listed companies in the fiscal from ₹ 19,833 crore a year ago, according to exchange data and analysts.

**Source** *Business-standards*

(a) What will be the formula for the calculating the change in the profits of the company?

(b) What is the percentage change in the profits in a year? **(Analysis) [1]**

(iv) Every corporation needs reliable access to capital to stay in business. Positive cash flow allows businesses to cover expenses, plan growth initiatives and reward long-term shareholders.

**Source** *money.usnews.com*

In context to this news

Fanny Ltd. redeemed 1,500, 12% debentures of ₹ 100 each at a premium of 10%. What will be the amount of cash flow from financing activity? **(Analysis) [1]**

(v) McDonald's Corp. cash provided by operations decreased from 2021 to 2022 but then increased from 2022 to 2023 exceeding 2021 level. Also McDonald's Corp. cash used for investing activities decreased from 2021 to 2022 and from 2022 to 2023.

Cash provided by operations totaled $9.6 billion in 2023, an increase of $2.2 billion or 30%. Free cash flow was $7.3 billion in 2023, an increase of $1.8 billion or 32%. The company's free cash flow conversion rate was 86% in 2023 and 89% in 2022. Cash provided by operations increased in 2023 compared to 2022 primarily due to improved operating results.

**Source** *Stock analysis-on*

Based on the above news what could be the reason involved for such improvement? **(Analysis) [1]**

**Que 12.**

From the following extract of the statement of profit and loss for the years ended 31st March, 2022 and 2023 of PQR Ltd. prepare a comparative statement of profit and loss. **(Application) [3]**

| Particulars | Note No. | 31st March, 2023 | 31 March, 2022 |
|---|---|---|---|
| Revenue from Operations | | ₹ 48,00,000 | ₹ 30,00,000 |
| Employee Benefit Expenses | | ₹ 22,00,000 | ₹ 18,00,000 |
| Other Expenses | | ₹ 2,00,000 | ₹ 4,00,000 |
| Tax Rate | | 40% | 40% |

SP-02

**Que 13.**

Read the following information and answer the questions that follow

| Particulars | Note No. | 31st March, 2021 (₹) | 31st March, 2020 (₹) |
|---|---|---|---|
| **I. EQUITY AND LIABILITIES** | | | |
| 1. **Shareholders' Funds** | | | |
| (i) Share Capital | | 4,00,000 | 3,00,000 |
| (ii) Reserves and Surplus | 1 | 10,000 | 85,000 |
| 2. **Non-current Liabilities** | | | |
| 10% Secured Loan | | 1,75,000 | 1,00,000 |
| 3. **Current Liabilities** | | | |
| (i) Sundry Creditors | | 2,95,000 | 3,10,000 |
| (ii) Short-term Provisions | | — | — |
| (iii) Provision for Taxation | | 1,35,000 | 80,000 |
| **Total** | | 10,15,000 | 8,75,000 |

| Particulars | Note No. | 31st March, 2021 (₹) | 31st March, 2020 (₹) |
|---|---|---|---|
| II. ASSETS | | | |
| 1. **Non-current Assets** | | | |
| Property, Plant and Equipment | | 5,50,000 | 4,00,000 |
| 2. **Current Assets** | | | |
| (i) Inventories | | 2,25,000 | 2,00,000 |
| (ii) Debtors | | 1,75,000 | 2,10,000 |
| (iii) Bills Receivables | | 55,000 | 35,000 |
| (iv) Cash and Cash Equivalents | | 10,000 | 30,000 |
| **Total** | | 10,15,000 | 8,75,000 |

**Notes to Accounts**

| Particulars | 31st December, 2021 (₹) | 31st December, 2020 (₹) |
|---|---|---|
| 1. **Reserves and Surplus** | | |
| Balance in Statement of Profit and Loss | 50,000 (Cr) | 45,000 (Dr) |
| Securities Premium | 60,000 | 40,000 |

**Additional Information**

(i) Proposed dividend 2021 ₹ 45,000; 2020 ₹ 45,000.

(ii) A machine included in property, plant and equipment whose book value on the date of sale was ₹ 50,000 was sold at 20% loss. Depreciation charged on the machine was ₹ 1,00,000.

(a) What is the cash flow from operations before working capital changes? [2]

(b) What is the cash flow from investing activity? [2]

(c) What is the cash flow from financing activity? (Evaluate) [2]

*Or*

Prepare a cash flow statement on the basis of the information given in the Balance Sheet of Privotel Ltd. as at 31st March, 2022 and 2021. (Application) [6]

| Particulars | Note No. | 31st March, 2022 (₹) | 31st March, 2021 (₹) |
|---|---|---|---|
| I. EQUITY AND LIABILITIES | | | |
| 1. **Shareholders' Funds** | | | |
| (i) Share Capital | | 1,00,000 | 75,000 |
| (ii) Reserves and Surplus | 1 | 45,000 | 37,500 |
| 2. **Non-current Liabilities** | | | |
| Long-term Borrowings | | 43,750 | 43,750 |
| 3. **Current Liabilities** | | | |
| Trade Payables | | 5,000 | 38,000 |
| **Total** | | 1,93,750 | 1,94,250 |
| II. ASSETS | | | |
| 1. **Non-current Assets** | | | |
| (i) Property, Plant & Equipment and Intangible Assets | | | |
| (a) Property, Plant and Equipment | | 93,750 | 70,000 |
| (ii) Non-current Investments | | 52,750 | 51,250 |
| 2. **Current Assets** | | | |
| (i) Current Investments (Marketable) | | 6,250 | 16,750 |
| (ii) Inventories | | 2,000 | 2,750 |
| (iii) Trade Receivables | | 4,750 | 11,500 |
| (iv) Cash and Cash Equivalents | | 34,250 | 42,000 |
| **Total** | | 1,93,750 | 1,94,250 |

SP-02

**Notes to Accounts**

| Particulars | 31st March, 2022 (₹) | 31st March, 2021 (₹) |
|---|---|---|
| 1. **Reserves and Surplus**<br>Surplus (Balance in Statement of Profit and Loss) | 45,000 | 37,500 |

**Que 14.**

From the following information, calculate any three given below (Application) [6]

(i) Liquid ratio
(ii) Working capital turnover ratio
(iii) Gross profit ratio
(iv) Proprietary ratio

Information are given below

| | |
|---|---|
| Paid-up capital | ₹ 8,00,000 |
| Current assets | ₹ 5,00,000 |
| Credit revenue from operations | ₹ 3,00,000 |
| Cash revenue from operations | 75% of credit revenue from operations |
| 9% debentures | ₹ 3,40,000 |
| Current liabilities | ₹ 2,90,000 |
| Cost of revenue from operations | ₹ 6,80,000 |
| Inventory | ₹ 65,000 |

# Solutions *in Topper's Style*

My Commitment *I affirm that I am reviewing these solutions only after I have solved the Sample Question Paper 2 on my own. My purpose of looking the solutions is solely to verify whether my answers/solutions were correct or not and to identify my mistakes in case my solutions were wrong or I could not solve that.*

1. (i) (*c*) Debit Bank A/c and Credit HFC Global Bank by ₹ 1,20,000

(ii) (*b*) debited to A's capital account

(iii) (*a*) Discount on Issue of Debentures = $30,00,000 \times 5/100 = 1,50,000$

Premium on Redemption of Debentures = $30,00,000 \times \frac{6}{100}$ = ₹ 1,80,000

Therefore, Loss on Issue of Debentures = 1,50,000 + 1,80,000 = ₹ 3,30,000

Now, entry to write-off loss on issue of debentures will be

| | | | |
|---|---|---|---|
| Securities Premium A/c | Dr | 90,000 | |
| General Reserve A/c | Dr | 2,00,000 | |
| Statement of Profit and Loss | Dr | 40,000 | |
| To Loss on Issue of Debentures A/c | | | 3,30,000 |

(iv) (*b*) B, C, D, A

(v) (a) Firm gets reconstituted and new partnership agreement among continuing partners comes into existence.

(b) A partner may retire in accordance with an express agreement by the partners.

(vi) Chetan's Capital A/c Dr 4,000

To Bhramit's Capital A/c 4,000

(Being goodwill adjustment made with 2/60 share as only Bhramit is sacrificing and Chetan is gaining)

(vii) (*c*) In order to issue forfeited shares at discount, it is not necessary to issue them as ESOPs. They can be issued at a discount which cannot exceed profit on forfeiture.

(viii) Amount to be paid to C = 21,000 + 4,500 + 1,500 = ₹ 27,000

(ix) **JOURNAL**

| Date | Particulars | | LF | Amt (Dr) | Amt (Cr) |
|---|---|---|---|---|---|
| 2022 Mar 31 | Raj's Capital A/c | Dr | | 4,000 | |
| | To Interest on Drawings A/c | | | | 4,000 |
| | (Being interest on drawing charged on Raj's capital account) | | | | |

(x) Short-term provision will come under the heads current liabilities.

2. **JOURNAL**

| Date | Particulars | | LF | Amt (Dr) | Amt (Cr) |
|---|---|---|---|---|---|
| | Bank A/c | Dr | | 6,30,000 | |
| | To Debenture Application and Allotment A/c | | | | 6,30,000 |
| | (Being the application money received with premium) | | | | |
| | Debenture Application and Allotment A/c | Dr | | 6,30,000 | |
| | Loss on Issue of Debentures A/c | Dr | | 60,000 | |
| | To 12% Debentures A/c | | | | 6,00,000 |
| | To Securities Premium A/c | | | | 30,000 |
| | To Premium on Redemption of Debentures A/c | | | | 60,000 |
| | (Being the debentures issued at premium and redeemable at premium) | | | | |
| | Securities Premium A/c | Dr | | 30,000 | |
| | Statement of Profit and Loss | Dr | | 30,000 | |
| | To Loss on Issue of Debentures A/c | | | | 60,000 |
| | (Being the loss on issue of debentures written-off) | | | | |

*Or* (i) (a) Amount to be transferred to debenture redemption reserve

= 10% of the nominal value of debentures issued

= 10% of 15,00,000 = ₹ 1,50,000

(b) Amount transferred to debenture reserve investment

= 15% of the nominal value of debentures = 15% of 15,00,000 = ₹ 2,25,000

(ii) **JOURNAL**

| Date | Particulars | | LF | Amt (Dr) | Amt (Cr) |
|---|---|---|---|---|---|
| | **At the Time of Issue of Debentures** | | | | |
| | Bank A/c | Dr | | 16,50,000 | |
| | To 10% Debenture Application and Allotment A/c | | | | 16,50,000 |
| | (Being receipt of application money) | | | | |
| | 10% Debenture Application and Allotment A/c | Dr | | 16,50,000 | |
| | To 10% Debentures A/c | | | | 15,00,000 |
| | To Securities Premium A/c | | | | 1,50,000 |
| | (Being issue of 15,000, 10% debentures at 10% premium, repayable at par) | | | | |

**Common Mistake** Students usually miscalculate amount related to debenture redemption reserve and debenture redemption investment. It should be noted that amount transferred to DRR and DRI are 10% and 15% of the nominal value of debentures respectively.

**3.** (i) **Calculation of Gaining Ratio**

$B = \frac{1}{2} - \frac{3}{8} = \frac{4-3}{8} = \frac{1}{8}$; $C = \frac{1}{2} - \frac{1}{8} = \frac{4-1}{8} = \frac{3}{8}$; Gaining Ratio $= \frac{1}{8} : \frac{3}{8} = 1:3$

(ii) **Calculation of A's Share of Goodwill**

Total of last three years profit = 1,05,000 + 30,000 + 84,000 = ₹ 2,19,000

A's share in last three years profit = 2,19,000 × 4/8 = ₹ 1,09,500

A's share of goodwill $= 1{,}09{,}500 \times \frac{50}{100} =$ ₹ 54,750

A's share of goodwill will be contributed by B and C in their gaining ratio of 1 : 3 as under

$B = 54{,}750 \times \frac{1}{4} =$ ₹ 13,688 ; $C = 54{,}750 \times \frac{3}{4} =$ ₹ 41,062

**Common Mistake** Students sometimes ignore the fact that goodwill will be computed based on 'three year's profits' since 5 year's profits are given. It is important to read the question carefully and use the profits of previous years as per the requirement of question only.

**4.** Dr **Partners' Capital Account** Cr

| Particulars | N (₹) | S (₹) | B (₹) | Particulars | N (₹) | S (₹) | B (₹) |
|---|---|---|---|---|---|---|---|
| To B's Capital A/c | 5,250 | 1,750 | — | By Balance b/d | 30,000 | 30,000 | 28,000 |
| To Balance c/d | 34,230 | 31,410 | 41,320 | By Reserves A/c | 6,000 | 2,000 | 4,000 |
| | | | | By Revaluation A/c (Profit) | 3,480 | 1,160 | 2,320 |
| | | | | By N's Capital A/c | — | — | 5,250 |
| | | | | By S's Capital A/c | — | — | 1,750 |
| | 39,480 | 33,160 | 41,320 | | 39,480 | 33,160 | 41,320 |
| To B's Loan A/c | — | — | 41,320 | By Balance b/d | 34,230 | 31,410 | 41,320 |
| To S's Current A/c (Balancing figure) | — | 15,000 | — | By N's Current A/c (Balancing figure) | 15,000 | — | — |
| To Balance c/d | 49,230 | 16,410 | — | | | | |
| | 49,230 | 31,410 | 41,320 | | 49,230 | 31,410 | 41,320 |

**Working Notes**

1. Old ratio = 3 : 1 : 2. As there is no information how B's share has been taken, it is assumed that his share has been taken by remaining partners in their old ratio.

   ∴ Gaining and new ratio between N and S will be 3 : 1.

   B's share of goodwill = 21,000 ×1/3 = ₹ 7,000 (taken over by N and S in gaining ratio, i.e., 3 : 1)

2. Capital adjustment **Amt (₹)**

   N's capital after adjustment = 34,230

   S's capital after adjustment = 31,410

   65,640

   N's new capital $\left(65{,}640 \times \frac{3}{4}\right)$ = ₹ 49,230 ; S's new capital $\left(65{,}640 \times \frac{1}{4}\right)$ = ₹ 16,410

*Or*

**JOURNAL**

| Date | Particulars | LF | Amt (Dr) | Amt (Cr) |
|---|---|---|---|---|
| | Bank A/c Dr | | 3,36,000 | |
| | To Neena's Capital A/c | | | 2,40,000 |
| | To Premium for Goodwill A/c | | | 96,000 |
| | (Being the amount of capital and goodwill/premium brought in cash) | | | |
| | Premium for Goodwill A/c Dr | | 96,000 | |
| | To Aruna's Capital A/c | | | 64,000 |
| | To Karuna's Capital A/c | | | 32,000 |
| | (Being goodwill/premium credited to old partners in their sacrificing ratio i.e. 2 : 1) | | | |
| | Aruna's Capital A/c Dr | | 16,000 | |
| | Karuna's Capital A/c Dr | | 8,000 | |
| | To Bank A/c | | | 24,000 |
| | (Being 1/4th of the goodwill premium withdrawn by old partners in cash) | | | |

**Calculation of New Profit Sharing Ratio**

Neena takes his share from Aruna $= \frac{2}{3} \times \frac{1}{4} = \frac{2}{12} = \frac{1}{6}$; Neena takes his share from Karuna $= \frac{1}{3} \times \frac{1}{4} = \frac{1}{12}$

Therefore, Aruna's new share $= \frac{3}{5} - \frac{1}{6} = \frac{13}{30}$; Karuna's new share $= \frac{2}{5} - \frac{1}{12} = \frac{19}{60}$; Neena's share $= \frac{1}{4}$

Therefore, new profit sharing ratio of Aruna, Karuna and Neena $= \frac{13}{30} : \frac{19}{60} : \frac{1}{4} = \frac{26:19:15}{60} = 26:19:15$

5. **JOURNAL**

| Date | Particulars | LF | Amt (Dr) | Amt (Cr) |
|---|---|---|---|---|
| 2023 Jan 1 | Bank A/c Dr | | 1,90,000 | |
| | To Debenture Application and Allotment A/c | | | 1,90,000 |
| | (Being debenture application money on 2,000, 11% debentures @ ₹ 95 each, received) | | | |
| Jan 1 | Debenture Application and Allotment A/c Dr | | 1,90,000 | |
| | Discount on Issue of Debentures A/c Dr | | 10,000 | |
| | To 11% Debentures A/c | | | 2,00,000 |
| | (Being issue of 2,000, 11% debentures of ₹ 100 each at a discount of 5%) | | | |
| Dec 31 | Debenture Interest A/c Dr | | 22,000 | |
| | To Debentureholders' A/c | | | 22,000 |
| | (Being interest due on debenture, i.e. 2,00,000 × 11% for 1 year) | | | |
| Dec 31 | Debentureholders' A/c Dr | | 22,000 | |
| | To Bank A/c | | | 22,000 |
| | (Being interest paid) | | | |

| Date | Particulars | | LF | Amt (Dr) | Amt (Cr) |
|---|---|---|---|---|---|
| Dec 31 | Statement of Profit and Loss | Dr | | 32,000 | |
| | To Debenture Interest A/c | | | | 22,000 |
| | To Discount on Issue of Debentures A/c | | | | 10,000 |
| | (Being debenture interest transferred and discount on issue of debenture written-off) | | | | |

**6.** Dr **Revaluation Account** Cr

| Particulars | Amt (₹) | Particulars | Amt (₹) | Amt (₹) |
|---|---|---|---|---|
| To Land and Building A/c | 36,000 | By Creditors | | 9,000 |
| | | By Loss on Revaluation transferred to | | |
| | | Ashu's Capital A/c | 13,500 | |
| | | Pashu's Capital A/c | 9,000 | |
| | | Tashu's Capital A/c | 4,500 | 27,000 |
| | 36,000 | | | 36,000 |

Dr **Partners' Capital Account** Cr

| Particulars | Ashu (₹) | Pashu (₹) | Tashu (₹) | Particulars | Ashu (₹) | Pashu (₹) | Tashu (₹) |
|---|---|---|---|---|---|---|---|
| To Tashu's Capital A/c | 9,000 | 18,000 | — | By Balance b/d | 2,37,000 | 2,10,000 | 1,83,000 |
| To Revaluation A/c | 13,500 | 9,000 | 4,500 | By General Reserve A/c | 11,700 | 7,800 | 3,900 |
| To Bank A/c | — | — | 89,400 | By Ashu's Capital A/c (Goodwill) | — | — | 9,000 |
| To Tashu's Loan A/c | — | — | 1,20,000 | By Pashu's Capital A/c (Goodwill) | — | — | 18,000 |
| To Balance c/d | 2,26,200 | 1,90,800 | — | | | | |
| | 2,48,700 | 2,17,800 | 2,13,900 | | 2,48,700 | 2,17,800 | 2,13,900 |

**Working Note**

Gaining Ratio = New Ratio − Old Ratio

Ashu $= \frac{5}{9} - \frac{3}{6} = \frac{10-9}{18} = \frac{1}{18}$; Pashu $= \frac{4}{9} - \frac{2}{6} = \frac{8-6}{18} = \frac{2}{18}$; Gaining ratio $= \frac{1}{18} : \frac{2}{18}$ *or* 1:2

**Value Points**

- New provision created will reduce the general reserve and it will not be shown in the revaluation account.
- If a liability is paid by partner and he is not getting reimbursement, it will be shown on the credit side of the revaluation account, but not on the debit side of the respective partner's capital account.

*Or* (a) **Calculation of Sacrificing Ratio**

Sacrificing Ratio = Old Ratio − New Ratio

⇒ Bimal's sacrificing share = 3/5 − 2/5 = 1/5

Chetan's sacrificing share = 2/5 − 2/5 = 0

∴ Sacrificing ratio = 1 : 0, only Bimal will sacrifice.

(b)

Dr **Partners' Capital Account** Cr

| Particulars | Bimal (₹) | Chetan (₹) | Dinesh (₹) | Particulars | Bimal (₹) | Chetan (₹) | Dinesh (₹) |
|---|---|---|---|---|---|---|---|
| To Profit and Loss A/c | 3,000 | 2,000 | — | By Balance b/d | 30,000 | 20,000 | — |
| To Cash A/c | 3,750 | — | — | By Cash A/c | — | — | 15,000 |
| To Revaluation A/c (Loss) | 165 | 110 | — | By Premium for Goodwill A/c | 7,500 | — | — |
| To Cash A/c (Balancing figure) | 585 | — | — | By Cash A/c (Balancing figure) | — | 12,110 | — |
| To Balance c/d | 30,000 | 30,000 | 15,000 | | | | |
| | 37,500 | 32,110 | 15,000 | | 37,500 | 32,110 | 15,000 |

**Working Notes**

1. Dr **Revaluation Account** Cr

| Particulars | Amt (₹) | Particulars | | Amt (₹) |
|---|---|---|---|---|
| To Provision for Doubtful Debts A/c | 125 | By Sundry Creditors A/c | | 250 |
| To Provision for Legal Damages A/c | 400 | By Loss Transferred to | | |
| | | Bimal Capital's A/c | 165 | |
| | | Chetan Capital's A/c | 110 | 275 |
| | 525 | | | 525 |

2. **Calculation of New Capitals of Partners**

Dinesh's capital = ₹ 15,000 for 1/5 shares ⇒ Total capital of firm = $(15,000 \times 5/1)$ = ₹ 75,000

Bimal's new capital = $(75,000 \times 2/5)$ = ₹ 30,000 ; Chetan's new capital = $(75,000 \times 2/5)$ = ₹ 30,000

Dinesh's new capital = $(75,000 \times 1/5)$ = ₹ 15,000

7.

**Balance Sheet**
as at 31st March, 2023

| Particulars | Note No. | Amt (₹) |
|---|---|---|
| **I. EQUITY AND LIABILITIES** | | |
| 1. **Shareholders' Fund** | | |
| (i) Share Capital | 1 | 5,00,000 |
| (ii) Reserves and Surplus | 2 | 4,20,000 |
| 2. **Non-current Liabilities** | | |
| Long-term Borrowings | 3 | 3,00,000 |
| 3. **Current Liabilities** | | |
| Trade Payables | | 2,50,000 |
| **Total** | | 14,70,000 |
| **II. ASSETS** | | |
| 1. **Non-current Assets** | | |
| (i) Property, Plant & Equipment and Intangible Assets | | |
| (a) Property, Plant and Equipment | 4 | 8,30,000 |
| 2. **Current Assets** | | |
| (i) Inventories | | 64,000 |
| (ii) Trade Receivables | | 2,56,000 |
| (iii) Cash and Cash Equivalents | | 3,20,000 |
| **Total** | | 14,70,000 |

**Notes to Accounts**

| Particulars | Amt (₹) |
|---|---|
| 1. **Share Capital** | |
| Preference Share Capital | 5,00,000 |
| 2. **Reserves and Surplus** | |
| General Reserve | 3,00,000 |
| Balance in Statement of Profit and Loss | 1,20,000 |
| | 4,20,000 |
| 3. **Long-term Borrowings** | |
| 8% Debentures | 3,00,000 |
| 4. **Property, Plant and Equipment** | |
| Cost | 9,00,000 |
| (–) Depreciation | (70,000) |
| | 8,30,000 |

**8.** Dr **Realisation Account** Cr

| Particulars | | Amt (₹) | Particulars | | Amt (₹) |
|---|---|---|---|---|---|
| To Sundry Assets | | 15,200 | By Provision for Doubtful Debts | | 960 |
| To Furniture | | 800 | By Creditors | | 6,400 |
| To Stock | | 6,240 | By Loan | | 1,200 |
| To Debtors | | 19,360 | By P's Capital A/c | | |
| To P's Capital A/c (Creditors) | | 6,400 | Furniture | 640 | |
| To R's Capital A/c | | | Debtors | 13,760 | 14,400 |
| Loan | 1,200 | | By Q's Capital A/c | | |
| (+) Accrued Interest | 24 | 1,224 | Stock | 5,600 | |
| To Cash A/c (Expenses) | | 216 | Sundry Assets | 5,760 | 11,360 |
| | | | By R's Capital A/c | | |
| | | | Sundry Assets (WN) | | 7,840 |
| | | | By Cash A/c (Debtors) [(19,360 – 16,000) × 50%] | | 1,680 |
| | | | By Loss transferred to | | |
| | | | P's Capital A/c | 3,360 | |
| | | | Q's Capital A/c | 1,120 | |
| | | | R's Capital A/c | 1,120 | 5,600 |
| | | 49,440 | | | 49,440 |

Dr **Partners' Capital Account** Cr

| Particulars | P (₹) | Q (₹) | R (₹) | Particulars | P (₹) | Q (₹) | R (₹) |
|---|---|---|---|---|---|---|---|
| To Realisation A/c | 14,400 | 11,360 | 7,840 | By Balance b/d | 22,000 | 8,000 | 5,600 |
| To Realisation (Loss) | 3,360 | 1,120 | 1,120 | By Realisation A/c | 6,400 | — | 1,224 |
| To Cash A/c (Balancing figure) | 10,640 | — | — | By Cash A/c (Balancing figure) | — | 4,480 | 2,136 |
| | 28,400 | 12,480 | 8,960 | | 28,400 | 12,480 | 8,960 |

Dr **Cash Account** Cr

| Particulars | Amt (₹) | Particulars | Amt (₹) |
|---|---|---|---|
| To Balance b/d | 2,560 | By Realisation (Expenses) | 216 |
| To Realisation A/c | 1,680 | By P's Capital A/c | 10,640 |
| To Q's Capital A/c | 4,480 | | |
| To R's Capital A/c | 2,136 | | |
| | 10,856 | | 10,856 |

**Working Note**

| | Amt (₹) |
|---|---|
| Total sundry assets | 15,200 |
| (–) Sundry assets taken over by Q (5,760/90%) | (6,400) |
| Remaining sundry assets taken over by R | 8,800 |
| at an agreed value (8,800 × 90%) of | 7,920 |
| (–) Discount | (80) |
| | 7,840 |

**9.**

**In the Books of Tagmark India Ltd.**
**JOURNAL**

| Date | Particulars | | LF | Amt (Dr) | Amt (Cr) |
|---|---|---|---|---|---|
| (i) | Bank A/c (20,000 × 40) | Dr | | 8,00,000 | |
| | To Share Application A/c | | | | 8,00,000 |
| | (Being application money received on 20,000 shares) | | | | |

| Date | Particulars | | LF | Amt (Dr) | Amt (Cr) |
|---|---|---|---|---|---|
| (ii) | Share Application A/c | Dr | | 8,00,000 | |
| | To Share Capital A/c (15,000 × 30) | | | | 4,50,000 |
| | To Securities Premium A/c (15,000 × 10) | | | | 1,50,000 |
| | To Share Allotment A/c | | | | 1,00,000 |
| | To Bank A/c | | | | 1,00,000 |
| | (Being application money transferred to share capital account, securities premium account and the excess money transferred to share allotment account and returned to rejected applicants) | | | | |
| (iii) | Share Allotment A/c | Dr | | 4,50,000 | |
| | To Share Capital A/c (15,000 × 20) | | | | 3,00,000 |
| | To Securities Premium A/c (15,000 × 10) | | | | 1,50,000 |
| | (Being money due on allotment) | | | | |
| (iv) | Bank A/c (WN 2) | Dr | | 3,43,000 | |
| | To Share Allotment A/c | | | | 3,43,000 |
| | (Being amount received in allotment) | | | | |
| (v) | Share Capital A/c (300 × 50) | Dr | | 15,000 | |
| | Securities Premium A/c (300 × 10) | Dr | | 3,000 | |
| | To Share Allotment A/c (300 × 30 – 2,000 EM) | | | | 7,000 |
| | To Share Forfeiture A/c (300 × 30 + 2,000 EM) | | | | 11,000 |
| | (Being forfeiture of 300 shares of Rohan for non-payment of allotment money) | | | | |
| (vi) | Share First Call A/c (14,700 × 30) | Dr | | 4,41,000 | |
| | To Share Capital A/c | | | | 4,41,000 |
| | (Being first call money due on 14,700 shares) | | | | |
| (vii) | Bank A/c (WN 4) | Dr | | 4,27,500 | |
| | To Share First Call A/c | | | | 4,27,500 |
| | (Being first call money received on 14,250 shares) | | | | |
| (viii) | Share Capital A/c (450 × 80) | Dr | | 36,000 | |
| | To Share First Call A/c (450 × 30) | | | | 13,500 |
| | To Share Forfeiture A/c (450 × 50) | | | | 22,500 |
| | (Being forfeiture of 450 Aman's shares) | | | | |
| (ix) | Share Second and Final Call A/c | Dr | | 2,85,000 | |
| | To Share Capital A/c (14,250 × 20) | | | | 2,85,000 |
| | (Being second and final call money due on 14,250 shares) | | | | |
| (x) | Bank A/c | Dr | | 2,85,000 | |
| | To Share Second and Final Call A/c | | | | 2,85,000 |
| | (Being due money received) | | | | |
| (xi) | Bank A/c (500 × 80) | Dr | | 40,000 | |
| | Share Forfeiture A/c (500 × 20) | Dr | | 10,000 | |
| | To Share Capital A/c (500 × 100) | | | | 50,000 |
| | (Being re-issue of 500 forfeited shares) | | | | |
| (xii) | Share Forfeiture A/c (WN 5) | Dr | | 14,333 | |
| | To Capital Reserve A/c | | | | 14,333 |
| | (Being profit on 500 re-issued shares transferred to capital reserve) | | | | |

**Working Notes**

1. Excess amount received on Rohan's application

   Rohan has been allotted = 300 shares

   He must have applied for $\left(\frac{17,500}{15,000} \times 300\right) = 350$ shares

| | Amt (₹) |
|---|---|
| Amount received from Rohan (350 × 40) | 14,000 |
| Amount adjusted on application (300 × 40) | (12,000) |
| Amount adjusted on allotment | 2,000 |
| Money due on allotment (300 × 30) | 9,000 |
| Money adjusted | (2,000) |
| Balance due on allotment | 7,000 |

2. Amount received on allotment

| | |
|---|---|
| Total amount due on allotment (15,000 × 30) | 4,50,000 |
| Amount received on application | (1,00,000) |
| | 3,50,000 |
| Amount not received on Rohan's share | (7,000) |
| | 3,43,000 |

3. Aman's allotted shares $= 525 \times \frac{15,000}{17,500} = 450$ shares

4. Money received on first call

| | |
|---|---|
| First call money due on 14,700 shares (14,700 × 30) | 4,41,000 |
| Application money not received on 450 shares (450 × 30) | (13,500) |
| | 4,27,500 |

5. 500 shares have been re-issued including 450 shares of Aman and balance 50 shares of Rohan

| | |
|---|---|
| Profit on 50 shares (11,000/300 × 50) | 1,833 |
| Profit on 450 shares | 22,500 |
| | 24,333 |
| (–) Loss on issue of 500 shares | (10,000) |
| | 14,333 |

*Or* (i) Number of shares allotted to Ram $= 360 \times \frac{5}{6} = 300$ shares

(ii) $(300 \times 2) =$ ₹ 600

(iii) **Amount Forfeited on Ram's shares**

Number of shares applied by Ram = 360

Amount paid by Ram on application = 360 × 2 = 720 (forfeited amount)

(iv) Calculation of the amount due but not paid on allotment

(a) Total number of shares applied = 360

(b) Total money paid on application (360 × 2) = ₹ 720

(c) Excess application money [720 – (300 × 2)] = ₹ 120

(d) Total amount due on allotment (300 × 5) = ₹ 1,500

(e) Amount due but not paid on allotment (1,500 – 120) = ₹ 1,380

(v) **JOURNAL**

| Date | Particulars | | LF | Amt (Dr) | Amt (Cr) |
|---|---|---|---|---|---|
| (a) | Share Capital A/c | Dr | | 3,000 | |
| | Securities Premium A/c | Dr | | 600 | |
| | To Forfeited Shares A/c | | | | 720 |
| | To Share Allotment A/c | | | | 1,380 |
| | To Share First and Final Call A/c | | | | 1,500 |
| | (Being 300 shares forfeited for non-payment of allotment and call money) | | | | |
| (b) | Bank A/c | Dr | | 900 | |
| | Forfeited Share A/c | Dr | | 100 | |
| | To Share Capital A/c | | | | 1,000 |
| | (Being 100 forfeited shares re-issued as fully paid-up for ₹ 9 share) | | | | |

| Date | Particulars | | LF | Amt (Dr) | Amt (Cr) |
|---|---|---|---|---|---|
| | Forfeited Share A/c | Dr | | 140 | |
| | To Capital Reserve A/c | | | | 140 |
| | (Being transfer of gain on re-issue to capital reserve) (WN) | | | | |

**Working Note**

Amount transferred to capital reserve

Amount forfeited on 300 shares = ₹ 720

∴ Amount forfeited on 100 shares (720/300 × 100) = 240

(–) Discount allowed on 100 shares re-issued = (100)

Gain on re-issue to be transferred to capital reserve = 140

**10.** (A) (a) Interest on Devakshi's Drawings $= 8{,}000 \times \frac{8}{100} \times \frac{6}{12} =$ ₹ 320

Interest on Ragini's Drawings $= 10{,}000 \times \frac{8}{100} \times \frac{6}{12} =$ ₹ 400

(b) **JOURNAL**

| Date | Particulars | | LF | Amt (Dr) | Amt (Cr) |
|---|---|---|---|---|---|
| | Interest on Devakshi's Loan A/c | Dr | | 1,200 | |
| | To Loan by Ragini A/c | | | | 1,200 |
| | (Being interest on loan provided) | | | | |
| | Profit and Loss A/c | Dr | | 1,200 | |
| | To Interest on Devakshi's Loan | | | | 1,200 |
| | (Being interest on loan transferred to profit and loss account) | | | | |

**Working Note**

₹ 1,200 is the amount of interest on loan to Devakshi on ₹ 20,000 @ 6% per annum as rate of interest was not stated in problem.

(c) Reserve will be computed on divisible profits and the amount of divisible profits would be 41,480 + 720 – 6,000 – 4,000 = ₹ 32,200

∴ Amount transferred to Reserve account = 32,200 × 10% = ₹ 3,220

**JOURNAL**

| Date | Particulars | | LF | Amt (Dr) | Amt (Cr) |
|---|---|---|---|---|---|
| | Profit and Loss Appropriation A/c | Dr | | 3,220 | |
| | To Reserve A/c | | | | 3,220 |
| | (Being amount transferred to reserve account) | | | | |

**JOURNAL**

(d)

| Date | Particulars | | LF | Amt (Dr) | Amt (Cr) |
|---|---|---|---|---|---|
| | Interest on Capital A/c | Dr | | 6,000 | |
| | To Devakshi's Capital A/c (60,000 × 6%) | | | | 3,600 |
| | To Ragini's Capital A/c (40,000 × 6%) | | | | 2,400 |
| | (Being interest allowed @ 6%) | | | | |
| | Profit and Loss Appropriation A/c | Dr | | 6,000 | |
| | To Interest on Capital A/c | | | | 6,000 |
| | (Being interest on capital transferred to profit and loss appropriation account) | | | | |

(B) **JOURNAL**

| Date | Particulars | | LF | Amt (Dr) | Amt (Cr) |
|---|---|---|---|---|---|
| | Profit and Loss Appropriation A/c | Dr | | 28,980 | |
| | To Devakshi's Capital A/c | | | | 14,490 |
| | To Ragini's Capital A/c | | | | 14,490 |
| | (Being profit transferred to partner's capital account) | | | | |

**Working Note**

**Profit and Loss Appropriation Account**
for the year ended ..........

| Dr Particulars | | Amt (₹) | Particulars | | Cr Amt (₹) |
|---|---|---|---|---|---|
| To Interest on Capital A/cs | | | By Net Profit as per Profit and Loss A/c (42,680 – 1,200) | | 41,480 |
| Devakshi | 3,600 | | | | |
| Ragini | 2,400 | 6,000 | By Interest on Drawings A/c | | |
| To Commission : Ragini (1,00,000 × 4%) | | 4,000 | Devakshi | 320 | |
| To Reserve A/c | | 3,220 | Ragini | 400 | 720 |
| To Net Profit transferred to | | | | | |
| Devakshi's Capital A/c | 14,490 | | | | |
| Ragini's Capital A/c | 14,490 | 28,980 | | | |
| | | 42,200 | | | 42,200 |

**Working Notes**

1. When question is silent upon sharing of profits, then it will be shared equally, i.e. 1 : 1.
2. Alternatively, interest on loan can be taken to the credit of Devakshi's loan account.

**Value Points**

- If interest rate on loan provided by the partner is not mentioned, it will be charged @ 6% p.a.
- If the question is silent about the time of drawings, average period will be assumed to be 6.

*Or* (A) (a) Interest on each partner's drawings $= 1{,}20{,}000 \times \frac{3}{100} \times \frac{6.5}{12} =$ ₹ 1,950

Total interest on drawings charged from the partners = 1,950 × 3 = ₹ 5,850

(b) **Profit and Loss Appropriation Account**
for the year ended 31st March, 2022

| Dr Particulars | | Amt (₹) | Particulars | | Cr Amt (₹) |
|---|---|---|---|---|---|
| To Interest on Capital A/c | | | By Profit and Loss A/c (Net profit) | | 7,00,000 |
| R | 72,000 | | By A's Capital A/c | | 1,00,000 |
| A | 60,000 | | By Interest on Drawings A/c | | |
| S | 60,000 | 1,92,000 | R | 1,950 | |
| To Salary to A | | 18,000 | A | 1,950 | |
| To Profit transferred to Capital A/c | | | S | 1,950 | 5,850 |
| R | 2,38,340 | | | | |
| A | 2,38,340 | | | | |
| S | 1,19,170 | 5,95,850 | | | |
| | | 8,05,850 | | | 8,05,850 |

**Working Note**

Firm's profit is ₹ 7,00,000 (i.e ₹ 1,00,000 less than the amount guaranteed by A). As such ₹ 1,00,000 will be debited to A's capital account and credited to profit and loss appropriation account.

(c) **A's Capital Account**

| Dr Particulars | Amt (₹) | Particulars | Cr Amt (₹) |
|---|---|---|---|
| To Profit and Loss Appropriation A/c | 1,00,000 | By Balance b/d | 10,00,000 |
| To Drawings A/c | 1,20,000 | By Interest on Capital A/c | 60,000 |
| To Interest on Drawings A/c | 1,950 | By Salary A/c | 18,000 |
| To Balance c/d | 10,94,390 | By Profit and Loss Appropriation A/c | 2,38,340 |
| | 13,16,340 | | 13,16,340 |

(B) Interest on capital (1,00,000) of Somil – ₹ 60,000 and Vomil – ₹ 40,000. Profit of ₹ 90,000 is not adequate enough to pay the interest on capital. Thus, profit will be credited to their respective capital account in the ratio of ₹ 60,000 : 40,000 is 3 : 2.

∴ Profit transferred to Somil $= 90{,}000 \times \frac{3}{5} =$ ₹ 54,000; Vomil $= 90{,}000 \times \frac{2}{5} =$ ₹ 36,000

**11.** (i) • Current ratio

• (*a*) Current ratio will improve because both current assets and the current liabilities are decreased by the same amount.

(ii) (*c*) High EPS indicates more profitability

(iii) (a) $\frac{\text{Absolute Change in Profit}}{\text{Previous Year Profit}} \times 100$ (b) $\frac{(30{,}767 - 19{,}833)}{19{,}833} \times 100 = 55\%$

(iv) Cash used in financing activity = 1,500 × 110 = ₹ 1,65,000

(v) Cash provided by operations increased in 2023 compared to 2022 primarily due to improved operating results.

Operating activity cash flows include transactions, adjustments and changes in value not defined as investing or financing activities.

**12.**

**Comparative Statement of Profit and Loss**

for the years ended 31st March, 2022 and 2023

| Particulars | Note No. | 31st March, 2022 (₹) | 31st March, 2023 (₹) | Absolute Change (₹) | % Change |
|---|---|---|---|---|---|
| I. Revenue from Operations | | 30,00,000 | 48,00,000 | 18,00,000 | 60 |
| II. (–) **Expenses** | | | | | |
| Employee's Benefit Expenses | | 18,00,000 | 22,00,000 | 4,00,000 | 22.2 |
| Other Expenses | | 4,00,000 | 2,00,000 | (2,00,000) | (50) |
| **Total Expenses** | | 22,00,000 | 24,00,000 | 2,00,000 | 9.09 |
| III. Profit before Tax (I – II) | | 8,00,000 | 24,00,000 | 16,00,000 | 200 |
| IV. (–) Tax | | 3,20,000 | 9,60,000 | 6,40,000 | 200 |
| V. Profit after Tax (III – IV) | | 4,80,000 | 14,40,000 | 9,60,000 | 200 |

**13.** (a)

| Particulars | | Amt (₹) |
|---|---|---|
| Net Profit before Tax (WN) | | 85,000 |
| Ajustments for | | |
| (+) Depreciation | 1,00,000 | |
| (+) Loss on Sale of Machine | 10,000 | |
| (+) Interest on Debentures | 10,000 | 1,20,000 |
| Operating Profit before Working Capital Changes | | 2,05,000 |

**Working Note**

| **Calculation of Net Profit before Tax** | **Amt (₹)** |
|---|---|
| Net Profit i.e. (–50,000 – 45,000) | (95,000) |
| (+) Proposed Dividend | 45,000 |
| (+) Proposed for Tax | 1,35,000 |
| | 85,000 |

(b) **Cash Flow from Investing Activities**

| Particulars | | Amt (₹) |
|---|---|---|
| **Cash Flow from Investing Activities** | | |
| Purchase of Machine | (3,00,000) | |
| Sale of Machine | 40,000 | |
| Cash Used in Investing Activities | | (2,60,000) |

**Working Note**

Dr **Property, Plant and Equipment (Machinery) Account** Cr

| Particulars | Amt (₹) | Particulars | Amt (₹) |
|---|---|---|---|
| To Balance b/d | 4,00,000 | By Depreciation A/c | 1,00,000 |
| To Bank A/c (Purchases) | 3,00,000 | By Cash A/c (Sales) | 40,000 |
| | | By Loss on Sales A/c | 10,000 |
| | | By Balance c/d | 5,50,000 |
| | 7,00,000 | | 7,00,000 |

(c) **Cash Flow from Financing Activities**

| Particulars | | Amt (₹) |
|---|---|---|
| **Cash Flow from Financing Activities** | | |
| Issue of Shares | 1,00,000 | |
| Securities Premium Reserve | 20,000 | |
| Issue of Debentures | 75,000 | |
| Interest Paid | (10,000) | |
| Dividend Paid | (45,000) | |
| Cash Flow from Financing Activities | | 1,40,000 |

*Or*

**Cash Flow Statement**
for the year ended 31st March, 2022

| Particulars | | Amt (₹) |
|---|---|---|
| I. **Cash Flow from Operating Activities** | | |
| Net Profit before Tax | | 7,500 |
| (+) Decrease in Current Assets and Increase in Current Liabilities | | |
| Decrease in Trade Receivables | 6,750 | |
| Decrease in Inventories | 750 | |
| (–) Increase in Current Assets and Decrease in Current Liabilities | | |
| Decrease in Trade Payables | (33,000) | (25,500) |
| Net Cash Used in Operating Activities | | (18,000) |
| II. **Cash Flow from Investing Activities** | | |
| Purchase of Property, Plant and Equipment | (23,750) | |
| Purchase of Non-current Investments | (1,500) | |
| Net Cash Used in Investing Activities | | (25,250) |
| III. **Cash Flow from Financing Activities** | | |
| Issue of Share Capital | 25,000 | |
| Net Cash from Financing Activities | | 25,000 |
| Net Decrease in Cash and Cash Equivalents (I + II + III) | | (18,250) |
| (+) Opening Balance of Cash and Cash Equivalents (42,000 + 16,750) | | 58,750 |
| Closing Balance of Cash and Cash Equivalents (34,250 + 6,250) | | 40,500 |

**14.** (i) Liquid Ratio $= \dfrac{\text{Liquid Assets}}{\text{Current Liabilities}} = \dfrac{4,35,000}{2,90,000} = 1.5:1$

Liquid Assets = Current Assets – Inventories

$= 5,00,000 - 65,000 = ₹\ 4,35,000$

(ii) Working Capital Turnover Ratio $= \frac{\text{Revenue from Operations}}{\text{Working Capital}} = \frac{5,25,000}{2,90,000} = 1.81$ times

Revenue from Operations = ₹ 5,25,000

Working Capital = Current Assets – Current Liabilities

= 5,00,000 – 2,90,000 = ₹ 2,10,000

(iii) Gross Profit Ratio $= \frac{\text{Gross Profit *}}{\text{Net Revenue from Operations (Sales)}} \times 100 = \frac{(-)\,1,55,000}{5,25,000} \times 100 = (-)\,29.52\%$

where,

Revenue from Operations = Credit Revenue from Operations + Cash Revenue from Operations

$= 3,00,000 + \frac{75}{100} \times 3,00,000 = 3,00,000 + 2,25,000 =$ ₹ 5,25,000

Gross Profit = Revenue from Operations – Cost of Revenue from Operations

= 5,25,000 – 6,80,000 = (₹ 1,55,000)

*Gross Profit = (₹ 1,55,000)

(iv) Proprietary Ratio $= \frac{\text{Shareholders' Funds}}{\text{Total Assets}} \times 100 = \frac{8,00,000}{14,30,000} \times 100 = 55.94\%$

Proprietary Ratio = 55.94%

Total Liabilities = Paid-up Capital + 9% Debentures + Current Liabilities

= 8,00,000 + 3,40,000 + 2,90,000 = ₹ 14,30,000

Total Assets = Total Liabilities

∴ Total Assets = ₹ 14,30,000

Shareholders' Funds = Paid-up Capital = ₹ 8,00,000

SQP Code : **PB-3/15** Series ***i*-Succeed 3-25/15** Roll No. | | | | | | | | |

# Sample Question Paper 03

## Accounts 12th (Code 858)

### General Instructions

1. Candidates are allowed additional 15 minutes for only reading the paper. They must not start writing during this time.
2. Section-A is compulsory for all candidates and has ten questions.
3. Candidates have to attempt all questions from either Section-B or Section-C*.
4. Internal choices have been provided in five questions in Section-A and one question in Section-B.
5. The intended marks for questions or parts of questions are given in the brackets [ ].
6. All calculations should be shown clearly.
7. All workings, including rough work, should be done on the same page as, and adjacent to, the rest of the answer.

*Section-C has not been covered.

**Time :** 3 Hrs.

**Max. Marks :** 80

## Section A Answer All Questions

[60 Marks]

**Que 1.**

In sub-parts (i) to (iv), choose the correct option and in sub-parts (v) to (x) answer the questions as instructed.

(i) What journal entry will be passed by the firm in case of dissolution when realisation expenses are paid by the firm on behalf of a partner? **(Application) [1]**

(a) Debit Realisation A/c and Credit Cash A/c
(b) Debit Realisation A/c and Credit Partner's Capital A/c
(c) Debit Partner's Capital A/c and Credit Cash A/c
(d) Debit Cash A/c and Credit Realisation A/c

(ii) A firm's balance sheet had a workmen compensation reserve of ₹ 40,000. Sandy, a new partner is admitted. The liability against the same was determined to be ₹ 30,000. What amount out of workmen compensation reserve will be distributed among old partners? **(Application) [1]**

(a) ₹ 10,000 (b) ₹ 70,000
(c) ₹ 30,000 (d) None of these

(iii) Choose the correct sequence of events for the forfeiture of shares.

I. Re-issue of shares
II. Amount transferred to capital reserve
III. Default on calls
IV. Forfeiture of shares **(Recall) [1]**

**Codes**

(a) I, III, IV, II (b) III, IV, I, II
(c) IV, I, III, II (d) III, II, I, IV

(iv) Employee provident fund, at the time of retirement of a partner, is transferred to **(Application) [1]**

(a) debit side of revaluation account
(b) credit side of partner's capital account
(c) new balance sheet prepared after partner's retirement
(d) debit side of partner's capital account

(v) **Assertion** (A) Rent to a partner is not shown in profit and loss appropriation account.
**Reason** (R) Rent to a partner is a charge against profit. **(Evaluate) [1]**

**Alternatives**

(a) Both Assertion (A) and Reason (R) are true and Reason (R) is the correct explanation of Assertion (A)

(b) Both Assertion (A) and Reason (R) are true, but Reason (R) is not the correct explanation of Assertion (A)

(c) Assertion (A) is true, but Reason (R) is false

(d) Assertion (A) is false, but Reason (R) is true

(vi) India's minister for technology said a multibillion-dollar chip venture between Taiwanese electronics manufacturer Foxconn Technology and resources conglomerate Vedanta ended due to internal issues.

**Source** *The Wall Street Journal*

(a) Based on the above statement, mention any one reason that can lead to dissolution of a partnership firm.

(b) What happens to the business if it becomes unlawful? (Recall) [1]

(vii) Vashya Ltd. issued 30,000, 10% debentures of ₹ 100 each as collateral security for a loan of ₹ 25,00,000 taken from Bank of India. Pass the journal entry for issue of debentures as a collateral security. (Application) [1]

(viii) A and B are partners sharing profits and losses in the ratio of 3 : 2. C is admitted as a new partner.

C gets 3/20th share from A and 1/20th share from B. Calculate old partners sacrificing ratio. (Application) [1]

(ix) X Ltd. purchased a building for ₹ 3,00,000 payable as 20% in cash and balance by allotment of 8% debentures of ₹ 100 each at a discount of 20%. Pass the journal entry for the above transaction. (Application) [1]

(x) Name an item that comes under the head non-current liabilities. (Understanding) [1]

## Que 2.

Amit, Anuj and Agraj are partners sharing profits and losses in the ratio of 4 : 3 : 1 respectively. Anju retires, selling his share of profit to Amit and Agraj for ₹ 8,10,000, ₹ 3,60,000 being paid by Amit and ₹ 4,50,000 by Agraj.

You are required to give necessary journal entry to record the above said sale of Anuj's share to Amit and Agraj. (Application) [3]

*Or*

P and Q are partners sharing profits and losses in the ratio of 3 : 2. They admit R into the firm for 1/4th share in profits which he takes 1/6th from P and 1/12 th from Q. R brings ₹ 9,000 as goodwill out of his share of ₹ 15,000. Pass necessary journal entries to record this arrangement. (Application)

## Que 3.

Kansal Ltd. issued 25,000, 10% debentures of ₹ 100 each.

(i) Give journal entry for issue of debentures when the debentures were issued at a premium of 20%.

(ii) Give the amount (in rupees) for securities premium per debenture.

(iii) Prepare an extract of balance sheet (liabilities) when debentures were issued as a collateral security. (Application) [3]

## Que 4.

On 1st April, 2019, Goyal Ltd. (a listed company) issued 2,000, 8% debentures of ₹ 100 each at a discount of 4%, redeemable at a premium of 5% after 5 years. The issue was fully subscribed. Debentures were redeemed on due date.

You are required to

(i) Give the amounts payable with

(a) Debenture redemption reserve.

(b) Debenture application and allotment. [2]

(ii) Prepare loss on issue of debentures account. (Application) [1]

*Or*

The following balance appeared in the books of King Ltd. on 1st April, 2023.

10% debentures ₹ 25,00,000

Debenture redemption reserve ₹ 2,50,000

Debentures are redeemable on 31st March, 2024 at premium of 2%. Debenture redemption investment purchased on 1st April, 2023 realised 101% on the date of redemption and the debentures were redeemed on the due date.

You are required to prepare

(i) Debentureholders' account

(ii) Debenture redemption investment account

**(Application) [3]**

**Que 5.**

Meet and Neeta were partners in a firm, sharing profits in the ratio of 3:1. Their balance sheet on 31st March, 2023 was as follows

**Balance Sheet**

as at 31st March, 2023

| Liabilities | | Amt (₹) | Assets | | Amt (₹) |
|---|---|---|---|---|---|
| Creditors | | 1,20,000 | Cash in Hand | | 16,000 |
| Bills Payables | | 4,000 | Debtors | 2,00,000 | |
| General Reserve | | 64,000 | (–) Provision for Doubtful Debts | (20,000) | 1,80,000 |
| Outstanding Salary | | 12,000 | Bills Receivables | | 40,000 |
| Capital A/cs | | | Patents | | 4,000 |
| Meet | 2,40,000 | | Machinery | | 1,60,000 |
| Neeta | 80,000 | 3,20,000 | Stock | | 1,20,000 |
| | | 5,20,000 | | | 5,20,000 |

They admit Geet as a new partner on this date. New profit sharing ratio is agreed as 3 : 2 : 3. Geet brings in proportionate capital after the following adjustment

(i) Geet brings ₹ 64,000 as her share of goodwill.

(ii) Provision for doubtful debts is to be reduced by ₹ 8,000.

(iii) There is an old typewriter valued at ₹ 9,600. It does not appear in the books of the firm. It is now to be recorded.

(iv) Patents are valueless.

(v) A liability of ₹ 20,000 included in creditors is not likely to arise.

You are required to calculate

(a) Sacrificing ratio

(b) Geet's capital contribution

**(Application) [3]**

**Que 6.**

SP-03 Nandini and Rohit are partners in a firm sharing profits and losses in the ratio of 3 : 2. Their balance sheet as at 31st March, 2023 was as follows

**Balance Sheet of Nandini and Rohit**

at as 31st March, 2023

| Liabilities | | Amt (₹) | Assets | Amt (₹) |
|---|---|---|---|---|
| Sundry Creditors | | 40,000 | Cash | 24,000 |
| Provision for Bad Debts | | 4,000 | Debtors | 36,000 |
| General Reserve | | 6,000 | Stock | 40,000 |
| Outstanding Salary | | 10,000 | Furniture | 80,000 |
| Capitals | | | Plant and Machinery | 80,000 |
| Nandini | 1,20,000 | | | |
| Rohit | 80,000 | 2,00,000 | | |
| | | 2,60,000 | | 2,60,000 |

Kartik was admitted for 1/6th share in the profits on the following terms

(i) Kartik will bring ₹ 60,000 as his capital and ₹ 20,000 for his share of goodwill premium, half of which will be withdrawn by Nandini and Rohit.

(ii) Debtors of ₹ 3,000 will be written-off as bad debts and provision of 5% will be created on debtors for bad and doubtful debts.

(iii) Investments of ₹ 5,000 not mentioned in balance sheet were to be taken into account.

(iv) Outstanding salary will be paid-off.

(v) A creditor of ₹ 4,200, not recorded in the books was to be taken into account.

(vi) Stock to be depreciated by 10%, furniture by ₹ 1,000 and plant and machinery by 8%.

Pass necessary journal entries for the above transactions in the books of the firm, at the time of Kartik's admission. (Application) [6]

*Or*

Following is the balance sheet of P, Q and R as at 31st December, 2023, sharing profits in the ratio of 5 : 3 : 2.

**Balance Sheet**
as at 31st December, 2023

| Liabilities | | Amt (₹) | Assets | Amt (₹) |
|---|---|---|---|---|
| Creditors | | 7,000 | Cash | 13,000 |
| Reserve Fund | | 10,000 | Debtors | 8,000 |
| Capital A/cs | | | Machinery | 30,000 |
| P | 30,000 | | Stock | 10,000 |
| Q | 25,000 | | Patents | 6,000 |
| R | 15,000 | 70,000 | Buildings | 20,000 |
| | | 87,000 | | 87,000 |

P died on 1st July, 2024. The partnership deed provided for the following on the death of a partner

(i) Patents are to be valued at ₹ 8,000, machinery at ₹ 28,000 and buildings at ₹ 30,000.

(ii) Interest on capital is to be provided at 10% per annum.

(iii) Goodwill of the firm is valued at 2 years' purchase of the average profits of the last five years, which were

2019 – ₹ 15,000; 2020 – ₹ 13,000; 2021 – ₹ 12,000; 2022 – ₹ 15,000; 2023 – ₹ 20,000

(iv) P's share of profit for the year 2023 has been accrued on the same scale as in 2023.

(v) P's executor is to be paid ₹ 11,500 and balance transferred to his loan account.

You are required to

(a) Calculate P's share in goodwill [1]

(b) Prepare P's capital account (Application) [5]

SP-03

**Que 7.**
Erica, Aditi and Tarini were partners in a firm sharing profits and losses in the ratio of 5 : 3 : 2. Due to difference of opinion, they decided to dissolve the partnership with effect from 1st April, 2023, on which date the firm's balance sheet was as follows

**Balance Sheet of Erica, Aditi and Tarini**
as at 1st April, 2023

| Liabilities | | Amt (₹) | Assets | | Amt (₹) |
|---|---|---|---|---|---|
| Employees' Provident Fund | | 8,000 | Cash at Bank | | 20,000 |
| Sundry Creditors | | 10,000 | Debtors | 22,000 | |
| Investment Fluctuation Reserve | | 4,000 | (–) Provision for Bad Debts | (2,000) | 20,000 |
| Current A/cs | | | Stock | | 12,000 |
| Erica | 8,000 | | Plant and Machinery | | 30,000 |
| Aditi | 10,000 | 18,000 | Land and Building | | 45,000 |

| Liabilities | | Amt (₹) | Assets | Amt (₹) |
|---|---|---|---|---|
| Capital A/cs | | | Investments | 35,000 |
| Erica | 60,000 | | Advertisement Suspense A/c | 3,000 |
| Aditi | 40,000 | | Current A/c | |
| Tarini | 30,000 | 1,30,000 | Tarini | 5,000 |
| | | 1,70,000 | | 1,70,000 |

The following additional information was given

(i) Plant and machinery costing ₹ 20,000 was taken over by Erica at ₹ 16,000 and the remaining machineries realised ₹ 9,000.

(ii) Land and building realised ₹ 42,000.

(iii) Investments were taken over by Aditi at ₹ 28,000.

(iv) Sundry debtors included a bad debt for ₹ 1,000 and the amount was realised from the good debtors subject to a cash discount of 10%.

(v) A creditor for ₹ 2,000 was untraceable and other creditors accepted payments allowing 10% discount.

(vi) Erica was allowed to retain the whole of the stock as her remuneration for services rendered by her in the course of dissolution of the firm.

You are required to prepare

(a) Realisation account (b) Partners' capital account **(Application) [6]**

**Que 8.**

From the following information, prepare the balance sheet of Satya Ltd. as at 31st March, 2023 as per provisions of Schedule III, Part I of the Companies Act, 2013. **(Application) [6]**

| Particulars | Amt (₹) | Particulars | Amt(₹) |
|---|---|---|---|
| General Reserve | 18,00,000 | Trade Payable | 15,00,000 |
| 8% Debentures (1/4 of the debentures to be redeemed on 31st March, 2024) | 18,00,000 | Trade Receivable | 15,36,000 |
| | | Plant and Machinery | 30,00,000 |
| Depreciation on Plant and Machinery | 4,20,000 | Land and Building | 24,00,000 |
| Balance of Statement of Profit and Loss | 7,20,000 | Equity Share Capital | 30,00,000 |
| | | Inventories | 3,84,000 |
| | | Cash and Cash Equivalents | 19,20,000 |



**Que 9.**

(A) Anu, Manu and Tanu were partners in a firm, sharing profits in the ratio of 1 : 2 : 2. After the division of profits of the year ended 31st March, 2023, thin capital stood at

| | |
|---|---|
| Anu | ₹ 6,00,000 |
| Manu | ₹ 8,00,000 |
| Tanu | ₹ 9,20,000 |

Their partnership deed contains the following clauses

(i) Manu was to be given salary @ ₹ 10,000 for 4 months.

(ii) Interest on capital to be allowed @ ₹ 10% per annum.

**Additional Information**

- During the year Anu, Manu and Tanu withdrew ₹ 80,000 each.
- The profit for the year was ₹ 4,00,000.

While preparing final accounts, interest on capitals and salary to Manu were not allowed. You are required to

(i) Calculate opening capital of partner's. [1½]

(ii) Pass necessary adjustment entry. [4 ½]

(iii) Prepare the partners' capital account as on 1st April, 2023. (Application) [2]

(B) Calculate interest on Manu's drawings if he has withdrawn ₹ 2,00,000 during the year and interest on drawing is charged @ 10%. (Application) [2]

*Or*

A and B decided to start a partnership firm. Their capital contribution was A — ₹ 2,00,000, B — ₹ 1,00,000 and C — Nil.

On 1st October, 2021, B granted a loan of ₹ 1,20,000 to the firm.

The terms of partnership were as follows

(i) A, B and C share profits in the ratio of 2 : 2 : 1.

(ii) Interest on capital @ 6% per annum. Interest on drawings @ 5%.

(iii) A to get a monthly salary of ₹ 6,000 and B to get salary of ₹ 4,000 per quarter.

(iv) 10% of the net profits are to be transferred to general reserve.

The profit of the firm for the year ended 31st March, 2022 was ₹ 3,37,800. Drawings of A and B were ₹ 50,000 and ₹ 40,000 respectively.

Due to shortage of capital, A contributed ₹ 50,000 on 30th September, 2021 and B contributed ₹ 20,000 on 1st January, 2022 as additional capital. Calculate

(i) Interest on capital of A and B. (Application) [2]

(ii) Pass necessary journal entries to record

(a) Charging interest on B's loan. (Recall) [2]

(b) Additional capital introduced by A. (Application) [2]

(c) Transfer of profit to general reserve. (Application) [2]

(d) Calculate interest on drawings charged from A. (Application) [2]

**Que 10.**

Sandhya Ltd. invited applications for issuing 10,000 equity shares of ₹ 10 each. The amount payable as ₹ 1 on application, ₹ 2 on allotment and ₹ 3 on first call and balance on final call.

The issue was fully subscribed. Ravi to whom 100 shares were allotted, failed to pay the allotment money and his shares were forfeited immediately after allotment. Amit to whom 150 shares were allotted, failed to pay the first call. His shares were also forfeited after the first call. Afterwards the second and final call was made. Sabi to whom 50 shares were allotted, failed to pay the second and final call his shares were also forfeited. All the forfeited shares were reissued at ₹ 9 per share fully paid-up. Pass the necessary journal entries in the books of Sandhya Ltd. (Application) [10]



*Or*

Sarthak Ltd. issued 10,000 equity shares of ₹ 40 each payable ₹ 10 on application, ₹ 15 on allotment, ₹ 10 on first call and ₹ 5 on the final call.

In all, applications for 16,000 equity shares were received out of these applications for 4,000 equity shares were rejected and allotment was made to others on pro-rata basis. Every shareholder paid the money as and when due, except Sohan who was allotted 400 equity shares and who did not pay the allotment money. His shares were forfeited immediately after allotment. These shares were re-issued for ₹ 30 per share as ₹ 35 paid-up after making the first call.

Give journal entries for issue, forfeiture and re-issue of forfeited shares.

(i) How much amount was received on application? [1]

(ii) What are the number of shares Sohan applied for? [1]

(iii) What is the amount forfeited on Sohan's shares? [1]

(iv) What is the amount received on allotment? [3]

(v) You are required to

(a) Pass the entry for the forfeiture of Sohan's share. [2]

(b) Pass the entry for the re-issue. (Application) [2]

## Section B

**[20 Marks]**

**Que 11.**

(i) A positive cash flow from these activities can either be good or bad, depending on the context. Positive cash flow from these activities means a company is selling more assets in value than it is acquiring. This can involve savvy cost-cutting measures and allow a company to focus on fewer projects. However, other corporations sell assets to cover unsustainable dividend payments or to cover debt obligations. A negative cash flow from these activities combined with a positive cash flow from operating activities can be a good sign, but investors still need more context.

**Source** *US News (edited)*

Based on the information with respect to cash flow statement

- Which activity is being discussed here? **(Analysis) [1]**
- Which of the following activities are related to the acquisition and disposal of long-term assets and other investments not included in cash equivalents? **(Recall) [1]**

(a) Operating activities (b) Investing activities

(c) Financing activities (d) None of these

(ii) India Inc's operating profit margin narrowed by a sharp 2.37 per cent in the December quarter to 16.3 per cent on an annual basis due to inflation and rising energy costs, a domestic ratings agency said on Monday.

**Source** *Business Standard*

Based on the following statement, which of the following is not a consequence of falling operating profit ratio? **(Understanding) [1]**

(a) High operating cost (b) High non-operating cost

(c) Both (a) and (b) (d) None of these

SP-03

(iii) The purpose of measuring the performance of local government financial management is to improve government performance, but performance measurement will help improve the ultimate effectiveness of local financial management.

**Source** *Finance news*

State how qualitative aspects are ignored in financial statement analysis. **(Analysis) [1]**

(iv) DLF Ltd's current ratio for the fiscal year 2022–23 was 2.3, which is an improvement over the previous year. This is higher than the average current ratio of 2.18 over the past five years. The current ratio measures a company's ability to pay its short-term liabilities and obligations, especially those that are due within 12 months. A current ratio above 1.00 generally indicates that a company can pay its current debts as they come due.

(a) What is the formula for calculating the aforementioned ratio?

(b) Suppose for the financial year, DLF Ltd. reported current assets as ₹ 26593.04 crore and current liabilities as ₹ 12869.13 crore, what will be the current ratio? **(Analysis) [1]**

(v) General Motors Co. engages in the designing, manufacturing and selling of trucks, crossovers, cars and automobile parts and in providing software-enabled services and subscriptions.

It operates through the following segments: GMNA, GMI, Cruise, and GM Financial. The company was founded by William C. Durant on 16th September, 1908 and is headquartered in Detroit, GM's free cash flow for Q2 2024 was $3.41B. For the 2024 fiscal year, GM's free cash flow was decreased by $3.16B and operating cash flow was $5.98B.

**Source** *Businesswise*

Based on the above news, state what could be the possible reason for this decrease?

(Application) [1]

**Que 12.**

Complete the common size income statement of Ajanta Ltd. from the given information.

(Application) [3]

**Common Size Income Statement**

for the years ended 31st March 2023 and 2023

| Particulars | 31st March, 2023 (₹) | 31st March, 2022 (₹) | Absolute Change (₹) | Percentage Change (%) |
|---|---|---|---|---|
| I. Revenue from Operations | 3,12,500 | ... | 62,500 | 25% |
| II. **Expenses** | | | | |
| (a) Purchase of Stock-in-trade | ... | 1,80,000 | ... | 21% |
| (b) Cost of Material Consumed | 15,000 | 20,000 | (5,000) | ... |
| **Total Expenses** | 2,32,500 | 2,00,000 | 32,500 | 16.25% |
| III. Profit before Tax | 80,000 | 50,000 | ... | ... |

**Que 13.**

Following are the extracts of Hindustan Unilever Ltd. balance sheet for the year ending 31st March, 2022

| Particulars | 2021-22 (₹) | 2020-21 (₹) |
|---|---|---|
| Equity Share Capital | 13,00,000 | 12,00,000 |
| Long-term Borrowings (10% Bank Loan) | 60,000 | 1,00,000 |
| **Property, Plant & Equipment and Intangible Assets** | | |
| Plant and Machinery | 1,70,000 | 1,40,000 |
| (–) Accumulated Depreciation | (24,000) | (40,500) |
| | 1,46,000 | 99,500 |
| Non-current Investments | 1,00,000 | 20,000 |
| Land (At cost) | 5,00,000 | 7,00,000 |
| Goodwill | 30,000 | 40,000 |

**Additional Information**

(i) The loan instalment and interest on loan was paid at the end of the financial year.

(ii) During the year 2021-22,

(a) The company provided depreciation on plant and machinery amounting to ₹ 13,500.

(b) The company sold 70% of its non-current investments which it held in the beginning of the year, at a profit of 20% on its book value.

| | 2021-22 (₹) | 2020-21 (₹) |
|---|---|---|
| (iii) Proposed dividend | 20,000 | 21,000 |

You are required to answer the following

(a) What is the cash flow from financing activities? [2]

(b) Prepare non-current investments account for the year ended 31st March, 2022. [2]

(c) Prepare plant and machinery account for the year ended 31st March, 2022. (Evaluate) [2]

SP-03

*Or*

From the following information, calculate cash flow from operating and investing activities of Balaji Ltd.

**Balance Sheet**
as at 31st March, 2023 and 2022

| Particulars | Note No. | 31st March, 2023 (₹) | 31st March, 2022 (₹) |
|---|---|---|---|
| I. **EQUITY AND LIABILITIES** | | | |
| 1. **Shareholders' Funds** | | | |
| (i) Share Capital | | 3,50,000 | 2,50,000 |
| (ii) Reserves and Surplus | 1 | 5,000 | 20,000 |
| 2. **Non-current Liabilities** | | | |
| Long-term Borrowings : 12% Debentures | | 1,00,000 | 60,000 |
| 3. **Current Liabilities** | | 1,25,000 | 1,50,000 |
| **Total** | | 5,80,000 | 4,80,000 |
| II. **ASSETS** | | | |
| 1. **Non-current Assets** | | | |
| (i) Property, Plant & Equipment and Intangible Assets | | 2,80,000 | 2,00,000 |
| (ii) Investments | | 1,00,000 | 1,00,000 |
| 2. **Current Assets** | | | |
| (i) Trade Receivables | | 1,60,000 | 1,50,000 |
| (ii) Cash and Cash Equivalents | | 40,000 | 30,000 |
| **Total** | | 5,80,000 | 4,80,000 |

**Notes to Accounts**

| Particulars | 31st March, 2023 (₹) | 31st March, 2022 (₹) |
|---|---|---|
| 1. **Reserves and Surplus** | | |
| Securities Premium | 25,000 | – |
| Surplus, i.e. Balance in Statement of Profit and Loss | (20,000) | 20,000 |
| | 5,000 | 20,000 |



**Additional Information**

(i) Debentures were issued on 1st April, 2022.

(ii) During the year, machine included in property, plant and equipment and intangible assets costing ₹ 1,20,000 was purchased and another machine having book value of ₹ 30,000 was sold at a loss of ₹ 2,000.

**(Application) [6]**

**Que 14.**

Answer any three of the following questions. **(Application) [6]**

(i) From the following information, calculate inventory turnover ratio

| | |
|---|---|
| Revenue from Operations | ₹ 32,000 |
| Average Inventory | ₹ 4,400 |
| Gross Loss | 5% |

(ii) Calculate net profit ratio from the following statement of profit and loss of ABC Ltd. for the year ended 31st March, 2023.

| Particulars | Note No. | 31st March, 2023 (₹) |
|---|---|---|
| I. Revenue from Operations | | 1,20,600 |
| II. Expenses | | 1,02,400 |
| III. Profit before Tax (I-II) | | 18,200 |
| IV. Tax @ 50% | | 9,100 |
| V. Profit after Tax (III-IV) | | 9,100 |

(iii) From the following information calculate current ratio and liquid ratio.

| | Amt (₹) |
|---|---|
| Liquid Assets | 75,000 |
| Working Capital | 60,000 |
| Current Liabilities | 40,000 |

(iv) From the following information compute total asset to debt ratio.

| | Amt (₹) |
|---|---|
| Long-term Borrowings | 3,00,000 |
| Long-term Provisions | 1,50,000 |
| Current Liabilities | 75,000 |
| Non-current Assets | 5,40,000 |
| Current Assets | 1,35,000 |

# Solutions *in Topper's Style*

**My Commitment** *I affirm that I am reviewing these solutions only after I have solved the Sample Question Paper 3 on my own. My purpose of looking the solutions is solely to verify whether my answers/solutions were correct or not and to identify my mistakes in case my solutions were wrong or I could not solve that.*

**1.** (i) (*c*) Debit Partner's Capital A/c and Credit Cash A/c

(ii) (*a*) 40,000 – 30,000 = ₹ 10,000 (to be distributed among old partners).

(iii) (*b*) III, IV, I, II

(iv) (*c*) new balance sheet prepared after partner's retirement

(v) (*a*) Both Assertion (A) and Reason (R) are true and Reason (R) is the correct explanation of Assertion (A)

(vi) (*a*) When the term for which the partnership firm was constituted, has expired.

(b) When the business of the firm becomes unlawful, it may lead to dissolution of the business firm.

(vii) **JOURNAL**

| Date | Particulars | | LF | Amt (Dr) | Amt (Cr) |
|---|---|---|---|---|---|
| | Debenture Suspense A/c | Dr | | 30,00,000 | |
| | To 10% Debentures A/c | | | | 30,00,000 |
| | (Being ₹ 30,00,000; 10% debentures issued as a collateral security for a loan of ₹ 25,00,000) | | | | |

(viii) Share sacrificed by A in favour of C = $\frac{3}{20}$

Share sacrificed by B in favour of C = $\frac{1}{20}$

∴ Sacrificing ratio = 3: 1

(ix) **JOURNAL**

| Date | Particulars | | LF | Amt (Dr) | Amt (Cr) |
|---|---|---|---|---|---|
| | Building A/c | Dr | | 3,00,000 | |
| | Loss on Issue of Debentures A/c (3,000 × 20) | Dr | | 60,000 | |
| | To 8% Debentures A/c (3,000 × 100) | | | | 3,00,000 |
| | To Cash A/c | | | | 60,000 |
| | (Being 8% debentures issued for the building purchased) | | | | |

**Working Note**

Amount payable in the form of debentures = 3,00,000 × 80/100 = ₹ 2,40,000

Issue price of debentures = 100 – 20 = ₹ 80

Number of debentures issued = 2,40,000/80 = 3,000 debentures

(x) Long-term borrowings

**2.** **JOURNAL**

| Date | Particulars | | LF | Amt (Dr) | Amt (Cr) |
|---|---|---|---|---|---|
| | Amit's Capital A/c | Dr | | 3,60,000 | |
| | Agraj's Capital A/c | Dr | | 4,50,000 | |
| | To Anuj's Capital A/c | | | | 8,10,000 |
| | (Being the sale of Anuj's share to Amit and Agraj for ₹ 8,10,000) | | | | |

**Working Note**

Amit and Agraj purchased Anuj's share for ₹ 8,10,000 out of which Amit pays ₹ 3,60,000 and Agraj pays ₹ 4,50,000 i.e., Amit and Agraj will share Anuj's share of profit in the ratio of 3,60,000 : 4,50,000 = 4 : 5.

*Or*

**JOURNAL**

| Date | Particulars | | LF | Amt (Dr) | Amt (Cr) |
|---|---|---|---|---|---|
| | Cash A/c | Dr | | 9,000 | |
| | To Premium for Goodwill A/c | | | | 9,000 |
| | (Being amount of goodwill premium brought in by new partner) | | | | |
| | Premium for Goodwill A/c | Dr | | 9,000 | |
| | R's Current A/c | Dr | | 6,000 | |
| | To P's Capital A/c | | | | 10,000 |
| | To Q's Capital A/c | | | | 5,000 |
| | (Being premium for goodwill distributed among old partners in sacrificing ratio) | | | | |

**Working Note**

Calculation of Sacrificing Ratio

P's sacrifice $= \frac{1}{6} \times \frac{2}{2} = \frac{2}{12}$; Q's sacrifice $= \frac{1}{12}$

Sacrificing ratio = 2 : 1

**Value Points**

- 1/6th and 1/12th will be the sacrificing ratio of old partners.
- Since R is unable to bring his entire share of goodwill in cash, the balance amount will be transferred to R's current account.

3. (i) **In the Books of Kansal Ltd.**

**JOURNAL**

| Date | Particulars | | LF | Amt (Dr) | Amt (Cr) |
|---|---|---|---|---|---|
| | Debenture Application and Allotment A/c | Dr | | 30,00,000 | |
| | To 10% Debentures A/c | | | | 25,00,000 |
| | To Securities Premium A/c | | | | 5,00,000 |
| | (Being the issue of 25,000 debentures of ₹ 100 each at a premium of 20%) | | | | |

(ii) Securities premium per debenture = $100 \times 20\%$ = ₹ 20

(iii) **In the Books of Kansal Ltd.**

**Balance Sheet** (An extract)

as at ..........

| Particulars | Note No. | Amt (₹) |
|---|---|---|
| I. **EQUITY AND LIABILITIES** | | |
| 1. **Non-current Liabilities** | | |
| Long-term Borrowings | 1 | 25,00,000 |

**Notes to Accounts**

| Particulars | Amt (₹) |
|---|---|
| 1. **Long-term Borrowings** | |
| Loan from Bank (Secured by issue of 25,000, 10% debentures @ ₹ 100 each as collateral security) | 25,00,000 |

4. (i) (a) There is no requirement of creation of DRR in case of a listed company.

(b) ₹ 1,92,000 (2,000 × 96)

(ii) Dr **Loss on Issue of Debentures Account** Cr

| Date | Particulars | Amt (₹) | Date | Particulars | Amt (₹) |
|---|---|---|---|---|---|
| 2019 | | | 2020 | | |
| Apr 1 | To Discount on Issue of Debentures A/c | 8,000 | Mar 31 | By Statement of Profit and Loss A/c | 18,000 |
| Apr 1 | To Premium on Redemption of Debentures A/c | 10,000 | | | |
| | | 18,000 | | | 18,000 |

*Or* (i) Dr **Debentureholders' Account** Cr

| Date | Particulars | Amt (₹) | Date | Particulars | Amt (₹) |
|---|---|---|---|---|---|
| 2024 | | | 2024 | | |
| Mar 31 | To Bank A/c | 25,50,000 | Mar 31 | By 10% Debenture A/c | 25,00,000 |
| | | | | By Premium on Redemption of Debentures A/c | 50,000 |
| | | 25,50,000 | | | 25,50,000 |

(ii) Dr **Debenture Redemption Investment Account** Cr

| Date | Particulars | Amt (₹) | Date | Particulars | Amt (₹) |
|---|---|---|---|---|---|
| 2023 | | | | | |
| Apr 1 | To Bank A/c (15% of 25,00,000) | 3,75,000 | | | |
| 2024 | | | 2024 | | |
| Mar 31 | To Profit on Sale of Investment (1% of 3,75,000) | 3,750 | Mar 31 | By Bank A/c | 3,78,750 |
| | | 3,78,750 | | | 3,78,750 |

**5.** (a) **Calculation of Sacrificing Ratio**

Meet's sacrifice $= \frac{3}{4} - \frac{3}{8} \Rightarrow \frac{6-3}{8} = \frac{3}{8}$; Neeta's sacrifice $= \frac{1}{4} - \frac{2}{8} = \frac{2-2}{8} = 0$

$\therefore$ Sacrificing ratio = 3 : 0

(b) **Calculation of Geet's capital**

| | Amt (₹) |
|---|---|
| Total adjusted capital | |
| Capital of Meet after adjustment | 3,77,200 |
| Capital of Neeta after adjustment | 1,04,400 |
| | 4,81,600 |

Calculation of total capital of new firm

Geet joins the firm for $\frac{3}{8}$th share

Therefore, Meet and Neeta will share $\frac{5}{8}$th $\left(1-\frac{3}{8}\right)$ of the firm's profit

$$\text{Total Capital of the Firm} = \frac{\text{Adjusted Combined Capital of Old Partners}}{\text{Combined Share of Profit of the Old Partners}}$$

$$= 4,81,600 \times \frac{8}{5} = ₹\ 7,70,560$$

$$\text{Geet's capital} = \left(7,70,560 \times \frac{3}{8}\right) = ₹\ 2,88,960$$

6. **JOURNAL**

| Date | Particulars | | LF | Amt (Dr) | Amt (Cr) |
|---|---|---|---|---|---|
| 2023 | | | | | |
| Mar 31 | General Reserve A/c | Dr | | 10,000 | |
| | To Nandini's Capital A/c | | | | 6,000 |
| | To Rohit's Capital A/c | | | | 4,000 |
| | (Being general reserve distributed among partners in the ratio 3 : 2) | | | | |
| | Cash A/c | Dr | | 80,000 | |
| | To Kartik's Capital A/c | | | | 60,000 |
| | To Premium for Goodwill A/c | | | | 20,000 |
| | (Being cash received as Kartik's capital and premium for goodwill) | | | | |
| | Premium for Goodwill A/c | Dr | | 20,000 | |
| | To Nandini's Capital A/c | | | | 12,000 |
| | To Rohit's Capital A/c | | | | 8,000 |
| | (Being premium for goodwill credited to old partner's capital account in sacrificing ratio) | | | | |
| | Nandini's Capital A/c | Dr | | 6,000 | |
| | Rohit's Capital A/c | Dr | | 4,000 | |
| | To Cash A/c | | | | 10,000 |
| | (Being half of premium for goodwill amount withdrawn by old partners) | | | | |
| | Bad Debts A/c | Dr | | 3,000 | |
| | To Debtorss A/c | | | | 3,000 |
| | (Being bad debts written-off). | | | | |
| | Provision for Bad and Doubtful Debts A/c | Dr | | 3,000 | |
| | To Bad Debts A/c | | | | 3,000 |
| | (Being provision for bad and doubtful debts utilised) | | | | |
| | Revaluation A/c | Dr | | 650 | |
| | To Provision for Bad and Doubtful Debts | | | | 650 |
| | (Being provision for bad debts created) | | | | |
| | Outstanding Salary A/c | Dr | | 6,000 | |
| | To Cash A/c | | | | 6,000 |
| | (Being outstanding salary paid) | | | | |
| | Revaluation A/c | Dr | | 11,400 | |
| | To Stock A/c | | | | 4,000 |
| | To Furniture A/c | | | | 1,000 |
| | To Plant and Machinery A/c | | | | 6,400 |
| | (Being decrease in assets recorded in revaluation account) | | | | |
| | Investments A/c | Dr | | 5,000 | |
| | To Revaluation A/c | | | | 5,000 |
| | (Being increase in investments recorded) | | | | |
| | Revaluation A/c | Dr | | 4,200 | |
| | To Creditors A/c | | | | 4,200 |
| | (Being increase in creditors recorded) | | | | |
| | Nandini's Capital A/c | Dr | | 6,750 | |
| | Rohit's Capital A/c | Dr | | 4,500 | |
| | To Revaluation A/c | | | | 11,250 |
| | (Being loss on revaluation transferred to partner's capital accounts) | | | | |

*Or* (a) **Calculation of P's share of goodwill**

$$\text{Average Profit} = \frac{\text{Total Profit}}{\text{Number of Years}} = \frac{15{,}000 + 13{,}000 + 12{,}000 + 15{,}000 + 20{,}000}{5} = ₹\ 15{,}000$$

$$\text{Goodwill} = \text{Average Profit} \times \text{Number of Years' Purchase} = 15{,}000 \times 2 = ₹\ 30{,}000$$

$$\text{P's share of goodwill} = 30{,}000 \times \frac{5}{10} = ₹\ 15{,}000 \text{ (to be divided in gaining ratio 3 : 2)}$$

(b) Dr **P's Capital Account** Cr

| Particulars | Amt (₹) | Particulars | Amt (₹) |
|---|---|---|---|
| To P's Executors A/c | 61,500 | By Balance b/d | 30,000 |
| (Balance transferred) | | By Reserve Fund A/c | 5,000 |
| | | By Q's Capital A/c | 9,000 |
| | | By R's Capital A/c | 6,000 |
| | | By Revaluation A/c | 5,000 |
| | | By Profit and Loss Suspense A/c | 5,000 |
| | | By Interest on Capital A/c | 1,500 |
| | 61,500 | | 61,500 |

**Working Notes**

1. Interest on capital $\left(30{,}000 \times \frac{10}{100} \times \frac{6}{12}\right) = ₹\ 1{,}500$
2. Reserve fund $\left(10{,}000 \times \frac{5}{10}\right) = ₹\ 5{,}000$
3. P's share of profit $\left(20{,}000 \times \frac{5}{10} \times \frac{6}{12}\right) = ₹\ 5{,}000$ (for 6 months)
4. Dr **Revaluation Account** Cr

| Particulars | | Amt (₹) | Particulars | Amt (₹) |
|---|---|---|---|---|
| To Machinery A/c | | 2,000 | By Patents A/c | 2,000 |
| To Profit transferred to | | | By Buildings A/c | 10,000 |
| P's Capital A/c | 5,000 | | | |
| Q's Capital A/c | 3,000 | | | |
| R's Capital A/c | 2,000 | 10,000 | | |
| | | 12,000 | | 12,000 |

**7.** (a) Dr **Realisation Account** Cr

| Particulars | | Amt (₹) | Particulars | | Amt (₹) |
|---|---|---|---|---|---|
| To Sundry Assets | | | By Sundry Liabilities | | |
| Debtors | 22,000 | | Employee's Provident Fund | 8,000 | |
| Stock | 12,000 | | Creditors | 10,000 | |
| Plant and Machinery | 30,000 | | Investment Fluctuation Reserve | 4,000 | 22,000 |
| Land and Building | 45,000 | | By Provision for Doubtful Debts A/c | | 2,000 |
| Investments | 35,000 | 1,44,000 | By Erica's Capital A/c (Plant and machinery) | | 16,000 |
| To Bank A/c (Creditors) | | 7,200 | By Bank A/c | | |
| To Bank A/c (Employee's provident fund) | | 8,000 | Plant and Machinery | 9,000 | |
| | | | Land and Building | 42,000 | |
| | | | Debtors | 18,900 | 69,900 |
| | | | By Aditi's Capital A/c | | 28,000 |
| | | | By Loss on Realisation to | | |
| | | | Erica's Capital A/c | 10,650 | |
| | | | Aditi's Capital A/c | 6,390 | |
| | | | Tarini's Capital A/c | 4,260 | 21,300 |
| | | 1,59,200 | | | 1,59,200 |

(b) Dr **Partners' Capital Account** Cr

| Particulars | Erica (₹) | Aditi (₹) | Tarini (₹) | Particulars | Erica (₹) | Aditi (₹) | Tarini (₹) |
|---|---|---|---|---|---|---|---|
| To Current A/c | — | — | 5,000 | By Balance b/d | 60,000 | 40,000 | 30,000 |
| To Advertisement Suspense A/c | 1,500 | 900 | 600 | By Current A/c | 8,000 | 10,000 | — |
| To Realisation A/c | 16,000 | 28,000 | — | | | | |
| To Realisation A/c (Loss) | 10,650 | 6,390 | 4,260 | | | | |
| To Bank A/c (Final payment) | 39,850 | 14,710 | 20,140 | | | | |
| | 68,000 | 50,000 | 30,000 | | 68,000 | 50,000 | 30,000 |

**Common Mistake** Students usually distribute the investment fluctuation reserve in partner's capital account since its a reserve. It should be noted that investment is given on the asset side, so investment fluctuation reserve will be transferred to realisation account.

8. **Balance Sheet**
as at 31st March, 2023

| Particulars | Note No. | Amt (₹) |
|---|---|---|
| I. **EQUITY AND LIABILITIES** | | |
| 1. **Shareholders' Funds** | | |
| (i) Share Capital | | 30,00,000 |
| (ii) Reserves and Surplus | 1 | 25,20,000 |
| 2. **Non-current Liabilities** | | |
| Long-term Borrowings | 2 | 13,50,000 |
| 3. **Current Liabilities** | | |
| (i) Short-term Borrowings | | 4,50,000 |
| (ii) Trade Payables | 3 | 15,00,000 |
| **Total** | | 88,20,000 |
| II. **ASSETS** | | |
| 1. **Non-current Assets** | | |
| (i) Property, Plant & Equipment and Intangible Assets | | |
| (a) Property, Plant and Equipment | 4 | 49,80,000 |
| 2. **Current Assets** | | |
| (i) Inventories | | 3,84,000 |
| (ii) Trade Receivables | | 15,36,000 |
| (iii) Cash and Cash Equivalents | | 19,20,000 |
| **Total** | | 88,20,000 |

**Notes to Accounts**

| Particulars | Amt (₹) |
|---|---|
| 1. **Reserves and Surplus** | |
| General Reserve | 18,00,000 |
| Balance of Statement of Profit and Loss | 7,20,000 |
| | 25,20,000 |
| 2. **Long-term Borrowing** | |
| 8% Debentures | 18,00,000 |
| (–) Mature Debentures | (4,50,000) |
| | 13,50,000 |

| Particulars | | Amt (₹) |
|---|---|---|
| 3. **Short-term Borrowing** | | |
| Mature Debentures (1/4 of 18,00,000) | | 4,50,000 |
| 4. **Property, Plant and Equipment** | | |
| Plant and Machinery | 30,00,000 | |
| (−) Depreciation | (4,20,000) | 25,80,000 |
| Land and Building | | 24,00,000 |
| | | 49,80,000 |

9. (A) (i) **Calculation of Opening Capitals**

| Particulars | Anu (₹) | Manu (₹) | Tanu (₹) |
|---|---|---|---|
| Closing Capitals | 6,00,000 | 8,00,000 | 9,20,000 |
| (+) Drawings already Adjusted | 80,000 | 80,000 | 80,000 |
| (–) Profit already adjusted (2,00,000 in 1 : 2 : 2) | (80,000) | (1,60,000) | (1,60,000) |
| Opening Capitals | 6,00,000 | 7,20,000 | 8,40,000 |

(ii) **JOURNAL**

| Date | Particulars | | LF | Amt (Dr) | Amt (Cr) |
|---|---|---|---|---|---|
| 2022 | | | | | |
| Apr 1 | Tanu's Capital A/c | Dr | | 18,400 | |
| | To Anu's Capital A/c | | | | 8,800 |
| | To Manu's Capital A/c | | | | 9,600 |
| | (Being interest on capital and salary omitted to be recorded, now adjusted) | | | | |

**Working Notes**

1. **Division of Profits as per Partnership Deed**

| | | Amt (₹) |
|---|---|---|
| Profit for the year | | 4,00,000 |
| (−) Interest on capitals to | | |
| Anu (6,00,000 ×10%) | = (60,000) | |
| Manu (7,20,000 ×10%) | = (72,000) | |
| Tanu (8,40,000 ×10%) | = (84,000) | (2,16,000) |
| (−) Salary to Seema (5,000 × 4) | | (40,000) |
| Divisible profits | | 1,44,000 |

Profit share of Anu = 1,44,000 ×1/5 = ₹ 28,800

Profit share of Manu = 1,44,000 × 2/5 = ₹ 57,600

Profit share of Tanu = 1,44,000 × 2/5 = ₹ 57,600

2. **Table Showing Adjustment**

| Particulars | Anu (₹) | Manu (₹) | Tanu (₹) |
|---|---|---|---|
| As per Note No. 2 | | | |
| (i) Interest on Capitals | 60,000 | 72,000 | 84,000 |
| (ii) Salary | — | 40,000 | — |
| (iii) Profit Share | 28,800 | 57,600 | 57,600 |
| Amount to be Credited | 88,800 | 1,69,600 | 1,41,600 |
| Amount to be Debited (4,00,000 in 1:2:2) | 80,000 | 1,60,000 | 1,60,000 |
| Difference (Dr/Cr) | 8,800 (Cr) | 9,600 (Cr) | 18,400 (Dr) |

(iii) Dr **Partners' Capital Account** Cr

| Particulars | Anu (₹) | Manu (₹) | Tanu (₹) | Particulars | Anu (₹) | Manu (₹) | Tanu (₹) |
|---|---|---|---|---|---|---|---|
| To Anu's Capital A/c | — | — | 8,800 | By Balance b/d | 6,00,000 | 7,20,000 | 8,40,000 |
| To Manu's Capital A/c | — | — | 9,600 | By Tanu's Capital A/c | 8,800 | 9,600 | — |
| To Balance c/d | 6,08,800 | 7,29,600 | 8,21,600 | | | | |
| | 6,08,800 | 7,29,600 | 8,40,000 | | 6,08,800 | 7,29,600 | 8,40,000 |

**Common Mistake** Students usually consider the capital balances as opening balances and use them to calculate interest on capital. They should check the date given in question carefully, i.e. here partners' capital provided is for the year ended 31st March, 2023, i.e., closing capitals.

(B) Calculation of interest on Manu's drawings $= 8,00,000 \times \frac{10}{100} = ₹\ 80,000$

*Or* (i) **Calculation of Interest on Capital**

**A** On 2,00,000 $= 2,00,000 \times \frac{6}{100} = ₹\ 12,000$; On 50,000 $= 50,000 \times \frac{6}{100} \times \frac{6}{12} = ₹\ 1,500$

Total interest on A's capital $= 12,000 + 1,500 = ₹\ 13,500$

**B** On 1,00,000 $= 1,00,000 \times \frac{6}{100} = ₹\ 6,000$; On 20,000 $= 20,000 \times \frac{6}{100} \times \frac{3}{12} = ₹\ 300$

Total interest on B's capital $= 6,000 + 300 = ₹\ 6,300$

(ii) **JOURNAL**

| Date | Particulars | | LF | Amt (Dr) | Amt (Cr) |
|---|---|---|---|---|---|
| (a) | B's Capital A/c | Dr | | 3,600 | |
| | To Interest on loan (WN 1) | | | | 3,600 |
| | (Being interest on B's loan) | | | | |
| (b) | Cash A/c | Dr | | 50,000 | |
| | To A's Capital A/c | | | | 50,000 |
| | (Being additional capital introduced by A) | | | | |
| (c) | Profit and Loss Appropriation A/c | Dr | | 33,420 | |
| | To General Reserve (WN 2) | | | | 33,420 |
| | (Being 10% profit transferred to general reseve) | | | | |

(d) **Calculation of interest on drawings**

$A = 50,000 \times \frac{5}{100} \times \frac{6}{12} = ₹\ 1,250$

**Working Notes**

1. Interest on loan $= 1,20,000 \times 6/100 \times 6/12 = ₹\ 3,600$
2. Transfer to reserve $= 10\% \times 3,34,200 = ₹\ 33,420$

**Common Mistake** Students usually forget to consider average period while calculating interest on drawings. Average period needs to be applied in the formula in the absence of any information.

**10.** **JOURNAL**

| Date | Particulars | | LF | Amt (Dr) | Amt (Cr) |
|---|---|---|---|---|---|
| (i) | Bank A/c | Dr | | 10,000 | |
| | To Share Application A/c | | | | 10,000 |
| | (Being application money received on 10,000 shares @ ₹ 1) | | | | |
| (ii) | Share Application A/c | Dr | | 10,000 | |
| | To Share Capital A/c | | | | 10,000 |
| | (Being application money transferred to share capital) | | | | |
| (iii) | Share Allotment A/c | Dr | | 20,000 | |
| | To Share Capital A/c | | | | 20,000 |
| | (Being allotment money due on 10,000 shares @ ₹ 2) | | | | |
| (iv) | Bank A/c | Dr | | 19,800 | |
| | Calls-in-arrears A/c | Dr | | 200 | |
| | To Share Allotment A/c | | | | 20,000 |
| | (Being money due on allotment received except on 100 shares) | | | | |
| (v) | Share Capital A/c | Dr | | 300 | |
| | To Calls-in-arrears A/c | | | | 200 |
| | To Share Forfeited A/c | | | | 100 |
| | (Being 100 shares forfeited for non-payment of allotment money) | | | | |
| (vi) | Share First Call A/c | Dr | | 29,700 | |
| | To Share Capital A/c | | | | 29,700 |
| | (Being share first call due on 9,900 shares @ ₹ 3) | | | | |
| (vii) | Bank A/c | Dr | | 29,250 | |
| | Call-in-arrears A/c | | | 450 | |
| | To Share First Call A/c | | | | 29,700 |
| | (Being money due to first call received except on 150 shares) | | | | |
| (viii) | Share Capital A/c | Dr | | 900 | |
| | To Calls-in-arrears A/c | | | | 450 |
| | To Share Forfeited A/c | | | | 450 |
| | (Being 150 shares forfeited for non-payment of first call money) | | | | |
| (ix) | Share Second and Final Call A/c | Dr | | 39,000 | |
| | To Share Capital A/c | | | | 39,000 |
| | (Being second and final call due on 9,750 share @ ₹ 4) | | | | |
| (x) | Bank A/c | Dr | | 38,800 | |
| | Calls-in-arrears A/c | Dr | | 200 | |
| | To Share Second and Final Call A/c | | | | 39,000 |
| | (Being money received on share second and final call except on 50 shares) | | | | |
| (xi) | Share Capital A/c | Dr | | 500 | |
| | To Calls-in-Arrears A/c | | | | 200 |
| | To Shares Forfeited A/c | | | | 300 |
| | (Being 50 shares forfeited) | | | | |
| (xii) | Bank A/c | Dr | | 2,700 | |
| | Share Forfeited A/c | Dr | | 300 | |
| | To Share Capital A/c | | | | 3,000 |
| | (Being 300 shares (100 + 150 + 50) shares reissued) | | | | |
| (xiii) | Share Forfeited A/c | Dr | | 550 | |
| | To Capital Reserve A/c | | | | 550 |
| | (Being profit on reissue transferred to capital reserve) | | | | |

*Or* (i) ₹ 1,60,000

(ii) $400 \times \frac{12,000}{10,000} = 480$

(iii) $480 \times 10 =$ ₹ 4,800

(iv) ₹ 1,24,800

**Working Note**

Money actually due on allotment ₹ 1,30,000

(Due 1,50,000 – 20,000 transferred from application)

Less ₹ 5,200 not paid by Sohan as follows

According to pro-rata = 5 : 6

Sohan applied for 480 equity shares $\left(400 \times \frac{6}{5}\right)$

| | Amt (₹) |
|---|---|
| Application money received on 480 shares (480 × 10) | = 4,800 |
| (–) Application money on 400 equity shares allotted to him (400 × 10) | = (4,000) |
| Surplus transferred to allotment | = 800 |
| Amount due on allotment (400 × 15) | = 6,000 |
| (–) Surplus adjusted here | = (800) |
| Calls-in-arrears on allotment | = 5,200 |

(v) (a) **JOURNAL**

| Date | Particulars | | LF | Amt (Dr) | Amt (Cr) |
|---|---|---|---|---|---|
| | Forfeiture of 400 shares of Sohan immediately after allotment | | | | |
| | Equity Share Capital Account (400 × 30) | Dr | | 10,000 | |
| | To Equity Share Forfeited Account (480 × 10) | | | | 4,800 |
| | (Amount paid on application) | | | | |
| | To Equity Share Allotment Account (Unpaid amount) | | | | 5,200 |
| | (Being 400 shares forfeited for non-payment of ₹ 5,200 on allotment) | | | | |

(b) **JOURNAL**

| Date | Particulars | | LF | Amt (Dr) | Amt (Cr) |
|---|---|---|---|---|---|
| | Re-issue of forfeited shares | | | | |
| | Bank A/c (400 × ₹ 30) | Dr | | 12,000 | |
| | Equity Shares Forfeited A/c (400 × 5) | Dr | | 2,000 | |
| | To Equity Share Capital A/c (400 × 35) | | | | 14,000 |
| | (Being 400 shares issued @ ₹ 30 per share as ₹ 35 paid-up) | | | | |
| | Equity Share Forfeited A/c | Dr | | 2,800 | |
| | To Capital Reserve A/c | | | | 2,800 |
| | (Being the balance in the shares forfeited account being profit on re-issue, transferred to capital reserve account i.e. 4,800 – 2,000) | | | | |

**Working Note**

| **Amount Expected to be Received on Allotment** | **Amt (₹)** |
|---|---|
| (1,50,000 – 20,000 received on application) | = 1,30,000 |
| (–) Arrears | = (5,200) |
| Amount actually received | 1,24,800 |

11. (i) • Investing activity • (*b*) Investing activities

(ii) (*d*) None of these

(iii) Financial statement analysis ignores qualitative elements as it is confined to the monetary matters only because quality cannot be measured in monetary terms.

(iv) (a) Current Ratio = Current Assets/Current Liabilities

(b) $\frac{26593.04}{12869.13} = 2.07$

(v) General motor's cash outflows stem from its enormous capital expenditures.

**12.** **Common Size Income Statement**

for the years ended 31st March, 2023 and 2022

| Particulars | 31st March, 2023 (₹) | 31st March, 2022 (₹) | Absolute Change (₹) | Percentage Change (%) |
|---|---|---|---|---|
| I. Revenue from Operations | 3,12,500 | **2,50,000** | 62,500 | 25% |
| II. **Expenses** | | | | |
| (a) Purchase of Stock-in-trade | **2,17,500** | 1,80,000 | **37,500** | 21% |
| (b) Cost of Material Consumed | 15,000 | 20,000 | (5,000) | **(25%)** |
| **Total Expenses** | 2,32,500 | 2,00,000 | 32,500 | 16.25% |
| III. Profit before Tax | 80,000 | 50,000 | **(30,000)** | **60%** |

**13.** (a) **Calculation of Cash Flow from Financing Activities**

| Particulars | Amt (₹) |
|---|---|
| Issue of Equity Shares | 1,00,000 |
| Repayment of Loan | (40,000) |
| Dividend Paid | (21,000) |
| Interest on Long-term Borrowings Paid (WN) | (10,000) |
| Net Cash Inflow from Financing Activities | 29,000 |

**Working Note**

Interest on long-term borrowings = $1,00,000 \times \frac{10}{100} =$ ₹ 10,000

(b) Dr **Non-current Investments Account** Cr

| Particulars | Amt (₹) | Particulars | Amt (₹) |
|---|---|---|---|
| To Balance b/d | 20,000 | By Bank A/c (Sales) | 16,800 |
| To Statement of Profit and Loss (Profit) | 2,800 | By Balance c/d | 1,00,000 |
| To Bank A/c (Purchase) (Balancing figure) | 94,000 | | |
| | 1,16,800 | | 1,16,800 |

(c) Dr **Property, Plant and Equipment** (Plant and Machinery) **Account** Cr

| Particulars | Amt (₹) | Particulars | Amt (₹) |
|---|---|---|---|
| To Balance b/d | 1,40,000 | By Accumulated Depreciation A/c (WN) | 30,000 |
| To Bank A/c (Purchase) (Balancing figure) | 60,000 | By Balance c/d | 1,70,000 |
| | 2,00,000 | | 2,00,000 |

**Working Note**

Dr **Accumulated Depreciation Account** Cr

| Particulars | Amt (₹) | Particulars | Amt (₹) |
|---|---|---|---|
| To Plant and Machinery A/c (Balancing figure) | 30,000 | By Balance b/d | 40,500 |
| | | By Statement of Profit and Loss | 13,500 |
| To Balance c/d | 24,000 | | |
| | 54,000 | | 54,000 |

*Or*

**Cash Flow from Operating and Investing Activities**

| Particulars | Amt (₹) |
|---|---|
| I. **Cash Flow from Operating Activities** | |
| Net Profit before Tax | (40,000) |
| (+) Adjustment for Non-cash and Non-operating Items | |
| Interest on Debentures | 12,000 |
| Depreciation on Property, Plant and Equipment and Intangible Assets | 10,000 |
| Loss on Sale of Machinery | 2,000 |
| Operating Profit before Working Capital Changes | (16,000) |
| (+) Increase in Current Liabilities and Decrease in Current Assets | — |
| (–) Decrease in Current Liabilities and Increase in Current Assets | |
| Current Liabilities | (25,000) |
| Trade Receivables | (10,000) |
| Cash Generated from Operating Activities | (51,000) |
| (–) Tax Paid | — |
| Cash Used in Operating Activities | (51,000) |
| II. **Cash Flow from Investing Activities** | |
| Purchase of Machinery | (1,20,000) |
| Sale of Machinery | 28,000 |
| Cash Used in Investing Activities | (92,000) |

**Working Note**

Dr **Property, Plant & Equipment and Intangible Assets Account** Cr

| Particulars | Amt (₹) | Particulars | Amt (₹) |
|---|---|---|---|
| To Balance b/d | 2,00,000 | By Bank A/c (Sale) | 28,000 |
| To Bank A/c (Purchase) | 1,20,000 | By Profit and Loss A/c (Loss on sale) | 2,000 |
| | | By Depreciation A/c (Balancing figure) | 10,000 |
| | | By Balance c/d | 2,80,000 |
| | 3,20,000 | | 3,20,000 |

**14.** (i) Inventory Turnover Ratio $= \dfrac{\text{Cost of Revenue from Operations}^*}{\text{Average Inventory}} = \dfrac{33,600}{4,400} = 7.63$

*Cost of Revenue from Operations = Revenue from Operations + Gross Loss

$= 32,000 + 1,600 (32,000 \times 5\%) = ₹\ 33,600$

(ii) Net Profit Ratio $= \dfrac{\text{Net Profit after Tax}}{\text{Revenue from Operations}} \times 100$

Net Profit (After Tax) $= \dfrac{9,100}{1,20,600} \times 100 = 7.55\%$

(iii) Current Assets = Working Capital + Current Liabilities = 60,000 + 40,000 = ₹ 1,00,000

Current Ratio $= \dfrac{\text{Current Assets}}{\text{Current Liabilities}} = \dfrac{1,00,000}{40,000} = 2.5 : 1$

Quick Ratio $= \dfrac{\text{Quick Assets}}{\text{Current Liabilities}} = \dfrac{75,000}{40,000} = 1.875 : 1$

(v) Total Assets to Debt Ratio $= \dfrac{\text{Total Assets}}{\text{Debt}}$

where $= \dfrac{6,75,000}{4,50,000} = 1.5 : 1$

Total Assets = Non-current Assets + Current Assets

$= 5,40,000 + 1,35,000 = ₹\ 6,75,000$

Debt = Long-term Borrowings + Long-term Provisions = 3,00,000 + 1,50,000 = ₹ 4,50,000

SQP Code : **PB-4/15** | Series ***i*-Succeed 4-25/15** | Roll No.

# Sample Question Paper 04

## Accounts 12$^{th}$ (Code 858)

### General Instructions

1. Candidates are allowed additional 15 minutes for only reading the paper. They must not start writing during this time.
2. Section-A is compulsory for all candidates and has ten questions.
3. Candidates have to attempt all questions from either Section-B or Section-C*.
4. Internal choices have been provided in five questions in Section-A and one question in Section-B.
5. The intended marks for questions or parts of questions are given in the brackets [ ].
6. All calculations should be shown clearly.
7. All workings, including rough work, should be done on the same page as, and adjacent to, the rest of the answer.

*Section-C has not been covered.

Time : 3 Hrs.
Max. Marks : 80

## Section A Answer All Questions

[60 Marks]

**Que 1.**

In sub-parts (i) to (iv), choose the correct option and in sub-parts (v) to (x) answer the questions as instructed.

(i) What will be the journal entry, when at the time of dissolution, land and building (book value ₹ 1,60,000) was sold for ₹ 3,00,000 at a brokerage of 2% on the deal? (Application) [1]

| | | | |
|---|---|---|---|
| (a) Cash A/c | Dr | 2,94,000 | |
| To Realisation A/c | | | 2,94,000 |
| (b) Realisation A/c | Dr | 3,06,000 | |
| To Cash A/c | | | 3,06,000 |
| (c) Realisation A/c | Dr | 2,94,000 | |
| To Cash A/c | | | 2,94,000 |
| (d) Cash A/c | Dr | 3,00,000 | |
| To Realisation A/c | | | 3,00,000 |

(ii) When debentures of ₹2,00,000 are issued at par but redeemable at a premium of 5%, the premium payable is debited to (Understanding) [1]

(a) discount on issue of debenture account
(b) debentures account
(c) debentures suspense account
(d) premium on redemption of debentures account

(iii) What will be the correct order of capital to be shown in notes to accounts? (Recall) [1]

A—Called-up capital
B—Authorised capital
C—Issued capital
D—Subscribed capital

**Codes**

(a) A, B, C, D
(b) A, B, D, C
(c) B, C, D, A
(d) C, D, B, A

(iv) Sunlight Ltd. purchased furniture for ₹ 2,70,000. As per the agreement payment is to be made by issuing sufficient number of 5% debentures of ₹ 100 each at a premium of 10% and if required a part of the purchase consideration in cash. How much will be purchase consideration discharged in cash? (Application) [1]

(a) ₹ 60 (b) ₹ 120
(c) ₹ 2,70,000 (d) ₹ 2,45,000

(v) List any four items which are shown under the heading 'current assets' as per Schedule III of the Companies Act, 2013. (Understanding) [1]

(vi) X and Y share profits in the ratio of 3 : 2. Z was admitted as a partner who gets 1/5 share. What will be new profit sharing ratio, if Z acquires 3/20 from X and 1/20 from Y? (Application) [1]

(vii) **Assertion** (A) Partners in a partnership firm distribute profits/losses in their profit sharing ratio and not in their capital ratio.

**Reason** (R) According to the Partnership Act, if appropriations are more than the amount of available profits, profit is distributed in the ratio of capital. (Evaluate) [1]

**Alternatives**

(a) Both Assertion (A) and Reason (R) are true and Reason (R) is the correct explanation of Assertion (A)
(b) Both Assertion (A) and Reason (R) are true, but Reason (R) is not the correct explanation of Assertion (A)
(c) Assertion (A) is true, but Reason (R) is false
(d) Assertion (A) is false, but Reason (R) is true

(viii) Reserve is an amount set aside out of profit to strengthen the financial position of the firm or to meet an unforseen liability.

**Source** *Business New*

(a) What are reserves?
(b) Mention the reserve created for unforseen liabilities. (Recall) [1]

(ix) At the time of retirement of a partner, the profit on revaluation of assets and liabilities is distributed amongst the partners. Pass necessary journal entry. (Application) [1]

(x) An unrecorded assets of ₹ 10,000 is taken by the partner at ₹ 6,000. What will be the journal entry of this transaction? (Application) [1]

**Que 2.**
Rani and Suman are in partnership with capitals of ₹ 80,000 and ₹ 60,000 respectively. During the year 2021-2022, Rani withdrew ₹ 10,000 from her capital and Suman ₹ 15,000. Profit before charging interest on capital was ₹ 50,000. Rani and Suman shared profits in the ratio of 3:2.

(i) Calculate the opening capitals of Rani and Suman.
(ii) Calculate the amount of interest on their capitals @ 12% p.a. for the year ended 31st March, 2022. (Application) [3]

SP-04

**Que 3.**
X,Y and Z were partners sharing profits in the ratio of 4 : 3 : 2. Their balance sheet as at 31st March, 2022 was as follows

**Balance Sheet**
as at 31st March, 2022

| Liabilities | | Amt (₹) | Assets | Amt (₹) |
|---|---|---|---|---|
| Capital A/cs | | | Cash | 1,600 |
| X | 80,000 | | Bank | 6,400 |
| Y | 48,000 | | Stock | 32,000 |
| Z | 24,000 | 1,52,000 | Debtors | 64,000 |
| Creditors | | 23,200 | Land | 80,000 |
| Workmen Compensation Reserve | | 6,400 | | |
| Provision for Doubtful Debts | | 2,400 | | |
| | | 1,84,000 | | 1,84,000 |

Y died on 12th June, 2022 and it was agreed that X and Z will share future profits in the ratio of 5 : 4. The following was agreed upon

(i) Goodwill is to be valued at 2.5 years purchase of average profits of last 3 years. The average profit was ₹ 28,800.
(ii) Y's share of profit till the date of his death will be calculated on the basis of average profits of last 3 years.
(iii) Land was undervalued by ₹ 19,200 and stock was overvalued by ₹ 6,880.
(iv) Provision for doubtful debts is to be made at 5% on debtors.
(v) Claim on workmen compensation was estimated at ₹ 1,900.

You are required to prepare

(a) Prepare revaluation account **[1]**

(b) Calculate • Y's share of goodwill • Y's share of profit **(Application) [2]**

*Or*

X and Y are partners in a firm. They admit Z as a new partner with 1/5th share in the profits of the firm. Z brings ₹ 5,00,000 as his share of capital. The value of the total assets of the firm was ₹ 15,00,000 and outside liabilities were valued at ₹ 5,00,000 on that date. Give the necessary journal entry to record goodwill at the time of Z's admission. Also, show your workings. **(Application) [3]**

**Que 4.**

Prepare debentureholder's account and general reserve account for the redemption of debentures when 15,000, 10% debentures of ₹ 100 each issued at 10% premium, repayable at par. Assume that company has sufficient funds in DRR and has already made investment. **(Application) [3]**

**Que 5.**

You are required to pass journal entries to record the following issues of debentures (exclude entries related to writing-off any capital losses).

(i) Zola Ltd. issues 5,000, 13% debentures of ₹ 100 each at a discount of 10% to be redeemed at par after 7 years.
(ii) Emerald Ltd. issues 3,000, 9% debentures of ₹ 100 each at a discount of 7% to be redeemed at a premium of 10% after 4 years. **(Application) [3]**

*Or*

XYZ Industries Ltd. issued 2,000, 10% debentures of ₹ 100 each, at a premium of ₹ 10 per debenture payable as follows



On application ₹ 50, On allotment ₹ 60. The debentures were fully subscribed and all money was duly received. Record the journal entries in the books of company. **(Application)**

**Que 6.**

Following is the trial balance of Evergreen Ltd. as at 31st March, 2023.

| Names of Accounts | Debit Balance (₹) | Credit Balance (₹) |
|---|---|---|
| Machinery | 3,20,000 | – |
| Land and Building | 13,48,000 | – |
| Depreciation on Machinery | 32,000 | – |
| Purchases of Raw Materials (Adjusted) | 8,00,000 | – |
| Closing Stock | 3,00,000 | – |
| Wages | 2,40,000 | – |
| Sales | – | 20,00,000 |
| Salaries | 1,60,000 | – |
| Bank Overdraft | | 4,00,000 |
| 10% Debentures (Issued on 1st April, 2022) | – | 2,00,000 |

| Names of Accounts | Debit Balance (₹) | Credit Balance (₹) |
|---|---|---|
| Equity Share Capital – 4,000 Shares of ₹ 100 each (Fully paid) | — | 4,00,000 |
| Preference Share Capital – 2,000, 6% Preference Shares of ₹ 100 each (Fully paid) | — | 2,00,000 |
| | 32,00,000 | 32,00,000 |

The Board of Directors of Evergreen Ltd. has decided to make the following appropriations

(i) To pay an equity dividend @ 10% on paid-up capital as approved by shareholders.
(ii) To pay dividend on the preference share capital in full.
(iii) To transfer ₹ 4,00,000 to general reserve.

You are required to prepare balance sheet of the company for the year ended 31st March, 2023 as per Schedule III of the Companies Act, 2013. (Application) [6]

**Note** Ignore the income tax.

**Que 7.**
Vyom, Dev and Saanchi were partners sharing profits in the ratio of 2 :1:1. Vyom withdrew ₹ 3,000 every month and Dev withdrew ₹ 4,000 every month. Interest on drawings @ 6% p.a. was charged. Partnership deed was silent about interest on drawings. Pass the necessary adjustment entry and show your working clearly. (Application) [6]

*Or*

On 31st March, 2022, the balance in the capital accounts of Aakash, Nishant and Ravi after making adjustments for profit and drawings were ₹ 1,60,000, ₹ 1,40,000 and ₹ 1,00,000 respectively. It was discovered that interest on capital and interest on drawings had not been charged/provided.

The partners were entitled to interest on capital @ 10% p.a and interest on drawings were also to been charged @ 10% p.a. The drawings during the year were Aakash ₹ 50,000; Nishant ₹ 60,000 and Ravi ₹ 30,000. The net profit for the year ending 31st March, 2023 amounted to ₹ 1,00,000. The profit sharing ratio was 2 : 2 : 1. Pass the necessary adjustment entry. (Application)

**Que 8.**
P, Q and R were carrying on business and sharing profits and losses in the ratio of 2 : 2 : 1. They dissolved their firm as on 31st December, 2022. On that date, their balance sheet was as follows

**Balance Sheet**
as at 31st December, 2022



| Liabilities | | Amt (₹) | Assets | Amt (₹) |
|---|---|---|---|---|
| Trade Creditors | | 8,12,000 | Cash | 1,80,000 |
| Reserve Fund | | 4,00,000 | Spare Parts | 6,40,000 |
| Investment Fluctuation Reserve | | 3,20,000 | Investments | 4,40,000 |
| Capital A/cs | | | Debtors | 4,00,000 |
| P | 6,00,000 | | Leasehold | 12,12,000 |
| Q | 6,00,000 | | | |
| R | 1,20,000 | 13,20,000 | | |
| Provision for Doubtful Debts | | 20,000 | | |
| | | 28,72,000 | | 28,72,000 |

All assets (except cash and investments) were taken over by a company for ₹ 26,00,000. The investments were sold at ₹ 4,52,000, trade creditors at ₹ 7,80,000, realisation expenses amounted to ₹ 1,20,000.

A bill was received from Mr. Z worth ₹ 40,000, which was under discount, now as Mr. Z has become insolvent, a dividend of 50% was received from his estate.

On the date of dissolution, firm upon realisation of assets and settlement of liabilities made a profit of ₹ 5,92,000.

(i) Prepare partners' capital account [1]
(ii) Prepare cash account (Application) [5]

**Que 9.**

Narang, Suri and Bajaj are partners in a firm, sharing profits and losses in proportion of 1/2, 1/6 and 1/3 respectively. The balance sheet as at 31st March, 2023 was as follows

**Balance Sheet**
as at 31st March, 2023

| Liabilities | | Amt (₹) | Assets | | Amt (₹) |
|---|---|---|---|---|---|
| Bills Payable | | 12,000 | Freehold Premises | | 40,000 |
| Sundry Creditors | | 18,000 | Machinery | | 30,000 |
| Reserves | | 12,000 | Furniture | | 12,000 |
| Capital A/cs | | | Stock | | 22,000 |
| Narang | 30,000 | | Sundry Debtors | 20,000 | |
| Suri | 30,000 | | (–) Provision for Doubtful Debts | (1,000) | 19,000 |
| Bajaj | 28,000 | 88,000 | Cash | | 7,000 |
| | | 1,30,000 | | | 1,30,000 |

Bajaj retires from the business and the partners agree to the following

(i) Freehold premises and stock are to be appreciated by 20% and 15% respectively.
(ii) Machinery and furniture are to be depreciated by 10% and 7% respectively.
(iii) Provision for doubtful debts is to be increased to ₹ 1,500.
(iv) Goodwill is valued at ₹ 21,000 on Bajaj's retirement.

(A) You are required to calculate the following
(a) What will be the gaining ratio of Narang and Suri? [2]
(b) What will be the share of revaluation profit/loss of Narang, Suri and Bajaj on revaluation? [2]
(c) Prepare partners' capital account of Bajaj. [2]
(d) What is the amount required to be transferred of to Bajaj capital account as his share of goodwill? (Recall) [2]

SP-04

(B) The continuing partners have decided to adjust their capitals in their new profit sharing ratio after retirement of Bajaj. Surplus/deficit, if any, in their capital accounts will be adjusted through current accounts.
What is the amount transferred to Narang's and Suri's capital account? (Application) [2]

*Or*

The following was the balance sheet of Arun, Bablu and Chetan sharing profits and losses in the ratio of $\frac{6}{14}:\frac{5}{14}:\frac{3}{14}$ respectively.

| Liabilities | | Amt (₹) | Assets | Amt (₹) |
|---|---|---|---|---|
| Creditors | | 9,000 | Land and Buildings | 24,000 |
| Bills Payable | | 3,000 | Furniture | 3,500 |
| Capital A/cs | | | Stock | 14,000 |
| Arun | 19,000 | | Debtors | 12,600 |
| Bablu | 16,000 | | Cash | 900 |
| Chetan | 8,000 | 43,000 | | |
| | | 55,000 | | 55,000 |

They agreed to take Deepak into partnership and give him a share of 1/8 on the following terms

(i) Deepak should bring in ₹ 4,200 as goodwill and ₹ 7,000 as his capital.

(ii) Furniture be depreciated by 12%.

(iii) Stock be depreciated by 10%.

(iv) A reserve of 5% be created for doubtful debts.

(v) The value of land and buildings having appreciated be brought upto ₹ 31,000.

(vi) After making the adjustments, capital accounts of the old partners (who continue to share in the same proportion as before) be adjusted on the basis of the proportion of Deepak's capital to his share in the business i.e., actual cash to be paid-off to or brought in by the old partners as the case may be.

(A) You are required to prepare

(a) profit and loss adjustment account (revaluation account). [1½]

(b) Partners' capial account. [4½]

(c) Opening balance sheet of the new firm. [2]

(B) A and B are partner in a firm. They admit C as a new partner with $\frac{1}{5}$th share in the profits of the firm. C brings ₹ 2,50,000 and ₹ 50,000 as his share of capital and goodwill respectively. Give the necessary journal entry to record goodwill at the time of C's admission. (Application) [2]

**Que 10.**

Rahul Ltd. invited applications for issuing 1,60,000 equity shares of ₹ 10 each at a premium of ₹ 6 per share. The amount was payable as follows

On application—₹ 4 per share (including premium ₹ 1 per share)

On allotment—₹ 6 per share (including premium ₹ 3 per share)

On first and final call—Balance amount

Applications for 3,20,000 shares were received. Applications for 80,000 shares were rejected and application money was refunded. Shares were allotted on pro-rata basis to the remaining applicants. Excess money received with applications was adjusted towards sums due on allotment. 'R' holding 800 shares failed to pay the allotment money. His shares were forfeited immediately after allotment. Afterwards the final call was made.

'S' who had applied for 1,200 shares failed to pay the final call. His shares were also forfeited. Out of the forfeited shares, 1,000 shares were re-issued at ₹ 8 per share fully paid-up.

The re-issued shares included all the forfeited shares of R.

Pass necessary journal entries for the above transactions in the books of Rahul Ltd. (Application) [10]

*Or*

Ganga Ltd. issued 10,000 equity shares of ₹ 20 each payable ₹ 5 on application, ₹ 8 on allotment ₹ 4 on first call and ₹ 3 on the final call. 15,000 applications were received and allotment was made as follows

(i) Applicants for 10,000 equity shares were allotted 6,000 equity shares. (Pro-rata)

(ii) Applicants for 5,000 equity shares were allotted 4,000 equity shares. (Pro-rata)

All applicants paid the money as and when due except Jagan and Mohan. They did not pay anything after application money. Jagan belonged to first category and was allotted 144 shares and Mohan belonged to the second category and he had applied for 120 equity shares.

Their shares were forfeited after first call. Out of these 100 equity shares (including 50 equity shares of Jagan) were re-issued after final call at ₹ 16 per share fully paid-up.

(i) How much amount was received on application? [1]

(ii) What are the number of shares allotted to Mohan? [1]

(iii) What is the amount forfeited on Mohan's shares? [1]

(iv) What is the amount not received from Mohan? [2]

(v) You are required to

(a) Pass the entry for the forfeiture of Jagan's share. [2]

(b) Pass the entry for the re-issue. [3]

## Section B

**[20 Marks]**

**Que 11.**

(i) As one of India's top fabric producers and clothing manufacturers, Raymond has a capacity of 38 million meters in wool and wool-blended fabrics, ranking in the top three fully integrated worsted suiting manufacturers in the world with a market share of over 60 per cent. The Raymond Company produces high value pure wool suiting fabrics in nearly 20,000 colours, designs and patterns for every age, occasion and style. In addition to the USA, Europe, Canada, Japan and the Middle East, Raymond exports products to over 55 countries.

**Source** *Khatabook*

- For a company manufacturing garments, procurement of raw material, sale of garments are classified as which type of activity? **(Recall)**

(a) Financing (b) Investing (c) Operating (d) None of these

- Procurement of raw material will be an inflow or outflow of cash. **(Analysis) [1]**

(ii) The financial statements of a company record important financial data on every aspect of a business activities. As such, they can be evaluated on the basis of past, current and projected performance.

**Source** *business.rev*

Which of the following is not a limitation of financial statements? **(Understanding) [1]**

(a) Window dressing (b) Lack of qualitative analysis

(c) Do not reflect price level changes (d) Measure short-term solvency of business

SP-04

(iii) One of the key concerns raised by Hindenburg Research in relation to Adani Group in its report released on 24th January is the excessive amount of debt that the Gautam Adani headed company has taken, thus making its future precarious and perilous.

**Source** *mintgenie.livemint.com*

Based on the above statement, what are the significance of high debt to equity ratio? **(Analysis) [1]**

(iv) Nestle India Limited reported earnings results for the first quarter ended 30th June, 2024. For the first quarter, the company reported revenue was ₹ 48,530.7 million compared to ₹ 46,824.8 million a year ago. Net income was ₹ 7, 466 million compared to ₹ 6,983.4 million a year ago. Basic earnings per share from continuing operations was ₹ 7.74 compared to ₹ 7.24 a year ago. Diluted earnings per share from continuing operations was ₹ 7.74 compared to ₹ 7.24 a year ago.

**Source** *Investopedia(edited)*

(a) What is the formula for calculating the earning per share?

(b) Calculate Earning per Share (EPS) from the following data,

Profit after Tax – ₹ 50,000

10 % Preference Share Capital (₹ 10 each) – ₹ 1,00,000

Equity share capital (₹ 10 per Share ) – ₹ 1,00,000 **(Analysis) [1]**

(v) The banking and finance companies in India provide various banking services like credit, deposits, small and big loans, investment advisory, and many other facilities. The BFSI companies are regulated by the Reserve Bank of India, which ensures risk management, best advisory, planning, etc., for the best interest of consumers.

**Source** *PwskillS*

Based on the above information state, dividend paid to shareholders by Ajay Ltd. a financing company is classified under which kind of activity while preparing cash flow statement? (Application) [1]

**Que 12.**

Prepare a comparative statement of profit and loss of XYZ Ltd., with the help of the following information (Application) [3]

| Particulars | 31st March, 2023 (₹) | 31st March, 2022 (₹) |
|---|---|---|
| Revenue from Operations | 4,00,000 | 2,50,000 |
| Purchase of Stock-in-trade | 2,10,000 | 1,20,000 |
| Changes in Inventories | 60,000 | 45,000 |
| Employee Benefit Expenses | 10,000 | 20,000 |
| Income Tax | 50% | 40% |

**Que 13.**

From the following balance sheet and the additional information of Quick Tubes Ltd, you are required to prepare cash flow statement as per AS-3.

| Particulars | Note No. | 31st March, 2024 (₹) | 31st March, 2023 (₹) |
|---|---|---|---|
| **I. EQUITY AND LIABILITIES** | | | |
| **1. Shareholders' Funds** | | | |
| (i) Share Capital | | 4,50,000 | 3,00,000 |
| (ii) Reserves and Surplus | | 1,85,000 | 70,000 |
| **2. Current Liabilities** | | | |
| (i) Sundry Creditors | | 95,000 | 80,000 |
| (ii) Bills Payable | | 40,000 | 25,000 |
| **Total** | | 7,70,000 | 4,75,000 |
| **II. ASSETS** | | | |
| **1. Non-current Assets** | | | |
| Property, Plant and Equipment | | 4,90,000 | 2,00,000 |
| **2. Current Assets** | | | |
| (i) Inventories | | 90,000 | 90,000 |
| (ii) Debtors | | 1,00,000 | 1,20,000 |
| (iii) Cash and Cash Equivalents | | 90,000 | 65,000 |
| **Total** | | 7,70,000 | 4,75,000 |

**Additional Information**

(i) Income tax paid during the year was ₹ 45,000.

(ii) Dividend paid during the year was 12%.

You are required to

(a) Calculate the value of cash flow from operating activities. [2]

(b) Calculate the value of cash flow from investing and financing activities. [2]

(c) Calculate the value of cash and cash equivalents at the end of the year. (Evaluate) [2]

SP-04

*Or* From the following summarised balance sheets of a company, prepare cash flow from investing and financing activities

| Particulars | 31st March, 2023 (₹) | 31st March, 2022 (₹) |
|---|---|---|
| **I. EQUITY AND LIABILITIES** | | |
| 1. **Shareholders' Funds** | | |
| (i) Equity Share Capital | 9,00,000 | 9,00,000 |
| (ii) Reserves and Surplus (Balance in Statement of Profit and Loss) | 2,40,000 | 1,50,000 |
| 2. **Non-current Liabilities** | | |
| 6% Debentures | 3,00,000 | 2,40,000 |
| 3. **Current Liabilities** | | |
| (i) Outstanding Expenses | 90,000 | 75,000 |
| (ii) Trade Payables | 15,000 | 75,000 |
| (iii) Other Current Liabilities | 75,000 | 60,000 |
| **Total** | 16,20,000 | 15,00,000 |
| **II. ASSETS** | | |
| 1. **Non-current Assets** | | |
| (i) Property, Plant & Equipment and Intangible Assets | 11,70,000 | 10,50,000 |
| (ii) Non-current Investments | 90,000 | 1,20,000 |
| 2. **Current Assets** | | |
| (i) Stock | 1,65,000 | 1,20,000 |
| (ii) Trade Receivables | 1,65,000 | 1,50,000 |
| (iii) Cash and Cash Equivalents | 30,000 | 60,000 |
| **Total** | 16,20,000 | 15,00,000 |

**Additional Information**

(i) A piece of machinery costing ₹ 1,50,000 on which depreciation of ₹ 60,000 had been charged, was sold for ₹ 75,000. Depreciation charged during the year was ₹ 1,71,000.

(ii) New debentures have been issued on 1st August, 2022. **(Application) [6]**

**Que 14.**

SP-04

A company's inventory turnover is 5 times. Inventory at the end of the year is ₹ 4,000 more than inventory at the beginning of the year. Revenue from operations during the year (all credit) were ₹ 3,00,000. Rate of gross profit is 25% on cost of revenue from operations. Current liabilities at the end of the year were ₹ 50,000.

Calculate

(i) Cost of revenue from operations

(ii) Opening inventory

(iii) Closing inventory **(Application) [6]**

# Solutions *in Topper's Style*

**My Commitment** *I affirm that I am reviewing these solutions only after I have solved the Sample Question Paper 4 on my own. My purpose of looking the solutions is solely to verify whether my answers/solutions were correct or not and to identify my mistakes in case my solutions were wrong or I could not solve that.*

**1.** (i) (*a*) Cash A/c Dr 2,94,000
To Realisation A/c 2,94,000

(ii) (*d*) premium on redemption of debentures account

(iii) (*c*) B, C, D, A

(iv) (*a*) Number of Debentures $= \frac{2,70,000}{110} = 2,454$

Total number of debentures that can be issued = 2,454

| | | |
|---|---|---|
| Amount of debenture = 2,454 × 100 | = | 2,45,400 |
| (+) Premium = 2,450 × 10 | = | 24,540 |
| | | 2,69,940 |

The balance amount of ₹ 60 (2,70,000 – 2,69,940) will be discharged in cash.

(v) Four items shows under the heading 'current assets' are

(a) Current investments
(b) Inventories
(c) Trade receivables
(d) Cash and cash equivalents

(vi) X's new share $= \frac{3}{5} - \frac{3}{20} = \frac{12-3}{20} = \frac{9}{20}$; Y's new share $= \frac{2}{5} - \frac{1}{20} = \frac{8-1}{20} = \frac{7}{20}$; Z's share $= \frac{1}{5} \times \frac{4}{4} = \frac{4}{20} \Rightarrow 9:7:4$

(vii) (*c*) Assertion (A) is true, but Reason (R) is false

(viii) (a) Reserves are funds that a company sets aside for specific purposes in the future.

(b) Workmen compensation reserve

(ix) **JOURNAL**

| Date | Particulars | LF | Amt (Dr) | Credit (Cr) |
|---|---|---|---|---|
| | Revaluation A/c Dr<br>To Old Partners' Capital A/c<br>(Being profit on revaluation is distributed amongst old partners) | | | |

(x) Debit partner's capital account and credit realisation account by ₹ 6,000.

**2.** (i) This question will be completely done on assumptions as

(a) The date of drawing from capital is not given, and

(b) It is not mentioned whether capital given is closing or opening, so we will assume these capitals as closing. Thus, opening capital will be calculated as follows

| Calculation of Opening Capital | Rani (₹) | Suman (₹) |
|---|---|---|
| Closing Capital | 80,000 | 60,000 |
| (+) Drawings | 10,000 | 15,000 |
| (–) Profit Share (50,000 in 3 : 2) | (30,000) | (20,000) |
| Opening Capital | 60,000 | 55,000 |

(ii) **Interest on Capital**

Rani $= 60,000 \times \frac{12}{100} =$ ₹ 7,200; Suman $= 55,000 \times \frac{12}{100} =$ ₹ 6,600

**3.** (a) Dr **Revaluation Account** Cr

| Particulars | | Amt (₹) | Particulars | Amt (₹) |
|---|---|---|---|---|
| To Stock | | 6,880 | By Land A/c | 19,200 |
| To Provision for Doubtful Debts | | 800 | | |
| To Profit transferred to | | | | |
| X's Capital A/c | 5,120 | | | |
| Y's Capital A/c | 3,840 | | | |
| Z's Capital A/c | 2,560 | 11,520 | | |
| | | 19,200 | | 19,200 |

(b) • **Y's Share of Goodwill**

Firm's Goodwill = Average Profit × Number of Years' Purchase = 28,800 × 2.5 = ₹ 72,000

Y's share of goodwill = 72,000 × 3/9 = ₹ 24,000 to be contributed by X and Z in their gaining ratio.

X's contribute = 24,000 × 1/3 = ₹ 8,000

Z's contribute = 24,000 × 2/3 = ₹ 16,000

Gaining Ratio = New Ratio – Old Ratio

X's gain $= \frac{5}{9} - \frac{4}{9} = \frac{1}{9}$; Z's gain $= \frac{4}{9} - \frac{2}{9} = \frac{2}{9}$; Gaining ratio = 1 : 2

• Y's share of profit $= 28{,}800 \times \frac{3}{9} \times \frac{73}{365} =$ ₹ 1,920

**Value Points**

- Old provision is given on the liabilities side, which will be considered while computing new provision.
- Since Y died on 12th June, current year's profit will be provided for 73 days, i.e. from 1st April to 12th June.

*Or* **Calculation of Adjusted Profit**

**JOURNAL**

| Date | Particulars | | LF | Amt (Dr) | Amt (Cr) |
|---|---|---|---|---|---|
| | Z's Capital A/c | Dr | | 2,00,000 | |
| | To X's Capital A/c | | | | 1,00,000 |
| | To Y's Capital A/c | | | | 1,00,000 |
| | (Being adjustment entry passed for goodwill) | | | | |

**Working Notes**

1. **Calculation of Z's Share of Goodwill**

New firm's capital on the basis of Z's capital and his profit share = 5,00,000 × 5/1 = ₹ 25,00,000

Adjusted Capital of Old Partners = Assets – Liabilities
= 15,00,000 – 5,00,000
= 10,00,000
(+) New Partner's Capital = 5,00,000
= ₹ 15,00,000

Value of hidden goodwill (1 – 2) = 25,00,000 – 15,00,000 = ₹ 10,00,000

Z's share = 10,00,000 × 1/5 = ₹ 2,00,000

Sacrificing ratio has been taken as equal as old partners' profit sharing ratio is not given.

**4.** Dr **General Reserve Account** Cr

| Date | Particulars | Amt (₹) | Date | Particulars | Amt (₹) |
|---|---|---|---|---|---|
| | To Bank A/c | 15,00,000 | | By 10% Debentures A/c | 15,00,000 |

Dr **Debentureholders' Account** Cr

| Date | Particulars | Amt (₹) | Date | Particular | Amt (₹) |
|---|---|---|---|---|---|
| | To Balance c/d | 15,00,000 | | By Debenture Redemption Reserve | 15,00,000 |

5. **JOURNAL**

| Date | Particulars | | LF | Amt (Dr) | Amt (Cr) |
|---|---|---|---|---|---|
| (i) | Bank A/c (5,000 × 90) | Dr | | 4,50,000 | |
| | To Debenture Application and Allotment A/c | | | | 4,50,000 |
| | (Being the application money received) | | | | |
| | Debenture Application and Allotment A/c (5,000 × 90) | Dr | | 4,50,000 | |
| | Discount on Issue of Debenture A/c (5,000 × 10) | Dr | | 50,000 | |
| | To 13% Debentures A/c (5,000 × 100) | | | | 5,00,000 |
| | (Being the application money transferred to debentures account issued at 10% discount and redeemable at par) | | | | |
| (ii) | Bank A/c | Dr | | 2,79,000 | |
| | To Debenture Application and Allotment A/c | | | | 2,79,000 |
| | (Being the application money received) | | | | |
| | Debenture Application and Allotment A/c | Dr | | 2,79,000 | |
| | Loss on Issue of Debentures A/c (21,000 + 30,000) | Dr | | 51,000 | |
| | To 9% Debentures A/c | | | | 3,00,000 |
| | To Premium on Redemption of Debentures A/c | | | | 30,000 |
| | (Being the application money transferred to debentures account issued at discount and redeemable at premium) | | | | |

*Or* **JOURNAL**

| Date | Particulars | | LF | Amt (Dr) | Amt (Cr) |
|---|---|---|---|---|---|
| | Bank A/c (2,000 × 50) | Dr | | 1,00,000 | |
| | To Debenture Application A/c | | | | 1,00,000 |
| | (Being application money on 10% debentures received) | | | | |
| | Debenture Application A/c | Dr | | 1,00,000 | |
| | To 10% Debentures A/c | | | | 1,00,000 |
| | (Being transfer of application money to debentures account) | | | | |
| | Debenture Allotment A/c (2,000 × 60) | Dr | | 1,20,000 | |
| | To 10% Debentures A/c (2,000 × 50) | | | | 1,00,000 |
| | To Securities Premium (2,000 × 10) | | | | 20,000 |
| | (Being allotment money due on debentures including the premium) | | | | |
| | Bank A/c | Dr | | 1,20,000 | |
| | To Debenture Allotment A/c | | | | 1,20,000 |
| | (Being allotment money received) | | | | |

6. **Balance Sheet**
as at 31st March, 2023

| Particulars | Note No. | Amt (₹) |
|---|---|---|
| I. **EQUITY AND LIABILITIES** | | |
| 1. **Shareholders' Funds** | | |
| (i) Share Capital | 1 | 6,00,000 |
| (ii) Reserves and Surplus | 2 | 6,96,000 |
| 2. **Non-current Liabilities** | | |
| Long-term Borrowings | 3 | 2,00,000 |
| 3. **Current Liabilities** | | |
| (i) Short-term Borrowings | 4 | 4,00,000 |
| (ii) Other Current Liabilities | 5 | 20,000 |
| (iii) Short-term Provisions | 6 | 52,000 |
| **Total** | | 19,68,000 |

| Particulars | Note No. | Amt (₹) |
|---|---|---|
| II. **ASSETS** | | |
| 1. **Non-current Assets** | | |
| (i) Property, Plant & Equipment and Intangible Assets | | |
| (a) Property, Plant and Equipment | 7 | 16,68,000 |
| 2. **Current Assets** | | |
| Inventories | | 3,00,000 |
| **Total** | | 19,68,000 |

## Notes to Accounts

| Particulars | | Amt (₹) |
|---|---|---|
| 1. **Share Capital** | | |
| **Subscribed Capital** | | |
| Subscribed and Fully Paid-up | | |
| 4,000, Equity Shares of ₹ 100 each | | 4,00,000 |
| 2,000, 6% Preference Shares of ₹ 100 each | | 2,00,000 |
| | | 6,00,000 |
| 2. **Reserves and Surplus** | | |
| General Reserve | | |
| Opening Balance | | – |
| (+) Transfer from Surplus, i.e., Balance in Statement of Profit and Loss | | 4,00,000 |
| | | 4,00,000 |
| Surplus, i.e., Balance in Statement of Profit and Loss | | |
| Profit for the Year | | 7,48,000 |
| (−) Appropriations | | |
| General Reserve | (4,00,000) | |
| Proposed Dividend | | |
| Equity | (40,000) | |
| Preference | (12,000) | (4,52,000) |
| | | 2,96,000 |
| 3. **Long-term Borrowings** | | |
| 10% Debentures | | 2,00,000 |
| 4. **Short-term Borrowings** | | |
| Bank Overdraft | | 4,00,000 |
| 5. **Other Current Liabilities** | | |
| Interest on Debentures | | 20,000 |
| 6. **Short-term Provisions** | | |
| Proposed Dividend | | |
| Equity | 40,000 | |
| Preference | 12,000 | 52,000 |
| 7. **Property, Plant and Equipment** | | |
| Machinery | | 3,20,000 |
| Land and Building | | 13,48,000 |
| | | 16,68,000 |

7.

### JOURNAL

| Date | Particulars | | LF | Amt (Dr) | Amt (Cr) |
|---|---|---|---|---|---|
| | Vyom's Capital A/c | Dr | | 180 | |
| | Saanchi's Capital A/c | Dr | | 630 | |
| | To Dev's Capital A/c | | | | 810 |
| | (Being adjustment entry for interest on drawings wrongly charged) | | | | |

**Working Note**

**Adjustment Table**

| Particulars | Vyom (₹) | Dev (₹) | Saanchi (₹) | Total (₹) |
|---|---|---|---|---|
| Interest on Drawings | 1,080 | 1,440 | — | 2,520 |
| Wrong Debited | — | — | — | 2,520 |
| Amount to be Debited (loss) [2 : 1 : 1] | (1,260) | (630) | (630) | — |
| Net Effect | 180 (Dr) | 810 (Cr) | 630 (Dr) | — |

**Interest on Drawings** Vyom $= (3{,}000 \times 12) \times \frac{6}{12} \times \frac{6}{100} =$ ₹ 1,080 ; Dev $= (4{,}000 \times 12) \times \frac{6}{12} \times \frac{6}{100} =$ ₹ 1,440

*Or*

**JOURNAL**

| Date | Particulars | | LF | Amt (Dr) | Amt (Cr) |
|---|---|---|---|---|---|
| | Nishant's Capital A/c | Dr | | 2,200 | |
| | To Aakash's Capital A/c | | | | 300 |
| | To Ravi's Capital A/c | | | | 1,900 |
| | (Being adjustment entry passed for the omission of interest on capital and interest on drawings) | | | | |

**Working Notes**

1. **Interest on Capital**

   Aakash = 1,60,000 × 10% = 16,000 ; Nishant = 1,40,000 × 10% = 14,000 ; Ravi = 1,00,000 × 10% = 10,000

2. **Adjustment Table**

| Particulars | Aakash (₹) | Nishant (₹) | Ravi (₹) | Total (₹) |
|---|---|---|---|---|
| Interest on Capital (Cr) | 16,000 | 14,000 | 10,000 | 40,000 |
| Interest on Drawing (Dr) | (2,500) | (3,000) | 1,500 | (7,000) |
| | 13,500 | 11,000 | 8,500 | 33,000 |
| Amount to be Credited (2 : 2 : 1) (Profit) | 13,200 | 13,200 | 6,600 | 33,000 |
| | 300 (Cr) | 2,200 (Dr) | 1,900 (Cr) | — |

**8.** (i) Dr **Partners' Capital Account** Cr

| Particulars | P (₹) | Q (₹) | R (₹) | Particulars | P (₹) | Q (₹) | R (₹) |
|---|---|---|---|---|---|---|---|
| To Balance c/d | 9,96,800 | 9,96,800 | 3,18,400 | By Balance b/d | 6,00,000 | 6,00,000 | 1,20,000 |
| | | | | By Reserve Fund A/c | 1,60,000 | 1,60,000 | 80,000 |
| | | | | By Realisation (Profit) | 2,36,800 | 2,36,800 | 1,18,400 |
| | 9,96,800 | 9,96,800 | 3,18,400 | | 9,96,800 | 9,96,800 | 3,18,400 |

(ii) Dr **Cash Account** Cr

| Particulars | Amt (₹) | Particulars | Amt (₹) |
|---|---|---|---|
| To Balance b/d | 1,80,000 | By Realisation A/c (Creditors) | 7,80,000 |
| To Realisation A/c (All assets) | 26,00,000 | By Realisation A/c (Expenses) | 1,20,000 |
| To Realisation A/c (Investment) | 4,52,000 | By Realisation A/c (Z's bill dishonoured) | 40,000 |
| To Realisation A/c (Z's bill realised) | 20,000 | By P's Capital A/c | 9,96,800 |
| | | By Q's Capital A/c | 9,96,800 |
| | | By R's Capital A/c | 3,18,400 |
| | 32,52,000 | | 32,52,000 |

**Common Mistake** Students usually do not record the cash received from the bill discounted which was dishonoured. It should be noted that in the given question, although the bill is dishonoured, 50% of the amount is received from his estate, which will increase the cash balance.

**9.** (A) (a) Old share = $\frac{1}{2}:\frac{1}{6}:\frac{1}{3}$; Old ratio = 3 : 1 : 2

As there is no information how Bajaj's share has been taken, it is assumed that his share has been taken by remaining partners in their old ratio.

∴ Gaining and new ratio between Narang and Suri will be 3 : 1.

(b) Dr **Revaluation Account** Cr

| Particulars | | Amt (₹) | Particulars | Amt (₹) |
|---|---|---|---|---|
| To Machinery A/c (30,000 × 10%) | | 3,000 | By Freehold Premises A/c (40,000 × 20%) | 8,000 |
| To Furniture A/c (12,000 × 7%) | | 840 | By Stock A/c (22,000 × 15%) | 3,300 |
| To Provision for Doubtful Debts A/c (1,500 – 1,000) | | 500 | | |
| To Profit transferred to | | | | |
| Narang's Capital A/c | 3,480 | | | |
| Suri's Capital A/c | 1,160 | | | |
| Bajaj's Capital A/c | 2,320 | 6,960 | | |
| | | 11,300 | | 11,300 |

(c) Dr **Bajaj's Capital Account** Cr

| Particulars | Amt (₹) | Particulars | Amt (₹) |
|---|---|---|---|
| To Bajaj's Capital A/c | – | By Balance b/d | 28,000 |
| To Balance c/d | 41,320 | By Reserves A/c | 4,000 |
| | | By Revaluation A/c (Profit) | 2,320 |
| | | By Narang's Capital A/c | 5,250 |
| | | By Suri's Capital A/c | 1,750 |
| | 41,320 | | 41,320 |
| To Bajaj's Loan A/c | 41,320 | By Balance b/d | 41,320 |
| To Suri's Current A/c (Balancing figure) | – | By Narang's Current A/c (Balancing figure) | – |
| To Balance c/d | – | | |
| | 41,320 | | 41,320 |

(d) Amount transferred as Bajaj's Share of goodwill

Bajaj's share of goodwill = 21,000 × $\frac{1}{3}$ = ₹ 7,000 (taken over by Narang and Suri in gaining ratio, i.e. 3 : 1)

(B)

| Capital adjustment | Amt (₹) |
|---|---|
| Narang's capital after adjustment | 34,230 |
| Suri's capital after adjustment | 31,410 |
| | 65,640 |

Narang's new capital $\left(65{,}640 \times \frac{3}{4}\right)$ = ₹ 49,230; Suri's new capital $\left(65{,}640 \times \frac{1}{4}\right)$ = ₹ 16,410

*Or* (A) (a) Dr **Revaluation Account** Cr

| Particulars | | Amt (₹) | Particulars | Amt (₹) |
|---|---|---|---|---|
| To Furniture | | 420 | By Land and Building | 7,000 |
| To Stock | | 1,400 | | |
| To Reserve for Bad Debt | | 630 | | |
| To Profit on Revaluation transferred to | | | | |
| Arun | 1,950 | | | |
| Bablu | 1,625 | | | |
| Chetan | 975 | 4,550 | | |
| | | 7,000 | | 7,000 |

(b) Dr **Partners' Capital Account** Cr

| Particulars | Arun (₹) | Bablu (₹) | Chetan (₹) | Deepak (₹) | Particulars | Arun (₹) | Bablu (₹) | Cheran (₹) | Deepak (₹) |
|---|---|---|---|---|---|---|---|---|---|
| To Bank (Bal fig) | 1,750 | 1,625 | — | — | By Balance b/d | 19,000 | 16,000 | 8,000 | — |
| To Balance c/d | 21,000 | 17,500 | 10,500 | 7,000 | By Bank | — | — | — | 7,000 |
| | | | | | By Goodwill | 1,800 | 1,500 | 900 | — |
| | | | | | By Profit on Revaluation | 1,950 | 1,625 | 975 | — |
| | | | | | By Bank (Blancing figure) | — | — | 625 | — |
| | 22,750 | 19,125 | 10,500 | 7,000 | | 22,750 | 19,125 | 10,500 | 7,000 |
| | | | | | By Balance b/d | 21,000 | 17,500 | 10,500 | 7,000 |

**Note** Firstly, calculate total capital of firm through Deepak's capital and his share in profit. Then, calculate capital of each partner as per new profit sharing ratio. Finally, use this capital as balance c/d in capital account and close the accounts. The difference, if any, will be cash withdrawn or deposit by the partner.

(c) **Balance Sheet** (New Firm)

| Liabilities | | Amt (₹) | Assets | | Amt (₹) |
|---|---|---|---|---|---|
| Creditors | | 9,000 | Land and Buildings | | 31,000 |
| Bills Payable | | 3,000 | Furniture | | 3,080 |
| Capital A/cs | | | Stock | | 12,600 |
| Arun | 21,000 | | Debtors | 12,600 | |
| Bablu | 17,500 | | (−) Reserve | (630) | 11,970 |
| Chetan | 10,500 | | Cash in Hand | | 9,350 |
| Deepak | 7,000 | 56,000 | | | |
| | | 68,000 | | | 68,000 |

**Working Notes**

1. Let total profit be 1.

Deepak's share $= \frac{1}{8}$; Remaining profit $= 1 - \frac{1}{8} = \frac{7}{8}$

Arun's new share $= \frac{7}{8} \times \frac{6}{14} = \frac{6}{16}$; Bablu's new share $= \frac{7}{8} \times \frac{5}{14} = \frac{5}{16}$

Chetan's new share $= \frac{7}{8} \times \frac{3}{14} = \frac{3}{16}$; Deepak's share $= \frac{1}{8} \times \frac{2}{2} = \frac{2}{16}$

∴ New profit sharing ratio = 6 : 5 : 3 : 2

2. Total capital of the new firm = 7,000 × 8/1 = ₹ 56,000

Arun's capital = 56,000 × 6/16 = ₹ 21,000; Bablu's capital = 56,000 × 5/16 = ₹ 17,500

Chetan's capital = 56,000 × 3/16 = ₹ 10,500; Deepak's capital = ₹ 7,000

(B) **JOURNAL**

| Date | Particulars | LF | Amt (Dr) | Amt (Cr) |
|---|---|---|---|---|
| | C's Current A/c Dr | | 50,000 | |
| | To A's Current A/c | | | 25,000 |
| | To B's Current A/c | | | 25,000 |
| | (Being C's goodwill adjusted to sacrificing partners equally through C's account) | | | |

**10.** **In the Books of Rahul Ltd.**

**JOURNAL**

| Date | Particulars | LF | Amt (Dr) | Amt (Cr) |
|---|---|---|---|---|
| (i) | Bank A/c Dr | | 12,80,000 | |
| | To Share Application A/c | | | 12,80,000 |
| | (Being share application money received) | | | |

| Date | Particulars | | LF | Amt (Dr) | Amt (Cr) |
|---|---|---|---|---|---|
| (ii) | Share Application A/c | Dr | | 12,80,000 | |
| | To Share Capital A/c | | | | 4,80,000 |
| | To Securities Premium A/c | | | | 1,60,000 |
| | To Share Allotment A/c | | | | 3,20,000 |
| | To Bank A/c | | | | 3,20,000 |
| | (Being share application money adjusted) | | | | |
| (iii) | Share Allotment A/c | Dr | | 9,60,000 | |
| | To Share Capital A/c | | | | 4,80,000 |
| | To Securities Premium A/c | | | | 4,80,000 |
| | (Being share allotment money due) | | | | |
| (iv) | Bank A/c | Dr | | 6,36,800 | |
| | Calls-in-arrear | Dr | | 3,200 | |
| | To Share Allotment A/c | | | | 6,40,000 |
| | (Being share allotment money received) (9,60,000 – 3,20,000 – 3,200) | | | | |
| (v) | Share Capital A/c | Dr | | 4,800 | |
| | Securities Premium A/c | Dr | | 2,400 | |
| | To Share Forfeiture A/c | | | | 4,000 |
| | To Share Allotment A/c | | | | 3,200 |
| | (Being 'R' share forfeited, 800 @ ₹ 6) | | | | |
| (vi) | Share First and Final Call A/c | Dr | | 9,55,200 | |
| | To Share Capital A/c | | | | 6,36,800 |
| | To Securities Premium A/c | | | | 3,18,400 |
| | (Being share first and final call money due on 1,59,200 shares) | | | | |
| (vii) | Bank A/c | Dr | | 9,50,400 | |
| | Calls-in-arrear | Dr | | 4,800 | |
| | To Share First and Final call A/c | | | | 9,55,200 |
| | (Being share first and final call money received on 1,59,200 – 800 = 1,58,400 shares) | | | | |
| (viii) | Share Capital A/c | Dr | | 8,000 | |
| | Securities Premium A/c | Dr | | 1,600 | |
| | To Share Forfeiture A/c | | | | 4,800 |
| | To Share First and Final Call A/c | | | | 4,800 |
| | (Being share forfeited) | | | | |
| | Bank A/c | Dr | | 8,000 | |
| | Share Forfeiture A/c | Dr | | 2,000 | |
| | To Share Capital A/c | | | | 10,000 |
| | (Being 1,000 shares re-issued) | | | | |
| | Share Forfeiture A/c | Dr | | 3,200 | |
| | To Capital Reserve A/c | | | | 3,200 |
| | (Being amount of forfeiture transferred to capital reserve) | | | | |

**Working Notes**

1. **Calculation of Calls-in-arears from 'R'**

| | |
|---|---|
| Number of shares applied by R = $800 \times \frac{2,40,000}{1,60,000}$ = | 1,200 |
| Amount received from 'R' on application (1,200 × 4) | 4,800 |
| Amount required from 'R' on application (800 × 4) | (3,200) |
| Excess amount received adjusted towards allotment | 1,600 |
| Amount to be paid by 'R' on allotment (800 × 6) | 4,800 |
| (–) Excess amount adjusted | (1,600) |
| Calls-in-arrears of 'R' | 3,200 |

2. **Calculation of Capital Reserve**

| | |
|---|---|
| Amount forefeited on 800 shares of 'R' | 4,000 |
| (+) Amount forfeited on 200 shares of 'S' 200 × 6 | 1,200 |
| | 5,200 |
| Discount allowed on re-issue of 800 and 200 shares of 'R' and 'S' respectively | (2,000) |
| Capital reserve | 3,200 |

*Or* (i) 15,000 × 5 = ₹ 75,000 (ii) $\frac{4,000}{5,000} \times 120 = 96$ (iii) 120 × 5 = ₹ 600 (iv) ₹ 1,032 [648 (WN) + 384]

**Working Note**

| | | | |
|---|---|---|---|
| Shares Applied by Mohan | = | | 120 |
| Pro-rata 4 : 5 | | | |
| Share allotted $\left(120 \times \frac{4}{5}\right)$ | = | | 96 |
| Amount paid on application (120 × 5) | = | ₹ | 600 |
| Application money on allotted shares (96 × 5) | = | ₹ | (480) |
| Surplus | = | ₹ | 120 |
| Amount due on allotment on shares (96 × 8) | = | ₹ | 768 |
| (–) Surplus as above | = | ₹ | (120) |
| Amount not paid on allotment (Calls-in-arrears) | = | ₹ | 648 |

(v) **JOURNAL**

| Date | Particulars | | LF | Amt (Dr) | Amt (Cr) |
|---|---|---|---|---|---|
| (a) | Forfeiture of Jagan's shares | | | | |
| | Equity Share Capital A/c (144 × 17) | Dr | | 2,448 | |
| | To Equity Share Forfeited A/c (240 × 5) | | | | 1,200 |
| | To Equity Share Allotment A/c (WN) | | | | 672 |
| | To Equity Share First Call A/c (144 × 4) | | | | 576 |
| | (Being Jagan's 144 shares forfeited for non-payment of allotment and first call money) | | | | |
| (b) | Bank A/c (100 × 16) | Dr | | 1,600 | |
| | Equity Share Forfeited A/c | Dr | | 400 | |
| | To Equity Share Capital Account (100 × 20) | | | | 2,000 |
| | (Being 100 forfeited shares re-issued at ₹ 16 per share fully paid-up including 50 shares of Jagan and 50 of Mohan) | | | | |
| | Equity Share Forfeited A/c | Dr | | 330 | |
| | To Capital Reserve A/c | | | | 330 |
| | (Being the unutilised money i.e. profit on re-issue transferred to capital reserve account) | | | | |

**Working Note**

| | | | |
|---|---|---|---|
| Share allotted to Jagan = 144 | | | |
| Pro-rata 3 : 5 | | | |
| Share applied by Jagan $\left(144 \times \frac{5}{3}\right)$ | = | | 240 |
| Application money (240 × 5) | = | ₹ | 1,200 |
| (–) Application money on allotted shares (144 × 5) | = | ₹ | (720) |
| Surplus | = | ₹ | 480 |
| Amount due on allotment on (144 × 8) | = | ₹ | 1,152 |
| (–) Surplus as above | = | ₹ | (480) |
| Amount not paid on allotment (Calls-in-arrears) | = | ₹ | 672 |

**11.** (i) • (c) Operating • Outflow of cash

(ii) (*d*) Measure short-term solvency of business

(iii) A high debt to equity ratio signifies that the company is depending more on borrowed funds in comparison to shareholders' fund.

(iv) (a) Earning Per Share $= \frac{\text{Net Profit after Tax and Preference Dividend}}{\text{Number of Equity Shares}}$ (b) Earning Per Share $= \frac{50,000 - 40,000}{10,000} = 1$

(v) Cash outflow under financing activities

**12.**

**Comparative Statement of Profit and Loss**
for the years ended 31st March, 2022 and 2023

| Particulars | Note No. | 2022 (₹) | 2023 (₹) | Absolute Change (Increase or Decrease) (₹) | Percentage Change (Increase or Decrease) (%) |
|---|---|---|---|---|---|
| (1) | | (2) | (3) | (4) | (5) |
| | | A | B | (B – A = C) | C/A × 100 = D |
| I. Revenue from Operations | | 2,50,000 | 4,00,000 | 1,50,000 | 60.00 |
| II. **Expenses** | | | | | |
| (a) Purchase of Stock-in-trade | | 1,20,000 | 2,10,000 | 90,000 | 75.00 |
| (b) Change in Inventories | | 45,000 | 60,000 | 15,000 | 33.33 |
| (c) Employee Benefit Expenses | | 20,000 | 10,000 | (10,000) | (50.00) |
| **Total Expenses** | | 1,85,000 | 2,80,000 | 95,000 | 51.35 |
| III. **Profit before Tax** (I – II) | | 65,000 | 1,20,000 | 55,000 | 84.62 |
| IV. (–) Tax | | (26,000) | (60,000) | (34,000) | 130.77 |
| V. **Profit after Tax** (III – IV) | | 39,000 | 60,000 | 21,000 | 53.85 |

**13.** (a)

**Cash Flow from Operating Activities**

| Particulars | | Amt (₹) |
|---|---|---|
| Cash Flow from Operating Activities | | |
| Net Profit before Tax and Extraordinary Items | | 1,96,000 |
| (+) Decrease in Current Assets and Increase in Current Liabilities | | |
| Debtors | 20,000 | |
| Sundry Creditors | 15,000 | |
| Bills Payable | 15,000 | 50,000 |
| Cash Generated from Operations | | 2,46,000 |
| (−) Income Tax Paid | | (45,000) |
| Net Cash Flow from Operating Activities | | 2,01,000 |

**Working Note**

**Calculation of Net Profit before Tax and Extraordinary Items**

| Particulars | Amt (₹) |
|---|---|
| Net Profit as per Profit and Loss Statement (1,85,000 – 70,000) | 1,15,000 |
| (+) Provision for Tax | 45,000 |
| Dividend Paid (Proposed) (12% × 3,00,000) | 36,000 |
| | 1,96,000 |

(b)

**Cash Flow from Investing and Financing Activities**

| Particulars | | Amt (₹) |
|---|---|---|
| **Cash Flow from Investing Activities** | | |
| Purchase of Property, Plant and Equipment | (2,90,000) | |
| Net Cash Used in Investing Activities | | (2,90,000) |
| **Cash Flow from Financing Activities** | | |
| Issue of Share Capital | 1,50,000 | |
| Dividend Paid | (36,000) | |
| Net Cash Flow from Financing Activities | | 1,14,000 |

(c)

| Particulars | Amt (₹) |
|---|---|
| Net Increase in Cash and Cash Equivalents (2,01,000 – 2,90,000 + 1,14,000) | 25,000 |
| (+) Opening Cash and Cash Equivalents | 65,000 |
| Closing Cash and Cash Equivalents | 90,000 |

*Or*

**Cash Flow from Investing and Financing Activities**

| Particulars | | Amt (₹) |
|---|---|---|
| **Cash Flow from Investing Activities** | | |
| Sale of Machinery | 75,000 | |
| Purchase of Machinery | (3,81,000) | |
| Sale of Non-current Investment | 30,000 | |
| Net Cash used in Investing Activities | | (2,76,000) |
| **Cash Flow from Financing Activities** | | |
| Issue of Debentures | 60,000 | |
| Interest on Debentures (WN1) | (16,800) | |
| Net Cash Flow from Financing Activities | | 43,200 |

**Working Notes**

1. Interest on debentures $= 2,40,000 \times \frac{6}{100} =$ ₹ $14,400 = 60,000 \times \frac{6}{100} \times \frac{8}{12} =$ ₹ 2,400

Total interest on debentures = 14,400 + 2,400 = ₹ 16,800

2. Dr **Property, Plant & Equipment and Intangible Assets Account** Cr

| Particulars | Amt (₹) | Particulars | Amt (₹) |
|---|---|---|---|
| To Balance b/d | 10,50,000 | By Depreciation | 1,71,000 |
| To Cash (Purchase of machinery) (Balancing figure) | 3,81,000 | By Cash A/c (Sale of machinery) | 75,000 |
| | | By Statement of Profit and Loss (Loss on sale) | 15,000 |
| | | By Balance c/d | 11,70,000 |
| | 14,31,000 | | 14,31,000 |

**14.** (i) Let cost of revenue from operations be $x$.

Revenue from Operations = Cost of Revenue from Operations + Gross Profit

$$3,00,000 = x + x \times \frac{25}{100} \Rightarrow 3,00,000 = x + \frac{x}{4}$$

$$3,00,000 = \frac{5x}{4} \Rightarrow \frac{3,00,000 \times 4}{5} = x$$

Cost of revenue from operations $(x) =$ ₹ 2,40,000

(ii) Let inventory in the beginning be ₹ $x$.

Inventory at the end = ₹ $(x + 4,000)$

$$\text{Inventory Turnover Ratio} = \frac{\text{Cost of Revenue from Operations}}{\text{Average Inventory}}$$

$$5 = \frac{2,40,000}{\text{Average Inventory}}$$

$$\text{Average Inventory} = \frac{2,40,000}{5} = ₹\ 48,000$$

$$\text{Average Inventory} = \frac{\text{Opening Inventory} + \text{Closing Inventory}}{2}$$

$$48,000 = \frac{x + x + 4,000}{2} \Rightarrow 48,000 = \frac{2x + 4,000}{2}$$

$$\Rightarrow 48,000 = x + 2,000 \Rightarrow x = 48,000 - 2,000 = ₹\ 46,000$$

Opening inventory $(x) =$ ₹ 46,000

(iii) Closing inventory = ₹ $(x + 4,000)$ and opening inventory $(x) =$ ₹ 46,000

∴ Closing inventory = 46,000 + 4,000

Closing inventory = ₹ 50,000

| SQP Code : **PB-5/15** | Series *i*-**Succeed 5-25/15** | Roll No. | | | | | | | |
|---|---|---|---|---|---|---|---|---|---|

# Sample Question Paper 05

## Accounts 12th (Code 858)

### General Instructions

1. Candidates are allowed additional 15 minutes for only reading the paper. They must not start writing during this time.
2. Section-A is compulsory for all candidates and has ten questions.
3. Candidates have to attempt all questions from either Section-B or Section-C*.
4. Internal choices have been provided in five questions in Section-A and one question in Section-B.
5. The intended marks for questions or parts of questions are given in the brackets [ ].
6. All calculations should be shown clearly.
7. All workings, including rough work, should be done on the same page as, and adjacent to, the rest of the answer.

*Section-C has not been covered.

**Time : 3 Hrs.**

**Max. Marks : 80**

## Section A Answer All Questions [60 Marks]

**Que 1.**

In sub-parts (i) to (iv), choose the correct option and in sub-parts (v) to (x) answer the questions as instructed.

(i) When a company issue fully paid shares to promoter for their services, the journal entry will be (Application) [1]

(a) Bank A/c Dr
  To Share Capital A/c

(b) Underwriter's A/c Dr
  To Share Capital A/c

(c) Promoter's A/c Dr
  To Share Capital A/c

(d) Promotion Expenses A/c Dr
  To Share Capital A/c

(ii) Choose the correct order of the following in relation to the division of profits. (Recall) [1]

A – Rent paid to partner

B – Transfer of profit to profit and loss appropriation account

C – Transfer to general reserve

D – Distribution of profit among the partners

**Codes**

(a) A, B, D, C (b) C, D, B, A

(c) A, B, C, D (d) D, B, C, A

(iii) G India Ltd. issued 5,000, 12% debentures of ₹ 100 each at a discount of 5% redeemable at the premium of 6%. What amount will be transferred to loss on issue of debentures account? (Application) [1]

(a) ₹ 60,000 (b) ₹ 55,000 (c) ₹ 50,000 (d) ₹ 30,000

(iv) Manoj, Mohan and Mayank were partners in a firm sharing profits in the ratio of 2:1:1. They decided to dissolve the firm with effect from 31st March, 2022.

While paying-off their liabilities, creditors (₹ 36,000) decided to take the furniture of the firm (₹ 70,000) and the remaining amount was paid by the creditors. The journal entry passed will be (Application) [1]

(a) Creditors A/c Dr 36,000
  To Furniture 36,000

(b) Furniture A/c Dr 70,000
    To Creditors A/c 70,000
(c) Bank A/c Dr 34,000
    To Realisation A/c 34,000
(d) Realisation A/c Dr 34,000
    To Bank A/c 34,000

(v) When debentures are issued at a discount and are redeemable at a premium, which account is debited at the time of issue to show amount of discount on issue of debentures and premium on redemption of debentures? (Understanding) [1]

(vi) **Assertion** (A) Goodwill is the present value of a firm's anticipated expected earnings.

**Reason** (R) The capitalised value attached to the differential profit capacity of a business is called goodwill. (Evaluate) [1]

**Alternatives**

(a) Both Assertion (A) and Reason (R) are true and Reason (R) is the correct explanation of Assertion (A)
(b) Both Assertion (A) and Reason (R) are true, but Reason (R) is not the correct explanation of Assertion (A)
(c) Assertion (A) is true, but Reason (R) is false
(d) Assertion (A) is false, but Reason (R) is true

(vii) M, S and G are partners in a firm with profit sharing ratio of 2:1:1. S retired on 31st March, 2022. M and G decided that the new firm's capital will be fixed at ₹ 2,40,000. The capital accounts of M and G show a credit balance of ₹ 1,64,000 and ₹ 82,000 after making all the adjustments relating to revaluation, goodwill and accumulated profit etc. What will be the actual cash to be brought in by M and G? (Application) [1]

(viii) Admission of a partner is the reconstitution of the firm because with the admission of a partner, existing agreement ends and a new agreement among all the partners comes into existence.

**Source** *Accounting statement*

(a) At the time of admission of partner, does the new partner is liable for any profit on loss occurred before his admission?
(b) Based on the above statement, state the mode(s) through which a partner can be admitted into the firm. (Recall) [1]

(ix) A, B and C are partners in a firm. Their balance sheet showed sundry assets of ₹ 2,69,100 at the time of dissolution of the firm.

B is to take over some of the sundry assets at ₹ 1,65,600 (being 10% less than the book value).

C is to take over remaining sundry assets at 80% of the book value.

You are required to pass the journal entry for sundry assets taken over by C. (Application) [1]

(x) The Ministry of Corporate Affairs (MCA) has levied a penalty on SMP Constructions Private Limited for not attaching cash flow statement along with the financial statements.

**Source** *Study cafe*

Based on the above statement, apart from cash flow statement, name the other elements of financial statements of a company. (Understanding) [1]

**Que 2.**

The partnership agreement between Maneesh and Girish provides that

(i) Profits will be shared equally.
(ii) Maneesh will be allowed a salary of ₹ 400 per month.
(iii) Girish who manages the sales department will be allowed a commission equal to 10% of the net profits, after allowing Maneesh's salary.
(iv) 7% interest will be allowed on partners' fixed capital.
(v) 5% interest will be charged on partners' annual drawings.
(vi) The fixed capitals of Maneesh and Girish are ₹ 1,00,000 and ₹ 80,000 respectively. Their annual drawings were ₹ 16,000 and ₹ 14,000 respectively. The net profit for the year ending 31st March, 2024 amounted to ₹ 40,000.

You are required to

(a) Calculate the amount of Girish's commission.
(b) Prepare firm's profit and loss appropriation account. (Application) [3]

**Que 3.**

Vimal Ltd. issued 58,000, 11% debentures of ₹ 100 each at a premium of 25%. Further, company purchased furniture of ₹ 11,00,000 from M/s Malhotra Furnitures. 50% of the amount was paid to Malhotra Furnitures by accepting a bill of exchange and for the balance, the company issued 11% debentures of ₹ 100 each at a premium of 10% in favour of Malhotra Furnitures.

You are required to pass journal entries to record

(i) The amount received on application and allotment.

(ii) The transfer of application money to debentures account.

(iii) For the settlement of purchase consideration for the purchase of furniture from Malhotra Furnitures.

Show working notes clearly. **(Application) [3]**

**Que 4.**

PQRS are partners in a firm sharing profits in 2 : 1 : 2 : 1 ratio. On the retirement of R, the goodwill was valued at ₹ 2,16,000. P, Q and S decided to share future profits equally.

(i) Calculate gaining ratio of the partners.

(ii) Calculate R's share of goodwill and pass the necessary journal entry.

**(Application) [3]**

*Or*

SP-05

X, Y and Z are partners sharing profits in the ratio of 4 : 3 : 2. On the 1st April, 2023. Y gave a notice to retire from the firm. X and Z decided to share future profits in the ratio of 1 : 1. The capital accounts of X and Z after all adjustments showed a balance of ₹ 21,500 and ₹ 40,250 respectively.

The total amount to be paid to Y was ₹ 47,750. This amount was to be paid by X ₹ 33,250 and by Z ₹ 14,500.

Pass necessary journal entries in the books of the firm for the above transactions.

**Que 5.**

Raghav Ltd. offered 20,00,000, 10% debentures of ₹ 200 each at a discount of 14% redeemable at premium of 8% after 9 years.

(i) You are required to **[2]**

(a) Give the amount received on application.

(b) Give the amount transferred to the loss on issue of debentures account.

(ii) Pass the journal entry for the transfer of debenture application money of debenture account. **(Application) [1]**

*Or*

Nand Pvt. Ltd. issued 10,000, 9% debentures of ₹ 100 each to the public at 10% discount on 1st April, 2022. These debentures are redeemable after 6 years at a premium of 10%.

Pass the necessary journal entries for issue of debentures. **(Application) [3]**

**Que 6.**

From the following information prepare balance sheet of Sagarika **(Application) [6]**

| Particulars | 31st March, 2023 (₹) |
|---|---|
| Share Capital | 50,00,000 |
| Long-term Borrowings | 30,00,000 |
| Short-term Borrowings | 4,80,000 |
| Reserves and Surplus | 12,00,000 |
| Other Current Liabilities | 1,10,000 |
| Trade Payables | 4,50,000 |
| Short-term Provisions | 60,000 |
| Property, Plant and Equipment | 72,00,000 |
| Inventories | 11,00,000 |
| Non-current Investment | 10,00,000 |
| Cash and Cash Equivalents | 3,50,000 |
| Trade Receivables | 6,00,000 |
| Other Current Assets | 50,000 |

**Que 7.**

A, B and C are partners sharing profits in the ratio of 3 : 1 : 1. On 31st March, 2024 they decided to dissolve their firm. On that date the balance sheet was as follows

**Balance Sheet**
as at 31st March, 2024

| Liabilities | | Amt (₹) | Assets | | Amt (₹) |
|---|---|---|---|---|---|
| Capital A/cs | | | Sundry Assets | | 76,000 |
| A | 1,10,000 | | Furniture | | 4,000 |
| B | 40,000 | | Stock | | 31,200 |
| C | 28,000 | 1,78,000 | Debtors | 96,800 | |
| Creditors | | 32,000 | (–) Provision for Doubtful Debts | (4,800) | 92,000 |
| Loan Account | | 6,000 | Cash | | 12,800 |
| | | 2,16,000 | | | 2,16,000 |

It is agreed that

(i) A is to take over the furniture at ₹ 3,200 and debtors amounting to ₹ 80,000 at ₹ 68,800 and also he agreed to pay the creditors of ₹ 32,000.

(ii) B is to take over the stock at ₹ 28,000 and part of sundry assets at ₹ 28,800 which is 10% less than the book value.

(iii) C is to take over the remaining sundry assets at 90% of the book value, less ₹ 400 as discount and also agreed to pay the loan along with accrued interest of ₹ 120 which has not been recorded in the books.

(iv) The dissolution expenses were ₹ 1,080.

(v) The remaining debtors were sold to a debt collecting agency for 50% of the book value.

(vi) On the date of dissolution, the firm made a loss of ₹ 28,000 on account of realisation of assets and settlement of liabilities.

You are required to prepare

(a) Partners' capital account [5]

(b) Cash account (Application) [1]

**Que 8.**

A, J and S are partners in a firm. Their capital accounts on 1st April, 2023 stood at ₹ 6,00,000, ₹ 4,80,000 and ₹ 3,60,000 respectively. Each partner withdrew ₹ 30,000 during the financial year 2023-24.

As per the provisions of their partnership deed

(i) J was entitled to a salary of ₹ 6,000 per month.

(ii) Interest on capital was to be allowed @ 10% per annum.

(iii) Interest on drawings was to be charged @ 4% per annum.

(iv) Profits and losses were to be shared in the ratio of their capitals.

The net profit of ₹ 4,50,000 for the year ended 31st March, 2024 was divided equally amongst the partners without providing for the terms of the deed.

You are required to pass a single adjusting journal entry to rectify the error. Show the working clearly. (Application) [6]

*Or*

Aman, Raman and Chaman are partners with fixed capitals of ₹ 4,00,000, ₹ 3,00,000 and ₹ 2,00,000 respectively. The balance of current accounts on 1st January, 2021 were Aman ₹ 20,000 (Cr), Raman ₹ 8,000 (Cr) and Chaman ₹ 6,000 (Dr).

Aman gave a loan to the firm of ₹ 50,000 on 1st July, 2021. The partnership deed provided for the following

(i) Interest on capital at 6%.

(ii) Interest on drawings at 9%. Each partner drew ₹ 12,000 on 1st July, 2021.

(iii) ₹ 50,000 is to be transferred in a reserve account.

(iv) Profit sharing ratio is 5 : 3 : 2 upto ₹ 1,60,000 and above ₹ 1,60,000 equally. Net profit of the firm before above adjustments was ₹ 3,96,720.

Prepare profit and loss appropriation account and show your workings clearly. (Application)

**Que 9.**

(A) Megha and Deepa are partners in a firm, sharing profits and losses in the ratio of 5 : 3. Their balance sheet as at 31st December, 2022 was as follows

**Balance Sheet**
as at 31st December, 2022

| Liabilities | | Amt (₹) | Assets | | Amt (₹) |
|---|---|---|---|---|---|
| Sundry Creditors | | 52,500 | Cash at Bank | | 17,500 |
| Provident Fund | | 35,000 | Sundry Debtors | 70,000 | |
| Workmen's Compensation Fund | | 20,300 | (–) Provision for Doubtful Debts | (2,100) | 67,900 |
| Capital A/cs | | | Stock of Goods | | 87,500 |
| Megha | 2,45,000 | | Property, Plant and Equipment | | 2,80,000 |
| Deepa | 1,08,500 | 3,53,500 | Profit and Loss A/c | | 8,400 |
| | | 4,61,300 | | | 4,61,300 |

They admitted Rahul into partnership with 1/8th share in profits. Rahul brings ₹ 70,000 as his capital and ₹ 42,000 for goodwill in cash. He acquires his share entirely from Megha.

Following revaluations are also made

(i) Provident fund is to be increased by ₹ 17,500.
(ii) Debtors are all good.
(iii) Stock includes ₹ 10,500 for obsolete items.
(iv) Creditors are to be paid ₹ 3,500 more.
(v) Property, plant and equipment are to be revalued at ₹ 2,45,000.

You are required to prepare

(a) Revaluation account [4½]
(b) Partners' capital account [1½]
(c) Balance sheet (Application) [2]

(B) Neel, Angad and Sugreev were partners in a firm, sharing profits and losses in the ratio of 4 : 3 : 2. Angad retires from the firm and his share is taken up by Neel and Sugreev in the ratio of 3 : 2.

At the time of retirement, the goodwill was valued at ₹ 60,000 and the same is recorded without raising goodwill account in the books of the firm. Calculate new profit sharing ratio and Angad's share of goodwill. (Application) [2]

SP-05

*Or*

The balance sheet of Raj, Neel and Kamal as at 31st December, 2022 was as follows

**Balance Sheet**
as at 31st December, 2022

| Liabilities | | Amt (₹) | Assets | Amt (₹) |
|---|---|---|---|---|
| Bills Payables | | 2,000 | Bank Balance | 5,800 |
| Sundry Creditors | | 5,000 | Bills Receivable | 800 |
| General Reserve | | 6,000 | Stock | 9,000 |
| Loans | | 7,100 | Sundry Debtors | 16,000 |
| Capital A/cs | | | Furniture | 2,000 |
| Raj | 22,750 | | Plant and Machinery | 6,500 |
| Neel | 15,250 | | Buildings | 30,000 |
| Kamal | 12,000 | 50,000 | | |
| | | 70,100 | | 70,100 |

The profit sharing ratio was 3:2:1. Kamal died on 30th April, 2023, the partnership deed provides that

(i) Goodwill is to be calculated on the basis of 3 years' purchase of the 4 years' average profits. The profits were

| | | |
|---|---|---|
| 2022 | — | ₹ 14,000 |
| 2021 | — | ₹ 16,000 |
| 2020 | — | ₹ 20,000 |
| 2019 | — | ₹ 10,000 |

(ii) The deceased partner to be given share of profit upto date of death on the basis of profits for previous year.

(iii) The assets have been revalued as under Stock ₹ 10,000, debtors ₹ 15,000, furniture ₹ 1,500, plant and machinery ₹ 5,000, building ₹ 35,000. A bill for ₹ 600 was found worthless.

(a) You are required to provide
- The entry for the adjustment of Kamal's share of goodwill. (Recall) [2]
- The entry for the transfer of general reserve. (Application) [2]
- The adjusting entry for the revaluation of assets and liabilities. (Application) [2]
- The entry for transfer of profit/loss on revaluation to partner's capital account. (Recall) [2]

(b) A sum of ₹ 12,900 was paid immediately to Kamal's executors and the balance to be paid in two equal annual instalments together with interest at 10% on the amount outstanding.
You are required to pass entries for the transfer of amount to Kamal's executors. (Application) [2]

**Que 10.**

Sita Ltd. had authorised capital of 20,000 equity shares of ₹ 100 each. It issued 8,000 equity shares of ₹ 100 each fully paid up to the vendors of a machine. It issued 10,000 equity shares to the public which were fully subscribed. During the first year only ₹ 60 were called up payable ₹ 20 on application, ₹ 20 on allotment, ₹ 10 on first call and ₹ 10 on second call. In respect of these shares, the amount were received as follows

(i) On 8,000 equity shares full money called.
(ii) On 1,200 equity shares ₹ 50 per share.
(iii) On 500 equity shares ₹ 40 per share.
(iv) On 300 equity shares ₹ 20 per share.

It was decided to forfeit 800 equity shares on which less than ₹ 50 were received. Out of these forfeited shares 600 equity shares were re-issued including all the shares of category (d) at ₹ 40 per share as ₹ 60 paid-up.

(i) Identify the shares on which less than ₹ 50 have been paid. [1]
(ii) Find out how much amount has been received on these shares. [1]
(iii) What is the amount of calls-in-arrears of other than the aforementioned shares? [1]
(iv) Workout the calls-in-arrears by preparing the table on these shares of categories (c) and (d) which are forfeited. [2]
(v) You are required to
(a) Pass the entry for the forfeiture of shares on which less than ₹ 50 are recieved. [2]
(b) Pass the entry for the re-issue. (Application) [3]

*Or*

Ajanta Limited invited applications for 4,00,000 of its equity shares of ₹ 10 each on the following terms

| | **Amt (₹)** |
|---|---|
| Payable on Application | 5 per share |
| Payable on Allotment | 3 per share |
| Payable on First and Final | 2 per share |

Application for 5,00,000 shares were received. It was decided

(i) to refuse allotment to the applicants for 20,000 shares;
(ii) to allot in full to applicants for 80,000 shares;
(iii) to allot the balance of the available shares pro-rata among the other applicants; and
(iv) to utilise excess application money in part as payment of allotment money.

One applicant, whom shares had been allotted on pro-rata basis, did not pay the amount due on allotment and on the call and his 400 shares were forfeited.
The shares were re-issued @ ₹ 9 per share.
Show the journal and prepare cash book to record the above. (Application) [10]

## Section B

**[20 Marks]**

**Que 11.**

(i) The global financial crisis has had a positive fallout. Leading corporates have learnt to be more efficient in managing their finances. According to a study conducted by management consultancy firm Booz and Co, companies reduced their working capital by 2% even as sales increased by 20% in 2008-09.

**Source** *Economic times (edited)*

- What is the formula to calculate working capital? **(Analysis)**
- The working capital of IAN Ltd. is ₹ 2,00,000 and its current assets are ₹ 6,00,000. What is its current ratio? **(Recall) [1]**

(a) 1.5 : 1 (b) 2 : 1
(c) 1 : 2 (d) 1 : 1.5

(ii) It is crucial to have cash flowing in the business and maintaining a proactive and disciplined approach to create cash flow statements as it will give you a better understanding of your business's cash position and how to best manage cash flows.

**Source** *Yahoo finance*

Based on the above statement, which of the following is not the importance of preparation of cash flow statement? **(Understanding) [1]**

(a) It helps in capital budgeting decisions
(b) It facilitates in ascertaining cash flow from various activities
(c) It helps in ascertaining the net profit after tax
(d) None of the above

(iii) The common size balance sheet shows the makeup of a company's various assets and liabilities through the presentation of percentages, in addition to absolute dollar values.

This affords the ability to quickly compare the historical trend of various line items or categories and provides a baseline for comparison of two firms of different market capitalisations.

Additionally, the relative percentages may be compared across companies and industries.

**Source** *Investopedia*

Which item is assumed to be 100 in case of common size statement of profit and loss and in the case of common size balance sheet? **(Analysis) [1]**

(iv) Imagine a bustling boardroom packed with executives and stakeholders awaiting the release of the company's financial performance. The room falls silent as the CEO proceeds to present the financial statements.

A financial statement is like the GPS of an organisation one that provides you with a picture of its financial performance. The documents can reveal a company's true health and trajectory. They provide a comprehensive snapshot of an enterprise's financial activities and position.

**Source** *happay.com*

What is the main objective of analysis of financial statements ? **(Application) [1]**

(v) In 24th March, our net debt came down to ₹ 3,700 crore, which is a nearly ₹ 800 crore deduction or nearly 18% net reduction. This is also leading us to a debt equity ratio of 0.80 to 1, which is certainly a good deleveraging.

This was attained by a very consistent focused policy and strategy that we did, that infusion of capital into the company at two stages and this has helped us to lower debt.

**Source** *Jk Tyres, Raghupati Singhania economic times*

(a) What is formula for debt equity ratio?
(b) The debt equity ratio of a company is 1.7:1. State with reason whether interest received on calls-in-advance ₹ 5,000 will improve reduce or will not change the debt equity ratio? **(Application) [1]**

SP-05

**Que 12.**

Prepare a comparative statement of profit and loss from the following (Application) [3]

| Particulars | 31st March, 2020 (₹) | 31st March, 2019 (₹) |
|---|---|---|
| Revenue from Operations | 25,00,000 | 20,00,000 |
| Cost of Material Consumed | 13,00,000 | 10,00,000 |
| Other Expenses | 1,20,000 | Nil |
| Tax Rate | 50% | 50% |

**13.** Balance sheets of Jaiswal Ltd. as at 31st March, 2022 and 2021 were as follows

| Particulars | Note No. | 31st March, 2022 (₹) | 31st March, 2021 (₹) |
|---|---|---|---|
| **I. EQUITY AND LIABILITIES** | | | |
| 1. **Shareholders' Fund** | | | |
| (i) Share Capital | | 10,00,000 | 7,00,000 |
| (ii) Reserves and Surplus | | 2,50,000 | 1,50,000 |
| **Total** | | 12,50,000 | 8,50,000 |
| **II. ASSETS** | | | |
| 1. **Non-current Assets** | | | |
| Property, Plant & Equipment and Intangible Assets | 1 | 8,00,000 | 5,00,000 |
| 2. **Current Assets** | | | |
| (i) Inventory | | 1,00,000 | 75,000 |
| (ii) Cash and Cash Equivalents | | 3,50,000 | 2,75,000 |
| **Total** | | 12,50,000 | 8,50,000 |

**Notes to Accounts**

| Particulars | 31st March, 2022 (₹) | 31st March, 2021 (₹) |
|---|---|---|
| 1. **Property, Plant & Equipment and Intangible Assets** | | |
| Plant and Machinery | 8,00,000 | 5,00,000 |

**Additional Information**

(i) ₹ 50,000 depreciation has been charged to plant and machinery during the year 2021-22.

(ii) A piece of machinery costing ₹ 12,000 (book value ₹ 5,000) was sold at 60% profit on book value.

SP-05

(iii) Proposed dividend for the year ended 31st March, 2021 and 2022 was ₹ 40,000 and ₹ 50,000 respectively.

(a) What is the value of net profit before tax? [2]

(b) Calculate the cash flow from financing acitivity. [2]

(c) Prepare plant and machinery account. (Evaluate) [2]

*Or*

Prepare a cash flow statement on the basis of the information given in the Balance Sheet of Grasim Industries Ltd. as at 31st March, 2020 and 2019 (Application) [6]

| Particulars | Note No. | 31st March, 2020 (₹) | 31st March, 2019 (₹) |
|---|---|---|---|
| **I. EQUITY AND LIABILITIES** | | | |
| 1. **Shareholders' Funds** | | | |
| (i) Share Capital | | 2,00,000 | 1,50,000 |
| (ii) Reserves and Surplus | 1 | 90,000 | 75,000 |

| Particulars | Note No. | 31st March, 2020 (₹) | 31st March, 2019 (₹) |
|---|---|---|---|
| 2. **Non-current Liabilities** | | | |
| Long-term Borrowings | | 87,500 | 87,500 |
| 3. **Current Liabilities** | | | |
| Trade Payables | | 10,000 | 76,000 |
| **Total** | | 3,87,500 | 3,88,500 |
| II. ASSETS | | | |
| 1. **Non-current Assets** | | | |
| (i) Property, Plant & Equipment and Intangible Assets | | | |
| (a) Property, Plant and Equipment | | 1,87,500 | 1,40,000 |
| (ii) Non-current Investments | | 1,05,500 | 1,02,500 |
| 2. **Current Assets** | | | |
| (i) Current Investments (Marketable) | | 12,500 | 33,500 |
| (ii) Inventories | | 4,000 | 5,500 |
| (iii) Trade Receivables | | 9,500 | 23,000 |
| (iv) Cash and Cash Equivalents | | 68,500 | 84,000 |
| **Total** | | 3,87,500 | 3,88,500 |

**Notes to Accounts**

| Particulars | 31st March, 2020 (₹) | 31st March, 2019 (₹) |
|---|---|---|
| 1. **Reserves and Surplus** | | |
| Surplus (Balance in statement of profit and loss) | 90,000 | 75,000 |

**Que 14.**

From the following information, calculate any three out of the following (upto two decimal places)

**(Application) [6]**

(i) Gross profit ratio (ii) Operating ratio

(iii) Inventory turnover ratio

Cash revenue from operations ₹ 5,00,000, credit revenue from operations ₹ 2,50,000, return inwards ₹ 50,000, opening inventory of goods ₹ 1,20,000, closing inventory of goods ₹ 1,80,000 purchase of goods ₹ 4,20,000, office expenses ₹ 40,000, selling expenses ₹ 20,000.

SP-05

(iv) Debt to capital employed ratio, using the following information

| Particulars | Note No. | Amt (₹) |
|---|---|---|
| I. EQUITY AND LIABILITIES | | |
| 1. **Shareholders' Funds** | | |
| (i) Share Capital | | 4,00,000 |
| (ii) Reserves and Surplus (Balance in statement of profit and loss) | | 1,00,000 |
| 2. **Non-current Liabilities** | | |
| Long-term Borrowings | | 1,50,000 |
| 3. **Current Liabilities** | | 50,000 |
| **Total** | | 7,00,000 |
| II. ASSETS | | |
| 1. **Non-current Assets** | | |
| (i) Property, Plant and Equipment | | 4,00,000 |
| (ii) Non-current Investments | | 1,00,000 |
| 2. **Current Assets** | | 2,00,000 |
| **Total** | | 7,00,000 |

# Solutions in Topper's Style

*My Commitment I affirm that I am reviewing these solutions only after I have solved the Sample Question Paper 5 on my own. My purpose of looking the solutions is solely to verify whether my answers/solutions were correct or not and to identify my mistakes in case my solutions were wrong or I could not solve that.*

1. (i) (*c*) Promoter's A/c Dr
   To Share Capital A/c

   (ii) (*c*) A, B, C, D

   (iii) (*b*) Premium on redemption $= 5{,}000 \times (100 \times 6\%) = 30{,}000$
   Discount on issue of debentures $= 5{,}000 \times (100 \times 5\%) = 25{,}000$
   Total loss $= 30{,}000 + 25{,}000 =$ ₹ 55,000

   (iv) (*c*) Bank A/c Dr 34,000
   To Realisation A/c 34,000
   Amount to be received from the creditors $= 70{,}000 - 36{,}000 =$ ₹ 34,000

   (v) Loss on issue of debentures account is debited to show amount of discount on issue of debentures.

   (vi) (*b*) Both Assertion (A) and Reason (R) are true, but Reason (R) is not the correct explanation of Assertion (A)

   (vii) New capitals of M and G
   M $= 2{,}40{,}000 \times 2/3 =$ ₹ 1,60,000; G $= 2{,}40{,}000 \times 1/3 =$ ₹ 80,000
   Cash brought in by M $= 1{,}64{,}000 - 1{,}60{,}000 =$ ₹ 4,000; Cash brought in by G $= 82{,}000 - 80{,}000 =$ ₹ 2,000

   (viii) (a) No, new partner is not liable for any profit or loss occured before his admission.
   (b) Concent of all the existing partners

   (ix) **JOURNAL**

| Date | Particulars | | LF | Amt (Dr) | Amt (Cr) |
|---|---|---|---|---|---|
| | C's Capital A/c | Dr | | 68,080 | |
| | To Realisation A/c | | | | 68,080 |
| | (Being the remaining sundry assets taken over by C) | | | | |

**Working Note**

Book value of assets taken over by B $= \dfrac{1{,}65{,}600 \times 100}{90} =$ ₹ 1,84,000

Value of asset taken over by C $= (2{,}69{,}100 - 1{,}84{,}000) \times \dfrac{80}{100} =$ ₹ 68,080

   (x) Other elements of financial statements apart from cash flow statement are
   (a) Statement of profit and loss (b) Balance sheet

2. (a) Girish's commission = ₹ 3,520 $\left[(40{,}000 - 4{,}800) \times \dfrac{10}{100}\right]$

   (b) **Profit and Loss Appropriation Account**
   for the year ended...

Dr | | Cr

| Particulars | | Amt (₹) | Particulars | | Amt (₹) |
|---|---|---|---|---|---|
| To Maneesh's Current A/c (Salary) (400 × 12) | | 4,800 | By Net Profit as per Profit and Loss A/c | | 40,000 |
| To Girish's Current A/c (Commission) | | 3,520 | By Interest on Drawings | | |
| To Interest on Capital | | | Maneesh's Current A/c $\left(16{,}000 \times \dfrac{5}{100}\right)$ | 800 | |
| Maneesh's Current A/c $\left(1{,}00{,}000 \times \dfrac{7}{100}\right)$ | 7,000 | | | | |
| Girish's Current A/c $\left(80{,}000 \times \dfrac{7}{100}\right)$ | 5,600 | 12,600 | Girish's Current A/c $\left(14{,}000 \times \dfrac{5}{100}\right)$ | 700 | 1,500 |
| To Profit transferred to | | | | | |
| Maneesh's Current A/c | 10,290 | | | | |
| Girish's Current A/c | 10,290 | 20,580 | | | |
| | | 41,500 | | | 41,500 |

**Common Mistake** Students usually get confused in calculating partner's commission. Here, only Maneesh's salary will be deducted from net profit in order to calculate Girish's commission.

3. **JOURNAL**

| Date | Particulars | | LF | Amt (Dr) | Amt (Cr) |
|---|---|---|---|---|---|
| (i) | Bank A/c (58,000 × 125) | Dr | | 72,50,000 | |
| | To Debenture Application and Allotment A/c | | | | 72,50,000 |
| | (Being the application and allotment money received) | | | | |
| (ii) | Debentures Application and Allotment A/c | Dr | | 72,50,000 | |
| | To 11% Debentures A/c (58,000 × 100) | | | | 58,00,000 |
| | To Securities Premium A/c (58,000 × 25) | | | | 14,50,000 |
| | (Being the application money transferred to debentures account) | | | | |
| (iii) | M/s Malhotra Furnitures A/c | Dr | | 11,00,000 | |
| | To Bills Payable A/c | | | | 5,50,000 |
| | To 11% Debentures A/c | | | | 5,00,000 |
| | To Securities Premium A/c | | | | 50,000 |
| | (Being the bill of exchange and 11% debentures issued with premium to Malhotra Furnitures) | | | | |

**Working Note**

$$\text{Number of Debentures Issued} = \frac{5,50,000}{(100+10)} = 5,000 \text{ Debentures}$$

4. (i) Calculation of Gaining Ratio

Gaining Ratio = New Share – Old Share

$$P = \frac{1}{3} - \frac{2}{6} = \frac{2-2}{6} = \frac{0}{6} = 0; \quad Q = \frac{1}{3} - \frac{1}{6} = \frac{2-1}{6} = \frac{1}{6}; \quad S = \frac{1}{3} - \frac{1}{6} = \frac{2-1}{6} = \frac{1}{6}$$

Gaining ratio of Q and S = 1 : 1

(ii) R's share of goodwill = $2,16,000 \times \frac{2}{6}$ = ₹ 72,000

**JOURNAL**

| Date | Particulars | | LF | Amt (Dr) | Amt (Cr) |
|---|---|---|---|---|---|
| | Q's Capital A/c | Dr | | 36,000 | |
| | S's Capital A/c | Dr | | 36,000 | |
| | To R's Capital A/c | | | | 72,000 |
| | (Being R's share of goodwill adjusted to remaining partners) | | | | |

*Or*

**JOURNAL**

| Date | Particulars | | LF | Amt (Dr) | Amt (Cr) |
|---|---|---|---|---|---|
| 2023 | | | | | |
| Apr 1 | Cash A/c | Dr | | 47,750 | |
| | To X's Capital A/c | | | | 33,250 |
| | To Z's Capital A/c | | | | 14,500 |
| | (Being cash to be paid to Y brought in by X and Z) | | | | |
| Apr 1 | Y's Capital A/c | Dr | | 47,750 | |
| | To Cash A/c | | | | 4,7750 |
| | (Being cash paid to Y for his capital) | | | | |

**5.** (i) (a) ₹ 37,20,00,000 [20,00,000 × 186] (b) ₹ 6,00,00,000 [3,20,00,000 + 2,80,00,000]

(ii) **JOURNAL**

| Date | Particulars | | LF | Amt (Dr) | Amt (Cr) |
|---|---|---|---|---|---|
| | 10% Debenture Application and Allotment A/c | Dr | | 37,20,00,000 | |
| | Loss on Issue of Debenture A/c | Dr | | 6,00,00,000 | |
| | To 10% Debentures A/c | | | | 40,00,00,000 |
| | To Premium on Redemption of Debentures A/c | | | | 3,20,00,000 |
| | (Being allotment of 20,00,000 debenture @ ₹ 200 each at 14% discount with the term of 8% premium on redemption) | | | | |

*Or*

**In the Books of Nand Pvt. Ltd.**
**JOURNAL**

| Date | Particulars | | LF | Amt (Dr) | Amt (Cr) |
|---|---|---|---|---|---|
| 2022 | | | | | |
| Apr 1 | Bank A/c (10,000 × 90) | Dr | | 9,00,000 | |
| | To 9% Debentures A/c | | | | 9,00,000 |
| | (Being money received on 10,000, 9% debentures @ 10% discount) | | | | |
| Apr 1 | 9% Debentures A/c | Dr | | 9,00,000 | |
| | Discount on Issue of Debentures A/c | Dr | | 1,00,000 | |
| | Loss on Issue of Debentures A/c | Dr | | 1,00,000 | |
| | To 9% Debentures A/c (10,000 × 100) | | | | 10,00,000 |
| | To Premium on Redemption of Debentures A/c (10,000 × 10) | | | | 1,00,000 |
| | (Being money is transferred to 9% debentures account with the term of issue and redemption) | | | | |

**6.** **Balance Sheet**
as at 31st March, 2023

| Particulars | Note No. | 31st March, 2023 (₹) |
|---|---|---|
| **I. EQUITY AND LIABILITIES** | | |
| 1. **Shareholders' Funds** | | |
| (i) Share Capital | | 50,00,000 |
| (ii) Reserves and Surplus | | 12,00,000 |
| 2. **Non-current Liabilities** | | |
| Long-term Borrowings | | 30,00,000 |
| 3. **Current Liabilities** | | |
| (i) Short-term borrowings | | 4,80,000 |
| (ii) Trade Payables | | 4,50,000 |
| (iii) Other Current Liabilities | | 1,10,000 |
| (iv) Short-term Provisions | | 60,000 |
| **Total** | | 1,03,00,000 |
| **II. ASSETS** | | |
| 1. **Non-current Assets** | | |
| (i) Property, Plant & Equipment and Intangible Assets | | |
| Property, Plant and Equipment | | 72,00,000 |
| (ii) Non-current Investments | | 10,00,000 |
| 2. **Current Assets** | | |
| (i) Inventories | | 11,00,000 |
| (ii) Trade Receivables | | 6,00,000 |
| (iii) Cash and Cash Equivalents | | 3,50,000 |
| (iv) Other Current Assets | | 50,000 |
| **Total** | | 1,03,00,000 |

7. (a) Dr **Partners' Capital Account** Cr

| Particulars | A (₹) | B (₹) | C (₹) | Particulars | A (₹) | B (₹) | C (₹) |
|---|---|---|---|---|---|---|---|
| To Realisation A/c | 72,000 | 56,800 | 39,200 | By Balance b/d | 1,10,000 | 40,000 | 28,000 |
| To Realisation (Loss) | 16,800 | 5,600 | 5,600 | By Realisation A/c | 32,000 | — | 6,120 |
| To Cash A/c (Balancing figure) | 53,200 | — | — | By Cash A/c (Balancing figure) | — | 22,400 | 10,680 |
| | 1,42,000 | 62,400 | 44,800 | | 1,42,000 | 62,400 | 44,800 |

**Working Note**

| | Amt (₹) |
|---|---|
| Total sundry assets | 76,000 |
| (–) Sundry assets taken over by B $\left(\frac{28,800}{90\%}\right)$ | (32,000) |
| Remaining sundry assets taken over by C | 44,000 |
| at an agreed value (44,000 × 90%) | 39,600 |
| (–) Discount | (400) |
| | 39,200 |

(b) Dr **Cash Account** Cr

| Particulars | Amt (₹) | Particulars | Amt (₹) |
|---|---|---|---|
| To Balance b/d | 12,800 | By Realisation (Expenses) | 1,080 |
| To Realisation A/c [Debtors realised (16,800 × 50%)] | 8,400 | By A's Capital A/c | 53,200 |
| To B's Capital A/c | 22,400 | | |
| To C's Capital A/c | 10,680 | | |
| | 54,280 | | 54,280 |

8. **In the Books of A, J and S**
**JOURNAL**

| Date | Particulars | | LF | Amt (Dr) | Amt (Cr) |
|---|---|---|---|---|---|
| 2012 Apr 1 | S's Capital A/c | Dr | | 55,650 | |
| | To A's Capital A/c | | | | 7,650 |
| | To J's Capital A/c | | | | 48,000 |
| | (Being adjustment entry for interest on capital, salary, interest on drawings and distribution of profit) | | | | |

**Working Notes**

1. **Statement of Adjustment**

| Particulars | A (₹) | J (₹) | S (₹) | Total (₹) |
|---|---|---|---|---|
| **Amount to be Debited** | | | | |
| Interest on Drawings (WN3) | 600 | 600 | 600 | 1,800 |
| Net Profit Wrongly Distributed | 1,50,000 | 1,50,000 | 1,50,000 | 4,50,000 |
| | 1,50,600 | 1,50,600 | 1,50,600 | 4,51,800 |
| **Amount to be Credited** | | | | |
| Interest on Capital | 60,000 | 48,000 | 36,000 | 1,44,000 |
| Salary | — | 72,000 | — | 72,000 |
| Corrected Net Profit (WN2) | 98,250 | 78,600 | 58,950 | 2,35,800 |
| | 1,58,250 | 1,98,600 | 94,950 | 4,51,800 |
| **Net Effect** | 7,650 (Cr) | 48,000 (Cr) | 55,650 (Dr) | Nil |

2. **Profit and Loss Appropriation Account**

Dr for the year ended 2011, 12 Cr

| Particulars | | Amt (₹) | Particulars | | Amt (₹) |
|---|---|---|---|---|---|
| To J's Salary (1,000 × 12) | | 72,000 | By Profit and Loss A/c (Net Profit) | | 4,50,000 |
| To Interest on Capital A/cs | | | By Interest on Drawings A/cs | | |
| A | 60,000 | | Alex | 600 | |
| J | 48,000 | | John | 600 | |
| S | 36,000 | 1,44,000 | Sam | 600 | 1,800 |
| To Profit transferred to Capital A/cs | | | | | |
| A | 98,250 | | | | |
| J | 78,600 | | | | |
| S | 58,950 | 2,35,800 | | | |
| | | 4,51,800 | | | 4,51,800 |

3. Interest on drawings $= 30{,}000 \times \frac{4}{100} \times \frac{6}{12} =$ ₹ 600

*Or*

**Profit and Loss Appropriation Account**

Dr for the year ended 31st December, 2021 Cr

| Particulars | | Amt (₹) | Particulars | | Amt (₹) |
|---|---|---|---|---|---|
| To Interest on Capital A/cs | | | By Net Profit as per Profit and Loss A/c [3,96,720 – 1,500 (Interest on loan)] | | 3,95,220 |
| Aman (4,00,000 × 6%) | 24,000 | | By Interest on Drawings A/c | | |
| Raman (3,00,000 × 6%) | 18,000 | | | | |
| Chaman (2,00,000 × 6%) | 12,000 | 54,000 | Aman $\left(12{,}000 \times \frac{9}{100} \times \frac{6}{12}\right)$ | 540 | |
| To Reserve A/c (Profit transferred) | | 50,000 | | | |
| To Net Profit transferred to | | | Raman $\left(12{,}000 \times \frac{9}{100} \times \frac{6}{12}\right)$ | 540 | |
| Aman's Capital A/c | 1,24,280 | | | | |
| Raman's Capital A/c | 92,280 | | Chaman $\left(12{,}000 \times \frac{9}{100} \times \frac{6}{12}\right)$ | 540 | 1,620 |
| Chaman's Capital A/c | 76,280 | 2,92,840 | | | |
| | | 3,96,840 | | | 3,96,840 |

**Working Notes**

1. Interest on Loan to Aman $= 50{,}000 \times \frac{6}{100} \times \frac{6}{12} =$ ₹ 1,500
2. Division of profits among partners
   Divisible profits = ₹ 2,92,840
   Profit upto ₹ 1,60,000 will be shared in 5 : 3 : 2, as
   Aman's share = 1,60,000 × 5/10 = ₹ 80,000 ; Raman's share = 1,60,000 × 3/10 = ₹ 48,000
   Chaman's share $= 1{,}60{,}000 \times \frac{2}{10} =$ ₹ 32,000
3. Remaining profits, i.e. (2,92,840 – 1,60,000) = ₹ 1,32,840, shall be divided equally as
   Aman's share = 1,32,840 × 1/3 = ₹ 44,280 ; Raman's share = 1,32,840 × 1/3 = ₹ 44,280
   Chaman's share = 1,32,840 × 1/3 = ₹ 44,280
4. Total profit share
   Aman = 80,000 + 44,280 = ₹ 1,24,280; Raman = 48,000 + 44,280 = ₹ 92,280; Chaman = 32,000 + 44,280 = ₹ 76,280

9. (A) (a) Dr **Revaluation Account** Cr

| Particulars | Amt (₹) | Particulars | | Amt (₹) |
|---|---|---|---|---|
| To Provident Fund A/c | 17,500 | By Provision for Doubtful Debts A/c | | 2,100 |
| To Stock A/c | 10,500 | By Loss transferred to | | |
| To Creditors A/c | 3,500 | Megha's Capital A/c | 40,250 | |
| To Property, Plant and Equipment A/c | 35,000 | Deepa's Capital A/c | 24,150 | 64,400 |
| | 66,500 | | | 66,500 |

(b) Dr **Partners' Capital Account** Cr

| Particulars | Megha (₹) | Deepa (₹) | Rahul (₹) | Particulars | Megha (₹) | Deepa (₹) | Rahul (₹) |
|---|---|---|---|---|---|---|---|
| To Profit and Loss A/c | 5,250 | 3,150 | — | By Balance b/d | 2,45,000 | 1,08,500 | — |
| To Revaluation A/c | 40,250 | 24,150 | — | By Workmen's Compensation Fund A/c | 12,688 | 7,612 | — |
| To Balance c/d | 2,54,188 | 88,812 | 70,000 | By Bank A/c | — | — | 70,000 |
| | | | | By Premium for Goodwill A/c | 42,000 | — | — |
| | 2,99,688 | 1,16,112 | 70,000 | | 2,99,688 | 1,16,112 | 70,000 |

(c) **Balance Sheet**
as at 31st December, 2022

| Liabilities | | Amt (₹) | Assets | Amt (₹) |
|---|---|---|---|---|
| Sundry Creditors | | 56,000 | Cash at Bank | 87,500 |
| Provident Fund | | 52,500 | Sundry Debtors | 70,000 |
| Capital A/cs | | | Stock | 77,000 |
| Megha | 2,54,188 | | Property, Plant and Equipment | 2,45,000 |
| Deepa | 88,812 | | Goodwill | 42,000 |
| Rahul | 70,000 | 4,13,000 | | |
| | | 5,21,500 | | 5,21,500 |

**Value Points**

- Provident fund is a liability and not a reserve, so it will not be distributed.
- Debtors are all good means that provisions for doubtful debts are no longer required.

(B) Calculation of new profit sharing ratio

Neel's old profit share = 4/9 ⇒ Neel obtains share from Angad $= \frac{3}{9} \times \frac{3}{5} = \frac{9}{45}$

Neel's New Profit Share = Old Share + Gain Share $= \frac{4}{9} + \frac{9}{45} = \frac{20+9}{45} = \frac{29}{45}$

Sugreev's old profit share = 2/9 ⇒ Sugreev obtains profit share from Angad $= \frac{3}{9} \times \frac{2}{5} = \frac{6}{45}$

Sugreev's New Profit Share = Old Share + Gain Share $= \frac{2}{9} + \frac{6}{45} = \frac{10+6}{45} = \frac{16}{45}$

New profit sharing ratio = 29 : 16 ; Angad's share of goodwill = 60,000 × 3/9 = ₹ 20,000

*Or* (a) **JOURNAL**

| Date | Particulars | | LF | Amt (Dr) | Amt (Cr) |
|---|---|---|---|---|---|
| 2022 Apr 30 | Raj's Capital A/c | Dr | | 4,500 | |
| | Neel's Capital A/c | Dr | | 3,000 | |
| | To Kamal's Capital A/c | | | | 7,500 |
| | (Being Kamal's share of goodwill adjusted into Raj and Neel in their gaining ratio of 3 : 2) | | | | |
| Apr 30 | General Reserve A/c | Dr | | 6,000 | |
| | To Raj's Capital A/c (6,000 × 3/6) | | | | 3,000 |
| | To Neel's Capital A/c (6,000 × 2/6) | | | | 2,000 |
| | To Kamal's Capital A/c (6,000 × 1/6) | | | | 1,000 |
| | (Being general reserve divided in 3 : 2 : 1 between all partners) | | | | |
| Apr 30 | Stock A/c | Dr | | 1,000 | |
| | Building A/c | Dr | | 5,000 | |
| | To Revaluation A/c | | | | 6,000 |
| | (Being increase in value of assets recorded) | | | | |

| Date | Particulars | | LF | Amt (Dr) | Amt (Cr) |
|---|---|---|---|---|---|
| Apr 30 | Revaluation A/c | Dr | | 3,600 | |
| | To Provision for Doubtful Debts A/c | | | | 1,000 |
| | To Furniture A/c | | | | 500 |
| | To Plant and Machinery A/c | | | | 1,500 |
| | To Bills Receivable A/c | | | | 600 |
| | (Being decrease in the value of assets) | | | | |
| Apr 30 | Revaluation A/c | Dr | | 2,400 | |
| | To Raj's Capital A/c | | | | 1,200 |
| | To Neel's Capital A/c | | | | 800 |
| | To Kamal's Capital A/c | | | | 400 |
| | (Being profit on revaluation transferred to partners' capital account) | | | | |

(b) **JOURNAL**

| Date | Particulars | | LF | Amt (Dr) | Amt (Cr) |
|---|---|---|---|---|---|
| Apr 30 | Kamal's Capital A/c | Dr | | 21,678 | |
| | To Kamal's Executor's A/c | | | | 21,678 |
| | (Being amount due to Kamal transferred to his executor account) | | | | |
| Apr 30 | Kamal's Executor's A/c | Dr | | 12,900 | |
| | To Bank A/c | | | | 12,900 |
| | (Being amount due and paid partly) | | | | |

**Working Notes**

1. Share of profit $\left(14{,}000 \times \frac{1}{6} \times \frac{4}{12}\right) = ₹ 778$
2. Valuation of goodwill

   Total profit = 14,000 + 16,000 + 20,000 + 10,000 = ₹ 60,000 ⇒ Average profit = $\frac{60{,}000}{4}$ = ₹ 15,000

   Hence, goodwill of the firm (15,000 × 3) = ₹ 45,000
3. Kamal's share of goodwill (45,000 × 1/6) = ₹ 7,500

**10.** (i) Category (c) 500 equity shares and (d) 300 shares. Only 800 equity shares will be forfeited.

(ii) ₹ 26,000

**Working Note**

Category (c) 500 × 40 @ = ₹ 20,000 Category (d) 300 × 20 @ = ₹ 6,000

(iii) There are also ₹ 12,000 calls-in-arrears on, 1200 shares of category (b).

(iv)

| | Allotment @ 20 (₹) | First Call @ 10 (₹) | Second Call @ 10 (₹) | Total |
|---|---|---|---|---|
| (c) 500 equity share | Nil | 5,000 | 5,000 | 10,000 |
| (d) 300 equity shares | 6,000 | 3,000 | 3,000 | 12,000 |
| | 6,000 | 8,000 | 8,000 | 22,000 |

(v) **JOURNAL**

| Date | Particulars | | LF | Amt (Dr) | Amt (Cr) |
|---|---|---|---|---|---|
| (a) | Forfeiture of 800 shares on which less than ₹ 50 were received | | | | |
| Jan 16 | Equity Share Capital A/c (800 × 60) | Dr | | 48,000 | |
| | To Equity Share Forfeited A/c (500 × 40 and 300 × 20) | | | | 26,000 |
| | To Equiaty Share Allotment A/c (unpaid) (300 × 210) C/A | | | | 6,000 |
| | To Equity Share First Call A/c (unpaid) (800 × 10) C/A | | | | 8,000 |
| | To Equity Share Second Call A/c (unpaid) (800 × 10) C/A | | | | 8,000 |
| | (Being the forfeiture of 800 shares, on which less than ₹ 50) | | | | |
| (b) | Bank A/c (600 × 400) | Dr | | 24,000 | |
| | Equity Shares Forfeiture A/c (600 × 20) | Dr | | 12,000 | |
| | To Equity Share Capital A/c (60 × 60) | | | | 36,000 |
| | (Being 600 shares re-issued at ₹ 40 as ₹ 60 paid-up) | | | | |

| Date | Particulars | | LF | Amt (Dr) | Amt (Cr) |
|---|---|---|---|---|---|
| | Equity Share Forfeited A/c | Dr | | 6,000 | |
| | To Capital Reserve A/c | | | | 6,000 |
| | (Being the amount of gain on re-issue of forfeited shares transferred to capital reserve) | | | | |

*Or*

**In the Books of Ajanta Ltd.**
**JOURNAL**

| Date | Particulars | | LF | Amt (Dr) | Amt (Cr) |
|---|---|---|---|---|---|
| (i) | Share Application A/c (5,00,000 × 5) | Dr | | 25,00,000 | |
| | To Share Capital A/c (4,00,000 × 5) | | | | 20,00,000 |
| | To Share Allotment A/c | | | | 5,00,000 |
| | (Being share application money adjusted) | | | | |
| (ii) | Share Allotment A/c | Dr | | 12,00,000 | |
| | To Share Capital A/c | | | | 12,00,000 |
| | (Being share allotment money due) | | | | |
| (iii) | Share First and Final Call A/c | Dr | | 8,00,000 | |
| | To Share Capital A/c | | | | 8,00,000 |
| | (Being share first and final call due) | | | | |
| (iv) | Share Capital A/c | Dr | | 4,000 | |
| | To Share Allotment A/c | | | | 700 |
| | To Share First and Final Call A/c | | | | 800 |
| | To Share Forfeiture A/c | | | | 2,500 |
| | (Being 400 shares forfeited) | | | | |
| (v) | Share Forfeiture A/c | Dr | | 400 | |
| | To Share Capital A/c | | | | 400 |
| | (Being share reissued and loss on issue charged from share forfeiture account) | | | | |
| (vi) | Share Forfeiture A/c (2,500 – 400) | Dr | | 2,100 | |
| | To Capital Reserve A/c | | | | 2,100 |
| | (Being share forfeiture account transferred to capital reserve account) | | | | |

Dr **Cash Book** (Bank Column) Cr

| Date | Particulars | JF | Amt (₹) | Date | Particulars | JF | Amt (₹) |
|---|---|---|---|---|---|---|---|
| | To Share Application (5,00,000 × 5) | | 25,00,000 | | By Shares Allotment | | 1,00,000 |
| | To Share Allotment (WN 3) | | 7,99,300 | | By Balance b/d | | 40,02,100 |
| | To Share First and Final Call (WN 4) | | 7,99,200 | | | | |
| | To Share Capital (400 × 9) | | 3,600 | | | | |
| | | | 41,02,100 | | | | 41,02,100 |

**Working Notes**

1. **Calculation of Amount Received on Allotment**

| | Amt (₹) |
|---|---|
| Money received on application (5,00,000 × 5) | 25,00,000 |
| (–) Money transferred to capital (4,00,000 × 5) | (20,00,000) |
| | 5,00,000 |
| (–) Money refunded for shares rejected (20,000 × 5) | (1,00,000) |
| Amount to be taken as allotment advance | 4,00,000 |

2. **Amount of Arrear on Allotment for 400 Shares Unpaid**

Shares applied = 4,00,000/3,20,000 × 400 = 500 shares

| | |
|---|---|
| Money received on application from applicant (500 × 5) | 2,500 |
| (–) Money transferred to share capital (400 × 5) | (2,000) |
| Taken as allotment advance | (500) |
| Amount due on allotment for 400 shares (400 × 3) | 1,200 |
| (–) Money received on application as advance | (500) |
| Arrear on 400 shares on allotment | 700 |

3. **Calculation for Money Received on Allotment**

| | |
|---|---|
| Money due on allotment (4,00,000 × 3) | 12,00,000 |
| (–) Received as advance on application | (4,00,000) |
| Money to be received on allotment | 8,00,000 |
| (–) Arrear of 400 shares to be forfeited | (700) |
| Net amount received on allotment | 7,99,300 |

4. **Calculation of Money Received on First Call**

| | |
|---|---|
| Money due (4,00,000 × 2) | 8,00,000 |
| (–) Amount of arrear (400 × 2) | (800) |
| Net amount received on final call | 7,99,200 |

11. (i) • Working Capital = Current Assets – Current Liabilities

• (*a*) Current Liabilities = Current Assets – Working Capital = 6,00,000 – 2,00,000 = ₹ 4,00,000

Current Ratio = Current Assets/Current Liabilities = 6,00,000/4,00,000 = 1.5

(ii) (*c*) It helps in ascertaining the net profit after tax

(iii) In case of common size statement, net sales figure is assumed to be 100 and in case of common size balance sheet, total assets/total liabilities are assumed to be 100.

(iv) To assess the current profitability and operational efficiency of the firm as a whole as well as its different departments so as to judge the financial health of the firm.

(v) (a) Debt Equity ratio = $\frac{\text{Debt/Long-term Debt}}{\text{Equity/Shareholders' Funds}}$

(b) Interest received on calls-in-advance will increase the equity of the company and will reduce the debt-equity ratio.

12. **Comparative Statement of Profit and Loss**

for the years ended 31st March, 2019 and 2020

| Particulars | Note No. | 2018-19 (₹) | 2019-20 (₹) | Absolute Change (₹) | Percentage (%) |
|---|---|---|---|---|---|
| I. Revenue from Operations | | 20,00,000 | 25,00,000 | 5,00,000 | 25.0 |
| II. Total Revenue | | 20,00,000 | 25,00,000 | 5,00,000 | 25.0 |
| III. **Expenses** | | | | | |
| Cost of Material Consumed | | 10,00,000 | 13,00,000 | 3,00,000 | 30.00 |
| Other Expenses | | — | 1,20,000 | 1,20,000 | — |
| Total Expenses | | 10,00,000 | 14,20,000 | 4,20,000 | 42.00 |
| IV. Profit before Tax (II – III) | | 10,00,000 | 10,80,000 | 80,000 | 8.00 |
| (–) Tax @ 50% | | (5,00,000) | (5,40,000) | (40,000) | (8.00) |
| V. Profit after Tax (IV–V) | | 5,00,000 | 5,40,000 | 40,000 | 8.00 |

13. (a) Net profit before tax

| | Amt (₹) |
|---|---|
| Profit as per balance sheet (2,50,000 – 1,50,000) | 1,00,000 |
| (+) Proposed dividend | 40,000 |
| | 1,40,000 |

(b) **Cash Flow from Financing Activities**

| Particulars | | Amt (₹) |
|---|---|---|
| **Cash Flow from Financing Activities** | | |
| Issue of Share Capital | 3,00,000 | |
| Proposed Dividend Paid | (40,000) | |
| Net Cash Flow from Financing Activities | | 2,60,000 |

(c) Dr **Plant and Machinery Account** Cr

| Particulars | Amt (₹) | Particulars | Amt (₹) |
|---|---|---|---|
| To Balance b/d | 5,00,000 | By Depreciation A/c | 50,000 |
| To Statement of Profit and Loss (Profit) | 3,000 | By Bank A/c (Sale) (5,000 + 60% × 5,000) | 8,000 |
| To Bank A/c (Purchase) (Balancing figure) | 3,55,000 | By Balance c/d | 8,00,000 |
| | 8,58,000 | | 8,58,000 |

*Or*

**Cash Flow Statement**
for the year ended 31st March, 2020

| Particulars | | Amt (₹) |
|---|---|---|
| I. **Cash Flow from Operating Activities** | | |
| Net Profit before Tax | | 15,000 |
| (+) Decrease in Current Assets and Increase in Current Liabilities | | |
| Decrease in Trade Receivables | 13,500 | |
| Decrease in Inventories | 1,500 | |
| (–) Increase in Current Assets and Decrease in Current Liabilities | | |
| Decrease in Trade Payables | (66,000) | (51,000) |
| Net Cash Used in Operating Activities | | (36,000) |
| II. **Cash Flow from Investing Activities** | | |
| Purchase of Property, Plant and Equipment | (47,500) | |
| Purchase of Non-current Investments | (3,000) | |
| Net Cash Used in Investing Activities | | (50,500) |
| III. **Cash Flow from Financing Activities** | | |
| Issue of Share Capital | 50,000 | |
| Net Cash Flow from Financing Activities | | 50,000 |
| Net Decrease in Cash and Cash Equivalents (I + II + III) | | (36,500) |
| (+) Opening Balance of Cash and Cash Equivalents (84,000 + 33,500) | | 1,17,500 |
| Closing Balance of Cash and Cash Equivalents (68,500 + 12,500) | | 81,000 |

**14.** (i) Gross Profit Ratio $= \dfrac{\text{Gross Profit}}{\text{Revenue from Operations}} \times 100 = \dfrac{3,40,000}{7,00,000} \times 100 = 48.57\ \%$

**Working Note**

Revenue from Operations = Cash Revenue from Operations + Credit Revenue from Operations – Return Inwards

= 5,00,000 + 2,50,000 – 50,000 = ₹ 7,00,000

Cost of Revenue from Operations = Opening Inventory + Net Purchases – Closing Inventory

= 1,20,000 + 4,20,000 – 1,80,000 = ₹ 3,60,000

Gross Profit = Revenue from Operations – Cost of Revenue from Operations

= 7,00,000 – 3,60,000 = ₹ 3,40,000

(ii) Operating Ratio $= \dfrac{\text{Cost of Revenue from Operations + Operating Costs}}{\text{Revenue from Operations}} \times 100$

$= \dfrac{3,60,000 + 60,000}{7,00,000} = \dfrac{4,20,000}{7,00,000} \times 100 = 60\%$

**Working Note**

Operating Expenses = Office Expenses + Selling Expenses = 40,000 + 20,000 = ₹ 60,000

(iii) Inventory Turnover Ratio $= \dfrac{\text{Cost of Revenue from Operations}}{\text{Average Inventory}} = \dfrac{3,60,000}{\frac{1,20,000 + 1,80,000}{2}} = \dfrac{3,60,000}{1,50,000} = 2.4$ Times

(iv) Debt to Capital Employed Ratio $= \dfrac{\text{Long-term Debts*}}{\text{Capital Employed**}} = \dfrac{1,50,000}{6,50,000} = 0.23 : 1$

*Long-term Debts = Long-term Borrowings = ₹ 1,50,000

Shareholders' Funds or Equity = Share Capital + Reserves and Surplus = 4,00,000 + 1,00,000 = ₹ 5,00,000

**Capital Employed = Shareholders' Funds + Long-term Borrowings = 5,00,000 + 1,50,000 = ₹ 6,50,000

SQP Code : **PB-6/15** Series *i*-**Succeed 6-25/15** Roll No. |  |  |  |  |  |  |  |  |

# Sample Question Paper 06

## Accounts 12th (Code 858)

### General Instructions

1. Candidates are allowed additional 15 minutes for only reading the paper. They must not start writing during this time.
2. Section-A is compulsory for all candidates and has ten questions.
3. Candidates have to attempt all questions from either Section-B or Section-C*.
4. Internal choices have been provided in five questions in Section-A and one question in Section-B.
5. The intended marks for questions or parts of questions are given in the brackets [ ].
6. All calculations should be shown clearly.
7. All workings, including rough work, should be done on the same page as, and adjacent to, the rest of the answer.

*Section-C has not been covered.

**Time :** 3 Hrs.

**Max. Marks :** 80

## Section A Answer All Questions [60 Marks]

**Que 1.**

In sub-parts (i) to (iv), choose the correct option and in sub-parts (v) to (x) answer the questions as instructed.

(i) Which of the following is the journal entry of salary to a partner when capital's are fluctuating? (Understanding) [1]

(a) Partner's Capital A/c Dr
 To Profit and Loss Appropriation A/c

(b) Profit and Loss A/c Dr
 To Partner's Capital A/c

(c) Profit and Loss Appropriation A/c Dr
 To Partner's Current A/c

(d) Profit and Loss Appropriation A/c Dr
 To Partner's Capital A/c

(ii) What will be the correct sequence of following events? (Recall) [1]

I. Default of calls
II. Re-issue of shares
III. Forfeiture of shares
IV. Amount transferred to capital reserve

**Codes**

(a) I, III, II, IV
(b) I, II, III, IV
(c) I, IV, II, III
(d) I, IV, III, II

(iii) A, B and C are partners in a firm sharing profits in the ratio of 5 : 3 : 2. They decided to share profits equally from 1st April, 2023.

The goodwill for this purpose was valued at ₹ 1,20,000. What will be journal entry? (Application) [1]

(a) B's Capital A/c Dr 4,000
 C's Capital A/c Dr 16,000
 To A's Capital A/c 20,000

(b) A's Capital A/c Dr 20,000
 B's Capital A/c Dr 4,000
 To C's Capital A/c 24,000

(c) A's Capital A/c Dr 16,000
 To B's Capital A/c 16,000

(d) A's Capital A/c Dr 4,000
 To C's Capital A/c 4000

(iv) A, B and C are partners in a firm. They decided to dissolve the firm. The firm had stock ₹ 80,000. A took over 50% of the stock at a discount of 20% while the remaining stock was sold off at a profit of 30% on cost. Calculate the total amount received from sale of stock. **(Application) [1]**

(a) ₹ 52,000 (b) ₹ 84,000
(c) ₹ 80,000 (d) ₹ 40,000

(v) "Borrowings shall further be sub-classified as secured and unsecured. Nature of security shall be specified separately in each case."
**Source** *Companies Act, 2013 – Schedule III*
In the light of the given statement
(a) What are short-term borrowings?
(b) Name an item that can be classified as short-term borrowings. **(Recall) [1]**

(vi) **Assertion** (A) No partner is entitled to claim interest on capital as a matter of right.
**Reason** (R) Interest on capital is only allowed when it is expressly agreed to by the partners. **(Evaluate) [1]**
**Alternatives**
(a) Both Assertion (A) and Reason (R) are true and Reason (R) is the correct explanation of Assertion (A)
(b) Both Assertion (A) and Reason (R) are true, but Reason (R) is not the correct explanation of Assertion (A)
(c) Assertion (A) is false, but Reason (R) is true
(d) Assertion (A) is true, but Reason (R) is false

(vii) On the basis of the following data, how much final payment will be made to a partner on firm's dissolution?
Credit balance of capital account of the partner was ₹ 1,30,000. Share of loss on realisation amounted to ₹ 70,000. Firm's liability taken over by him was of ₹ 27,000. **(Application) [1]**

SP-06

(viii) Sam Ltd. issued 10,000, 9% debentures of ₹ 100 each as collateral security for a loan of ₹ 6,00,000 taken from Saandi Bank. Pass the necessary journal entry for the issue of debentures as collateral security. **(Application) [1]**

(ix) What will be the journal entry to distribute workmen compensation reserve of ₹ 1,20,000 at the link of retirement of Swati, when there is no claim against it?
The firm had three partners Anamika, Swati and Kavita. **(Application) [1]**

(x) Name any two items that come under the head non-current liabilities. **(Understanding) [1]**

**Que 2.**
A, B and C are partners in a business sharing profits as 3/4, 1/8 and 1/8 respectively and their balance sheet as at 31st March, 2022 was as follows

**Balance Sheet**
as at 31st March, 2022

| Liabilities | | Amt (₹) | Assets | Amt (₹) |
|---|---|---|---|---|
| Capital A/cs | | | Machinery | 30,00,000 |
| A | 30,00,000 | | Debtors | 21,00,000 |
| B | 18,00,000 | | Stock | 12,00,000 |
| C | 15,00,000 | 63,00,000 | Bank | 15,00,000 |
| Creditors | | 15,00,000 | | |
| | | 78,00,000 | | 78,00,000 |

C died on 31st December, 2022. The partnership deed provided for the following on the death of a partner

(i) The deceased partner will be entitled to his share of profits upto the date of death, calculated on the basis of previous year's profits, i.e. ₹ 12,00,000.
(ii) He will be entitled to his share of goodwill which was ₹ 11,25,000.
(iii) His drawings amounted to ₹ 1,08,000 upto the date of death.
(iv) Interest on capital was to be allowed and on drawings to be charged @ 5% p.a. respectively. (On total amount in case of drawings).

(a) You are required to give the share of goodwill contributed by A and B. [1]
(b) C's share of profit. [1]
(c) Prepare C's capital account **(Application) [1]**

*Or*

Varun, Chetan and Nitin are in partnership sharing profits in the ratio of 5:3:2. Nitin retires and the following balances appeared in their books.

| Particulars | Amt (Dr) | Amt (Cr) |
|---|---|---|
| Capitals A/cs | | |
| Varun | — | 20,000 |
| Chetan | — | 10,000 |
| Nitin | — | 9,000 |
| Creditors | — | 7,000 |
| Goodwill | 6,000 | — |
| Bank Balance | 5,000 | — |
| Other Assets | 35,000 | — |
| **Total** | 46,000 | 46,000 |

Goodwill is agreed at ₹ 15,000. Sufficient money is to be introduced so that Nitin is paid-off leaving bank balance of ₹ 2,000. Varun and Chetan are to provide such sum as it will make their capitals proportionate to their share of profits.

You are required to pass journal entries to record

(i) The adjustment of the goodwill

(ii) Cash brought in and brought out by Varun and Chetan to pay of Nitin.

(iii) Payment made to Nitin. (Application) [3]

**Que 3.**

Following balances have been extracted from the books of Vardhman Ltd. on 31st March, 2023.

Equity share capital (2,00,000 equity shares of ₹ 10 each) ₹ 20,00,000, securities premium ₹ 4,00,000, 12% debentures ₹ 10,00,000, trade payables ₹ 4,00,000, provision for tax ₹ 1,00,000, surplus, i.e. balance in statement of profit and loss (debit) ₹ 1,00,000, plant and machinery ₹ 18,00,000, government bonds ₹ 10,00,000, capital work-in-progress (building) ₹ 7,00,000, discount on issue of 12% debentures ₹ 2,00,000, cash at bank ₹ 1,00,000.

Debentures were issued on 1st April, 2019 redeemable after 5 years, i.e. on 31st March, 2024. Surplus, i.e. balance in statement of profit and loss is before writing-off discount on issue of debentures.

Prepare the balance sheet of the company as per Schedule III, Part I of the Companies Act, 2013. (No need to prepare notes to accounts) (Application) [3]

**Que 4.**

On 1st April, 2023, Moly, Poly and Dolly entered into partnership with capitals of ₹ 3,00,000, ₹ 2,50,000 and ₹ 1,50,000 respectively. Dolly advanced ₹ 50,000 as loan to the partnership on 1st October, 2023. The partnership deed consisted of the following provisions

(i) Interest on capital and on drawings shall be @ 6% per annum.

(ii) Each partner drew ₹ 20,000 at the end of each quarter commencing from 30th June, 2023.

(iii) Moly and Poly are to get a salary of ₹ 1,000 and ₹ 1,500 per month respectively.

(iv) Interest on loan was allowed to Dolly @ 6% per annum.

(v) Profit and losses are to be shared in the ratio of 2 : 2 : 1.

Net profit of the firm for the year ended 31st March, 2024 (before making the above adjustments) was ₹ 5,55,000.

Prepare profit and loss appropriation account. (Application) [3]

**Que 5.**

Name the major heads and sub-heads under which of the following items will be presented in the balance sheet of a company as per Schedule III of the Companies Act, 2013. (Application) [3]

(i) Loose tools

(ii) Copyrights and patents

(iii) Land and building

(iv) Sundry creditors

(v) Securities premium

(vi) Public deposits

(vii) Provision for tax

(viii) Stock-in-trade

(ix) Government securities

*Or*

Name the major heads and sub-heads under which of the following items will be presented in the balance sheet of a Company as per Schedule III of the Companies Act, 2013. (Application)

(i) Outstanding salary

(ii) Debentures

(iii) Livestock

(iv) Forfeited shares account

(v) Trademarks (vi) Land

(vii) Trade payables (viii) Tax reserve

(ix) Stores and spares

**Que 6.**

On 31st March, 2023 the balance in the capital accounts of Abhir, Bobby and Vineet, after making adjustments for profits and drawings were ₹ 8,00,000, ₹ 6,00,000 and ₹ 4,00,000 respectively.

Subsequently, it was discovered that interest on capital and interest on drawings had been omitted.

The partners were entitled to interest on capital @ 10% p.a. and were to be charged interest on drawings @ 6% p.a. The drawings during the year were: Abhir ₹ 20,000 drawn at the end of each month, Bobby ₹ 50,000 drawn at the beginning of every half year and Vineet ₹ 1,00,000 withdrawn on 31st October, 2022. The net profit for the year ended 31st March, 2023 was ₹ 1,50,000. The profit sharing ratio was 2 : 2 : 1.

Pass necessary adjusting entry for the above adjustments in the books of the firm. Also, show your workings clearly. **(Application) [6]**

**Que 7.**

Arihant Ltd. issued 80,000, 9% debentures of ₹ 100 each at a discount of 4% on 1st April, 2021, payable ₹ 30 on application and the balance on allotment. The debentures are redeemable after 5 years.

(i) Calculate the amount transferred to discount on issue of debentures acccount. **[1]**

(ii) Prepare the balance sheet as at 31st March, 2022. Ignore interest. **(Application) [5]**

*Or*

(i) Rajan Ltd. purchased assets of Surya Ltd. as under Plant of ₹ 10,00,000 at ₹ 9,00,000, land and buildings of ₹ 15,00,000 at ₹ 21,00,000 for purchase consideration of ₹ 27,50,000 and paid ₹ 5,00,000 in cash and remaining by issue of 10% debentures of ₹ 100 each at a premium of 20%. Record necessary entries in the books of Rajan Ltd.

(ii) Arihant Ltd. secured a loan of ₹ 1,60,000 from Punjab National Bank issuing 2,000, 9% debentures of ₹ 100 each as collateral security. How will you show issue of debentures in the balance sheet when journal entry is passed? **(Application) [6]**

**Que 8.**

X, Y and Z are partners. Their balance sheet as at 31st March, 2023 was

**Balance Sheet**
as at 31st March, 2023

| Liabilities | | Amt (₹) | Assets | Amt (₹) |
|---|---|---|---|---|
| Capital A/cs | | | Bank | 21,000 |
| X | 35,000 | | Building | 56,000 |
| Y | 28,000 | | Investment | 14,000 |
| Z | 21,000 | 84,000 | Debtors | 7,000 |
| Creditors | | 14,000 | Stock | 10,500 |
| Profit and Loss A/c | | 10,500 | | |
| | | 1,08,500 | | 1,08,500 |

The partnership was dissolved on the above date. X took over the investment at a value of ₹ 13,300. Cash realised was as follows

Building ₹ 63,000
Debtors ₹ 6,300
Stock ₹ 9,800

Creditors were paid at a discount of 5%. Expenses of realisation come to ₹ 1,400.

Prepare necessary ledger accounts to close the books. **(Application) [6]**

SP-06

**Que 9.**

(A) Rahil and Maahi were partners in a firm sharing profits in the ratio of 3 : 2. On 1st April, 2022 their balance sheet was as follows

**Balance Sheet**
as at 1st April, 2022

| Liabilities | | Amt (₹) | Assets | | Amt (₹) |
|---|---|---|---|---|---|
| Creditors | | 17,000 | Cash | | 6,000 |
| General Reserve | | 4,000 | Debtors | 15,000 | |
| Workmen Compensation Reserve | | 9,000 | (−) Provision for Doubtful Debts | (2,000) | 13,000 |
| Investment Fluctuation Reserve | | 11,000 | Investment | | 20,000 |
| Capital A/cs | | | Plant | | 14,000 |
| Rahil | 30,000 | | Land and Building | | 38,000 |
| Maahi | 20,000 | 50,000 | | | |
| | | 91,000 | | | 91,000 |

On the above date, Neha was admitted for 1/4th share in the profits of the firm on the following terms

(i) Neha will bring ₹ 20,000 for her capital and ₹ 4,000 for her share of goodwill premium.
(ii) All debtors were considered good.
(iii) The market value of investments was ₹ 15,000.
(iv) There was a liability of ₹ 6,000 for workmen compensation.
(v) Capital accounts of Rahil and Maahi are to be adjusted on the basis of Neha's capital by opening current accounts.

(a) Calculate the amount of premium for goodwill to be transferred to Rahil's and Maahi's capital account. [2]
(b) Prepare revaluation account. [1½]
(c) Prepare partners' capital account. (Application) [4½]

*Or*

Asha and Aditi are partners in a firm sharing profits and losses in the ratio of 3:2. They admit Raghav as a partner for 1/4th share in the profits of the firm. Raghav brings ₹ 6,00,000 as his capital and his share of goodwill in cash. Goodwill of the firm is to be valued at two years' purchase of average profits of the last four years.

The profits of the firm during the last four years are given below

| Year | 2013-14 | 2014-15 | 2015-16 | 2016-17 |
|---|---|---|---|---|
| Profit (₹) | 3,50,000 | 4,75,000 | 6,70,000 | 7,45,000 |

The following additional information is given

(i) To cover management cost, an annual charge of ₹ 56,250 should be made for the purpose of valuation of goodwill.
(ii) The closing stock for the year ended 31st March, 2017 was overvalued by ₹ 15,000.

The general reserve account showed a balance of ₹ 30,000.

You are required to

(a) Calculate average profit of last five years. (Application) [2]
(b) Calculate Raghav's share of goodwill. (Application) [2]
(c) Pass the journal entry for the transfer of general reserve. (Recall) [2]
(d) Pass the journal entry for the capital and goodwill brought in by Raghav. (Application) [2]

(B) P, Q and R are partners sharing profit and loss in the ratio of 2 : 2 : 1. Q retires from the firm on 31st March, 2023.

On the date of Q's retirement, the following balances appeared in the books of the firm.

| | Amt (₹) |
|---|---|
| General reserve | 30,000 |
| Investment fluctuation reserve | 40,000 |

Pass the necessary journal entries for the adjustment of these items on B's retirement. (Application) [2]

SP-06

(e) Pass the journal entry for the transfer of premium of goodwill. (Application) [2]

**Que 10.**

AB Ltd. invited applications for 1,00,000 equity shares of ₹ 10 each, payable as ₹ 2 on application, ₹ 3 on allotment and the balance on first and final call. Applications were received for 3,00,000 shares and the shares were allotted on a pro-rata basis. The excess application money was to be adjusted against allotment only.

(i) What is the amount received on application adjusted towards allotment? [1]

(ii) What is the amount received on application adjusted towards final call? [1]

(iii) What is the amount refunded to the shareholders? [1]

(iv) M, a shareholder, who had applied for 3,000 shares, failed to pay the call money and his shares were accordingly forfeited and re-issued @ ₹ 8 per share as fully paid.

Show the amount refunded to M after adjustment in allotment money of 'M'. [2]

(v) Pass necessary journal entries for

(a) Forfeiture of 'M's' share. [2]

(b) Re-issue of M's share. (Application) [3]

*Or*

Patromax Ltd. issued 50,000 shares of ₹ 10 each at a premium of ₹ 2 per share payable as ₹ 3 on application, ₹ 5 including premium on allotment and balance in equal instalments over two calls. Applications were received for 92,000 shares and the allotment was done as under

(i) Applications of 40,000 shares — Allotted 30,000 shares

(ii) Applications of 40,000 shares — Allotted 20,000 shares

(iii) Applications of 12,000 shares — Nil

Suresh who had applied for 2,000 shares of category (i) did not pay any money other than application money. Chandar who was allotted 800 shares of category (ii) paid the call money due alongwith allotment. All other allottees paid their dues as per schedule.

Pass necessary journal entries in the books of Patromax Ltd. for the above transactions.

(Application) [10]

## Section B

[20 Marks]

**Que 11.**

(i) **Balance Sheet** (Extract)

| Particulars | 2023 (₹) | 2022 (₹) |
|---|---|---|
| **Non-current Assets** | | |
| (i) Property, Plant & Equipment and Intangible Asset | | |
| Property, Plant and Equipment | 24,00,000 | 18,00,000 |

**Additional Information**

Depreciation charged on property, plant and equipment was ₹ 2,40,000.

How much amount will be shown in investing activities? (Understanding) [1]

(a) ₹ 6,00,000 (b) ₹ 3,60,000
(c) ₹ 8,40,000 (d) ₹ 3,00,000

(ii) The quick ratio of a company is 1 : 1. State whether the following would improve, reduce or not change the ratio.

- Purchase of machinery for cash
- Sale of goods at a profit (Recall) [1]

(a) Improve, improve
(b) Reduce, improve
(c) Reduce, no change
(d) No change, improve

(iii) The current ratio of two or higher is considered good, indicating that the company can meet its short-term obligations. But if the current ratio is higher than three, it also could mean that the company is not utilising its current assets efficiently. And the cash or bank balance may be remained because of the fewer investment opportunities. The current of 2 : 1 is considered satisfactory because, first of all, it means the current assets are double in amount of its current liabilities, so the company will not face problems to cover current obligations. And secondly, it can provide for losses and delays.

SP-06

Some types of companies with a current ratio below one can operate steadily and comfortably if their inventory turns into cash quickly and continuously than accounts payables due.

**Source** *Topstock (edited)*

- What does a low current ratio indicates? (Analysis)
- If inventory is ₹ 6,00,000 current assets ₹ 48,00,000 and current liabilities ₹ 24,00,000 then what will be the current ratio? (Application) [1]

(iv) Financial distress is a condition where the company experiences a decline in its financial condition before bankruptcy. To avoid this condition, the company must pay attention to its financial condition both in terms of its balance sheet and income statement using financial statement analysis techniques.

**Source** *Researchin*

State any two tools of analysis of financial statements. (Analysis) [1]

(v) India Inc generated strong cash flows in financial year 2024, with cash and bank balances shooting up 18% to nearly ₹ 10 trillion, the fastest pace in four years. A universe of 1,350 large companies for which comparative data is available, generated operating cash flows of nearly ₹ 15 trillion.

**Source** *Financial Express (edited)*

Based on the above news of cash flows suppose

A company sold a plant for ₹ 12,000. The book value of the plant was ₹ 14,000. What amount will be transferred to operating activity? (Analysis) [1]

**Que 12.**

From the following statement of profit and loss of Neetu Ltd., for the year ended 31st March, 2022 and 31st March, 2023, prepare common size statement. (Application) [3]

| Particulars | Note No. | 2023 | 2022 |
|---|---|---|---|
| Revenue from Operations | | ₹ 50,00,000 | ₹ 40,00,000 |
| Employees benefit Expenses | | ₹ 20,00,000 | ₹ 14,00,000 |
| Other Expenses | | ₹ 2,00,000 | ₹ 3,00,000 |
| Tax Rate | | 40% | 40% |

**Que 13.**

Answer any three from the following (Application) [6] SP-06

(i) From the following information, calculate return on investment

Equity share capital ₹ 50,000, general reserve ₹ 5,000, balance of statement of profit and loss after interest and tax ₹ 15,000, 9% debentures ₹ 20,000, creditors ₹ 15,000, land and building ₹ 65,000, equipments ₹ 15,000, debtors ₹ 14,500, cash ₹ 5,500, revenue from operations, i.e. sales for the year ended 31st March, 2021 was ₹ 50,000, tax rate is 50%.

(ii) Calculate closing inventory of a company from the following information

Inventory turnover ratio = 4 times

Revenue from operations = ₹ 3,00,000

Gross profit ratio = 25%

Current liabilities = ₹ 40,000

Quick ratio = 0.75 : 1

Closing inventory was ₹ 20,000 more than opening inventory

(iii) Calculate proprietory ratio from the following information

| | |
|---|---|
| Long-term borrowings | ₹ 2,00,000 |
| Long-term provisions | ₹ 1,00,000 |

Current liabilities ₹ 50,000
Non-current Assets ₹ 3,60,000
Current Assets ₹ 90,000

(iv) Calculate debt equity ratio from the following information

Total assets ₹ 350,000
Total debts ₹ 250,000
Current liabilities ₹ 80,000

**Que 14.**

You are required to prepare a cash flow from operating activities for the year 2023-24 from the following balance sheet.

**Balance Sheets of Aashram Ltd.**
as at 31st March, 2024 and 31st March, 2023

| Particulars | Note No. | 31st March, 2024 (₹) | 31st March, 2023 (₹) |
|---|---|---|---|
| **I. EQUITY AND LIABILITIES** | | | |
| **1. Shareholders' Funds** | | | |
| (i) Share Capital (Equity share capital) | | 7,00,000 | 5,00,000 |
| (ii) Reserves and Surplus (Statement of P & L) | | 2,50,000 | 2,00,000 |
| **2. Non-current Liabilities** | | | |
| Long-term Borrowings (10% debentures) | | 2,50,000 | 70,000 |
| **3. Current Liabilities** | | | |
| (i) Short-term Borrowings (Bank overdraft) | | 10,000 | 15,000 |
| (ii) Trade Payables (Creditors) | | 50,000 | 30,000 |
| (iii) Short-term Provisions | 1 | 30,000 | 15,000 |
| **Total** | | 12,90,000 | 8,30,000 |
| **II. ASSETS** | | | |
| **1. Non-current Assets** | | | |
| (i) Property, Plant & Equipment and Intangible Assets | | | |
| (a) Property, Plant and Equipment | 2 | 8,00,000 | 4,50,000 |
| (b) Intangible (Goodwill) | | 70,000 | 1,00,000 |
| **2. Current Assets** | | | |
| (i) Inventories | | 1,25,000 | 1,00,000 |
| (ii) Trade Receivables | | 2,50,000 | 1,50,000 |
| (iii) Cash and Bank Balance (Cash at bank) | | 45,000 | 30,000 |
| **Total** | | 12,90,000 | 8,30,000 |

## Notes to Accounts

| Particulars | 31st March, 2024 (₹) | 31st March, 2023 (₹) |
|---|---|---|
| **1. Short-term Provisions** | | |
| Provision for Taxation | 30,000 | 15,000 |
| **2. Property, Plant and Equipment** | | |
| Plant and Machinery | 8,80,000 | 5,00,000 |
| (−) Accumulated Depreciation | (80,000) | (50,000) |
| | 8,00,000 | 4,50,000 |

SP-06

### Additional Information

During the year 2023-24

(i) A part of the machine, costing ₹ 25,000 accumulated depreciation thereon being ₹ 10,000, was sold for ₹ 9,000.

(ii) Tax paid ₹ 10,000.

(iii) Interest of ₹ 25,000 paid on debentures. (Application) (6)

*Or* Following are the balance sheet of Mittal Ltd. as at 31st March, 2021 and 2022

| Particulars | Note No. | 2022 (₹) | 2021 (₹) |
|---|---|---|---|
| I. **EQUITY AND LIABILITIES** | | | |
| 1. **Shareholders' Funds** | | | |
| (i) Share Capital | | 14,00,000 | 10,00,000 |
| (ii) Reserves and Surplus | 1 | 5,00,000 | 4,00,000 |
| 2. **Non-current Liabilities** | | | |
| Long-term Borrowings | 2 | 6,00,000 | 2,00,000 |
| 3. **Current Liabilities** | | | |
| Short-term Provisions | 3 | 80,000 | 60,000 |
| **Total** | | 25,80,000 | 16,60,000 |
| II. **ASSETS** | | | |
| 1. **Non-current Assets** | | | |
| (i) Property, Plant & Equipment and Intangible Assets | | | |
| (a) Property, Plant and Equipment | 4 | 16,00,000 | 9,00,000 |
| (b) Intangible Assets | 5 | 1,40,000 | 2,00,000 |
| 2. **Current Assets** | | | |
| (i) Inventories | | 2,50,000 | 2,00,000 |
| (ii) Trade Receivables | | 5,00,000 | 3,00,000 |
| (iii) Cash and Cash Equivalents | | 90,000 | 60,000 |
| **Total** | | 25,80,000 | 16,60,000 |

**Notes to Accounts**

| Particulars | 31st March, 2022 (₹) | 31st March, 2021 (₹) |
|---|---|---|
| 1. **Reserves and Surplus** | | |
| Balance in Statement of Profit and Loss | 5,00,000 | 4,00,000 |
| 2. **Long-term Borrowings** | | |
| 9% Deposits | 6,00,000 | 2,00,000 |
| 3. **Short-term Provisions** | | |
| Provision for Tax | 80,000 | 60,000 |
| 4. **Property, Plant and Equipment** | | |
| Machinery | 16,00,000 | 9,00,000 |
| 5. **Intangible Assets** | | |
| Goodwill | 1,40,000 | 2,00,000 |

SP-06

### Additional Information

(i) Fresh deposits was issued on 30th June, 2021.

(ii) Depreciation provided on machinery during the year ₹ 2,00,000.

(a) Calculate the value of cash flow from operations before tax paid. [2]

(b) Prepare property, plant and equipment (machinery) account. [2]

(c) Calculate the value of cash flow from financing activity. (Evaluate) [2]

# Solutions in Topper's Style

***My Commitment*** *I affirm that I am reviewing these solutions only after I have solved the Sample Question Paper 6 on my own. My purpose of looking the solutions is solely to verify whether my answers/solutions were correct or not and to identify my mistakes in case my solutions were wrong or I could not solve that.*

**1.** (i) (*d*) Profit and Loss appropriation A/c Dr
To Partner's Capital A/c

(ii) (*a*) I, III, II, IV

(iii) (a) B's Capital A/c Dr 4,000
C's Capital A/c Dr 16,000
To A's Capital A/c 20,000

(iv) (*a*) Cash received from sale of stock $= 40{,}000 + \left(40{,}000 \times \frac{30}{100}\right) =$ ₹ 52,000

(v) (a) Short-term borrowings are the borrowings undertaken for a short period to meet immediately monetary requirement.
(b) Current maturities of long-term borrowing.

(vi) (*a*) Both Assertion (A) and Reason (R) are true and Reason (R) is the correct explanation of Assertion (A)

(vii) Dr **Partners' Capital Account** Cr

| Particulars | Amt (₹) | Particulars | Amt (₹) |
|---|---|---|---|
| To Realisation A/c (Loss) | 70,000 | By Balance b/d | 1,30,000 |
| To Bank A/c (Final payment) | 87,000 | By Realisation A/c (Liability taken over) | 27,000 |
| | 1,57,000 | | 1,57,000 |

(viii) **JOURNAL**

| Date | Particulars | LF | Amt (Dr) | Amt (Cr) |
|---|---|---|---|---|
| | Debenture Suspense A/c Dr | | 10,00,000 | |
| | To 9% Debentures A/c | | | 10,00,000 |
| | (Being issue of 9% debentures as a collateral security for a loan of ₹ 6,00,000) | | | |

(ix) **JOURNAL**

| Date | Particulars | LF | Amt (Dr) | Amt (Cr) |
|---|---|---|---|---|
| | Workmen Compensation Reserve A/c Dr | | 1,20,000 | |
| | To Anamika's Capital A/c | | | 40,000 |
| | To Swati's Capital A/c | | | 40,000 |
| | To Kavita's Capital A/c | | | 40,000 |
| | (Being workmen compensation reserve distributed to old partners in old ratio) | | | |

**Note** Since the profit sharing ratio is not given, it is distributed equally.

(x) Items that comes under the head non-current liabilities are (any two)
(a) Long-term borrowings
(b) Deferred tax liability (net)
(c) Other long-term liabilities
(d) Long-term provisions

**2.** (a) Share of goodwill contributed by
A $\left(11{,}25{,}000 \times \frac{6}{7}\right) =$ ₹ 9,64,286; B $\left(11{,}25{,}000 \times \frac{1}{7}\right) =$ ₹ 1,60,714

(b) C's share of profit $= 12{,}00{,}000 \times \frac{1}{8} \times \frac{9}{12} =$ ₹ 1,12,500

(c) Dr **C's Capital Account** Cr

| Particulars | Amt (₹) | Particulars | Amt (₹) |
|---|---|---|---|
| To Drawings A/c | 1,08,000 | By Balance b/d | 15,00,000 |
| To Interest on Drawings A/c | 4,050 | By Profit and Loss Suspense A/c | 1,12,500 |
| To C's Executors A/c | 26,81,700 | By A's Capital A/c | 9,64,286 |
| | | By B's Capital A/c | 1,60,714 |
| | | By Interest on Capital A/c | 56,250 |
| | 27,93,750 | | 27,93,750 |

**Working Notes**

1. Interest on capital $= 15,00,000 \times \frac{5}{100} \times \frac{9}{12} =$ ₹ 56,250
2. Interest on drawings $= 1,08,000 \times \frac{5}{100} \times \frac{9}{12} =$ ₹ 4,050

**Common Mistake** Students usually get confused regarding the average period to be taken while calculating interest on drawings. Since he died after 9 months, interest will be calculated for 9 months.

*Or*

**JOURNAL**

| Date | Particulars | | LF | Amt (Dr) | Amt (Cr) |
|---|---|---|---|---|---|
| (i) | Varun's Capital A/c | Dr | | 3,000 | |
| | Chetan's Capital A/c | Dr | | 1,800 | |
| | Nitin's Capital A/c | Dr | | 1,200 | |
| | To Goodwill A/c | | | | 6,000 |
| | (Being the goodwill in the books written-off) | | | | |
| | Varun's Capital A/c | Dr | | 1,875 | |
| | Chetan's Capital A/c | Dr | | 1,125 | |
| | To Nitin's Capital A/c | | | | 3,000 |
| | (Being the amount of goodwill due to retiring partner adjusted) | | | | |
| (ii) | Bank A/c | Dr | | 7,800 | |
| | To Varun's Capital A/c | | | | 3,625 |
| | To Chetan's Capital A/c | | | | 4,175 |
| | (Being the cash brought in by the partners) | | | | |
| (iii) | Nitin's Capital A/c | Dr | | 10,800 | |
| | To Bank A/c | | | | 10,800 |
| | (Being the retiring partner paid-off) | | | | |

**Working Notes**

1.

| Particulars | Varun (₹) | Chetan (₹) | Nitin (₹) |
|---|---|---|---|
| Capital | 20,000 | 10,000 | 9,000 |
| (–) Old Goodwill Write-off | (3,000) | (1,800) | (1,200) |
| | 17,000 | 8,200 | 7,800 |
| Adjustment for Goodwill | (1,875) | (1,125) | 3,000 |
| | 15,125 | 7,075 | 10,800 |

2.

| | Amt (₹) |
|---|---|
| Varun's Captial | 15,125 |
| Chetan's Capital | 7,075 |
| Nitin's Capital | 10,800 |
| | 33,000 |
| (+) Bank Balance to be Left | 2,000 |
| | 35,000 |
| (–) Bank Balance already Available | (5,000) |
| | 30,000 |

to be divided between Varun and Chetan.

**Cash Brought in by Partners**

Varun = 30,000 × 5/8 = 18,750 – 15,125 = ₹ 3,625 ; Chetan = 30,000 × 3/8 = 11,250 – 7,075 = ₹ 4,175

3. **Balance Sheet**
as at 31st March, 2023

| Particulars | Note No. | Year Ended 31st March, 2023 (₹) |
|---|---|---|
| **I. EQUITY AND LIABILITIES** | | |
| 1. **Shareholders' Funds** | | |
| (i) Share Capital | | 20,00,000 |
| (ii) Reserves and Surplus | | 1,00,000 |
| 2. **Non-current Liabilities** | | |
| Long-term Borrowings | | 10,00,000 |
| 3. **Current Liabilities** | | |
| (i) Trade Payables | | 4,00,000 |
| (ii) Short-term Provisions | | 1,00,000 |
| **Total** | | 36,00,000 |
| **II. ASSETS** | | |
| 1. **Non-current Assets** | | |
| (i) Property, Plant & Equipment and Intangible Assets | | |
| (a) Property, Plant and Equipment | | 18,00,000 |
| (b) Capital Work-in-progress | | 7,00,000 |
| (ii) Non-current Investments | | 10,00,000 |
| 2. **Current Assets** | | |
| Cash and Cash Equivalents | | 1,00,000 |
| **Total** | | 36,00,000 |

4. **Profit and Loss Appropriation Account**
for the year ended 31st March, 2024

Dr | Cr

| Particulars | | Amt (₹) | Particulars | | Amt (₹) |
|---|---|---|---|---|---|
| To Interest on Capital A/cs | | | By Net Profit as per Profit and Loss A/c (5,55,000 – 1,500 being interest on loan) | | 5,53,500 |
| Moly (3,00,000 × 6/100) | 18,000 | | By Interest on Drawings A/c | | |
| Poly (2,50,000 × 6/100) | 15,000 | | Moly $\left(20{,}000 \times 4 \times \frac{6}{100} \times \frac{4.5}{12}\right)$ | 1,800 | |
| Dolly (1,50,000 × 6/100) | 9,000 | 42,000 | Poly $\left(20{,}000 \times 4 \times \frac{6}{100} \times \frac{4.5}{12}\right)$ | 1,800 | |
| To Salaries A/c | | | Dolly $\left(20{,}000 \times 4 \times \frac{6}{100} \times \frac{4.5}{12}\right)$ | 1,800 | 5,400 |
| Moly (1,000 × 12) | 12,000 | | | | |
| Poly (1,500 × 12) | 18,000 | 30,000 | | | |
| To Profit transferred to Capital A/cs | | | | | |
| Moly | 1,94,760 | | | | |
| Poly | 1,94,760 | | | | |
| Dolly | 97,380 | 4,86,900 | | | |
| | | 5,58,900 | | | 5,58,900 |

**Value Points**

- Since Dolly advanced loan on 1st October, interest will be charged for 6 months only.
- Since interest on loan is a charge against profit, it will be deducted from the profit provided in the question.

5.

| S.No. | Particulars | Major Heads | Sub-heads |
|---|---|---|---|
| (i) | Loose Tools | Current Assets | Inventories |
| (ii) | Copyrights and Patents | Non-current Assets | Property, Plant & Equipment and Intangible Assets : Intangible Assets |
| (iii) | Land and Building | Non-current Assets | Property, Plant & Equipment and Intangible Assets : Property, Plant and Equipment |

| S.No. | Particulars | Major Heads | Sub-heads |
|---|---|---|---|
| (iv) | Sundry Creditors | Current Liabilities | Trade Payable |
| (v) | Securities Premium | Shareholders Funds | Reserves and Surplus |
| (vi) | Public Deposits | Non-current Liabilities | Long-term Borrowings |
| (vii) | Provision for Tax | Current Liabilities | Short-term Provisions |
| (viii) | Stock-in-trade | Current Assets | Inventories |
| (ix) | Government Securities | Non-current Assets | Non-current Investments |

*Or*

| S. No. | Particulars | Major Heads | Sub-heads |
|---|---|---|---|
| (i) | Outstanding Salary | Current Liabilities | Other Current Liabilities |
| (ii) | Debentures | Non-current Liabilities | Long-term Borrowings |
| (iii) | Livestock | Non-current Assets | Property, Plant & Equipment and Intangible Assets : Property, Plant and Equipment |
| (iv) | Forfeited Shares Account | Shareholders' Funds | Subscribed Capital (shown as an addition) |
| (v) | Trademarks | Non-current Assets | Property, Plant & Equipment and Intangible Assets : Intangible Assets |
| (vi) | Land | Non-current Assets | Property, Plant & Equipment and Intangible Assets : Property, Plant and Equipment |
| (vii) | Trade Payables | Current Liabilities | Trade Payables |
| (viii) | Tax Reserve | Current Liabilities | Short-term Provisions |
| (ix) | Stores and Spares | Current Assets | Inventories |

**6.**

**JOURNAL**

| Date | Particulars | | LF | Amt (Dr) | Amt (Cr) |
|---|---|---|---|---|---|
| 2023 | | | | | |
| Apr 1 | Bobby's Capital A/c | Dr | | 14,402 | |
| | To Abhir's Capital A/c | | | | 10,112 |
| | To Vineet's Capital A/c | | | | 4,290 |
| | (Being an adjustment entry passed for past adjustment) | | | | |

**Calculation of Opening Capital**

| Particulars | Abhir (₹) | Bobby (₹) | Vineet (₹) |
|---|---|---|---|
| Capital at the End | 8,00,000 | 6,00,000 | 4,00,000 |
| (+) Drawings | 2,40,000 | 1,00,000 | 1,00,000 |
| | 10,40,000 | 7,00,000 | 5,00,000 |
| (–) Profit | (60,000) | (60,000) | (30,000) |
| Capital at the Beginning | 9,80,000 | 6,40,000 | (4,70,000) |

**Calculation of Interest on Drawings**

Abhir $= 20{,}000 \times 12 \times \frac{6}{100} \times \frac{5.5}{12} =$ ₹ 6,600 ; Bobby $= 50{,}000 \times 2 \times \frac{6}{100} \times \frac{9}{12} =$ ₹ 4,500

Vineet $= 1{,}00{,}000 \times \frac{6}{100} \times \frac{5}{12} =$ ₹ 2,500

**Calculation of Amount to be Adjusted**

| Particulars | Abhir (₹) | Bobby (₹) | Vineet (₹) | Total (₹) |
|---|---|---|---|---|
| **Amount to be Debited** | | | | |
| Profit | 60,000 | 60,000 | 30,000 | 1,50,000 |
| Interest on Drawings | 6,600 | 4,500 | 2,500 | 13,600 |
| | 66,600 | 64,500 | 32,500 | 1,63,600 |
| **Amount to be Credited** | | | | |
| Interest on Capital @ 10% p.a. | 76,712 | 50,098 | 36,790 | 1,63,600 |
| Interest on Capital will be allowed to the Extent of Maximum Profit Available | 10,112 (Cr) | 14,402 (Dr) | 4,290 (Cr) | Nil |

**7.** (i) ₹ 3,20,000 [80,000 × 4]

(ii)

**Balance Sheet** (Extract)
as at 31st March, 2022

| Particulars | Note No. | Amt (₹) |
|---|---|---|
| **I. EQUITY AND LIABILITIES** | | |
| 1. **Shareholders' Funds** | | |
| Reserves and Surplus | | (3,20,000) |
| 2. **Non-current Liabilities** | | |
| Long-term Borrowings | 1 | 80,00,000 |
| **Total** | | 76,80,000 |
| **II. ASSETS** | | |
| 1. **Current Assets** | | |
| Cash and Cash Equivalents | 2 | 76,80,000 |
| **Total** | | 76,80,000 |

**Notes to Accounts**

| Particulars | Amt (₹) |
|---|---|
| 1. **Long-term Borrowings** | |
| 80,000, 9% Debentures of ₹ 100 each | 80,00,000 |
| 2. **Cash and Cash Equivalents** | |
| Cash at Bank | 76,80,000 |

*Or* (i)

**JOURNAL**

| Date | Particulars | | LF | Amt (Dr) | Amt (Cr) |
|---|---|---|---|---|---|
| | Plant A/c | Dr | | 9,00,000 | |
| | Land and Building A/c | Dr | | 21,00,000 | |
| | To Surya Ltd. | | | | 27,50,000 |
| | To Capital Reserve (Balancing figure) | | | | 2,50,000 |
| | (Being purchase of assets of Surya Ltd.) | | | | |
| | Surya Ltd. | Dr | | 5,00,000 | |
| | To Bank A/c | | | | 5,00,000 |
| | (Being part payment of agreed purchase consideration paid in cash) | | | | |
| | Surya Ltd. | Dr | | 22,50,000 | |
| | To 10% Debentures A/c | | | | 18,75,000 |
| | To Securities Premium A/c | | | | 3,75,000 |
| | (Being issue of 18,750 debentures of ₹ 100 each at 20% premium) | | | | |

**Working Note**

Number of debentures issued to Surya Ltd. $= \dfrac{27{,}50{,}000 - 5{,}00{,}000}{100 + 20} = 18{,}750$ debentures

(ii)

**JOURNAL**

| Date | Particulars | | LF | Amt (Dr) | Amt (Cr) |
|---|---|---|---|---|---|
| | Debenture Suspense A/c | Dr | | 2,00,000 | |
| | To 9% Debentures A/c | | | | 2,00,000 |
| | (Being the issue of 2,000, 9% debentures of ₹ 100 each as collateral security for a loan from a bank as per board's resolution) | | | | |

**Balance Sheet** (Extract)
as at...

| Particulars | Note No. | Amt (₹) |
|---|---|---|
| **I. EQUITY AND LIABILITIES** | | |
| 1. **Non-current Liabilities** | | |
| Long-term Borrowings | 1 | 1,60,000 |
| | | 1,60,000 |

**Notes to Accounts**

| Particulars | | Amt (₹) |
|---|---|---|
| 1. **Long-term Borrowings** | | |
| Loan from Punjab National Bank | | 1,60,000 |
| 2,000, 9% Debentures of Par Value of ₹ 100 each Issued as Collateral Security | 2,00,000 | |
| (–) Debenture Suspense | (2,00,000) | — |
| | | 1,60,000 |

8. Dr **Realisation Account** Cr

| Particulars | | Amt (₹) | Particulars | | Amt (₹) |
|---|---|---|---|---|---|
| To Sundry Assets | | | By Sundry Liabilities | | |
| Building | 56,000 | | Creditors | | 14,000 |
| Investment | 14,000 | | By X's Capital A/c (Investment) | | 13,300 |
| Debtors | 7,000 | | By Bank A/c | | |
| Stock | 10,500 | 87,500 | Building | 63,000 | |
| To Bank A/c (Creditors) | | 13,300 | Debtors | 6,300 | |
| To Bank A/c (Expenses) | | 1,400 | Stock | 9,800 | 79,100 |
| To Profit transferred to | | | | | |
| X's Capital A/c | 1,400 | | | | |
| Y's Capital A/c | 1,400 | | | | |
| Z's Capital A/c | 1,400 | 4,200 | | | |
| | | 1,06,400 | | | 1,06,400 |

Dr **Partners' Capital Account** Cr

| Particulars | X (₹) | Y (₹) | Z (₹) | Particulars | X (₹) | Y (₹) | Z (₹) |
|---|---|---|---|---|---|---|---|
| To Realisation A/c | 13,300 | — | — | By Balance b/d | 35,000 | 28,000 | 21,000 |
| To Bank A/c | 26,600 | 32,900 | 25,900 | By Profit and Loss A/c | 3,500 | 3,500 | 3,500 |
| | | | | By Realisation A/c | 1,400 | 1,400 | 1,400 |
| | 39,900 | 32,900 | 25,900 | | 39,900 | 32,900 | 25,900 |

Dr **Bank Account** Cr

| Particulars | Amt (₹) | Particulars | Amt (₹) |
|---|---|---|---|
| To Balance b/d | 21,000 | By Realisation A/c | 13,300 |
| To Realisation (Assets realised) | 79,100 | By Realisation A/c | 1,400 |
| | | By X's Capital A/c | 26,600 |
| | | By Y's Capital A/c | 32,900 |
| | | By Z's Capital A/c | 25,900 |
| | 1,00,100 | | 1,00,100 |

9. (A) (a) **Distribution of Goodwill**

Rahil $= 4{,}000 \times \frac{3}{5} = ₹\ 2{,}400$ ; Maahi $= 4{,}000 \times \frac{2}{5} = ₹\ 1{,}600$

**Working Notes**

1. **Calculation of New Profit Sharing Ratio**

Old Ratio $= 3:2$

Let the profit of the firm $= 1$

Remaining profit of the firm after Neha's share $= 1 - \frac{1}{4} = \frac{3}{4}$

Rahil's new share $= \frac{3}{5} \times \frac{3}{4} = \frac{9}{20}$; Maahi'snew share $= \frac{2}{5} \times \frac{3}{4} = \frac{6}{20}$

$\therefore$ New profit sharing ratio $= \frac{9}{20} : \frac{6}{20} : \frac{1}{4} = 9:6:5$

2. **Calculation of Sacrificing Ratio**

Old Ratio = 3 : 2 ; New Ratio = 9 : 6 : 5

Sacrificing Ratio = Old Share – New Share

Rahil $= \frac{3}{5} - \frac{9}{20} = \frac{12-9}{20} = \frac{3}{20}$; Maahi $= \frac{2}{5} - \frac{6}{20} = \frac{8-6}{20} = \frac{2}{20}$

(b) Dr **Revaluation Account** Cr

| Particulars | | Amt (₹) | Particulars | Amt (₹) |
|---|---|---|---|---|
| To Profit transferred to Capital A/cs | | | By Provision for Doubtful Debts | 2,000 |
| Rahil | 1,200 | | | |
| Maahi | 800 | 2,000 | | |
| | | 2,000 | | 2,000 |

(c) Dr **Partners' Capital Account** Cr

| Particulars | Rahil (₹) | Maahi (₹) | Neha (₹) | Particulars | Rahil (₹) | Maahi (₹) | Neha (₹) |
|---|---|---|---|---|---|---|---|
| To Current A/c | 5,400 | 3,600 | — | By Balance b/d | 30,000 | 20,000 | — |
| To Balance c/d (Balancing figure) | 36,000 | 24,000 | 20,000 | By General Reserve A/c | 2,400 | 1,600 | — |
| | | | | By Workmen Compensation Reserve A/c | 1,800 | 1,200 | — |
| | | | | By Investment Fluctuation Reserve A/c | 3,600 | 2,400 | — |
| | | | | By Revaluation (Profit) | 1,200 | 800 | — |
| | | | | By Cash A/c | — | — | 20,000 |
| | | | | By Premium for Goodwill A/c | 2,400 | 1,600 | — |
| | 41,400 | 27,600 | 20,000 | | 41,400 | 27,600 | 20,000 |

**Working Note**

Neha's capital for $\frac{1}{4}$ th share = ₹ 20,000 ; Total capital of firm $= 20,000 \times \frac{4}{1} =$ ₹ 80,000

New profit sharing ratio = 9 : 6 : 5

Rahil's new capital $= 80,000 \times \frac{9}{20} =$ ₹ 36,000 ; Maahi's new capital $= 80,000 \times \frac{6}{20} =$ ₹ 24,000

Neha's new capital $= 80,000 \times \frac{5}{20} =$ ₹ 20,000

[B] **JOURNAL**

| Date | Particulars | | LF | Amt (Dr) | Amt (Cr) |
|---|---|---|---|---|---|
| 2018 | | | | | |
| Mar 31 | General Reserve A/c | Dr | | 30,000 | |
| | Investment Fluctuation Reserve A/c | Dr | | 40,000 | |
| | To P's Capital A/c (70,000 × 2/5) | | | | 28,000 |
| | To Q's Capital A/c (70,000 × 2/5) | | | | 28,000 |
| | To R's Capital A/c (70,000 × 1/5) | | | | 14,000 |
| | (Being the general reserve and investment fluctuation reserve transferred to capital accounts on Q's retirement) | | | | |

*Or* (a) **Calculation of Average Profit**

2013-14 — 3,50,000 – 56,250 = ₹ 2,93,750

2014-15 — 4,75,000 – 56,250 = ₹ 4,18,750

2015-16 — 6,70,000 – 56,250 = ₹ 6,13,750

2016-17 — 7,45,000 – 56,250 – 15,000 = ₹ 6,73,750

Total profit = 2,93,750 + 4,18,750 + 6,13,750 + 6,73,750 = ₹ 20,00,000

Average profit $= \frac{20,00,000}{4} =$ ₹ 5,00,000

(b) **Calculation of Raghav's Share of Goodwill**

Goodwill = Average Profit × Number of Years Purchase = 5,00,000 × 2 = ₹ 10,00,000

Raghav's share of goodwill = $10,00,000 \times \frac{1}{4}$ = ₹ 2,50,000 to be shared by Asha and Aditi in 3:2 ratio.

(c) **JOURNAL**

| Date | Particulars | | LF | Amt (Dr) | Amt (Cr) |
|---|---|---|---|---|---|
| | General Reserve A/c | Dr | | 30,000 | |
| | To Asha's Capital A/c | | | | 18,000 |
| | To Aditi's Capital A/c | | | | 12,000 |
| | (Being transfer of general reserve to old partners) | | | | |

(d) **JOURNAL**

| Date | Particulars | | LF | Amt (Dr) | Amt (Cr) |
|---|---|---|---|---|---|
| 2017 | | | | | |
| Apr 1 | Cash A/c | Dr | | 8,50,000 | |
| | To Raghav's Capital A/c | | | | 6,00,000 |
| | To Premium for Goodwill A/c | | | | 2,50,000 |
| | (Being Raghav brought his share of capital and goodwill premium in cash) | | | | |

(e) **JOURNAL**

| Date | Particulars | | LF | Amt (Dr) | Amt (Cr) |
|---|---|---|---|---|---|
| Apr 1 | Premium for Goodwill A/c | Dr | | 2,50,000 | |
| | To Asha's Capital A/c | | | | 1,50,000 |
| | To Aditi's Capital A/c | | | | 1,00,000 |
| | (Being premium distributed among the partners) | | | | |

**10.** (i) ₹ 3,00,000

| **Working Note** | | **Amt (₹)** |
|---|---|---|
| Total money received (3,00,000 × 2) | = | 6,00,000 |
| (–) Application money (1,00,000 × 2) | = | (2,00,000) |
| Call money | = | 4,00,000 |
| (–) Money kept for allotment (1,00,000 × 3) | = | (3,00,000) |
| Money refunded | = | 1,00,000 |

(ii) None

(iii) ₹ 1,00,000 [WN of point (i)]

(iv) The amount refunded to M after adjustment in allotment money = ₹ 1,000 (4,000 – 3,000)

**Working Note**

Number of shares allotted to M = $\frac{1,00,000}{3,00,000} \times 3,000 = 1,000$ shares

(v) **JOURNAL**

| Date | Particulars | | LF | Amt (Dr) | Amt (Cr) |
|---|---|---|---|---|---|
| (a) | Equity Share Capital A/c (1,000 × 10) | Dr | | 10,000 | |
| | To Forfeited Shares A/c (1,000 × 5) | | | | 5,000 |
| | To Equity Share First and Final Call A/c (1,000 × 5) | | | | 5,000 |
| | (Being the shares forfeited due to non-payment of call money) | | | | |
| (b) | Bank A/c (1,000 × 8) | Dr | | 8,000 | |
| | Forfeited Shares A/c (1,000 × 2) | Dr | | 2,000 | |
| | To Equity Share Capital A/c | | | | 10,000 |
| | (Being the re-issue of 1,000 shares @ ₹ 8 per share as fully paid) | | | | |

| Date | Particulars | LF | Amt (Dr) | Amt (Cr) |
|---|---|---|---|---|
| | Forfeited Shares A/c Dr | | 3,000 | |
| | To Capital Reserve A/c (WN) | | | 3,000 |
| | (Being the amount of forfeited shares account transferred to capital reserve) | | | |

**Working Note**

Amount transferred to capital reserve = 5,000 – 2,000 = ₹ 3,000

*Or*

**JOURNAL**

| Date | Particulars | LF | Amt (Dr) | Amt (Cr) |
|---|---|---|---|---|
| | Bank A/c Dr | | 2,76,000 | |
| | To Share Application A/c (92,000 × 3) | | | 2,76,000 |
| | (Being share application money received on 92,000 shares @ ₹ 3 per share) | | | |
| | Share Application A/c Dr | | 2,76,000 | |
| | To Share Capital A/c ( 50,000 × 3) | | | 1,50,000 |
| | To Share Allotment A/c (30,000 × 3) | | | 90,000 |
| | To Bank A/c (12,000 × 3) | | | 36,000 |
| | (Being share application money transferred) | | | |
| | Share Allotment A/c (50,000 × 5) Dr | | 2,50,000 | |
| | To Share Capital A/c (50,000 × 3) | | | 1,50,000 |
| | To Securities Premium A/c (50,000 × 2) | | | 1,00,000 |
| | (Being allotment money due on 50,000 shares @ ₹ 5 per share including premium of ₹ 2 each) | | | |
| | Bank A/c (WN) Dr | | 1,57,200 | |
| | To Equity Share Allotment A/c | | | 1,54,000 |
| | To Calls-in-advance A/c | | | 3,200 |
| | (Being allotment money received and calls-in-advance on 800 shares @ ₹ 4 per share) | | | |
| | Share First Call A/c Dr | | 1,00,000 | |
| | To Share Capital A/c (50,000 × 2) | | | 1,00,000 |
| | (Being first call money due on 50,000 shares @ ₹ 2 per share) | | | |
| | Bank A/c Dr | | 95,400 | |
| | Calls-in-advance A/c (800 × 2) Dr | | 1,600 | |
| | To Share First Call A/c (48,500 × 2) | | | 97,000 |
| | (Being first call money received on 48,500 shares @ ₹ 2 per share) | | | |
| | Share Final Call A/c Dr | | 1,00,000 | |
| | To Share Capital A/c (50,000 × 2) | | | 1,00,000 |
| | (Being final call money due on 50,000 shares @ ₹ 2 per share) | | | |
| | Bank A/c Dr | | 95,400 | |
| | Calls-in-advance A/c Dr | | 1,600 | |
| | To Share Final Call A/c | | | 97,000 |
| | (Being final call money received on 48,500 shares @ ₹ 2 per share) | | | |

**Working Note**

| Applied Shares | Allotted Shares | |
|---|---|---|
| 40,000 | 30,000 | (Pro-rata allotment) |
| 40,000 | 20,000 | (Pro-rata allotment) |
| 12,000 | Nil | |
| 92,000 | 50,000 | |

Number of shares allotted to Suresh = $2{,}000 \times \frac{30{,}000}{40{,}000}$ = 1,500 shares

| **Surplus towards Allotment on Suresh's Shares** | | **Amt (₹)** |
|---|---|---|
| Application money received (2,000 × 3) | | 6,000 |
| (–) Application money required (1,500 × 3) | | (4,500) |
| Surplus towards allotment | | 1,500 |
| **Calculation of Amount Received on Allotment** | | |
| Allotment money due (50,000 × 5) | | 2,50,000 |
| (–) Excess received with application (30,000 × 3) | | (90,000) |
| | | 1,60,000 |
| (–) Calls-in-arrears (Suresh) | | |
| Due (1,500 × 5) | 7,500 | |
| (–) Surplus | (1,500) | (6,000) |
| | | 1,54,000 |
| (+) Calls-in-advance (Chandar) | | |
| First call (800 × 2) | 1,600 | |
| Final call (800 × 2) | 1,600 | 3,200 |
| Amount received with allotment | | 1,57,200 |

11. (i) (*c*) ₹ 8,40,000 [24,00,000 – (18,00,000 – 2,40,000)]

(ii) (*b*) • Reduce

**Reason** Due to payment in cash to vendor of machine, the quick assets will reduce and thus the quick ratio also reduce.

• Improve

**Reason** The quick assets will increase by the sales amount, thus quick ratio will improve.

(iii) • The low current ratio indicates a weak liquidity position for the company. It means that the company is insufficient to pay-off current liabilities.

• Current Ratio $\frac{\text{Current Assets}}{\text{Current Liabilities}} = \frac{48,00,000}{24,00,000} = 2:1$

(iv) Tools of analysis of financial statements are

(a) Ratio analysis

(b) Cash flow statement

(v) Loss on sale of plant = ₹ 2,000

12. **Common Size Statement**

for the year ending 31st March, 2023 and 2022

| Particulars | Note No. | Absolute Amount | | (%) of Revenue from Operations | |
|---|---|---|---|---|---|
| | | 31st March, 2022 (₹) | 31st March, 2023 (₹) | 31st March, 2022 (%) | 31st March, 2023 (%) |
| I. Revenue from Operations | | 40,00,000 | 50,00,000 | 100 | 100 |
| (+) Other Incomes | | — | — | — | — |
| Total Revenue | | 40,00,000 | 50,00,000 | 100 | 100 |
| II. **Expenses** | | | | | |
| Employees benefit Expenses | | 14,00,000 | 20,00,000 | 35 | 40 |
| Other Expenses | | 6,00,000 | 4,00,000 | 15 | 8 |
| Total Expenses | | 20,00,000 | 24,00,000 | 50 | 48 |
| Profit before Tax (I – II) | | 20,00,000 | 26,00,000 | 50 | 52 |
| (–) Tax @ 40% | | (8,00,000) | (10,40,000) | (20) | (20.8) |
| | | 12,00,000 | 15,60,000 | 30 | 31.2 |

13. (i) Return on Investment $= \frac{\text{Profit before Interest, Tax and Preference Dividend}^{*}}{\text{Capital Employed}^{**}} \times 100 = \frac{31,800}{90,000} \times 100 = 35.33\%$

Profit before Tax $= \frac{\text{Profit after Tax}}{100 - \text{Tax Rate}} \times 100 = \frac{15,000 \times 100}{100 - 50} = \frac{15,000 \times 100}{50} =$ ₹ 30,000

Profit before interest and tax (interest on debentures) = 30,000 + 1,800 = ₹ 31,800

**Capital Employed = Equity Share Capital + General Reserve + Balance of Statement of Profit and Loss + 9% Debentures

= 50,000 + 5,000 + 15,000 + 20,000 = ₹ 90,000

(ii) Inventory Turnover Ratio = $\dfrac{\text{Cost of Revenue from Operations}}{\text{Average Inventory}}$

Gross profit = $3,00,000 \times \dfrac{25}{100}$ = ₹ 75,000

Cost of Revenue from Operations = Revenue from Operations – Gross Profit

= 3,00,000 – 75,000 = ₹ 2,25,000

Average Inventory = $\dfrac{\text{Opening Inventory} + \text{Closing Inventory}}{2}$

Let be the opening inventory = $x$

Closing inventory = $x$ + 20,000

Average inventory = $\dfrac{x + x + 20,000}{2} = \dfrac{2x + 20,000}{2} = x + 10,000$

Inventory turnover ratio = 4 times, so = $\dfrac{2,25,000}{x + 10,000} = 4$

⇒ $4x + 40,000 = 2,25,000$; $x$ = ₹ 46,250

∴ Opening inventory = ₹ 46,250

Closing inventory = 46,250 + 20,000 = ₹ 66,250

(iii) Proprietary Ratio = $\dfrac{\text{Shareholders' Funds}}{\text{Total Assets}} = \dfrac{1,00,000}{4,50,000} = 0.22 : 1$

Where,

Shareholders' Funds = Total Assets – (Current Liabilities + Long-term Borrowings + Long-term Provisions)

= (3,60,000 + 90,000) – (50,000 + 2,00,000 + 1,00,000)

= 4,50,000 – 3,50,000 = ₹ 1,00,000

(iv) Debt Equity Ratio = $\dfrac{\text{Long – term Debt}}{\text{Equity}} = \dfrac{1,70,000}{1,00,000} = 1.7 : 1$

Where,

Long-term Debt = Total Debt – Current Liabilities = 2,50,000 – 80,000 = ₹ 1,70,000

Equity/Shareholders' Funds = Total Assets – Total Debt = 3,50,000 – 2,50,000 = ₹ 1,00,000

**Common Mistake** Students usually gets confused whether gross profit is presented as percentage of net sales or percentage of cost of goods sold. In the absence of any information, gross profit will be taken as percentage of net sales.

**14.**

**In the Books of Aashram Ltd.**

**Cash Flow from Operating Activities**

| Particulars | Amt (₹) |
|---|---|
| A. **Cash Flow from Operating Activities** | |
| Net Profit before Taxation (WN 1) | 75,000 |
| (+) Adjustment for Non-cash and Non-operating Items | |
| Goodwill Written-off | 30,000 |
| Loss on Sale of Machinery | 6,000 |
| Depreciation on Machinery | 40,000 |
| Interest Paid on Debentures | 25,000 |
| Operating Profit before Working Capital Changes | 1,76,000 |
| (+) Decrease in Current Assets and Increase in Current Liabilities (Creditors) | 20,000 |
| | 1,96,000 |

| Particulars | | Amt (₹) |
|---|---|---|
| (–) Increase in Current Assets and Decrease in Current Liabilities | | |
| Stock | | (25,000) |
| Trade Receivable | | (1,00,000) |
| | | 71,000 |
| (–) Tax Paid | | (10,000) |
| **Net Cash from Operating Activities** | | 61,000 |

**Working Notes**

| | Amt (₹) |
|---|---|
| 1. Calculation of net profit before tax reserve and surplus balance on 31st March, 2024 | 2,50,000 |
| (–) Reserve and surplus balance on 31st March, 2023 | (2,00,000) |
| | 50,000 |
| (+) Provision for tax made during the year | 25,000 |
| | 75,000 |

2. Dr **Plant and Machinery Account** Cr

| Particulars | Amt (₹) | Particulars | Amt (₹) |
|---|---|---|---|
| To Balance b/d | 5,00,000 | By Bank A/c | 9,000 |
| To Bank A/c (Balancing figure being purchase) | 4,05,000 | By Accumulated Depreciation A/c | 10,000 |
| | | By Statement of Profit and Loss | 6,000 |
| | | By Balance c/d | 8,80,000 |
| | 9,05,000 | | 9,05,000 |

3. Dr **Accumulated Depreciation Account** Cr

| Particulars | Amt (₹) | Particulars | Amt (₹) |
|---|---|---|---|
| To Machine A/c | 10,000 | By Balance b/d | 50,000 |
| To Balance c/d | 80,000 | By Statement of Profit and Loss (Balancing figure) | 40,000 |
| | 90,000 | | 90,000 |

4. Dr **Provision for Taxation Account** Cr

| Particulars | Amt (₹) | Particulars | Amt (₹) |
|---|---|---|---|
| To Cash A/c | 10,000 | By Balance b/d | 15,000 |
| To Balance c/d | 30,000 | By Statement of Profit and Loss (Balancing figure) | 25,000 |
| | 40,000 | | 40,000 |

*Or* (a) **Cash Flow from Operating Activities**

| Particulars | | Amt (₹) |
|---|---|---|
| Net Profit before Tax (1,00,000 + 80,000) | | 1,80,000 |
| **Adjustments for** | | |
| (+) Depreciation on Machinery | 2,00,000 | |
| Interest on Deposits | 45,000 | |
| Goodwill Written-off | 60,000 | 3,05,000 |
| Operating Profit before Working Capital Changes | | 4,85,000 |
| (–) Increase in Current Assets and Decrease in Current Liabilities | | |
| Inventories | (50,000) | |
| Trade Receivables | (2,00,000) | (2,50,000) |
| Cash Flow from Operations before Tax Paid | | 2,35,000 |

(b)

Dr **Property, Plant and Equipment (Machinery) Account** Cr

| Particulars | Amt (₹) | Particulars | Amt (₹) |
|---|---|---|---|
| To Balance b/d | 9,00,000 | By Depreciation A/c | 2,00,000 |
| To Bank A/c (Purchases) (Balance transferred) | 9,00,000 | By Balance c/d | 16,00,000 |
| | 18,00,000 | | 18,00,000 |

(c)

| Particulars | | Amt (₹) |
|---|---|---|
| **Cash Flow from Financing Activities** | | |
| Issue of Shares | 4,00,000 | |
| 9% Deposits Raised | 4,00,000 | |
| Interest Paid | (45,000) | |
| Net Cash Generated from Financing Activities | | 7,55,000 |

**Working Note**

$$\text{Interest on Deposits} = \left(2{,}00{,}000 \times \frac{9}{100} \times \frac{3}{12}\right) + \left(6{,}00{,}000 \times \frac{9}{100} \times \frac{9}{12}\right)$$

$$= 4{,}500 + 40{,}500$$

$$= ₹\ 45{,}000$$

SQP Code : **PB-7/15**    Series ***i*-Succeed 7-25/15**    Roll No. | | | | | | | | |

# Sample Question Paper 07

## Accounts 12th (Code 858)

### General Instructions

1. Candidates are allowed additional 15 minutes for only reading the paper. They must not start writing during this time.
2. Section-A is compulsory for all candidates and has ten questions.
3. Candidates have to attempt all questions from either Section-B or Section-C*.
4. Internal choices have been provided in five questions in Section-A and one question in Section-B.
5. The intended marks for questions or parts of questions are given in the brackets [ ].
6. All calculations should be shown clearly.
7. All workings, including rough work, should be done on the same page as, and adjacent to, the rest of the answer.

*Section-C has not been covered.

**Time :** 3 Hrs.

**Max. Marks :** 80

## Section A Answer All Questions [60 Marks]

**Que 1.**

In sub-parts (i) to (iv), choose the correct option and in sub-parts (v) to (x) answer the questions as instructed.

(i) What will be the journal entry for allowing interest on capital to the partners? (Application) [1]

(a) Debit Partners' Capital A/c and Credit Interest on Capital A/c

(b) Debit Partners' Capital A/c and Credit Profit and Loss Appropriation A/c

(c) Debit Profit and Loss Appropriation A/c and Credit Partners' Capital A/c

(d) Debit Interest on Capital A/c and Credit Partners' Capital A/c

(ii) Choose the correct order of steps required for valuation of goodwill using weighted average profit method. (Recall) [1]

A – Assign weights to each years' profit/loss

B – Find goodwill

C – Calculate weighted average profit

D – Calculate normal profit

**Codes**

(a) D, A, C, B  (b) A, D, C, B

(c) D, A, B, C  (d) A, C, B, D

(iii) Excess value of net assets over purchase consideration at the time of purchase of business is (Understanding) [1]

(a) credited to the vendor's account

(b) credited to the capital reserve

(c) debited to the goodwill account

(d) credited to the general reserve

(iv) The balance sheet of ABCD partnership firm showed ₹ 20,000 debit balance of profit and loss account. Calculate the goodwill on 2 years' purchase of average profits of last two years if the company earned ₹ 30,000 profit in the previous year. (Application) [1]

(a) ₹ 30,000  (b) ₹ 20,000

(c) ₹ 10,000  (d) Can't say

(v) **Assertion** (A) The DRR is shown under the head 'reserves and surplus' of a company.

**Reason** (R) After redemption, DRR is transferred to general reserve. (Evaluate) [1]

**Alternatives**

(a) Both Assertion (A) and Reason (R) are true and Reason (R) is the correct explanation for Assertion (A)

(b) Both Assertion (A) and Reason (R) are true, but Reason (R) is not the correct explanation for Assertion (A)

(c) Assertion (A) is true, but Reason (R) is false

(d) Both Assertion (A) and Reason (R) are false

(vi) Name any two sources that are available for redemption of debentures. (Understanding) [1]

(vii) In a partnership firm, a partner withdrew ₹ 24,000 per month on the last day of each month during the year for personal use. If interest on drawings is charged @ 8% p.a. what will be the interest on drawings? (Application) [1]

(viii) Three partnership firms – VG Panneerdas & Company, VGP Investments and VGP Beach Housing – belonging to the famous Chennai-based VGP group have been ordered to be dissolved by an interim award given on 18th March, 2021, by Arbitrator Justice K Kannan (Retd), who was appointed by the Madras High Court.

**Source** *The Hindu business line*

(a) Which mode of dissolution is being adopted here? (Recall)

(b) Name other modes of dissolution of a partnership firm. (Recall) [1]

(ix) Ramya Ltd. issued 20,000, 12% debentures of ₹ 100 each as a collateral security for a loan of ₹ 12,00,000 taken from Sia Bank. Pass the journal entry for the same. (Application) [1]

(x) What will be the journal entry for the furniture worth ₹ 1,00,000 being taken over by 'B' a partner for cash payment at 5% less than the book value? (Application) [1]

**Que 2.**

Anil, Jatin and Ramesh were partners, sharing profits in the ratio of 2:1:1. Their balance sheet as at 31st December, 2022 stood as follows

**Balance Sheet**
as at 31st December, 2022

| Liabilities | | Amt (₹) | Assets | | Amt (₹) |
|---|---|---|---|---|---|
| Creditors | | 24,400 | Cash | | 1,00,000 |
| Bank Loan | | 10,000 | Debtors | 20,000 | |
| Profit and Loss A/c | | 18,000 | (–) Provision for Doubtful Debts | (1,600) | 18,400 |
| Bills Payables | | 2,000 | Stock | | 10,000 |
| Capital A/cs | | | Building | | 20,000 |
| Anil | 50,000 | | Investment | | 36,000 |
| Jatin | 40,000 | | | | |
| Ramesh | 40,000 | 1,30,000 | | | |
| | | 1,84,400 | | | 1,84,400 |

Ramesh died on 31st March, 2023. The following adjustments were agreed upon

(i) Goodwill be valued at 2 years' purchase of the average profit of the past 5 years.

(ii) Ramesh's share of profit to the death be calculated on the basis of the profit of the preceding year. Profits for the years 2018, 2019, 2020 and 2021 were ₹ 26,000, ₹ 22,000, ₹ 20,000 and ₹ 24,000 respectively.

(a) Prepare Ramesh's capital account.

(b) Ramesh's executors' account immediately after Ramesh's death assuming that ₹ 18,425 be paid immediately to his executors and balance to be left to the Ramesh's executor's account. (Application) [3]

SP-07

**Que 3.**
Amit, Sumit and Ramit formed a partnership on the following terms

(i) Profit shall be divided in the ratio of 2 : 2 : 1.
(ii) Amit's share of profit guaranteed to be not less than ₹ 1,25,000 in any year.
(iii) Ramit gives guarantee to the effect that the gross fee earned by him for the firm shall not be less than average fees of preceding four years when he was carrying on the profession alone.
(iv) Their capital accounts shall be fixed.

The profits for the first year of partnership are ₹ 2,51,250. The gross fees earned by Ramit for the firm is ₹ 40,000. Gross fees earned by Ramit during last four years were ₹ 40,000, ₹ 60,000, ₹ 30,000 and ₹ 35,000 respectively.

You are required to

(a) Give the amount of shortage of guaranteed fees by Ramit, if any.
(b) Deficiency in Amit's guaranteed amount.
(c) Prepare profit and loss appropriation account. (Application) [3]

**Que 4.**
XYZ Ltd. has 20,000, 9% debentures of ₹ 100 each outstanding in the books of accounts as on 31st March, 2020, to be redeemed on 31st March, 2025. Show how will you disclose debentures in the balance sheet. (Application) [3]

*Or*

Nand Ram Ltd. issued 1,00,000, 8% debentures of ₹ 10 each at ₹ 12 on 1st April, 2020. The issue was fully subscribed. In terms of the issue of debentures, interest was payable at the end of the financial year.

You are required to calculate

(i) Amount of interest payable on 8% debentures. [1]
(ii) Amount transferred to statement of profit and loss and bank account. (Application) [2]

**Que 5.**
Pass necessary journal entries relating to the issue of debentures for the following

(i) Issued ₹ 2,00,000, 10% debentures of ₹ 100 each at a premium of 8%, redeemable at 10% premium.
(ii) Issued ₹ 3,00,000, 10% debentures of ₹ 100 each at par, repayable at a premium of 10%. (Application) [3]

*Or*

Deepak Ltd. Company purchased furniture ₹ 2,20,000 from M/s Furniture Mart, 50% of the amount was paid to Furniture Mart by accepting a bill of exchange and for the balance the company issued 9% debentures of ₹ 100 each at a premium of 10% in favour of Furniture Mart. Pass necessary journal entries in the books of Deepak Ltd.

(i) For the purchase of furniture.
(ii) For the acceptance of bills.
(iii) For the issuance of debentures in lieu of part payment. (Application)

**Que 6.**

(i) Parul, Payal and Priyanka are partners. They decided to dissolve the firm. Pass the necessary journal entries for the following after the various assets (other than cash and bank) and outside liabilities have been transferred to realisation account.
   (a) There were total debtors of ₹ 76,000. A provision for bad and doubtful debts also stood in the books at ₹ 6,000. ₹ 12,000 debtors proved bad and rest paid the amount due.
   (b) Parul agreed to pay off her husband's loan of ₹ 7,000 at a discount of 5%.
   (c) A machine which is not recorded in the books was taken over by Payal at ₹ 3,000 whereas its expected value was ₹ 5,000.

SP-07

(ii) Lal and Pal were partners in a firm sharing profits in the ratio of 3 : 7. On 1st April, 2021 their firm was dissolved. After transferring assets (other than cash) and outsider's liabilities to realisation account, you are given the following information
   (a) A creditor of ₹ 3,60,000 accepted machinery valued at ₹ 5,00,000 and paid to the firm ₹ 1,40,000.
   (b) A second creditor for ₹ 50,000 accepted stock at ₹ 45,000 in full settlement of his claim.

(c) A third creditor amounting to ₹ 90,000 accepted ₹ 45,000 in cash and investments worth ₹ 43,000 in full settlement of his claim.

Pass necessary journal entries for the above transactions in the books of firm assuming that all payments were made by cheque. **(Application) [6]**

**Que 7.**

Bimal and Chetan are partners in a firm. The partnership deed provides for the following

(i) Interest on capital @ 10% per annum.
(ii) Salary to Bimal ₹ 5,000 per month.
(iii) Remaining profits will be shared in the ratio of 3 : 2.

The balance of capital accounts as at 1st April, 2018 were ₹ 5,00,000 and ₹ 3,50,000 respectively. The net profit for the year 2018-19 was ₹ 2,40,000. At the end of the year, it was found that interest on capital was duly recorded and given but without considering salary to Bimal, remaining profit was shared in the ratio of 2 : 3. You are required to

(a) Calculate the actual divisible profit. [1]
(b) Rectify the situation by means of adjustment entry and show your workings clearly. **(Application) [5]**

**Que 8.**

Under what heads and sub-heads, the following items will appear in the balance sheet of a company as per Schedule III of the Companies Act, 2013.

SP-07

(i) Premium on redemption of debentures
(ii) Loose tools (iii) Balance with banks
(iv) General reserve
(v) Stores and spares
(vi) Mining rights (vii) Subsidy reserve
(viii) Preliminary expenses **(Application) [6]**

*Or*

Innara Ltd. has the following balances in reserves and surplus

Debenture redemption ₹ 10,00,000

Securities premium ₹ 12,00,000

Surplus, i.e. balance in statement of profit and loss (₹ 3,00,000)

During the year ended 31st March, 2022, it earned a profit after tax of ₹ 10,00,000. It decided to appropriate ₹ 2,00,000 towards debenture redemption reserve ₹ 2,50,000 towards general reserve and declare a final dividend of ₹ 1,50,000.

(i) Show how it will be shown in the notes to accounts on reserves and surplus?
(ii) Show how will proposed dividend be shown in the balance sheet assuming that it is approved by the shareholders? **(Application)**

**Que 9.**

The directors of Super Star Ltd. invited applications for 2,00,000 equity shares of ₹ 10 each to be issued at 20% premium. The money payable on shares is

On application ₹ 5, on allotment ₹ 4 (including premium of ₹ 2), first call ₹ 2 and final call ₹ 1.

Applications were received for 2,40,000 shares and allotment was made as

(i) To applicants for 1,00,000 shares — In full
(ii) To applicants for 80,000 shares — 60,000 shares
(iii) To applicants for 60,000 shares — 40,000 shares

Applicants of 1,000 shares falling in category (i) and allottees of 1,200 shares falling in category (ii) failed to pay allotment money. These shares were forfeited, on failure to pay first call.

Holders of 1,200 shares falling in category (iii) failed to pay first and final call and these shares were forfeited after final call. 1,300 shares [1,000 of category (i) and 300 of category (ii)] were re-issued at ₹ 8 per share as fully paid.

(a) What are the numbers of applied and allotted shares of defaulters? [1]
(b) Calculate the amount not received on allotment. [1]
(c) What is the total amount of calls-in-arrears? [1]
(d) Prepare a table showing allotment of shares. [2]
(e) Give the journal entries for
- Forfeiture of the shares [2]
- Re-issue of the shares **(Application) [3]**

*Or*

SK Ltd. invited applications for issuing 3,20,000 equity shares of ₹ 10 each at a premium of ₹ 5 per share. The amount was payable as follows

On application – ₹ 3 per share (including premium ₹ 1 per share)

On allotment – ₹ 5 per share (including premium ₹ 2 per share)

On first and final call – Balance amount

Applications for 4,00,000 shares were received. Applications for 40,000 shares were rejected and application money refunded. Shares were alloted on pro-rata basis to the remaining applicants. Excess money received with applications was adjusted towards sums due on allotment. Jeevan holding 800 shares failed to pay the allotment money and his shares were immediately forfeited. Afterwards final call was made, Ganesh who had applied for 2,700 shares failed to pay the final call. His shares were also forfeited. Out of the forfeited shares 1,500 shares were re-issued at ₹ 8 per share fully paid up. The re-issued shares included all the forfeited shares of Jeevan.

Pass necessary journal entries for the above transactions in the books of the company. (Application) [10]

**Que 10.**

(A) P, N and S are partners, sharing profits in the ratio of 3 : 2 : 1. N retired from the firm due to his illness. On that date, the balance sheet of the firm was as follows

**Balance Sheet**

as at 31st March, 2023

| Liabilities | | Amt (₹) | Assets | | Amt (₹) |
|---|---|---|---|---|---|
| General Reserve | | 24,000 | Bank | | 15,200 |
| Sundry Creditors | | 30,000 | Sundry Debtors | 12,000 | |
| Bills Payable | | 24,000 | (–) Provision for Doubtful Debts | (800) | 11,200 |
| Outstanding Salary | | 4,400 | Stock | | 18,000 |
| Provision for Legal Damages | | 12,000 | Furniture | | 82,000 |
| Capital A/cs | | | Premises | | 1,60,000 |
| P | 92,000 | | | | |
| N | 60,000 | | | | |
| S | 40,000 | 1,92,000 | | | |
| | | 2,86,400 | | | 2,86,400 |

**Additional Information**

(i) Premises have appreciated by 20%, stock depreciated by 10% and provision for doubtful debts was to be made at 5% on debtors. Further, provision for legal damages is to be made for ₹ 2,400 and furniture to be brought upto ₹ 90,000.

(ii) Goodwill of the firm be valued at ₹ 84,000.

(iii) ₹ 52,000 from N's capital account be transferred to his loan account and balance be paid through bank, if required, necessary loan may be obtained from bank.

(iv) New profit sharing ratio of P and S is decided to be 5 : 1.

You are required to

(a) Prepare revaluation account. [1½]

(b) Prepare Partners' capital account. [4½]

(c) Prepare balance sheet as at 1st April, 2023. (Application) [2]

(B) R, S and N are partners sharing profit in the ratio of 1 : 2 : 3. N retires and her capital, after making adjustments for reserves and profits on revaluation stands at ₹ 2,20,000.
R and S agreed to pay her ₹ 2,50,000 in full settlement of her claim. Record necessary journal entry for the treatment of goodwill, if the new profit sharing ratio is decided at 1 : 3. (Application) [2]

SP-07

*Or*

On the date of N's admission, an extract of the balance sheet of L and M sharing profits and losses in the ratio of 3 : 2 was as under

**Balance Sheet** (Extract)
as at ...

| Liabilities | Amt (₹) | Assets | Amt (₹) |
|---|---|---|---|
| General Reserve | 15,000 | Investments (Market value ₹ 57,000) | 60,000 |
| Contingencies Reserve | 1,350 | Machinery Replacement Fund Investment | 3,000 |
| Profit and Loss A/c | 9,000 | Advertisement Expenditure (Deferred Revenue) | 3,000 |
| Investment Fluctuation Reserve | 4,500 | | |
| Machinery Replacement Fund | 3,000 | | |
| Workmen's Compensation Reserve | 3,600 | | |
| Employees' Provident Fund | 6,000 | | |

New partner N was admitted for 1/5th share of profits. A claim on account of workmen's compensation is estimated at ₹ 450 only. Pass the necessary journal entries to adjust accumulated profits and losses.

You are required to

(i) Pass the journal entry for the transfer of general reserve and balance of profit and loss account. **(Application) [2]**

(ii) Pass the journal entry for the investment fluctuation reserve and contingency reserve. **(Application) [2]**

(iii) Pass the journal entry for the machinery replacement fund. **(Recall) [2]**

(iv) Pass the journal entry for the transfer advertisement expenditure. **(Application) [2]**

(v) Pass the journal entry for the workmen compensation reserve. **(Application) [2]**

## Section B

**[20 Marks]**

**Que 11.**

(i) Analysing the profitability ratios of the Adani Group reveals fluctuations and trends in its profitability over the years. First, let's consider the PBDIT (Profit Before Depreciation, Interest and Taxes) margin, which increased from 4.57% in 2020 to 10.44% in 2022, signaling an improvement in the group's operational efficiency and profitability. However, it dipped to 7.13% in 2023, suggesting a potential decrease in profitability or increased operating expenses.

**Source** *Annual report-2023 (edited)*

- What kind of measure ratio analysis provides regarding performance of a company? **(Analysis)**

(a) Qualitative (b) Quantitative (c) Cross (d) Relative

- Name any one profitability ratio. **(Recall) [1]**

(ii) Cash flow is important to a small business because it shows how much money is actually moving in and out of your company, not how much money you're awaiting from accounts receivable.

**Source** *Business news daily*

Based on the above statement, which of the following is/are objective(s) of cash flow statement? **(Understanding) [1]**

A. To determine the sources of cash B. To determine the application of cash

C. To determine net change in cash and cash equivalents

D. None of the above

**Codes**

(a) A, B and C (b) A and B (c) A and C (d) Only A

SP-07

(iii) Reviewing financial statements before making important decisions is important because these documents offer a comprehensive snapshot of a company's fiscal health and performance. Financial statements provide vital insights into its profitability, liquidity, solvency and overall stability. By analysing income statements, balance sheets and cash flow statements, stakeholders can study the company's past and current financial standings, identify trends and predict future trajectories.

**Source** *acc.review (edited)*

Briefly explain the interest of investors and management in the analysis of financial statements. (Analysis) [1]

(iv) The investing section of cash flow statement sheds light on cash flow from asset investments, like property or equipment. Lastly, the financing section elucidates cash movements linked to capital structure, encompassing actions such as issuing stock, paying dividends or acquiring loans. This statement is pivotal for investors and stakeholders, providing insights beyond profitability by illuminating a company's ability to generate cash and meet its financial obligations.

**Source** *Knowldge.com(edited)*

Interest received by a non-financial enterprise will be shown under which activity in cash flow statements? (Understanding) [1]

(v) The ratio of current assets ₹ 6,00,000 to current liabilities ₹ 4,00,000 is 1.5 : 1. The accountant of the firm is intended in maintaining a current ratio of 2:1, by paying-off a part of current liabilities. What will be the amount of current liabilities that should be paid so that the current ratio at level of 2:1 may be maintained? (Application) [1]

**Que 12.**

Prepare comparative income statement from the following (Application) [3]

| Particulars | 31st March, 2023 (₹) | 31st March, 2022 (₹) |
|---|---|---|
| Revenue from Operations | 15,00,000 | 10,00,000 |
| Expenses | 10,50,000 | 6,00,000 |
| Other Income | 1,80,000 | 2,00,000 |
| Income Tax | 50% | 50% |

**Que 13.**

Following are the balance sheets of Arihant Tiles Ltd. as at 31st March, 2022 and 31st March, 2023.



**Balance Sheet**
as at 31st March, 2023 and 2022

| Particulars | Note No. | 2022-23 (₹) | 2021-22 (₹) |
|---|---|---|---|
| I. **EQUITY AND LIABILITIES** | | | |
| 1. **Shareholders' Funds** | | | |
| (i) Share Capital | | 9,00,000 | 8,25,000 |
| (ii) Reserve and Surplus | 1 | 2,25,000 | 1,50,000 |
| 2. **Non-current Liabilities** | | | |
| Long-term Borrowings | | 1,80,000 | 1,27,500 |
| 3. **Current Liabilities** | | | |
| (i) Trade Payables | | 1,34,250 | 1,53,000 |
| (ii) Short-term Provision | | 37,500 | 57,750 |
| **Total** | | 14,76,750 | 13,13,250 |

| Particulars | Note No. | 2022-23 (₹) | 2021-22 (₹) |
|---|---|---|---|
| **II. ASSETS** | | | |
| **1. Non-current Assets** | | | |
| (i) Property, Plant & Equipment and Intangible Assets | | | |
| (a) Property, Plant and Equipment | 2 | 8,02,500 | 6,37,500 |
| (b) Intangible Assets | 3 | 30,000 | 84,000 |
| **2. Current Assets** | | | |
| (i) Current Investments | | 1,80,000 | 1,12,500 |
| (ii) Inventories | | 96,750 | 90,750 |
| (iii) Trade Receivables | | 1,27,500 | 1,07,250 |
| (iv) Cash and Cash Equivalents | | 2,40,000 | 2,81,250 |
| **Total** | | 14,76,750 | 13,13,250 |

## Notes to Accounts

| Particulars | 2022-23 (₹) | 2021-22 (₹) |
|---|---|---|
| 1. **Reserves and Surplus** | | |
| Surplus, i.e. Balance in Statement of Profit and Loss | 2,25,000 | 1,50,000 |
| 2. **Property, Plant and Equipment** | | |
| Machinery | 9,52,500 | 7,50,000 |
| (−) Accumulated Depreciation | (1,50,000) | (1,12,500) |
| | 8,02,500 | 6,37,500 |
| 3. **Intangible Assets** | | |
| Goodwill | 30,000 | 84,000 |

## Additional Information

During the year, a piece of machinery costing ₹ 18,000 on which accumulated depreciation was ₹ 12,000, was sold for ₹ 4,500. Prepare cash flow statement. **(Application) [6]**

*Or*

Following are the balance sheets of Mittal Ltd, as at 31st March, 2022 and 2023

| Particulars | Note No. | 2023 (₹) | 2022 (₹) |
|---|---|---|---|
| **I. EQUITY AND LIABILITIES** | | | |
| 1. **Shareholders' Funds** | | | |
| (i) Share Capital | | 7,00,000 | 5,00,000 |
| (ii) Reserves and Surplus | 1 | 2,50,000 | 2,00,000 |
| 2. **Non-current Liabilities** | | | |
| Long-term Borrowings | 2 | 3,00,000 | 1,00,000 |
| 3. **Current Liabilities** | | | |
| Short-term Provisions | 3 | 40,000 | 30,000 |
| **Total** | | 12,90,000 | 8,30,000 |
| **II. ASSETS** | | | |
| 1. **Non-current Assets** | | | |
| (i) Property, Plant & Equipment and Intangible Assets | | | |
| (a) Property, Plant and Equipment | 4 | 8,00,000 | 4,50,000 |
| (b) Intangible Assets | 5 | 70,000 | 1,00,000 |
| 2. **Current Assets** | | | |
| (i) Inventories | | 1,25,000 | 1,00,000 |
| (ii) Trade Receivables | | 2,50,000 | 1,50,000 |
| (iii) Cash and Cash Equivalents | | 45,000 | 30,000 |
| **Total** | | 12,90,000 | 8,30,000 |

**Notes to Accounts**

| Particulars | 31st March, 2023 (₹) | 31st March, 2022 (₹) |
|---|---|---|
| 1. **Reserves and Surplus** | | |
| Balance in Statement of Profit and Loss | 2,50,000 | 2,00,000 |
| 2. **Long-term Borrowings** | | |
| 9% Deposits | 3,00,000 | 1,00,000 |
| 3. **Short-term Provisions** | | |
| Provision for Tax | 40,000 | 30,000 |
| 4. **Property, Plant and Equipment** | | |
| Machinery | 8,00,000 | 4,50,000 |
| 5. **Intangible Assets** | | |
| Goodwill | 70,000 | 1,00,000 |

## Additional Information

(i) The company paid interest ₹ 22,500 on its deposits.
(ii) Depreciation provided on machinery during the year ₹ 1,00,000.
(a) Prepare property, plant and equipment (machinery) account. [2]
(b) Calculate the value of cash flow from operations. [2]
(c) Calculate the value of cash flow from financing activities. (Evaluate) [2]

**Que 14.**

Answer any three from the following (Application) [6]

From the following information, calculate

(i) Inventory turnover ratio (ii) Operating ratio
(iii) Net profit ratio (iv) Operating profit ratio

**Statement of Profit and Loss**
for the year ended 31st March, 2023

| Particulars | | Amt (₹) |
|---|---|---|
| I. Revenue from Operations (Sales) | 5,40,000 | |
| (–) Returns | (40,000) | 5,00,000 |
| II. Other Incomes | | 60,000 |
| III. Total Revenue | | 5,60,000 |
| Expenses | | |
| Purchases | | 2,50,000 |
| Change in Inventories (Opening Inventory – Closing Inventory) | | 8,000 |
| Carriage | | 20,000 |
| Wages | | 58,000 |
| Other Expenses | | 30,000 |
| IV. Total Expenses | | 3,66,000 |
| V. Net Profit before Tax (III – IV) | | 1,94,000 |
| VI. Profit for Tax | | (58,200) |
| VII. Net Profit after Tax (V – VI) | | 1,35,800 |

## Additional Information

(a) Other incomes include discount received ₹ 5,000.
(b) Opening inventory was ₹ 60,000 and closing inventory was ₹ 68,000.
(c) Other expenses include interest @ 10% on long-term borrowings ₹ 20,000 and remaining expenses relate to office and selling purposes.
(d) Shareholders' funds stood at ₹ 8,70,000.

SP-07

# Solutions *in Topper's Style*

My Commitment *I affirm that I am reviewing these solutions only after I have solved the Sample Question Paper 7 on my own. My purpose of looking the solutions is solely to verify whether my answers/solutions were correct or not and to identify my mistakes in case my solutions were wrong or I could not solve that.*

1. (i) (*d*) Debit Interest on Capital A/c and Credit Partners' Capital A/c

(ii) (*a*) D, A, C, B

(iii) (*b*) credited to the capital reserve

(iv) (*c*) Average Profits $= \dfrac{(20{,}000) + 30{,}000}{2} = ₹\ 5{,}000$

Goodwill $= 2 \times 5{,}000 = ₹\ 10{,}000$

(v) (*b*) Both Assertion (A) and Reason (R) are true, but Reason (R) is not the correct explanation for Assertion (A)

(vi) Two sources available for redemption of debentures are

(a) Redemption out of capital

(b) Redemption out of profits

(vii) Interest on drawings $= 24{,}000 \times 12 \times \dfrac{8}{100} \times \dfrac{5.5}{12} = ₹\ 10{,}560$

(viii) (a) Dissolution of partnership firm by court order.

(b) Other modes of dissolution of a partnership firm are (any one)

- Dissolution on happening of a certain event.
- Dissolution by notice.
- Dissolution by mutual agreement.

(ix) **JOURNAL**

| Date | Particulars | | LF | Amt (Dr) | Amt (Cr) |
|---|---|---|---|---|---|
| | Debenture Suspense A/c | Dr | | 20,00,000 | |
| | To 9% Debentures A/c | | | | 20,00,000 |
| | (Being 20,000 debentures were issued as a collateral security) | | | | |

(x) **JOURNAL**

| Date | Particulars | | LF | Amt (Dr) | Amt (Cr) |
|---|---|---|---|---|---|
| | Realisation A/c | Dr | | — | |
| | To Cash A/c | | | | — |
| | (Being furniture taken over by 'B' for cash) | | | | |

2. (a) Dr **Ramesh's Capital Account** Cr

| Particulars | Amt (₹) | Particulars | Amt (₹) |
|---|---|---|---|
| To Ramesh's Executor's A/c | 56,625 | By Balance b/d | 40,000 |
| | | By Profit and Loss A/c (18,000 × 1/4) | 4,500 |
| | | By Profit and Loss Suspense A/c | 1,125 |
| | | By Anil's Capital A/c | 7,333 |
| | | By Jatin's Capital A/c | 3,667 |
| | 56,625 | | 56,625 |

**Working Notes**

1. Adjustment of goodwill

Average Profit = Total Profit/Number of Years

$$= \frac{26{,}000 + 22{,}000 + 20{,}000 + 24{,}000 + 18{,}000}{5} = \frac{1{,}10{,}000}{5} = ₹\ 22{,}000$$

Goodwill = Average Profit × Number of Years' Purchase = 22,000 × 2 = ₹ 44,000

Ramesh's share of goodwill = 44,000 × 1/4 = ₹ 11,000 (to be borne by Anil and Jatin in the gaining ratio, i.e. 2 : 1)

Amount of goodwill borne by Anil = 11,000 × 2/3 = ₹ 7,333

Amount of goodwill borne by Jatin = 11,000 × 1/3 = ₹ 3,667

2. Ramesh's share in profit = $18,000 \times \frac{1}{4} \times \frac{3}{12}$ = ₹ 1,125

(b) Dr **Ramesh's Executor's Account** Cr

| Particulars | Amt (₹) | Particulars | Amt (₹) |
|---|---|---|---|
| To Cash A/c | 18,425 | By Ramesh's Capital A/c | 56,625 |
| To Balance c/d | 38,200 | | |
| | 56,625 | | 56,625 |

**Common Mistake** Students sometimes mistakenly take the profit of last year (2021 in Q.) given in the adjustment in order to calculate deceased partner's share in profits. But profits of last balance sheet (2022 in Q.) will be used to calculate Ramesh's share in profits.

3. (a) **Calculation of Shortage of Guaranteed Fees**

Average Fees of Last Four Years = $\frac{40,000 + 60,000 + 30,000 + 35,000}{4} = \frac{1,65,000}{4}$ = ₹ 41,250

Shortage of Fees = 41,250 − 40,000 = ₹ 1,250

(b) Deficiency in Amit's guaranteed amount ₹ 24,000 (1,25,000 − 1,01,000) shall be borne by Sumit and Ramit in their profit sharing ratio, i.e. 2 : 1.

Share of Amit = (2,51,250 + 1,250) $\times \frac{2}{5}$ = ₹ 1,01,000

(c) **Profit and Loss Appropriation Account**

Dr for the year ended... Cr

| Particulars | | Amt (₹) | Particulars | Amt (₹) |
|---|---|---|---|---|
| To Profit transferred to | | | By Net Profit as per Profit and Loss A/c | 2,51,250 |
| Amit's Current A/c (2,52,500 × 2/5) | 1,01,000 | | By Ramit's Current A/c (Shortage of guarantee fees) | 1,250 |
| (+) Deficiency from Sumit | 16,000 | | | |
| Deficiency from Ramit | 8,000 | 1,25,000 | | |
| Sumit's Current A/c (2,52,500 × 2/5) | 1,01,000 | | | |
| (−) Guarantee to Amit | (16,000) | 85,000 | | |
| Ramit's Current A/c (2,52,500 × 1/5) | 50,500 | | | |
| (−) Guarantee to Amit | (8,000) | 42,500 | | |
| | | 2,52,500 | | 2,52,500 |

4. In the balance sheet, they are shown as follows

**Balance Sheet**

as at 31st March, 2020 (Relevant part only)

| Particulars | Note No. | Amt (₹) |
|---|---|---|
| I. **EQUITY AND LIABILITIES** | | |
| 1. **Non-current Liabilities** | | |
| Long-term Borrowings | 1 | 20,00,000 |
| | | 20,00,000 |

**Notes to Accounts**

| Particulars | Amt (₹) |
|---|---|
| 1. **Long-term Borrowings** | |
| 20,000, 9% Debentures of ₹ 100 each | 20,00,000 |

*Or* (i) Interest on debentures = 10, 00, 000 × 8% = ₹ 80,000

(ii) Amount transferred to statement of profit and loss will be same as of debenture interest, i.e. 80, 000 and Bank account = ₹ 11,20,000 (12,00, 000 − 80, 000)

**5.**

**JOURNAL**

| Date | Particulars | LF | Amt (Dr) | Amt (Cr) |
|---|---|---|---|---|
| (i) | Bank A/c (2,000 × 108) Dr | | 2,16,000 | |
| | To Debenture Application and Allotment A/c | | | 2,16,000 |
| | (Being debenture application money received) | | | |
| | Debenture Application and Allotment A/c Dr | | 2,16,000 | |
| | Loss on Issue of Debentures A/c (2,000 × 10) Dr | | 20,000 | |
| | To 10% Debentures A/c (2,000 × 100) | | | 2,00,000 |
| | To Securities Premium A/c (2,000 × 8) | | | 16,000 |
| | To Premium on Redemption of Debentures A/c (2,000 × 10) | | | 20,000 |
| | (Being issue of 10% debentures of ₹ 100 each at 8% premium redeemable at a premium of 10%) | | | |
| (ii) | Bank A/c (3,000 × 100) Dr | | 3,00,000 | |
| | To Debenture Application and Allotment A/c | | | 3,00,000 |
| | (Being debentures application money received) | | | |
| | Debenture Application and Allotment A/c Dr | | 3,00,000 | |
| | Loss on Issue of Debentures A/c (3,000 × 10) Dr | | 30,000 | |
| | To 10% Debentures A/c (3,000 × 100) | | | 3,00,000 |
| | To Premium on Redemption of Debentures A/c (3,000 × 10) | | | 30,000 |
| | (Being issue of 10% debentures of ₹ 100 each at par, repayable at a premium of 10%) | | | |

*Or*

**JOURNAL**

| Date | Particulars | LF | Amt (Dr) | Amt (Cr) |
|---|---|---|---|---|
| (i) | Furniture A/c Dr | | 2,20,000 | |
| | To M/s Furniture Mart | | | 2,20,000 |
| | (Being furniture purchased) | | | |
| (ii) | M/s Furniture Mart Dr | | 1,10,000 | |
| | To Bills Payable A/c | | | 1,10,000 |
| | (Being bills payable accepted in part payment) | | | |
| (iii) | M/s Furniture Mart Dr | | 1,10,000 | |
| | To 9% Debentures A/c (1,000 × 100) | | | 1,00,000 |
| | To Securities Premium A/c (1,000 × 10) | | | 10,000 |
| | (Being debentures issued to Furniture Mart in part payment) | | | |

**Working Note**

$$\text{Number of Debentures Issued} = \frac{\text{Amount due to M/s Furniture Mart}}{\text{Issue Price per Debenture}} = \frac{1,10,000}{110} = 1,000 \text{ debentures}$$

**6.** (i)

**JOURNAL**

| Date | Particulars | LF | Amt (Dr) | Amt (Cr) |
|---|---|---|---|---|
| (a) | Bank A/c (76,000 − 12,000) Dr | | 64,000 | |
| | To Realisation A/c | | | 64,000 |
| | (Being the debtors realised) | | | |
| (b) | Realisation A/c Dr | | 6,650 | |
| | To Parul's Capital A/c (7,000 × 95%) | | | 6,650 |
| | (Being husband's loan paid off by Parul) | | | |
| (c) | Payal's Capital A/c Dr | | 3,000 | |
| | To Realisation A/c | | | 3,000 |
| | (Being unrecorded machine taken by Payal) | | | |

**Value Points**

- Bad debts will decrease the debtors and the remaining amount will be received by the firm.
- Unrecorded assets are recorded at their realised value and not at their expected value.

(ii) **JOURNAL**

| Date | Particulars | | LF | Amt (Dr) | Amt (Cr) |
|---|---|---|---|---|---|
| (a) | Bank A/c | Dr | | 1,40,000 | |
| | To Realisation A/c | | | | 1,40,000 |
| | (Being payment received from creditors) | | | | |
| (b) | No Entry | | | | |
| (c) | Realisation A/c | Dr | | 45,000 | |
| | To Bank A/c | | | | 45,000 |
| | (Being partial payment made to creditors through cheque) | | | | |

7. (a) Division of profits as per partnership deed

Net profit for the year 2018-19 = ₹ 2,40,000

(–) Interest on capital to

Bimal $(5,00,000 \times 10\%)$ 50,000

Chetan $(3,50,000 \times 10\%)$ 35,000 = ₹ (85,000)

(–) Salary to Bimal $(5,000 \times 12)$ = ₹ (60,000)

Divisible profit = ₹ 95,000

Profit share of Bimal $= 95,000 \times 3/5 =$ ₹ 57,000; Profit share of Chetan $= 95,000 \times 2/5 =$ ₹ 38,000

Bimal's share $= 50,000 + 60,000 + 57,000 =$ ₹ 1,67,000; Chetan's share $= 35,000 + 38,000 =$ ₹ 73,000

(b) **JOURNAL**

| Date | Particulars | | LF | Amt (Dr) | Amt (Cr) |
|---|---|---|---|---|---|
| | Chetan's Capital A/c | Dr | | 55,000 | |
| | To Bimal's Capital A/c | | | | 55,000 |
| | (Being omission of salary and profits divided in wrong proportion, adjusted) | | | | |

**Working Note**

Division of profits without considering the provisions of partnership deed

Profit for the year 2018-19 = ₹ 2,40,000

(–) Interest on capitals to Bimal $(5,00,000 \times 10\%)$ 50,000

Chetan $(3,50,000 \times 10\%)$ 35,000 = ₹ (85,000)

Divisible profits = ₹ 1,55,000

Profit share of Bimal $\left(1,55,000 \times \frac{2}{5}\right) =$ ₹ 62,000; Profit share of Chetan $\left(1,55,000 \times \frac{3}{5}\right) =$ ₹ 93,000

Bimal's share $= (50,000 + 62,000) =$ ₹ 1,12,000; Chetan's share $= (35,000 + 93,000) =$ ₹ 1,28,000

8.

| S.No. | Items | Major Heads | Sub-heads |
|---|---|---|---|
| (i) | Premium on Redemption of Debentures | Non-current Liabilities | Other Long-term Liabilities |
| (ii) | Loose Tools | Current Assets | Inventories |
| (iii) | Balance with Banks | Current Assets | Cash and Cash Equivalents |
| (iv) | General Reserve | Shareholders' Funds | Reserves and Surplus |
| (v) | Stores and Spares | Current Assets | Inventories |
| (vi) | Mining Rights | Non-current Assets | Property, Plant & Equipment and Intangible Assets: Intangible Assets |
| (vii) | Subsidy Reserve | Shareholders' Funds | Reserves and Surplus |
| (viii) | Preliminary Expenses | Reserves and Surplus | Deducted from Securities Premium Reserve |

*Or* (i) **Notes to Accounts**

| Particulars | | | 31st March, 2022 (₹) |
|---|---|---|---|
| **Reserves and Surplus** | | | |
| (i) **Debenture Redemption Reserve** | | | |
| Opening Balance | | 10,00,000 | |
| (+) Transfer from Surplus i.e. Balance in Statement of Profit and Loss | | 2,00,000 | 12,00,000 |
| (ii) **Securities Premium** | | | |
| Opening Balance | | | 12,00,000 |
| (iii) **General Reserve** | | | |
| Opening Balance | | 0 | |
| (+) Transfer from Surplus i.e. Balance in Statement of Profit and Loss | | 2,50,000 | 2,50,000 |
| (iv) **Surplus i.e. Balance in Statement of Profit and Loss** | | | |
| Opening Balance | (3,00,000) | | |
| (+) Profit for the year | 10,00,000 | 7,00,000 | |
| (–) Appropriations : Debenture Redemption Reserve | 2,00,000 | | |
| General Reserve | 2,50,000 | | |
| Proposed Dividend | 1,50,000 | (6,00,000) | 1,00,000 |
| **Total** (i + ii + iii + iv) (To be shown in the Balance Sheet against Reserves and Surplus) | | | 27,50,000 |

(ii) Proposed dividend will be shown in equity and liabilities part of balance sheet as under

| Particulars | Amt (₹) |
|---|---|
| **Current Liabilities** | |
| Short-term Provisions | |
| Proposed Dividend | 1,50,000 |

**Common Mistake** Students usually forget to decrease the amount of profit after tax as various reserves are being created. It should be noted that the amount of increase in a reserve will reduce the profit after tax.

**9.** (a) Applied and allotted shares of defaulters

| | Category (i) | Category (ii) | Category (iii) |
|---|---|---|---|
| Applied shares | 1,000 | $1,200 \times \frac{4}{3} = 1,600$ | $1,200 \times \frac{3}{2} = 1,800$ |
| Allotted shares | 1,000 | 1,200 | 1,200 |

(b) Arrears on allotment

| Particulars | Category (i) | Category (ii) |
|---|---|---|
| Due on allotment | 4,000 | 4,800 |
| (–) Excess money | Nil | (2,000) |
| | ₹ 4,000 | ₹ 2,800 |

Total arrears on allotment (4,000 + 2,800) = ₹ 6,800

(c) Total calls-in-arrears = 6,800 + 6,800 + 1,200 = ₹ 14,800

where, Arrears on allotment = ₹ 6,800

Arrears on first call (3,400 ×2) = ₹ 6,800

Arrears on second and final call (1,200 ×1) = ₹ 1,200

(d) Allotment of shares

| Categories | Applied Shares | Allotted Shares | Ratio |
|---|---|---|---|
| (i) | 1,00,000 | 1,00,000 | 1 : 1 |
| (ii) | 80,000 | 60,000 | 4 : 3 |
| (iii) | 60,000 | 40,000 | 3 : 2 |
| | 2,40,000 | 2,00,000 | |

(e)

**JOURNAL**

| Date | Particulars | | LF | Amt (Dr) | Amt (Cr) |
|---|---|---|---|---|---|
| • | Share Capital A/c (2,200 × 9) | Dr | | 19,800 | |
| | Securities Premium A/c (2,200 × 2) | Dr | | 4,400 | |
| | To Share Forfeiture A/c (1,000 × 5 +1,200 × 5 + 2,000) | | | | 13,000 |
| | To Share Allotment A/c (2,200 × 4 – 2,000) | | | | 6,800 |
| | To Share First Call A/c (2,200 × 2) | | | | 4,400 |
| | (Being 2,200 shares forfeited issued at a premium of ₹ 2 per share for non-payment of allotment and first call) | | | | |
| | Share Capital A/c (1,200 × 10) | Dr | | 12,000 | |
| | To Share Forfeiture A/c (1,200 × 7) | | | | 8,400 |
| | To Share First Call A/c (1,200 × 2) | | | | 2,400 |
| | To Share Second and Final Call A/c (1,200 × 1) | | | | 1,200 |
| | (Being 1,200 shares forfeited for non-payment of first and final call) | | | | |
| • | Bank A/c (1,300 × 8) | Dr | | 10,400 | |
| | Share Forfeiture A/c (1,300 × 2) | Dr | | 2,600 | |
| | To Share Capital A/c (1,300 × 10) | | | | 13,000 |
| | (Being 1,300 shares re-issued at ₹ 8 per share, fully paid-up) | | | | |
| | Share Forfeiture A/c | Dr | | 4,400 | |
| | To Capital Reserve A/c | | | | 4,400 |
| | (Being profit on forfeitures transferred to capital reserve account) | | | | |

**Working Note**

**Calculation of Capital Reserve**

| Particulars | Amt (₹) |
|---|---|
| Amount forfeited on 1,000 shares @ ₹ 5 | 5,000 |
| Amount forfeited on 300 shares $\left(\frac{8,000}{1,200} \times 300\right)$ | 2,000 |
| Amount forfeited on re-issue of forfeited shares | 7,000 |
| (–) Loss on re-issue of forfeited shares | (2,600) |
| Net gain after re-issue | 4,400 |

*Or*

**JOURNAL**

| Date | Particulars | | LF | Amt (Dr) | Amt (Cr) |
|---|---|---|---|---|---|
| | Bank A/c (4,00,000 × 3) | Dr | | 12,00,000 | |
| | To Equity Share Application A/c | | | | 12,00,000 |
| | (Being application money received on 4,00,000 shares) | | | | |
| | Equity Share Application A/c | Dr | | 12,00,000 | |
| | To Equity Share Capital A/c (3, 20,000 × 2) | | | | 6,40,000 |
| | To Securities Premium A/c (3, 20,000 × 1) | | | | 3,20,000 |
| | To Equity Share Allotment A/c | | | | 1,20,000 |
| | To Bank A/c (40,000 × 3) | | | | 1,20,000 |
| | (Being amount of application money transferred to share capital and excess money is adjusted towards allotment) | | | | |

| Date | Particulars | | LF | Amt (Dr) | Amt (Cr) |
|---|---|---|---|---|---|
| | Equity Share Allotment A/c (3, 20,000 × 5) | Dr | | 16,00,000 | |
| | To Equity Share Capital A/c (3, 20,000 × 3) | | | | 9,60,000 |
| | To Securities Premium A/c (3, 20, 000 × 2) | | | | 6,40,000 |
| | (Being amount due on allotment) | | | | |
| | Bank A/c (16,00,000 – 1,20,000 – 3,700) | Dr | | 14,76,300 | |
| | To Equity Share Allotment A/c | | | | 14,76,300 |
| | (Being amount received on allotment) | | | | |
| | Equity Share Capital A/c (800 × 5) | Dr | | 4,000 | |
| | Securities Premium A/c (800 × 2) | Dr | | 1,600 | |
| | To Share Forfeited A/c | | | | 1,900 |
| | To Share Allotment A/c | | | | 3,700 |
| | (Being 800 shares of Jeevan forfeited due to non-payment of allotment money) | | | | |
| | Equity Share First and Final Call A/c (3,19, 200 × 7) | Dr | | 22,34,400 | |
| | To Equity Share Capital A/c (3,19, 200 × 5) | | | | 15,96,000 |
| | To Securities Premium A/c (3,19, 200 × 2) | | | | 6,38,400 |
| | (Being amount due on first and final call on 3,19,200 shares) | | | | |
| | Bank A/c ( 22,34,400 – 16,800) | Dr | | 22,17,600 | |
| | To Equity Share First and Final Call A/c | | | | 22,17,600 |
| | (Being amount received on first and final call account) | | | | |
| | Equity Share Capital A/c | Dr | | 24,000 | |
| | Securities Premium A/c | Dr | | 4,800 | |
| | To Equity Share Forfeited A/c | | | | 12,000 |
| | To Equity Share First and Final Call A/c | | | | 16,800 |
| | (Being Ganesh's shares forfeited) | | | | |
| | Bank A/c (1,500 × 8) | Dr | | 12,000 | |
| | Share Forfeiture A/c (1,500 × 2) | Dr | | 3,000 | |
| | To Equity Share Capital A/c (1,500 × 10) | | | | 15,000 |
| | (Being forfeited shares re-issued @ ₹ 8 per share fully paid-up) | | | | |
| | Equity Share Forfeiture A/c | Dr | | 2,400 | |
| | To Capital Reserve A/c | | | | 2,400 |
| | (Being excess amount on forfeiture transferred to capital reserve) | | | | |

**Working Note**

**Computation Table**

| Categories | Shares applied | Shares allotted | Money received on application @ ₹ 3 each | Money transferred to share capital @ ₹ 2 each | Money transferred to securities premium @ ₹ 1 each | Excess application money | Amount adjusted on allotment | Money refunded |
|---|---|---|---|---|---|---|---|---|
| I | 40,000 | – | 1,20,000 | – | – | 1,20,000 | – | 1,20,000 |
| II | 3,60,000 | 3,20,000 | 10,80,000 | 6,40,000 | 3,20,000 | 1,20,000 | 1,20,000 | – |
| | 4,00,000 | 3,20,000 | 12,00,000 | 6,40,000 | 3,20,000 | 2,40,000 | 1,20,000 | 1,20,000 |

**Calculation of Amount Unpaid on Allotment**

Shares applied by Jeevan $\left(\frac{3,60,000}{3,20,000} \times 800\right) = 900$ shares

Excess money received from Jeevan (100 × 3) = ₹ 300

| | | |
|---|---|---|
| Amount due on allotment (800 × 3) | = ₹ | 2,400 |
| (–) Excess application money | = ₹ | (300) |
| Amount unpaid on allotment | = ₹ | 2,100 |
| Amount unpaid on securities premium reserve (800 × 2) | = ₹ | 1,600 |
| Total amount unpaid on allotment | = ₹ | 3,700 |

**Calculation of Amount Received from Jeevan**

Amount received on application = 1,600 $(800 \times 2)$ excluding premium

(+) Excess application money = 300

1,900

**Unpaid Amount of First and Final Call**

Shares allotted to Ganesh $= \frac{3,20,000}{3,60,000} \times 2,700 = 2,400$ shares

Unpaid amount on first and final call $(2,400 \times 7) =$ ₹ 16,800

**Calculation of Amount Received from Gupta**

Amount received on application = ₹ 4,800 $(2,400 \times 2)$ excluding premium

(+) Amount received on allotment = ₹ 7,200 $(2,400 \times 3)$

= ₹ 12,000

**Calculation of Capital Reserve**

(i) 800 shares of Jeevan

Share forfeiture (Cr) = ₹ 1,900

(–) Share forfeiture (Dr) = ₹ (1,600) $(800 \times 2)$

Capital reserve 300

(ii) 200 shares of Ganesh

Share forfeiture (Cr) = ₹ 3,500 $\left(\frac{12,000}{2,400} \times 700\right)$

(–) Share forfeiture (Dr) = ₹ (1,400) $(700 \times 2)$

Capital reserve ₹ 2,100

Total capital reserve = ₹ 2,400 (2,100 + 300)

10. (A) (a) Dr **Revaluation Account** Cr

| Particulars | | Amt (₹) | Particulars | Amt (₹) |
|---|---|---|---|---|
| To Stock A/c | | 1,800 | By Premises A/c | 32,000 |
| To Provision for Legal Damages A/c | | 2,400 | By Provision for Doubtful Debts A/c | 200 |
| To Profit transferred to | | | By Furniture A/c | 8,000 |
| P's Capital A/c | 18,000 | | | |
| N's Capital A/c | 24,000 | | | |
| S's Capital A/c | 6,000 | 36,000 | | |
| | | 40,200 | | 40,200 |

(b) Dr **Partners' Capital Account** Cr

| Particulars | P (₹) | N (₹) | S (₹) | Particulars | P (₹) | N (₹) | S (₹) |
|---|---|---|---|---|---|---|---|
| To N's Capital A/c | 28,000 | — | — | By Balance b/d | 92,000 | 60,000 | 40,000 |
| To N's Loan A/c | — | 52,000 | — | By General Reserve A/c | 12,000 | 8,000 | 4,000 |
| To Bank A/c | — | 56,000 | — | By Revaluation A/c (Profit) | 18,000 | 12,000 | 6,000 |
| To Balance c/d | 94,000 | — | 50,000 | By P's Capital A/c | — | 28,000 | — |
| | 1,22,000 | 1,08,000 | 50,000 | | 1,22,000 | 1,08,000 | 50,000 |

**Working Notes**

1. Gaining ratio of remaining partners

$P\text{'s gain} = \frac{5}{6} - \frac{3}{6} = \frac{5-3}{6} = \frac{2}{6};$ $\quad S\text{'s gain} = \frac{1}{6} - \frac{1}{6} = 0$

Only P has gained on N's retirement. Hence, contribution of goodwill for retiring partner will be made by P.

2. General reserve is to be distributed among all the partners in old ratio.

3. N's share of goodwill $= 84,000 \times 2/6 =$ ₹ 28,000

(c) **Balance Sheet**
as at 1st April, 2023

| Liabilities | | Amt (₹) | Assets | | Amt (₹) |
|---|---|---|---|---|---|
| Sundry Creditors | | 30,000 | Sundry Debtors | 12,000 | |
| Bills Payable | | 24,000 | (–) Provision for Doubtful Debts | (600) | 11,400 |
| Outstanding Salary | | 4,400 | Stock | | 16,200 |
| Provision for Legal Damages | | 14,400 | Furniture | | 90,000 |
| Bank Loan | | 40,800 | Premises | | 1,92,000 |
| N's Loan | | 52,000 | | | |
| Capital A/cs | | | | | |
| P | 94,000 | | | | |
| S | 50,000 | 1,44,000 | | | |
| | | 3,09,600 | | | 3,09,600 |

(B) **JOURNAL**

| Date | Particulars | | LF | Amt (Dr) | Amt (Cr) |
|---|---|---|---|---|---|
| | R's Capital A/c (30,000 × 1/6) | Dr | | 5,000 | |
| | S's Capital A/c (30,000 × 5/6) | Dr | | 25,000 | |
| | To N's Capital A/c | | | | 30,000 |
| | (Being N's share of goodwill adjusted to the capital accounts of R and S in their gaining ratio of 1 : 5) | | | | |

**Working Notes**

1. **Calculation of Gaining Ratio**

   Gaining Ratio = New Share – Old Share

   $R = \frac{1}{4} - \frac{1}{6} = \frac{3-2}{12} = \frac{1}{12}$; $S = \frac{3}{4} - \frac{2}{6} = \frac{9-4}{12} = \frac{5}{12}$; Gaining ratio $= \frac{1}{12} : \frac{5}{12}$ *or* 1 : 5

2. **Calculation of Hidden Goodwill**

| | Amt (₹) |
|---|---|
| Amount agreed to be paid in full settlement | 2,50,000 |
| (–) N's capital after all adjustments | (2,20,000) |
| Hidden goodwill | 30,000 |

*Or* (i)

| Date | Particulars | | LF | Amt (Dr) | Amt (Cr) |
|---|---|---|---|---|---|
| | General Reserve A/c | Dr | | 15,000 | |
| | Profit and Loss A/c | Dr | | 9,000 | |
| | To L's Capital A/c | | | | 14,400 |
| | To M's Capital A/c | | | | 9,600 |
| | (Being transfer of general reserve and profit to old partners) | | | | |

(ii)

| Date | Particulars | | LF | Amt (Dr) | Amt (Cr) |
|---|---|---|---|---|---|
| | Investment Fluctuation Reserve A/c [4,500 – (60,000 – 57,000)] | Dr | | 1,500 | |
| | Contingency Reserve A/c | Dr | | 1,350 | |
| | To L's Capital A/c | | | | 1,710 |
| | To M's Capital A/c | | | | 1,140 |
| | (Being transfer of investment fluctuation reserve and contingency reserve to old partners) | | | | |

(iii) No entry required. Machinery replacement fund is in the nature of accumulated depreciation and not in nature of accumulated profits and hence is not distributed among the partners.

(iv)

| Date | Particulars | | LF | Amt (Dr) | Amt (Cr) |
|---|---|---|---|---|---|
| | L's Capital A/c | Dr | | 1,800 | |
| | M's Capital A/c | Dr | | 1,200 | |
| | To Advertisement Expenditure A/c | | | | 3,000 |
| | (Being the transfer of deferred expenditure losses to old partners in their old profits sharing ratio) | | | | |

(v)

| Date | Particulars | | LF | Amt (Dr) | Amt (Cr) |
|---|---|---|---|---|---|
| | Workmen Compensation Reserve A/c [3,600 – 450] | Dr | | 3,150 | |
| | To L's Capital A/c | | | | 1,890 |
| | To M's Capital A/c | | | | 1,260 |
| | (Being transfer of general reserve and profit to old partners) | | | | |

11. (i) • (*d*) Relative • Net profit ratio
(ii) (*a*) A, B and C
(iii) Investors are interested in analysing financial statements to assess the safety of their investment and ensuring of returns regularly. Management is interested in analysing financial statements to know the performance of the business as a whole and short-term and long-term solvency position of the business firm.
(iv) Investing activities
(v) Let the amount of current liabilities to be paid = ₹ $x$

Current ratio after making payment = 2 : 1

$$\text{Current Ratio} = \frac{\text{Current Assets}}{\text{Current Liabilities}}$$

$$\frac{2}{1} = \frac{6,00,000 - x}{4,00,000 - x}$$

$$8,00,000 - 2x = 6,00,000 - x$$

$$8,00,000 - 6,00,000 = 2x - x$$

$$₹\ 2,00,000 = x$$

∴ Current liabilities to be paid-off is ₹ 2,00,000

12.

**Comparative Statement of Profit and Loss**

for the year ended 31st March, 2022-23

| Particulars | Absolute Figures | | Change | |
|---|---|---|---|---|
| | 31st March, 2022 (₹) | 31st March, 2023 (₹) | 31st March, 2023 (₹) | (%) |
| I. Revenue from Operations | 10,00,000 | 15,00,000 | 5,00,000 | 50% |
| II. Other Incomes | 2,00,000 | 1,80,000 | (20,000) | (10%) |
| III. Total Revenue (I + II) | 12,00,000 | 16,80,000 | 4,80,000 | 40% |
| IV. Expenses | 6,00,000 | 10,05,000 | 4,50,000 | 75% |
| V. Profit before Tax (III – IV) | 6,00,000 | 6,30,000 | 30,000 | 5% |
| VI. Tax (50%) | (3,00,000) | (3,15,000) | (15,000) | (5%) |
| VII. Profit after Tax (V – VI) | 3,00,000 | 3,15,000 | 15,000 | 5% |

13.

**Cash Flow Statement**

for the year ending 31st March, 2023

| Particulars | | Amt (₹) |
|---|---|---|
| A. **Cash Flow from Operating Activities** | | |
| Net Profit before Tax and Extraordinary Items | | 75,000 |
| (+) Non-cash and Non-operating Expenses | | |
| Goodwill Written-off | 54,000 | |
| Depreciation on Machinery | 49,500 | |
| Loss on Sale of Machinery | 1,500 | 1,05,000 |

| Particulars | | Amt (₹) |
|---|---|---|
| Operating Profit before Working Capital Changes | | 1,80,000 |
| (−) Increase in Current Assets and Decrease in Current Liabilities | | |
| Trade Receivables | (20,250) | |
| Inventories | (6,000) | |
| Trade Payables | (18,750) | |
| Short-term Provisions | (20,250) | (65,250) |
| Cash Flow from Operating Activities | | 1,14,750 |
| B. **Cash Flow from Investing Activities** | | |
| Purchase of Machinery | (2,20,500) | |
| Sale of Machinery | 4,500 | |
| Cash Used in Investing Activities | | (2,16,000) |
| C. **Cash Flow from Financing Activities** | | |
| Issue of Share Capital | 75,000 | |
| Money Raised from Borrowings | 52,500 | |
| Cash Flow from Financing Activities | | 1,27,500 |
| D. Net Increase in Cash and Cash Equivalents (A + B + C) | | 26,250 |
| E. Opening Balance of Cash and Cash Equivalents | | |
| Current Investments | 1,12,500 | |
| Cash and Cash Equivalents | 2,81,250 | 3,93,750 |
| F. Closing Balance of Cash and Cash Equivalents | | |
| Current Investments | 1,80,000 | |
| Cash and Cash Equivalents | 2,40,000 | 4,20,000 |

**Working Notes**

1. Dr **Machinery Account** Cr

| Particulars | Amt (₹) | Particulars | Amt (₹) |
|---|---|---|---|
| To Balance b/d | 7,50,000 | By Bank A/c (Sale) | 4,500 |
| To Bank A/c (Purchase) (Balancing figure) | 2,20,500 | By Accumulated Depreciation A/c | 12,000 |
| | | By Loss on Sale of Machinery A/c | 1,500 |
| | | By Balance c/d | 9,52,500 |
| | 9,70,500 | | 9,70,500 |

2. Dr **Accumulated Depreciation Account** Cr

| Particulars | Amt (₹) | Particulars | Amt (₹) |
|---|---|---|---|
| To Machinery A/c | 12,000 | By Balance b/d | 1,12,500 |
| To Balance c/d | 1,50,000 | By Depreciation A/c (Balancing figure) | 49,500 |
| | 1,62,000 | | 1,62,000 |

*Or* (a) Dr **Property, Plant and Equipment** (Machinery) **Account** Cr

| Particulars | Amt (₹) | Particulars | Amt (₹) |
|---|---|---|---|
| To Balance b/d | 4,50,000 | By Depreciation A/c | 1,00,000 |
| To Bank A/c (Purchases)(Balance Transferred) | 4,50,000 | By Balance c/d | 8,00,000 |
| | 9,00,000 | | 9,00,000 |

(b)

| Particulars | | Amt (₹) |
|---|---|---|
| **Cash Flow from Operations before Tax** | | |
| Net Profit before Tax [(2,50,000 − 2,00,000) + 40,000] | | 90,000 |
| **Adjustments for** | | |
| (+) Depreciation on Machinery | 1,00,000 | |
| Interest on Deposits | 22,500 | |
| Goodwill Written-off | 30,000 | 1,52,500 |
| Operating Profit before Working Capital Changes | | 2,42,500 |

| Particulars | | Amt (₹) |
|---|---|---|
| (–) Increase in Current Assets and Decrease in Current Liabilities | | |
| Inventories | (25,000) | |
| Trade Receivables | (1,00,000) | (1,25,000) |
| Cash Flow from Operations | | 1,17,500 |

(c)

| Particulars | | Amt (₹) |
|---|---|---|
| **Cash Flow from Financing Activities** | | |
| Issue of Shares | 2,00,000 | |
| 9% Deposits Raised | 2,00,000 | |
| Interest Paid | (22,500) | |
| Net Cash Generated from Financing Activities | | 3,77,500 |

**14.** (i) Inventory Turnover Ratio $= \frac{\text{Cost of Revenue from Operations}}{\text{Average Inventory}} = \frac{3,20,000}{64,000}$

Inventory Turnover Ratio = 5 times

Cost of Revenue from Operations = Opening Inventory + Net Purchases + Carriage + Wages – Closing Inventory
= 60,000 + 2,50,000 + 20,000 + 58,000 – 68,000 = ₹ 3,20,000

Average Inventory $= \frac{\text{Opening Inventory} + \text{Closing Inventory}}{2} = \frac{60,000 + 68,000}{2} =$ ₹ 64,000

(ii) Operating Ratio $= \frac{\text{Cost of Revenue from Operations} + \text{Other Operating Expenses} - \text{Operating Incomes}}{\text{Net Revenue from Operations}} \times 100$

$= \frac{3,20,000 + 10,000 - 5,000}{5,00,000} \times 100$

∴ Operating Ratio = 65%

Cost of revenue from operations = ₹ 3,20,000

Other operating expenses = Office and selling expenses = 30,000 – 20,000 = ₹ 10,000

Other operating incomes = Discount received = ₹ 5,000

(iii) Net Profit Ratio $= \frac{\text{Net Profit}}{\text{Revenue from Operations}} \times 100 = \frac{1,35,800}{5,00,000} \times 100 = 27.16\%$

(iv) Operating Profit Ratio + Operating Ratio = 100%

Operating Profit Ratio = 100% – 65% = 35%

SQP Code : **PB-8/15** Series ***i*-Succeed 8-25/15** Roll No. | | | | | | | | |

# Sample Question Paper 08

## Accounts 12th (Code 858)

**General Instructions**

1. Candidates are allowed additional 15 minutes for only reading the paper. They must not start writing during this time.
2. Section-A is compulsory for all candidates and has ten questions.
3. Candidates have to attempt all questions from either Section-B or Section-C*.
4. Internal choices have been provided in five questions in Section-A and one question in Section-B.
5. The intended marks for questions or parts of questions are given in the brackets [ ].
6. All calculations should be shown clearly.
7. All workings, including rough work, should be done on the same page as, and adjacent to, the rest of the answer.

*Section-C has not been covered.

**Time : 3 Hrs.**

**Max. Marks : 80**

## Section A Answer All Questions [60 Marks]

**Que 1.**

In sub-parts (i) to (iv), choose the correct option and in sub-parts (v) to (x) answer the questions as instructed.

(i) Natsya Ltd. issued 2,000, 10% debentures of ₹ 100 each at a discount of 10%, redeemable at a premium of 10% after 4 years on 1st April, 2023. Interest is payable on 31st March every year.

The journal entry for the accruing of interest amount to debentureholders' on 31st March, 2024 will be (Application) [1]

| | | | | |
|---|---|---|---|---|
| (a) | Interest A/c | Dr | 20,000 | |
| | To Debentureholders' A/c | | | 20,000 |
| (b) | Debentureholders' A/c | Dr | 10,000 | |
| | To Interest A/c | | | 10,000 |
| (c) | Debentureholders' A/c | Dr | 25,000 | |
| | To Interest A/c | | | 25,000 |
| (d) | Interest A/c | Dr | 10,000 | |
| | To Debentureholders' A/c | | | 10,000 |

(ii) Choose the correct order for the following in relation to their appearance in the balance sheet.

A – Short-term Provision
B – Trade Payables
C – Reserves and Surplus
D – Non-current Assets (Recall) [1]

**Codes**

(a) C, B, A, D (b) A, B, C, D
(c) D, C, A, B (d) B, C, D, A

(iii) As a purchase consideration of a machinery of ₹ 7,20,000, debentures of ₹ 100 each were issued at a premium of ₹ 25 by the company. The number of debentures issued by the company is (Application) [1]

(a) 7,000 (b) 5,700
(c) 5,760 (d) 7,200

(iv) Court cannot pass the order to dissolve the firm, when ……… . (Understanding) [1]

(a) partners' become incapable permanently
(b) partnership agreement persistently followed by partners

(c) business of the firm cannot be carried except at a loss

(d) partner transfer whole of its interest to a third party

(v) At the time of dissolution of partnership firm, what will be the journal entry for the settlement of loan advanced by the firm to a partner? (Application) [1]

(vi) **Assertion** (A) The relevant provisions of the Indian Companies Act, 2013 become applicable if partnership deed is silent regarding remuneration to the partners.

**Reason** (R) If a partner has given loan to the firm, he is entitled to interest on such amount @ 6% p.a., if the partnership deed is silent. (Evaluate) [1]

**Alternatives**

(a) Both Assertion (A) and Reason (R) are true and Reason (R) is the correct explanation of Assertion (A)

(b) Both Assertion (A) and Reason (R) are true, but Reason (R) is not the correct explanation of Assertion (A)

(c) Assertion (A) is false, but Reason (R) is true

(d) Assertion (A) is true, but Reason (R) is false

(vii) Jinn Limited purchased a machinery of ₹ 21,00,000 from Dinn Limited and issued equity shares of ₹ 100 each at a premium of 5% for the purchase consideration. Pass the entry for shares issued to Dinn Limited by Jinn Limited. (Application) [1]

(viii) If the retiring partner is not paid the full amount due to him immediately on retirement, how should his capital account be shown in the subsequent balance sheet? (Understanding) [1]

(ix) Capital reserves are an essential aspect of financial statements that reflect the financial fitness and legitimacy of a corporation.

Adequate liquidity and profitability make an enterprise stand out in the competition, and proper management of these reserves plays a critical role in their success.

**Source** *Live mint*

(a) What are capital reserves?

(b) Apart from capital reserves, name other reserves that a company can maintain. (Recall) [1]

(x) Goodwill of firm is ₹ 1,07,500. Find the number of years' purchased if the average profits are ₹ 43,000. (Application) [1]

**Que 2.**

ITI Ltd. issued 2,00,000, 8% debentures of ₹ 10 each at ₹ 12 on 1st April, 2021. The issue was fully subscribed. In terms of the issue of debentures, interest was payable at the end of the financial year. Pass the journal entries for the above transaction. (Application) [3]

*Or*

On 1st May, 2017 Solar Energy Ltd. issued 50,000, 9% debentures of ₹ 100 each at a discount of 10% redeemable at par after five years. All the debentures were subscribed.

It has a balance of ₹ 3,00,000 in securities premium which the company decided to use for writing-off the loss and also decided to write-off the remaining discount in the first year itself.

You are required to

(i) Pass the journal entries for issue of debentures.

(ii) Pass the journal entry for writing-off the discount.

(iii) Prepare discount on issue of debentures account. (Application)

**Que 3.**

Nutan, Sumit and Shiba are partners in a firm, sharing profits in the ratio of 5 : 3 : 2. On 31st December, 2021, their balance sheet was as under

**Balance Sheet**

as at 31st December, 2021

| Liabilities | | Amt (₹) | Assets | Amt (₹) |
|---|---|---|---|---|
| Creditors | | 52,000 | Building | 60,000 |
| Reserve Fund | | 15,000 | Plant | 50,000 |
| Capital A/cs | | | Stock | 27,000 |
| Nutan | 60,000 | | Debtors | 25,000 |
| Sumit | 45,000 | | Cash | 10,000 |
| Shiba | 30,000 | 1,35,000 | Bank | 30,000 |
| | | 2,02,000 | | 2,02,000 |

Nutan died on 1st July, 2022. It was agreed between her executor and the remaining partners that

(i) Goodwill to be valued at 2½ years' purchase of the average profits of the last 4 years, which were 2018 ₹ 25,000; 2019 ₹ 20,000; 2020 ₹ 40,000 and 2021 ₹ 35,000.

(ii) Building is valued at ₹ 70,000, plant at ₹ 46,000 and stock at ₹ 32,000.

(iii) Profit for the year 2022 be taken as having accrued at the same rate as that of the previous year.

(iv) Interest on capital is provided at 9% per annum.

(v) On 1st July, 2022, her drawings account showed a balance of ₹ 20,000.

(a) Prepare revaluation account.

(b) Prepare Nutan's capital account as at 1st July, 2022. (Application) [3]

**Que 4.**

Anmol Ltd. company issued debentures of ₹ 1,00,000 which were issued as follows

(i) For cash at 90% ₹ 50,000 (nominal).

(ii) To vendor ₹ 40,000 against asset purchased (Nominal value ₹ 50,000).

Pass journal entries. (Application) [3]

**Que 5.**

On 1st April, 2020, Brij and Nandan entered into partnership to construct toilets in government girls schools in the remote areas of Uttarakhand. Brij contributed capital of ₹ 10,00,000. Their profit sharing ratio was 2 : 3 and interest allowed on capital as provided in the partnership deed was 12% per annum. Salary of ₹ 1,80,000 was payable to Nandan. During the year ended 31st March, 2023, the firm earned a profit of ₹ 2,00,000.

SP-08

You are required to

(i) Give the amount of

(a) Interest on capital of Brij to be transferred to profit and loss appropriation account.

(b) Amount of Nandan's salary to be transferred to profit and loss appropriation account. [2]

(ii) Prepare profit and loss appropriation account of Brij and Nandan for the year ended 31st March, 2023. (Application) [1]

*Or*

Nitin, Megha, Priyanka and Ankit are partners. Their capital accounts on 1st April, 2022 were ₹ 60,000, ₹ 1,00,000, ₹ 1,60,000 and ₹ 2,00,000 respectively.

After the accounts for the year ended 31st March, 2023 have been prepared, it is discovered that interest @ 5% as provided in the partnership agreement has not been credited to partners' capital accounts before distributing profits.

So, it is decided to make adjusting entry at the beginning of the next year.

You are required to

(i) State the profit sharing ratio of the partners.

(ii) Give the necessary journal entry along with working notes. (Application) [3]

**Que 6.**

Ashish and Kanav were partners in a firm sharing profits and losses in the ratio of 3 : 2. On 31st March, 2022 their balance sheet was as follows

**Balance Sheet of Ashish and Kanav**
as at 31st March, 2022

| Liabilities | | Amt (₹) | Assets | Amt (₹) |
|---|---|---|---|---|
| Trade Creditors | | 42,000 | Bank | 35,000 |
| Empolyees' Provident Fund | | 60,000 | Stock | 24,000 |
| | | | Debtors | 19,000 |
| Mrs. Ashish's Loan | | 9,000 | Furniture | 40,000 |
| Kanav's Loan | | 35,000 | Plant | 2,10,000 |
| Workmen's Compensation Fund | | 20,000 | Investments | 32,000 |
| Investment Fluctuation Reserve | | 4,000 | Profit and Loss A/c | 10,000 |
| Capital A/cs | | | | |
| Ashish | 1,20,000 | | | |
| Kanav | 80,000 | 2,00,000 | | |
| | | 3,70,000 | | 3,70,000 |

On the above date, they decided to dissolve the firm.

(i) Ashish agreed to take over furniture at ₹ 38,000 and pay-off Mrs. Ashish's loan.

(ii) Debtors realised ₹ 18,500 and plant realised 10% more.

(iii) Kanav took over 40% of the stock at 20% less than the book value. Remaining stock was sold at a gain of 10%.

(iv) Trade creditors took over investments in full settlement.

(v) Kanav agreed to take over the responsibility of completing dissolution at an agreed remuneration of ₹ 12,000 and to bear realisation expenses. Actual expenses of realisation amounted to ₹ 8,000.

Prepare realisation account. (Application) [6]

**Que 7.**

Rinki, Pinki and Dinki are partners in a firm. Their capital accounts stood at ₹ 2,00,000, ₹ 1,50,000 and ₹1,00,000 respectively on 1st April, 2021. They shared profits and losses in the ratio of 3 : 2 : 1 respectively.

Partners are entitled to interest on capital @ 6% per annum and salary to Pinki and Dinki @ ₹ 1,000 per month and ₹ 1,500 per quarter respectively, as per the provisions of partnership deed. Pinki's share of profit including interest on capital but excluding salary is guaranteed at a minimum of ₹ 20,500 per annum. Any deficiency arising on that account shall be met by Dinki. Profit for the year ended 31st March, 2022 amounted to ₹ 78,000.

You are required to

(i) Ascertain the Pinki's deficiency amount. [1]

(ii) Prepare profit and loss appropriation account for the year ended 31st March, 2022. (Application) [5]

*Or*

Praveen, Sahil and Riya are partners having fixed capitals of ₹ 2,00,000, ₹ 1,60,000 and ₹ 1,20,000 respectively. They share profits in the ratio of 3 : 1 : 1. The partnership deed provided for the following which were not recorded in the books

(i) Interest on capital @ 5% per annum.

(ii) Salary to Praveen ₹ 1,500 per month and to Riya ₹ 1,000 per month.

(iii) Transfer of profit to general reserve ₹ 10,000. Net profit for the year ended 31st March, 2021 was ₹ 1,00,000.

Pass necessary rectifying entry for the above adjustments in the books of the firm. Also show your workings clearly. (Application) [6]

**Que 8.**

(i) From the following information extracted from the books of ABC Ltd. prepare the balance sheet of the company as at 31st March, 2022 as per Schedule III of the Companies Act, 2013.

Long-term Provisions ₹ 30,000; Short-term Borrowings ₹ 12,000; Other Current Liabilities ₹ 6,000; Short-term Provisions ₹ 18,000; Share Capital ₹ 26,000; Property, Plant and Equipment ₹ 42,000; Inventories ₹ 8,000; Other Current Assets ₹ 9,000; Cash and Cash Equivalents ₹ 11,000; Short-term loan and advances ₹ 22,000.

(ii) From the following information, prepare relevant notes to accounts.

Buildings ₹ 80,000, Plant and Equipment ₹ 1,00,000, Furniture and Fixtures ₹ 50,000, Goodwill ₹ 30,000, Securities Premium ₹ 60,000, Revaluation Reserve ₹ 45,000, Finished Goods ₹ 25,000, Stores and Spares ₹ 15,000, Capital Advances ₹ 30,000, Security Deposits ₹ 12,000, Provision for Doubtful Debts ₹ 15,000 and Provision for Tax ₹ 40,000. (Application) [6]

SP-08

**Que 9.**

(A) Following is the balance sheet of Daksh, Taksh and Harsh as on 31st March, 2021, who have agreed to share profits and losses in proportion to their capital

**Balance Sheet**

as at 31st March, 2021

| Liabilities | | Amt (₹) | Assets | | Amt (₹) |
|---|---|---|---|---|---|
| Capital A/cs | | | Building | | 1,20,000 |
| Daksh | 1,20,000 | | Machinery | | 1,80,000 |
| Taksh | 1,80,000 | | Stock | | 60,000 |
| Harsh | 1,20,000 | 4,20,000 | Debtors | 66,000 | |
| Employees Provident Fund | | 21,000 | (–) Provision for Doubtful Debts | (6,000) | 60,000 |
| Workmen Compensation Reserve | | 9,000 | Bank | | 60,000 |
| Creditors | | 30,000 | | | |
| | | 4,80,000 | | | 4,80,000 |

On 31st March, 2021, Daksh retired from the firm and the remaining partners decided to carry on the business. It was agreed to revalue the assets and reassess the liabilities on that date, on the following basis

(i) Building be appreciated by 30%.
(ii) The claim against workmen compensation was ₹ 4,500.
(iii) There were bad debts of ₹ 10,500.
(iv) Machinery be depreciated by 30%.
(v) Taksh and Harsh will share future profits in the ratio of 3 : 4.
(vi) Firms goodwill was valued at ₹ 84,000.
(vii) Capital of the new firm in total will be the same as before the retirement of Daksh and will be in the new profit sharing ratio of the continuing partners.
(viii) Amount due to Daksh will be settled by paying ₹ 30,000 in cash and balance by transferring to his loan account.

(a) Prepare revaluation account. [1½]
(b) Prepare partners' capital account. [4½]
(c) Prepare balance sheet of the new firm. (Application) [2]

(B) M, N and O are partners sharing profits in the ratio of 5 : 3 : 2. They have admitted P into the partnership on 1st April, 2023 for 1/4th share. An extract of their balance sheet on this date is as follows

**Balance Sheet**
**as at 1st April, 2023**

| Liabilities | Amt (₹) | Assets | Amt (₹) |
|---|---|---|---|
| Investment Fluctuation Reserve | 27,000 | Investment (Cost) | 3,00,000 |

Show the accounting treatment if the market value of investment is ₹ 2,70,000. (Application) [2]

*Or*

W and R are partners in a firm sharing profits in the ratio of 3 : 2. Their balance sheet as at 31st March, 2016 was as follows

**Balance Sheet**
**as at 31st March, 2016**

| Liabilities | | Amt (₹) | Assets | Amt (₹) |
|---|---|---|---|---|
| Sundry Creditors | | 20,000 | Cash | 12,000 |
| Provision for Bad Debts | | 2,000 | Debtors | 18,000 |
| Outstanding Salary | | 3,000 | Stock | 20,000 |
| General Reserve | | 5,000 | Furniture | 40,000 |
| Capital A/cs | | | Plant and Machinery | 40,000 |
| W | 60,000 | | | |
| R | 40,000 | 1,00,000 | | |
| | | 1,30,000 | | 1,30,000 |

On the above date, C was admitted for 1/6th share in the profits on the following terms

(i) C will bring ₹ 30,000 as his capital and ₹ 10,000 for his share of goodwill premium, half of which will be withdrawn by W and R.
(ii) Debtors ₹ 1,500 will be written-off as bad debts and a provision of 5% will be created for bad and doubtful debts.
(iii) Outstanding salary will be paid-off.

(iv) Stock will be depreciated by 10%, furniture by ₹ 500 and plant and machinery by 8%.
(v) Investments ₹ 2,500 not mentioned in the balance sheet were to be taken into account.

You are required to

(a) Pass the journal entries for the adjustment of goodwill. (Application) [2]

(b) Pass the journal entry for the transfer of general reserve. (Application) [2]

(c) Pass the journal entry for the transfer of outstanding salary. (Recall) [2]

(d) Pass the journal entries for the transfer of effects on revaluation account. (Application) [2]

(e) Pass the journal entry for the transfer of profit/ loss on revaluation to the partners' capital accounts. (Application) [2]

**Que 10.**

In 2023, Vayu Ltd. was registered with an authorised capital of ₹ 4,00,000 in equity shares of ₹ 10 each. Of these, 16,000 equity shares were issued as fully paid to vendors for the purchase of plant and machinery and the remaining 24,000 shares were subscribed for, by the public for cash. During the first year, ₹ 6 per equity share was called-up, on these 24,000 shares payable ₹ 3 on application, ₹ 1 on allotment and ₹ 2 on the first call.

The amount received in respect of these shares was as follows

On 20,000 shares, the full amount called

On 2,400 shares ₹ 4 per share

On 1,600 shares ₹ 3 per share

The company forfeited all those shares on which only ₹ 3 had been received and re-issued them at ₹ 4 per share, ₹ 6 paid-up. Journalise the transactions in the books of the company and prepare a calls-in-arrears account. (Application) [10]

*Or*

Sriram Finance India Ltd. has an authorised capital of ₹ 15,00,000 divided into 1,00,000 equity shares of ₹ 10 each and 50,000, 9% preference shares of ₹ 10 each. The company invited applications for all the preference shares but only 90,000 equity shares. All the preference shares were subscribed, called and paid while subscriptions were received for only 85,000 equity shares.

During the first year, ₹ 8 per share were called. Ram holding 1,000 shares and Shyam holding 2,000 shares did not pay first call of ₹ 2. Shyam's shares were forfeited after the first call and later on 1,500 of the forfeited shares were re-issued at ₹ 6 per share ₹ 8 called-up.

SP-08

(i) What is the amount of application and allotment received on equity shares? [1]

(ii) Calculate the amount of capital reserve, to be shown in the balance sheet. [1]

(iii) Calculate the amount of total issued capital. [1]

(iv) Show share capital in the balance sheet as per Schedule III as at 31st March, 2022. [2]

(v) Prepare relevant 'notes to accounts' showing

(a) Authorised capital [2]

(b) Subscribed capital (Application) [3]

## Section B

**[20 Marks]**

**Que 11.**

(i) A cash flow statement is a good tool for examining your past financial decisions, but it doesn't help you predict your business's future.

**Source** *Business.com*

Based on the above statement, which of the following is a limitation of cash flow statement? **(Recall) [1]**

(a) Non-cash transactions are not shown

(b) Facilitates comparative study

(c) Determines net change in cash and cash equivalent

(d) Ascertains liquidity and solvency

(ii) According to the legendary investor Peter Lynch, one can consider paying premium PE for high growth stocks. But he mentioned that a company with a PE of X must have EPS growth prospects of X % annually. Hence, I prefer avoiding HUL and Nestle stocks.

Hence, I can't justify buying them when I am seeing other good growth stocks available at reasonable PEs. Even if HUL and Nestle do keep going up forever, the fact that these stocks are already overbought implies that there is a very low chance that you will get great returns. At best, I will buy them only when there is a significant correction in price not before that at all.

**Source** *business daily*

As the above discussion is stating about the PE ratio, you are required to answer the following

- What is PE ratio? **(Recall)**
- Choose the correct formula for PE ratio. **(Recall) [1]**

(a) $\frac{\text{Net Profit after Tax and Preference Dividend}}{\text{Number of Equity Shares}}$ (b) $\frac{\text{Market Value of an Equity Share}}{\text{Earning per Share}}$

(c) $\frac{\text{Net Profit before Interest and Tax}}{\text{Capital Employed}} \times 100$ (d) None of these

(iii) Mahindra & Mahindra Limited reported earnings results for the first quarter ended 30th June, 2024. For the first quarter, the company reported sales was INR 370,100.6 million compared to INR 334,064.4 million a year ago. Revenue was INR 376,264.9 million compared to INR 346,986.8 million a year ago. Net income was INR 32,826.3 million compared to INR 35,084.1 million a year ago. Basic earnings per share from continuing operations was INR 29.44 compared to INR 31.5 a year ago. Diluted earnings per share from continuing operations was INR 29.32 compared to INR 31.37 a year ago.

**Source** *Stockpedia (edited)*

You are required to

(a) Give the formula to calculate the percentage change in net income. **(Recall)**

(b) Calculate the percentage change in net income in comparison with the last year. **(Application) [1]**

(iv) In recent years, there has been an increase in the number cases of financial statement correction following the revelation of accounting irregularities (including window dressing and inappropriate accounting). There have also been cases in which companies voluntarily correct their financial statements even if they have not committed fraud. Credit risk can appear inordinately low when calculated based on pre-correction financial statements that paint a rosier picture than those created with more realistic figures. If a given company goes bankrupt as a result, there will be a significant impact on overall future credit management.

SP-08

**Source** *business news (edited)*

How is window dressing a limitation of financial statement analysis? (Understanding) [1]

(v) Anil Ltd. is involved in the business of trading cars, invested ₹ 50, 00,000 in the equity shares of Sonam Ltd, a manufacturing company. Dividend received from Sonam Ltd will be treated under which activity while preparing cash flow statement? (Understanding) [1]

**Que 12.**

Fill in the missing information in the common size balance sheet. (Application) [3]

**Common Size Balance Sheet**
as at 31st March, 2022 and 2023

| Particulars | Absolute Amounts | | % of Balance Sheet | |
|---|---|---|---|---|
| | 2022 (₹) | 2023 (₹) | 2022 (₹) | 2023 (₹) |
| **I. EQUITY AND LIABILITIES** | | | | |
| 1. Shareholders' Funds | ........... | ........... | 50 | 50 |
| 2. Non-current Liabilities | 6,00,000 | 15,00,000 | ...... | 31.25 |
| 3. Current Liabilities | 6,00,000 | 9,00,000 | ...... | 18.75 |
| **Total** | 24,00,000 | ........... | 100 | 100 |
| **II. ASSETS** | | | | |
| 1. Non-current Assets | ........... | 30,00,000 | 62.5 | 62.5 |
| 2. Current Assets | 9,00,000 | ........... | ...... | 37.5 |
| **Total** | 24,00,000 | 48,00,000 | 100 | 100 |

**Que 13.**

Answer any three of the following questions.

From the following information, calculate (Application) [6]

(i) Debt to equity ratio
(ii) Proprietary ratio
(iii) Current ratio
(iv) Acid test ratio

**Information given**

| | |
|---|---|
| Long-term borrowings | ₹ 1,00,000 |
| Long-term provision | ₹ 50,000 |
| Current liabilities | ₹ 25,000 |
| Non-current assets | ₹ 1,80,000 |
| Current assets | ₹ 45,000 |
| Inventory | ₹ 20,000 |



**Que 14.**

From the following balance sheet of Alpha Ltd. prepare (Application) [6]

(i) Cash flow from operating activities.
(ii) Cash flow from investing activities.
(iii) Cash flow from financing activities.

| Particulars | Note No. | 31st March, 2022 (₹) | 31st March, 2021 (₹) |
|---|---|---|---|
| **I. EQUITY AND LIABILITIES** | | | |
| 1. **Shareholders' Funds** | | | |
| (i) Share Capital | | 4,00,000 | 3,00,000 |
| (ii) Reserves and Surplus | 1 | 10,000 | 85,000 |
| 2. **Non-current Liabilities** | | | |
| 10% Secured Loan | | 1,75,000 | 1,00,000 |

| Particulars | Note No. | 31st March, 2022 (₹) | 31st March, 2021 (₹) |
|---|---|---|---|
| 3. **Current Liabilities** | | | |
| (i) Sundry Creditors | | 2,95,000 | 3,10,000 |
| (ii) Short-term Provisions | | — | — |
| (iii) Provision for Taxation | | 1,95,000 | 1,25,000 |
| **Total** | | 10,75,000 | 9,20,000 |
| II. **ASSETS** | | | |
| 1. **Non-current Assets** | | | |
| Property, Plant and Equipment | | 5,50,000 | 4,00,000 |
| 2. **Current Assets** | | | |
| (i) Inventories | | 2,25,000 | 2,00,000 |
| (ii) Debtors | | 1,90,000 | 2,10,000 |
| (iii) Bills Receivables | | 1,00,000 | 80,000 |
| (iv) Cash and Cash Equivalents | | 10,000 | 30,000 |
| **Total** | | 10,75,000 | 9,20,000 |

### Notes to Accounts

| Particulars | 31st March, 2022 (₹) | 31st March, 2021 (₹) |
|---|---|---|
| 1. **Reserves and Surplus** | | |
| Balance in Statement of Profit and Loss | 50,000 (Dr) | 45,000 (Cr) |
| Securities Premium Reserve | 60,000 | 40,000 |
| | 10,000 | 85,000 |
| 2. **Contingent Liability** | | |
| Proposed Dividend | 60,000 | — |

### Additional Information

A part of property, plant and equipment whose book value on the date of sale was ₹ 50,000 was sold at 20% loss. Depreciation charged on the property, plant and equipment was ₹ 1,00,000.

*Or*

SP-08 From the following information answer the questions given below in relation to the cash flow statement of the Amit Ltd. for the year 2023.

**Balance Sheet** (An Extract)

| Particulars | Note No. | 31st March, 2023 (₹) | 31st March, 2022 (₹) |
|---|---|---|---|
| 1. Property, Plant & Equipment and Intangible Assets | | | |
| (i) Property, Plant and Equipment | 1 | 6,20,000 | 6,00,000 |
| (ii) Intangible Assets | 2 | 3,20,000 | 5,60,000 |

### Notes of Accounts (Extract)

| Particulars | Note No. | 31st March, 2023 (₹) | 31st March, 2022(₹) |
|---|---|---|---|
| 1. **Property, Plant and Equipment** | | | |
| Machinery | | 8,40,000 | 8,00,000 |
| (–) Accumulated Depreciation | | 2,20,000 | 2,00,000 |
| | | 6,20,000 | 6,00,000 |
| 2. **Intangible Assets** | | | |
| Patents | | 3,20,000 | 5,60,000 |

**Additional Information**

(i) During the year, a machine costing ₹ 80,000, accumulated depreciation ₹ 48,000, was sold for ₹ 40,000.

(ii) Patents were written-off to the extent of ₹ 80,000 and some patents were sold at a profit of ₹ 40,000.

(a) Prepare accumulated depreciation account. [2]

(b) Give the sale proceeds from sale of patents. [2]

(c) How much payment is made for purchase of machinery? (Application) [2]

# Solutions *in Topper's Style*

My Commitment *I affirm that I am reviewing these solutions only after I have solved the Sample Question Paper 8 on my own. My purpose of looking the solutions is solely to verify whether my answers/solutions were correct or not and to identify my mistakes in case my solutions were wrong or I could not solve that.*

1. (i) (*a*) Interest A/c Dr 20,000
 To Debentureholders' A/c 20,000

(ii) (*a*) C, B, A, D

(iii) (*c*) No. of Debentures $= \frac{7,20,000}{125} = 5,760$

(iv) (*b*) Court can pass order to dissolve the firm if partnership agreement is breached constantly by a partner or partners.

(v) Debit Bank A/c and Credit Loan to Partner A/c

(vi) (*c*) The relevant provisions of Indian partnership are applicable in the absence of deed.

(vii) **JOURNAL**

| Date | Particulars | LF | Amt (Dr) | Amt (Cr) |
|---|---|---|---|---|
| | Dinn Limited A/c Dr | | 21,00,000 | |
| | To Equity Share Capital A/c (2,00,000 × 100) | | | 20,00,000 |
| | To Securities Premium A/c (20,000 × 5) | | | 100,000 |
| | (Being 20,000 shares issued for the purchase of machinery from Dinn Limited) | | | |

**Working Note**

Face value of share = ₹ 100
Premium 5% of ₹ 100 = ₹ 5
No. of shares issued = 21,00,000/105 = 20,000 shares

(viii) If the retiring partner is not paid fully immediately on retirement, the remaining balance of his capital account will be transferred to his loan account and will be shown as his loan on the liabilities side of the balance sheet of the firm.

(ix) (a) Capital reserve is the amount kept aside to cover company's unexpected expenses or losses.

(b) Other reserves that a company can maintain are (any one)

- General reserve
- Revaluation reserve
- Debenture redemption reserve

(x) Goodwill = Number of Years' Purchase × Average Profits

1,07,500 = Number of Years' Purchase × 43,000

Number of Years' Purchase $= \frac{1,07,500}{43,000} = 2.5$

2. **JOURNAL**

| Date | Particulars | LF | Amt (Dr) | Amt (Cr) |
|---|---|---|---|---|
| 2021 | | | | |
| Apr 1 | Bank A/c (2,00,000 × 12) Dr | | 24,00,000 | |
| | To Debenture Application A/c | | | 24,00,000 |
| | (Being the application money received on 2,00,000, 8% debentures @ ₹ 12) | | | |

| Date | Particulars | | LF | Amt (Dr) | Amt (Cr) |
|---|---|---|---|---|---|
| | Debenture Application A/c | Dr | | 24,00,000 | |
| | To 8% Debentures A/c (2,00,000 × 10) | | | | 20,00,000 |
| | To Securities Premium Reserve (2,00,000 × 2) | | | | 4,00,000 |
| | (Being 2,00,000, 8% debentures allotted to debenture applicants) | | | | |
| 2022 | | | | | |
| Mar 31 | Debenture Interest A/c (20,00,000 × 8%) | Dr | | 1,60,000 | |
| | To Debentureholders' A/c | | | | 1,60,000 |
| | (Being the interest payable on 8% debentures provided) | | | | |
| Mar 31 | Statement of Profit and Loss | Dr | | 1,60,000 | |
| | To Interest on Debentures A/c | | | | 1,60,000 |
| | (Being the interest on debentures transferred to statement of profit and loss) | | | | |

**Note** Interest is calculated @ 8% per annum on the face value of the debentures, i.e. ₹ 20,00,000.

*Or* (i) **JOURNAL**

| Date | Particulars | | LF | Amt (Dr) | Amt (Cr) |
|---|---|---|---|---|---|
| 2017 | | | | | |
| May 1 | Bank A/c (50,000 × 90) | Dr | | 45,00,000 | |
| | To Debenture Application and Allotment A/c | | | | 45,00,000 |
| | (Being the applications received for 50,000, 9% debentures of ₹ 100 each @ ₹ 90 per debenture) | | | | |
| | Debenture Application and Allotment A/c | Dr | | 45,00,000 | |
| | Discount on Issue of Debentures A/c | Dr | | 5,00,000 | |
| | To 9% Debentures A/c | | | | 50,00,000 |
| | (Being 50,000, 9% debentures allotted) | | | | |

(ii) **JOURNAL**

| Date | Particulars | | LF | Amt (Dr) | Amt (Cr) |
|---|---|---|---|---|---|
| 2018 | | | | | |
| Mar 31 | Securities Premium A/c | Dr | | 3,00,000 | |
| | Statement of Profit and Loss (Finance cost) | Dr | | 2,00,000 | |
| | To Discount on Issue of Debentures A/c | | | | 5,00,000 |
| | (Being the discount on issue of debentures written-off) | | | | |

(iii) Dr **Discount on Issue of Debentures Account** Cr

| Date | Particulars | Amt (₹) | Date | Particulars | Amt (₹) |
|---|---|---|---|---|---|
| 2017 May 1 | To 9% Debentures A/c | 5,00,000 | 2018 Mar 31 | By Securities Premium A/c | 3,00,000 |
| | | | | By Statement of Profit and Loss | 2,00,000 |
| | | 5,00,000 | | | 5,00,000 |

**3.** (a) Dr **Revaluation Account** Cr

| Particulars | | Amt (₹) | Particulars | Amt (₹) |
|---|---|---|---|---|
| To Plant | | 4,000 | By Building | 10,000 |
| To Profit transferred to | | | By Stock | 5,000 |
| Sumit's Capital A/c | 5,500 | | | |
| Shiba's Capital A/c | 3,300 | | | |
| Nutan's Capital A/c | 2,200 | 11,000 | | |
| | | 15,000 | | 15,000 |

(b) Dr **Nutan's Capital Account** Cr

| Particulars | Amt (₹) | Particulars | Amt (₹) |
|---|---|---|---|
| To Drawings A/c | 20,000 | By Balance b/d | 60,000 |
| To Nutan's Executor's A/c (Balance transferred) | 1,01,950 | By Sumit's Capital A/c (Goodwill) | 22,500 |
| | | By Shiba's Capital A/c (Goodwill) | 15,000 |
| | | By Revaluation A/c (Gain) | 5,500 |
| | | By Profit and Loss Suspense A/c (Profit upto date of death) | 8,750 |
| | | By Interest on Capital A/c $\left(60,000 \times \frac{9}{100} \times \frac{6}{12}\right)$ | 2,700 |
| | | By Reserve Fund A/c $\left(15,000 \times \frac{5}{10}\right)$ | 7,500 |
| | 1,21,950 | | 1,21,950 |

**Working Notes**

1. Calculation of Nutan's share of goodwill

$$\text{Average Profit} = \frac{\text{Total Profit}}{\text{Number of Years}} = \frac{25,000 + 20,000 + 40,000 + 35,000}{4} = ₹\,30,000$$

Goodwill = Average Profit × Number of Years' Purchase = 30,000 × 2.5 = ₹ 75,000

$$\text{Nutan's share of goodwill} = 75,000 \times \frac{5}{10} = ₹\,37,500$$

2. Calculation of profit upto date of death Nutan's share $= 35,000 \times \frac{5}{10} \times \frac{6}{12} = ₹\,8,750$

**Common Mistake** Students mistakenly calculate interest on capital for the whole year. Since Nutan worked for 6 months in current year, interest on capital will be calculated for 6 months only.

**4.** **JOURNAL**

| Date | Particulars | | LF | Amt (Dr) | Amt (Cr) |
|---|---|---|---|---|---|
| (i) | Bank A/c (50,000 × 90%) | Dr | | 45,000 | |
| | To Debenture Application and Allotment A/c | | | | 45,000 |
| | (Being application money received) | | | | |
| | Debenture Application and Allotment A/c | Dr | | 45,000 | |
| | Discount on Debentures A/c | Dr | | 5,000 | |
| | To Debentures A/c | | | | 50,000 |
| | (Being application money transferred to debentures account) | | | | |
| (ii) | Fixed Assets A/c | Dr | | 40,000 | |
| | To Vendor Co. A/c | | | | 40,000 |
| | (Being amount spent for purchase of fixed assets) | | | | |
| | Vendor Co. A/c | Dr | | 40,000 | |
| | Discount on Debentures A/c | Dr | | 10,000 | |
| | To Debentures A/c | | | | 50,000 |
| | (Being debentures issued to vendor at discount) | | | | |

**5.** (i) (a) Brij will get $= \frac{1,20,000}{3,00,000} \times 2,00,000 = ₹\ 80,000$

(b) Nandan will get $= \frac{1,80,000}{3,00,000} \times 2,00,000 = ₹\ 1,20,000$

(ii) Dr **Profit and Loss Appropriation Account** for the year ended 31st March, 2023 Cr

| Particulars | Amt (₹) | Particulars | Amt (₹) |
|---|---|---|---|
| To Interest on Capital A/c (Brij) | 80,000 | By Net Profit as per Profit and Loss A/c | 2,00,000 |
| To Salary to Nandan | 1,20,000 | | |
| | 2,00,000 | | 2,00,000 |

**Working Note**

Interest on Capital (Brij) = 10,00,000 × 12/100 = ₹ 1,20,000

Salary to Nandan = ₹ 1,80,000

= ₹ 3,00,000

But profit earned = ₹ 2,00,000

**Value Point**

When profit is less than appropriation of interest on capital and salary, then the profit is distributed in interest on capital and salary ratio.

*Or* (i) 1 : 1 : 1 : 1 (In the absence of any information in connection with profit sharing ratio, it is presumed to be equal)

(ii) **JOURNAL**

| Date | Particulars | | LF | Amt (Dr) | Amt (Cr) |
|---|---|---|---|---|---|
| 2022 | | | | | |
| Apr 1 | Nitin's Capital A/c | Dr | | 3,500 | |
| | Megha's Capital A/c | Dr | | 1,500 | |
| | To Priyanka's Capital A/c | | | | 1,500 |
| | To Ankit's Capital A/c | | | | 3,500 |
| | (Being the adjustment of interest on capital omitted in previous year) | | | | |

**Working Notes**

**Statement Showing Adjustment**

| Particulars | Nitin (₹) | Megha (₹) | Priyanka (₹) | Ankit (₹) | Total (₹) |
|---|---|---|---|---|---|
| **Amount to be Credited** | | | | | |
| Interest on Capital @ 5% | 3,000 | 5,000 | 8,000 | 10,000 | 26,000 |
| **Amount to be Debited** | | | | | |
| Share of profit (26,000 in 1 : 1 : 1 : 1) | 6,500 | 6,500 | 6,500 | 6,500 | 26,000 |
| | 3,500 (Dr) | 1,500 (Dr) | 1,500 (Cr) | 3,500 (Cr) | – |

**6.** Dr **Realisation Account** Cr

| Particulars | | Amt (₹) | Particulars | | Amt (₹) |
|---|---|---|---|---|---|
| To Sundry Assets | | | By Sundry Liabilities | | |
| Stock | 24,000 | | Creditors | 42,000 | |
| Debtors | 19,000 | | Employees Provident Fund | 60,000 | |
| Furniture | 40,000 | | Mrs. Ashish's loan | 9,000 | |
| Plant | 2,10,000 | | Investment Fluctuation Reserve | 4,000 | 1,15,000 |
| Investments | 32,000 | 3,25,000 | By Ashish's Capital (Furniture) | | 38,000 |
| To Ashish's Capital A/c (Mrs. Ashish Loan) | | 9,000 | By Kanav's Capital (40% Stock) | | 7,680 |
| To Bank – Employees Provident Fund | | 60,000 | By Bank | | |
| To Kanav's Capital A/c | | 12,000 | Debtors | 18,500 | |
| (Realisation expenses) | | | Plant | 2,31,000 | |
| To Profit transferred to | | | 60% Stock | 15,840 | 2,65,340 |
| Ashish's Capital A/c | 12,012 | | | | |
| Kanav's Capital A/c | 8,008 | 20,020 | | | |
| | | 4,26,020 | | | 4,26,020 |

**Working Notes**

1. 40% Stock = 24,000 × 40% = ₹ 9,600
   (–) 20% = ₹ (1,920)
   = ₹ 7,680

2. 60% Stock = 24,000 × 60% = ₹ 14,400
   (+) 10% = ₹ 1,440
   = ₹ 15,840

**Value Points**

- Asset taken over by a creditor will not be recorded.
- Only the remuneration agreed will be recorded in the books, irrespective of the original expense.

7. (i) Pinki's guaranteed amount = ₹ 20,500

| | | |
|---|---|---|
| Pinki's share of profit | = | ₹ 11,000 |
| (+) Interest on capital | = | ₹ 9,000 |
| | | ₹ 20,000 |

∴ Deficiency amount of Pinki to be borne by Dinki (20,500 – 20,000) = ₹ 500

(ii) **Profit and Loss Appropriation Account**
for the year ended 31st March, 2022

Dr Cr

| Particulars | | Amt (₹) | Particulars | Amt (₹) |
|---|---|---|---|---|
| To Interest on Capital A/cs | | | By Net Profit as per Profit and Loss A/c | 78,000 |
| Rinki | 12,000 | | | |
| Pinki | 9,000 | | | |
| Dinki | 6,000 | 27,000 | | |
| To Salary A/cs | | | | |
| Pinki | 12,000 | | | |
| Dinki | 6,000 | 18,000 | | |
| To Net Profit transferred to | | | | |
| Rinki's Capital A/c (33,000 × 3/6) | | 16,500 | | |
| Pinki's Capital A/c (33,000 × 2/6) | 11,000 | | | |
| (+) Deficiency to be Borne by Dinki | 500 | 11,500 | | |
| Dinki's Capital A/c | 5,500 | | | |
| (–) Deficiency Borne | (500) | 5,000 | | |
| | | 78,000 | | 78,000 |

*Or*

**JOURNAL**

| Date | Particulars | | LF | Amt (Dr) | Amt (Cr) |
|---|---|---|---|---|---|
| | Praveen's Current A/c | Dr | | 10,400 | |
| | Sahil's Current A/c | Dr | | 4,800 | |
| | To Riya's Current A/c | | | | 5,200 |
| | To General Reserve A/c | | | | 10,000 |
| | (Being the adjustment entry passed) | | | | |

**Adjustment Table**

| Particulars | Praveen (₹) | Sahil (₹) | Riya (₹) | Total (₹) |
|---|---|---|---|---|
| I. **Amount Already Recorded** | | | | |
| Share of Profit, i.e. ₹ 1,00,000 in 3 : 1 : 1 | 60,000 | 20,000 | 20,000 | 1,00,000 |
| II. **Amount which should have been Recorded** | | | | |
| Interest on Capital | 10,000 | 8,000 | 6,000 | 24,000 |
| Salary | 18,000 | — | 12,000 | 30,000 |
| Share of Profit, i.e. 36,000 in 3 : 1 : 1 | 21,600 | 7,200 | 7,200 | 36,000 |
| | 49,600 | 15,200 | 25,200 | 90,000 |
| **Net Effect** (I–II) | 10,400 (Dr) | 4,800 (Dr) | 5,200 (Cr) | 10,000 (Cr) |

**Working Notes**

1. **Calculation of Interest on Capital**

Praveen = $2,00,000 \times \frac{5}{100}$ = ₹ 10,000; Sahil = $1,60,000 \times \frac{5}{100}$ = ₹ 8,000; Riya = $1,20,000 \times \frac{5}{100}$ = ₹ 6,000

Salary : Praveen (1,500 × 12) = ₹ 18,000; Riya (1,000 × 12) = ₹ 12,000

2. **Calculation of Adjusted Profits**

Adjusted Profits = Given Profit – Transfer to Reserve – Interest on Capital – Salary
= 1,00,000 – 10,000 – 24,000 (10,000 + 8,000 + 6,000) – 30,000 (18,000 + 12,000) = ₹ 36,000

**8.** (i)

**ABC Ltd. Balance Sheet**
as at 31st March, 2022

| Particulars | Note No. | Amt (₹) |
|---|---|---|
| **I. EQUITY AND LIABILITIES** | | |
| 1. **Shareholders' Funds** | | |
| Share Capital | | 26,000 |
| 2. **Non-current Liabilities** | | |
| Long-term Provision | | 30,000 |
| 3. **Current Liabilities** | | |
| (i) Short-term Borrowings | | 12,000 |
| (ii) Short-term Provisions | | 18,000 |
| (iii) Other Current Liabilities | | 6,000 |
| **Total** | | 92,000 |
| **II. ASSETS** | | |
| 1. **Non-current Assets** | | |
| (i) Property, Plant & Equipment and Intangible Assets | | |
| Property, Plant and Equipment | | 42,000 |
| 2. **Current Assets** | | |
| (i) Inventories | | 8,000 |
| (ii) Cash and Cash Equivalents | | 11,000 |
| (iii) Short-term Loan and Advances | | 22,000 |
| (iv) Other Current Assets | | 9,000 |
| **Total** | | 92,000 |

(ii) **Notes to Accounts**

| Particulars | Amt (₹) |
|---|---|
| 1. **Reserves and Surplus** | |
| (i) Securities Premium | 60,000 |
| (ii) Revaluation Reserve | 45,000 |
| | 1,05,000 |
| 2. **Short-term Provisions** | |
| (i) Provision for Doubtful Debts | 15,000 |
| (ii) Provision for Tax | 40,000 |
| | 55,000 |
| 3. **Property, Plant and Equipment** | |
| (i) Buildings | 80,000 |
| (ii) Plant and Equipment | 1,00,000 |
| (iii) Furniture and Fixtures | 50,000 |
| | 2,30,000 |
| 4. **Intangible Assets** | |
| Goodwill | 30,000 |
| 5. **Inventories** | |
| (i) Finished Goods | 25,000 |
| (ii) Stores and Spares | 15,000 |
| | 40,000 |

**Value Points**

- Finished goods are inventories and stores and spares are a part of inventories.
- Provision for doubtful debts is a short-term provision and will be shown accordingly.

9. (A) (a) Dr **Revaluation Account** Cr

| Particulars | Amt (₹) | Particulars | | Amt (₹) |
|---|---|---|---|---|
| To Bad Debts | 4,500 | By Building | | 36,000 |
| To Machinery | 54,000 | By Loss transferred to | | |
| | | Daksh's Capital A/c | 6,429 | |
| | | Taksh's Capital A/c | 9,642 | |
| | | Harsh's Capital A/c | 6,429 | 22,500 |
| | 58,500 | | | 58,500 |

(b) Dr **Partners' Capital Account** Cr

| Particulars | Daksh (₹) | Taksh (₹) | Harsh (₹) | Particulars | Daksh (₹) | Taksh (₹) | Harsh (₹) |
|---|---|---|---|---|---|---|---|
| To Daksh's Capital A/c | — | — | 24,000 | By Balance b/d | 1,20,000 | 1,80,000 | 1,20,000 |
| To Revaluation (Loss) | 6,429 | 9,642 | 6,429 | By Workmen Compensation Reserve A/c | 1,286 | 1,928 | 1,286 |
| To Bank A/c | 30,000 | — | — | | | | |
| To Daksh's Loan A/c | 1,08,857 | — | — | By Harsh's Capital A/c | 24,000 | — | — |
| To Balance c/d | — | 1,80,000 | 2,40,000 | By Bank A/c (Balancing Figure) | — | 7,714 | 1,49,143 |
| | 1,45,286 | 1,89,642 | 2,70,429 | | 1,45,286 | 1,89,642 | 2,70,429 |

**Working Notes**

1. Calculation of sacrificing or gaining ratio

   Sacrificing Ratio = Old Ratio – New Ratio

   Taksh $= \frac{3}{7} - \frac{3}{7} =$ Nil; Harsh $= \frac{2}{7} - \frac{4}{7} = \left(\frac{2}{7}\right)$

   Only Harsh gains

2. Firm's goodwill = ₹ 84,000

   Daksh's share of goodwill $= 84{,}000 \times \frac{2}{7} =$ ₹ 24,000 to be contributed by gaining partner, i.e. Harsh.

3. Firm's total capital = 1,20,000 + 1,80,000 + 1,20,000 = ₹ 4,20,000

   Taksh's new capital $= 4{,}20{,}000 \times \frac{3}{7} =$ ₹ 1,80,000 ; Harsh's new capital $= 4{,}20{,}000 \times \frac{4}{7} =$ ₹ 2,40,000

(c) **Balance Sheet**

as at 31st March, 2021

| Liabilities | | Amt (₹) | Assets | Amt (₹) |
|---|---|---|---|---|
| Capital A/cs | | | Building | 1,56,000 |
| Taksh | 1,80,000 | | Machinery | 1,26,000 |
| Harsh | 2,40,000 | 4,20,000 | Stock | 60,000 |
| Daksh's Loan A/c | | 1,08,857 | Debtors | 55,500 |
| Claim against Workmen Compensation Reserve | | 4,500 | Bank | 1,86,857 |
| Employees Provident Fund | | 21,000 | | |
| Creditors | | 30,000 | | |
| | | 5,84,357 | | 5,84,357 |

(B) **JOURNAL**

| Date | Particulars | | LF | Amt (Dr) | Amt (Cr) |
|---|---|---|---|---|---|
| | Investment Fluctuation Reserve A/c | Dr | | 27,000 | |
| | Revaluation A/c | Dr | | 3,000 | |
| | To Investment A/c | | | | 30,000 |
| | (Being fall in the book value of investments credited to investment account and excess charged to revaluation account) | | | | |
| | M's Capital A/c | Dr | | 1,500 | |
| | N's Capital A/c | Dr | | 900 | |
| | O's Capital A/c | Dr | | 600 | |
| | To Revaluation A/c | | | | 3,000 |
| | (Being loss on revaluation debited to partners capital account in their old profit sharing ratio) | | | | |

*Or* (a)

**JOURNAL**

| Date | Particulars | | LF | Amt (Dr) | Amt (Cr) |
|---|---|---|---|---|---|
| 2016 Mar 31 | Cash A/c | Dr | | 40,000 | |
| | To C's Capital A/c | | | | 30,000 |
| | To Premium for Goodwill A/c | | | | 10,000 |
| | (Being cash and premium for goodwill brought in by C) | | | | |
| | Premium for Goodwill A/c | Dr | | 10,000 | |
| | To W's Capital A/c | | | | 6,000 |
| | To R's Capital A/c | | | | 4,000 |
| | (Being premium for goodwill shared by old partners in sacrificing ratio) | | | | |
| | W's Capital A/c | Dr | | 3,000 | |
| | R's Capital A/c | Dr | | 2,000 | |
| | To Cash A/c | | | | 5,000 |
| | (Being half goodwill withdrawn by W and R in old ratio) | | | | |

(b)

| Date | Particulars | | LF | Amt (Dr) | Amt (Cr) |
|---|---|---|---|---|---|
| | General Reserve A/c | Dr | | 5,000 | |
| | To W's Capital A/c | | | | 3,000 |
| | To R's Capital A/c | | | | 2,000 |
| | (Being general reserve distributed among old partners in old ratio) | | | | |

(c)

| Date | Particulars | | LF | Amt (Dr) | Amt (Cr) |
|---|---|---|---|---|---|
| | Outstanding Salary A/c | Dr | | 3,000 | |
| | To Cash A/c | | | | 3,000 |
| | (Being outstanding salary paid) | | | | |

(d)

| Date | Particulars | | LF | Amt (Dr) | Amt (Cr) |
|---|---|---|---|---|---|
| | Revaluation A/c | Dr | | 8,125 | |
| | To Provision for Doubtful Debts A/c | | | | 325 |
| | To Stock A/c | | | | 2,000 |
| | To Furniture A/c | | | | 500 |
| | To Plant and Machinery A/c | | | | 3,200 |
| | To Creditors A/c | | | | 2,100 |
| | (Being the decrease in the value of assets and increase in value of liabilities and unrecorded liability recorded) | | | | |
| | Investment A/c | Dr | | 2,500 | |
| | To Revaluation A/c | | | | 2,500 |
| | (Being increase in the value of asset recorded) | | | | |

(e)

| Date | Particulars | | LF | Amt (Dr) | Amt (Cr) |
|---|---|---|---|---|---|
| | W's Capital A/c (5,625 × 3/5) | Dr | | 3,375 | |
| | R's Capital A/c (5,625 × 2/5) | Dr | | 2,250 | |
| | To Revaluation A/c | | | | 5,625 |
| | (Being loss on revaluation transferred to partners' capital accounts) | | | | |

**Working Notes**

1. **Distribution of Goodwill in Sacrificing Ratio**

   W's share $= 10{,}000 \times \frac{3}{5} =$ ₹ 6,000;  R's share $= 10{,}000 \times \frac{2}{5} =$ ₹ 4,000

   **Note** It has been assumed that W and R sacrifice in ratio 3 : 2 (equal to old profit sharing ratio).

2. **Provision for Bad and Doubtful Debts**

| | Amt (₹) |
|---|---|
| Debtors | 18,000 |
| (–) Bad debts, to be adjusted against provision for bad debts | (1,500) |
| | 16,500 |
| Provision for doubtful debts @ 5% on 16,500 | 825 |
| (–) Existing provision after adjusting bad debts (2,000 – 1,500) | (500) |
| Amount to be debited to revaluation account | 325 |

10.

**JOURNAL**

| Date | Particulars | | LF | Amt (Dr) | Amt (Cr) |
|---|---|---|---|---|---|
| (i) | Plant and Machinery A/c | Dr | | 1,60,000 | |
| | To Vendor A/c | | | | 1,60,000 |
| | (Being plant and machinery purchased) | | | | |
| (ii) | Vendor A/c | Dr | | 1,60,000 | |
| | To Equity Share Capital A/c | | | | 1,60,000 |
| | (Being 16,000 equity shares @ ₹ 10 issued as fully paid) | | | | |
| (iii) | Bank A/c (24,000 × 3) | Dr | | 72,000 | |
| | To Share Application A/c | | | | 72,000 |
| | (Being application amount received on 24,000 equity shares @ ₹ 3) | | | | |
| (iv) | Share Application A/c | Dr | | 72,000 | |
| | To Equity Share Capital A/c | | | | 72,000 |
| | (Being application amount transferred to equity share capital) | | | | |
| (v) | Share Allotment A/c | Dr | | 24,000 | |
| | To Equity Share Capital A/c (24,000 × 1) | | | | 24,000 |
| | (Being allotment amount due on 24,000 equity shares @ ₹ 1) | | | | |
| (vi) | Bank A/c (22,400 × 1) | Dr | | 22,400 | |
| | Calls-in-arrears A/c (1,600 × 1) | Dr | | 1,600 | |
| | To Share Allotment A/c | | | | 24,000 |
| | (Being allotment amount received on 22,400 shares @ ₹ 1) | | | | |
| (vii) | Share First Call A/c | Dr | | 48,000 | |
| | To Equity Share Capital A/c (24,000 × 2) | | | | 48,000 |
| | (Being first call due on 24,000 equity shares @ ₹ 2) | | | | |
| (viii) | Bank A/c (20,000 × 2) | Dr | | 40,000 | |
| | Calls-in-arrears A/c (4,000 × 2) | Dr | | 8,000 | |
| | To Share First Call A/c | | | | 48,000 |
| | (Being first call amount received on 20,000 equity shares @ ₹ 2) | | | | |
| (ix) | Equity Share Capital A/c (1,600 × 6) | Dr | | 9,600 | |
| | To Calls-in-arrears A/c (1,600 × 3) | | | | 4,800 |
| | To Share Forfeiture A/c (1,600 × 3) | | | | 4,800 |
| | (Being 1,600 equity shares forfeited for non-payment of allotment and first call) | | | | |
| (x) | Bank A/c (1,600 × 4) | Dr | | 6,400 | |
| | Share Forfeiture A/c (1,600 × 2) | Dr | | 3,200 | |
| | To Equity Share Capital A/c | | | | 9,600 |
| | (Being 1,600 forfeited equity shares re-issued @ ₹ 4, ₹ 6 paid-up) | | | | |
| (xi) | Share Forfeiture A/c | Dr | | 1,600 | |
| | To Capital Reserve A/c | | | | 1,600 |
| | (Being balance of forfeited shares account transferred to capital reserve) | | | | |

Dr **Calls-in-arrears Account** Cr

| Date | Particulars | Amt (₹) | Date | Particulars | Amt (₹) |
|---|---|---|---|---|---|
| | To Share Allotment A/c | 1,600 | | By Equity Share Capital A/c | 4,800 |
| | To Share First Call A/c | 8,000 | | By Balance c/d | 4,800 |
| | | 9,600 | | | 9,600 |
| | To Balance b/d | 4,800 | | | |

*Or* (i) 85,000 × 6 = ₹ 5,10,000

(ii) Profit on forfeiture of 2,000 shares = 2,000 × 6 = ₹ 12,000

Loss on re-issue = 1,500 × 2 = ₹ 3,000

$$\text{Capital reserve} = \left[\left(\frac{12,000}{2,000} \times 1,500\right) - 3,000\right] = 9,000 - 3,000 = ₹\ 6,000$$

(iii) Issued Capital = ₹ 14,00,000

**Working Note**

| | | |
|---|---|---|
| 90,000 Equity Shares @ 10 each | = | 9,00,000 |
| (+) 50,000 Preference Shares @ 10 each | = | 5,00,000 |
| | | ₹ 14,00,000 |

(iv) **Balance Sheet**

as at 31st March, 2022 (Extract)

| Particulars | Note No. | 31st March, 2022 (₹) |
|---|---|---|
| I. **EQUITY AND LIABILITIES** | | |
| 1. **Shareholders' Funds** | | |
| (i) Share Capital | 1 | 11,77,000 |
| (ii) Reserves and Surplus | 2 | 6,000 |
| **Total** | | 11,83,000 |

(v) **Notes to Accounts**

| Particulars | | 31st March, 2022 (₹) |
|---|---|---|
| 1. **Share Capital** | | |
| **Authorised Capital** | | |
| 1,00,000 Equity Shares of ₹ 10 each | | 10,00,000 |
| 50,000, 9% Preference Shares of ₹ 10 each | | 5,00,000 |
| | | 15,00,000 |
| **Issued Capital** [Point (iii)] | | 14,00,000 |
| **Subscribed Capital** | | |
| **Subscribed and Fully Paid** | | |
| 50,000, 9% Preference Shares of ₹ 10 each | | 5,00,000 |
| **Subscribed but not Fully Paid** | | |
| 84,500 Equity Shares of ₹ 10 each ₹ 8 Called-up | 6,76,000 | |
| (−) Calls-in-arrears (1,000 × 2) | (2,000) | |
| (+) Shares Forfeited (500 × 6) | 3,000 | 6,77,000 |
| 2. **Reserves and Surplus** | | |
| Capital Reserve (1,500 × 4, i.e. ₹ 6 gain on forfeiture ₹ 2 loss on re-issue) | | 6,000 |

**11.** (i) (a) Non-cash transactions are not shown

(ii) • PE ratio is the price-to-earnings ratio. It measures a company's current share price relative to its per share earnings.

• (b) $\dfrac{\text{Market Value of an Equity Share}}{\text{Earing per Share}}$

(iii) (a) $\dfrac{\text{Absolute Change}}{\text{Base Year}} \times 100$

(b) $\dfrac{32{,}826.3 - 35{,}054.1}{35{,}084.1} \times 100 = \dfrac{(2{,}257.8)}{35{,}084.1} \times 100 = (6.435)\,\%$ (Decrease)

(iv) Firms manipulate the data contained in the financial statements, so as to cover up their weak financial position. Analysis based on such financial statements may be misleading due to manipulation.

(v) Cash flow from investing activities

12. **Common Size Balance Sheet**
as at 31st March, 2023 and 2022

| Particulars | Absolute Amounts | | % of Balance Sheet | |
|---|---|---|---|---|
| | 2022 (₹) | 2023 (₹) | 2022 (%) | 2023 (%) |
| I. **EQUITY AND LIABILITIES** | | | | |
| 1. Shareholders' Funds | **12,00,000** | **24,00,000** | 50 | 50 |
| 2. Non-current Liabilities | 6,00,000 | 15,00,000 | **25** | 31.25 |
| 3. Current Liabilities | 6,00,000 | 9,00,000 | **25** | 18.75 |
| **Total** | 24,00,000 | **48,00,000** | 100 | 100 |
| II. **ASSETS** | | | | |
| 1. Non-current Assets | **15,00,000** | 30,00,000 | 62.5 | 62.5 |
| 2. Current Assets | 9,00,000 | **18,00,000** | **37.5** | 37.5 |
| **Total** | 24,00,000 | 48,00,000 | 100 | 100 |

13. (i) Debt to Equity Ratio $= \dfrac{\text{Debt}}{\text{Equity}} = \dfrac{\text{Long-term Borrowings + Long-term Provisions}}{\text{Shareholders' Funds}}$

$$= \frac{1{,}00{,}000 + 50{,}000}{50{,}000} \Rightarrow \frac{1{,}50{,}000}{50{,}000}$$

Debt to Equity Ratio = 3 : 1

**Shareholders' Funds**
**Assets Approach**

| Particulars | Amt (₹) |
|---|---|
| Non-current Assets | 1,80,000 |
| Current Assets | 45,000 |
| Total Assets | 2,25,000 |
| (–) Current Liabilities | (25,000) |
| (–) Long-term Borrowings | (1,00,000) |
| (–) Long-term Provisions | (50,000) |
| | 50,000 |

(ii) Proprietary Ratio $= \dfrac{\text{Shareholders' Funds}}{\text{Total Assets}} = \dfrac{50{,}000}{2{,}25{,}000}$

Proprietary Ratio = 0.22 : 1

(iii) Current Ratio $= \dfrac{\text{Current Assets}}{\text{Current Liabilities}} = \dfrac{45{,}000}{25{,}000} = 1.8:1$

(iv) Acid Test Ratio $= \dfrac{\text{Liquid Assets}}{\text{Current Liabilities}} = \dfrac{25{,}000}{25{,}000} = 1:1$

Liquid Assets = Current Assets – Inventories = 45,000 – 20,000 = 25,000

**14.** (i)

## Cash Flow from Operating Activities

| Particulars | | Amt (₹) |
|---|---|---|
| **Cash Flow from Operating Activities** | | |
| Net Profit before Tax (WN) | | 1,00,000 |
| **Adjustments for** | | |
| (+) Depreciation | 1,00,000 | |
| Loss on Sale of Assets | 10,000 | |
| Interest on Debentures | 10,000 | 1,20,000 |
| Operating Profit before Working Capital Changes | | 2,20,000 |
| (–) Increase in Current Assets and Decrease in Current Liabilities | | |
| Sundry Creditors | (15,000) | |
| Inventories | (25,000) | |
| Bills Receivable | (20,000) | (60,000) |
| (+) Decrease in Current Assets and Increase in Current Liabilities | | |
| Debtors | | 20,000 |
| Cash Generated from Operations | | 1,80,000 |
| (–) Tax Paid | | (1,25,000) |
| Cash Flow from Operating Activities | | 55,000 |

**Working Note**

Calculation of net profit before tax and extraordinary items

| | |
|---|---|
| Net profit, i.e. (– 50,000 – 45,000) | ₹ (95,000) |
| (+) Provision for tax | ₹ 1,95,000 |
| | ₹ 1,00,000 |

(ii)

## Cash Flow from Investing Activities

| Particulars | | Amt (₹) |
|---|---|---|
| **Cash Flow from Investing Activities** | | |
| Purchase of Property, Plant and Equipment (WN) | (3,00,000) | |
| Sale of Property, Plant and Equipment | 40,000 | |
| Cash used in Investing Activities | | (2,60,000) |

**Working Note**

Dr **Property, Plant and Equipment Account** Cr

| Particulars | Amt (₹) | Particulars | Amt (₹) |
|---|---|---|---|
| To Balance b/d | 4,00,000 | By Depreciation A/c | 1,00,000 |
| To Bank A/c (Purchases) | 3,00,000 | By Cash A/c | 40,000 |
| | | By Loss on Sales A/c | 10,000 |
| | | By Balance c/d | 5,50,000 |
| | 7,00,000 | | 7,00,000 |

(iii)

## Cash Flow from Financing Activities

| Particulars | | Amt (₹) |
|---|---|---|
| **Cash Flow from Financing Activities** | | |
| Issue of Shares | 1,00,000 | |
| Securities Premium Reserve | 20,000 | |
| Issue of Debentures | 75,000 | |
| Interest Paid | (10,000) | |
| Cash Flow from Financing Activities | | 1,85,000 |

*Or* (a) Dr **Accumulated Depreciation Account** Cr

| Particulars | Amt (₹) | Particulars | Amt (₹) |
|---|---|---|---|
| To Machinery A/c<br>(Depreciation on machinery sold) | 48,000 | By Balance b/d | 2,00,000 |
| To Balance c/d | 2,20,000 | By Depreciation A/c<br>(Statement of profit and loss)<br>(Balancing figure) | 68,000 |
| | 2,68,000 | | 2,68,000 |

(b) Dr **Patents Account** Cr

| Particulars | Amt (₹) | Particulars | Amt (₹) |
|---|---|---|---|
| To Balance b/d | 5,60,000 | By Bank A/c (Sale) (Balancing figure) | 2,00,000 |
| To Profit on Sale of Patents A/c<br>(Statement of profit and loss)<br>(Given) | 40,000 | By Amortisation A/c<br>(Statement of profit and loss) | 80,000 |
| | | By Balance c/d | 3,20,000 |
| | 6,00,000 | | 6,00,000 |

∴ Sale Proceeds = ₹ 2,00,000

(c) Dr **Machinery Account** Cr

| Particulars | Amt (₹) | Particulars | Amt (₹) |
|---|---|---|---|
| To Balance b/d | 8,00,000 | By Bank A/c (Sale of machinery) | 40,000 |
| To Profit on Sale of Machinery A/c (WN)<br>(Statement of profit and loss) | 8,000 | By Accumulated Depreciation A/c<br>(Depreciation on machinery sold) | 48,000 |
| To Bank A/c (Purchases)<br>(Balancing figure) | 1,20,000 | By Balance c/d | 8,40,000 |
| | 9,28,000 | | 9,28,000 |

∴ Payment made for purchase of machinery = ₹ 1,20,000

**Working Note**

Profit on Sale of Machinery = Sale Price – Book Value of Machinery = 40,000 – 32,000 (80,000 – 48,000) = ₹ 8,000

SQP Code : **PB-9/15** Series *i*-**Succeed 9-25/15** Roll No. | | | | | | | | |

# Sample Question Paper 09

## Accounts 12th (Code 858)

### General Instructions

1. Candidates are allowed additional 15 minutes for only reading the paper. They must not start writing during this time.
2. Section-A is compulsory for all candidates and has ten questions.
3. Candidates have to attempt all questions from either Section-B or Section-C*.
4. Internal choices have been provided in five questions in Section-A and one question in Section-B.
5. The intended marks for questions or parts of questions are given in the brackets [ ].
6. All calculations should be shown clearly.
7. All workings, including rough work, should be done on the same page as, and adjacent to, the rest of the answer.

*Section-C has not been covered.

**Time : 3 Hrs.**

**Max. Marks : 80**

## Section A Answer All Questions

[60 Marks]

**Que 1.**

In sub-parts (i) to (iv), choose the correct option and in sub-parts (v) to (x) answer the questions as instructed.

(i) Samaira Ltd. purchased a building from Nahar Ltd. for ₹ 16,00,000. The consideration was paid by issue of 10% debentures of ₹ 100 each at a discount of 20%. The 10% debenture account will be credited with what amount? (Application) [1]

(a) ₹ 12,80,000 (b) ₹ 20,00,000

(c) ₹ 19,20,000 (d) ₹ 20,80,000

(ii) Choose the correct sequence of presentation in relation with the balance sheet as per the Schedule III of Companies Act, 2013. (Recall) [1]

A – Current Investments

B – Cash and Cash Equivalents

C – Inventories

D – Trade Receivables

**Codes**

(a) D, B, C, A (b) A, B, C, D

(c) B, C, A, D (d) A, C, D, B

(iii) What will be the journal entry if Neil takes over the loan payable to Mrs. Neil ₹10,000 ? (Application) [1]

(a) Loan A/c (Dr), Neil's Capital A/c (Cr)

(b) Bank A/c (Dr), Neil's Capital A/c (Cr)

(c) Realisation A/c (Dr), Bank A/c (Cr)

(d) Realisation A/c (Dr), Neil's Capital A/c (Cr)

(iv) A and B are partners in a firm sharing profits and losses in the ratio of 1 : 1. A new partner C is admitted for 1/5 th share and goodwill of the firm is valued at ₹ 1,20,000. What is the entry for goodwill, if C does not bring his share of goodwill in cash. (Application) [1]

(a) Premium for Goodwill A/c Dr 15,000
  To A's Capital A/c 7,500
  To B's Capital A/c 7,500

(b) C's Current A/c Dr 20,000
  To A's Capital A/c 10,000
  To B's Capital A/c 10,000

(c) Premium for Goodwill A/c Dr 12,000
  To A's Capital A/c 6,000
  To B's Capital A/c 6,000

(d) C's Current A/c Dr 24,000
To A's Capital 12,000
To B's Capital 12,000

(v) **Assertion** (A) Co-ownership of property is an example of partnership.
**Reason** (R) Since the element of business is present in co-ownership, it is considered as a partnership. (Evaluate) [1]

**Alternatives**
(a) Both Assertion (A) and Reason (R) are true and Reason (R) is the correct explanation of Assertion (A)
(b) Both Assertion (A) and Reason (R) are true, but Reason (R) is not the correct explanation of Assertion (A)
(c) Assertion (A) is true, but Reason (R) is false
(d) Both Assertion (A) and Reason (R) are false

(vi) "According to Amarjit Chopra, past President, Institute of Chartered Accountants of India, the provisions of the Banking Regulation Act allow the share premium account to be used for setting-off losses, provided due procedure is followed and approvals are given." (Recall) [1]
(a) What is securities premium?
(b) On the basis of above mentioned statement, state any one purpose where a company can utilise the amount of securities premium.

(vii) Journalise the following in case of dissolution (Application) [1]
Partner Z's loan was appearing on the liabilities side of the balance sheet ₹ 96,000. He accepted an unrecorded asset of ₹ 80,000 at ₹ 72,000 and the balance was paid to him in cash.

(viii) Sagar Ltd. issued 20,000, 9% debentures of ₹ 100 each at a discount of 10%, redeemable at a premium. On issue of these debentures. Loss on issue of debentures account was debited with ₹ 4,00,000. What will be premium on redemption of debentures? (Application) [1]

(ix) A, B and C were partners in a firm Sharing profits in the ratio of 4 : 3 : 1. C died and his share was taken entirely by A. What Will be the new profit sharing ratio of A and B? (Application) [1]

(x) Distribute general reserve of ₹ 80,000 at the time of admission of Z, when 25% of general reserve is to be transferred to provision for doubtful debts. The firm has two partners X and Y. (Application) [1]

## Que 2.

Raghav and Krishna are partners. Their profit sharing ratio is 3 : 2. Ram joins the partnership for 1/4th share in profits (of which he acquires 2/3 from Raghav and 1/4 from Krishna). Ram brings in ₹ 6,00,000 for capital and ₹ 2,40,000 for goodwill. 1/4th of the amount of goodwill is withdrawn by old partners.

(i) Find out new profit sharing ratio. (ii) Pass necessary journal entries (Application) [3]

*Or*

M, N and O were partners in a firm sharing profits and losses equally. Their balance sheet at 31st December, 2022 was as follows

**Balance Sheet**
as at 31st December, 2022

| Liabilities | | Amt (₹) | Assets | Amt (₹) |
|---|---|---|---|---|
| Capital A/cs | | | Plant and Machinery | 60,000 |
| M | 70,000 | | Stock | 30,000 |
| N | 70,000 | | Sundry Debtors | 95,000 |
| O | 70,000 | 2,10,000 | Cash at Bank | 40,000 |
| General Reserve | | 30,000 | Cash in Hand | 35,000 |
| Creditors | | 20,000 | | |
| | | 2,60,000 | | 2,60,000 |

N died on 14th March, 2023. According to the partnership deed, executors of the deceased partner are entitled to

(i) Balance of partners' capital accounts.
(ii) Interest on capital @ 5% per annum.
(iii) Share of goodwill calculated on the basis of twice the average of past 3 years' profits.
(iv) Share of profits from the closure of the last accounting year till the date of death on the basis of twice the average of three completed years' profits before death.

Profits for 2020, 2021 and 2022 were ₹ 80,000, ₹ 90,000 and ₹ 1,00,000 respectively.

You are required to pass journal entries to record

(i) The transfer of share of general reserve and interest on capital to N.
(ii) The N's share of adjusted goodwill
(iii) Payment made to N's executor.

(Application) [3]

**Que 3.**

P, Q and R were partners in a firm having capital of ₹ 18,000, ₹ 18,000 and ₹ 24,000 respectively. Their current account balances were ₹ 6,000, ₹ 3,000 and ₹ 1,200 (Dr) respectively. According to the partnership deed, the partners were entitled to interest on capital @ 5% per annum. R being the working partner was also entitled to a salary of ₹ 3,600 per annum. The profits were to be divided as follows

SP-09

(i) The first ₹ 12,000 in proportion to their capitals.
(ii) Next ₹ 18,000 in the ratio of 5 : 3 : 2.
(iii) Remaining profits to be shared equally.

The firm made a profit of ₹ 45,000 before charging any of the above items.

(i) Calculate the distribution of profit to P, Q and R.
(ii) Prepare the profit and loss appropriation account.

(Application) [3]

*Or*

S and P are two partners in a firm sharing profits and losses in the ratio of 3 : 2. At the time of distributing the net profit between the partners, interest on capital was credited @ 18% instead of 8% wrongly.

Partners' capitals are given on 1st April, 2023 as ₹ 5,00,000 and ₹ 3,00,000 respectively. Profit on 31st March, 2024 is ₹ 2,00,000.

(i) You are required to [2]
  (a) Give the amount that should have been recorded at the time of distribution of profit.
  (b) Give the net effect of the error rectified.
(ii) Pas the necessary journal entry.

(Application) [1]

**Que 4.**

Under which major head and sub-heads will the following items be placed in the balance sheet of the company as per Schedule III, Part I of the Companies Act, 2013? (Application) [3]

(i) Publishing Titles
(ii) Mining Rights
(iii) Loose Tools
(iv) Cheques and Bank Drafts in Hand
(v) Securities Premium
(vi) Sundry Debtors
(vii) Preliminary Expenses
(viii) Calls-in-arrears
(ix) Investment in Debentures

**Que 5.**

From the following information extracted from the books of Z Ltd. prepare Balance Sheet of the company as at 31st March, 2022 as per Schedule III of the Companies Act, 2013. (Application) [3]

| Particulars | Amt (₹) | Particulars | Amt (₹) |
|---|---|---|---|
| Long-term Borrowings | 20,000 | Property, Plant and Equipment | 32,000 |
| Trade Payables | 1,200 | Inventories | 800 |
| Share Capital | 16,000 | Trade Receivables | 3,200 |
| Reserves and Surplus | 3,600 | Cash and Cash Equivalents | 4,800 |

**Que 6.**

Sohan and Mohan, the two partners of a business firm, agreed to appropriate the profits of their firm on the following terms

(i) Interest is payable on capital @ 5% per annum.
(ii) Sohan to get a salary of ₹ 1,000 per month.

(iii) Interest on loan provided @ 10% per annum.

(iv) Interest and drawings to be charged @ 5% per annum.

(v) Mohan will get commission @ 1% on the sales made during the year.

(vi) Sohan is entitled to a rent of ₹ 50,000 per annum for allowing the firm to carry on the business in his premises.

The net profit of the firm for the year ended 31st March, 2023, was ₹ 3,60,000 before taking into account any of the above terms

| Particulars | Sohan (₹) | Mohan (₹) |
|---|---|---|
| Capital Balances on 1st April, 2022 | 3,00,000 | 2,80,000 |
| Loan Advanced on 1st October, 2022 | — | 2,00,000 |
| Drawings made during the Year | 80,000 | 60,000 |

During the year 2022-23, sales of the firm amounted to ₹ 14,00,000. Prepare profit and loss appropriation account and partners' capital accounts. (Application) [6]

**Que 7.**

The balance sheet of R and K as at 31st March, 2023, was as follows

**Balance Sheet of R and K**
as at 31st March, 2023

| Liabilities | Amt (₹) | Assets | Amt (₹) |
|---|---|---|---|
| Creditors | 5,000 | Cash | 1,400 |
| Investment Fluctuation Fund | 300 | Debtors | 4,700 |
| Capital A/cs | | Stock | 2,300 |
| R | 3,500 | Furniture | 50 |
| K | 2,750 | Property | 2,000 |
| | | Investment | 1,100 |
| | 11,550 | | 11,550 |

The partners shared profits in the ratio of 9:7. The partnership firm was dissolved on the date of the balance sheet subject to the following adjustments

(i) Property realised 75%.

(ii) Bad debts and discount amounted to ₹ 500.

(iii) Stock realised ₹ 2,525.

(iv) Creditors allowed a discount of 2%.

(v) Expenses of dissolution amounted to ₹ 75 which were paid by R.

You are required to prepare the realisation account. (Application) [6]

*Or*

Hanif and Jubed were partners in a firm sharing profits in the ratio of their capitals. On 31st March, 2021, their balance sheet was as follows

**Balance Sheet**
as at 31st March, 2021

| Liabilities | Amt (₹) | Assets | Amt (₹) |
|---|---|---|---|
| Creditors | 1,50,000 | Bank | 2,00,000 |
| Workmen's Compensation Fund | 3,00,000 | Debtors | 3,40,000 |
| General Reserve | 75,000 | Stock | 1,50,000 |
| Hanif's Current A/c | 25,000 | Furniture | 4,60,000 |

SP-09

| Liabilities | | Amt (₹) | Assets | Amt (₹) |
|---|---|---|---|---|
| Capital A/cs | | | Machinery | 8,20,000 |
| Hanif | 10,00,000 | | Jubed's Current A/c | 80,000 |
| Jubed | 5,00,000 | 15,00,000 | | |
| | | 20,50,000 | | 20,50,000 |

On the above date, the firm was dissolved.

(i) Debtors were realised at a discount of 5%. 50% of the stock was taken over by Hanif at 10% less than the book value. Remaining stock was sold for ₹ 65,000.

(ii) Furniture was taken over by Jubed for ₹ 1,35,000. Machinery was sold as scrap for ₹ 74,000.

(iii) Creditors were paid in full.

(iv) Expenses on realisation ₹ 8,000 were paid by Hanif.

Prepare realisation account. (Application)

**Que 8.**

On 1st April, 2023, Fast Computers Ltd. issued 20,000, 6% debentures of ₹ 100 each at a discount of 4% redeemable at a premium of 5% after 3 years. The amount was payable as follows

On application – ₹ 50 per debenture

Balance – On allotment

(i) Record the necessary journal entries for issue of debentures. [5]

(ii) Fast Computers Ltd. has a balance of ₹ 50,000 in securities premium and ₹ 1,00,000 in general reserve. How will loss on issue be written-off? (Application) [1]

**Que 9.**

Sudarshan Ltd invited applications for 1,00,000 equity shares of ₹ 10 each. The shares were issued at a premium of ₹ 5 per share. The amount was payable as follows

On application and allotment ₹ 8 per share (including premium ₹ 3).

Balance including premium on the first and final call.

Applications for 1,50,000 shares were received. Applications for 10,000 shares were rejected and pro-rata allotment was made to the remaining applicants on the following basis

(i) Applicants for 80,000 shares were allotted 60,000 shares.

SP-09 (ii) Applicants for 60,000 shares were allotted 40,000 shares.

Excess share application and allotment money could be utilised for calls.

X, who belonged to the category (i) and was allotted 300 shares, failed to pay the first call money. Y, who belonged to the (ii) category and was allotted 200 shares also failed to pay the first call money. Their shares were forfeited. The forfeited shares were re-issued @ ₹ 12 per share fully paid-up.

(a) Pass necessary journal entries (except cash related entries).

(b) Prepare cash book. (Application) [10]

*Or*

ABC Ltd. has been registered with an authorised capital of ₹ 4,00,000 divided into 4,000 shares of ₹ 100 of which 2,000 shares were offered for public subscription at a premium of ₹ 5 per share payable as under

| | |
|---|---|
| On Application | ₹ 10 |
| On Allotment | ₹ 25 (including premium) |
| On First call | ₹ 40 |
| On Final call | ₹ 30 |

Applications were received for 3,600 shares of which applications for 600 shares were rejected outright and the rest of the applications were allotted 2,000 shares of pro-rata basis. Excess application money was transferred to allotment.

All the money were duly received except from Rohit of 400 shares, who failed to pay allotment and first call money. His shares were later on forfeited and re-issued to Shyam at ₹ 60 per share as ₹ 70 paid-up. Final call has not been made.

(i) What are the number of shares applied by Rohit? [1]

(ii) What is the amount received on allotment? [1]

(iii) What is the excess amount adjusted on allotment? [1]

(iv) What is the amount of calls-in-arrears on allotment? [2]

(v) (a) Pass the journal entry for the forfeiture of shares. [2]

(b) Pass the journal entry for the re-issue of shares. [3]

**Que 10.**

(A) The balance sheet of Madan and Mohan, who were sharing profits and losses in the ratio of 3 : 2 on 31st March, 2021 was as follows

**Balance Sheet**
as at 31st March, 2021

| Liabilities | | Amt (₹) | Assets | | Amt (₹) |
|---|---|---|---|---|---|
| Creditors | | 28,000 | Cash at Bank | | 10,000 |
| Workmen's Compensation Fund | | 12,000 | Debtors | 65,000 | |
| General Reserve | | 20,000 | (–) Provision for Doubtful Debts | (5,000) | 60,000 |
| Capital A/cs | | | Stock | | 30,000 |
| Madan | 60,000 | | Investments | | 50,000 |
| Mohan | 40,000 | 1,00,000 | Patents | | 10,000 |
| | | 1,60,000 | | | 1,60,000 |

They decide to admit Gopal on 1st April, 2021 for 1/4th share on the following terms

(i) Gopal shall bring ₹ 25,000 as his share of premium for goodwill.

(ii) That unaccounted accrued income of ₹ 500 be provided for.

(iii) The market value of investments was ₹ 45,000.

(iv) A debtor whose dues of ₹ 1,000 were written-off as bad debts paid ₹ 800 in full settlement.

(v) A claim of ₹ 2,000 on account of workmen compensation to be provided for.

(vi) Patents are undervalued by ₹ 5,000.

(vii) Gopal to bring in capital equal to 1/4th of the total capital of a new firm after all adjustments.

(a) Prepare revaluation account. [1½]

(b) Prepare the capital account of the partners. [4½]

(c) Prepare the balance sheet of the new firm. (Application) [2]

(B) A and S are partners sharing profits in the ratio of 5 : 3. M joins the firm as a new partner. A gives 1/4th of his share and S gives 1/5th of his share to M. Find out new profit sharing ratio. (Application) [2]

*Or*

Sunaina and Tamanna are partners in a firm sharing profits and losses in the ratio of 3:2. Their balance sheet as at 31st March, 2020 stood as follows

SP-09

**Balance Sheet**
**as at 31st March, 2020**

| Liabilities | | Amt (₹) | Assets | | Amt (₹) |
|---|---|---|---|---|---|
| Capital A/cs | | | Plant and Machinery | | 1,20,000 |
| Sunaina | 60,000 | | Land and Building | | 1,40,000 |
| Tamanna | 80,000 | 1,40,000 | Debtors | 1,90,000 | |
| Current A/cs | | | (–) Provision for | | |
| Sunaina | 10,000 | | Doubtful Debts Debts | (40,000) | 1,50,000 |
| Tamanna | 30,000 | 40,000 | Stock | | 40,000 |
| General Reserve | | 1,20,000 | Cash | | 30,000 |
| Workmen's Compensation Reserve | | 50,000 | Goodwill | | 20,000 |
| Creditors | | 1,50,000 | | | |
| | | 5,00,000 | | | 5,00,000 |

They agreed to admit Pranav into partnership for 1/5th share of profits on 1st April, 2020, on the following terms

(i) All debtors are good.

(ii) Value of land and building to be increased to ₹ 1,80,000.

(iii) Value of plant and machinery to be reduced by ₹ 20,000.

(iv) The liability against workmen's compensation fund is determined at ₹ 20,000 which is to be paid later in the year.

(v) Mr. Anil, to whom ₹ 40,000 were payable (already included in above creditors), drew a bill of exchange for 3 months which was duly accepted.

(vi) Pranav to bring in capital of ₹ 1,00,000 and ₹ 10,000 as premium for goodwill in cash.

You are required to

(a) Pass the journal entries for the adjustment of goodwill. **(Application) [2]**

(b) Pass the journal entry for the transfer of general reserve. **(Application) [2]**

(c) Pass the journal entry for the transfer of workmen compensation reserve. **[Recall] [2]**

(d) Pass the journal entries for the transfer of effects on revaluation account. **(Application) [2]**

(e) Pass the journal entry for the transfer of profit/ loss on revaluation to the partners' capital accounts. **(Application) [2]**



## Section B **[20 Marks]**

**Que 11.**

(i) What will be the effect of issue of bonus shares on cash flow statement? **(Understanding) [1]**

(a) Inflow of cash (b) Outflow of cash

(c) No flow of cash (d) Either (a) or (b)

(ii) Amul reported revenue growth of 18.6% in FY22, after muted growth of just 1.9% in FY 21. Inflation in milk prices and strong volume growth across segments drove revenue growth for the company. Gross and EBITDA margins stood at 4.5% and 0.4%, respectively, in FY22. Profitability was stable YoY. Amul continued introducing new products across categories in FY22.

**Source** *Business news (edited)*

Based on the above statement **(Recall) [1]**

- Mention any one profitability ratio.
- Which of the following is the formula for gross profit?

(a) Gross Profit/Net Revenue from Operations × 100
(b) Gross Profit/Cost of Revenue from Operations × 100
(c) Net Profit/Cost of Revenue from Operations × 100
(d) Net Profit/Cost of Revenue from Operations × 100

(iii) Financial statement analysis involves a comprehensive examination of a company's financial statements, including the income statement, balance sheet and cash flow statement. Analysts assess revenue, earnings, assets, liabilities and cash flow to gauge financial health and performance.

**Source**: *Nism(edited)*

How is the financial statement analysis useful to finance manager? (Evaluate) [1]

(iv) "According to Accounting Scholar, ratios are the most frequently used accounting formulas in regard to business analysis. Analysing your finances with these ratios helps you identify trends and other data that guide important business decisions."

**Source** *Business news daily*

On the basis of above statement, give an advantage of accounting ratios. (Understanding) [1]

(v) Net profit after tax ₹ 70,000
Goodwill written-off ₹ 10,000
Loss on sale of machinery ₹ 3,000
Calculate the cash flow from financing activity. (Application) [1]

**Que 12.**
Fill in the missing figure in the following common size balance sheet. (Application) [3]

**Common Size Balance Sheet**
as at 31st March, 2023 and 2024

| Particulars | Note No. | Absolute Amounts | | % of Balance Sheet Total | |
|---|---|---|---|---|---|
| | | 2023 (₹) | 2024 (₹) | 2023 % | 2024 % |
| I. **EQUITY AND LIABILITIES** | | | | | |
| 1. **Shareholders' Funds** | | | | | |
| (i) Share Capital | | ... | ... | ... | ... |
| (ii) Reserves and Surplus | | ... | ... | 8 | 15 |
| 2. **Non-current Liabilities** | | 3,20,000 | 4,80,000 | ... | ... |
| 3. **Current Liabilities** | | | | | |
| (i) Trade Payables | | ... | ... | 16 | 20 |
| (ii) Short-term Provision | | 40,000 | 1,60,000 | ... | ... |
| **Total** | | ... | ... | 100 | 100 |
| II. **ASSETS** | | | | | |
| 1. **Non-current Assets** | | | | | |
| (i) Fixed Assets | | ... | ... | ... | ... |
| (ii) Non-current Investment | | ... | ... | 4 | 5 |
| 2. **Current Assets** | | 20,000 | 40,000 | 20 | 25 |
| **Total** | | ... | ... | 100 | 100 |

**Que 13.**
From the following, calculate the net cash flow from operating activities.

| Particulars | Note No. | 31st March, 2023 (₹) | 31st March, 2022 (₹) |
|---|---|---|---|
| I. **EQUITY AND LIABILITIES** | | | |
| 1. **Shareholders' Funds** | | | |
| (i) Share Capital | 1 | 3,75,000 | 3,75,000 |
| (ii) Reserves and Surplus | 2 | 1,55,000 | (10,000) |

SP-09

| Particulars | Note No. | 31st March, 2023 (₹) | 31st March, 2022 (₹) |
|---|---|---|---|
| 2. **Non-current Liabilities** (8% Debentures) | | 1,30,000 | 75,000 |
| 3. **Current Liabilities** | | | |
| (i) Short-term Borrowings (8% Bank loan) | | 20,000 | 25,000 |
| (ii) Trade Payables | | 60,000 | 55,000 |
| (iii) Short-term Provisions (Provision for tax) | | 25,000 | 20,000 |
| **Total** | | 7,65,000 | 5,40,000 |
| II. **ASSETS** | | | |
| 1. **Non-current Assets** | | | |
| (i) Property, Plant and Equipment | | 4,30,000 | 3,10,000 |
| (ii) Intangible Assets (Goodwill) | | 7,500 | 20,000 |
| (iii) Non-current Investments | | 62,500 | 40,000 |
| 2. **Current Assets** | | | |
| (i) Current Investments | | 2,500 | 7,500 |
| (ii) Inventories | | 97,500 | 50,000 |
| (iii) Trade Receivables | | 1,00,000 | 1,00,000 |
| (iv) Cash and Cash Equivalents | | 65,000 | 12,500 |
| **Total** | | 7,65,000 | 5,40,000 |

**Notes to Accounts**

| Particulars | 2023 (₹) | 2022 (₹) |
|---|---|---|
| 1. **Share Capital** | | |
| Equity Share Capital | 2,75,000 | 2,25,000 |
| 5% Preference Share Capital | 1,00,000 | 1,50,000 |
| | 3,75,000 | 3,75,000 |
| 2. **Reserves and Surplus** | | |
| General Reserve | 75,000 | 60,000 |
| Statement of Profit and Loss | 75,000 | (70,000) |
| Securities Premium Reserve | 5,000 | — |
| | 1,55,000 | (10,000) |

SP-09 **Additional Information**

During the year, a piece of machinery costing ₹ 30,000 on which depreciation charged was ₹ 10,000 was sold for ₹ 10,000. Depreciation provided on property, plant and equipment ₹ 30,000. Dividend on equity shares @ 8% was paid on opening balance. Income tax ₹ 22,500 was provided. Additional debentures were issued at par on 1st October, 2021 and bank loan was repaid on the same date. At the end of the year, preference shares were redeemed at a premium of 5%. **(Application) [6]**

*Or*

Following is the balance sheet of Ramesh Ltd. as at 31st March, 2022 and 2023.

| Particulars | Note No. | 31st March, 2023 (₹) | 31st March, 2022 (₹) |
|---|---|---|---|
| I. **EQUITY AND LIABILITIES** | | | |
| 1. **Shareholders' Funds** | | | |
| (i) Equity Share Capital | | 3,60,000 | 3,00,000 |
| (ii) Reserves and Surplus | 1 | 2,00,000 | 1,60,000 |

| Particulars | Note No. | 31st March, 2023 (₹) | 31st March, 2022 (₹) |
|---|---|---|---|
| 2. **Non-current Liabilities** | | | |
| Long-term Borrowings | 2 | 3,78,000 | 2,62,000 |
| 3. **Current Liabilities** | | | |
| (i) Trade Payables (Creditors) | | 20,000 | 16,000 |
| (ii) Cash Credit | | 8,000 | 12,000 |
| (iii) Other Current Liabilities (Outstanding expenses) | | 2,000 | 6,000 |
| **Total** | | 9,68,000 | 7,56,000 |
| II. **ASSETS** | | | |
| 1. **Non-current Assets** | | | |
| (i) Property, Plant & Equipment and Intangible Assets | | | |
| (a) Property, Plant and Equipment | 3 | 6,40,000 | 4,60,000 |
| (b) Intangible (Goodwill) | | 10,000 | 20,000 |
| 2. **Current Assets** | | | |
| (i) Inventories | | 34,000 | 40,000 |
| (ii) Trade Receivables | 4 | 1,68,000 | 1,36,000 |
| (iii) Other Current Assets (Prepaid expenses) | | 16,000 | 20,000 |
| (iv) Cash and Cash Equivalents (Cash at bank) | | 1,00,000 | 80,000 |
| **Total** | | 9,68,000 | 7,56,000 |

**Notes to Accounts**

| Particulars | 2023 (₹) | 2022 (₹) |
|---|---|---|
| 1. **Reserves and Surplus** | | |
| General Reserve | 60,000 | 60,000 |
| Balance of Statement of Profit and Loss | 1,40,000 | 1,00,000 |
| | 2,00,000 | 1,60,000 |
| 2. **Long-term Borrowings** | | |
| 12% Debentures | 1,38,000 | 1,02,000 |
| 12% Public Deposits | 2,40,000 | 1,60,000 |
| | 3,78,000 | 2,62,000 |
| 3. **Property, Plant and Equipment** | | |
| Building | 4,40,000 | 3,00,000 |
| Plant | 2,00,000 | 1,60,000 |
| | 6,40,000 | 4,60,000 |
| 4. **Trade Receivables** | | |
| Debtors | 1,50,000 | 1,20,000 |
| Bills Receivables | 18,000 | 16,000 |
| | 1,68,000 | 1,36,000 |

**Additional Information**

(i) Depreciation charged on building ₹ 20,000 and plant ₹ 10,000.

(ii) Interest paid on debentures ₹ 14,400. New debentures of ₹ 36,000 were issued on 1st October, 2022.

(iii) Interest paid on deposits from public ₹ 19,200 for the year.

(a) Calculate operating profit before working capital changes. [2]

(b) Prepare building and plant account. [2]

(c) Calculate cash flow from financing activity. **(Evaluate) [2]**

**Que 14.**

Answer any three of the following **(Application) [6]**

From the given informaton, calculate

(i) Operating ratio (ii) Inventory turnover ratio

(iii) Debt to equity ratio (iv) Gross profit ratio

| Particulars | Amt (₹) |
|---|---|
| Equity Share Capital | 5,00,000 |
| 9% Preference Share Capital | 4,00,000 |
| 12% Debenture (Non-current liabilites) | 2,40,000 |
| General Reserve | 40,000 |
| Revenue from Operations | 8,00,000 |
| Opening Stock | 48,000 |
| Puchases | 5,00,000 |
| Wages | 30,000 |
| Closing Stock | 52,000 |
| Selling and Distribution Expenses | 6,000 |
| Other Current Assets | 2,00,000 |
| Current Liabilities | 1,50,000 |

# Solutions *in Topper's Style*

**My Commitment** *I affirm that I am reviewing these solutions only after I have solved the Sample Question Paper 9 on my own. My purpose of looking the solutions is solely to verify whether my answers/solutions were correct or not and to identify my mistakes in case my solutions were wrong or I could not solve that.*

1. (i) (*b*) 10% debentures amount $= 20{,}000 \times 100 =$ ₹ 20,00,000

where, Number of Debentures $= \frac{16{,}00{,}000}{80} = 20{,}000$

(ii) (*d*) A, C, D, B

(iii) (*d*) Realisation A/c (Dr), Neil's capital A/c (Cr)

(iv) (*d*) C's Current A/c Dr 24,000
To A's Capital 12,000
To B's Capital 12,000

(v) (*d*) Element of business is not present in co-ownership.

(vi) (a) Securities premium represents the excess amount received from issuing shares above their face value.

(b) The amount of securities premium can be utilised for the following purposes (any one)

- Issuing fully paid-up bonus shares to the members.
- In purchasing its own shares (buy-back).

(vii) **JOURNAL**

| Date | Particulars | | Amt (Dr) | Amt (Cr) |
|---|---|---|---|---|
| | Z's Loan A/c | Dr | 96,000 | |
| | To Realisation A/c | | | 72,000 |
| | To Bank A/c | | | 24,000 |
| | (Being Z's loan was paid) | | | |

(viii) Discount on issue $= 20{,}000 \times 10 =$ ₹ 2,00,000

$\therefore$ Premium on redemption $= 4{,}00{,}000 - 2{,}00{,}000 =$ ₹ 2,00,000

(ix) A's New Share $= \frac{4}{8} + \frac{1}{8} = \frac{5}{8}$; B's New Share $= \frac{3}{8}$

$\therefore$ New Profit Sharing Ratio $= 5:3$

(x) **JOURNAL**

| Date | Particulars | | LF | Amt (Dr) | Amt (Cr) |
|---|---|---|---|---|---|
| | General Reserves A/c | Dr | | 80,000 | |
| | To Provision for Doubtful Debts A/c | | | | 20,000 |
| | To X's Capital A/c | | | | 30,000 |
| | To Y's Capital A/c | | | | 30,000 |
| | (Being amount of general reserve adjusted at the admission of Z) | | | | |

2. (i) **Calculation of New Profit Sharing Ratio**

Ram takes his share from Raghav $= \frac{2}{3} \times \frac{1}{4} = \frac{2}{12} = \frac{1}{6}$; Ram takes his share from Krishna $= \frac{1}{3} \times \frac{1}{4} = \frac{1}{12}$

Therefore, Raghav's new share $= \frac{3}{5} - \frac{1}{6} = \frac{13}{30}$; Krishna's new share $= \frac{2}{5} - \frac{1}{12} = \frac{19}{60}$; Ram's share $= \frac{1}{4}$

Therefore, new profit sharing ratio of Ragav, Krishna and Ram $= \frac{13}{30} : \frac{19}{60} : \frac{1}{4} = \frac{26:19:15}{60} = 26:19:15$

(ii) **JOURNAL**

| Date | Particulars | | LF | Amt (Dr) | Amt (Cr) |
|---|---|---|---|---|---|
| | Bank A/c | Dr | | 8,40,000 | |
| | To Ram's Capital A/c | | | | 6,00,000 |
| | To Premium for Goodwill A/c | | | | 2,40,000 |
| | (Being the amount of capital and goodwill/premium brought in cash) | | | | |

| Date | Particulars | | LF | Amt (Dr) | Amt (Cr) |
|---|---|---|---|---|---|
| | Premium for Goodwill A/c | Dr | | 2,40,000 | |
| | To Raghav's Capital A/c | | | | 1,60,000 |
| | To Krishna's Capital A/c | | | | 80,000 |
| | (Being goodwill/premium credited to old partners in their sacrificing ratio i.e. 2 : 1) | | | | |
| | Raghav's Capital A/c | Dr | | 40,000 | |
| | Krishna's Capital A/c | Dr | | 20,000 | |
| | To Bank A/c | | | | 60,000 |
| | (Being 1/4th of the goodwill premium withdrawn by old partners in cash) | | | | |

*Or* (i)

**JOURNAL**

| Date | Particulars | | LF | Amt (Dr) | Amt (Cr) |
|---|---|---|---|---|---|
| 2023 | | | | | |
| Mar 14 | General Reserve A/c | Dr | | 10,000 | |
| | To N's Capital A/c | | | | 10,000 |
| | (Being transfer of N's share of general reserve to his capital account) | | | | |
| | Interest on Capital A/c $\left(70{,}000 \times \frac{5}{100} \times \frac{73}{365}\right)$ | Dr | | 700 | |
| | To N's Capital A/c | | | | 700 |
| | (Being interest @ 5% per annum credited to N's capital account upto 14th March, 2023) | | | | |

(ii)

**JOURNAL**

| Date | Particulars | | LF | Amt (Dr) | Amt (Cr) |
|---|---|---|---|---|---|
| | M's Capital A/c | Dr | | 30,000 | |
| | O's Capital A/c | Dr | | 30,000 | |
| | To N's Capital A/c | | | | 60,000 |
| | (Being goodwill adjusted in gaining ratio, i.e. 1 : 1) | | | | |

(iii)

**JOURNAL**

| Date | Particulars | | LF | Amt (Dr) | Amt (Cr) |
|---|---|---|---|---|---|
| | N's Capital A/c | Dr | | 1,52,700 | |
| | To N's Executor's A/c | | | | 1,52,700 |
| | (Being the transfer of amount due to N's executor's account) | | | | |

**Working Notes**

1. Calculation of goodwill

   $$\text{Average Profit} = \frac{\text{Total Profit}}{\text{Number of Years}} = \frac{80{,}000 + 90{,}000 + 1{,}00{,}000}{3} = ₹\ 90{,}000$$

   $$\text{Goodwill of the Firm} = \text{Average Profit} \times \text{Number of Years' Purchase} = 90{,}000 \times 2 = ₹\ 1{,}80{,}000$$

   $$\text{N's share in goodwill} = 1{,}80{,}000 \times \frac{1}{3} = ₹\ 60{,}000$$

2. Time from the date of last balance sheet (31st December, 2022) to the date of death (14th March, 2023) = 31 days of January + 28 days of February (2023 is not a leap year) + 14 days of March = 73 days

   $$\text{N's Share in Profit} = 90{,}000 \times 2 \times \frac{73}{365} \times \frac{1}{3} = 12{,}000$$

3. Amount due to N = 70,000 + 10,000 + 700 + 60,000 + 12,000 = ₹ 1,52,700

**3.** (i)

| Particulars | P (₹) | Q (₹) | R (₹) |
|---|---|---|---|
| (i) ₹ 12,000 in the capital ratio, i.e. 3 : 3 : 4 | 3,600 | 3,600 | 4,800 |
| (ii) Next ₹ 18,000 in the ratio, 5 : 3 : 2 | 9,000 | 5,400 | 3,600 |
| (iii) Remaining equally, i.e. ₹ 8,400 | 2,800 | 2,800 | 2,800 |
| | 15,400 | 11,800 | 11,200 |

(ii)

**Profit and Loss Appropriation Account**
for the year ended ......

Dr | Cr

| Particulars | | Amt (₹) | Particulars | Amt (₹) |
|---|---|---|---|---|
| To Interest on Capital | | | By Profit | 45,000 |
| P's Current A/c | 900 | | | |
| Q's Current A/c | 900 | | | |
| R's Current A/c | 1,200 | 3,000 | | |
| To R's Current A/c (Salary) | | 3,600 | | |
| To Profit transferred to | | | | |
| P's Current A/c | 15,400 | | | |
| Q's Current A/c | 11,800 | | | |
| R's Current A/c | 11,200 | 38,400 | | |
| | | 45,000 | | 45,000 |

*Or* (i) (a) S – ₹ 48,000; P – ₹ 56,000
(b) S – ₹ 2,000; P – ₹ 2,000

**Working Note**

**Adjustment Table**

| Particulars | S (₹) | P (₹) | Total (₹) |
|---|---|---|---|
| I. **Amount already Recorded** | | | |
| Interest on Capital @ 18% | 90,000 | 54,000 | 1,44,000 |
| II. **Amount which should have been Recorded** | | | |
| Interest on Capital @ 8% | 40,000 | 24,000 | 64,000 |
| Share of Profit (1,44,000 – 64,000) in ratio of 3 : 2 | 48,000 | 32,000 | 80,000 |
| | 88,000 | 56,000 | 1,44,000 |
| Net Effect (I – II) | 2,000 | 2,000 | – |

(ii)

**JOURNAL**

| Date | Particulars | | LF | Amt (Dr) | Amt (Cr) |
|---|---|---|---|---|---|
| 2023 | | | | | |
| Apr 1 | S's Capital A/c | Dr | | 2,000 | |
| | To P's Capital A/c | | | | 2,000 |
| | (Being an adjusting entry passed) | | | | |

4.

| S.No. | Particulars | Major Heads | Sub-heads |
|---|---|---|---|
| (i) | Publising Titles | Non-current Assets | Property, Plant & Equipment and Intangible Assets: Intangible Assets |
| (ii) | Mining Rights | Non-current Assets | Property, Plant & Equipment and Intangible Assets : Intangible Assets |
| (iii) | Loosse Tools | Current Assets | Inventories |
| (iv) | Cheques and Bank Drafts in Hand | Current Assets | Cash and Cash Equivalents |
| (v) | Securities Premium | Shareholder's Funds | Reserves and Surplus |
| (vi) | Sundry Debtors | Current Assets | Trade Receivables |
| (vii) | Preliminary Expenses | Reserves and Surplus | Deducted from Security Premium Reserve |
| (viii) | Calls-in-arrears | Shareholder's Funds | Share Capital (Notes ot Accounts) |
| (ix) | Investments in Debentures | Non-current Assets | Non-current Investments |

**Common Mistake** Students usually record mining rights in 'properties, plant and equipment: tangible assets' as mines are a tangible asset. But "rights" given by government to mine is an intangible asset and will be shown under sub-head 'properties, plant and equipment: intangible assets'.

**5.**

**In the Books of Z Ltd.**
**Balance sheet**
as at 31st March, 2022

| Particulars | Note No. | Amt (₹) |
|---|---|---|
| I. **EQUITY AND LIABILITIES** | | |
| 1. **Shareholders' Fund** | | |
| (i) Share Capital | | 16,000 |
| (ii) Reserves and Surplus | | 3,600 |
| 2. **Non-current Liabilities** | | |
| Long-term Borrowings | | 20,000 |
| 3. **Current Liabilities** | | |
| Trade Paybles | | 1,200 |
| **Total** | | 40,800 |
| II. **ASSETS** | | |
| 1. **Non-current Assets** | | |
| (i) Proprerty, Plant & Equipment and Intangible Assets | | 32,000 |
| 2. **Current Assets** | | |
| (i) Inventories | | 800 |
| (ii) Trade Receivables | | 3,200 |
| (iii) Cash and Cash Equivalents | | 4,800 |
| **Total** | | 40,800 |

**6.**

**Profit and Loss Appropriation Account**
for the year ended 31st March, 2023

Dr | Cr

| Particulars | | Amt (₹) | Particulars | | Amt (₹) |
|---|---|---|---|---|---|
| To Interest on Capital A/cs | | | By Net Profit as per Profit and Loss A/c | 3,60,000 | |
| Sohan (3,00,000 × 5%) | 15,000 | | (−) Rent to Sohan | (50,000) | |
| Mohan (2,80,000 × 5%) | 14,000 | 29,000 | (−) Interest on Loan (Mohan) | (10,000) | 3,00,000 |
| To Salary – Sohan (1,000 × 12) | | 12,000 | By Interest on Drawings A/c | | |
| To Commission to Mohan | | 14,000 | Sohan $\left(80,000 \times \frac{5}{100} \times \frac{6}{12}\right)$ | 2,000 | |
| To Net Profit transferred to | | | Mohan $\left(60,000 \times \frac{5}{100} \times \frac{6}{12}\right)$ | 1,500 | 3,500 |
| Sohan's Capital A/c | 1,24,250 | | | | |
| Mohan's Capital A/c | 1,24,250 | 2,48,500 | | | |
| | | 3,03,500 | | | 3,03,500 |

**Partners' Capital Account**

Dr | Cr

| Particulars | Sohan (₹) | Mohan (₹) | Particulars | Sohan (₹) | Mohan (₹) |
|---|---|---|---|---|---|
| To Drawings A/c | 80,000 | 60,000 | By Balance b/d | 3,00,000 | 2,80,000 |
| To Interest on Drawings A/c | 2,000 | 1,500 | By Interest on Capital A/c | 15,000 | 14,000 |
| To Balance c/d | 4,19,250 | 3,80,750 | By Salary A/c | 12,000 | — |
| | | | By Commission A/c | — | 14,000 |
| | | | By Rent A/c | 50,000 | — |
| | | | By Interest on Loan A/c | — | 10,000 |
| | | | By Profit and Loss Appropriation A/c (Profit) | 1,24,250 | 1,24,250 |
| | 5,01,250 | 4,42,250 | | 5,01,250 | 4,42,250 |

**Note** Rent payable to Sohan and interest on loan payable to Mohan may also be shown on the liabilities side.

**Value Points**

- For interest on drawings, average period will be 6 in the absence of any information.
- Rent to Sohan is a charge against profit and will be charged to profit and loss account and not to profit and loss appropriation account

**7.** Dr **Realisation Account** Cr

| Particulars | Amt (₹) | Particulars | | Amt (₹) |
|---|---|---|---|---|
| To Debtors | 4,700 | By Creditors | | 5,000 |
| To Stock | 2,300 | By Investment Fluctuation Fund | | 300 |
| To Furniture | 50 | By Cash A/c (Assets realised) | | |
| To Property | 2,000 | Property | 1,500 | |
| To Investment | 1,100 | Stock | 2,525 | |
| To Cash A/c (Creditors) | 4,900 | Debtors | 4,200 | |
| To R's Capital A/c | 75 | Furniture | 50 | |
| | | Investment | 1,100 | 9,375 |
| | | By Loss on Realisation transferred to | | |
| | | R's Capital A/c | 253 | |
| | | K's Capital A/c | 197 | 450 |
| | 15,125 | | | 15,125 |

*Or* Dr **Realisation Account** Cr

| Particulars | | Amt (₹) | Particulars | | Amt (₹) |
|---|---|---|---|---|---|
| To Sundry Assets A/c | | | By Sundry Liabilities A/c | | |
| Debtors | 3,40,000 | | Creditors | | 1,50,000 |
| Stock | 1,50,000 | | By Bank A/c (Assets realised) | | |
| Furniture | 4,60,000 | | Debtors | 3,23,000 | |
| Machinery | 8,20,000 | 17,70,000 | Stock | 65,000 | |
| To Bank A/c (Liabilities paid) | | | Machinery | 74,000 | 4,62,000 |
| Creditors | | 1,50,000 | By Hanif's Current A/c (Stock) (75,000 – 7,500) | | 67,500 |
| To Hanif's Current A/c (Realisation expenses) | | 8,000 | By Jubed's Current A/c (Furniture) | | 1,35,000 |
| | | | By Loss transferred to Current A/cs | | |
| | | | Hanif | 7,42,333 | |
| | | | Jubed | 3,71,167 | 11,13,500 |
| | | 19,28,000 | | | 19,28,000 |

**8.** (i) **JOURNAL**

| Date | Particulars | | LF | Amt (Dr) | Amt (Cr) |
|---|---|---|---|---|---|
| 2023 | | | | | |
| Apr 1 | Bank A/c (20,000 × 50) | Dr | | 10,00,000 | |
| | To Debenture Application A/c | | | | 10,00,000 |
| | (Being receipt of application money on 20,000 debentures @ ₹ 50 each) | | | | |
| Apr 1 | Debenture Application A/c | Dr | | 10,00,000 | |
| | To 6% Debentures A/c | | | | 10,00,000 |
| | (Being application money transferred to 6% debentures account) | | | | |
| Apr 1 | Debenture Allotment A/c (20,000 × 46) | Dr | | 9,20,000 | |
| | Loss on Issue of Debentures A/c (80,000 + 1,00,000) | Dr | | 1,80,000 | |
| | To 6% Debentures A/c (20,000 × 50) | | | | 10,00,000 |
| | To Premium on Redemption of Debentures A/c (20,000 × 5) | | | | 1,00,000 |
| | (Being amount due @ ₹ 46 each on 20,000 debentures issued at 4% discount and redeemable at 5% premium) | | | | |

| Date | Particulars | | LF | Amt (Dr) | Amt (Cr) |
|---|---|---|---|---|---|
| Apr 1 | Bank A/c | Dr | | 9,20,000 | |
| | To Debenture Allotment A/c | | | | 9,20,000 |
| | (Being allotment money received) | | | | |

(ii)

| Date | Particulars | | LF | Amt (Dr) | Amt (Cr) |
|---|---|---|---|---|---|
| 2024 | | | | | |
| Mar 31 | Securities Premium A/c | Dr | | 50,000 | |
| | General Reserve A/c | Dr | | 1,00,000 | |
| | Statement of Profit and Loss | Dr | | 30,000 | |
| | To Loss on Issue of Debentures A/c | | | | 1,80,000 |
| | (Being loss on issue of debentures written-off) | | | | |

**9.** (a) **JOURNAL**

| Date | Particulars | | LF | Amt (Dr) | Amt (Cr) |
|---|---|---|---|---|---|
| | Equity Share Application and Allotment A/c | Dr | | 11,20,000 | |
| | To Equity Share Capital A/c (1,00,000 × 5) | | | | 5,00,000 |
| | To Securities Premium A/c (1,00,000 × 3) | | | | 3,00,000 |
| | To Calls-in-advance A/c (40,000 × 8) | | | | 3,20,000 |
| | (Being transfer of application and allotment money) | | | | |
| | Equity Share First and Final Call A/c (1,00,000 × 7) | Dr | | 7,00,000 | |
| | To Equity Share Capital A/c (1,00,000 × 5) | | | | 5,00,000 |
| | To Securities Premium A/c (1,00,000 × 2) | | | | 2,00,000 |
| | (Being first and final call due on 1,00,000 shares) | | | | |
| | Calls-in-arrears A/c (WN1) | Dr | | 1,900 | |
| | To Equity Share First and Final Call A/c | | | | 1,900 |
| | (Being amount not received on call) | | | | |
| | Calls-in-advance A/c | Dr | | 3,20,000 | |
| | To Equity Share First and Final Call A/c | | | | 3,20,000 |
| | (Being calls-in-advance adjusted to share first and final call account) | | | | |
| | Equity Share Capital A/c (500 × 10) | Dr | | 5,000 | |
| | Securities Premium A/c (500 × 2) | Dr | | 1,000 | |
| | To Calls-in-arrears A/c (1,300 + 600) | | | | 1,900 |
| | To Share Forfeiture A/c | | | | 4,100 |
| | (Being forfeiture of 300 shares of X and 200 shares of Y for non-payment of call money) | | | | |
| | Share Forfeiture A/c | Dr | | 4,100 | |
| | To Capital A/c | | | | 4,100 |
| | (Being balance of share forfeiture transferred to capital reserve) | | | | |

**Working Notes**

1. (i) Number of shares applied by X $= \frac{80,000}{60,000} \times 300 = 400$

Number of shares applied by Y $= \frac{60,000}{40,000} \times 200 = 300$

Excess amount received from X = 400 shares – 300 shares = 100 shares × 8 = ₹ 800

Excess amount received from Y = 300 shares – 200 shares = 100 shares × 8 = ₹ 800

(ii) Amount due from X and Y on first and final call

| | Amt (₹) |
|---|---|
| X = 300 shares @ ₹ 7 | 2,100 |
| Y = 200 shares @ ₹ 7 | 1,400 |
| | 3,500 |
| (–) Excess received on application and allotment from X and Y (800 + 800) | (1,600) |
| Amount due but not paid on first and final call | 1,900 |

2. Since, the question is silent as to the utilisation of excess application and allotment money from X and Y, it has been assumed that the entire excess application and allotment money is exclusively for share capital and hence, securities premium account has been debited in the entry for forfeiture.

(b) Dr **Cash Book** Cr

| Particulars | Amt (₹) | Particulars | Amt (₹) |
|---|---|---|---|
| To Equity Share Application and Allotment A/c (1,50,000 × 8) | 12,00,000 | By Equity Share Application and Allotment A/c (Refund of applications for 10,000 shares @ ₹ 8 per share) | 80,000 |
| To Equity Share First and Final Call A/c (7,00,000 – 3,20,000 – 1,900) | 3,78,100 | By Balance c/d | 15,04,100 |
| To Equity Share Capital A/c | 5,000 | | |
| To Securities Premium A/c | 1,000 | | |
| | 15,84,100 | | 15,84,100 |

*Or* (i) Number of shares applied by Rohit $= 400 \times \frac{3,000}{2,000} = 600$ shares

(ii) **Calculation of Amount Received at Allotment**

| | Amt (₹) |
|---|---|
| Amount due on allotment (2,000 × 25) | 50,000 |
| (–) Excess amount received on application | (10,000) |
| (–) Calls-in-arrears on allotment | 40,000 |
| Amount received on allotment | (8,000) |
| | 32,000 |

| | |
|---|---|
| (iii) Amount received on application (600 × 10) | 6,000 |
| Amount due on application (400 × 10) | (4,000) |
| Excess amount to be adjusted on allotment | 2,000 |
| (iv) Amount due on allotment (400 × 25) | 10,000 |
| (–) Amount adjusted on allotment | (2,000) |
| Calls-in-arrears on allotment | 8,000 |
| Calls-in-arrears on first call (400 × 40) | 16,000 |

∴ Total calls-in-arrears = 8,000 + 16,000 = ₹ 24,000

(v)

| Date | Particulars | | LF | Amt (Dr) | Amt (Cr) |
|---|---|---|---|---|---|
| (a) | Share Capital A/c (400 × 70) | Dr | | 28,000 | |
| | Securities Premium A/c (400 × 5) | | | 2,000 | |
| | To Share Allotment A/c | | | | 8,000 |
| | To Share First Call A/c (400 × 40) | | | | 16,000 |
| | To Share Forfeiture A/c | | | | 6,000 |
| | (Being 400 share forfeited for the non-payment of allotment and share first call) | | | | |
| (b) | Bank A/c (400 × 60) | Dr | | 24,000 | |
| | Share Forfeiture A/c (400 × 10) | Dr | | 4,000 | |
| | To Share Capital A/c (400 × 70) | | | | 28,000 |
| | (Being re-issued of forfeited shares at ₹ 60 per share @ ₹ 70 paid-up) | | | | |
| | Share Forfeiture A/c | Dr | | 2,000 | |
| | To Capital Reserve A/c | | | | 2,000 |
| | (Being transfer of share forfeiture to capital reserve account) | | | | |

**10.** (A)

(a) Dr **Revaluation Account** Cr

| Particulars | | Amt (₹) | Particulars | Amt (₹) |
|---|---|---|---|---|
| To Investment A/c | | 5,000 | By Accrued Income A/c | 500 |
| To Profit transferred to | | | By Bad Debts Recovered A/c | 800 |
| Madan's Capital A/c | 780 | | By Patents A/c | 5,000 |
| Mohan's Capital A/c | 520 | 1,300 | | |
| | | 6,300 | | 6,300 |

(b) Dr **Partners' Capital Account** Cr

| Particulars | Madan (₹) | Mohan (₹) | Gopal (₹) | Particulars | Madan (₹) | Mohan (₹) | Gopal (₹) |
|---|---|---|---|---|---|---|---|
| To Balance c/d | 93,780 | 62,520 | 52,100 | By Balance b/d | 60,000 | 40,000 | — |
| | | | | By Premium for Goodwill A/c | 15,000 | 10,000 | — |
| | | | | By General Reserve A/c | 12,000 | 8,000 | — |
| | | | | By Workmen Compensation Fund A/c | 6,000 | 4,000 | — |
| | | | | By Revaluation A/c (Profit) | 780 | 520 | — |
| | | | | By Bank A/c | — | — | 52,100 |
| | 93,780 | 62,520 | 52,100 | | 93,780 | 62,520 | 52,100 |

**Working Notes**

1. Let the profits be ₹ 1

   Remaining share $= 1 - \frac{1}{4} = \frac{3}{4}$

   Madan's new share $= \frac{3}{5} \times \frac{3}{4} = \frac{9}{20}$; Mohan's new share $= \frac{2}{5} \times \frac{3}{4} = \frac{6}{20}$

   Gopal's share $= \frac{1}{4} \times \frac{5}{5} = \frac{5}{20}$

   New ratio $= 9:6:5$

2. Calculation of adjustment of capital

| | Amt (₹) |
|---|---|
| Adjusted capital of Madan | 93,780 |
| Adjusted capital of Mohan | 62,520 |
| | 1,56,300 |

   Gopal's share in new firm $= \frac{1}{4}$th

   Remaining share $= 1 - \frac{1}{4} = \frac{4-1}{4} = \frac{3}{4}$

   Capital of Madan and Mohan for $\frac{3}{4}$th share = ₹ 1,56,300

   So, total capital $= 1{,}56{,}300 \times \frac{4}{3} =$ ₹ 2,08,400

   Gopal's capital $= 2{,}08{,}400 \times \frac{1}{4} =$ ₹ 52,100

(c) **Balance Sheet**
**as at 1st April, 2021**

| Liabilities | | Amt (₹) | Assets | | Amt (₹) |
|---|---|---|---|---|---|
| Workmen Compensation Fund | | 2,000 | Accrued Income | | 500 |
| Creditors | | 28,000 | Investment | 50,000 | |
| Capital A/cs | | | (−) Decrease in Value | (5,000) | 45,000 |
| Madan | 93,780 | | Patents | 10,000 | |
| Mohan | 62,520 | | (+) Undervalued | 5,000 | 15,000 |
| Gopal | 52,100 | 2,08,400 | Bank | | 87,900 |

| Liabilities | Amt (₹) | Assets | | Amt (₹) |
|---|---|---|---|---|
| | | Debtors | 65,000 | |
| | | (–) Provision for Doubtful Debts | (5,000) | 60,000 |
| | | Stock | | 30,000 |
| | 2,38,400 | | | 2,38,400 |

**Working Note**

Dr **Bank Account** Cr

| Particulars | Amt (₹) | Particulars | Amt (₹) |
|---|---|---|---|
| To Balance b/d | 10,000 | By Balance c/d | 87,900 |
| To Bad Debts Recovered A/c | 800 | | |
| To Premium for Goodwill A/c | 25,000 | | |
| To Gopal's Capital A/c | 52,100 | | |
| | 87,900 | | 87,900 |

**Common Mistake** Students may deduct ₹ 1,000 as bad debts from debtors. These bad debts are not of current year, hence it is previously recorded as bad debts and should not be deducted from the debtors and ₹ 800 will be added back to cash at bank.

(B) (ii) A's sacrifice $= \frac{5}{8} \times \frac{1}{4} = \frac{5}{32}$; A's new share $= \frac{5}{8} - \frac{5}{32} = \frac{20-5}{32} = \frac{15}{32} \times \frac{5}{5} = \frac{75}{160}$; S's sacrifice $= \frac{3}{8} \times \frac{1}{5} = \frac{3}{40}$

S's new share $= \frac{3}{8} - \frac{3}{40} = \frac{15-3}{40} = \frac{12}{40} \times \frac{4}{4} = \frac{48}{160}$; M's share $= \frac{5}{32} + \frac{3}{40} = \frac{25+12}{160} = \frac{37}{160}$

New ratio = 75 : 48 : 37

*Or* (a)

**JOURNAL**

| Date | Particulars | | LF | Amt (Dr) | Amt (Cr) |
|---|---|---|---|---|---|
| Apr 1 | Sunaina's Current A/c (20,000 × 3/5) | Dr | | 12,000 | |
| | Tamanna's Current A/c (20,000 × 2/5) | Dr | | 8,000 | |
| | To Goodwill A/c | | | | 20,000 |
| | (Being goodwill written-off) | | | | |
| Apr 1 | Cash A/c | Dr | | 1,10,000 | |
| | To Pranav's Capital A/c | | | | 1,00,000 |
| | To Premium for Goodwill A/c | | | | 10,000 |
| | (Being capital and premium brought-in by new partner) | | | | |
| Apr 1 | Premium for Goodwill A/c | Dr | | 10,000 | |
| | To Sunaina's Current A/c (10,000 x 3/5) | | | | 6,000 |
| | To Tamanna's Current A/c (10,000 x 2/5) | | | | 4,000 |
| | (Being premium distributed among sacrificing partners in sacrificing ratio) | | | | |
| | (Being plant and machinery revalued) | | | | |

(b)

**JOURNAL**

| Date | Particulars | | LF | Amt (Dr) | Amt (Cr) |
|---|---|---|---|---|---|
| Apr 1 | General Reserve A/c | Dr | | 1,20,000 | |
| | To Sunaina's Current A/c (1,20,000 × 3/5) | | | | 72,000 |
| | To Tamanna's Current A/c (1,20,000 × 2/5) | | | | 48,000 |
| | (Being reserve distributed among old partners) | | | | |

(c)

**JOURNAL**

| Date | Particulars | | LF | Amt (Dr) | Amt (Cr) |
|---|---|---|---|---|---|
| Apr 1 | Workmen Compensation Reserve A/c | Dr | | 50,000 | |
| | To Claim for Workmen Compensation A/c | | | | 20,000 |
| | To Sunaina's Current A/c (30,000 × 3/5) | | | | 18,000 |
| | To Tamanna's Current A/c (30,000 × 2/5) | | | | 12,000 |
| | (Being provision for workmen compensation provided and balance reserve distributed among old partners) | | | | |

(d)

**JOURNAL**

| Date | Particulars | | LF | Amt (Dr) | Amt (Cr) |
|---|---|---|---|---|---|
| Apr 1 | Revaluation A/c | Dr | | 20,000 | |
| | To Plant and Machinery A/c | | | | 20,000 |
| | (Being plant and machinery revalued) | | | | |
| Apr 1 | Land and Building A/c | Dr | | 40,000 | |
| | Provision for Doubtful Debts A/c | Dr | | 40,000 | |
| | To Revaluation A/c | | | | 80,000 |
| | (Being land and building revalued and provision for doubtful debts written back) | | | | |

(e)

**JOURNAL**

| Date | Particulars | | LF | Amt (Dr) | Amt (Cr) |
|---|---|---|---|---|---|
| Apr 1 | Revaluation A/c | Dr | | 60,000 | |
| | To Sunaina's Current A/c (60,000 × 3/5) | | | | 36,000 |
| | To Tamanna's Current A/c (60,000 x 2/5) | | | | 24,000 |
| | (Being profit on revaluation credited to partners current account) | | | | |

11. (i) (*c*) The issue of bonus shares will not effect while preparing cash flow statement as there is no flow of cash.

(ii) • Gross profit ratio

• (*a*) Gross Profit/Net Revenue from Operations × 100

(iii) Financial statement analysis is useful to finance manager for taking financial decisions for the business. It provided adequate information for financial planning.

(iv) Accounting ratios are useful for intra-firm analysis.

(v)

| | |
|---|---|
| Net profit after tax | 70,000 |
| (+) Goodwill written-off | 10,000 |
| Loss on sale of machinery | 3,000 |
| | ₹ 83,000 |

12.

**Common Size Balance Sheet**

as at 31st March, 2023 and 2024

| Particulars | Note No. | Absolute Amounts | | % of Balance Sheet Total | |
|---|---|---|---|---|---|
| | | 2023 (₹) | 2024 (₹) | 2023 (%) | 2024 (%) |
| **I. EQUITY AND LIABILITIES** | | | | | |
| **1. Shareholders' Funds** | | | | | |
| (i) Share Capital | | 4,00,000 | 4,00,000 | 40 | 25 |
| (ii) Reserves and Surplus | | 80,000 | 2,40,000 | 8 | 15 |
| **2. Non-current Liabilities** | | 3,20,000 | 4,80,000 | 32 | 30 |
| **3. Current Liabilities** | | | | | |
| (i) Trade Payables | | 1,60,000 | 3,20,000 | 16 | 20 |
| (ii) Short-term Provision | | 40,000 | 1,60,000 | 4 | 10 |
| **Total** | | 10,00,000 | 16,00,000 | 100 | 100 |
| **II. ASSETS** | | | | | |
| **1. Non-current Assets** | | | | | |
| (i) Fixed Assets | | 7,60,000 | 11,20,000 | 76 | 70 |
| (ii) Non-current investments | | 40,000 | 80,000 | 4 | 5 |
| **2. Current Assets** | | 2,00,000 | 4,00,000 | 20 | 25 |
| **Total** | | 10,00,000 | 16,00,000 | 100 | 100 |

13.

**Calculation of Net Cash Flow from Operating Activities**

| Particulars | Amt (₹) |
|---|---|
| **Cash Flow from Operating Activities** | |
| Net Profit before Tax (WN 1) | 2,08,000 |

| Particulars | | Amt (₹) |
|---|---|---|
| **Adjustments for** | | |
| (+) Depreciation on Property, Plant and Equipment | 30,000 | |
| Loss on Sale of Machinery (WN 2) | 10,000 | |
| Interest on Debentures [ $(75,000 \times 8/100) + (55,000 \times 8/100 \times 6/12)$] | 8,200 | |
| Interest on Bank Loan [$(25,000 \times 8/100 \times 6/12) + (20,000 \times 8/100 \times 6/12)$] | 1,800 | |
| Goodwill Amortised | 12,500 | |
| Premium on Redemption of Preference Shares | 2,500 | 65,000 |
| Operating Profit before Working Capital Changes | | 2,73,000 |
| (+) Decrease in Current Assets and Increase in Current Liabilities | | |
| Trade Payables | 5,000 | |
| (–) Increase in Current Assets and Decrease in Current Liabilities | | |
| Inventories | (47,500) | (42,500) |
| Net Cash Flow from Operating Activities before Tax | | 2,30,500 |
| (–) Tax Paid (WN 3) | | (17,500) |
| Net Cash Inflow from Operating Activities after Tax | | 2,13,000 |

**Working Notes**

1. **Calculation of Net Profit before Tax**

| Particulars | Amt (₹) |
|---|---|
| Net Profit as per Statement of Profit and Loss (75,000 + 70,000) | 1,45,000 |
| (+) Transfer to Reserve | 15,000 |
| (+) Dividend on Equity Shares | 18,000 |
| (+) Dividend on Preference Shares | 7,500 |
| (+) Provision for Tax | 22,500 |
| Net Profit before Tax | 2,08,000 |

2. Dr **Property, Plant and Equipment Account** Cr

| Particulars | Amt (₹) | Particulars | Amt (₹) |
|---|---|---|---|
| To Balance b/d | 3,10,000 | By Depreciation A/c | 30,000 |
| To Bank A/c (Purchases) (Balancing figure) | 1,70,000 | By Bank A/c (Sale) | 10,000 |
| | | By Loss on Sale A/c (Statement of profit and loss) | 10,000 |
| | | By Balance c/d | 4,30,000 |
| | 4,80,000 | | 4,80,000 |

3. Dr **Provision for Tax Account** Cr

| Particulars | Amt (₹) | Particulars | Amt (₹) |
|---|---|---|---|
| To Bank A/c (Balancing figure) | 17,500 | By Balance b/d | 20,000 |
| To Balance c/d | 25,000 | By Provision for Tax A/c (Statement of profit and loss) | 22,500 |
| | 42,500 | | 42,500 |

*Or* (a)

| Particulars | | Amt (₹) |
|---|---|---|
| Net Profit as per Statement of Profit and Loss (1,40,000 – 1,00,000) | | 40,000 |
| **Adjustments for** | | |
| (+) Goodwill Written-off | 10,000 | |
| Depreciation on Building | 20,000 | |
| Depreciation on Plant | 10,000 | |
| Interest on Debentures | 14,400 | |
| Interest on Public Deposits | 19,200 | 73,600 |
| Operating Profit before Working Capital Changes | | 1,13,600 |

(b) Dr **Building Account** Cr

| Particulars | Amt (₹) | Particulars | Amt (₹) |
|---|---|---|---|
| To Balance b/d | 3,00,000 | By Depreciation A/c | 20,000 |
| To Bank A/c (Purchase) (Balancing figure) | 1,60,000 | By Balance c/d | 4,40,000 |
| | 4,60,000 | | 4,60,000 |

Dr **Plant Account** Cr

| Particulars | Amt (₹) | Particulars | Amt (₹) |
|---|---|---|---|
| To Balance b/d | 1,60,000 | By Depreciation A/c | 10,000 |
| To Bank A/c (Purchase) (Balancing figure) | 50,000 | By Balance c/d | 2,00,000 |
| | 2,10,000 | | 2,10,000 |

(c) **Cash Flow from Financing Activities**

| Particulars | | Amt (₹) |
|---|---|---|
| **Cash Flow from Financing Activities** | | |
| Decrease in Cash Credit | (4,000) | |
| Cash Proceeds from Issue of Equity Shares | 60,000 | |
| Cash Proceeds from Issue of Debentures | 36,000 | |
| Cash Proceeds from Public Deposits | 80,000 | |
| Interest on Debentures Paid | (14,400) | |
| Interest on Public Deposits Paid | (19,200) | |
| Net Cash from Financing Activities | | 1,38,400 |

**14.** (i) $\text{Operating Ratio} = \dfrac{\text{Operating Cost}}{\text{Net Revenue from Operations}} \times 100 = \dfrac{5{,}32{,}000}{8{,}00{,}000} \times 100$

Operating Ratio = 66.5%

where,

Operating Cost = Cost of Revenue from Operations + Operating Expenses

*or* = Opening Inventory + Net Purchases + Direct Expenses − Closing Inventory + Selling and Distribution Expenses

= 48,000 + 5,00,000 + 30,000 − 52,000 + 6,000 = ₹ 5,32,000

(ii) $\text{Inventory Turnover Ratio} = \dfrac{\text{Cost of Revenue from Operations}}{\text{Average Inventory}} = \dfrac{5{,}26{,}000}{50{,}000}$

Inventory Turnover Ratio = 10.52 times

where,

Cost of Revenue from Operations

= Opening Inventory + Purchases + Wages − Closing Inventory

= 48,000 + 5,00,000 + 30,000 − 52,000 = ₹ 5,26,000

$\text{Average Stock} = \dfrac{\text{Opening Inventory} + \text{Closing Inventory}}{2} = \dfrac{48{,}000 + 52{,}000}{2} = ₹\ 50{,}000$

(iii) $\text{Debt to Equity Ratio} = \dfrac{\text{Debt}}{\text{Equity}} = \dfrac{2{,}40{,}000}{9{,}40{,}000} = 0.26 : 1$

Debt = ₹ 2,40,000

Equity = 5,00,000 + 4,00,000 + 40,000 = ₹ 9,40,000

(iv) $\text{Gross Profit Ratio} = \dfrac{\text{Gross Profit}}{\text{Net Sales}} \times 100 = \dfrac{2{,}74{,}000}{8{,}00{,}000} \times 100 = 34.25\%$

Net Sales = ₹ 8,00,000

Gross Profit = Net Sales − Cost of Revenue from Operations

= 8,00,000 − 5,26,000 = ₹ 2,74,000

SQP Code : **PB-10/15** Series ***i*-Succeed 10-25/15** Roll No. 

# Sample Question Paper 10

## Accounts 12th (Code 858)

### General Instructions

1. Candidates are allowed additional 15 minutes for only reading the paper. They must not start writing during this time.
2. Section-A is compulsory for all candidates and has ten questions.
3. Candidates have to attempt all questions from either Section-B or Section-C*.
4. Internal choices have been provided in five questions in Section-A and one question in Section-B.
5. The intended marks for questions or parts of questions are given in the brackets [ ].
6. All calculations should be shown clearly.
7. All workings, including rough work, should be done on the same page as, and adjacent to, the rest of the answer.

*Section-C has not been covered.

**Time :** 3 Hrs.

**Max. Marks :** 80

## Section A Answer All Questions [60 Marks]

**Que 1.**

In sub-parts (i) to (iv), choose the correct option and in sub-parts (v) to (x) answer the questions as instructed.

(i) In case of dissolution of a partnership, outstanding liability previously unrecorded, is now realised in cash.
The journal entry passed will be (Understanding) [1]

(a) Debit Realisation Account and Credit Unrecorded Liability
(b) Debit Unrecorded Liability and Credit Realisation Account
(c) No entry will be passed
(d) Debit Realisation Account and Credit Cash Account

(ii) What will be the correct sequence of the following events?

A – Re-issue of shares
B – Incorporation of company
C – Forfeiture of shares
D – Inviting applications from public (Recall) [1]

**Codes**

(a) B, A, D, C
(b) D, C, B, A
(c) D, B, C, A
(d) B, D, C, A

(iii) Balance sheet of A and B showed ₹ 12,000 profit and loss account debit balance, at the time of admission of new partner C with 1/4th share.

What journal entry will be passed for the debit balance of profit and loss account of ₹ 12,000? (Application) [1]

| | | | | |
|---|---|---|---|---|
| (a) | Revaluation A/c | Dr | 12,000 | |
| | To Profit and Loss A/c | | | 12,000 |
| (b) | Profit and Loss A/c | Dr | 12,000 | |
| | To A's Capital A/c | | | 6,000 |
| | To B's Capital A/c | | | 6,000 |
| (c) | A's Capital A/c | Dr | 6,000 | |
| | B's Capital A/c | Dr | 6,000 | |
| | To Profit and Loss A/c | | | 2,000 |
| (d) | Profit and Loss A/c | Dr | 12,000 | |
| | To C's Capital A/c | | | 12,000 |

(iv) X Co Ltd. purchased assets worth ₹ 28,80,000.
It issued debentures of ₹ 100 each at a discount of 4 per cent in full satisfaction of the purchase consideration. The number of debentures issued to vendor is (Application) [1]

(a) 30,000 (b) 28,800
(c) 32,000 (d) 40,000

(v) **Assertion** (A) Goodwill is the present value of a firm's anticipated expected earnings.

**Reason** (R) The capitalised value attached to the differential profit capacity of a business is called goodwill. (Evaluate) [1]

**Alternatives**

(a) Both Assertion (A) and Reason (R) are true and Reason (R) is the correct explanation of Assertion (A)
(b) Both Assertion (A) and Reason (R) are true, but Reason (R) is not the correct explanation of Assertion (A)
(c) Assertion (A) is true, but Reason (R) is false
(d) Assertion (A) is false, but Reason (R) is true

(vi) A company purchases building for ₹ 3,60,000 and issued debentures as a payment in debentures at 20% premium. Pass the requried journal entry to record the transaction. (Application) [1]

(vii) The value of furniture is reduced up to ₹ 45,000. The book value of the furniture was ₹ 55,000. What journal entry will be passed for change in the value of furniture? (Application) [1]

(viii) "Reserve is an amount set aside out of profit to strengthen the financial position of the firm or to meet an unforeseen liability."

(a) What are reserves?
(b) Based on the statement, name the reserve that is created to meet an unforeseen liability. (Recall) [1]

(ix) At the time of dissolution of a firm, debtors (before deducting provision) and provision for doubtful debts were ₹ 18,000 and ₹ 3,000. Debtors worth ₹ 6,000 proved bad. Calculate the amount realised from debtors. (Application) [1]

(x) What are trade payables? (Understanding) [1]

**Que 2.**

Amar, Barun, Chand and Daler are partners. Their capital accounts on 1st April, 2021 were as follows

Amar – ₹ 10,000, Barun – ₹ 15,000, Chand – ₹ 20,000 and Daler – ₹ 25,000. After the accounts for the year ended 31st March, 2022 have been prepared, it is discovered that interest @ 5% p.a. as provided for in the partnership agreement has not been credited to the partners' capital accounts before distributing profits.

It is decided to make an adjustment entry in the beginning of next year.

You are required to

(i) Prepare statement showing amount to be adjusted.
(ii) Pass necessary journal entry. (Application) [3]

*Or*

Ram, Shyam and Mohan are partners in a firm sharing profits and losses in the ratio of 2 : 2 : 1. They started business on 1st October, 2022 with ₹ 3,00,000, ₹ 2,00,000 and ₹ 1,50,000 respectively as their capitals.

During the year ended 31st March, 2023, Ram withdrew ₹ 1,000 in the beginning of each month, Mohan withdrew ₹ 2,000 at the end of each month while Shyam withdrew ₹ 9,000 during the period of six months.

(i) Partners are allowed interest on capital @ 5% p.a. Interest on drawings is charged @ 6% p.a.
(ii) Mohan is to get salary of ₹ 2,500 per month.
(iii) Ram is to get commission @ 5% of the net profit of the firm.
(iv) Shyam is to get commission of 5% of the net profit of the firm after charging such commission.

During the period ended 31st March, 2023, profit of the firm was ₹ 10,35,000 after charging Mohan's salary which had been debited to wages and salaries account.

You are required to

(a) Calculate the commission of Ram.
(b) Give adjusting entry for Shyam's commission.
(c) Give rectifying and closing entry for Mohan's salary. (Application)

SP-10

**Que 3.**

Under which major headings and sub-headings will the following items be presented in the balance sheet of a company as per Schedule III, Part I of the Companies Act, 2013?

(i) Interest accrued and due on debentures
(ii) Loose tools
(iii) Accrued interest on calls-in-advance
(iv) Interest due on calls-in-arrears
(v) Trademarks
(vi) Premium on redemption of debentures
(vii) Plant and machinery
(viii) Patents (Application) [3]

**Que 4.**

Kiran and Arun were partners in a firm sharing profits and losses in the ratio of 3 : 2. Their balance sheet as at 31st March, 2021 was as follows

**Balance Sheet**
as at 31st March, 2021

| Liabilities | | Amt (₹) | Assets | Amt (₹) |
|---|---|---|---|---|
| Creditors | | 42,000 | Current Assets | 2,00,000 |
| Employee's Provident Fund | | 20,000 | Investments | 50,000 |
| Contingency Reserve | | 30,000 | Furniture | 20,000 |
| Profit and Loss A/c | | 45,000 | Machinery | 90,000 |
| Workmen's Compensation Reserve | | 18,000 | Advertisement Expenditure | 20,000 |
| Investment Fluctuation Reserve | | 25,000 | (Deferred revenue expenditure) | |
| Capital A/cs | | | | |
| Kiran | 1,20,000 | | | |
| Arun | 80,000 | 2,00,000 | | |
| | | 3,80,000 | | 3,80,000 |

They admit Mukesh into partnership on the above date and the new profit sharing ratio is agreed at 2:1:1. It is estimated that

- Claim on account of workmen's compensation is estimated at ₹ 10,000.
- Market value of investments is ₹ 46,000.

You are required to

(i) Find the amount payable to distribute advertisement expenditure to partners' capital account. [1]

(ii) Pass the entries for contigency reserve, profit and loss, workmen compensation reserve, investment fluctuation reserve. (Application) [2]

*Or*

A, B and C were in partnership sharing profits and losses in the ratio of 3 : 2 : 1. Their balance sheet as at 31st March, 2022 was as follows

**Balance Sheet**
as at 31st March, 2022

| Liabilities | | Amt (₹) | Assets | | Amt (₹) |
|---|---|---|---|---|---|
| Capital A/cs | | | Bank | | 6,448 |
| A | 9,600 | | Debtors | 4,960 | |
| B | 4,800 | | (–) Provision for Doubtful Debts | (480) | 4,480 |
| C | 2,400 | 16,800 | Stock | | 3,680 |
| Current A/cs | | | Plant and Machinery | | 7,520 |
| A | 768 | | Building | | 4,800 |
| B | 672 | | | | |
| C | 448 | 1,888 | | | |
| A's Loan A/c | | 2,000 | | | |
| Creditors | | 6,240 | | | |
| | | 26,928 | | | 26,928 |

A retired on 31st March, 2022 and B and C decided to share future profits in the ratio of 2 : 1. A's loan was repaid on 1st April, 2022 and it was agreed that the remaining balance due to him, other than the current account should remain as loan to the partnership.

For the purpose of A's retirement, it was agreed that

(i) Building be revalued at ₹ 9,600 and plant and machinery at ₹ 6,320.
(ii) Provision for doubtful debts was to be increased by ₹ 160.
(iii) A provision of ₹ 200 included in creditors is not likely to be paid.
(iv) ₹ 480 was to be written-off from the stock.
(v) A provision of ₹ 1,696 be made in respect of outstanding legal charges.
(vi) Firms goodwill be valued at ₹ 5,760.

You are required to prepare revaluation account at the time of A's retirement.

**(Application) [3]**

**Que 5.**

Prepare the balance sheet of XYZ Ltd. as per Schedule III of the Companies Act, 2013 for the below items

Share Capital ₹ 13,000, Deferred Tax Assets ₹ 7,000, Non-current Investments ₹ 9,000, Reserves and Surplus ₹ 9,000, Long-term Borrowings ₹ 21,000, Other Non-current Assets ₹ 11,000, Short-term Provisions ₹ 7,000, Property, Plant and Equipment ₹ 12,000, Deferred Tax Liabilities ₹ 5,000, Trade Payables ₹ 12,000, Trade Receivables ₹ 8,000, Current Investments ₹ 12,000, Cash and Cash Equivalents ₹ 6,000, Other Current Assets ₹ 2,000.

**(Application) [3]**

**Que 6.**

Chand Limited issued 10,000, 12% debentures of ₹ 100 each on 1st April, 2018 at par redeemable at a premium of 5%. Interest on these debentures is paid half-yearly, i.e. on 30th September and 31st March. Pass necessary journal entries for the year ended 31st March, 2019 assuming income tax is deducted @ 20% on the amount of interest.

**(Application) [6]**

**Que 7.**

What journal entries will be passed in the books of A and B sharing profits and losses in the ratio of 3:1, for the following transactions on dissolution of the firm?

It is assumed that all the assets (other than cash) and outsider's liabilities are transferred to realisation account.

(i) An unrecorded asset realised ₹ 2,500.
(ii) Stock of ₹ 20,000 was taken by a partner A at 75%.
(iii) B to bear realisation expenses for which he will get ₹ 3,000. The actual expenses paid by B were ₹ 2,000.
(iv) There was a balance of ₹ 40,000 in the general reserve account on the date of dissolution.
(v) A creditor for ₹ 3,000 accepted machinery valued at ₹ 2,800 in full settlement of his claim.
(vi) A provision for doubtful debts was ₹ 16,000 in the books. ₹ 24,000 debtors proved bad. Total debtors were ₹ 59,000.

**(Application) [6]**

*Or*

Reeta and Meeta were partners from 1st April, 2022 with capitals of ₹ 2,40,000 and ₹ 1,60,000 respectively. They shared profits and losses in the ratio of 3 : 2.

They carried on business for two years. In the first year ended 31st March, 2023, they earned a profit of ₹ 2,00,000 but in the second year ended 31st March, 2024, a loss of ₹ 80,000 was incurred. As the business was no longer profitable, they dissolved the firm on 31st March, 2024.

Their balance sheet was as follows

**Balance Sheet**
as at 31st March, 2024

| Liabilities | | Amt (₹) | Assets | Amt (₹) |
|---|---|---|---|---|
| Creditors | | 80,000 | Sundry Assets | 4,72,000 |
| Capital A/cs | | | | |
| Reeta | 2,48,000 | | | |
| Meeta | 1,44,000 | 3,92,000 | | |
| | | 4,72,000 | | 4,72,000 |

Sundry assets realised ₹ 4,00,000 and expenses on realisation were ₹ 12,000.

Prepare realisation account, partners' capital account and cash account.

**(Application)**

**Que 8.**

A and B are partners with capitals of ₹ 45,00,000 and ₹ 30,00,000 respectively. They agree to share profits in the ratio of 3:2. Show how the following transactions will be recorded in the capital accounts of the partners in case

(i) The capitals are fixed [5]

(ii) The capitals are fluctuating (Application) [1]

The books are closed on 31st December every year.

| Particulars | A (₹) | B (₹) |
|---|---|---|
| Additional Capital Contributed on 1st July, 2018 | 9,00,000 | 6,00,000 |
| Interest on Capital | 5% | 5% |
| Drawings (during 2018-19) | 90,000 | 60,000 |
| Interest on Drawings | 5,400 | 3,600 |
| Salary | 60,000 | 21,000 |
| Commission | 3,000 | — |
| Share in Loss for the Year 2019 | 1,80,000 | 1,20,000 |

**Que 9.**

(A) A, B and C are partners. They share profits in capital ratio. Their balance sheet is given below

**Balance Sheet**
as at 31st December, 2022

| Liabilities | | Amt (₹) | Assets | | Amt (₹) |
|---|---|---|---|---|---|
| Creditors | | 2,00,000 | Cash in Hand | | 80,000 |
| Bank Overdraft | | 1,00,000 | Debtors | 82,000 | |
| Reserves | | 60,000 | (–) Provision for Doubtful Debts | (2,000) | 80,000 |
| Expenses Due | | 40,000 | Land and Building | | 4,00,000 |
| Capital A/cs | | | Machinery | | 40,000 |
| A | 80,000 | | | | |
| B | 80,000 | | | | |
| C | 40,000 | 2,00,000 | | | |
| | | 6,00,000 | | | 6,00,000 |

SP-10

**Additional Information**

(i) B takes retirement.

(ii) New ratio of A and C is 1 : 1.

(iii) Goodwill of the firm ₹ 1,20,000.

(iv) Make 5% provision for debtors.

(v) Building increased by 10%.

(vi) Make provision for claim for damages of ₹ 12,000.

(vii) ₹ 20,000 paid to B in cash. Balance transferred to his loan account.

(a) Pass the journal entries for adjustment of B's share of goodwill. [1½]

(b) Prepare revaluation account. [2]

(c) Prepare partners' capital account. (Application) [4½]

(B) U, V and W are partners sharing profits in the ratio of 2 : 2 :1. V retires and his share is taken by W. Calculate new profit sharing ratio of U and W. (Application) [2]

*Or*

P and Q sharing profits in the ratio of 3 : 2 had the following balance sheet as at 31st March, 2022.

**Balance Sheet**
as at 31st March, 2022

| Liabilities | | Amt (₹) | Assets | | Amt (₹) |
|---|---|---|---|---|---|
| Creditors | | 1,50,000 | Cash | | 50,000 |
| General Reserve | | 1,20,000 | Debtors | 2,00,000 | |
| Capital A/cs | | | (–) Provision for Doubtful Debts | (8,000) | 1,92,000 |
| P | 5,40,000 | | Patents | | 1,48,000 |
| Q | 3,60,000 | 9,00,000 | Investments | | 80,000 |
| Current A/cs | | | Machinery | | 7,20,000 |
| P | 1,00,000 | | Goodwill | | 1,00,000 |
| Q | 20,000 | 1,20,000 | | | |
| | | 12,90,000 | | | 12,90,000 |

On 1st April, 2022, they decided to admit R on the following terms

(i) A provision of 5% is to be created on debtors.

(ii) Accrued income of ₹ 15,000 does not appear in the books and ₹ 50,000 are outstanding for salaries.

(iii) The present market value of investments is ₹ 60,000. P takes over the investments at this value.

(iv) The new profit sharing ratio of partners will be 4 : 3 : 2.

(v) R will bring in ₹ 2,00,000 as his capital.

(vi) R is to pay in cash an amount equal to his share in the firm's goodwill valued at twice the average profit of the last three years which were ₹ 2,50,000, ₹ 2,60,000 and ₹ 3,00,000 respectively.

(vii) Half the amount of goodwill is withdrawn by the old partners.

(a) Calculate R's share of goodwill. **(Application) [2]**

(b) Pass journal entries related to R's capital and premium for goodwill. **(Recall) [2]**

(c) Prepare revaluation account. **(Application) [2]**

SP-10 (d) Prepare partners' capital account. **Application) [2]**

(e) Prepare partners' current account. **(Application) [2]**

**Que 10.**

In 2023, Ganga Ltd. was registered with an authorised capital of ₹ 1,00,000 in equity shares of ₹ 10 each. Of these, 4,000 equity shares were issued as fully paid to vendors for the purchase of plant and machinery and the remaining 6,000 shares were subscribed for, by the public for cash. During the first year, ₹ 6 per equity share was called-up, on these 6,000 shares payable ₹ 3 on application, ₹ 1 on allotment and ₹ 2 on the first call.

The amount received in respect of these shares was as follows

On 5,000 shares, the full amount called

On 600 shares ₹ 4 per share

On 400 shares ₹ 3 per share

The company forfeited all those shares on which only ₹ 3 had been received and re-issued them at ₹ 4 per share, ₹ 6 paid-up. Journalise the transactions in the books of the company and prepare a calls-in-arrears account. **(Application) [10]**

*Or*

Grand Hotels Ltd. issued 10,000 equity shares of ₹ 10 each at a premium of ₹ 3 per share payable as On Application—₹ 4, On Allotment—₹ 5 (including premium), On First Call—₹ 2. The balance as and when decided by the board of directors.

Applications were received for 12,000 shares. The company made pro-rata allotment to all the applicants.

One shareholder who was allotted 900 shares paid the total outstanding amount with allotment while another shareholder who had applied for 1,200 shares, did not pay the allotment money and on his subsequent failure to pay the first call his shares were forfeited.

Of the forfeited shares, 800 were re-issued at ₹ 7 per share.

You are required to

(i) Calculate amount of excess application money adjusted on allotment. [1]

(ii) Calculate the amount received on allotment. [1]

(iii) Prepare share allotment account. [1]

(iv) Prepare securities premium account. [2]

(v) Prepare calls-in-arrears account. [2]

(vi) Prepare share forfeiture account. (Application) [3]

## Section B [20 Marks]

**Que 11.**

(i) The cash flow statement paints a picture as to how a company's operations are running, where its money comes from and how money is being spent. Also known as the statement of cash flows, the CFS helps its creditors determine how much cash is available (referred to as liquidity) for the company to fund its operating expenses and pay down its debts.

**Source** *Investopedia (edited)*

Based on the above statement

- State any one cash equilavent considered in cash flow statement. (Recall)
- Which of the following statement presents the importance of cash flow statement? (Analysis) [1]
  (a) It helps in ascertaining the profitability of the business
  (b) It helps in ascertaining the liquidity and solvency of the business
  (c) It helps in ascertaining the operating cycle of the business
  (d) It helps in ascertaining the operating efficiency of the business

(ii) For investors, the strength of a company's balance sheet can be evaluated by examining three financial metrics: working capital adequacy, asset performance and capitalisation structure.

In this article, we'll start with a comprehensive look at how best to assess the company's working capital position.

In simple terms, this entails measuring the liquidity and managerial efficiency related to a company's current position.

**Source** *Investopedia (edited)*

What will be the impact of increase in current liabilities on working capital turnover ratio? (Understanding) [1]

(a) Working capital turnover ratio will increase
(b) Working capital turnover ratio will decrease
(c) Working capital turnover ratio will not change
(d) Either (a) or (b)

(iii) The revenues of HCL technologies stood at ₹ 10,28,180 m in financial year 2023, which was up 18.6% compared to ₹ 8,67,220 m reported in financial year 2022. HCL technologies' revenue has grown from ₹ 6,13,800 m in financial year 2019 to ₹ 10,28,180 m in financial year 2023.

Over the past 5 years, the revenue of HCL technologies has grown at a CAGR (Compound Annual Growth Rate) of 13.8%.

**Source** *Equitymaster (edited)*

Based on the above information
- State the percentage change in revenue of HCL technologies of the year 2023 and 2019.
- State whether there is an increase in the revenue or decrease. **(Analysis) [1]**

(iv) **Balance Sheet** (Extract)

| Liabilities | Amt (₹) | Assets | Amt (₹) |
|---|---|---|---|
| Borrowings: 10% Debentures | 6,00,000 | Inventories | 4,80,000 |
| Trade Payables | 9,36,000 | Trade Receivables | 3,60,000 |
| Short-term Provisions | 24,000 | Cash and Cash Equivalents | 91,200 |

**Additional Information**

50% of the debentures are repaid by issuing shares amounting to ₹ 3,00,000.

Based on the above information, the liquid ratio for the company will be ........ . **(Application) [1]**

(v) Goodwill is an accounting measure of a business popularity and strength in its market. While goodwill's value on a company's books may be decreased due to market conditions, the only way this asset can be increased is through the business acquisition of a subsidiary. It is the subsidiary transaction that will affect the cash flow statement, but only if the business used cash to pay for at least part of the acquisition price.

**Source** *smallbusiness-chron (edited)*

If net profit after writing-off goodwill of ₹ 20,000 is ₹ 1,00,000, then find out the cash flow from operating activities. **(Analysis) [1]**

**Que 12.**

From the following balance sheet of Hemkunt Ltd. as at 31st March, 2021, prepare a common size balance sheet. **(Application) [3]**

**Common Size Balance Sheet**
as at 31st March, 2024

| Particulars | Note No. | Absolute Amt (₹) | Percentage of Balance Sheet Total (%) |
|---|---|---|---|
| I. EQUITY AND LIABILITIES | | | |
| 1. **Shareholders' Funds** | | | |
| (i) Share Capital | | ... | 60 |
| (ii) Reserves and Surplus | | ... | 8 |
| 2. **Non-current Liabilities** | | | |
| Long-term Borrowings | | 10,00,000 | ... |
| 3. **Current Liabilities** | | | |
| Trade Payables | | 6,00,000 | ... |
| **Total** | | 50,00,000 | 100 |
| II. ASSETS | | | |
| 1. **Non-current Assets** | | | |
| (i) Property, Plant & Equipment and Intangible Assets | | | |
| (a) Property, Plant and Equipment | | 30,00,000 | ... |
| (b) Intangible Assets | | ... | 12 |
| 2. **Current Assets** | | | |
| (i) Inventories | | ... | 20 |
| (ii) Cash and Cash Equivalents | | ... | 8 |
| **Total** | | 50,00,000 | 100 |

**Que 13.**

(i) Answer any three of the following **(Application) [6]**

From the following information, calculate stock turnover ratio

Net revenue from operations ₹ 8,00,000

SP-10

| | |
|---|---|
| Opening inventory | ₹ 20,000 |
| Closing inventory | ₹ 6,000 less than opening inventory |
| Net purchases | 80% of net revenue from operations |
| Direct expenses | ₹ 40,000 |

(ii) Calculate debt-equity ratio from the following information

| | |
|---|---|
| Current assets | ₹ 2,00,000 |
| Prepaid expenses | ₹ 6,000 |
| Current liabilities | ₹ 1,20,000 |
| 10% debentures | ₹ 8,00,000 |
| Bank loan (long-term) | ₹ 3,00,000 |
| Equity share capital | ₹ 16,00,000 |
| 9% preference share capital | ₹ 6,00,000 |

(iii) Calculate earning per share from the following information

| | |
|---|---|
| Profit before tax | ₹ 20,00,000 |
| 10% preference shares | ₹ 10,00,000 |
| Equity shares 30,000 of ₹ 100 each | ₹ 30,00,000 |
| Current market price of the equity share | ₹ 200 |

Tax rate for the company is 35%

(iv) From the following information, calculate working capital turnover ratio

**Additional Information**

Paid-up share capital ₹ 8,00,000, current assets ₹ 5,00,000, credit revenue from operations ₹ 3,00,000, cash revenue from operations 75% of credit revenue from operations, 9% debentures ₹ 3,40,000, current liabilities ₹ 2,90,000, cost of revenue from operations ₹ 1,80,000.

**Que 14.**

From the following summarised balance sheets of a company, prepare

(i) Machinery account [2]

(ii) Cash flow from investing activities. [2]

(iii) Cash flow from financing activities. (Evaluate) [2]

| Particulars | 31st March, 2022 (₹) | 31st March, 2021 (₹) |
|---|---|---|
| I. **EQUITY AND LIABILITIES** | | |
| 1. **Shareholders' Funds** | | |
| (i) Equity Share Capital | 3,00,000 | 3,00,000 |
| (ii) Reserves and Surplus (Balance in statement of profit and loss) | 80,000 | 50,000 |
| 2. **Non-current Liabilities** | | |
| 6% Debentures | 1,00,000 | 80,000 |
| 3. **Current Liabilities** | | |
| (i) Outstanding Expenses | 30,000 | 25,000 |
| (ii) Trade Payables | 5,000 | 25,000 |
| (iii) Other Current Liabilities | 25,000 | 20,000 |
| **Total** | 5,40,000 | 5,00,000 |
| II. **ASSETS** | | |
| 1. **Non-current Assets** | | |
| (i) Property, Plant & Equipment and Intangible Assets | 3,90,000 | 3,50,000 |
| (ii) Non-current Investments | 30,000 | 40,000 |

| Particulars | 31st March, 2022 (₹) | 31st March, 2021 (₹) |
|---|---|---|
| 2. **Current Assets** | | |
| (i) Stock | 55,000 | 40,000 |
| (ii) Trade Receivables | 55,000 | 50,000 |
| (iii) Cash and Cash Equivalents | 10,000 | 20,000 |
| **Total** | 5,40,000 | 5,00,000 |

## Additional Information

(a) A piece of machinery costing ₹ 50,000 on which depreciation of ₹ 20,000 had been charged, was sold for ₹ 25,000. Depreciation charged during the year was ₹ 57,000.

(b) New debentures have been issued on 1st August, 2021.

*Or*

From the following balance sheet of Vikas Ltd. as on 31st March, 2023 and 2022, prepare a cash flow statement

**Balance Sheet**

as at 31st March, 2021 and 2023

| Particulars | Note No. | 31st March, 2023 (₹) | 31st March, 2022 (₹) |
|---|---|---|---|
| I. **EQUITY AND LIABILITIES** | | | |
| 1. **Shareholders' Funds** | | | |
| (i) Share Capital | | 1,30,000 | 90,000 |
| (ii) Reserves and Surplus | 1 | 84,000 | 48,000 |
| 2. **Current Liabilities** | | | |
| Trade Payables | | 22,000 | 17,400 |
| **Total** | | 2,36,000 | 1,55,400 |
| II. **ASSETS** | | | |
| 1. **Non-current Assets** | | | |
| (i) Property, Plant & Equipment and Intangible Assets | | | |
| (a) Property, Plant and Equipment | | 1,66,000 | 93,400 |
| 2. **Current Assets** | | | |
| (i) Inventories | | 26,000 | 22,000 |
| (ii) Trade Receivables | | 39,000 | 36,000 |
| (iii) Cash and Cash Equivalents | | 5,000 | 4,000 |
| **Total** | | 2,36,000 | 1,55,400 |

**Notes to Accounts**

| Particulars | 2023 (₹) | 2023 (₹) |
|---|---|---|
| 1. **Reserves and Surplus** | | |
| General Reserve | 55,000 | 30,000 |
| Balance of Statement of Profit and Loss | 30,000 | 20,000 |
| Preliminary Expenses | (1,000) | (2,000) |
| | 84,000 | 48,000 |

## Additional Information

(i) Depreciation charged on property, plant and equipment for the year 2022-23 was ₹ 20,000.

(ii) Income tax ₹ 5,000 has been paid during the year.

**(Application) [6]**

SP-10

# Solutions in Topper's Style

*My Commitment* *I affirm that I am reviewing these solutions only after I have solved the Sample Question Paper 10 on my own. My purpose of looking the solutions is solely to verify whether my answers/solutions were correct or not and to identify my mistakes in case my solutions were wrong or I could not solve that.*

1. (i) (*d*) Debit Realisation Account and Credit Cash Account

(ii) (*d*) B, D, C, A

(iii) (*c*) A's Capital A/c Dr 6,000

B's Capital A/c Dr 6,000

To Profit and Loss A/c 12,000

(iv) (*a*) Number of Debentures Issued $= \frac{28,80,000}{100-4} = 30,000$ Debentures

(v) (*b*) Both Assertion (A) and Reason (R) are true, but Reason (R) is not the correct explanation of Assertion (A)

(vi) Building A/c Dr 3,60,000

To Debentures A/c 3,00,000

To Security Premium A/c 60,000

**Working Note**

Number of Debentures $= \frac{\text{Purchase Consideration}}{\text{Face Value + Premium}} = \frac{3,60,000}{100+20} = 3,000$ Debentures

(vii) Debit Revaluation A/c and Credit Furniture A/c by ₹ 10,000

(viii) (a) Reserves are part of profits that have been allotted for a specific purpose.

(b) Workmen compensation reserve is created to meet unforeseen liability of the firm related to claims of the staff.

(ix) Amount realised from debtor 18,000 – 6,000 = ₹ 12,000

(x) Trade payables refer to the amount due on account of goods purchased or services received in the normal course of business.

2. (i) **Statement Showing Amount to be Adjusted**

| Particulars | Amar (₹) | Barun (₹) | Chand (₹) | Daler (₹) | Total (₹) |
|---|---|---|---|---|---|
| Interest on Capital to be Credited | 500 | 750 | 1,000 | 1,250 | 3,500 |
| Share of Profit to be Debited | 875 | 875 | 875 | 875 | 3,500 |
| | 375 (Dr) | 125 (Dr) | 125 (Cr) | 375 (Cr) | Nil |

(ii) **JOURNAL**

| Date | Particulars | | LF | Amt (Dr) | Amt (Cr) |
|---|---|---|---|---|---|
| 2022 Apr 1 | Amar's Capital A/c | Dr | | 375 | |
| | Barun's Capital A/c | Dr | | 125 | |
| | To Chand's Capital A/c | | | | 125 |
| | To Daler's Capital A/c | | | | 375 |
| | (Being amount of interest on capital adjusted) | | | | |

*Or* (a) Commission A/c (Ram's Capital A/c)

[5/100 of (10,35,000 + 15,000)] = ₹ 52,500

(b) **Adjusting Entry**

| Date | Particulars | | LF | Amt (Dr) | Amt (Cr) |
|---|---|---|---|---|---|
| | Commission A/c | Dr | | 50,000 | |
| | To Shyam's Capital A/c | | | | 50,000 |
| | (Being Shyam's commission adjusted) | | | | |

(c) **JOURNAL**

| Date | Particulars | | LF | Amt (Dr) | Amt (Cr) |
|---|---|---|---|---|---|
| | **Rectification Entry** | | | | |
| | Salary A/c (Partner's) | Dr | | 15,000 | |
| | To Wages and Salaries A/c | | | | 15,000 |
| | (Being the partner's salary wrongly debited to wages and salaries account, now rectified) | | | | |
| | **Closing Entry** | | | | |
| | Profit and Loss Appropriation A/c | Dr | | 15,000 | |
| | To Salary A/c (Partner's) | | | | 15,000 |
| | (Being the salary to partner transferred to profit and loss appropriation account) | | | | |

**3.**

| S. No. | Major Headings | Sub-heading |
|---|---|---|
| (i) | Current Liabilities | Other Current Liabilities |
| (ii) | Current Assets | Inventories |
| (iii) | Current Liabilities | Other Current Liabilities |
| (iv) | Current Assets | Other Current Assets |
| (v) | Non-current Assets | Property, Plant & Equipment and Intangible Assets: Intangible Assets |
| (vi) | Non-current Liabilities | Other Non-current Liabilities |
| (vii) | Non-current Assets | Property, Plant & Equipment and Intangible Assets: Property, Plant and Equipment |
| (viii) | Non-current Assets | Property, Plant & Equipment and Intangible Assets: Intangible Assets |

**Value Points**

- Interest accrued and due on any borrowings is part of current liabilities.
- 'Loose tools' and 'stores and spares' are part of inventory.

**4.** (i) Kiran's Capital = ₹ 12,000 and Arun's Capital = ₹ 8,000
(Accumulated loss transferred to old partners in their old profit sharing ratio)

(ii) **JOURNAL**

| Date | Particulars | | LF | Amt (Dr) | Amt (Cr) |
|---|---|---|---|---|---|
| Mar 31 | Contingency Reserve A/c | Dr | | 30,000 | |
| | Profit and Loss A/c | Dr | | 45,000 | |
| | Workmen's Compensation Reserve A/c (18,000 – 10,000) | Dr | | 8,000 | |
| | Investment Fluctuation Reserve A/c (25,000 – 4,000) | Dr | | 21,000 | |
| | To Kiran's Capital A/c | | | | 62,400 |
| | To Arun's Capital A/c | | | | 41,600 |
| | (Being accumulated profits transferred to old partners in their old profit sharing ratio, i.e. 3 : 2) | | | | |

**Value Points**

- Since workmen compensation reserve is maintained by the firm, claim against workmen compensation will be paid using that.
- Since market value of the investment is decreasing, the loss will be written-off using investment fluctuating reserve.

*Or*

Dr **Revaluation Account** Cr

| Particulars | Amt (₹) | Particulars | Amt (₹) |
|---|---|---|---|
| To Plant and Machinery A/c | 1,200 | By Building A/c | 4,800 |
| To Provision for Doubtful Debts A/c | 160 | By Creditors A/c | 200 |
| To Stock A/c | 480 | | |
| To Outstanding Legal Charges A/c | 1,696 | | |

| Particulars | | Amt (₹) | Particulars | Amt (₹) |
|---|---|---|---|---|
| To Profit transferred to | | | | |
| A's Current A/c | 732 | | | |
| B's Current A/c | 488 | | | |
| C's Current A/c | 244 | 1,464 | | |
| | | 5,000 | | 5,000 |

5.

**Balance Sheet**

as at...........

| Particulars | Note No. | Amt (₹) |
|---|---|---|
| I. **EQUITY AND LIABILITIES** | | |
| 1. **Shareholders' Funds** | | |
| (i) Share Capital | | 13,000 |
| (ii) Reserves and Surplus | | 9,000 |
| 2. **Non-current Liabilities** | | |
| (i) Long-term Borrowings | | 21,000 |
| (ii) Deferred Tax Liabilities | | 5,000 |
| 3. **Current Liabilities** | | |
| (i) Short-term Provisions | | 7,000 |
| (ii) Trade Payables | | 12,000 |
| **Total** | | 67,000 |
| II. **ASSETS** | | |
| 1. **Non-current Assets** | | |
| (i) Property, Plant & Equipment and Intangible Assets | | |
| (a) Property, Plant and Equipment | | 12,000 |
| (ii) Non-current Investments | | 9,000 |
| (iii) Deferred Tax Assets | | 7,000 |
| (iv) Other Non-current Assets | | 11,000 |
| 3. **Current Assets** | | |
| (i) Current Investments | | 12,000 |
| (ii) Trade Receivables | | 8,000 |
| (iii) Cash and Cash Equivalents | | 6,000 |
| (iv) Other Current Assets | | 2,000 |
| **Total** | | 67,000 |

6.

**JOURNAL**

| Date | Particulars | | LF | Amt (Dr) | Amt (Cr) |
|---|---|---|---|---|---|
| 2018 Apr 1 | Bank A/c (10,000 × 100) | Dr | | 10,00,000 | |
| | To Debenture Application and Allotment A/c | | | | 10,00,000 |
| | (Being amount received on application) | | | | |
| Apr 1 | Debenture Application and Allotment A/c | Dr | | 10,00,000 | |
| | Loss on Issue of Debentures A/c (10,000 × 5) | Dr | | 50,000 | |
| | To 12% Debentures A/c (10,000 × 100) | | | | 10,00,000 |
| | To Premium on Redemption of Debentures A/c (10,000 × 5) | | | | 50,000 |
| | (Being issue of debentures at par and redeemable at 5% premium) | | | | |
| Sep 30 | Interest on Debentures A/c $\left(10,00,000 \times \frac{12}{100} \times \frac{6}{12}\right)$ | Dr | | 60,000 | |
| | To Debentures A/c | | | | 48,000 |
| | To Income Tax Payable A/c (60,000 × 20%) | | | | 12,000 |
| | (Being half-yearly interest due on debentures and tax deducted at source) | | | | |

| Date | Particulars | | LF | Amt (Dr) | Amt (Cr) |
|---|---|---|---|---|---|
| Sep 30 | Debentureholders' A/c | Dr | | 48,000 | |
| | To Bank A/c | | | | 48,000 |
| | (Being payment of interest) | | | | |
| Sep 30 | Income Tax Payable A/c | Dr | | 12,000 | |
| | To Bank A/c | | | | 12,000 |
| | (Being TDS deposited with income tax authorities) | | | | |
| 2019 Mar 31 | Interest on Debentures A/c $\left(10,00,000 \times \frac{12}{100} \times \frac{6}{12}\right)$ | Dr | | 60,000 | |
| | To Debentureholders' A/c | | | | 48,000 |
| | To Income Tax Payable A/c $\left(60,000 \times \frac{20}{100}\right)$ | | | | 12,000 |
| | (Being half-yearly interest due on debentures and tax deducted at source) | | | | |
| Mar 31 | Debentureholders' A/c | Dr | | 48,000 | |
| | To Bank A/c | | | | 48,000 |
| | (Being payment of interest) | | | | |
| Mar 31 | Income Tax Payable A/c | Dr | | 12,000 | |
| | To Bank A/c | | | | 12,000 |
| | (Being TDS deposited with income tax authorities) | | | | |
| Mar 31 | Statement of Profit and Loss | Dr | | 1,20,000 | |
| | To Interest on Debentures A/c (60,000 + 60,000) | | | | 1,20,000 |
| | (Being interest transferred to statement of profit and loss) | | | | |

7. **JOURNAL**

| Date | Particulars | | LF | Amt (Dr) | Amt (Cr) |
|---|---|---|---|---|---|
| (i) | Bank A/c | Dr | | 2,500 | |
| | To Realisation A/c | | | | 2,500 |
| | (Being an unrecorded asset realised) | | | | |
| (ii) | A's Capital A/c | Dr | | 15,000 | |
| | To Realisation A/c | | | | 15,000 |
| | (Being stock taken over by A at 75%) | | | | |
| (iii) | Realisation A/c | Dr | | 3,000 | |
| | To B's Capital A/c | | | | 3,000 |
| | (Being realisation expenses paid to B) | | | | |
| (iv) | General Reserve A/c | Dr | | 40,000 | |
| | To A's Capital A/c | | | | 30,000 |
| | To B's Capital A/c | | | | 10,000 |
| | (Being general reserve distributed among partners) | | | | |
| (v) | No Entry | | | | |
| (vi) | Bank A/c | Dr | | 35,000 | |
| | To Realisation A/c | | | | 35,000 |
| | (Being ₹ 24,000 debtors proved bad and rest paid the amount) | | | | |

**Common Mistake** Students usually get confused that which amount will be recorded if the actual realisation expenses paid by the partner is given. It doesn't matter how much amount is paid by partner B, the firm will record the amount that is paid to B, which is ₹ 3,000 in this question.

*Or* Dr **Realisation Account** Cr

| Particulars | Amt (₹) | Particulars | | Amt (₹) |
|---|---|---|---|---|
| To Sundry Assets A/c | 4,72,000 | By Creditors | | 80,000 |
| To Cash A/c (Creditors) | 80,000 | By Cash A/c (Assets realised) | | 4,00,000 |
| To Cash A/c (Expenses) | 12,000 | By Loss transferred to | | |
| | | Reeta's Capital A/c | 50,400 | |
| | | Meeta's Capital A/c | 33,600 | 84,000 |
| | 5,64,000 | | | 5,64,000 |

Dr **Partners' Capital Account** Cr

| Particulars | Retta (₹) | Meeta (₹) | Particulars | Reeta (₹) | Meeta (₹) |
|---|---|---|---|---|---|
| To Realisation A/c (Loss) | 50,400 | 33,600 | By Balance b/d | 2,48,000 | 1,44,000 |
| To Cash A/c | 1,97,600 | 1,10,400 | | | |
| | 2,48,000 | 1,44,000 | | 2,48,000 | 1,44,000 |

Dr **Cash Account** Cr

| Liabilities | Amt (₹) | Particulars | Amt (₹) |
|---|---|---|---|
| To Realisation A/c (Assets realised) | 4,72,000 | By Realisation A/c (Creditors) | 80,000 |
| | | By Realisation A/c (Expenses) | 12,000 |
| | | By Reeta's Capital A/c | 1,97,600 |
| | | By Meeta's Capital A/c | 1,10,400 |
| | 4,00,000 | | 4,00,000 |

8. (i) **Fixed Capital Method**

Dr **Partners' Capital Account** Cr

| Date | Particulars | LF | A (₹) | B (₹) | Date | Particulars | LF | A (₹) | B (₹) |
|---|---|---|---|---|---|---|---|---|---|
| | To Balance c/d | | 54,00,000 | 36,00,000 | | By Balance b/d | | 45,00,000 | 30,00,000 |
| | | | | | | By Bank A/c (Additional capital) | | 9,00,000 | 6,00,000 |
| | | | 54,00,000 | 36,00,000 | | | | 54,00,000 | 36,00,000 |

Dr **Partners' Current Account** Cr

| Date | Particulars | LF | A (₹) | B (₹) | Date | Particulars | LF | A (₹) | B (₹) |
|---|---|---|---|---|---|---|---|---|---|
| | To Drawings A/c | | 90,000 | 60,000 | | By Interest on Capital A/c | | 2,47,500 | 1,65,000 |
| | To Interest on Drawings A/c | | 5,400 | 3,600 | | By Partners' Salary A/c | | 60,000 | 21,000 |
| | To Profit and Loss Appropriation A/c (Loss) | | 1,80,000 | 1,20,000 | | By Commission A/c | | 30,000 | — |
| | To Balance c/d | | 62,100 | 2,400 | | | | | |
| | | | 3,37,500 | 1,86,000 | | | | 3,37,500 | 1,86,000 |

**Working Note**

| **Calculation of Interest on Capital** | **Amt (₹)** |
|---|---|
| **A** 5% on ₹ 45,00,000 for 1 year = $45{,}00{,}000 \times 5/100$ | 2,25,000 |
| 5% on ₹ 9,00,000 for 6 months = $9{,}00{,}000 \times \frac{6}{12} \times \frac{5}{100}$ | 22,500 |
| | 2,47,500 |
| **B** 5% on ₹ 30,00,000 for 1 year = $30{,}00{,}000 \times \frac{5}{100}$ | 1,50,000 |
| 5% on ₹ 6,00,000 for 6 months = $6{,}00{,}000 \times \frac{6}{12} \times \frac{5}{100}$ | 15,000 |
| | 1,65,000 |

**(ii) Fluctuating Capital Method**

Dr **Partners' Capital Account** Cr

| Date | Particulars | LF | A (₹) | B (₹) | Date | Particulars | LF | A (₹) | B (₹) |
|---|---|---|---|---|---|---|---|---|---|
| | To Drawings A/c | | 90,000 | 60,000 | | By Balance b/d | | 45,00,000 | 30,00,000 |
| | To Interest on Drawings A/c | | 5,400 | 3,600 | | By Bank A/c (Additional capital) | | 9,00,000 | 6,00,000 |
| | To Profit and Loss A/c | | 1,80,000 | 1,20,000 | | By Interest on Capital A/c | | 2,47,500 | 1,65,000 |
| | To Balance c/d | | 54,62,100 | 36,02,400 | | By Salary A/c | | 60,000 | 21,000 |
| | | | | | | By Commission A/c | | 30,000 | — |
| | | | 57,37,500 | 37,86,000 | | | | 57,37,500 | 37,86,000 |

**9.** (A) (a) **JOURNAL**

| Date | Particulars | | LF | Amt (Dr) | Amt (Cr) |
|---|---|---|---|---|---|
| | A's Capital A/c | Dr | | 12,000 | |
| | C's Capital A/c | Dr | | 36,000 | |
| | To B's Capital A/c | | | | 48,000 |
| | (Being B's share of goodwill transferred to A and B in gaining ratio) | | | | |

Gaining Ratio = New Share – Old Share A $=\frac{1}{2}-\frac{2}{5}=\frac{5-4}{10}=\frac{1}{10}$; C $=\frac{1}{2}-\frac{1}{5}=\frac{5-2}{10}=\frac{3}{10}$

∴ Gaining Ratio = 1 : 3

(b) Dr **Revaluation Account** Cr

| Particulars | | Amt (₹) | Particulars | Amt (₹) |
|---|---|---|---|---|
| To Provision for Doubtful Debts A/c | | 2,100 | By Building A/c | 40,000 |
| To Provision for Claim for Damages A/c | | 12,000 | | |
| To Profit transferred to | | | | |
| A's Capital A/c | 10,360 | | | |
| B's Capital A/c | 10,360 | | | |
| C's Capital A/c | 5,180 | 25,900 | | |
| | | 40,000 | | 40,000 |

(c) Dr **Partners' Capital Account** Cr

| Particulars | A (₹) | B (₹) | C (₹) | Particulars | A (₹) | B (₹) | C (₹) |
|---|---|---|---|---|---|---|---|
| To B's Capital A/c | 12,000 | — | 36,000 | By Balance b/d | 80,000 | 80,000 | 40,000 |
| To Cash A/c | — | 20,000 | — | By Reserve A/c | 24,000 | 24,000 | 12,000 |
| To B's Loan A/c | — | 1,42,360 | — | By Revaluation A/c | 10,360 | 10,360 | 5,180 |
| To Balance c/d | 1,02,360 | — | 21,180 | By A's Capital A/c | — | 12,000 | — |
| | | | | By C's Capital A/c | — | 36,000 | — |
| | 1,14,360 | 1,62,360 | 57,180 | | 1,14,360 | 1,62,360 | 57,180 |

B's share in Goodwill = 1,20,000 × 2 / 5 = ₹ 48,000, which is contributed by A and B in gaining ratio, i.e. 1 : 3.

**Working Note**

Dr **Cash Account** Cr

| Particulars | Amt (₹) | Particulars | Amt (₹) |
|---|---|---|---|
| To Balance b/d | 80,000 | By B's Capital A/c | 20,000 |
| | | By Balance c/d | 60,000 |
| | 80,000 | | 80,000 |

(B) Share taken by W from V $= \frac{2}{5}$

W's New Share = Old Share + Share taken from V

W's New Share $= \frac{1}{5} + \frac{2}{5} = \frac{3}{5}$; U's New Share $= \frac{2}{5}$ (unchanged)

New ratio of U and W $= \frac{2}{5} : \frac{3}{5} = 2:3$

*Or* (a) **Calculation of Goodwill**

Average Profit $= \frac{2,50,000 + 2,60,000 + 3,00,000}{3} =$ ₹ 2,70,000

Goodwill = 2,70,000 × 2 = ₹ 5,40,000

R brings in his share of goodwill in cash.

Therefore, the amount of goodwill brought in by R = 5,40,000 × 2/9 = ₹ 1,20,000

(b) **JOURNAL**

| Date | Particulars | | LF | Amt (Dr) | Amt (Cr) |
|---|---|---|---|---|---|
| | Cash A/c | Dr | | 3,20,000 | |
| | To R's Capital A/c | | | | 2,00,000 |
| | To Premium for Goodwill A/c (WN) | | | | 1,20,000 |
| | (Being capital and goodwill brought in by R) | | | | |
| | Premium for Goodwill A/c | Dr | | 1,20,000 | |
| | To P's Current A/c | | | | 84,000 |
| | To Q's Current A/c | | | | 36,000 |
| | (Being goodwill distributed between P and Q) | | | | |
| | P's Current A/c | Dr | | 42,000 | |
| | Q's Current A/c | Dr | | 18,000 | |
| | To Cash A/c | | | | 60,000 |
| | (Being half amount of goodwill withdrawn by P and Q) | | | | |

**Working Note**

Sacrificing ratio of P $= \frac{3}{5} - \frac{4}{9} = \frac{27-20}{45} = \frac{7}{45}$; Q $= \frac{2}{5} - \frac{3}{9} = \frac{18-15}{45} = \frac{3}{45}$ *or* 7 : 3

(c) Dr **Revaluation Account** Cr

| Particulars | Amt (₹) | Particulars | | Amt (₹) |
|---|---|---|---|---|
| To Provision for Doubtful Debts A/c | 2,000 | By Accrued Income A/c | | 15,000 |
| To Outstanding Salaries A/c | 50,000 | By Loss transferred to | | |
| To Investments A/c | 20,000 | P's Current A/c | 34,200 | |
| | | Q's Current A/c | 22,800 | 57,000 |
| | 72,000 | | | 72,000 |

(d) Dr **Partners' Capital Account** Cr

| Particulars | P (₹) | Q (₹) | R (₹) | Particulars | P (₹) | Q (₹) | R (₹) |
|---|---|---|---|---|---|---|---|
| To Balance c/d | 5,40,000 | 3,60,000 | 2,00,000 | By Balance b/d | 5,40,000 | 3,60,000 | – |
| | | | | By Cash A/c | – | – | 2,00,000 |
| | 5,40,000 | 3,60,000 | 2,00,000 | | 5,40,000 | 3,60,000 | 2,00,000 |

(e) Dr **Partners' Current Account** Cr

| Particulars | P (₹) | Q (₹) | Particulars | P (₹) | Q (₹) |
|---|---|---|---|---|---|
| To Investments A/c | 60,000 | – | By Balance b/d | 1,00,000 | 20,000 |
| To Revaluation A/c | 34,200 | 22,800 | By General Reserve A/c | 72,000 | 48,000 |

| Particulars | P (₹) | Q (₹) | Particulars | P (₹) | Q (₹) |
|---|---|---|---|---|---|
| To Goodwill A/c | 60,000 | 40,000 | By Premium for Goodwill A/c | 84,000 | 36,000 |
| To Cash A/c | 42,000 | 18,000 | | | |
| To Balance c/d | 59,800 | 23,200 | | | |
| | 2,56,000 | 1,04,000 | | 2,56,000 | 1,04,000 |

**Working Note**

Goodwill appearing in the balance sheet is written-off by the old partners in their old profit sharing ratio.

**10.**

**JOURNAL**

| Date | Particulars | | LF | Amt (Dr) | Amt (Cr) |
|---|---|---|---|---|---|
| (i) | Plant and Machinery A/c | Dr | | 40,000 | |
| | To Vendor A/c | | | | 40,000 |
| | (Being plant and machinery purchased) | | | | |
| (ii) | Vendor A/c | Dr | | 40,000 | |
| | To Equity Share Capital A/c | | | | 40,000 |
| | (Being 4,000 equity shares @ ₹ 10 issued as fully paid) | | | | |
| (iii) | Bank A/c (6,000 × 3) | Dr | | 18,000 | |
| | To Share Application A/c | | | | 18,000 |
| | (Being application amount received on 6,000 equity shares @ ₹ 3) | | | | |
| (iv) | Share Application A/c | Dr | | 18,000 | |
| | To Equity Share Capital A/c | | | | 18,000 |
| | (Being application amount transferred to equity share capital) | | | | |
| (v) | Share Allotment A/c | Dr | | 6,000 | |
| | To Equity Share Capital A/c (6,000 × 1) | | | | 6,000 |
| | (Being allotment amount due on 6,000 equity shares @ ₹ 1) | | | | |
| (vi) | Bank A/c (5,600 × 1) | Dr | | 5,600 | |
| | Calls-in-arrears A/c (400 × 1) | Dr | | 400 | |
| | To Share Allotment A/c | | | | 6,000 |
| | (Being allotment amount received on 5,600 shares @ ₹ 1) | | | | |
| (vii) | Share First Call A/c | Dr | | 12,000 | |
| | To Equity Share Capital A/c (6,000 × 2) | | | | 12,000 |
| | (Being first call due on 6,000 equity shares @ ₹ 2) | | | | |
| (viii) | Bank A/c (5,000 × 2) | Dr | | 10,000 | |
| | Calls-in-arrears A/c (1,000 × 2) | Dr | | 2,000 | |
| | To Share First Call A/c | | | | 12,000 |
| | (Being first call amount received on 5,000 equity shares @ ₹ 2) | | | | |
| (ix) | Equity Share Capital A/c (400 × 6) | Dr | | 2,400 | |
| | To Calls-in-arrears A/c (400 × 3) | | | | 1,200 |
| | To Share Forfeiture A/c (400 × 3) | | | | 1,200 |
| | (Being 400 equity shares forfeited for non-payment of allotment and first call) | | | | |
| (x) | Bank A/c (400 × 4) | Dr | | 1,600 | |
| | Share Forfeiture A/c (400 × 2) | Dr | | 800 | |
| | To Equity Share Capital A/c | | | | 2,400 |
| | (Being 400 forfeited equity shares re-issued @ ₹ 4, ₹ 6 paid-up) | | | | |
| (xi) | Share Forfeiture A/c | Dr | | 400 | |
| | To Capital Reserve A/c | | | | 400 |
| | (Being balance of forfeited shares account transferred to capital reserve) | | | | |

Dr **Calls-in-arrears Account** Cr

| Date | Particulars | Amt (₹) | Date | Particulars | Amt (₹) |
|---|---|---|---|---|---|
| | To Share Allotment A/c | 400 | | By Equity Share Capital A/c | 1,200 |
| | To Share First Call A/c | 2,000 | | By Balance c/d | 1,200 |
| | | 2,400 | | | 2,400 |
| | To Balance b/d | 1,200 | | | |

*Or* (i) Excess application money adjusted on allotment = (12,000 – 10,000) ×4 = ₹ 8,000

(ii) Amount received on allotment = ₹ 37,800

**Working Note**

| **Calculation of Amount received on Allotment** | **Amt (₹)** |
|---|---|
| Total allotment money due (10,000 × 5) | 50,000 |
| (–) Excess application money adjusted (WN 1) | (8,000) |
| | 42,000 |
| (–) Allotment money due but not received (WN 2) | (4,200) |
| Amount received on allotment | 37,800 |

(iii) Dr **Share Allotment Account** Cr

| Date | Particulars | Amt (₹) | Date | Particulars | Amt (₹) |
|---|---|---|---|---|---|
| | To Share Capital A/c (10,000 × 2) | 20,000 | | By Share Application A/c | 8,000 |
| | To Securities Premium A/c (10,000 × 3) | 30,000 | | By Bank A/c | 37,800 |
| | | | | By Calls-in-arrears A/c | 4,200 |
| | | 50,000 | | | 50,000 |

(iv) Dr **Securities Premium Account** Cr

| Date | Particulars | Amt (₹) | Date | Particulars | Amt (₹) |
|---|---|---|---|---|---|
| | To Calls-in-arrears A/c (1,000 × 3) | 3,000 | | By Share Allotment A/c (10,000 × 3) | 30,000 |
| | To Balance c/d | 27,000 | | | |
| | | 30,000 | | | 30,000 |

(v) Dr **Calls-in-arrears Account** Cr

| Date | Particulars | Amt (₹) | Date | Particulars | Amt (₹) |
|---|---|---|---|---|---|
| | To Share Allotment A/c | 4,200 | | By Share Capital A/c | 3,200 |
| | To Share First Call A/c | 2,000 | | By Securities Premium A/c | 3,000 |
| | | 6,200 | | | 6,200 |

(vi) Dr **Share Forfeiture Account** Cr

| Date | Particulars | Amt (₹) | Date | Particulars | Amt (₹) |
|---|---|---|---|---|---|
| | To Share Capital A/c (Discount on re-issue of 800 shares) | 800 | | By Share Capital A/c (1,200 × 4) | 4,800 |
| | To Capital Reserve A/c (WN 2) | 3,040 | | | |
| | To Balance c/d (4,800/1,000 × 200) | 960 | | | |
| | | 4,800 | | | 4,800 |

**Working Notes**

1. Amount not received from defaulter shareholders (Calls-in-arrears)

   (i) Shares allotted to him $= \frac{10,000}{12,000} \times 1,200 = 1,000$

   (ii) Application money received = 1,200 × 4 = ₹ 4,800

   (iii) Application money due on shares allotted = 1,000 × 4 = ₹ 4,000

   (iv) Excess application money adjusted on allotment = 4,800 – 4,000 = ₹ 800

(v) Allotment money due on shares allotted = 1,000 × 5 = ₹ 5,000

(vi) Allotment money due but not received (Calls-in-arrears) = 5,000 – 800 = ₹ 4,200

2. **Calculation of Amount transferred to Capital Reserve**

| Particulars | Amt (₹) |
|---|---|
| Amount forfeited on re-issued shares (4,800/1,000 × 800) | 3,840 |
| (–) Re-issue discount (800 × 1) | (800) |
| Gain on re-issue transferred to capital reserve | 3,040 |

**11.** (i) • Marketable securities

• (*b*) It helps in ascertaining the liquidity and solvency of the business.

(ii) (*a*) Working capital turnover ratio will increase because increase in current liabilities will result in decrease in working capital.

(iii) • 67.51% • Considerable increase

(iv) $\text{Liquid Ratio} = \dfrac{\text{Liquid Assets}}{\text{Current Liabilities}} = \dfrac{3,60,000 + 91,200}{9,36,000 + 24,000} = \dfrac{4,51,200}{9,60,000} = 0.47 : 1$

(v) Cash Flow from Operating Activities = Net Profit + Non-operating Expenses (Goodwill written-off)
= 1,00,000 + 20,000 = ₹1,20,000

**12.** **Common Size Balance Sheet**
as at 31st March, 2024

| Particulars | Note No. | Absolute Amount (₹) | Percentage of Balance Sheet Total (%) |
|---|---|---|---|
| I. **EQUITY AND LIABILITIES** | | | |
| 1. **Shareholders' Funds** | | | |
| (i) Share Capital | | **30,00,000** | 60 |
| (ii) Reserves and Surplus | | **4,00,000** | 8 |
| 2. **Non-current Liabilities** | | | |
| Long-term Borrowings | | 10,00,000 | **20** |
| 3. **Current Liabilities** | | | |
| Trade Payables | | 6,00,000 | **12** |
| **Total** | | 50,00,000 | 100 |
| II. **ASSETS** | | | |
| 1. **Non-current Assets** | | | |
| (i) Property, Plant & Equipment and Intangible Assets | | | |
| (a) Property, Plant and Equipment | | 30,00,000 | **60** |
| (b) Intangible Assets | | **6,00,000** | 12 |
| 2. **Current Assets** | | | |
| (i) Inventories | | **10,00,000** | 20 |
| (ii) Cash and Cash Equivalents | | **4,00,000** | 8 |
| **Total** | | 50,00,000 | 100 |

**13.** (i) $\text{Stock/Inventory Turnover Ratio} = \dfrac{\text{Cost of Revenue from Operations, i.e. Cost of Goods Sold}}{\text{Average Inventory}} = \dfrac{6,86,000}{17,000}$

Stock Turnover Ratio = 40.35 times

Net Purchases = 80% of Net Revenue from Operations

$= \dfrac{80}{100} \times 8,00,000 = ₹\ 6,40,000$

Opening inventory = ₹ 20,000

Closing inventory = 20,000 – 6,000 = ₹ 14,000

Cost of Revenue from Operations = Opening Inventory + Net Purchases + Direct Expenses – Closing Inventory
= 20,000 + 6,40,000 + 40,000 – 14,000

Cost of Revenue from Operations = ₹ 6,86,000

$\text{Average Inventory} = \dfrac{\text{Opening Inventory + Closing Inventory}}{2} = \dfrac{20,000 + 14,000}{2}$

∴ Average Inventory = ₹ 17,000

(ii) $\text{Debt-equity Ratio} = \dfrac{\text{Debt (Long-term)}}{\text{Equity/Shareholders' Funds}} = \dfrac{\text{10\% Debentures + Bank Loan}}{\text{Equity Share Capital + 9\% Preference Share Capital}}$

$$= \frac{8,00,000 + 3,00,000}{16,00,000 + 6,00,000} = \frac{11,00,000}{22,00,000}$$

Debt-equity Ratio = 0.5 : 1

(iii) $\text{Equity Per Share (EPS)} = \dfrac{\text{Net Profit after Tax and Preference Dividend}}{\text{Number of Equity Shares}}$

$$= \frac{20,00,000 - (7,00,000) - (1,00,000)}{30,000} = \frac{12,00,000}{30,000} = ₹\,40$$

(iv) $\text{Working Capital Turnover Ratio} = \dfrac{\text{Revenue from Operations}^{**}}{\text{Working Capital}^{*}} = \dfrac{5,25,000}{2,10,000} = 2.5 \text{ times}$

*Working Capital = Current Assets – Current Liabilities = 5,00,000 – 2,90,000 = ₹ 2,10,000

**Revenue from Operations = Cash Revenue from Operations + Credit Revenue from Operations

= 2,25,000 + 3,00,000 = ₹ 5,25,000

**Common Mistake** Student sometimes only calculate net profit after tax to calculate EPS. It should be noted that preference dividnd will also be deducted from net profit after tax.

14. (i) Dr **Property, Plant and Equipment** (Machinery) **Account** Cr

| Particulars | Amt (₹) | Particulars | Amt (₹) |
|---|---|---|---|
| To Balance b/d | 3,50,000 | By Depreciation | 57,000 |
| To Cash (Purchase of machinery) | 1,27,000 | By Cash A/c (Sale of machinery) | 25,000 |
| (Balancing figure) | | By Statement of Profit and Loss (Loss on sale) | 5,000 |
| | | By Balance c/d | 3,90,000 |
| | 4,77,000 | | 4,77,000 |

(ii) **Cash Flow from Investing Activities**

| Particulars | | Amt (₹) |
|---|---|---|
| **Cash Flow from Investing Activities** | | |
| Sale of Machinery | 25,000 | |
| Purchase of Machinery | (1,27,000) | |
| Sale of Non-current Investment | 10,000 | |
| Net Cash used in Investing Activities | | (92,000) |

(iii) **Cash Flow from Financing Activities**

| Particulars | | Amt (₹) |
|---|---|---|
| **Cash Flow from Financing Activities** | | |
| Issue of Debentures | 20,000 | |
| Interest on Debentures (WN1) | (5,600) | |
| Net Cash Flow from Financing Activities | | 14,400 |

**Working Note**

Interest on debentures $= 80,000 \times \dfrac{6}{100} = ₹\,4,800$ ; $20,000 \times \dfrac{6}{100} \times \dfrac{8}{12} = ₹\,800$

Total interest on debentures = 4,800 + 800 = ₹ 5,600

*Or*

**Cash Flow Statement**
for the year ended 31st March, 2023

| Particulars | | 31st March, 2023 (₹) |
|---|---|---|
| **I. Cash Flow from Operating Activities** | | |
| Net Profit before Tax and Extraordinary Items | | 40,000 |
| **Adjustments for** | | |
| (+) Depreciation | 20,000 | |
| Preliminary Expenses Written-off | 1,000 | 21,000 |
| Operating Profit before Working Capital Changes | | 61,000 |
| (+) Increase in Current Liabilities and Decrease in Current Assets | | |
| Trade Creditors | 4,600 | |
| (−) Increase in Current Assets and Decrease in Current Liabilities | | |
| Stock | (4,000) | |
| Debtors | (3,000) | (2,400) |
| Cash Flow from Operating Activities before Tax | | 58,600 |
| (−) Income Tax Paid | | (5,000) |
| Cash Flow from Operating Activities after Tax | | 53,600 |
| **II. Cash Flow from Investing Activities** | | |
| Purchase of Property, Plant and Equipment | (92,600) | |
| Net Cash Used in Investing Activities | | (92,600) |
| **III. Cash Flow from Financing Activities** | | |
| Issue of Share Capital | 40,000 | |
| Cash Flow from Financing Activities | | 40,000 |
| Net Increase in Cash and Cash Equivalent (I + II + III) | | 1,000 |
| (+) Cash and Cash Equivalent at the Beginning of the Period | | 4,000 |
| Cash and Cash Equivalent at the End of the Period | | 5,000 |

**Working Notes**

1. Dr **Property, Plant and Equipment Account** Cr

| Particulars | Amt (₹) | Particulars | Amt (₹) |
|---|---|---|---|
| To Balance b/d | 93,400 | By Depreciation A/c | 20,000 |
| To Bank A/c (Purchase) (Balancing figure) | 92,600 | By Balance c/d | 1,66,000 |
| | 1,86,000 | | 1,86,000 |

2. **Calculation of Net Profit before Tax and Extraordinary Items**

| | Amt (₹) |
|---|---|
| Profit as per Balance Sheet (30,000 – 20,000) | 10,000 |
| (+) Income Tax Paid | 5,000 |
| (+) Transfer to General Reserve | 25,000 |
| | 40,000 |

SQP Code : **PB-11/15** Series ***i*-Succeed 11-25/15** Roll No.

# Sample Question Paper 11

## Accounts 12th (Code 858)

### General Instructions

1. Candidates are allowed additional 15 minutes for only reading the paper. They must not start writing during this time.
2. Section-A is compulsory for all candidates and has ten questions.
3. Candidates have to attempt all questions from either Section-B or Section-C*.
4. Internal choices have been provided in five questions in Section-A and one question in Section-B.
5. The intended marks for questions or parts of questions are given in the brackets [ ].
6. All calculations should be shown clearly.
7. All workings, including rough work, should be done on the same page as, and adjacent to, the rest of the answer.

*Section-C has not been covered.

**Time :** 3 Hrs.

**Max. Marks :** 80

## Section A Answer All Questions [60 Marks]

**Que 1.**

In sub-parts (i) to (iv), choose the correct option and in sub-parts (v) to (x) answer the questions as instructed.

(i) When debentures are issued as collateral security against a loan, the entry for issue of debentures will be (Understanding) [1]

(a) Credit Debentures A/c and Debit Bank A/c
(b) Debit Debenture Suspense A/c and Credit Bank A/c
(c) Debit Debenture Suspense A/c and Credit Debentures A/c
(d) Debit Cash A/c and Credit Bank A/c

(ii) Choose the correct order in relation to the partnership deed. (Recall) [1]

A – Name and address of the partners and firm

B – Profit and loss sharing ratio

C– Capital contributed by each partner

**Codes**

(a) A, B, C (b) A, C, B
(c) B, C, A (d) C, A, B

(iii) 'A' has given guarantee to 'C', for minimum ₹ 10,000 profit. At year end, the firm suffered loss and C's share in the loss was ₹ 2,000. Calculate amount of deficiency to be borne by 'A'. (Application) [1]

(a) ₹ 8,000 (b) ₹ 12,000
(c) ₹ 10,000 (d) ₹ 14,000

(iv) Gobind carried out dissolution of the firm for a remuneration of ₹ 20,000. He later agreed to take stock valued at ₹ 18,000 in settlement of his remuneration. The journal entry for the same will be (Application) [1]

| | | | | |
|---|---|---|---|---|
| (a) | Gobind's Capital A/c | Dr | 20,000 | |
| | To Realisation A/c | | | 20,000 |
| (b) | Gobind's Capital A/c | Dr | 20,000 | |
| | To Stock A/c | | | 18,000 |
| | To Realisation A/c | | | 20,000 |
| (c) | Realisation A/c | Dr | 18,000 | |
| | To Stock A/c | | | 18,000 |
| (d) | No entry | | | |

(v) An operating cycle is the time between the acquisition of assets for processing and then realisation in cash or cash equivalents.

State the duration when a normal operating cycle cannot be identified. **(Understanding) [1]**

(vi) Priya, Teena and Beena were partners in a firm sharing profits and losses in the ratio of 3 : 2 : 1. On 31st March, 2021, Priya retired from the partnership firm.

Firm's goodwill valued at ₹ 84,000 on the date of her retirement.

Pass the necessary journal entry for adjustment of goodwill. **(Application) [1]**

(vii) **Assertion** (A) Losses, including deficiencies of capital, shall be paid first out of profits.

**Reason** (R) The amount realised from assets will be utilised first to pay-off the third party liabilities of the firm. **(Evaluate) [1]**

**Alternatives**

(a) Both Assertion (A) and Reason (R) are true and Reason (R) is the correct explanation of Assertion (A)

(b) Both Assertion (A) and Reason (R) are true, but Reason (R) is not the correct explanation of Assertion (A)

(c) Assertion (A) is false, but Reason (R) is true

(d) Assertion (A) is true, but Reason (R) is false

(viii) Neel, Nitin and Mukesh were partners in a firm. On 31st March, 2023, Mukesh retired. The amount payable to Mukesh ₹ 2,17,000 was transferred to his loan account. Mukesh agreed to receive interest on this amount as per the provisions of Partnership Act, 1932. State the rate at which interest will be paid to Mukesh. **(Application) [1]**

SP-11

(ix) Stock warrants are an alien concept to many investors, but for seasoned investors, they can be one of the most lucrative ways to invest in a stock. Like options, they offer leverage on a stock's price.

However, unlike options, they are directly issued by the underlying business.

**Source** *The motley fool*

(a) On the basis of above statement, elaborate the meaning of share warrants.

(b) State the head under which this is shown. **(Recall) [1]**

(x) Chandu Limited issued 10,000, 12% debentures of ₹ 100 each on 1st April, 2019 at par redeemable at a premium of 5%. Interest on these debentures is paid half-yearly i.e. on 30th September and 31st March.

You are required to pass necessary journal entry for interest on debentures on 30th September assuming that income tax is deducted @ 20% on the amount of interest. **(Application) [1]**

**2.** Gokul Foods Ltd. offered 20,000, 8% debentures of ₹ 500 each at a premium of 10% payable as ₹ 200 on application (including premium) and balance on allotment, redeemable at par after 8 years. But applications are received for 30,000 debentures and the allotment is made on pro-rata basis. All the money due on application and allotment is received.

You are required to pass journal entries to record

(i) Transfer of application money to debenture account.

(ii) Payment due on allotment.

(iii) Receipt of allotment money. **(Application) [3]**

**Que 3.**

Following is the balance sheet of Daksh, Taksh and Harsh as on 31st March, 2021, who have agreed to share profits and losses in proportion to their capital

**Balance Sheet**
as at 31st March, 2021

| Liabilities | | Amt (₹) | Assets | Amt (₹) |
|---|---|---|---|---|
| Capital A/cs | | | Building | 1,20,000 |
| Daksh | 1,20,000 | | Machinery | 1,80,000 |
| Taksh | 1,80,000 | | Stock | 60,000 |
| Harsh | 1,20,000 | 4,20,000 | | |

| Liabilities | Amt (₹) | Assets | | Amt (₹) |
|---|---|---|---|---|
| Employees Provident Fund | 21,000 | Debtors | 66,000 | |
| Workmen Compensation Reserve | 9,000 | (–) Provision for Doubtful Debts | (6,000) | 60,000 |
| Creditors | 30,000 | Bank | | 60,000 |
| | 4,80,000 | | | 4,80,000 |

On 31st March, 2021, Daksh retired from the firm and the remaining partners decided to carry on the business. It was agreed to revalue the assets and reassess the liabilities on that date, on the following basis

(i) Building to be appreciated by 30%.

(ii) The claim against workmen compensation was ₹ 4,500.

(iii) There were bad debts of ₹ 10,500.

(iv) Machinery to be depreciated by 30%.

Prepare revaluation account. (Application) [3]

*Or*

Lal and Bal are partners. They agree to admit Pal as a partner w.e.f. 1st April, 2019. They agreed to value goodwill at 2 years' purchase by super profit method for which they decided to take average of last 5 years profits. The profits for the last 5 years were

| Years | Amt (₹) | |
|---|---|---|
| 2014-15 | 40,000 | (including gain of ₹ 5,000 from sale of fixed assets) |
| 2015-16 | 34,000 | (including abnormal loss of ₹ 10,000) |
| 2016-17 | 42,000 | |
| 2017-18 | 46,000 | |
| 2018-19 | 50,000 | |

Capital employed in the firm is ₹ 3,00,000 and normal rate of return in similar business is 10%. You are required to

(i) Give the amount of corrected profit. [1]

(ii) Calculate the value of goodwill. [Application] [2]

SP-11

**Que 4.**

On 1st April, 2017, Abhinav Ltd. (an unlisted company) issued 60,000, 12% debentures of ₹ 100 each at a premium of 10% redeemable after three years at a premium of 5%. The company decided to transfer the minimum required amount to debenture redemption reserve on 31st March, 2019.

It also made the required investment in government securities earning interest @ 10% p.a. on 1st April, 2019. Tax was deducted on interest earned @ 10%.

Ignoring entries relating to interest paid on debentures, pass the necessary journal entries to record redemption of debentures. (Application) [3]

**Que 5.**

Vikas and Riyansh are partners and the balance sheet as at 31st March, 2021 was as follows

| Liabilities | | Amt (₹) | Assets | Amt (₹) |
|---|---|---|---|---|
| Capital A/cs | | | Sundry Assets | 5,80,000 |
| Vikas | 2,00,000 | | | |
| Riyansh | 1,60,000 | 3,60,000 | | |

| Liabilities | | Amt (₹) | Assets | Amt (₹) |
|---|---|---|---|---|
| Current A/cs | | | | |
| Vikas | 40,000 | | | |
| Riyansh | 20,000 | 60,000 | | |
| General Reserve | | 80,000 | | |
| Workmen Compensation Reserve | | 80,000 | | |
| | | 5,80,000 | | 5,80,000 |

Profit for the year ended 31st March, 2021 was ₹ 20,000. As per the partnership deed, partners are entitled to interest on capital @ 12% per annum.

Prepare profit and loss appropriation account after taking into account the following necessary adjustments.

(i) Partners will get interest on capital in full.

(ii) The workmen compensation reserve was not utilised during the year so it was decided by the partners to transfer 50% of this reserve back to profit.

(iii) A fine of ₹ 1,000 was charged from Riyansh for competing with the firm.

(iv) Vikas and Riyansh will share profits of ₹ 14,400 each.

In case of any deficiency, the firm may utilise its general reserve. **(Application) [3]**

*Or*

A and B are partners in a firm sharing profits and losses in the ratio of 2:3. Their fixed capitals as on 1st April, 2018 were ₹ 3,00,000 and ₹ 4,00,000 respectively.

As per partnership deed, both partners partners are to get monthly salary of ₹ 12,500 each and interest on capital @ 8% p.a. They are to be charged interest on drawings @ 10% p.a. Drawings during the year ended 31st March, 2019 were A ₹ 5,000 per month and B ₹ 60,000 during the year. Firm incurred a loss of ₹ 50,000 during the year before above adjustments.

Prepare an account showing the distribution of profit/loss. **(Application)**

**Que 6.**

A, B and C are partners in a firm. Their capital accounts on 1st April, 2021 stood at ₹ 2,00,000, ₹ 1,60,000 and ₹ 1,20,000 respectively.

SP-11

Each partner withdrew ₹ 10,000 during the financial year 2021-22. As per the provisions of their partnership deed

(i) B was entitled to a salary of ₹ 2,000 per month.

(ii) Interest on capital was to be allowed @ 10% per annum.

(iii) Interest on drawings was to be charged @ 4% per annum.

(iv) Profits and losses were to be shared in the ratio of their capitals.

The net profits of ₹ 1,50,000 for the year ended 31st March, 2022 was divided equally amongst the partners without providing for the terms of the deed.

Pass a single adjusting journal entry to rectify the error. Show working notes clearly. **(Application) [6]**

*Or*

On 31st March, 2021 the balance in the capital accounts of Eluin, Monu and Ahmed, after making adjustments for profits, drawing, etc. were ₹ 80,000, ₹ 60,000 and ₹ 40,000 respectively. Subsequently, it was discovered that interest on capital and interest on drawings has been omitted.

The partners were entitled to interest on capital @ 5% pa. The drawings during the year Eluin ₹ 20,000, Monu ₹ 15,000 and Ahmed ₹ 9,000. Interest on drawings chargeable to partners were Eluin ₹ 500, Monu ₹ 360 and Ahmed ₹ 200.

The net profit during the year amounted to ₹ 1,20,000. The profit sharing ratio was 3 : 2 : 1.

You are required to

(i) Calculate opening capital of partners. [1]

(ii) Pass necessary adjustment entry. (Application) [5]

**Que 7.**

Following is the balance sheet of Arun and Varun as at 31st March, 2021

**Balance Sheet**

as at 31st March, 2021

| Liabilities | | Amt (₹) | Assets | | Amt (₹) |
|---|---|---|---|---|---|
| Sundry Creditors | | 60,000 | Cash in Hand | | 1,000 |
| Bills Payable | | 16,000 | Cash at Bank | | 16,000 |
| Mrs Arun's Loan | | 10,000 | Stock-in-trade | | 10,000 |
| Mrs Varun's Loan | | 20,000 | Investments | | 20,000 |
| General Reserve | | 20,000 | Debtors | 40,000 | |
| Investments Fluctuation Fund | | 2,000 | (−) Provision for Doubtful Debts | (4,000) | 36,000 |
| Capital A/cs | | | Plant and Machinery | | 40,000 |
| Arun | 20,000 | | Building | | 30,000 |
| Varun | 20,000 | 40,000 | Goodwill | | 8,000 |
| | | | Profit and Loss A/c | | 7,000 |
| | | 1,68,000 | | | 1,68,000 |

The firm was dissolved on 31st March, 2021 and following was agreed

(i) Arun promised to pay Mrs Arun's loan and took stock-in-trade at ₹ 8,000.

(ii) Varun took half the investment @ 10% discount.

(iii) Debtors realised ₹ 38,000.

(iv) Creditors and bills payable were due on an average basis of one month after 31st March but they were paid immediately on 31st March @ 6% discount per annum.

(v) Plant realised ₹ 50,000, building ₹ 80,000, goodwill ₹ 12,000 and remaining investments at ₹ 9,000.

(vi) There was an old typewriter in the firm which had been written-off completely from the books. It is now estimated to realise ₹ 600. It was taken away by Varun at this estimated price.

(vii) Realisation expenses were ₹ 2,000.

From the following information prepare realisation account and partners' capital account . (Application) [6]



**Que 8.**

Prepare balance sheet of Shambhu Ltd. as per Schedule III Part I of the Companies Act, 2013 from the following information as on 31st March, 2023.

Plant and machinery ₹ 4,00,000, shares in Shin Ltd. ₹ 2,00,000, bill receivables ₹ 20,000, stock-in-trade ₹ 1,60,000, 10% debentures ₹ 1,20,000, short-term loan from bank ₹ 20,000, provision for taxation ₹ 20,000, prepaid expenses ₹ 20,000, share capital ₹ 4,00,000, capital redemption reserve ₹ 2,40,000. (Application) [6]

**Que 9.**

(A) Sarthak and Vansh are partners, sharing profits in the ratio of 2 : 1. They admit Mansi into partnership for 1/3rd share in profits. She brings ₹ 60,000 for goodwill and proportionate capital. At the time of admission of Mansi, the balance sheet of Sarthak and Vansh are as under

**Balance Sheet**
as at ...

| Liabilities | | Amt (₹) | Assets | | Amt (₹) |
|---|---|---|---|---|---|
| Capital A/cs | | | Plant | | 66,000 |
| Sarthak | 70,000 | | Furniture | | 30,000 |
| Vansh | 60,000 | 1,30,000 | Investments | | 40,000 |
| General Reserve | | 18,000 | Stock | | 46,000 |
| Bank Loan | | 18,000 | Debtors | 38,000 | |
| Creditors | | 72,000 | (–) Provision for Doubtful Debts | (4,000) | 34,000 |
| | | | Cash | | 22,000 |
| | | 2,38,000 | | | 2,38,000 |

It was decided to

(i) Reduce the value of stock by ₹ 10,000.
(ii) Plant is to be valued at ₹ 80,000.
(iii) An amount of ₹ 3,000 included in creditors was not payable.
(iv) Half of the investments were taken over by Sarthak and remaining were valued at ₹ 25,000.

You are required to

(a) Prepare revaluation account. [1½]
(b) Prepare partners' capital account and cash account of the reconstituted firm. [4 ½]
(c) Prepare balance sheet. [2]

(B) A, B, C and D were partners in a firm sharing profits and losses in the ratio of 1 : 2 : 3 : 4. On 31st March, 2022, C retired from the firm and his share was acquired by A and B in the ratio of 3 : 2. Calculate the new profit sharing ratio of A, B and D. **(Application) [2]**

*Or*

The balance sheet of Gupta, Verma and Sharma who are sharing profits in the ratio of 2 : 3 : 4 is as follows

**Balance Sheet**
as at ...

| Liabilities | | Amt (₹) | Assets | | Amt (₹) |
|---|---|---|---|---|---|
| Creditors | | 17,500 | Plant and Machinery | | 1,50,000 |
| General Reserve | | 22,500 | Patents | | 10,000 |
| Capital A/cs | | | Stock | | 2,00,000 |
| Gupta | 65,000 | | Debtors | 75,000 | |
| Verma | 1,75,000 | | (–) Provision for Doubtful Debts | (10,000) | 65,000 |
| Sharma | 2,20,000 | 4,60,000 | Bank Balance | | 75,000 |
| | | 5,00,000 | | | 5,00,000 |

Gupta retires from the firm on the following terms

(i) Plant and machinery be depreciated by 20%.
(ii) Patents are valueless.
(iii) Stock is estimated at the value of ₹ 1,92,500.
(iv) Provision for doubtful debts be kept at 10% on debtors.
(v) Goodwill of the firm be valued at ₹ 63,000 and Gupta's share of goodwill be adjusted into the accounts of Verma and Sharma.
(vi) Amount due to Gupta is to be paid on the date of his retirement.
(vii) The capital of the new firm be fixed at ₹ 3,50,000.

SP-11

You are required to give

(a) The entry for the transfer of revaluation profit/loss. (Recall) [2]

(b) The entry for transfer of general reserve. (Application) [2]

(c) The entry for adjustment of goodwill. (Application) [2]

(d) Prepare capital account. (Application) [2]

(e) Prepare the balance sheet. (Application) [2]

**Que 10.**

Disney Dreams Ltd. issued 1,00,000 equity shares of ₹ 15 each at par. The money was payable as follows On application ₹ 5 per share, on allotment ₹ 4 per share, on first and final call ₹ 6 per share. Applications were received for 1,02,500 shares. Excess applications were rejected and full allotment was made. Donald, who held 5,000 shares failed to pay the allotment money and the call. His shares were forfeited after the final call.

(i) How much amount was received on application? [1]

(ii) What is the amount received on allotment? [1]

(iii) What is the amount forfeited on Donald's shares? [1]

(iv) What is the total calls-in-arrear? [2]

(v) You are required to

(a) Pass the entry for the forfeiture of Donald's share. [2]

(b) Pass the entry for the final call being made. (Recall) [3]

*Or*

Meena Ltd. issued 60,000 shares of ₹ 10 each at a premium of ₹ 2 per share payable as ₹ 3 on application, ₹ 5 on allotment (including premium) and balance on the first and final call. Applications were received for 1,02,000 shares. The directors resolved to allot as follows

(i) Applicants of 60,000 shares – 30,000 shares

(ii) Applicants of 40,000 shares – 30,000 shares

(iii) Applicants of 2,000 shares – Nil

Nikhil who had applied for 1,000 shares in category (i) and Vish, who was allotted 600 shares in category (ii) failed to pay the allotment money.

(a) Calculate the amount received allotment.

(b) Journalise the above transactions. (Application) [10]

## Section B

**[20 Marks]**

**Que 11.**

(i) Net working capital compares a company's operating current assets (excluding cash and cash equivalents) to its operating current liabilities (excluding debt and interest bearing securities). The formula to calculate net working capital subtracts operating current liabilities from operating current assets. A positive value implies the company can pay-off its short-term obligations by liquidating its current assets, while a negative Net Working Capital (NWC) compares a company's operating current assets (excluding cash and cash equivalents) to its operating current liabilities (excluding debt and interest bearing securities).

**Source** *wallstreetprep.(edited)*

- Mention the formula to calculate net working capital. (Recall) [1]
- What will be the current ratio of a company whose net working capital is zero?(Analysis) [1]

(a) 1 : 2 (b) 2 : 1
(c) 1 : 1 (d) 0

(ii) State which of the following would result in inflow/outflow of cash or cash equivalents?

- Issue of shares against purchase of fixed assets.
- Sale of furniture (book value ₹ 10,000) for ₹ 8,000 in cash. (Understanding) [1]

(a) No effect, inflow
(b) Inflow, outflow
(c) Outflow, inflow
(d) No effect, no effect

(iii) Employers must design benefits packages that align with the needs of their employees, are affordable and comply with legal requirements. Some benefits, like health insurance and retirement plans, are commonly offered, while others, such as flexible work arrangements and wellness programmes, are gaining popularity. In fact, approximately 60% of people say benefits and perks are a significant consideration when deciding whether to accept a job.

**Source** *onsurity (edited)*

With respect to the above information which benefit is mentioned here? **(Analysis) [1]**

(iv) Reviewing financial statements before making important decisions is important because these documents offer a comprehensive snapshot of a company's fiscal health and performance.

Financial statements provide vital insights into its profitability, liquidity, solvency and overall stability. By analysing income statements, balance sheets and cash flow statements, stakeholders can study the company's past and current financial standings, identify trends and predict future trajectories.

**Source** *Nism (edited)*

After reviewing the aforementioned information , state cash receipts from sale of goods and rendering of services, royalties and commission received are example of which activity? **(Analysis) [1]**

(v) Liquidity is important because it shows how flexible a company is in meeting its financial obligations and unexpected costs.

**Source** *Business insider*

Based on the above statement, write the correct formula of liquid assets. **(Application) [1]**

**Que 12.**

From the following statement of profit and loss of CCC Ltd. prepare a comparative statement of profit and loss. **(Application) [3]**

| Particulars | 31st March, 2022 (₹) | 31st March, 2021 (₹) |
|---|---|---|
| Revenue from Operations | 32,500 | 25,000 |
| Cost of Materials Consumed | 16,590 | 11,850 |
| Employees Benefit Expenses | 4,910 | 1,150 |
| Profit before Tax | 11,000 | 12,000 |

SP-11

**Que 13.**

Following are the balance sheets of Jindal Saw Ltd. as at 31st March, 2018 and 2019

| Particulars | Note No. | 2018-19 (₹) | 2017-18 (₹) |
|---|---|---|---|
| I. **EQUITY AND LIABILITIES** | | | |
| 1. **Shareholders' Funds** | | | |
| (i) Share Capital | | 7,00,000 | 6,00,000 |
| (ii) Reserves and Surplus | 1 | 2,00,000 | 1,10,000 |
| 2. **Non-current Liabilities** | | | |
| Long-term Borrowings | | 3,30,000 | 2,25,000 |
| **Total** | | 12,30,000 | 9,35,000 |

| Particulars | Note No. | 2018-19 (₹) | 2017-18 (₹) |
|---|---|---|---|
| II. **ASSETS** | | | |
| 1. **Non-current Assets** | | | |
| (i) Property, Plant & Equipment and Intangible Assets | | | |
| (a) Property, Plant and Equipment | 2 | 11,00,000 | 8,00,000 |
| 2. **Current Assets** | | | |
| (i) Inventories | | 70,000 | 60,000 |
| (ii) Trade Receivables | | 32,000 | 40,000 |
| (iii) Cash and Cash Equivalents | | 28,000 | 35,000 |
| **Total** | | 12,30,000 | 9,35,000 |

**Notes to Accounts**

| Particulars | 31st March, 2019 (₹) | 31st March, 2018 (₹) |
|---|---|---|
| 1. **Reserves and Surplus** | | |
| Surplus (Balance in Statement of Profit and Loss) | 2,00,000 | 1,10,000 |
| 2. **Property, Plant and Equipment** | | |
| Plant and Machinery | 11,00,000 | 8,00,000 |

**Additional Information**

A piece of machinery of the book value of ₹ 80,000 was sold for ₹ 65,000 at the beginning of the year. Depreciation provided on plant and machinery during the year amounted to ₹ 2,00,000. From the following information prepare

(i) Cash flow from operating activities.
(ii) Cash flow from investing activities.
(iii) Cash flow from financing activities. **(Application) [6]**

*Or*

Following is the information of Radha Ltd. as at 31st March, 2023. Based on this, answer the questions given below in relation to the cash flow statement.

| Particulars | 31st March, 2023 (₹) | 31st March, 2022 (₹) |
|---|---|---|
| Inventories | 69,000 | 72,000 |
| Trade Receivables | 94,000 | 61,000 |
| Prepaid Expenses | 14,000 | 3,000 |
| Trade Payable | 82,000 | 78,000 |
| Provision for Tax | 13,000 | 19,000 |

The net profit after tax of Radha Ltd. for the year ended 31st March, 2023 was ₹ 3,40,000.

**Additional Information**

(i) Depreciation charged on plant and machinery ₹ 49,000.
(ii) Insurance claim received ₹ 20,000.
(iii) Gain on sale of investments of ₹ 8,000 appeared in the statement of profit and loss.

(a) What is the amount of tax paid during the year? [2]
(b) What will be the treatment for the gain on sale of investments? [2]
(c) What is the net operating profit before working capital changes? **(Evaluate) [2]**

**Que 14.**

Following particulars are given to you

| Particulars | 31st March, 2023 (₹) | 31st March, 20232 (₹) |
|---|---|---|
| Revenue from Operations | 2,19,000 | 1,82,500 |
| Cost of Revenue from Operations | 1,69,000 | 1,42,500 |

SP-11

**Balance Sheet**
as at ...

| Particulars | Note No. | 31st March, 2023 (₹) | 31st March, 2022 (₹) |
|---|---|---|---|
| **I. EQUITY AND LIABILITIES** | | | |
| **1. Shareholders' Funds** | | | |
| (i) Share Capital | | 1,50,000 | 1,50,000 |
| (ii) Reserves and Surplus | | 40,000 | 30,000 |
| **2. Non-current Liabilities** | | | |
| Long-term Borrowings | | 1,30,000 | 70,000 |
| **3. Current Liabilities** | | | |
| Trade Payables | | 80,000 | 50,000 |
| **Total** | | 4,00,000 | 3,00,000 |
| **II. ASSETS** | | | |
| **1. Non-current Assets** | | | |
| Property, Plant & Equipment and Intangible Assets | | 2,08,000 | 2,10,000 |
| **2. Current Assets** | | | |
| (i) Inventory | | 72,000 | 50,000 |
| (ii) Trade Receivables | | 60,000 | 30,000 |
| (iii) Cash and Cash Equivalents | | 50,000 | 5,000 |
| (iv) Other Current Assets : Prepaid Expenses | | 10,000 | 5,000 |
| **Total** | | 4,00,000 | 3,00,000 |

Calculate any three of the following ratios
(i) Acid test ratio
(ii) Trade receivables turnover ratio
(iii) Working capital turnover ratio
(iv) Debt equity ratio **(Application) [6]**

# Solutions in Topper's Style

My Commitment *I affirm that I am reviewing these solutions only after I have solved the Sample Question Paper 11 on my own. My purpose of looking the solutions is solely to verify whether my answers/solutions were correct or not and to identify my mistakes in case my solutions were wrong or I could not solve that.*

1. (i) (*c*) Debit Debenture Suspense A/c and Credit Debentures A/c

(ii) (*b*) A, C, B

(iii) (*b*) Amount of deficiency to be borne by 'A' = Guaranteed Amount + Actual Share of Loss

$= 10{,}000 + 2{,}000 = ₹\ 12{,}000$

(iv) (d) No entry

(v) 12 months

(vi) **JOURNAL**

| Date | Particulars | | LF | Amt (Dr) | Amt (Cr) |
|---|---|---|---|---|---|
| | Teena's Capital A/c | Dr | | 28,000 | |
| | Beena's Capital A/c | Dr | | 14,000 | |
| | To Priya's Capital A/c | | | | 42,000 |
| | (Being the Priya's share of goodwill adjusted in gaining ratio i.e. 2 : 1) | | | | |

**Working Note**

Priya's Share of Goodwill $= 84{,}000 \times \frac{3}{6} = ₹\ 42{,}000$

(vii) (*b*) Both Assertion (A) and Reason (R) are true, but Reason (R) is not the correct explanation of Assertion (A)

(viii) As per the provisions of Partnership Act, 1932 interest on loan to be payable to Mukesh is 6% p.a.

(ix) (a) Share warrants are the financial instruments which give holder the right to acquire equity shares at a specified date and at a specified time.

(b) Shareholder's funds.

(x) **JOURNAL**

| Date | Particulars | | LF | Amt (Dr) | Amt (Cr) |
|---|---|---|---|---|---|
| 2019 | | | | | |
| Sept 30 | Interest on Debentures A/c $\left(10{,}00{,}000 \times \frac{12}{100} \times \frac{6}{12}\right)$ | Dr | | 60,000 | |
| | To Debentureholders' A/c | | | | 48,000 |
| | To Income Tax Payable A/c (60,000 × 20%) | | | | 12,000 |
| | (Being the half-yearly interest due to debentures and tax deducted at source) | | | | |
| Sept 30 | Debentureholders' A/c | Dr | | 48,000 | |
| | To Bank A/c | | | | 48,000 |
| | (Being the payment made of interest) | | | | |

2. **JOURNAL**

| Date | Particulars | | LF | Amt (Dr) | Amt (Cr) |
|---|---|---|---|---|---|
| (i) | Bank A/c (30,000 × 200) | Dr | | 60,00,000 | |
| | To Debenture Application A/c | | | | 60,00,000 |
| | (Being application money received) | | | | |
| | Debenture Application A/c | Dr | | 60,00,000 | |
| | To 8% Debentures A/c (20,000 × 150) | | | | 30,00,000 |
| | To Security Premium A/c (20,000 × 50) | | | | 10,00,000 |
| | To Debenture Allotment A/c (10,000 × 200) | | | | 20,00,000 |
| | (Being application money transferred to debenture account and excess adjusted on allotment) | | | | |
| (ii) | Debenture Allotment A/c (20,000 × 350) | Dr | | 70,00,000 | |
| | To 8% Debentures A/c | | | | 70,00,000 |
| | (Being allotment due) | | | | |

| Date | Particulars | | LF | Amt (Dr) | Amt (Cr) |
|---|---|---|---|---|---|
| (iii) | Bank A/c (70,00,000 – 20,00,000) | Dr | | 50,00,000 | |
| | To Debentures Allotment A/c | | | | 50,00,000 |
| | (Being allotment money received) | | | | |

3. Dr **Revaluation Account** Cr

| Particulars | Amt (₹) | Particulars | | Amt (₹) |
|---|---|---|---|---|
| To Bad Debts | 4,500 | By Building | | 36,000 |
| To Machinery | 54,000 | By Loss transferred to | | |
| | | Daksh's Capital A/c | 6,429 | |
| | | Taksh's Capital A/c | 9,642 | |
| | | Harsh's Capital A/c | 6,429 | 22,500 |
| | 58,500 | | | 58,500 |

**Common Mistake** Students mostly record bad debts by the amount given in additional information (₹ 10,500 in Q.) on debit side of the revaluation account. But since the firm has maintained provision for doubtful debts (₹ 6,000 in Q.), so here only ₹ 4,500 will be recorded as bad debts.

*Or* (i) **Calculation of Correct Profit**

| Year | Profit (₹) | Correct Profit (₹) |
|---|---|---|
| 2014-15 | 40,000 – 5,000 | 35,000 |
| 2015-16 | 34,000 + 10,000 | 44,000 |
| 2016-17 | 42,000 | 42,000 |
| 2017-18 | 46,000 | 46,000 |
| 2018-19 | 50,000 | 50,000 |
| | | 2,17,000 |

(ii) Average profit $= \frac{2,17,000}{5} =$ ₹ 43,400

Capital = ₹ 3,00,000

Normal profit $= 3,00,000 \times \frac{10}{100} =$ ₹ 30,000

Super Profit = Average Profit – Normal Profit = 43,400 – 30,000 = ₹ 13,400

Goodwill = Super Profit × Number of Years' Purchase = 13,400 × 2 = ₹ 26,800

4. **JOURNAL**

| Date | Particulars | | LF | Amt (Dr) | Amt (Cr) |
|---|---|---|---|---|---|
| 2019 | | | | | |
| Mar 31 | Surplus, i.e. Balance in Statement of Profit and Loss | Dr | | 6,00,000 | |
| | To Debenture Redemption Reserve A/c | | | | 6,00,000 |
| | (Being the debenture redemption reserve created out of profits) | | | | |
| Apr 1 | 10% Debenture Redemption Investments A/c | Dr | | 9,00,000 | |
| | To Bank A/c | | | | 9,00,000 |
| | (Being the debenture redemption investment purchased) | | | | |
| 2020 | | | | | |
| Mar 31 | Bank A/c | Dr | | 81,000 | |
| | TDS Collected/Deposited A/c | Dr | | 9,000 | |
| | To Interest on Debenture Redemption Investments A/c | | | | 90,000 |
| | (Being the interest received on debenture redemption investments) | | | | |
| Mar 31 | Bank A/c | Dr | | 9,00,000 | |
| | To 10% Debenture Redemption Investments A/c | | | | 9,00,000 |
| | (Being the debenture redemption investments sold) | | | | |
| Mar 31 | 12% Debentures A/c | Dr | | 60,00,000 | |
| | Premium on Redemption of Debentures A/c | Dr | | 3,00,000 | |
| | To Debentureholders' A/c | | | | 63,00,000 |
| | (Being the amount payable to debentureholders on redemption) | | | | |

| Date | Particulars | | LF | Amt (Dr) | Amt (Cr) |
|---|---|---|---|---|---|
| Mar 31 | Debentureholders' A/c | Dr | | 63,00,000 | |
| | To Bank A/c | | | | 63,00,000 |
| | (Being the debenture redeemed) | | | | |
| Mar 31 | Interest on Debenture Redemption Investments A/c | Dr | | 90,000 | |
| | To Statement of Profit and Loss | | | | 90,000 |
| | (Being the interest on debenture redemption investments transferred to statement of profit and loss) | | | | |
| Mar 16 | Debenture Redemption Reserve A/c | Dr | | 6,00,000 | |
| | To General Reserve A/c | | | | 6,00,000 |
| | (Being the debenture redemption reserve transferred to general reserve) | | | | |

5.

**Profit and Loss Appropriation Account**

for the year ended 31st March, 2021

Dr Cr

| Particulars | | Amt (₹) | Particulars | Amt (₹) |
|---|---|---|---|---|
| To Interest on Capital A/c | | | By Profit | 20,000 |
| Vikas | 24,000 | | By Workmen Compensation on Reserve | 40,000 |
| Riyansh | 19,200 | 43,200 | By Riyansh's Capital A/c (Fine) | 1,000 |
| To Profit transferred to Current A/cs | | | By General Reserve (Balancing figure) | 11,000 |
| Vikas | 14,400 | | | |
| Riyansh | 14,400 | 28,800 | | |
| | | 72,000 | | 72,000 |

**Working Note**

**Calculation of Interest on Capital**

Vikas $= 2,00,000 \times \frac{12}{100} = ₹\,24,000$; Riyansh $= 1,60,000 \times \frac{12}{100} = ₹\,19,200$

**Value Points**

- Transferring the workmen compensation reserve to profits will increase the profit and it will be recorded on the credit side of appropriation account.
- Fine charged on a partner will also increase the profits of the firm.

*Or*

**Profit and Loss Appropriation Account**

for the year ended 31st March, 2019

Dr Cr

| Particulars | Amt (₹) | Particulars | | Amt (₹) |
|---|---|---|---|---|
| To Profit and Loss A/c (Net loss) | 50,000 | By Interest on Drawings A/cs | | |
| | | A | 3,000 | |
| | | B | 3,000 | 6,000 |
| | | By Loss transferred to | | |
| | | A's Current A/c (2/5) | 17,600 | |
| | | B's Current A/c (3/5) | 26,400 | 44,000 |
| | 50,000 | | | 50,000 |

**Working Notes**

1. **Interest on Drawings**

   A's Drawings $= 5,000 \times 12 = 60,000 \times \frac{10}{100} \times \frac{6}{12} = ₹\,3,000$; B's Drawings $= 60,000 \times \frac{10}{100} \times \frac{6}{12} = ₹\,3,000$

   In the absence of actual date of drawings, interest thereon has been calculated for an average period of 6 months.
2. Salary and interest on capital will not be provided in case of loss.
3. Although, profit and loss appropriation account is not prepared in case of loss, it has been prepared in this question because 'Interest on Drawings' is to be credited to this account.

**6.** **Calculation of Amount to be Adjusted**

| Particulars | A (₹) | B (₹) | C (₹) | Total (₹) |
|---|---|---|---|---|
| Salary | — | 24,000 | — | 24,000 |
| Interest on Capital | 20,000 | 16,000 | 12,000 | 48,000 |
| Profit | 32,750 | 26,200 | 19,650 | 78,600 |
| | 52,750 | 66,200 | 31,650 | 1,50,600 |
| (−) Interest on Drawings | (200) | (200) | (200) | (600) |
| Amount to be Credited | 52,550 | 66,000 | 31,450 | 1,50,000 |
| Amount to be Debited (Profit wrongly divided equally) | (50,000) | (50,000) | (50,000) | 1,50,000 |
| | 2,550 (Cr) | 16,000 (Cr) | 18,550 (Dr) | Nil |

**JOURNAL**

| Date | Particulars | | LF | Amt (Dr) | Amt (Cr) |
|---|---|---|---|---|---|
| | C's Capital A/c | Dr | | 18,550 | |
| | To A's Capital A/c | | | | 2,550 |
| | To B's Capital A/c | | | | 16,000 |
| | (Being an adjustment entry passed) | | | | |

**Working Note**

Dr **Profit and Loss Appropriation Account** Cr

| Particulars | | Amt (₹) | Particulars | | Amt (₹) |
|---|---|---|---|---|---|
| To Salary (B's Capital A/c) (2,000 × 12) | | 24,000 | By Profit and Loss A/c | | 1,50,000 |
| To Interest on Capital | | | By Interest on Drawings | | |
| A's Capital A/c | 20,000 | | A's Capital A/c | 200 | |
| B's Capital A/c | 16,000 | | B's Capital A/c | 200 | |
| C's Capital A/c | 12,000 | 48,000 | C's Capital A/c | 200 | 600 |
| To Profit transferred to | | | | | |
| A's Capital A/c | 32,750 | | | | |
| B's Capital A/c | 26,200 | | | | |
| C's Capital A/c | 19,650 | 78,600 | | | |
| | | 1,50,600 | | | 1,50,600 |

*Or* (i) **Calculation of Opening Capital**

| Particulars | Eluin (₹) | Monu (₹) | Ahmed (₹) |
|---|---|---|---|
| Capital as on 31st March, 2021 | 80,000 | 60,000 | 40,000 |
| (+) Drawings | 20,000 | 15,000 | 9,000 |
| (−) Profits (1,20,000 in 3 : 2 : 1) | (60,000) | (40,000) | (20,000) |
| Capital as on 1st April, 2020 | 40,000 | 35,000 | 29,000 |

(ii) **JOURNAL**

| Date | Particulars | | LF | Amt (Dr) | Amt (Cr) |
|---|---|---|---|---|---|
| | Eliun's Capital A/c | Dr | | 570 | |
| | To Monu's Capital A/c | | | | 10 |
| | To Ahmed's Capital A/c | | | | 560 |
| | (Being profit adjusted among all partners) | | | | |

**Working Note**

| Statement for Adjustment | | Eluin (₹) | Monu (₹) | Ahmed (₹) |
|---|---|---|---|---|
| Amount Already Credited | | 60,000 | 40,000 | 20,000 |
| | A | 60,000 | 40,000 | 20,000 |

| Statement for Adjustment | | Eluin (₹) | Monu (₹) | Ahmed (₹) |
|---|---|---|---|---|
| **Amount to be Credited** | | | | |
| (+) Interest on Capital | | 2,000 | 1,750 | 1,450 |
| (−) Interest on Drawings Share of Profit | | (500) | (360) | (200) |
| (1,20,000 + 1,060 − 5,200) in 3 : 2 : 1 | | 57,930 | 38,620 | 19,310 |
| | B | 59,430 | 40,010 | 20,560 |
| Difference (B − A) | | (570) Dr | (10) Cr | (560) Cr |

**Note** Negative is debit.

7\. Dr **Realisation Account** Cr

| Particulars | | Amt (₹) | Particulars | | Amt (₹) |
|---|---|---|---|---|---|
| To Sundry Assets A/c | | | By Sundry Liabilities A/c | | |
| Stock-in-trade | 10,000 | | Sundry Creditors | 60,000 | |
| Investments | 20,000 | | Bills Payable | 16,000 | |
| Debtors | 40,000 | | Mrs Arun's Loan | 10,000 | |
| Plant and Machinery | 40,000 | | Mrs Varun's Loan | 20,000 | |
| Building | 30,000 | | Investments Fluctuation Fund | 2,000 | |
| Goodwill | 8,000 | 1,48,000 | Provision for Doubtful Debts | 4,000 | 1,12,000 |
| To Arun's Capital A/c (Mrs Arun's Loan) | | 10,000 | By Arun's Capital A/c (Stock) | | 8,000 |
| To Bank A/c (Liabilities paid) | | | By Varun's Capital A/c (Investments) | | 9,000 |
| Creditors (60,000 − 300) (WN) | 59,700 | | By Bank A/c (Assets realised) | | |
| Bills Payable (16,000 − 80) (WN) | 15,920 | | Debtors | 38,000 | |
| Realisation Expenses | 2,000 | | Plant and Machinery | 50,000 | |
| Mrs Varun's Loan | 20,000 | 97,620 | Building | 80,000 | |
| To Profit transferred to | | | Goodwill | 12,000 | |
| Arun's Capital A/c | 31,490 | | Investments | 9,000 | 1,89,000 |
| Varun's Capital A/c | 31,490 | 62,980 | By Varun's Capital A/c (Typewriter) | | 600 |
| | | 3,18,600 | | | 3,18,600 |

Dr **Partners' Capital Account** Cr

| Particulars | Arun (₹) | Varun (₹) | Particulars | Arun (₹) | Varun (₹) |
|---|---|---|---|---|---|
| To Realisation A/c | 8,000 | 9,000 | By Balance b/d | 20,000 | 20,000 |
| To Realisation A/c | — | 600 | By Realisation A/c | 10,000 | — |
| To Profit and Loss A/c | 3,500 | 3,500 | By Realisation A/c (Profit) | 31,490 | 31,490 |
| To Bank A/c (Final settlement) | 59,990 | 48,390 | By General Reserve | 10,000 | 10,000 |
| | 71,490 | 61,490 | | 71,490 | 61,490 |

**Working Note**

Discount on Creditors $= 60,000 \times 6/100 \times 1/12 =$ ₹ 300 ; Discount on Bills Payable $= 16,000 \times 6/100 \times 1/12 =$ ₹ 80

**Value Points**

- Since creditors and bills payables are paid one month early, it will be paid 6% less for 1 month only, i.e. discount on creditors and bills payables $= (60,000 + 16,000) \times 6/100 \times 1/12$.
- Unrecorded asset will be directly transferred to credit side of the realisation account as realised.

**8.**

**Balance Sheet of Shambhu Ltd.**
as at 31st March, 2023

| Particulars | Note No. | 31st March, 2023 (₹) |
|---|---|---|
| **I. EQUITY AND LIABILITIES** | | |
| 1. **Shareholders' Funds** | | |
| (i) Share Capital | 1 | 4,00,000 |
| (ii) Reserves and Surplus | 2 | 2,40,000 |
| 2. **Non-current Liabilities** | | |
| Long-term Borrowings | 3 | 1,20,000 |
| 3. **Current Liabilities** | | |
| (i) Short-term Borrowings | 4 | 20,000 |
| (ii) Short-term Provisions | 5 | 20,000 |
| **Total** | | 8,00,000 |
| **II. ASSETS** | | |
| 1. **Non-current Assets** | | |
| (i) Property, Plant & Equipment and Intangible Assets | | |
| (a) Property, Plant and Equipment | 6 | 4,00,000 |
| (ii) Non-current Investments | 7 | 20,000 |
| 2. **Current Liabilities** | | |
| (i) Inventories | 8 | 1,60,000 |
| (ii) Trade Receivables | 9 | 2,00,000 |
| (iii) Other Current Assets | 10 | 20,000 |
| **Total** | | 8,00,000 |

**Notes to Accounts**

| Particulars | Amt (₹) |
|---|---|
| 1. **Share Capital Paid-up** | |
| Subscribed and Capital | 4,00,000 |
| 2. **Reserves and Surplus** | |
| Capital Redemption Reserve | 2,40,000 |
| 3. **Long-term Borrowings** | |
| 10% Debentures | 1,20,000 |
| 4. **Short-term Loan from Bank** | |
| Short-term Loan from Bank | 20,000 |
| 5. **Short-term Provisions** | |
| Provision for Taxation | 20,000 |
| 6. **Property, Plant and Equipment** | |
| Plant and Machinery | 4,00,000 |
| 7. **Non-current Investments** | |
| Shares in Shin Ltd. | 2,00,000 |
| 8. **Inventories** | |
| Stock-in-trade | 1,60,000 |
| 9. **Trade Receivables** | |
| Bill Receivables | 20,000 |
| 10. **Other Current Assets** | |
| Prepaid Expenses | 20,000 |

9. (A) (a) Dr **Revaluation Account** Cr

| Particulars | | Amt (₹) | Particulars | Amt (₹) |
|---|---|---|---|---|
| To Stock | | 10,000 | By Plant | 14,000 |
| To Profit transferred to | | | By Creditors | 3,000 |
| Sarthak's Capital A/c | 8,000 | | By Investments | 5,000 |
| Vansh's Capital A/c | 4,000 | 12,000 | | |
| | | 22,000 | | 22,000 |

(b) Dr **Partners' Capital Account** Cr

| Particulars | Sarthak (₹) | Vansh (₹) | Mansi (₹) | Particulars | Sarthak (₹) | Vansh (₹) | Mansi (₹) |
|---|---|---|---|---|---|---|---|
| To Investments | 20,000 | — | — | By Balance b/d | 70,000 | 60,000 | — |
| To Balance c/d | 1,10,000 | 90,000 | 1,00,000 | By General Reserve A/c | 12,000 | 6,000 | — |
| | | | | By Revaluation (Profit) | 8,000 | 4,000 | — |
| | | | | By Premium for Goodwill | 40,000 | 20,000 | — |
| | | | | By Cash A/c | — | — | 1,00,000 |
| | 1,30,000 | 90,000 | 1,00,000 | | 1,30,000 | 90,000 | 1,00,000 |

Dr **Cash Account** Cr

| Particulars | Amt (₹) | Particulars | Amt (₹) |
|---|---|---|---|
| To Balance b/d | 22,000 | By Balance c/d | 1,82,000 |
| To Premium for Goodwill | 60,000 | | |
| To Mansi's Capital A/c | 1,00,000 | | |
| | 1,82,000 | | 1,82,000 |

**Working Note**

**Mansi's Capital** Total capital of the new firm $= 1,10,000 + 90,000 =$ ₹ 2,00,000

2/3rd share capital = ₹ 2,00,000 ; 1/3 rd share capital $= 2,00,000 \times 3/2 \times 1/3 =$ ₹ 1,00,000

(c) **Balance Sheet**

as at ......

| Liabilities | | Amt (₹) | Assets | | Amt (₹) |
|---|---|---|---|---|---|
| Bank Loan | | 18,000 | Stock | | 36,000 |
| Creditors | | 69,000 | Plant | | 80,000 |
| Capital A/cs | | | Furniture | | 30,000 |
| Sarthak | 1,10,000 | | Investments | | 25,000 |
| Vansh | 90,000 | | Debtors | 38,000 | |
| Mansi | 1,00,000 | 3,00,000 | (–) Provision for Doubtful Debts | (4,000) | 34,000 |
| | | | Cash | | 1,82,000 |
| | | 3,87,000 | | | 3,87,000 |

**Common Mistake** Students usually reduce the amount of investment which is taken over by partner (Sarthak in this case) by debiting it to revaluation account. Since Sarthak is taking over the asset at its book value, this portion of investment will not be recorded in the revaluation account.

(B) Old ratio between A, B, C and D = 1 : 2 : 3 : 4

C's share acquired by A and B in the ratio = 3 : 2

A acquires C's share $= \frac{3}{10} \times \frac{3}{5} = \frac{9}{50}$; B acquires C's share $= \frac{3}{10} \times \frac{2}{5} = \frac{6}{50}$

**Calculation of New Ratio**

$A = \frac{1}{10} + \frac{9}{50} = \frac{5+9}{50} = \frac{14}{50}$; $B = \frac{2}{10} + \frac{6}{50} = \frac{10+6}{50} = \frac{16}{50}$; $D = \frac{4}{10} \times \frac{5}{5} = \frac{20}{50}$

∴ New ratio = 14 : 16 : 20 *or* 7 : 8 : 10

*Or*

**JOURNAL**

| Date | Particulars | | LF | Amt (Dr) | Amt (Cr) |
|---|---|---|---|---|---|
| (a) | Gupta's Capital A/c | Dr | | 10,000 | |
| | Verma's Capital A/c | Dr | | 15,000 | |
| | Sharma's Capital A/c | Dr | | 20,000 | |
| | To Revaluation A/c | | | | 45,000 |
| | (Being revaluation loss transferred to partners' capital account) | | | | |
| (b) | General Reserve A/c | Dr | | 22,500 | |
| | To Gupta's Capital A/c | | | | 5,000 |
| | To Verma's Capital A/c | | | | 7,500 |
| | To Sharma's Capital A/c | | | | 10,000 |
| | (Being general reserve transferred to partners' capital account) | | | | |
| (c) | Verma's Capital A/c | Dr | | 6,000 | |
| | Sharma's Capital A/c | Dr | | 8,000 | |
| | To Gupta's Capital A/c | | | | 14,000 |
| | (Being adjustment of goodwill made) | | | | |

(d) Dr **Partners' Capital Account** Cr

| Particulars | Gupta (₹) | Verma (₹) | Sharma (₹) | Particulars | Gupta (₹) | Verma (₹) | Sharma (₹) |
|---|---|---|---|---|---|---|---|
| To Revaluation A/c (Loss) | 10,000 | 15,000 | 20,000 | By Balance b/d | 65,000 | 1,75,000 | 2,20,000 |
| To Gupta's Capital A/c | — | 6,000 | 8,000 | By General Reserve A/c | 5,000 | 7,500 | 10,000 |
| To Bank A/c | 74,000 | 11,500 | 2,000 | By Verma's Capital A/c | 6,000 | — | — |
| To Balance c/d | — | 1,50,000 | 2,00,000 | By Sharma's Capital A/c | 8,000 | — | — |
| | 84,000 | 1,82,500 | 2,30,000 | | 84,000 | 1,82,500 | 2,30,000 |

**Working Notes**

1. Adjustment of goodwill

   Gupta's share of goodwill $= 63{,}000 \times \frac{2}{9} =$ ₹ 14,000

   As there is no agreement on the ratio, old ratio of remaining partners shall be taken as gaining ratio as well as new ratio.

   $\therefore$ Gaining ratio $\Rightarrow$ 3 : 4 $\Leftarrow$ New ratio

   Verma will bear for goodwill $= 14{,}000 \times \frac{3}{7} =$ ₹ 6,000;  Sharma will bear for goodwill $= 14{,}000 \times \frac{4}{7} =$ ₹ 8,000

2. Capital adjustments

   New capital of Verma and Sharma = ₹ 3,50,000

   Verma's new capital $\left(3{,}50{,}000 \times \frac{3}{7}\right) =$ ₹ 1,50,000;  Sharma's new capital $\left(3{,}50{,}000 \times \frac{4}{7}\right) =$ ₹ 2,00,000

(e) **Balance Sheet**

as at ...

| Liabilities | | Amt (₹) | Assets | | Amt (₹) |
|---|---|---|---|---|---|
| Capital A/cs | | | Plant and Machinery (1,50,000 – 30,000) | | 1,20,000 |
| Verma | 1,50,000 | | Stock | | 1,92,500 |
| Sharma | 2,00,000 | 3,50,000 | Debtors | 75,000 | |
| Creditors | | 17,500 | (–) Provision for Doubtful Debts | (7,500) | 67,500 |
| Bank Overdraft (WN 3) | | 12,500 | | | |
| | | 3,80,000 | | | 3,80,000 |

**Working Note**

Dr **Bank Account** Cr

| Particulars | Amt (₹) | Particulars | Amt (₹) |
|---|---|---|---|
| To Balance b/d | 75,000 | By Gupta's Capital A/c | 74,000 |
| To Balance c/d (Balancing figure) | 12,500 | By Verma's Capital A/c | 11,500 |
| | | By Sharma's Capital A/c | 2,000 |
| | 87,500 | | 87,500 |

10. (i) ₹ 5,12,500 (1,02,500 × 5) (ii) ₹ 3,80,000 (95,000 × 4)
(iii) ₹ 25,000 (5,000 × 5) (iv) ₹ 50,000 (30,000 + 20,000)
(v) **JOURNAL**

| Date | Particulars | | Amt (Dr) | Amt (Cr) |
|---|---|---|---|---|
| (a) | Equity Share Capital A/c | Dr | 75,000 | |
| | To Calls-in-arrears A/c | | | 50,000 |
| | To Share Forfeiture A/c | | | 25,000 |
| | (Being 5,000 shares of Donald forfeited on passing the required resolution) | | | |
| (b) | Equity Share First and Final Call A/c | Dr | 6,00,000 | |
| | To Equity Share Capital A/c (1,00,000 × 6) | | | 6,00,000 |
| | (Being final call made due) | | | |
| | Bank A/c (95,000 × 6) | Dr | 5,70,000 | |
| | Calls-in-arrears A/c (5,000 × 6) | Dr | 30,000 | |
| | To Equity Share First and Final Call A/c | | | 6,00,000 |
| | (Being final call money received, with the exception on 5,000 shares) | | | |

*Or* (a)

| **Calculation of Amount Received on Allotment** | | **Amt (₹)** |
|---|---|---|
| Allotment money due (60,000 × 5) | | 3,00,000 |
| (–) Excess received with application (40,000 × 3) | | (1,20,000) |
| (–) Calls-in-arrears (Nikhil) | | |
| Due (500 × 5) | 2,500 | |
| (–) Surplus (WN) | (1,500) | (1,000) |
| (–) Calls-in-arrears (Vish) | | |
| Due (600 × 5) | 3,000 | |
| (–) Surplus (WN) | (600) | (2,400) |
| Amount received with allotment | | 1,76,600 |

**Working Note**

| | Applied Shares | Allotted Shares | |
|---|---|---|---|
| 1. | 60,000 | 30,000 | (Pro-rata allotment) |
| 2. | 40,000 | 30,000 | (Pro-rata allotment) |
| 3. | 2,000 | Nil | |
| | 1,02,000 | 60,000 | |

Number of shares allotted to Nikhil $= 1{,}000 \times \frac{30{,}000}{60{,}000} = 500$ shares

| **Surplus towards Allotment on Nikhil's Shares** | **Amt (₹)** |
|---|---|
| Application money received (1,000 × 3) | 3,000 |
| (–) Application money required (500 × 3) | (1,500) |
| Surplus towards allotment | 1,500 |

Number of shares applied by Vish $= 600 \times \frac{40{,}000}{30{,}000} = 800$ shares

**Surplus towards Allotment on Vish's Shares**

| | |
|---|---|
| Application money received (800 × 3) | 2,400 |
| (–) Application money required (600 × 3) | (1,800) |
| Surplus towards allotment | 600 |

(b) **JOURNAL**

| Date | Particulars | | LF | Amt (Dr) | Amt (Cr) |
|---|---|---|---|---|---|
| | Bank A/c (1,02,000 × 3) | Dr | | 3,06,000 | |
| | To Share Application A/c | | | | 3,06,000 |
| | (Being application money received on 1,02,000 shares) | | | | |
| | Share Application A/c | Dr | | 3,06,000 | |
| | To Share Capital A/c (60,000 × 3) | | | | 1,80,000 |
| | To Share Allotment A/c (40,000 × 3) | | | | 1,20,000 |
| | To Bank A/c (2,000 × 3) | | | | 6,000 |
| | (Being application money transferred to share capital at the time of allotment and excess adjusted towards allotment and refunded) | | | | |
| | Share Allotment A/c | Dr | | 3,00,000 | |
| | To Share Capital A/c (60,000 × 3) | | | | 1,80,000 |
| | To Securities Premium A/c (60,000 × 2) | | | | 1,20,000 |
| | (Being allotment made due) | | | | |
| | Bank A/c | Dr | | 1,76,600 | |
| | To Share Allotment A/c (Point a) | | | | 1,76,600 |
| | (Being allotment money received) | | | | |
| | Share First and Final Call A/c | Dr | | 2,40,000 | |
| | To Share Capital A/c (60,000 × 4) | | | | 2,40,000 |
| | (Being final call made due) | | | | |
| | Bank A/c | Dr | | 2,35,600 | |
| | To Share First and Final Call A/c | | | | 2,35,600 |
| | (Being final call money received with the exception of 1,100 shares) | | | | |

**Note** In the absence of any given information, it is assumed that if a shareholder has defaulted in the payment of allotment, then he had also defaulted in making payments towards the calls.

**11.** (i) • Net Working Capital (NWC) = Operating Current Assets – Operating Current Liabilities

• (*c*) Net working capital = 0 Current Assets – Current Liabilities = 0

So, Current Assets = Current Liabilities ....(i)

Current Ratio = Current Assets/Current Liabilities

Using Eq.(i); Current Ratio = Current Liabilities/Current Liabilities = 1

(ii) (*a*) • No effect – Cash is not affected as it is not a cash transaction.

• Inflow – Cash is increased by ₹ 8,000.

(iii) Employee benefit expenses

(iv) Operating activity

(v) Current assets – Prepaid expenses – Inventories

**12.**

**Comparative Statement of Profit and Loss**
for the years ended 31st March, 2022 and 2021

| Particulars | 31st March, 2021 (₹) | 31st March, 2022 (₹) | Absolute Change (Increase/ Decrease) (₹) | Percentage Change (Increase/ Decrease) (%) |
|---|---|---|---|---|
| I. Revenue from Operations | 25,000 | 32,500 | 7,500 | 30.00 |
| II. Expenses | | | | |
| Cost of Materials Consumed | 11,850 | 16,590 | 4,740 | 40.00 |
| Employees Benefit Expenses | 1,150 | 4,910 | 3,760 | 327.00 |
| Total Expenses | 13,000 | 21,500 | 8,500 | 65.38 |
| III. Profit before Tax (I – II) | 12,000 | 11,000 | (1,000) | (8.33) |

13. (i)

| Particulars | | Amt (₹) |
|---|---|---|
| **Cash Flow from Operating Activities** | | |
| Net Profit before Tax | | 90,000 |
| Adjustments for | | |
| (+) Depreciation on Machinery | 2,00,000 | |
| Loss on Sale of Machinery | 15,000 | 2,15,000 |
| Operating Profit before Working Capital Changes | | 3,05,000 |
| (+) Decrease in Current Assets and Increase in Current Liabilities | | |
| Trade Receivables | | 8,000 |
| (–) Increase in Current Assets and Decrease in Current Liabilities | | |
| Inventory | | (10,000) |
| Net Cash Generated from Operating Activities | | 3,03,000 |

(ii)

| Particulars | | Amt (₹) |
|---|---|---|
| **Cash Flow from Investing Activities** | | |
| Machinery Purchased | (5,80,000) | |
| Machinery Sold | 65,000 | |
| Net Cash Used in Investing Activities | | (5,15,000) |

(iii)

| Particulars | | Amt (₹) |
|---|---|---|
| Cash Flow from Financing Activities | | |
| Issue of Shares | 1,00,000 | |
| Long-term Borrowings | 1,05,000 | |
| Net Cash Generated from Financing Activities | | 2,05,000 |

**Working Note**

Dr **Plant and Machinery Account** Cr

| Particulars | Amt (₹) | Particulars | Amt (₹) |
|---|---|---|---|
| To Balance b/d | 8,00,000 | By Cash A/c | 65,000 |
| To Cash A/c (Balancing figure) | 5,80,000 | By Loss on Sale of Machinery A/c | 15,000 |
| | | By Depreciation A/c | 2,00,000 |
| | | By Balance c/d | 11,00,000 |
| | 13,80,000 | | 13,80,000 |

*Or* (a) Amount of tax paid during the year will be ₹ 19,000.

**Working Note**

In the absence of any other information, current year's provision for tax is treated as provision for tax made during the year. It is preserved that previous year's provision for taxation is paid during the year and current year's provision is made during the year.

(b) Gain of sale of investment ₹ 8,000 will be deducted from the net profit before tax and extraordinary items.

(c)

| Particulars | Amt (₹) |
|---|---|
| Net Profit after Tax as per Statement of Profit and Loss | 3,40,000 |
| (+) Provision for Tax (Current Year) | 13,000 |
| | 3,53,000 |
| (–) Extraordinary Item | |
| Insurance Claim Received | (20,000) |
| **Net Profit before Tax and Extraordinary Items** | 3,33,000 |
| (+)/(–) Non-Cash and Non-Operating Items | |
| (+) Depreciation on Plant and Machinery | 49,000 |
| | 3,82,000 |
| (–) Gain (Profit) on Sale of Investments | (8,000) |
| **Operating Profit before Working Capital Changes** | 3,74,000 |

**14.** (i) $\text{Acid Test Ratio} = \dfrac{\text{Quick Assets}}{\text{Current Liabilities}}$

$\text{Acid Test Ratio (2022)} = \dfrac{35,000}{50,000} = 0.7 : 1$

$\text{Acid Test Ratio (2023)} = \dfrac{1,10,000}{80,000} = 1.375 : 1$

(ii) $\text{Trade Receivable Turnover Ratio} = \dfrac{\text{Credit Revenue from Operations}}{\text{Average Trade Receivables}}$

$\text{Trade Receivable Turnover Ratio (2022)} = \dfrac{1,82,500}{30,000} = 6.08 \text{ times}$

$\text{Trade Receivable Turnover Ratio (2023)} = \dfrac{2,19,000}{60,000} = 3.65 \text{ times}$

(iii) $\text{Working Capital Turnover Ratio} = \dfrac{\text{Revenue from Operations}}{\text{Working Capital}}$

$\text{Working Capital Turnover Ratio (2022)} = \dfrac{1,82,500}{40,000} = 4.56 \text{ times}$

$\text{Working Capital Turnover Ratio (2023)} = \dfrac{2,19,000}{1,12,000} = 1.96 \text{ times}$

**Working Note**

Working Capital = Current Assets − Current Liabilities

Working Capital (2022) = 90,000 − 50,000 = ₹ 40,000

Working Capital (2023) = 1,92,000 − 80,000 = ₹ 1,12,000

(iv) $\text{Debt Equity Ratio} = \dfrac{\text{Debt}}{\text{Equity}}$

$(2022) = \dfrac{70,000}{1,80,000} = 0.39 : 1$

$(2023) = \dfrac{1,30,000}{1,90,000} = 0.68 : 1$

where, Debt = Long-term borrowings

Debt (2022) = ₹ 70,000

Debt (2023) = ₹ 1,30,000

Equity = Shareholders' funds

(2022) = ₹ 1,80,000

(2023) = ₹ 1,90,000

SQP Code : **PB-12/15** Series ***i*-Succeed 12-25/15** Roll No. [ ]

# Sample Question Paper 12

## Accounts 12th (Code 858)

### General Instructions

1. Candidates are allowed additional 15 minutes for only reading the paper. They must not start writing during this time.
2. Section-A is compulsory for all candidates and has ten questions.
3. Candidates have to attempt all questions from either Section-B or Section-C*.
4. Internal choices have been provided in five questions in Section-A and one question in Section-B.
5. The intended marks for questions or parts of questions are given in the brackets [ ].
6. All calculations should be shown clearly.
7. All workings, including rough work, should be done on the same page as, and adjacent to, the rest of the answer.

*Section-C has not been covered.

**Time :** 3 Hrs.
**Max. Marks :** 80

## Section A Answer All Questions [60 Marks]

**Que 1.**

In sub-parts (i) to (iv), choose the correct option and in sub-parts (v) to (x) answer the questions as instructed.

(i) What will be the correct sequence of the following in realisation to the dissolution of partnership firm? (Recall) [1]

A – Payment of outsiders liabilities.
B – Payment of partner's loan.
C – Payment of partner's capital due.
D – Surplus, if any distributed amongst partners.

**Codes**

(a) D, B, C, A (b) A, B, C, D
(c) A, C, B, D (d) C, A, B, D

(ii) B Ltd. purchased a furniture worth ₹ 4,00,000 from G Ltd. and payment is done by issuing 11% debentures at par. What journal entry will be passed in the books of B Ltd. for purchase of furniture? (Understanding) [1]

(a) Debit G Ltd. and Credit 11% Debentures A/c
(b) Debit Furniture A/c and Credit G Ltd. A/c
(c) Debit G Ltd. A/c and Credit Furniture A/c
(d) None of the above

(iii) Sameer, Yasmin and Saloni are partners sharing profits in the ratio of 4 : 3 : 3. Sameer retires and the new profit sharing ratio between Yasmin and Saloni will be 3 : 2.

The goodwill of the firm is valued at ₹ 5,40,000. Sameer's share of goodwill will be adjusted (Application) [1]

(a) by debiting Yasmin's capital and Saloni's capital account with ₹ 1,08,000 each
(b) by debiting only Yasmin's capital account with ₹ 2,16,000
(c) by debiting Yasmin's capital and Saloni's capital account with ₹ 1,29,600 and ₹ 86,400 respectively
(d) by debiting Yasmin's capital and Saloni's capital account with ₹ 1,62,000 and ₹ 54,000 respectively

(iv) If applicants for 80,000 shares were allotted 60,000 shares on pro-rata basis, the shareholder who was allotted 1,200 shares must have applied for (Application) [1]

(a) 900 shares (b) 3,600 shares
(c) 1,600 shares (d) 4,800 shares

(v) Risk-averse investors tend to favour companies with higher ratios of current assets, because such businesses will always have the cash on hand needed to pay salaries, move product and keep the wheels of business rolling.

**Source** *Investopedia*

(a) What are current assets?

(b) Based on the above statement, apart from cash, name any two items that comes under the head current assets. (Recall) [1]

(vi) After the redemption of debentures, the debenture redemption reserve is transferred to which account? (Understanding) [1]

(vii) **Assertion** (A) The gain or loss on revaluation is transferred to all partners' capital account in new ratio.

**Reason** (R) It is necessary to show that true position of the firm at the time of admission of a new partner. (Evaluate) [1]

**Alternatives**

(a) Both Assertion (A) and Reason (R) are true and Reason (R) is the correct explanation of Assertion (A)
(b) Both Assertion (A) and Reason (R) are true, but Reason (R) is not the correct explanation of Assertion (A)
(c) Assertion (A) is false, but Reason (R) is true
(d) Assertion (A) is true, but Reason (R) is false

(viii) Deepak, a partner is to carry out dissolution and he gets ₹ 1,50,000 as remuneration. Realisation expenses of ₹ 1,25,000 are paid by the firm. Realisation account will be debited with how much amount? (Application) [1]

(ix) During the year 2019-20, Network 10 Ltd. issued 12% debentures of ₹ 100 each as per the details given.

A machine was purchased for ₹ 2,18,500. The vendor was paid by the issue of 1,900 debentures at a premium of 15%, to be redeemed at par.

Pass the necessary journal entry for the payment. (Application) [1]

(x) Capital employed by a partnership firm is ₹ 10,00,000. If its average profit is ₹ 1,20,000 and the normal rate of return is similar type of business is 10%, what is the amount of super profit? (Application) [1]

**Que 2.**

You are required to pass journal entries for the issue of debentures in the following conditions

(i) Sunfeast Biscuits Ltd. issued 5,000, 12% debentures of ₹ 100 each at par, redeemable at 5% premium after 5 years.

(ii) Reliance Securities Ltd. issued 30,000, 7% debentures of ₹ 100 each to a creditor for ₹ 25,000 in full satisfaction of his claim. The company had purchased machinery from him. (Application) [3]

*Or*

You are required to pass journal entries for the issue of debentures in the following conditions

(i) Supertech Cements Ltd. issued ₹ 2,00,000, 12% debentures of ₹ 100 each at a discount of 2% redeemable at a premium of 5% after 10 years.

(ii) Hamdard India Ltd. issued 6,000, 12% debentures of ₹ 100 each at a premium of 5%, redeemable at a premium of 10% after 6 years. (Application)

**Que 3.**

A business has average profit of ₹ 2,00,000 during last few years and the normal rate of return is 10%.

The assets and the external liabilities of the business ₹ 20,00,000 and ₹ 3,60,000 respectively.

You are required to find out the value of goodwill by

(i) Capitalisation of super profit method.

(ii) Super profit method, if the goodwill is valued at 3 years' purchases of super profit. (Application) [3]

**Que 4.**

ABC a banking company issued 10,000, 9% debentures of ₹ 100 each on 1st April, 2017. The debentures were due for redemption on 31st March, 2023

You are required to pass journal entries to record

(i) The amount of debenture redemption reserve to be created.

(ii) The journal entries for redemption of debentures. (Application) [3]

**Que 5.**

Madhu and Neha were partners in a firm sharing profits and losses in the ratio of 3 : 5. Their fixed capitals were ₹ 4,00,000 and ₹ 6,00,000 respectively.

On 1st January, 2020, Tina was admitted as a new partner for 1/4th share in the profits. Tina acquired her share of profit from Neha. Tina brought ₹ 4,00,000 as her capital which was to be kept fixed like the capitals of Madhu and Neha.

You are required to calculate

(i) (a) the goodwill of the firm on Tina's admission.

(b) the new profit sharing ratio of Madhu, Neha and Tina. [2]

(ii) Pass necessary journal entry for the treatment of goodwill on Tina's admission considering that Tina did not bring her share of goodwill premium in cash. (Application) [1]

*Or*

On 31st March, 2019 the balance sheet of D, E and F who are sharing profits and losses in proportion to their capital stood as follows

**Balance Sheet**
as at 31st March, 2019

| Liabilities | | Amt (₹) | Assets | | Amt (₹) |
|---|---|---|---|---|---|
| Creditors | | 2,00,000 | Bank | | 1,02,000 |
| Capital A/cs | | | Debtors | 1,00,000 | |
| D | 6,00,000 | | (–) Provision for Doubtful Debts | (2,000) | 98,000 |
| E | 4,00,000 | | Stock | | 2,00,000 |
| F | 2,00,000 | 12,00,000 | Machinery | | 4,00,000 |
| | | | Land and Building | | 6,00,000 |
| | | 14,00,000 | | | 14,00,000 |

E retires from the firm on the same date and partners agreed that

(i) ₹ 40,000 of insurance premium paid to be carried forward as unexpired insurance.

(ii) Land and building be appreciated by 10% and machinery be depreciated by 5%.

(iii) Reserve for doubtful debts be brought upto 10% on debtors.

(iv) A provision for ₹ 36,000 be made in respect of an outstanding bill for repairs.

You are required to

(a) Calculate the amount to be shown in the debtors in the balance sheet.

(b) Prepare revaluation account. (Application) [3]

SP-12

**Que 6.**

Diya and Riya were partners sharing profits and losses equally. On 31st March, 2021, the balance sheet of the firm was as follows

**Balance Sheet**
as at 31st March, 2021

| Liabilities | Amt (₹) | Assets | | Amt (₹) |
|---|---|---|---|---|
| Sundry Creditors | 1,20,000 | Cash | | 50,000 |
| Riya's Loan | 30,000 | Debtors | 84,000 | |
| General Reserve | 30,000 | (–) Provision for Doubtful Debts | (12,000) | 72,000 |

| Liabilities | Amt (₹) | Assets | Amt (₹) |
|---|---|---|---|
| Investment Fluctuation Fund | 4,000 | Stock | 24,000 |
| Riya's Capital | 60,000 | Investments | 36,000 |
| Diya's Capital | 20,000 | Plant and Machinery | 78,000 |
| | | Diya's Loan | 4,000 |
| | 2,64,000 | | 2,64,000 |

Their firm was dissolved on above date and the assets and liabilities were settled as follows

(i) The creditors were paid-off by giving them the plant and machinery at a discount of 10% and the balance in cash.
(ii) Riya's loan was paid with interest of ₹ 1,000.
(iii) Debtors realised 10% less of the amount due from them.
(iv) Stock was taken over by Riya at ₹ 14,000.
(v) Investments realised 80% of their book value.
(vi) Realisation expenses ₹ 1,200 were paid by Diya.

You are required to prepare realisation account and partners' capital account. **(Application) [6]**

*Or*

Adil and Muneer, who were sharing profits and losses in the ratio of 3 : 1 respectively, decided to dissolve the firm on 31st March, 2023.

Their balance sheet is as follows

**Balance Sheet**
as at 31st March, 2023

| Liabilities | Amt (₹) | Assets | Amt (₹) |
|---|---|---|---|
| Trade Creditors | 15,000 | Cash at Bank | 1,000 |
| Loan from Mrs. Adil | 5,000 | Muneer's Capital | 5,000 |
| Adil's Capital | 50,000 | Profit and Loss A/c | 4,000 |
| | | Other Sundry Assets | 60,000 |
| | 70,000 | | 70,000 |

The assets (other than cash at bank) realised ₹ 55,000 and all creditors including loan from Mrs. Adil were paid-off less 5% discount. Realisation expenses amounted to ₹ 500. Prepare the realisation account, bank account and the capital account of the partners assuming that both the partners are solvent. **(Application)**



**Que 7.**

Prepare the balance sheet for Dishant Ltd. as at 31st March, 2022 from the following information as per provisions of Schedule III Part I of the Companies Act, 2013. **(Application) [6]**

**Balance Sheet**
as at 31st December, 2022

| Particulars | Amt (₹) |
|---|---|
| General Reserve | 9,00,000 |
| 8% Debentures | 9,00,000 |
| Balance of Statement of Profit and Loss (Credit) | 3,60,000 |
| Depreciation of Property, Plant and Equipment and Intangible Assets | 2,10,000 |
| Property, Plant and Equipment | 27,00,000 |
| Trade Payables | 7,50,000 |
| Equity Share Capital | 15,00,000 |
| Inventories | 1,92,000 |
| Trade Receivables | 7,68,000 |
| Cash and Cash Equivalents | 9,60,000 |

**Que 8.**

A, B and C are partners sharing profits in the ratio of 4 : 3 : 1. Their balance sheet as at 31st March, 2021 is as follows

**Balance Sheet**
as at 31st March, 2021

| Liabilities | | Amt (₹) | Assets | | Amt (₹) |
|---|---|---|---|---|---|
| Creditors | | 70,000 | Cash in Hand | | 80,000 |
| Bills Payable | | 30,000 | Cash at Bank | | 20,000 |
| Workmen Compensation Reserve | | 20,000 | Stock | | 75,000 |
| General Reserve | | 80,000 | Debtors | 1,30,000 | |
| Capital A/cs | | | (−)Provision for Doubtful Debts | (5,000) | 1,25,000 |
| A | 2,00,000 | | Motor Car | | 1,50,000 |
| B | 3,00,000 | | Investments | | 1,00,000 |
| C | 2,00,000 | 7,00,000 | Plant and Machinery | | 1,20,000 |
| | | | Building | | 2,30,000 |
| | | 9,00,000 | | | 9,00,000 |

On 1st April, 2021, B retires from the firm, selling his share of profit to A for ₹ 36,000 and to C for ₹ 45,000 in the ratio of 4 : 5. For the purpose of B's retirement, it was agreed that

(i) Stock is to be appreciated by 20% and building by 10%.
(ii) Motor car is to be valued at ₹ 70,000.
(iii) Provision for doubtful debts is increased to 10%.
(iv) Investments are sold for ₹ 2,30,000.
(v) Claim on account of workmen compensation is ₹ 12,000.
(vi) Amount due to B is to be settled on the following basis 50% on retirement and the balance 50% within one year.
(vii) The capital of the newly constituted firm is fixed at ₹ 6,00,000 to be divided between A and C in the profit sharing ratio. Adjustment is to be made in cash.

You are required to

(i) Calculate new profit sharing ratio of partners. [1]
(ii) Prepare partners' capital account. (Application) [5]

SP-12

**Que 9.**

Mohan Bakers Ltd. invited applications of 10,00,000 equity shares of ₹ 10 each at a premium of ₹ 2 per share. The amount was payable as follows

| | |
|---|---|
| On Application | ₹ 5 (including premium) |
| On Allotment | ₹ 4 |
| On First and Final Call | ₹ 3 |

Applications for 15,00,000 shares were received. Application of 3,00,000 shares were rejected and pro-rata allotment was made to the remaining applicants. Excess application money was utilised towards sum due on allotment. Giri who had applied for 24,000 shares, failed to pay allotment and call money. His shares were forfeited. Out of the forfeited shares, 10,000 shares were issued for ₹ 8 per share fully paid-up.

(i) Pass necessary journal entries in the books of the company.
(ii) Prepare share forfeiture account. [10]

*Or*

Raunak Cotton Ltd. issued a prospectus inviting application for 6,000 equity shares of ₹ 100 each at a premium of ₹ 20 per shares, payable as follows

On Application ₹ 20
On Allotment ₹ 50 (including premium)
On First Call ₹ 30
On Final Call ₹ 20

Applications were received for 10,000 shares and allotment was made pro-rata to the applicants of 8,000 shares, the remaining applications being refused. Money received in excess on the application was adjusted toward the amount due on allotment.

Rohit, to whom 300 shares were allotted failed to pay allotment and calls money, his shares were forfeited. Itika, who applied for 600 shares, failed to pay the two calls and her share were also forfeited. All these shares were sold to Kartika as fully paid for ₹ 80 per shares.

(i) What are the number of shares allotted to Itika? [1]
(ii) What is the amount received on allotment? [1]
(iii) What is the amount adjusted on allotment for the shares of Rohit? [1]
(iv) What is the amount of total calls-in-arrears of Rohit? [2]
(v) Give the journal entries passed by the company for
  (a) forfeiture of shares [2]
  (b) re-issue of shares (Application) [3]

**Que 10.**

(A) Lokesh and Azad are partners sharing profits in the ratio 3 : 2, with capitals of ₹ 50,000 and ₹ 30,000 respectively. Interest on capital is agreed to be paid @ 6% p.a. Azad is allowed a salary of ₹ 2,500 p.a. During 2023, the profits prior to the calculation of interest on capital but after charging Azad's salary amounted to ₹ 12,500. A provision of 5% of profits is to be made in respect of manager's commission.

You are required to
  (i) Calculate the interest on capital allowed to Lokesh and Azad and amount of provision for manager's commission during the year 2023. [2]
  (ii) Prepare profit and loss appropriation account. [4½]
  (iii) Prepare partners' capital account. (Application) [1½]

(B) Mickey, Tom and Jerry were partners in the ratio of 5 : 3 : 2. On 31st March, 2021, their books reflected a net profit of ₹ 2,10,000. As per the terms of the partnership deed they were entitled for interest on capital which amounted to ₹ 80,000, ₹ 60,000 and ₹ 40,000 respectively.

SP-12

Besides this a salary of ₹ 60,000 each was payable to Mickey and Tom. Calculate the ratio in which the profits would be appropriated. (Application) [2]

*Or*

A, B and C entered into partnership on 1st January, 2018 to share profits in the ratio of 2 : 1 : 1. Partners have given a guarantee that C's share of profit will not be less than ₹ 70,000 per annum. The loss for the year ended 31st December, 2018 was ₹ 2,00,000 before allowing interest ₹ 8,000 on A's loan which is due for the current year.

You are required to
(i) Mention the amount of loss to be transferred. [2]
(ii) Pass the adjusting journal entry for opening and closing of interest of loan to A. [2]
(iii) Pass the journal entry for the transfer of loss. [2]
(iv) Calculate the amount of deficiency of C. [2]
(v) Pass the journal entry for the adjustment of deficiency of C. (Recall) [2]

## Section B [20 Marks]

**Que 11.**

(i) A company must understand how well it is generating cash and how much it has. That way, it can take corrective action, if needed. When you track your finances, including where cash comes from and where it goes, you can place yourself in a better position to plan business activities and company operations that lead to profits and growth.

**Source** *Investopedia (edited)*

- Give an example of outflow of cash. (Recall)
- While calculating cash from operating activities which among the following will be added to net profit? (Analysis) [1]

(a) Loss on issue of debentures (b) Depreciation
(c) Goodwill (d) All of these

(ii) Liquidity is the lifeblood of a business. If a company doesn't have enough liquid assets to meet its current financial obligations, it might need to declare bankruptcy. Liquidity ratios help to determine if a company has adequate liquidity to cover its current liabilities.

**Source** *The motley fool*

Based on the above statement, which of the following is the correct formula for calculating liquid ratio? (Understanding) [1]

(a) Current assets/Current liabilities (b) Liquid assets/Liquid liabilities
(c) Liquid assets/Current liabilities (d) None of these

(iii) State why shareholders are interested in financial statement analysis. (Analysis) [1]

(iv) **Balance Sheet** (Extract)

| Particulars | 31st March, 2020 (₹) | 31st March, 2019 (₹) |
|---|---|---|
| **EQUITY AND LIABILITIES** | | |
| 12% Debentures | 1,60,000 | 2,00,000 |

**Additional Information**

Interest on debentures is paid on half-yearly basis on 30th September and 31st March each year. Debentures were redeemed on 30th September, 2019. How much amount (related to above information) will be shown in financing activity for cash flow statement prepared on 31st March, 2020? [1]

SP-12

(v) The ratio/financial analysis of HDFC Bank reveals: Net interest margin declined from 4.3% in financial year 2021 to 4.1% in financial year 2022. Net profit margins grew from 24.8% in financial year 2021 to 28.0% in financial year 2022. Debt to equity ratio for financial year 2022 stood at 7.2 as compared to 7.2 in financial year 2021. The net profit of HDFC Bank stood at ₹ 3,80, 528 m in financial year 2022, which was up 19.5% compared to ₹ 3,18,332 m reported in financial year 2022. This compares to a net profit of ₹ 2,72,540 m in financial year 2020 and a net profit of ₹ 2,23,324 m in financial year 2019. Over the past 5 years, HDFC Bank's net profit has grown at a CAGR of 19.7%.

The bank's debt to equity ratio increased and stood at 7.23 × during financial year 2022, from 7.20 × during financial year 2021.

**Source** *Equity master (edited)*

- What does the debt-equity ratio of bank depicts?
- Mention any two ratios to measure the short-term solvency of the firm. (Application) [1]

**12.** Prepare common size balance sheet from the following information. **(Application) [3]**

| Particulars | 31st March, 2023 (₹) | 31st March, 2022 (₹) |
|---|---|---|
| Shareholders' Funds | 1,80,000 | 1,20,000 |
| Non-current Liabilities | 60,000 | 60,000 |
| Current Liabilities | 60,000 | 20,000 |
| Non-current Assets | 2,10,000 | 1,40,000 |
| Current Assets | 90,000 | 60,000 |

**13.** Prepare a cash flow statement from the following balance sheets of Surya Vanaspati Ltd. **(Application) [6]**

| Particulars | Note No. | 31st March, 2023 (₹) | 31st March, 2022 (₹) |
|---|---|---|---|
| **I. EQUITY AND LIABILITIES** | | | |
| **1. Shareholders' Funds** | | | |
| (i) Share Capital | | 2,50,000 | 2,00,000 |
| (ii) Reserves and Surplus | | 72,000 | 50,000 |
| **2. Current Liabilities** | | | |
| (i) Trade Payables | | 1,13,000 | 1,30,000 |
| (ii) Short-term Provision | 1 | 24,000 | 20,000 |
| **Total** | | 4,59,000 | 4,00,000 |
| **II. ASSETS** | | | |
| **1. Non-current Assets** | | | |
| Property, Plant & Equipment and Intangible Assets | 2 | 2,52,000 | 1,50,000 |
| **2. Current Assets** | | | |
| (i) Inventory | | 41,000 | 93,000 |
| (ii) Trade Receivables | | 1,40,000 | 1,40,000 |
| (iii) Other Current Assets | 3 | 6,000 | 5,000 |
| (iv) Cash and Cash Equivalents | | 20,000 | 12,000 |
| **Total** | | 4,59,000 | 4,00,000 |

SP-12

**Notes to Accounts**

| Particulars | 2023 (₹) | 2022 (₹) |
|---|---|---|
| **1. Short-term Provision** | | |
| Provision for Taxation | 24,000 | 20,000 |
| **2. Property, Plant & Equipment and Intangible Assets** | | |
| Building | 2,00,000 | 1,00,000 |
| Machinery | 1,00,000 | 90,000 |
| (–) Accumulated Depreciation | (48,000) | (40,000) |
| | 2,52,000 | 1,50,000 |
| **3. Other Current Assets** | | |
| Prepaid Rent | – | 2,000 |
| Prepaid Insurance | 6,000 | 3,000 |
| | 6,000 | 5,000 |

*Or* Following are the balance sheets of Jindal Saw Ltd. as at 31st March, 2022 and 2023

| Particulars | Note No. | 2022-23 (₹) | 2021-22 (₹) |
|---|---|---|---|
| **I. EQUITY AND LIABILITIES** | | | |
| 1. **Shareholders' Funds** | | | |
| (i) Share Capital | | 7,00,000 | 6,00,000 |
| (ii) Reserves and Surplus | 1 | 2,00,000 | 1,10,000 |
| 2. **Non-current Liabilities** | | | |
| Long-term Borrowings | | 3,30,000 | 2,25,000 |
| **Total** | | 12,30,000 | 9,35,000 |
| **II. ASSETS** | | | |
| 1. **Non-current Assets** | | | |
| (i) Property, Plant & Equipment and Intangible Assets | | | |
| (a) Property, Plant and Equipment | 2 | 11,00,000 | 8,00,000 |
| 2. **Current Assets** | | | |
| (i) Inventories | | 70,000 | 60,000 |
| (ii) Trade Receivables | | 32,000 | 40,000 |
| (iii) Cash and Cash Equivalents | | 28,000 | 35,000 |
| **Total** | | 12,30,000 | 9,35,000 |

**Notes to Accounts**

| Particulars | 31st March, 2023 (₹) | 31st March, 2022 (₹) |
|---|---|---|
| 1. **Reserves and Surplus**<br>Surplus, i.e. Balance in Statement of Profit and Loss | 2,00,000 | 1,10,000 |
| 2. **Property, Plant and Equipment**<br>Plant and Machinery | 11,00,000 | 8,00,000 |

## Additional Information

A piece of machinery of the book value of ₹ 80,000 was sold for ₹ 65,000 at the beginning of the year.

Depreciation provided on plant and machinery during the year amounted to ₹ 2,00,000.

(i) What is the amount of machinery purchased during the year? [2]

(ii) How much was the inflow/outflow of cash from financing activities? [2]

(iii) Calculate cash flow from operating activities. (Evaluate) [2]

14. Answer any three of the following (Application) [6]

(i) Calculate net profit ratio

Give the answer upto two decimal places.

| Particulars | Amt (₹) |
|---|---|
| Cost of Revenue from Operations | 6,00,000 |
| Operating Expenses | 50,000 |
| Revenue from Operations | 8,00,000 |
| Sales Returns | 10,000 |
| Total Current Assets | 3,00,000 |
| Total Current Liabilities | 1,00,000 |
| Total Assets | 7,00,000 |
| Closing Inventory | 30,000 |
| Prepaid Insurance | 5,000 |

SP-12

(ii) Calculate debt equity ratio from the following information.

| | Amt (₹) |
|---|---|
| Long-term Borrowing | 4,00,000 |
| Long-term Provisions | 2,00,000 |
| Current Liabilities | 1,00,000 |
| Non-current Assets | 7,20,000 |
| Current Assets | 1,80,000 |

(iii) From the following information, calculate current ratio
Working Capital ₹ 1,20,000, Total Debts ₹ 5,40,000, Long-term Borrowings ₹ 4,80,000.

(iv) From the information given below calculate interest coverage ratio.

| | Amt (₹) |
|---|---|
| Long-term Loans from Banks | 1,50,000 |
| 10% Debentures | 1,50,000 |
| 8% Preference Shares | 2,10,000 |
| 30,000 Equity Shares @ ₹ 10 | 3,00,000 |
| Interest on Long-term Loans from Bank | 15,000 |
| Profit after Tax | 2,25,000 |
| Tax | 27,000 |

# Answers

**1.** (i) (b) (ii) (b) (iii) (d) (iv) (c) (vii) (c)
(viii) Realisation account will be debited = ₹ 2,75,000
(x) Super profit = ₹ 20,000

**3.** (i) Goodwill = ₹ 3,60,000
(ii) Goodwill = ₹ 10,80,000

**4.** (i) Debenture Redemption Reserve = Nil

**5.** (i) (a) Hidden Goodwill = ₹ 2,00,000
(b) New Profit Sharing Ratio = 3 : 3 : 2

*Or* (i) ₹ 90,000

**6.** Loss on Realisation = ₹ 19,600
Final Payment to Riya = ₹ 51,200;
Diya = ₹ 22,400

*Or* Loss on Realisation on = ₹ 4,500
Final Payment to Adil = ₹ 43,625
Cash brought in by Muneer = ₹ 7,125

**7.** Total of Balance Sheet = ₹ 44,10,000

**8.** (i) 2 : 1
(ii) Balance in Capital Accounts A = ₹ 4,00,000; C = ₹ 2,00,000

**9.** (ii) Transfer to Capital Reserve = ₹ 20,000

*Or* (i) 450 shares (ii) ₹ 2,47,000
(iii) ₹ 6,000 (iv) ₹ 15,000

**10.** (A)
(i) Interest on Capital : Azad = ₹ 1,800, Lokesh ₹ 3,000
Provision for Manager's Commission = ₹ 750
(ii) Profit transferred to Capital A/cs
Lokesh's = ₹ 4,170; Azad's = ₹ 2,780
(iii) Partners' Capital Account Lokesh = ₹ 57,170 ; Azad = ₹ 37,080

(B) Ratio = 7 : 6 : 2

**11.** (i) • Purchase of machinery • (d) (ii) (c)
(iv) Cash used in Financing Activities = ₹ 61,600

**13.** Cash Flow from Operating Activities = ₹ 68,000
Cash used in Investing Activities = ₹ (1,10,000)
Cash Flow from Financing Activities = ₹ 50,000

*Or* (i) Balance of Plant and Machinery Account = ₹ 5,80,000
(ii) Cash Flow from Financing Activities = ₹ 2,05,000
(iii) Cash Flow from Operating Activities = ₹ 3,03,000

**14.** (i) Net Profit Ratio = 17.72%
(ii) Debt Equity Ratio = 3 : 1
(iii) Current Ratio = 3 : 1
(iv) Interest Coverage Ratio = 9.4 times

For explanations scan the given QR Code

SP-12

SQP Code : **PB-13/15** Series ***i*-Succeed 13-25/15** Roll No.

# Sample Question Paper 13

## Accounts 12th (Code 858)

### General Instructions

1. Candidates are allowed additional 15 minutes for only reading the paper. They must not start writing during this time.
2. Section-A is compulsory for all candidates and has ten questions.
3. Candidates have to attempt all questions from either Section-B or Section-C*.
4. Internal choices have been provided in five questions in Section-A and one question in Section-B.
5. The intended marks for questions or parts of questions are given in the brackets [ ].
6. All calculations should be shown clearly.
7. All workings, including rough work, should be done on the same page as, and adjacent to, the rest of the answer.

*Section-C has not been covered.

**Time :** 3 Hrs.

**Max. Marks :** 80

## Section A Answer All Questions [60 Marks]

**Que 1.**

In sub-parts (i) to (iv), choose the correct option and in sub-parts (v) to (x) answer the questions as instructed.

(i) Choose the correct sequence where new partner is to bring proportionate capital. (Recall) [1]

A – Preparation of revaluation account.

B – Calculation of capital to be brought by the new partner.

C – Calculate of capital balance of old partners.

D – Determination of revaluation gain/loss.

**Codes**

(a) A, B, C, D (b) A, D, C, B

(c) D, A, B, C (d) A, D, B, C

(ii) When a liability is taken over by a partner, his capital account will be (Understanding) [1]

(a) debited

(b) credited

(c) No entry

(d) None of the above

(iii) What journal entry is passed when the profit of forfeiture is transferred to capital reserve? (Application) [1]

(a) Debit Capital Reserve A/c and Credit Share Forfeiture A/c

(b) Debit Capital Reserve A/c and Credit Defaulter's A/c

(c) Debit Share Forfeiture A/c and Credit Calls-in-arrears A/c

(d) Debit Share Forfeiture A/c and Credit Capital Reserve A/c

(iv) Aggarwal Limited (an unlisted company) issued 40,000, 7½% debentures of ₹ 100 each 31st December, 2010, redeemable as follows

| | |
|---|---|
| On 31st March, 2017 | 20,000 |
| On 31st March, 2018 | 10,000 |
| On 31st March, 2019 | 5,000 |
| On 31st March, 2020 | 5,000 |

The board of directors decided to transfer to debenture redemption reserve ₹ 2,50,000 on 31st March, 2015 and balance required to be transferred to debenture redemption reserve on 31st March, 2016.

Identify the amount transferred to general reserve on 31st March, 2017. (Application) [1]

(a) ₹ 2,50,000 (b) ₹ 2,00,000
(c) ₹ 4,00,000 (d) ₹ 3,50,000

(v) Raghu, Parul and Manish were partners in a firm sharing profits and losses in the ratio of 4 : 3 : 3. Parul decided to retire from the firm. On the date of her retirement, land and building worth ₹ 40,000 appreciated by 30%, plant and machinery to be depreciated to 70% (book value ₹ 30,000) and bad debts ₹ 3,000 to be written-off. Ascertain the profit/loss on account of revaluation of assets and reassessment of liabilities. (Application) [1]

(vi) Vibhuti Ltd. a listed NBFC, had outstanding 50,000, 7% debentures of ₹ 100 each, due for redemption on 31st March, 2022. As per the provisions of the Companies Act, 2013, what amount, if any, does the company need to transfer to debenture redemption reserve, before it can redeem the debentures? (Application) [1]

(vii) Following is the extract of the balance sheet of Rahul, Raj, Raghav who are partners in a firm with profit sharing ratio 3 : 2 : 1 respectively.

| Liabilities | Amt (₹) | Assets | Amt (₹) |
|---|---|---|---|
| Workmen Compensation Reserve | 24,000 | | |

At the time of retirement of Raghav, if liability for workmen compensation to the extent of ₹ 12,000 is to be created, what amount will the workmen compensation reserve be shown in new balance sheet? (Application) [1]

(viii) **Assertion** (A) It is necessary to revalue the assets and liabilities of a firm when a new partner is admitted.

**Reason** (R) The incoming partner should neither be put to an advantage nor to disadvantage due to change in the volume of assets and liabilities. (Evaluate) [1]

**Alternatives**

(a) Both Assertion (A) and Reason (R) are true and Reason (R) is the correct explanation of Assertion (A)
(b) Both Assertion (A) and Reason (R) are true, but Reason (R) is not the correct explanation of Assertion (A)
(c) Assertion (A) is false, but Reason (R) is true
(d) Assertion (A) is true, but Reason (R) is false

(ix) As of 2018, companies can keep deferred tax assets on their balance sheets indefinitely, meaning they can save them for the precise time they need them. They just can't be used on taxes that have already been filed.

**Source** *Finance yahoo*

(a) What do you mean by deferred tax?
(b) Based on the above statement, name the main head and sub-head of deferred tax asset. (Recall) [1]

(x) Rolly and Golly were two partners in a firm. They decided to dissolve their firm on 31st March, 2020.

At the time of dissolution, loan from Golly stood at ₹ 2,00,000 while her capital account showed a debit balance of ₹ 2,25,000. You are required to pass necessary journal entry for settlement of Golly's loan at the time of dissolution. (Application) [1]

SP-13

**Que 2.**

Sanjana and Alok were partners in a firm sharing profits and losses in the ratio 3:2. On 31st March, 2018, their balance sheet was as follows

**Balance Sheet of Sanjana and Alok**
as on 31st March, 2018

| Liabilities | | Amt (₹) | Assets | | Amt (₹) |
|---|---|---|---|---|---|
| Creditors | | 60,000 | Cash | | 1,66,000 |
| Workmen's Compensation Fund | | 60,000 | Debtors | 1,46,000 | |
| Capitals A/c | | | (–) Provision for Doubtful Debts | (2,000) | 1,44,000 |
| Sanjana | 5,00,000 | | Stock | | 1,50,000 |
| Alok | 4,00,000 | 9,00,000 | Investments | | 2,60,000 |
| | | | Furniture | | 3,00,000 |
| | | 10,20,000 | | | 10,20,000 |

On 1st April, 2018, they admitted Nidhi as a new partner for 1/4th share in the profits on the following terms

(i) Goodwill of the firm was valued at ₹ 4,00,000 and Nidhi brought the necessary amount in cash for her share of goodwill premium, half of which was withdrawn by the old partners.

(ii) Stock was to be increased by 20% and furniture was to be reduced to 90%.

(iii) Investments were to be value at ₹ 3,00,000. Alok took over investment at this value.

(iv) Nidhi brought ₹ 3,00,000 as her capital and the capitals of Sanjana and Alok were adjusted in the new profit sharing ratio.

You are required to

(a) Calculate Nidhi's share of goodwill. [1]

(b) Prepare partners' capital account.

(Application) [2]

*Or*

M, N and S were partners in a firm sharing profits in the ratio of 1 : 2 : 1. The firm closes its books on 31st March every year. On 30th September, 2021 N died.

On that date his capital account showed a debit balance of ₹ 5,000. There was a debit balance of ₹ 30,000 in the profit and loss account. The goodwill of the firm was valued at ₹ 3,80,000.

N's share of profit in the year of his death was to be calculated on the basis of average profit of last 5 years, which was ₹ 90,000.

You are required to pass journal entries to record

(i) The adjustment of goodwill.

(ii) The settlement of profits.

(iii) Payment made to the executor.

(Application) [3]

**Que 3.**

Raghav Ltd. offered 20,00,000, 12% debentures of ₹ 200 each at a discount of 7% redeemable at premium of 8% after 9 years. Record necessary entries in the books of Raghav Ltd.

(Application) [3]

**Que 4.**

Anuj Ltd. a listed company, issued 25,000, 10% debentures of ₹ 10 each on 1st April, 2016 redeemable at par on 30th June, 2018. The company received applications for 27,500 debentures and the allotment was made to the applicants on pro-rata basis. The debentures were redeemed on due date. Investment was made on 1st April of the financial year in which redemption is due.

Prepare

(i) Debentureholders account.

(ii) Debenture redemption investment account. (Application) [3]

*Or*

Apurva Ltd. company purchased furniture ₹ 8,80,000 from Anshu Ltd. 50% of the amount was paid to Anshu Ltd. by accepting a bill of exchange and for the balance the company issued 12% debentures of ₹ 100 each at a premium of 10% in favour of Anshu Ltd.

Pass necessary journal entries in the books of Apurva Ltd. company for above transactions.

(Application)

**Que 5.**

B and M are partners in a firm. Their profit sharing ratio is 5 : 3. They admit S into partnership for 1/4th share. B and M decide to share profits equally in future. S brings in ₹ 6,00,000 as his capital and ₹ 3,00,000 as premium.

(i) Calculate the sacrificing ratio

(ii) Record the necessary journal entries on the assumption that the amount of premium brought in by S is retained in business.

(Application) [3]

**Que 6.**

David and Bimal are partners sharing profits and losses in the ratio of 3 : 2. Their balance sheet as at 31st March, 2018 was as follows

**Balance Sheet**
as at 31st March, 2018

| Liabilities | | Amt (₹) | Assets | | Amt (₹) |
|---|---|---|---|---|---|
| Sundry Creditors | | 82,000 | Cash | | 32,000 |
| General Reserve | | 3,000 | Stock | | 15,000 |
| Capital A/cs | | | Debtors | 9,400 | |
| David | 18,000 | | (−) Provision for Doubtful Debts | (400) | 9,000 |
| Bimal | 12,000 | 30,000 | Building | | 55,000 |
| | | | Furniture | | 4,000 |
| | | 1,15,000 | | | 1,15,000 |

They admitted Chander as a new partner on 1st April, 2018 and the new profit sharing ratio becomes 5 : 3 : 2. Chander introduced a capital of ₹ 16,000.

Chander was unable to bring any cash for goodwill and so it was decided to value the goodwill on the basis of this share in the profits and the capital contributed by him. The following revaluations were made at the time of Chander's admission

(i) Stock had been overvalued by ₹ 750 and furniture by ₹ 500.

(ii) Provision for doubtful debts to be increased by ₹ 100.

(ii) A creditor for ₹ 2,350 was paid-off by Bimal privately for which he was not to be reimbursed.

You are required to

(a) Calculate sacrificing ratio. [1]

(b) Prepare partners' capital account. (Application) [5]

**Que 7.**

Anjali, Bheem and Chetan sharing profits equally, dissolved their firm on 30th June, 2021, at which date their balance sheet was as follows

| Liabilities | Amt (₹) | Assets | Amt (₹) |
|---|---|---|---|
| Sundry Creditors | 62,000 | Bank | 12,600 |
| Reserve for Contingency | 36,000 | Debtors | 1,10,000 |
| Profit and Loss A/c | 24,000 | Stock | 1,62,000 |
| Anjali's Husband Loan | 24,000 | Furniture | 40,000 |
| Bank Loan at 12% | 40,000 | Plant | 1,07,400 |
| Capital A/cs | | Current A/c – Chetan | 44,000 |
| Anjali | 1,20,000 | | |
| Bheem | 1,00,000 | | |
| Chetan | 40,000 | | |
| Current A/cs | | | |
| Anjali | 20,000 | | |
| Bheem | 10,000 | | |
| | 4,76,000 | | 4,76,000 |

(i) There is a bill for ₹ 10,000 under discount. This bill was received from 'Amit'. Amit proved insolvent and 60% were received from his estate.

(ii) It was found that an investment not recorded in the books is worth ₹ 16,000. This is taken over by one of the creditors at this value.

(iii) Anjali agreed to accept furniture in full settlement of her husband's loan.

(iv) Bank loan was repaid alongwith interest for nine months.

(v) Assets realised as follows – Debtors ₹ 49,000, stock ₹ 1,20,000, plant ₹ 56,000.

Prepare realisation account and partners' capital account. (Application) [6]

*Or*

Pass the necessary journal entries for the following transactions on the dissolution of the firm of Atul, Abhay and Anuj sharing profits in the ratio of 2 : 2 : 1, after the transfer of all assets (other than cash) and external liabilities to realisation account.

(i) Debtors were of ₹ 62,100. Atul takes over debtors amounted to ₹ 60,000 at ₹ 58,600 and the remaining debtors were sold to a debt collecting agency at 50% of the value.

(ii) Sundry assets were of ₹ 58,500. Abhya is to taken over some sundry assets of ₹ 36,000 (10% less than the book value). Anuj is to taken over remaining sundry assets at 80% of the book value.

(iii) Anuj assumes the responsibility of discharge of Mrs. Anuj's loan of ₹ 5,750 together with accrued interest of ₹ 1,150. (Application)

**Que 8.**

The trainee accountant of Fast Track and Company Ltd. who has gained a little knowledge of accounts, has drafted the following balance sheet

**Balance Sheet**

as at 31st March, 2023

| Liabilities | Amt (₹) | Assets | Amt (₹) |
|---|---|---|---|
| Capital – 36,000 Equity Shares of 10 each | | Building | 2,19,000 |
| Fully Called-up | 3,60,000 | Fixed Deposit Accepted | 30,000 |
| Preliminary Expenses | 44,000 | Furniture | 60,000 |
| 10% Debentures | 70,000 | Goodwill | 20,000 |
| Provision for Taxation | 72,000 | Inventories | 48,000 |
| Statement of Profit and Loss Balance (Cr) | 96,000 | Sundry Creditors | 18,000 |
| Investment in SCS Ltd. | 30,000 | Machinery | 50,000 |
| Bills Receivable | 14,000 | Cash | 76,000 |
| Debtors | 18,000 | Bills Payable | 14,000 |
| Unclaimed Dividend | 22,000 | Bank | 1,44,000 |
| Authorised Capital | | General Reserve | 24,000 |
| 40,000 Equity Shares of ₹ 10 each | | Calls-in-arrears (on 2,000 shares) | 4,000 |
| Share Forfeiture | 1,000 | Securities Premium | 20,000 |
| | 7,27,000 | | 7,27,000 |

**Note** Proposed dividend ₹ 28,000.

You are required to re-draft the balance sheet as per Schedule III, Part I of the Companies Act, 2013. (Application) [6]

SP-13

**Que 9.**

Shiv and Hari entered into partnership on 1st January, 2018, contributing ₹ 10,00,000 and ₹ 4,00,000 respectively. Hari also introduced ₹ 2,00,000 as additional capital on 1st April, 2018. They agreed to share profits and losses in the ratio of 3 : 2. Following information is provided regarding the partnership

(i) Shiv and Hari, each are allowed a salary of ₹ 10,000 per quarter.

(ii) Interest is to be allowed on capital @ 8% p.a. and charged on drawings at 10% p.a.

Drawings of Shiv and Hari during the year were ₹ 24,000 and ₹ 20,000 respectively. Profits as at 31st December, 2018 before the above mentioned adjustments was ₹ 3,92,000.

You are required to

(a) Pass the entry for interest on capital of Shiv and Hari. **(Application) [2]**

(b) Pass the entry for salary allowed to Shiv and Hari. **(Application) [2]**

(c) Pass the entry for interest on drawings of Shiv. **(Application) [2]**

(d) Pass the entry for adjusting and closing entry for drawings of Hari. **(Recall) [2]**

(e) Pass the entry for transfer of profit or loss among partners. **(Application) [2]**

*Or*

(A) Shankar and Vijay are partners in a firm sharing profits and losses in the ratio of 3 : 2. On 1st April, 2022, their fixed capital accounts showed a balance of ₹ 4,00,000 and ₹ 8,00,000 respectively.

On this date, their current account balances were ₹ 1,00,000 and ₹ 2,00,000 respectively. On 1st January, 2023, Shankar introduced additional capital of ₹ 4,00,000 while Vijay gave a loan of ₹ 3,00,000 to the firm.

The partnership deed provided for

(i) Interest on capital to be allowed at the rate of 10% p.a.

(ii) Interest on drawings to be charged at the rate of 12% p.a.

(iii) 10% of the correct net profit to be transferred to general reserve.

During the financial year 2022-23, both partners withdrew ₹ 12,000 each at the beginning of every quarter.

Net profit of the firm, before any interest, for the financial year 2022-23 was ₹ 10,00,000.

You are required to prepare

SP-13

(a) Profit and loss appropriation account [1½]

(b) Partners' fixed capital account [2]

(c) Partners' current account [4½]

(B) P and Q are partners. The net divisible profit as per profit and loss appropriation account is ₹ 5,00,000. The total interest on partners' drawings is ₹ 8,000. P's salary is ₹ 8,000 per quarter and Q's salary is ₹ 8,000 per annum. Calculate the net profit earned during the year. **(Application) [2]**

**Que 10.**

VXN Ltd. invited applications for issuing 50,000 equity shares of ₹ 10 each at a premium of ₹ 8 per share. The amount was payable as follows

On application ₹ 4 per share (including ₹ 2 premium)
On allotment ₹ 6 per share (including ₹ 3 premium)
On first call ₹ 5 per share (including ₹ 1 premium)
On second and final call Balance amount

The issue was fully subscribed. Gopal, a shareholder holding 200 shares, did not pay the allotment money and Madhav, a holder of 400 shares, paid his entire share money along with the allotment money. Gopal's shares were immediately forfeited after allotment.

Afterwards, the first call was made. Krishna, a holder of 100 shares, failed to pay the first call money and Girdhar, a holder of 300 shares, paid the second call money also along with the first call.

Krishna's shares were forfeited immediately after the first call. Second and final call was made afterwards and was duly received. All the forfeited shares were re-issued at ₹ 9 per share fully paid-up.

Pass necessary journal entries for the above transactions in the books of the company. (Application) [10]

*Or*

SK Ltd. invited applications for issuing 3,20,000 equity shares of ₹ 10 each at a premium of ₹ 5 per share. The amount was payable as follows

On application ₹ 3 per share (including premium ₹ 1 per share)

On allotment ₹ 5 per share (including premium ₹ 2 per share)

On first and final call Balance amount

Applications for 4,00,000 shares were received. Applications for 40,000 shares were rejected and application money refunded. Shares were alloted on pro-rata basis to the remaining applicants. Excess money received with applications was adjusted towards sums due on allotment.

Jeevan holding 800 shares failed to pay the allotment money and his shares were immediately forfeited. Afterwards final call was made, Ganesh who had applied for 2,700 shares failed to pay the final call. His shares were also forfeited. Out of the forfeited shares 1,500 shares were re-issued at ₹ 8 per share fully paid-up. The re-issued shares included all the forfeited shares of Jeevan.

(i) What is the amount unpaid on allotment? [1]

(ii) What is the amount received from Jeevan? [1]

(iii) What is the amount unpaid from first and final call? [1]

(iv) Calculate the amount received from Gupta. [2]

(v) Give the entries for

(a) The forfeiture of share [2]

(b) Re-issue of shares (Application) [3]

## Section B

[20 Marks]

**Que 11.**

(i) Measuring a company's liquidity ratio is like checking a car's fuel or electricity gauge. Even a zippy Lamborghini or top-of-the-line Tesla won't get you to your destination if it runs short of juice. Likewise, if a company runs out of cash-or assets to be converted to cash-to pay its short-term liabilities, well, that's potentially the end of the line for the company, right? Maybe or maybe not. But it certainly helps to know when a company appears to be running out of gas (liquidity).

**Source** *Britannica (edited)*

Based on the above statement

- Name any one liquidity ratio. (Recall)
- Liquid assets do not include (Analysis) [1]

(a) Bills receivable (b) Debtors (c) Inventory (d) Bank balance

(ii) Since the income statement and balance sheet are based on accrual accounting, those financials don't directly measure what happens to cash over a period. Therefore, companies typically provide a cash flow statement for management, analysts and investors to review.

**Source** *corporatedaily (edited)*

Which of the following is incorrect about the statement of cash flows? (Understanding) [1]

(a) It provides information about the cash receipt and cash payments of an enterprise

(b) It reconciles ending cash balance with the balance as per bank statement

(c) It provides information about the operating, investing and financing activities
(d) It explains the deviation of cash from earnings

(iii) The net profit of HCL technologies stood at ₹ 148,450 m in financial year 2023, which was up better as compared to ₹ 1,35,230 m reported in financial year 2022. This compares to a net profit of ₹ 1,11,690 m in financial year 2021 and a net profit of ₹ 1,10,570 m in financial year 2020. Over the past 5 years, HCL technologies net profit has grown at a CAGR of 10.1%.

**Source** *Equitymasters*

Based on the above information

(a) Find out the percentage increase or decrease in the net profit of the year 2022-23.
(b) Find out the percentage increase or decrease in the net profit of the year 2021-22. **(Evaluate) [1]**

(iv) 'Net decrease in working capital' other than cash and cash equivalents will increase, decrease or not change the cash flow of operating activities. Give reason. **(Understanding) [1]**

(v) The average collection period should be lower as a higher ratio means that the company is taking too long to collect the receivables and hence is unfavourable for the operations of the company.

**Source** *Tradebrains*

Based on the above statement, give the formula to calculate the average collection period. **(Recall) [1]**

**Que 12.**

Fill in the missing information in the comparative statement of profit and loss. **(Application) [3]**

**Comparative Statement of Profit and Loss**
for the year ended 31st March, 2022 and 2021

| Particulars | 31st March, 2021 (₹) | 31st March, 2022 (₹) | Absolute Increase/ Decrease (₹) | Percentage Increase/ Decrease (%) |
|---|---|---|---|---|
| **I. Revenue from Operations** | 40,00,000 | 50,00,000 | 10,00,000 | ... |
| (+) Other Income | ... | 2,50,000 | ... | 25 |
| Total Revenue | 42,00,000 | 52,50,000 | 10,50,000 | 25 |
| **II. Expenses** | | | | |
| Purchase of Stock-in-trade | 30,00,000 | 40,00,000 | 10,00,000 | ... |
| Change in Inventory | ... | 10,00,000 | ... | 25 |
| Other Expenses | 4,00,000 | ... | 1,00,000 | 25 |
| Total Expenses | 42,00,000 | 55,00,000 | 13,00,000 | 30.95 |
| **Profit after Tax (I – II)** | — | (2,50,000) | (2,50,000) | — |

**Que 13.**

From the following balance sheet and the additional information of Pomi Wires Ltd. you are required to prepare cash flow statement as per AS-3.

| Particulars | Note No. | 31st March, 2023 (₹) | 31st March, 2022 (₹) |
|---|---|---|---|
| **I. EQUITY AND LIABILITIES** | | | |
| 1. **Shareholders' Funds** | | | |
| (i) Share Capital | | 6,50,000 | 5,00,000 |
| (ii) Reserves and Surplus | | 1,65,000 | 50,000 |
| 2. **Current Liabilities** | | | |
| (i) Sundry Creditors | | 90,000 | 75,000 |
| (ii) Bills Payable | | 45,000 | 30,000 |
| **Total** | | 9,50,000 | 6,55,000 |

SP-13

| Particulars | Note No. | 31st March, 2023 (₹) | 31st March, 2022 (₹) |
|---|---|---|---|
| **II. ASSETS** | | | |
| 1. **Non-current Assets** | | | |
| Property, Plant & Equipment and Intangible Assets | | 5,90,000 | 3,00,000 |
| 2. **Current Assets** | | | |
| (i) Inventories | | 1,20,000 | 1,20,000 |
| (ii) Debtors | | 1,20,000 | 1,40,000 |
| (iii) Cash and Cash Equivalents | | 1,20,000 | 95,000 |
| **Total** | | 9,50,000 | 6,55,000 |

**Additional Information**

(i) Income tax paid during the year was ₹ 55,000.

(ii) Dividend paid during the year was 12%.

(a) Show the calculation of net profit before tax. [2]

(b) Calculate the cash flow from operating activities. [2]

(c) Calculate the cash flow from financing activities. (Evaluate) [2]

*Or*

The balance sheet of Rajneesh Ltd. for the years ending at 31st March, 2023 and 2022 were as follows

| Particulars | Note No. | 31st March, 2023 (₹) | 31st March, 2022 (₹) |
|---|---|---|---|
| **I. EQUITY AND LIABILITIES** | | | |
| 1. **Shareholders' Funds** | | | |
| (i) Share Capital | | 1,25,000 | 1,00,000 |
| (ii) Reserves and Surplus | 1 | 33,800 | 30,250 |
| 2. **Non-current Liabilities** | | | |
| Long-term Borrowings | | 7,500 | 10,000 |
| 3. **Current Liabilities** | | | |
| (i) Short-term Borrowings | 2 | — | 35,000 |
| (ii) Trade Payables | | 72,600 | 75,000 |
| **Total** | | 2,38,900 | 2,50,250 |
| **II. ASSETS** | | | |
| 1. **Non-current Assets** | | | |
| Property, Plant & Equipment and Intangible Assets | 3 | 1,82,000 | 1,75,000 |
| 2. **Current Assets** | | | |
| (i) Inventories | | 20,500 | 35,000 |
| (ii) Trade Receivables | | 32,100 | 40,000 |
| (iii) Cash and Cash Equivalents | 4 | 4,300 | 250 |
| **Total** | | 2,38,900 | 2,50,250 |

**Notes to Accounts**

| Particulars | 31st March, 2023 (₹) | 31st March, 2022 (₹) |
|---|---|---|
| 1. **Reserves and Surplus** | | |
| Balance in Statement of Profit and Loss | 33,800 | 30,250 |

SP-13

| Particulars | 31st March, 2023 (₹) | 31st March, 2022 (₹) |
|---|---|---|
| **2. Short-term Borrowings** | | |
| Bank Overdraft | — | 35,000 |
| **3. Property, Plant & Equipment and Intangible Assets** | | |
| Land and Buildings | 95,000 | 1,00,000 |
| Plant and Machinery | 87,000 | 75,000 |
| | 1,82,000 | 1,75,000 |
| **4. Cash and Cash Equivalents** | | |
| Cash in Hand | 300 | 250 |
| Bank Balance | 4,000 | — |
| | 4,300 | 250 |
| **5. Contingent Liability** | | |
| Proposed Dividend | 15,000 | 15,000 |

## Additional Information

Depreciation written-off on land and buildings during the year 2022-23 was ₹ 6,000.

Calculate the cash flow from operating and financing activities. **(Application) [6]**

**Que 14.**

Answer any three of the following **(Application) [6]**

(i) The current ratio of Raj Ltd. is 2 : 1. State with reason, which of the following transactions on would increase, decrease or not change the ratio.

(a) Company purchased machinery of ₹ 90,000. The vendor was paid by issue of equity shares of ₹ 10 each at par.

(b) Trade receivables included debtors of ₹ 80,000 which were received.

(ii) From the given information calculate the cost of revenue from operations.
Inventory turnover ratio 6 times, inventory at the end is ₹ 6,000 more than the inventory in the beginning, revenue from operations (credit) ₹ 2,40,000, gross profit 25% on cost, current liabilities ₹ 80,000, quick ratio 0.80 : 1.

(iii) Calculate operating ratio when revenue from operations ₹ 6,80,000, rate of gross profit on cost 25%, selling expenses ₹ 1,44,000, administrative expenses ₹ 73,000.

SP-13 (iv) The following particulars are extracted from the balance sheet of Goodwill Enterprises Ltd. as at 31st March, 2021

| Particulars | Amt (₹) |
|---|---|
| Equity Share Capital | 3,00,000 |
| 10% Preference Share Capital | 1,20,000 |
| Capital Reserve | 60,000 |
| Profit and Loss Balance | 1,20,000 |
| 12% Debentures | 50,000 |
| 10% Mortgage Loan | 1,50,000 |
| Current Liabilities | 2,80,000 |
| Non-current Assets | 4,80,000 |
| Current Assets | 6,00,000 |

Showing the full working, calculate the proprietary ratio

Net profit after interest and tax amounted to ₹ 63,000.

Rate of income tax was 50%. **(Application) [6]**

# Answers

1. (i) (b) (ii) (b) (iii) (d) (iv) (b) (v) Revaluation Account = ₹ 12,000 (viii) (a)
2. (a) Nidhi's Share of Goodwill = ₹ 1,00,000
   (b) Partners' Capital Account Balance Sanjana = ₹ 4,50,000 ; Alok = ₹ 3,00,000 ; Nidhi = ₹ 3,00,000
5. (i) Sacrificing Ratio: B = 2/8 ; M = Nil
6. (a) Sacrificing Ratio = 1 : 1
   (b) Partners' Capital Account Balance David = ₹ 23,400 ; Bimal = ₹ 16,600 ; Chander = ₹ 16,000
7. Loss on Realisation = ₹ 1,62,000 ; Final Payment to A = ₹ 1,06,000 ; B = ₹ 76,000
   Deficit brought in by C = ₹ 38,000
8. Total of Balance Sheet = ₹ 6,79,000
9. *Or* (A) (a) Profit on Profit and Loss Appropriation Account Shankar = ₹ 4,63,890 ; Vijay = ₹ 3,09,260
   (b) Partners' Capital Account Balance Shankar = ₹ 8,00,000 ; Vijay = ₹ 8,00,000
   (c) Partners' Capital Account Balance Shankar = ₹ 5,62,290 ; Vijay = ₹ 5,37,660
   (B) Net Profit = ₹ 5,32,000
10. *Or* (i) Amount Unpaid on Allotment = ₹ 3,700
    (ii) Amount received from Jeevan = ₹ 1,900
    (iii) Unpaid Amount on First and Final Call = ₹ 16,800
    (iv) Amount received from Gupta = ₹ 12,000
11. (i) • Current ratio (ii) (b)
    • (c)
    (iii) (a) 9.8% (b) 32.9%
13. (a) Net Profit before Tax = ₹ 2,30,000
    (b) Cash Flow from Operating Activities = ₹ 2,25,000
    (c) Cash Flow from Financing Activities = ₹ 90,000
    *Or* Net Cash Flow from Operating Activities = ₹ 44,550 ; Net Cash used in Financing Activities = ₹ (27,500)
14. (ii) Cost of Revenue from Operations = ₹ 1,92,000
    (iii) Operating Ratio = 111.91%
    (iv) Proprietary Ratio = 0.55 : 1

For explanations scan the given QR Code

SP-13

SQP Code : **PB-14/15** Series ***i*-Succeed 14-25/15** Roll No. | | | | | | | | |

# Sample Question Paper 14

## Accounts 12th (Code 858)

### General Instructions

1. Candidates are allowed additional 15 minutes for only reading the paper. They must not start writing during this time.
2. Section-A is compulsory for all candidates and has ten questions.
3. Candidates have to attempt all questions from either Section-B or Section-C*.
4. Internal choices have been provided in five questions in Section-A and one question in Section-B.
5. The intended marks for questions or parts of questions are given in the brackets [ ].
6. All calculations should be shown clearly.
7. All workings, including rough work, should be done on the same page as, and adjacent to, the rest of the answer.

*Section-C has not been covered.

Time : 3 Hrs.

Max. Marks : 80

## Section A Answer All Questions

[60 Marks]

**Que 1.**

In sub-parts (i) to (iv), choose the correct option and in sub-parts (v) to (x) answer the questions as instructed.

(i) First call amount received in advance from the shareholders before it is actually called-up by the directors is **(Understanding) [1]**

(a) debited to calls-in-advance account
(b) credited to share allotment account
(c) debited to first call account
(d) credited to calls-in-advance account

(ii) Choose the correct sequence in context to dissolution which amount realised from assets will be utilised to pay.

A – Partners' capital
B – Loan by partners'
C – Secured debts of the firm
D – Unsecured debts of the firm **(Recall) [1]**

**Codes**

(a) A, C, B, D (b) D, B, A, C
(c) A, C, D, B (d) C, D, B, A

(iii) P, Q and R are partners in a firm sharing profits and losses in the ratio of 3 : 2 : 1. At the time of retirement of R, investment fluctuation reserve appears in the books at ₹ 40,000 while investments (market value ₹ 2,40,000) appear at ₹ 4,00,000.
What will be the amount of investment fluctuation reserve credited to R's capital? **(Application) [1]**

(a) ₹ 2,60,000
(b) ₹ 1,60,000
(c) ₹ 2,00,000 (d) None

(iv) Geeta, Sunita and Anita were partners in a firm sharing profits in the ratio of 3 : 2 : 1. On 1st April, 2023, they admitted Yogita as a new partner on the following terms

- Goodwill of the firm to be valued at ₹ 3,00,000. Yogita brings her share of goodwill.
- New profit sharing ratio among Geeta, Sunita, Anita and Yogita will be 3 : 3 : 2 : 2.

Which of the following entry is correct on admission of Yogita? **(Application) [1]**

(a) Premium for Goodwill A/c Dr 60,000
To Geeta's Capital A/c 36,000
To Sunita's Capital A/c 24,000

(b) Premium for Goodwill A/c Dr 60,000
To Sunita's Capital A/c 40,000
To Anita's Capital A/c 20,000

(c) Premium for Goodwill A/c Dr 60,000
To Geeta's Capital A/c 30,000
To Sunita's Capital A/c 20,000
To Anita's Capital A/c 10,000

(d) Anita's Capital A/c Dr 10,000
Premium for Goodwill A/c Dr 60,000
To Geeta's Capital A/c 60,000
To Sunita's Capital A/c 10,000

(v) Pankaj Ltd. issued 70,000, 14% debentures of 100 each at a premium of 5% redeemable at a premium of 20%. Pass necessary journal entries at the time of issue of debentures. (Application) [1]

(vi) A reserve specifically represented by earmarked investments shall be termed as fund.
State where does the reserve comes in the balance sheet as per Schedule III. (Application) [1]

(vii) A and B are partners sharing profits in the ratio of 7 : 3. C was admitted for 3/7th share in the profits. What will be the new profit sharing ratio among A, B and C? (Application) [1]

(viii) **Assertion** (A) Profit or loss on revaluation is transferred to new partner's capital account.

**Reason** (R) Profit or loss on revaluation at the time of admission of a partners is distributed to old partners. (Evaluate) [1]

**Alternatives**

(a) Both Assertion (A) and Reason (R) are true and Reason (R) is the correct explanation of Assertion (A)
(b) Both Assertion (A) and Reason (R) are true, but Reason (R) is not the correct explanation of Assertion (A)
(c) Assertion (A) is false, but Reason (R) is true
(d) Assertion (A) is true, but Reason (R) is false

(ix) Sharma Ltd. (an unlisted company) has 20,000, 9% debentures of ₹ 100 each due for redemption on 31st March, 2020.

Debenture redemption reserve has a balance of ₹ 50,000 on 31st March, 2019. You are required to calculate the amount to be transferred to DRR. (Application) [1]

(x) The partnership agreement must specifically state how the partnership business is liquidated as the failure to do so could trigger disputes and even lawsuits in the future.

**Source** *Smallbusiness.chron.com*

(a) What is liquidation here?
(b) Based on the above statement, state the sequence in which the assets of a firm are applied. (Recall) [1]

**Que 2.**

Deepak Ltd. Company purchased furniture ₹ 2,20,000 from M/s Furniture Mart. 50% of the amount was paid to Furniture Mart by accepting a bill of exchange and for the balance the company issued 9% debentures of ₹ 100 each at a premium of 10% in favour of Furniture Mart. Pass necessary journal entries in the books of Deepak Ltd. company for above transactions. (Application) [3]

*Or*

Youth Ltd. took a loan of ₹ 15,00,000 from State Bank of India against the security of assets. In addition to principal security, it issued 10,000, 11% debentures of ₹ 100 each as collateral security.

Pass necessary journal entries for the above transactions, if the company decided to record the issue of 11% debentures as collateral security and show the presentation in the balance sheet of Youth Ltd. (Application)

**Que 3.**

Following is the balance sheet of Hari, Ram and Shyam as at 31st December, 2022.

**Balance Sheet**
as at 31st December, 2022

| Liabilities | | Amt (₹) | Assets | Amt (₹) |
|---|---|---|---|---|
| Sundry Creditors | | 3,000 | Tools | 1,000 |
| Reserve Fund | | 3,200 | Furniture | 8,000 |
| Capital A/cs | | | Stock | 6,000 |
| Hari | 10,000 | | Debtors | 6,000 |
| Ram | 5,000 | | Cash at Bank | 5,000 |
| Shyam | 5,000 | 20,000 | Cash in Hand | 200 |
| | | 26,200 | | 26,200 |

Ram died on 31st March, 2023. Under the partnership agreement, he was entitled to the following amounts

(i) Amount standing to the credit of his capital account.
(ii) Interest on capital, which amounted to ₹ 62.50.
(iii) His share of goodwill ₹ 3,500.

(a) You are required to calculate
- Ram's share of goodwill.
- Hari's and Shyam's share in Ram's goodwill. [2]

(b) Prepare Ram's capital account (Application) [1]

**Que 4.**

Rajan Ltd. purchased assets of Surya Ltd. as under Plant of ₹ 10,00,000 at ₹ 9,00,000, land and buildings of ₹ 15,00,000 at ₹ 21,00,000 for purchase consideration of ₹ 27,50,000 and paid ₹ 5,00,000 in cash and remaining by issue of 9% debentures of ₹ 100 each at a premium of 20%.

You are required to

(i) Calculate the number of debentures issued.
(ii) Record necessary entries in the books of Rajan Ltd. (Application) [3]

SP-14

**Que 5.**

Sharma, Gupta and Jain are partners in a firm sharing profits and losses in the ratio of 3 : 2 : 1. Jain retires from the firm on 1st April, 2023. On the date of Jain's retirement, following balances appeared in the books of the firm. General reserve ₹ 2,16,000; profit and loss account (Dr) ₹ 36,000; employees' provident fund ₹ 2,88,000. Workmen compensation reserve ₹ 28,800 which was no more required.

You are required to pass entry for

(i) Distribution of general reserve.
(ii) Distribution of profit and loss.
(iii) Distribution of workmen compensation. (Application) [3]

*Or*

Asha and Aditi are partners in a firm sharing profits and losses in the ratio of 3 : 2. They admit Raghav as a partner for 1/4th share in the profits of the firm. Raghav brings ₹ 6,00,000 as his capital and his share of goodwill in cash. Goodwill of the firm is to be valued at two years' purchase of average profits of the last four years.

The profits of the firm during the last four years are given below

| Year | Profit (₹) |
|---|---|
| 2019-20 | 3,50,000 |
| 2020-21 | 4,75,000 |
| 2021-22 | 6,70,000 |
| 2022-23 | 7,45,000 |

The following additional information is given

(i) To cover management cost, an annual charge of ₹ 56,250 should be made for the purpose of valuation of goodwill.

(ii) The closing stock for the year ended 31st March, 2023 was overvalued by ₹ 15,000.

Pass necessary journal entries on Raghav's admission showing the working notes clearly. (Application)

**Que 6.**

Following balances have been extracted from the books of Shalimar Ltd. as at 31st March, 2023.

| Particulars | Amt (₹) |
|---|---|
| Share Capital | 5,00,000 |
| Securities Premium | 50,000 |
| 11% Debentures | 2,50,000 |
| Trade Payables | 1,00,000 |
| Balance of Statement of Profit and Loss (Dr) | 25,000 |
| Livestock | 4,25,000 |
| Investment in Government Bonds | 2,00,000 |
| Work-in-progress | 2,00,000 |
| Discount on Issue of 11% Debentures | 50,000 |
| Patents | 20,000 |
| Unclaimed Dividend | 5,000 |
| Trade Receivables | 10,000 |
| Public Deposits | 25,000 |

Prepare the balance sheet of the company as per Schedule III under the Companies Act, 2013. (Application) [6]



**Que 7.**

Arnab, Ragini and Dhrupad are partners sharing profits in the ratio of 3: 1 : 1. On 31st March, 2021, they decided to dissolve their firm. On that date their balance sheet was as under

**Balance Sheet**
as at 31st March, 2021

| Liabilities | | Amt (₹) | Assets | | Amt (₹) |
|---|---|---|---|---|---|
| Creditors | | 60,000 | Bank | | 50,000 |
| Arnab's Brother's Loan | | 95,000 | Debtors | 1,70,000 | |
| Dhrupad's Loan | | 1,00,000 | (−) Provision for Bad Debts | (20,000) | 1,50,000 |
| Investment Fluctuation Fund | | 50,000 | Stock | | 1,50,000 |
| Capital A/cs | | | Investments | | 2,50,000 |
| Arnab | 2,75,000 | | Building | | 3,00,000 |
| Ragini | 2,00,000 | | Profit and Loss A/c | | 50,000 |
| Dhrupad | 1,70,000 | 6,45,000 | | | |
| | | 9,50,000 | | | 9,50,000 |

The assets were realised and the liabilities were paid as under

(i) Arnab agreed to pay his brother's loan.
(ii) Investments realised 20% less.
(iii) Creditors were paid at 10% less.
(iv) Building was auctioned for ₹ 3,55,000. Commission on auction was ₹ 5,000.
(v) 50% of the stock was taken over by Ragini at market price which was 20% less than the book value and the remaining was sold at market price.
(vi) Dissolution expenses were ₹ 8,000. ₹ 3,000 were to be borne by the firm and the balance by Dhrupad. The expenses were paid by him.

(a) Prepare realisation account. [5]
(b) Prepare partners' capital account. (Application) [1]

**Que 8.**

X, Y and Z were partners in a firm sharing profits in the ratio of 7 : 2 : 1. The balance sheet of the firm as at 31st March, 2021 was as follows

**Balance Sheet**
as at 31st March, 2023

| Liabilities | | Amt (₹) | Assets | Amt (₹) |
|---|---|---|---|---|
| Capital A/cs | | | Goodwill | 80,000 |
| X | 1,40,000 | | Land and Buildings | 1,20,000 |
| Y | 40,000 | | Machinery | 80,000 |
| Z | 20,000 | 2,00,000 | Stock | 14,000 |
| General Reserve | | 40,000 | Debtors | 24,000 |
| Loan from Y | | 60,000 | Cash | 10,000 |
| Creditors | | 28,000 | | |
| | | 3,28,000 | | 3,28,000 |

Y died on 24th August, 2021. Partnership deed provides for the settlement of claims on the death of a partner in addition to his capital as under

SP-14

(i) The share of profit of deceased partner to be computed upto the date of death on the basis of average profits of the past three years which were ₹ 1,60,000.
(ii) His share in profit/loss on revaluation of assets and reassessment of liabilities which were as follows

Land and buildings were revalued at ₹ 1,88,000, machinery at ₹ 76,000 and stock at ₹ 10,000. Provision of 2.5% was to be created on debtors for doubtful debts.

(iii) The net amount payable to Y's executors was transferred to his loan account, to be paid later on.

X and Z decided to continue the business keeping their capital balances in their new profit sharing ratio. Any surplus or deficit to be transferred to current account of the partners.

From the following, prepare revaluation account, partners' capital account and Y's executor's account. (Application) [6]

*Or*

X and Y sharing profits in the ratio of 3 : 2 had the following balance sheet as at 31st March, 2023

**Balance Sheet**
as at 31st March, 2023

| Liabilities | | Amt (₹) | Assets | | Amt (₹) |
|---|---|---|---|---|---|
| Creditors | | 1,80,000 | Cash | | 60,000 |
| General Reserve | | 1,44,000 | Debtors | 2,40,000 | |
| Capital A/cs | | | (–) Provision for Doubtful Debts | (9,600) | 2,30,400 |
| X | 6,48,000 | | Patents | | 1,77,600 |
| Y | 4,32,000 | 10,80,000 | Investments | | 96,000 |
| Current A/cs | | | Machinery | | 8,64,000 |
| X | 1,20,000 | | Goodwill | | 1,20,000 |
| Y | 24,000 | 1,44,000 | | | |
| | | 15,48,000 | | | 15,48,000 |

On 1st April, 2018, they decided to admit Z on the following terms

(i) A provision of 5% is to be created on debtors.
(ii) Accrued income of ₹ 18,000 does not appear in the books and ₹ 60,000 are outstanding for salaries.
(iii) The present market value of investments is ₹ 72,000. X takes over the investments at this value.
(iv) The new profit sharing ratio of partners will be 4 : 3 : 2.
(v) Z will bring in ₹ 2,40,000 as his capital.
(vi) Z is to pay in cash an amount equal to his share in the firm's goodwill valued at twice the average profit of the last three years which were ₹ 3,00,000, ₹ 3,12,000 and ₹ 3,60,000 respectively.
(vii) Half the amount of goodwill is withdrawn by the old partners.

Prepare revaluation account, partners' capital accounts and partners' current account. (Application)

**Que 9.**

(A) P, Q, R and S are partners sharing profits and losses in the ratio of 4 : 3 : 2 : 1. Their capitals as at 1st April, 2022 were ₹ 6,00,000, ₹ 5,00,000, ₹ 3,00,000 and ₹ 2,00,000 respectively.

S's share of profits excluding interest on capital has been guaranteed by the firm to be not less than ₹ 5,00,000.

R's share of profits including interest on capital and salary guaranteed by P is not less than ₹ 5,20,000. The profits for the year ended 31st March, 2023 were ₹ 18,00,000 before interest on capital @ 10% and salary to R @ ₹ 20,000 per month.

You are required to

(i) Calculate firm's deficiency. [1½]
(ii) Deficiency recovered by R from P. [2]
(iii) Prepare profit and loss appropriation account. [4½]

(B) Ram, Saumya and Hardik are partners in the ratio of 5 : 3 : 2. If Saumya's share of profit at the end of the year amounted to ₹ 1,50,000, what will be the Ram's share of profit? [2]

*Or*

On 31st March, 2018, the balance in the capital accounts of Abhir, Bobby and Vineet, after making adjustments for profits and drawings were ₹ 8,00,000, ₹ 6,00,000 and ₹ 4,00,000 respectively. Subsequently, it was discovered that interest on capital and interest on drawings had been omitted. The partners were entitled to interest on capital @ 10% p.a. and were to be charged interest on drawings @ 6% p.a. The drawings during the year were Abhir ₹ 20,000 drawn at the end of each month, Bobby ₹ 50,000 drawn at the beginning of every half year and Vineet ₹ 1,00,000 withdrawn on 31st October, 2017.

The net profit for the year ended 31st March, 2018 was ₹ 1,50,000. The profit sharing ratio was 2 : 2 : 1.

(i) Calculate the opening capitals of the partners. **(Application) [2]**

(ii) Calculate interest on drawings of all the partners. **(Application) [2]**

(iii) Calculate interest on capital of all the partners. **(Application) [2]**

(iv) Calculate amount to be adjusted. **(Application) [2]**

(v) Pass necessary journal entry. **(Recall) [2]**

**Que 10.**

Reliable Ltd. was registered with an authorised capital of ₹ 20,00,000 in ₹ 10 per equity share. It invited applications for issuing 1,00,000 equity shares at a premium of ₹ 2 per share. The amount was payable as follows

On application ₹ 4 per share (including premium)

On allotment ₹ 3 per share

Balance on first and final call

Applications were received for 1,30,000 shares. Applications for 10,000 shares were rejected and the application money received on them was refunded. Pro-rata allotment was made to the remaining applications.

Amount overpaid on these applications was adjusted towards the amount due on allotment. Sameer, who had applied for 1,200 shares, failed to pay the allotment and call money.

The company forfeited his shares, out of which, 800 shares were re-issued to Sanjay at ₹ 9 per share fully paid-up.

You are required to pass the journal entries in the books of the company through calls-in-arrears account and prepare the share allotment account. **(Application) [10]**

*Or*

Genix Ltd. forfeited 1,200 equity shares of ₹ 10 each issued at a premium of 20% to R who had applied for 1,440 equity shares, for non-payment of allotment money of ₹ 5 per equity share (including premium) and the first and final call of ₹ 5 per equity share. Out of these, 400 equity shares were re-issued to S credited as fully paid for ₹ 9 per equity share.

Genix Ltd. follows the policy of adjusting excess application money towards other sums due on equity shares.

(i) How much excess amount was received on application? [1]

(ii) What is the amount received on allotment? [1]

(iii) What is the amount forfeited on 400 shares? [1]

(iv) What is the amount due but not paid on allotment including premium? [2]

(v) You are required to

(a) Pass the entry for the forfeiture of these share. [2]

(b) Pass the entry for the re-issue. [3]



## Section B

**[20 Marks]**

**Que 11.**

(i) Retail and manufacturing companies often hold significant inventory levels. So you might deem the quick ratio, which excludes inventories, to be more relevant than the current ratio. Service companies, on the other hand, don't usually hold the same level of inventories, so perhaps the current ratio may be more relevant.

**Source** *Britannicamoney (edited)*

Based on the above information

- Which ratio determines the number of times stock is converted into revenue from operations during the year? **(Analysis)**

(a) Current ratio (b) Liquid ratio
(c) Inventory turnover ratio (d) All of these

- What is the correct formula for the ratio chosen? **(Recall) [1]**

(ii) Essentially, the accountant will convert net income to actual cash flow by de-accruing it through a process of identifying any non-cash expenses for the period from the income statement.

The most common and consistent of these are depreciation, the reduction in the value of an asset over time, and amortisation, the spreading of payments over multiple periods.

**Source** *hbsdaily (edited)*

While preparing cash flow statement, which of the following will not be classified as outflow of cash from financing activities? **(Understanding) [1]**

P – Redemption of debentures Q – Decrease in bank overdraft

R – Proposed dividend (current year) S – Interest on investment

**Codes**

(a) Q and R (b) R and S (c) Q, R and S (d) P, Q and R

(iii) The revenues of INFOSYS stood at ₹ 15,01,150 m in financial year 2023, which was up as compared to ₹ 12,39,360 m reported in financial year 2022. INFOSYS' revenue has grown from ₹ 8,55,570 m in financial year 2019 to ₹ 15,01,150 m in financial year 2023. Over the past 5 years, the revenue of INFOSYS has grown at a CAGR of 15.1%.

**Source** *Equitymaster( edited)*

Based on the above information

(a) State the percentage change in revenue of HCL technologies of the year 2023 and 2022.

(b) State whether there is an increase in the revenue or decrease. **(Analysis) [1]**

(iv) The current assets of APE Ltd. are ₹ 6,00,000 ; current liabilities are ₹ 2,00,000; inventories are ₹ 1,50,000; prepaid expenses are ₹ 50,000 and cash and cash equivalents are ₹ 1,00,000. What is its quick ratio? **(Application) [1]**

(v) **Balance Sheet** (An extract)

| Particulars | Note No. | 31st March, 2023 (₹) | 31st March, 2022 (₹) |
|---|---|---|---|
| I. **EQUITY AND LIABILITIES** | | | |
| 12% Debentures | | 80,000 | 1,00,000 |

**Additional Information**

Debentures were redeemed on 30th September, 2022. Interest on debentures is paid on half-yearly basis on 30th September and 31st March every year. State the amount shown in financing activity for cash flow statement. **(Evaluate) [1]**

**Que 12.**

From the following information, prepare a common size statement of profit and loss of KK Ltd. for the year ended 31st March, 2022 and 31st March, 2023. **(Application) [3]**

| Particulars | 2022-23 (₹) | 2021-22 (₹) |
|---|---|---|
| Revenue from Operations | 20,00,000 | 15,00,000 |
| Other Income | 2,00,000 | 1,50,000 |
| Expenses | 4,00,000 | 3,00,000 |
| Tax Rate @ 50% | | |

**Que 13.**

Following are the balance sheets of Jindal Saw Ltd. as at 31st March, 2022 and 2023

| Particulars | Note No. | 2023-22 (₹) | 2021-22 (₹) |
|---|---|---|---|
| I. **EQUITY AND LIABILITIES** | | | |
| 1. **Shareholders' Funds** | | | |
| (i) Share Capital | 1 | 7,00,000 | 6,00,000 |
| (ii) Reserves and Surplus | | 2,00,000 | 1,10,000 |

| Particulars | Note No. | 2023-22 (₹) | 2021-22 (₹) |
|---|---|---|---|
| **2. Non-current Liabilities** | | | |
| Long-term Borrowings | | 3,30,000 | 2,25,000 |
| **Total** | | 12,30,000 | 9,35,000 |
| **II. ASSETS** | | | |
| **1. Non-current Assets** | | | |
| (i) Property, Plant & Equipment and Intangible Assets | | | |
| (a) Property, Plant and Equipment | 2 | 11,00,000 | 8,00,000 |
| **2. Current Assets** | | | |
| (i) Inventories | | 70,000 | 60,000 |
| (ii) Trade Receivables | | 32,000 | 40,000 |
| (iii) Cash and Cash Equivalents | | 28,000 | 35,000 |
| **Total** | | 12,30,000 | 9,35,000 |

**Notes to Accounts**

| Particulars | 31st March, 2023 (₹) | 31st March, 2022 (₹) |
|---|---|---|
| **1. Reserves and Surplus** | | |
| Surplus (Balance in Statement of Profit and Loss) | 2,00,000 | 1,10,000 |
| **2. Property, Plant and Equipment** | | |
| Plant and Machinery | 11,00,000 | 8,00,000 |

## Additional Information

A piece of machinery of the book value of ₹ 80,000 was sold for ₹ 65,000 at the beginning of the year. Depreciation provided on plant and machinery during the year amounted to ₹ 2,00,000.

Calculate the following

(i) Machinery purchased during the year. [2]

(ii) Cash flow from operating activities. [2]

(iii) Cash flow from financing activities. (Evaluate) [2]

*Or* Following are the Balance Sheets of Good Luck Ltd. Prepare cash flow statement. (Application) [6]

| Particulars | Note No. | 31st March, 2023 (₹) | 31st March, 2022 (₹) |
|---|---|---|---|
| **I. EQUITY AND LIABILITIES** | | | |
| **1. Shareholders' Funds** | | | |
| (i) Share Capital | | 4,00,000 | 3,00,000 |
| (ii) Reserves and Surplus | 1 | 58,000 | 50,000 |
| **2. Non-current Liabilities** | | | |
| Long-term Borrowings (Mortgage loan) | | 1,40,000 | 1,70,000 |
| **3. Current Liabilities** | | | |
| Trade Payables | | 1,48,000 | 1,25,000 |
| **Total** | | 7,46,000 | 6,45,000 |
| **II. ASSETS** | | | |
| **1. Non-current Assets** | | | |
| Property, Plant & Equipment and Intangible Assets | 2 | 3,41,000 | 2,32,000 |
| **2. Current Assets** | | | |
| (i) Inventories | | 2,80,000 | 2,00,000 |
| (ii) Trade Receivables | | 1,07,000 | 1,30,000 |
| (iii) Other Current Assets (Share issue expenses) | | — | 3,000 |
| (iv) Cash and Cash Equivalents | 3 | 18,000 | 80,000 |
| **Total** | | 7,46,000 | 6,45,000 |

**Notes to Accounts**

| Particulars | 31st March, 2023 (₹) | 31st March, 2022 (₹) |
|---|---|---|
| 1. **Reserves and Surplus** | | |
| Surplus, i.e. Balance in Statement of Profit and Loss | 58,000 | 50,000 |
| 2. **Property, Plant & Equipment and Intangible Assets** | | |
| Property, Plant and Equipment : Plant | 2,96,000 | 1,72,000 |
| Intangible : Goodwill | 45,000 | 60,000 |
| | 3,41,000 | 2,32,000 |
| 3. **Cash and Cash Equivalents** | | |
| Cash in Hand | 16,000 | 50,000 |
| Cash at Bank | 2,000 | 30,000 |
| | 18,000 | 80,000 |

**Que 14.**

Answer any three of the following (Application) [6]

From the following information, calculate the following ratios (upto two decimal places)

(i) Debt-equity ratio (ii) Interest coverage ratio

(iii) Proprietary ratio (iv) Total asset to debt ratio

| Particulars | Amt (₹) |
|---|---|
| Equity Share Capital | 2,00,000 |
| 5% Preference Share Capital | 60,000 |
| General Reserve | 1,20,000 |
| Property, Plant and Equipment | 5,05,000 |
| Long-term Investments | 3,85,000 |
| Current Assets | 1,20,000 |
| Current Liabilities | 40,000 |
| Loan @ 10% Interest | 5,00,000 |
| Tax Paid During the Year | 30,000 |
| Profit for the Current Year after Interest and Tax | 90,000 |

SP-14

# Answers

1. (i) (d) (ii) (d) (iii) (d) (iv) (d) (vii) New Profit Sharing Ratio = 14 : 6 : 15
(viii) (c) (ix) ₹ 1,50,000

2. Number of Debentures Issued = 1,000

3. (a) Ram = ₹ 3,500 ; Hari = ₹ 1,750 ; Shyam = ₹ 1,750
(b) Transfer to Ram's Loan Account = ₹ 9,629.17

4. (i) Number of Debentures Issued = 18,750

6. Total of Balance Sheet = ₹ 8,55,000

7. (i) Profit on Realisation = ₹ 43,000
(ii) Final Payment to Arnab = ₹ 3,65,800 ; Ragini = ₹ 1,38,600 ; Dhrupad = ₹ 1,71,600

8. Profit on Revaluation = ₹ 59,400; Balance in Capital Accounts X = ₹ 1,53,580; Z = ₹ 21,940
Y's Executor's Loan Account = ₹ 1,16,680

*Or* Loss on Revaluation = ₹ 68,400 ; Balance in X's Current Account = ₹ 71,760
Balance in Y's Current Account = ₹ 27,840

9. (A) (i) ₹ 3,60,000 (ii) ₹ 5,20,000 (iii) ₹ 18,00,000
(B) ₹ 2,50,000

*Or* (i) Abhir = ₹ 9,80,000 ; Bobby = ₹ 6,40,000 ; Vineet = ₹ (4,70,000)
(ii) Abhir = ₹ 6,600 ; Bobby = ₹ 4,500 ; Vineet = ₹ 2,500
(iii) Abhir = ₹ 76,712 ; Bobby = ₹ 50,098 ; Vineet = ₹ 36,790
(iv) Abhir = ₹ 10,112 (Cr) ; Bobby = ₹ 14,402 (Dr) ; Vineet = ₹ 4,290 (Cr)

10. Share Allotment Account = ₹ 3,00,000

*Or* (i) ₹ 480 (ii) ₹ 5,520 (iii) ₹ 960 (iv) ₹ 1,840

11. (i) • (c) (ii) (b) (iii) (a) 21.1% (b) Increase
(iv) 2 (v) ₹ 30,800 (Outflow)

13. (i) ₹ 5,80,000 (ii) ₹ 3,03,000 (iii) ₹ 2,05,000

SP-14

*Or* Cash used in Operating Activities = ₹ (8,000); Cash used in Investing Activities = ₹ (1,24,000)
Cash Flow from Financing Activities = ₹ 70,000

14. (i) Debt-equity Ratio = 1.06 : 1 (ii) Interest Coverage Ratio = 3.4 times
(iii) Proprietary Ratio = 0.46 : 1 (iv) Total Assets to Debt Ratio = 2.02 : 1

For explanations scan the given QR Code

SQP Code : **PB-15/15** Series ***i*-Succeed 15-25/15** Roll No. | | | | | | | | |

# Sample Question Paper 15

## Accounts 12th (Code 858)

### General Instructions

1. Candidates are allowed additional 15 minutes for only reading the paper. They must not start writing during this time.
2. Section-A is compulsory for all candidates and has ten questions.
3. Candidates have to attempt all questions from either Section-B or Section-C*.
4. Internal choices have been provided in five questions in Section-A and one question in Section-B.
5. The intended marks for questions or parts of questions are given in the brackets [ ].
6. All calculations should be shown clearly.
7. All workings, including rough work, should be done on the same page as, and adjacent to, the rest of the answer.

*Section-C has not been covered.

**Time :** 3 Hrs.

**Max. Marks :** 80

## Section A Answer All Questions [60 Marks]

**Que 1.**

In sub-parts (i) to (iv), choose the correct option and in sub-parts (v) to (x) answer the questions as instructed.

(i) When an unrecorded asset is realised at the time of dissolution of the firm, which of the following entry will be passed? (Application) [1]

(a) Debit realisation account, credit cash account

(b) Debit concerned partner account, credit cash account

(c) Debit cash account, credit realisation account

(d) Debit realisation account, credit concerned partner account

(ii) A and B sharing profits and losses in equal ratio, decided to admit C as a new partner with effect from 1st April, 2023. Their balance sheet show workmen compensation fund ₹ 50,000. If claim on account of workmen compensation is ₹ 10,000, what journal entry will be passed? (Application) [1]

(a) Workmen Compensation Fund Dr 50,000
 To Workmen Compensation Claim A/c 50,000

(b) Workmen Compensation Fund Dr 50,000
 To Revaluation A/c 40,000
 To Workmen Compensation Claim A/c 10,000

(c) Workmen Compensation Fund Dr 50,000
 To Workmen Compensation Claim A/c 10,000
 To A's Capital A/c 20,000
 To B's Capital A/c 20,000

(d) Workmen Compensation Fund Dr 50,000
 To A's capital A/c 25,000
 To C's Capital A/c 25,000

(iii) Choose the correct order of allotment of shares.

A – Share call money due

B – Allotment money received

C – Inviting application from investors

D – Application money received (Recall) [1]

**Codes**

(a) D, C, B, A

(b) C, B, D, A

(c) C, D, B, A

(d) D, B, C, A

(iv) Sheena, Beena, Reena are partners sharing profits in the ratio of 3 : 2 : 1. Beena retired from the firm. On the date of her retirement, plant and machinery depreciated by ₹ 30,000, patents have become valueless (book value ₹ 10,000) and stock has been estimated at the value of ₹ 1,92,500 (book value ₹ 2,00,000).

Loss on account of revaluation account debited to Beena's account will be (Application) [1]

(a) ₹ 9,167
(b) ₹ 13,000
(c) ₹ 15,833
(d) None of the above

(v) XYZ Ltd. purchased fixed assets worth ₹ 25,00,000 and took over current liabilities of ₹ 4,00,000 and issued 8% debentures at a premium of 5% to the vendor in lieu of purchase consideration.

You are required to pass relevant journal entries in the books of XYZ Ltd. (Application) [1]

(vi) **Assertion** (A) A company can issue debentures at par, premium or at a discount.

**Reason** (R) Premium on redemption of debentures will be credited when debentures are issued at premium. (Evaluate) [1]

**Alternatives**

(a) Both Assertion (A) and Reason (R) are true and Reason (R) is the correct explanation of Assertion (A)
(b) Both Assertion (A) and Reason (R) are true, but Reason (R) is not the correct explanation of Assertion (A)
(c) Assertion (A) is false, but Reason (R) is true
(d) Assertion (A) is true, but Reason (R) is false

(vii) BMC Ltd. issued 5,000, 9% debentures of ₹ 100 each redeemable at a premium of 10%. Pass the journal entry regarding receipt of the amount. (Application) [1]

(viii) How is a debit balance on a partner's current account dealt with? (Understanding) [1]

(ix) On dissolution of a firm of partners X and Y after various assets (other than cash) and outside liabilities have been transferred to realisation account, debtors ₹ 5,28,000, provision for doubtful debts ₹ 48,000, ₹ 96,000 of the book debts proved bad. Debtors were realised for how much amount? (Application) [1]

(x) Non-current assets can lower cash flow and can signal to investors that the company is serious about growing their business and increasing the customers' trust as the company scale its line.

**Source** *Business news daily*

(a) What are non-current assets?
(b) Based on the above statement, name the items that comes under the head non-current assets. (Recall) [1]

SP-15

## Que 2.

R, S and M were in partnership sharing profits and losses in the proportions of 3 : 2 : 1. On 1st April, 2018, S retires from the firm. At that date, following adjustments were given

(i) Goodwill of the firm to be valued at 4 times of average super profits of last three years.

Taking into consideration the risk of the business, normal profits of the firm are estimated at ₹ 5,00,000 every year.

But actual profits of last three years ending 31st March were as 2016 – ₹ 6,00,000, 2017 – ₹ 5,50,000, 2018 – ₹ 5,75,000.

(ii) Workmen compensation reserve stood at ₹ 96,000 in balance sheet. Claim on account of workmen's compensation is ₹ 36,000.

(iii) Reserve fund stood in the balance sheet at ₹ 2,10,000.

You are required to pass journal entries to record

(a) The adjustment of S's share of goodwill.
(b) Distribution of workmen's compensation reserve.
(c) Distribution of reserve fund among partners. (Application) [3]

*Or*

The balance sheet of Sudha, Rahim and Kartik who were sharing profits in the ratio of 3 : 3 : 4 as at 31st March, 2018 was as follows

**Balance Sheet**
as at 31st March, 2018

| Liabilities | | Amt (₹) | Assets | Amt (₹) |
|---|---|---|---|---|
| General Reserve | | 10,000 | Cash | 16,000 |
| Bills Payable | | 5,000 | Stock | 44,000 |
| Loan | | 12,000 | Investments | 47,000 |
| Capital A/cs | | | Land and Buildings | 60,000 |
| Sudha | 60,000 | | Sudha's Loan | 10,000 |
| Rahim | 50,000 | | | |
| Kartik | 40,000 | 1,50,000 | | |
| | | 1,77,000 | | 1,77,000 |

Sudha died on 30th June, 2018. The partnership deed provided for the following on the death of a partner

(i) Goodwill of the firm be valued at two years' purchase of average profits for the last 3 years.

(ii) Sudha's share of profit or loss till the date of her death was to be calculated on the basis of sales.

Sales for the year ended 31st March, 2018 amounted to ₹ 4,00,000 and that from 1st April to 30th June, 2018 to ₹ 1,50,000.

The profit for the year ended 31st March, 2018 was ₹ 1,00,000.

(iii) Interest on capital was to be provided @ 6% per annum.

(iv) The average profits of the last 3 years were ₹ 42,000.

You are required to

(a) Give the amount of [2]

- Sudha's share of goodwill
- Sudha's share of profits

(b) Prepare Sudha's capital account

(Application) [1]

**Que 3.**

On 1st April, 2017, KK Ltd. (an unlisted company) invited applications for issuing 5,000, 10% debentures of ₹ 100 each at a discount of 6%. These debentures were repayable at the end of 3rd year at a premium of 10%.

The directors decided to transfer the minimum amount to debenture redemption reserve on 31st March, 2019. On 1st April, 2019, the company invested the necessary amount in 9% bank fixed deposit as per the provisions of the Companies Act, 2013.

Tax was deducted at source by bank @ 10% on interest.

Pass the necessary journal entries for redemption of debentures. Ignore entries relating to writing-off loss on issue of debentures and interest paid on debentures.

(Application) [3]

**Que 4.**

Goodwill is to be valued at 2.5 years' purchase of the average profits of last 3 years. Profits of the previous 5 years are given below

2023 – ₹ 1,80,000; 2022 – ₹ 1,20,000 ; 2021 – ₹ 3,30,000; 2020 – ₹ 1,20,000; 2019 – ₹ 1,20,000.

Capital investment of the firm is ₹ 3,00,000 and have a rate of return of 20%.

You are required to

(i) Calculate the average profit of last 3 years.

(ii) The value of goodwill by super profit method. (Application) [3]

SP-15

**Que 5.**

Asian Ltd. purchased assets of Goyal Ltd. as plant and machinery of ₹ 40,00,000 at ₹ 36,00,000 and buildings of ₹ 60,00,000 at ₹ 84,00,000 for purchase consideration of ₹ 1,10,00,000 and paid ₹ 20,00,000 in cash and remaining by issue of 8% debentures of ₹ 100 each at a premium of 20%, record necessary journal entries in the books of Asian Ltd. (Application) [3]

*Or*

State Bank of India issued, 50,000, 10% debentures of ₹ 100 each at a premium of 5% on 1st April, 2012 redeemable on 31st March, 2018.

The issue was fully subscribed. Pass necessary journal entries for the issue and redemption of debentures. (Application)

**Que 6.**

X and Y are in partnership sharing profits and losses in the ratio of 3 : 2. Their balance sheet as at 31st March, 2022, was as under

**Balance Sheet**
as at 31st March, 2022

| Liabilities | | Amt (₹) | Assets | | Amt (₹) |
|---|---|---|---|---|---|
| Creditors | | 15,000 | Cash | | 5,000 |
| General Reserve | | 12,000 | Debtors | 20,000 | |
| Capital A/cs | | | (−) Provision for Doubtful Debts | (800) | 19,200 |
| X | 60,000 | | Patents | | 14,800 |
| Y | 30,000 | 90,000 | Investments | | 8,000 |
| Current A/cs | | | Fixed Assets | | 72,000 |
| X | 10,000 | | Goodwill | | 10,000 |
| Y | 2,000 | 12,000 | | | |
| | | 1,29,000 | | | 1,29,000 |

They admit Z on the following terms

(i) A provision of 5% is to be created on debtors.
(ii) Accrued income of ₹1,500 does not appear in the books and ₹5,000 are for outstanding salaries.
(iii) Present market value of investments is ₹ 6,000. X takes over the investments at this value.
(iv) New profit sharing ratio of partners will be 4 : 3 : 2. Z will bring in ₹ 20,000 as his capital.
(v) Z is to pay in cash an amount equal to his share in firm's goodwill valued at twice the average profits of the last 3 years which were ₹ 30,000, ₹ 26,000 and ₹ 25,000 respectively.
(vi) Half the amount of goodwill is withdrawn by old partners.

You are required to

(a) Calculate sacrificing ratio of the partners. [1]
(b) Prepare revaluation account and partners' current account. (Application) [5]

**Que 7.**

What journal entries would be passed for the following transactions on the dissolution of a firm of partners X and Y, after various assets and third party liabilities have been transferred to realisation account?

**SP-15**

(i) Workmen compensation reserve stood at ₹ 3,000 and liability in respect of it was ascertained at ₹ 3,000.
(ii) There was no workmen compensation reserve and firm had to pay ₹ 750 as compensation to the workers.
(iii) Building (Book value ₹ 25,000) sold for ₹ 40,000 through a broker who charged 2% commission.
(iv) Investments (Book value ₹ 2,000) realised 150%. (Application) [6]

*Or*

A, B and C are partners sharing profits in the ratio of 3 : 1 : 1. On 31st March, 2018, they decided to dissolve their firm. On that date their balance sheet was as under

**Balance Sheet**
as at 31st March, 2018

| Liabilities | Amt (₹) | Assets | | Amt (₹) |
|---|---|---|---|---|
| Creditors | 36,000 | Bank | | 30,000 |
| A's Brother's Loan | 57,000 | Debtors | 1,02,000 | |
| C's Loan | 60,000 | (−) Provision for Bad Debts | (12,000) | 90,000 |

| Liabilities | | Amt (₹) | Assets | Amt (₹) |
|---|---|---|---|---|
| Investment Fluctuation Fund | | 30,000 | Stock | 90,000 |
| Capital A/cs | | | Investments | 1,50,000 |
| A | 1,65,000 | | Building | 1,80,000 |
| B | 1,20,000 | | Profit and Loss A/c | 30,000 |
| C | 1,02,000 | 3,87,000 | | |
| | | 5,70,000 | | 5,70,000 |

The assets were realised and the liabilities were paid as under

(i) A agreed to pay his brother's loan.
(ii) Investments realised 20% less.
(iii) Creditors were paid at 10% less.
(iv) Building was auctioned for ₹ 2,13,000. Commission on auction was ₹ 3,000.
(v) 50% of the stock was taken over by B at market price which was 20% less than the book value and the remaining was sold at market price.
(vi) Dissolution expenses were ₹ 4,800. ₹ 1,800 were to be borne by the firm and the balance by C. The expenses were paid by him.

Prepare realisation account and partners' capital accounts. (Application)

**Que 8.**

Under what heads the following items on the assets side of the balance sheet of a company will be presented? (Application) [6]

(i) Investments (ii) Mortgage Loan
(iii) Outstanding Salary
(iv) Share Issue Expenses (to be written-off in next 12 months)
(v) Premium on Redemption of Debentures
(vi) Loans Payable on Demand

**Que 9.**

Ali, Bimal and Deepak are partners in a firm. On 1st April, 2022 their capital accounts stood at ₹ 4,00,000, ₹ 3,00,000 and ₹ 2,00,000 respectively. They shared profits and losses in the proportion of 5 : 3 : 2. Partners are entitled to interest on capital @ 10% per annum and salary to Bimal and Deepak ₹ 2,000 per month and ₹ 3,000 per quarter respectively as per the provisions of the partnership deed.

Bimal's share of profit (excluding interest on capital but including salary) is guaranteed at a minimum of ₹ 50,000 per annum. Any deficiency arising on that account shall be met by Deepak. The profits of the firm for the year ended 31st March, 2023 amounted to ₹ 2,00,000.

You are required to give

(i) The entry for transfer of interest on capital of partners to the profit and loss appropriation account. (Application) [2]
(ii) The adjusting entry and closing entry for Bimal's salary. (Recall) [2]
(iii) The amount of shortfall in Bimal's guaranteed amount. (Application) [2]
(iv) Ali and Deepak's final share in profits. (Application) [2]
(v) The entry for the transfer of credit/debit balance of profit and loss appropriation account. (Application) [2]

*Or*

(A) Ramesh and Suresh were partners in a firm sharing profits in the ratio of their capitals contributed on commencement of business which were ₹ 80,000 and ₹ 60,000 respectively. The firm started business on 1st April, 2022. According to the partnership agreement, interest on capital and drawings are 12% and 10% p.a. respectively.

Ramesh and Suresh are to get a monthy salary of ₹ 2,000 and ₹ 3,000 respectively.

The profits for year ended 31st March, 2023 before making above appropriations was ₹ 1,00,300. The drawings of Ramesh and Suresh were ₹ 40,000 and ₹ 50,000 respectively. Interest on drawings amounted to ₹ 2,000 for Ramesh and ₹ 2,500 for Suresh.

You are required to

(i) Calculate Ramesh's and Suresh's interest on capitals. [1½]

(ii) Prepare profit and loss appropriation account. [4½]

(iii) Prepare partners' capital accounts, assuming that their capitals are fluctuating. (Application) [2]

(B) A and B are partners in a firm sharing profit in the ratio of 3 : 2. Their balance sheet as on 31st March, 2021 was as follows

| Liabilities | Amt (₹) | Assets | Amt (₹) | Amt (₹) |
|---|---|---|---|---|
| A's Capital | 30,000 | Drawings | | |
| B's Capital | 10,000 | A | 4,000 | |
| | | B | 2,000 | 6,000 |
| | | Other Assets | | 34,000 |
| | 40,000 | | | 40,000 |

Net profit of the year ended 31st March, 2021, ₹ 5,000 was divided without providing for interest on capital @ 10% p.a. What will be the amount of interest on A's capital? (Application) [2]

**Que 10.**

Suman Ltd. invited applications for issuing 50,000 equity shares of ₹ 10 each. The amount was payable as follows

| | |
|---|---|
| On application | ₹ 3 per share |
| On allotment | ₹ 4 per share |
| On first and final call | ₹ 3 per share |

Applications were received for 75,000 shares and pro-rata allotment was made as follows

(i) Applicants for 40,000 shares were allotted 30,000 shares on pro-rata basis.

(ii) Applicants for 35,000 shares were allotted 20,000 shares on pro-rata basis.

Pallav, to whom 1,200 shares were allotted, out of the group applying for 40,000 shares failed to pay the allotment money.

His shares were forfeited immediately after the allotment. Tanu, who had applied for 700 shares, out of the group applying for 35,000 shares, failed to pay the call, her shares were also forfeited.

Out of the forfeited shares, 1,000 shares were re-issued @ ₹ 8 per share as fully paid-up. The re-issued shares included all the forfeited shares of Tanu. Pass journal entries in the books of Suman Ltd. (Application) [10]

*Or*

Fox Chains Ltd. issued 75,000 equity shares of ₹ 30 each at face value, on which the amount was payable as ₹ 10 on application, ₹ 10 on allotment, ₹ 10 on first and final call.

Applications were received for 90,000 shares and proportionate allotment was made. Karan, who applied for 4,500 shares, failed to pay the allotment moneyand the call thereafter. (Application)

(i) How much amount is transferred to share capital on application? [1]

(ii) How many shares were allotted to Karan? [1]

(iii) What is the amount received on allotment? [2]

(iv) What is the amount of total calls-in-arrear? [1]

(v) You are required to

(a) Pass the entry for the reciept of allotment money. [2]

(b) Pass the entry for the final call being made. [3]



## Section B

[20 Marks]

**Que 11.**

(i) The Adani Group's decision to club non-current investments and security money put up against bank guarantees as part of cash equivalents has raised concerns among analysts about whether the new classification portrays an accurate picture of the group's ability to meet financial obligations.

**Source** *Livemint*

Based on the above statement, which of the following is not a part of cash and cash equivalent? (Recall) [1]

(a) Cheque in hand

(b) Draft in hand

(c) Cash at bank

(d) None of the above

(ii) Railways achieved highest ever total revenue of ₹ 2,40,177 crore in 2022-23 with operating ratio of 98.10%.

CAG report examined railways finances to end of March 2022 and made recommenda- tions. Railways' total receipts in 2020-21 were ₹ 1,91,367 crore, showing incremental revenues of ₹ 50,584 crore. Data from the minister reveals that railways spent ₹ 97.30 in 2018-19, ₹ 98.36 in 2019-2020, and ₹ 97.45 in 2020-2021 to earn ₹ 100. Covid-19 had a significant impact on railway operations in 2021-22 as well.

**Source** *Economictimes (edited)*

Keeping in view the above news, you are required to

- Mention the formula for operating ratio.
- What will be the operating ratio, if operating profit ratio is 21.42%? (Evaluate) [1]

(a) 50% (b) 100% (c) 71% (d) 78.58%

(iii) HERO MOTOCORP balance sheet analysis shows that the company's current liabilities during FY23 stood at ₹ 60 billion as compared to ₹ 55 billion in FY22, thereby witnessing an increase of 9.0%.Long-term debt down at ₹ 201 million as compared to ₹ 362 million during FY22, a fall of 44.5%.

Current assets fell 11% and stood at ₹ 94 billion, while fixed assets rose 21% and stood at ₹ 155 billion in FY23. Overall, the total assets and liabilities for FY23 stood at ₹ 249 billion as against ₹ 233 billion during FY22%.

**Source** *Equitymaster (edited)*

(a) You are required to give the formula to calculate the percentage change in total assets.

(b) Calculate the percentage change in total in comparison with the last year stating whether it was an increase or decrease. (Evaluate) [1]

(iv) Cash Flow from Financing Activities (CFF) details cash flows related to raising capital, repaying debts, issuing stocks or paying dividends.

Analysing these cash flows helps investors understand how a company funds its operations and growth.

It provides insights into the company's financing structure and its strategies for managing debt and equity. Positive cash flow from financing might indicate a company's ability to raise capital without solely relying on debt.

**Source** *Nism (edited)*

State with reason whether the issue of 10% debentures to vendors for the purchase of machinery of ₹ 90,000 will result in inflow or outflow of cash. (Understanding) [1]

(v) The financial year FY23 was a tough one for India Inc as skyrocketing inflation, hardening interest rates and deteriorating consumption resulted in a tough business environment.

Despite this, the deleveraging exercise continued, with as many as 121 companies bringing their debt further down in FY23 versus FY22, data analysed by ET Markets showed.

**Source** *Economic times (edited)*

What does the debt to equity ratio measures? (Recall) [1]



**Que 12.**

Present the following common size balance sheet in its complete term (Application) [3]

**Common Size Balance Sheet**
as at 31st March, 2023 and 2022

| Particulars | Absolute Amounts | | Percentage of Balance Sheet Total | |
|---|---|---|---|---|
| | 2022 (₹) | 2023 (₹) | 2022(%) | 2023 (%) |
| 1. **EQUITY AND LIABILITIES** | | | | |
| (i) Shareholders' Funds | ... | 18,00,000 | ... | 60 |
| (ii) Non-current Liabilities | 6,00,000 | 6,00,000 | 30 | ... |
| (iii) Current Liabilities | 2,00,000 | 6,00,000 | 10 | ... |
| **Total** | ... | 30,00,000 | 100 | 100 |

| Particulars | Absolute Amounts | | Percentage of Balance Sheet Total | |
|---|---|---|---|---|
| **2. ASSETS** | | | | |
| (i) Non-current Assets | 14,00,000 | 21,00,000 | ... | 70 |
| (ii) Current Assets | 6,00,000 | ... | 30 | 30 |
| **Total** | 20,00,000 | ... | 100 | 100 |

**Que 13.**

Following is the information available of Balaji Ltd.

**Balance Sheet**
as at 31st March, 2023 and 2022

| Particulars | Note No. | 31st March, 2023 (₹) | 31st March, 2022 (₹) |
|---|---|---|---|
| **I. EQUITY AND LIABILITIES** | | | |
| 1. **Shareholders' Funds** | | | |
| (i) Share Capital | | 3,50,000 | 2,50,000 |
| (ii) Reserves and Surplus | 1 | 5,000 | 20,000 |
| 2. **Non-current Liabilities** | | | |
| Long-term Borrowings : 12% Debentures | | 1,00,000 | 60,000 |
| 3. **Current Liabilities** | | 1,25,000 | 1,50,000 |
| **Total** | | 5,80,000 | 4,80,000 |
| **II. ASSETS** | | | |
| 1. **Non-current Assets** | | | |
| (i) Property, Plant & Equipment and Intangible Assets | | 2,80,000 | 2,00,000 |
| (ii) Investments | | 1,00,000 | 1,00,000 |
| 2. **Current Assets** | | | |
| (i) Trade Receivables | | 1,60,000 | 1,50,000 |
| (ii) Cash and Cash Equivalents | | 40,000 | 30,000 |
| **Total** | | 5,80,000 | 4,80,000 |

**Notes to Accounts**

| Particulars | 31st March, 2023 (₹) | 31st March, 2022 (₹) |
|---|---|---|
| 1. **Reserves and Surplus** | | |
| Securities Premium Reserve | 25,000 | – |
| Surplus, i.e. Balance in Statement of Profit and Loss | (20,000) | 20,000 |
| | 5,000 | 20,000 |

SP-15

**Additional Information**

(i) Debentures were issued on 1st April, 2022.

(ii) During the year, machine included in property, plant and equipment and intagible assets costing ₹ 1,20,000 was purchased and another machine having book value of ₹ 30,000 was sold at a loss of ₹ 2,000.

(a) Calculate the value of operating profit before working capital changes. [2]

(b) Calculate cash flow from investing activities. [2]

(c) Calculate cash flow from financing activities **(Evaluate) [2]**

*Or*

From the following Balance Sheets of Classic Ltd. as at 31st March, 2022 and 2023, prepare a cash flow from investing and financing activities. **(Application) [6]**

| Particulars | Note No. | 31st March, 2023 (₹) | 31st March, 2022 (₹) |
|---|---|---|---|
| I. **EQUITY AND LIABILITIES** | | | |
| 1. **Shareholders' Funds** | | | |
| (i) Equity Share Capital | | 7,20,000 | 6,00,000 |
| (ii) Reserves and Surplus | 1 | 4,00,000 | 3,20,000 |
| 2. **Non-current Liabilities** | | | |
| Long-term Borrowings | 2 | 7,56,000 | 5,24,000 |
| 3. **Current Liabilities** | | | |
| (i) Trade Payables (Creditors) | | 40,000 | 32,000 |
| (ii) Cash Credit | | 16,000 | 24,000 |
| (iii) Other Current Liabilities (Outstanding expenses) | | 4,000 | 12,000 |
| **Total** | | 19,36,000 | 15,12,000 |
| II. **ASSETS** | | | |
| 1. **Non-current Assets** | | | |
| (i) Property, Plant & Equipment and Intangible Assets | | | |
| (a) Property, Plant and Equipment | 3 | 12,80,000 | 9,20,000 |
| (b) Intangible (Goodwill) | | 20,000 | 40,000 |
| 2. **Current Assets** | | | |
| (i) Inventories (Stock) | | 68,000 | 80,000 |
| (ii) Trade Receivables | 4 | 3,36,000 | 2,72,000 |
| (iii) Other Current Assets (Prepaid expenses) | | 32,000 | 40,000 |
| (iv) Cash and Cash Equivalents (Cash at bank) | | 2,00,000 | 1,60,000 |
| **Total** | | 19,36,000 | 15,12,000 |

## Notes to Accounts

| Particulars | 31st March, 2023 (₹) | 31st March, 2022 (₹) |
|---|---|---|
| 1. **Reserves and Surplus** | | |
| General Reserve | 1,20,000 | 1,20,000 |
| Balance of Statement of Profit and Loss | 2,80,000 | 2,00,000 |
| | 4,00,000 | 3,20,000 |
| 2. **Long-term Borrowings** | | |
| 12% Debentures | 2,76,000 | 2,04,000 |
| 12% Public Deposits | 4,80,000 | 3,20,000 |
| | 7,56,000 | 5,24,000 |
| 3. **Property, Plant and Equipment and Intagible Assets** | | |
| Building | 8,80,000 | 6,00,000 |
| Plant | 4,00,000 | 3,20,000 |
| | 12,80,000 | 9,20,000 |
| 4. **Trade Receivables** | | |
| Debtors | 3,00,000 | 2,40,000 |
| Bills Receivables | 36,000 | 32,000 |
| | 3,36,000 | 2,72,000 |

## Additional Information

(i) Depreciation charged on building ₹ 40,000 and plant ₹ 20,000.
(ii) Interest paid on debentures ₹ 28,800. New debentures of ₹ 72,000 were issued on 1st Oct, 2022.
(iii) Interest paid on deposits from public ₹ 38,400 for the year.

**Que 14.**

From the following information, calculate any three of the following ratios (upto two decimal places)

(i) Debt-equity ratio (ii) Interest coverage ratio

(iii) Proprietary ratio (iv) Total asset to debt ratio (Application) [6]

| Particulars | Amt (₹) |
|---|---|
| Equity Share Capital | 2,00,000 |
| 5% Preference Share Capital | 60,000 |
| General Reserve | 1,20,000 |
| Property, Plant and Equipment | 5,05,000 |
| Long-term Investments | 3,85,000 |
| Current Assets | 1,20,000 |
| Current Liabilities | 40,000 |
| Loan @ 10% Interest | 5,00,000 |
| Tax Paid During the Year | 30,000 |
| Profit for the Current Year after Interest and Tax | 90,000 |

# Answers

**1.** (i) (c) (ii) (c) (iii) (c) (iv) (c) (vi) (d) (ix) ₹ 4,32,000

**2.** *Or* (a) Sudha's Share of Goodwill = ₹ 25,200 ; Sudha's Share of Profit = ₹ 11,250

(b) Amount given to Sudha's Executor = ₹ 90,350

**4.** (i) ₹ 2,10,000 (ii) ₹ 3,75,000

**6.** (a) Sacrificing Ratio = 7:3

(b) Loss on Revaluation Account X = ₹ 3,420, Y = ₹ 2,280

Balance in Current Account X = ₹ 5,980, Y = ₹ 2,320

**7.** *Or* Profit on Realisation = ₹ 25,800 ; Final Payment to A = ₹ 2,19,480, B = ₹ 83,160, C = ₹ 1,02,960

**9.** (iii) ₹ 3,800 (iv) Ali = ₹ 37,000 ; Deepak = ₹ 11,000

**SP-15** *Or* (A) (i) Ramesh = ₹ 9,600, Suresh = ₹ 7,200

(ii) Profit of profit and loss appropriation account = ₹ 28,000

(iii) Balance in capital account Ramesh = ₹ 87,600, Suresh = ₹ 62,700

(B) ₹ 3,100

**10.** *Or* (i) ₹ 7,50,000 (ii) ₹ 3,750 (iii) ₹ 5,70,000 (iv) ₹ 67,500

**11.** (i) (d) (ii) • (d) (iii) (b) 6.8%

**13.** (a) ₹ (16,000) (b) ₹ (92,000) (c) ₹ 1,53,000

*Or* Cash used in Investing Activities = ₹ (4,20,000); Cash Flow from Financing Activities = ₹ 2,76,800

**14.** (i) 1.06 : 1 (ii) 3.4 times (iii) 0.47 : 1 (iv) 2.02 : 1

For explanations scan the given QR Code

# Knowledge Booster Zone

## Welcome to the Knowledge Booster Zone !

This section is dedicated to enhancing your understanding of key concepts. Here, you will find chapter-wise revision notes designed to solidify your **foundational knowledge**. Use these notes to review and reinforce what you've learned, ensuring you're well-prepared for each topic.

Progress Tracker **Tick the chapters as you revise them.**

- ☐ Accounting for Partnership: Fundamentals
- ☐ Reconstitution of a Partnership Firm: Admission of a Partner
- ☐ Reconstitution of a Partnership Firm: Retirement/Death of a Partner
- ☐ Dissolution of a Partnership Firm
- ☐ Issue of Shares
- ☐ Issue and Redemption of Debentures
- ☐ Final Accounts of Companies
- ☐ Financial Statement Analysis
- ☐ Cash flow Statement
- ☐ Ratio Analysis

# Chapter 1 Accounting for Partnership : Fundamentals

**1. Meaning of Partnership**

According to Section 4 of the Indian Partnership Act, 1932, "Partnership is the relation between persons who have agreed to share the profits of a business carried on by all or any of them acting for all".

**2. Features of Partnership**

(i) Two or more persons
(ii) Agreement
(iii) Legal business
(iv) Mutual agency
(v) Sharing of profits
(vi) Limited liability of partner

Note Minimum number of partners in a partnership business must be 2 and maximum number of partners should be 50.

**3. Partnership Deed**

The document containing the agreement in writing among partners is called partnership deed.

**4. Importance of Partnership Deed**

A firm should have a partnership deed because

(i) It regulates the rights, duties and liabilities of the partners.
(ii) It avoids disputes in future by acting as a proof or guiding document.
(iii) It helps to avoid any misunderstanding among the partners.

**5. Rules Applicable in the Absence of Partnership Deed**

In the absence of partnership deed, the relevant provisions of the Indian Partnership Act, 1932 are as follows

(i) Sharing of profits/losses – Equally
(ii) Interest on capital – Not allowed
(iii) Salary/Commission to a partner – Not allowed
(iv) Interest on advances or loan by a partner – 6% per annum
(v) Interest on drawings – Not charged

Note
- Loan by a relative is not a loan from a partner. Hence, on such loan, this provision will not apply.
- In the absence of partnership deed, profits are to be shared equally, irrespective of the type of partner (active, sleeping) or the amount of capital contributed by them.
- Interest on capital is payable to a partner (if there is a provision in the agreement) but such interest is payable only out of profits except if it is allowed as a charge.

**6. Distribution of Profit among Partners: Profit and Loss Appropriation Account**

Profit and loss appropriation account is an extension of the profit and loss account. It is an account that is prepared to distribute the profits in accordance with the agreement among the partners. It is an account that shows appropriation or distribution of profits.

**7. Format of Profit and Loss Appropriation Account**

**Profit and Loss Appropriation Account**
for the year ended.........

Dr | | | Cr

| Particulars | | Amt (₹) | Particulars | | Amt (₹) |
|---|---|---|---|---|---|
| To Interest on Capital A/cs | | | By Profit and Loss A/c | | ... |
| A's Capital/Current A/c | ... | | (Net profit subject to appropriations) | | |
| B's Capital/Current A/c | ... | ... | By Interest on Drawings A/cs | | |
| To Partners' Salaries A/c | | ... | A's Capital/Current A/c | ... | |
| To Partners' Commission A/c | | ... | B's Capital/Current A/c | ... | ... |
| To Reserve A/c | | ... | | | |
| To Profit transferred to A's Capital A/c** (or A's Current A/c)*** | ... | | | | |

| Particulars | | Amt (₹) | Particulars | Amt (₹) |
|---|---|---|---|---|
| B's Capital A/c** (or B's Current A/c)*** | ... | | | |
| | | ... | | |
| | | ... | | ... |

**When capitals are fluctuating. ***When capitals are fixed.

## 8. Maintenance of Capital Accounts of Partners

**Capital Accounts of Panthers**

**Fixed Capital**
- Two accounts maintained, i.e. capital and current account
- Capital accounts of partners record only introduction and withdrawal of capital
- All other adjustment are made in current accounts Capital account-credit balance only current account-debit or credit balance

**Fluctuating Capital**
- Only one account maintained, i.e. capital account
- All the adjustments are made in capital accounts of partners

### (i) Format of Fixed Capital Method

Dr **Partners' Capital Accounts** Cr

| Particulars | X (₹) | Y (₹) | Z (₹) | Particulars | X (₹) | Y (₹) | Z (₹) |
|---|---|---|---|---|---|---|---|
| To Cash/Bank A/c (Withdrawal of capital) | ... | ... | ... | By Balance b/d | ... | ... | ... |
| To Balance c/d | ... | ... | ... | By Cash/Bank A/c (Additional capital introduced) | ... | ... | ... |
| | ... | ... | ... | | ... | ... | ... |

Dr **Partners' Current Accounts** Cr

| Particulars | X (₹) | Y (₹) | Z (₹) | Particulars | X (₹) | Y (₹) | Z (₹) |
|---|---|---|---|---|---|---|---|
| To Balance b/d (In case of debit opening balance) | ... | ... | ... | By Balance b/d (In case of credit opening balance) | ... | ... | ... |
| To Drawings A/c | ... | ... | ... | By Interest on Capital A/c | ... | ... | ... |
| To Interest on Drawings A/c | ... | ... | ... | By Commission A/c | ... | ... | ... |
| To Profit and Loss Appropriation A/c (Loss) | ... | ... | ... | By Salary A/c | ... | ... | ... |
| To Balance c/d* | ... | ... | ... | By Profit and Loss Appropriation A/c (Profit) | ... | ... | ... |
| | | | | By Balance c/d* | ... | ... | ... |
| | ... | ... | ... | | ... | ... | ... |

*Either of the two will appear.

### (ii) Format of Fluctuating Capital Method

Dr **Partners' Capital Accounts** Cr

| Particulars | X (₹) | Y (₹) | Z (₹) | Particulars | X (₹) | Y (₹) | Z (₹) |
|---|---|---|---|---|---|---|---|
| To Balance b/d (In case of debit opening balance) | ... | ... | ... | By Balance b/d (In case of credit opening balance) | ... | ... | ... |
| To Drawings A/c | ... | ... | ... | By Cash/Bank A/c (Additional capital introduced) | ... | ... | ... |
| To Interest on Drawings A/c | ... | ... | ... | | | | |
| To Profit and Loss Appropriation A/c (Loss) | ... | ... | ... | By Salary A/c | ... | ... | ... |
| | | | | By Interest on Capital A/c | ... | ... | ... |
| To Balance c/d* | ... | ... | ... | By Commission A/c | ... | ... | ... |
| | | | | By Profit and Loss Appropriation A/c (Profit) | ... | ... | ... |
| | | | | By Balance c/d* | ... | ... | ... |
| | ... | ... | ... | | ... | ... | ... |

* Either of the two will appear.

## 9. Classification of Transactions to be Shown Under the Fixed Capital Method and Fluctuating Capital Method

| Items | Fixed Capital Method | Fluctuating Capital Method |
|---|---|---|
| Introduction of Capital | Capital Account (Cr) | Capital Account (Cr) |
| Withdrawal of Capital (Drawings against capital) | Capital Account (Dr) | Capital Account (Dr) |
| Interest on Capital | Current Account (Cr) | Capital Account (Cr) |
| Salary or Commission to Partners | Current Account (Cr) | Capital Account (Cr) |
| Drawings (Against profits) | Current Account (Dr) | Capital Account (Dr) |
| Interest on Drawings | Current Account (Dr) | Capital Account (Dr) |
| Share of Profits | Current Account (Cr) | Capital Account (Cr) |
| Share of Losses | Current Account (Dr) | Capital Account (Dr) |

## 10. Interest on Capital

It is an appropriation of profits and is provided only if there is profit. It will be provided in case of loss also only if partnership deed so provides or it is to be treated as a charge against profits.

$$\text{Interest on capital} = \text{Amount of capital} \times \frac{\text{Rate}}{100} \times \frac{\text{Time}}{12}$$

## 11. Different Cases Related to Interest on Capital

The various cases related to interest on capital are

**Case I** When partnership agreement is silent about interest on capital – Not allowed

**Case II** When partnership agreement provides that interest on capital is to be allowed

(i) In case, there is a loss — Not provided

(ii) In case, there are sufficient profits — Fully allowed

(iii) If there are insufficient profits — Proportionately allowed to the extent of available profits

**Case III** When partnership agreement states that interest on capital is to be provided as a charge – Fully allowed irrespective of profits or losses.

**Note** Interest on capital is always calculated on the opening balance of capital in a year.

In case, the question gives closing capital, then opening capital will be calculated first by using the following formula

$$\text{Opening capital} = \text{Closing capital} - \text{Profits} + \text{Drawings} - \text{Additional capital}$$

## 12. Interest on Drawings

The amount withdrawn by the partners in cash or in kind for their personal use is termed as drawings. When the partnership deed is silent, no interest on drawings is charged. Interest on drawings is calculated with reference to the time period for which money was withdrawn.

**Case I** When fixed amount is withdrawn at fixed intervals

$$\text{Interest on drawings} = \text{Total drawings} \times \frac{\text{Rate of interest}}{100} \times \frac{\text{Time}}{12}$$

Value of time under different circumstances will be as under

| Circumstances | Monthly Drawings for 12 Months | Quarterly Drawings for 12 Months | Half-yearly Drawings for 12 Months | Monthly Drawings for 6 Months |
|---|---|---|---|---|
| • When drawings are made in the beginning of each period | 6.5 | 7.5 | 9 | 3.5 |
| • When drawings are made in the middle of each period | 6 | 6 | 6 | 3 |
| • When drawings are made in the end of each period | 5.5 | 4.5 | 3 | 2.5 |

***Case II*** *When unequal amount is withdrawn at different dates*

*Here, interest on drawings is calculated with the help of simple method or product method.*

*(i)* ***Simple Method*** *In this method, interest on drawings is calculated for every individual drawings considering the time for which it is used.*

$$\text{Interest on drawings} = \text{Amount of drawings} \times \frac{\text{Rate of interest}}{100} \times \frac{\text{Months remaining}}{12}$$

*(ii)* ***Product Method*** *In this method, individual drawings are multiplied by the months remaining in the year and interest for one month is calculated on the total of such products.*

$$\text{Interest on drawings} = \text{Total of products} \times \frac{\text{Rate of interest}}{100} \times \frac{1}{12} \text{ or } \frac{1}{365}$$

**Computation of Total Product**

| Date of Drawings (a) | Amount of Drawings (b) | Number of Months for which Drawings have been made (c) | Product (d) = (b) × (c) |
|---|---|---|---|
| XX – XX – XXXX | XXX | X | XXXX |
| XX – XX – XXXX | XXX | X | XXXX |
| XX – XX – XXXX | XXX | X | XXXX |
| | Total | | XXXX |

**Note**
- *When the rate of interest is given without the suffix per annum, interest will be charged without considering time or date of drawings.*
- *If the date of withdrawal is not given, in that case the interest on total drawings for the year is calculated for six months on an average basis.*

### 13. Accounting Treatment of Interest on Partner's Loan to the Firm

*Interest on partner's loan is a charge against the profits and not an appropriation out of profits and hence, must be transferred to the debit of profit and loss account and not to the debit of profit and loss appropriation account.*

**Note**
- *If there is an agreement as to the rate of interest, a partner is entitled to an interest on loan at an agreed rate of interest.*
- *If there is no agreement as to the rate of interest, partner is entitled to interest on loan @ 6% per annum.*
- *Interest on partner's loan is not recorded in the partner's capital/current account but it should be recorded to the credit side of partner's loan account.*

### 14. Accounting Treatment of Salary or Commission to a Partner

*Salary or commission to a partner is to be allowed, if the partnership agreement provides for the same. Salary or commission to a partner is an appropriation out of profits and not a charge against the profits, i.e. they are to be allowed only if there are profits and hence, must be transferred to the debit of profit and loss appropriation account and not to the debit of profit and loss account.*

*(i) Commission as percentage of net profit before charging such commission*

$$= \text{Net profit before commission} \times \frac{\text{Rate of commission}}{100}$$

*(ii) Commission as percentage of net profit after charging such commission*

$$= \text{Net profit before commission} \times \frac{\text{Rate of commission}}{100 + \text{Rate of commission}}$$

**Note** *Charges such as interest on partners' loan, manager's salary and commission must be deducted from profit before transferring it to profit and loss appropriation account.*

### 15. Transfer to Reserves

After the net profit is calculated as per profit and loss account, the balance in profit and loss appropriation account can be used to transfer profits to the general reserve or the specific reserve.

Journal entry to be passed will be

| Date | Particulars | LF | Amt (Dr) | Amt (Cr) |
|---|---|---|---|---|
| | Profit and Loss Appropriation A/c Dr | | ... | |
| | To Reserve A/c | | | ... |
| | (Being amount transferred to reserve account) | | | |

### 16. Interest on Current Account

Interest on current account is allowed in case of credit balance and charged in a case of debit balance on opening balance.

**Note** It is allowed or charged, if instructed in the question.

### 17. Rent Paid to a Partner

It is a charge against the profits and not an appropriation out of profits. It is therefore debited to profit and loss account and credited to partners' current accounts, in case of fixed capitals or to partners' capital account, when capitals are fluctuating.

### 18. Guarantee of Profits to a Partner

A partner may be admitted into the firm with a guarantee of minimum profits which means that if his share of profit is less than that of guaranteed profit, then he would be paid the guaranteed share of profit.

The deficiency (difference between guaranteed profit and actual profit) is borne by partner or partners who have guaranteed the profit in agreed ratio.

### 19. Different Cases Regarding Guarantee of Profits

**Guarantee of Profits**

- By one partner to another
- By the firm to a partner
- By a partner to the firm.
- Simultaneous guarantee - firm to partner
  - partner to firm

**Note** In case a question contains guarantee of profit by one partner to another partner, by the firm to a partner and by a partner to the firm, in such case following sequence should be followed

- First calculate the guarantee given by the partner to the firm.
- Then calculate the guarantee given by the firm to a partner.
- Then calculate the guarantee given by a partner to another partner.

### 20. Past Adjustments

If after closing the accounts of a partnership firm, some errors or omissions are discovered in the accounts, e.g. interest on capital or drawings may not have been allowed or charged; charged or allowed at a higher or lower rate, etc, then under such circumstances, the accounts once closed are not reopened.

Such errors and omissions are rectified by recording an adjusting entry. Such adjustments are called past adjustments as they relate to past period.

### 21. Goodwill

It is the good name or reputation of a business earned by a businessman through hard work and honesty which helps it to earn more profits than normal profits.

### 22. Nature of Goodwill

Goodwill is an intangible asset but not a fictitious asset because it has a realisable value. Fictitious assets don't have a realisable value.

### 23. Features of Goodwill

(i) It is an intangible and valuable asset.
(ii) It is helpful in earning excess profits.
(iii) Its value is liable to constant fluctuations.
(iv) It is relevant only when the entire business is sold.

### 24. Factors Affecting Goodwill

(i) Nature of business
(ii) Efficiency of management
(iii) Location
(iv) Market situation
(v) Special advantages

### 25. Classification of Goodwill

Goodwill can be classified into two categories

(i) **Purchased (Acquired) Goodwill** It is the goodwill that is acquired by a business after paying consideration in cash or in kind.

**Note** As per Accounting Standard (AS) 26, purchased goodwill is recorded in the books of accounts.

*(ii)* ***Self-generated Goodwill*** *It is internally generated or hard earned goodwill which arises due to continued hard work of the organisation, its better quality products, better customer service, etc.*

**Note** *As Per Accounting Standard (AS) 26, self-generated goodwill is not recorded in the books because no consideration is paid for it.*

### 26. Need for Valuation of Goodwill

*Need for valuation of goodwill arises in the following circumstances*

*(i) At the time of change in profit sharing ratio.*

*(ii) At the time of admission of a new partner.*

*(iii) At the time of retirement or death of a partner.*

### 27. Methods of Valuation of Goodwill

*(i)* ***Average Profit Method***

*This method is based on the assumption that a new business will not be able to earn profits during the initial years as compared to an established business.*

*Under this method, goodwill is ascertained by multiplying the average profits by a certain number of years' purchase.*

*(a) Simple average profit method*

*Value of goodwill = Average profit* × Number of years' purchase*

**Average profit*

$$= \frac{\text{Total actual profits of given number of years before abnormal and non-business items}}{\text{Given number of years}}$$

*(b) Weighted average profit method*

*Value of goodwill = Weighted average profit* × Number of years' purchase*

$$^{*}\text{Weighted average profit} = \frac{\text{Total of products}}{\text{Total of weights}}$$

*(ii)* ***Super Profit Method***

*In any business, a certain amount of percentage of profits is normally expected. But in practice, we may earn more than that normal profit or we may earn less than that normal profit.*

*Excess of actual profits over the normal profits is called super profits.*

*In this method, goodwill is calculated by multiplying super profit by a certain number of years given.*

*Value of goodwill = Super profit* × Number of years' purchase*

**Super profit = Average (Actual) profits − Normal profits***

$$^{**}\text{Normal profits} = \text{Capital employed}^{***} \times \frac{\text{Normal rate of return}}{100}$$

****Capital employed (Net assets) = Total assets (excluding goodwill, non-trade investments and fixed assets) − External liabilities*

*(iii)* ***Capitalisation Method***

*(a)* ***Capitalisation of average profit***

*Under the capitalisation of average profit method, the capitalised value of the business is determined by capitalising the average profit by the normal rate of return. Out of the value so determined, value of net assets is deducted to determine the value of goodwill.*

*Value of goodwill = Capitalised value of average profits* − Actual capital employed***

**Capitalised value of average profits*

$$= \text{Average profits} \times \frac{100}{\text{Normal rate of return}}$$

***Actual capital employed = Total assets (excluding goodwill, non-trade investments and fixed assets) − External liabilities*

*(b)* ***Capitalisation of super profit***

*In the capitalisation of super profit, goodwill is calculated by the capitalisation of super profit on the basis of normal rate of return.*

$$\text{Goodwill} = \text{Super profits} \times \frac{100}{\text{Normal rate of return}}$$

$$\text{Normal profits} = \text{Average capital employed} \times \frac{\text{Normal rate of return}}{100}$$

*Super profits = Average (Actual) profits − Normal profits*

# Chapter 2 Reconstitution of a Partnership Firm : Admission of a Partner

### 1. Reconstitution of a Partnership Firm

Any change in the existing agreement of partnership amounts to reconstitution of a firm.

### 2. Modes of Reconstitution of Partnership firm

- Change in profit-sharing ratio
- Admission of a partner
- Retirement/Death of a partner
- Amalgamation of two partnership firms

### 3. Change in the Profit Sharing Ratio

When one or more partners acquire an interest in the business from another existing partner(s), it is said to be a change in the profit sharing ratio in a partnership firm.

A change in the profit sharing ratio among the existing partners means, it is reconstitution of the firm without admission, retirement or death of a partner.

### 4. Adjustments Required at the Time of Change in Profit Sharing Ratio

Due to change in profit sharing ratio, following adjustments need to be incorporated in the books of accounts

(i) Calculation of each partners' sacrifice or gain.
(ii) Treatment of goodwill.
(iii) Treatment of revaluation of assets and liabilities.
(iv) Treatment of accumulated profits, reserves and losses.
(v) Preparation of capital account and revised balance sheet.

### 5. Calculation of Sacrifice or Gain of Partners

The sacrifice made or gain received by a partner is calculated by deducting the new share from the old share of partner.

Sacrifice/Gain share = Old profit share − New profit share

If difference found positive, then it is sacrifice share and in case of negative difference, it will be gain share.

### 6. Treatment of Goodwill

At the time of change in profit sharing ratio, the treatment of goodwill would be in the following manner

(i) For goodwill appearing in the balance sheet

| | | |
|---|---|---|
| All Partners' Capital A/c Dr | (Book value) | |
| To Goodwill A/c (in old ratio) | | (Book value) |

(ii) For recording of goodwill share without opening goodwill account

| | |
|---|---|
| Gaining Partners' Capital/Current A/c | Dr |
| To Sacrificing Partners' Capital/Current A/c | |

**Note** Capital accounts should be used in case capital accounts are maintained by fluctuating capital method and current accounts should be used in case of fixed capital method.

### 7. Treatment of Revaluation of Assets and Liabilities

Two alternatives available for this purpose are

(i) **When revised values are to be recorded in the books of accounts**

An account titled 'revaluation account' or 'profit and loss adjustment account' is opened for this purpose

**Format of Revaluation Account**

Dr **Revaluation Account** Cr

| Particulars | Amt (₹) | Particulars | Amt (₹) |
|---|---|---|---|
| To Decrease in Value of Assets (Loss) | .... | By Increase in Value of Assets (Profit) | .... |
| To Increase in Value of Liabilities (Loss) | .... | By Decrease in Value of Liabilities (Profit) | .... |
| To Unrecorded Liabilities (at an agreed value) | .... | By Unrecorded Assets (at an agreed value) | .... |
| To Profit transferred to Old Partners' Capital/Current A/c (in old ratio)* | .... | By Loss transferred to Old Partners' Capital/Current A/c (in old ratio)* | .... |
| | .... | | .... |

*Any one will appear.

***(ii) When revised values are not to be recorded in the books of accounts***

*(Adjustments of profits/losses on revaluation of assets and reassessment of liabilities through the capital accounts only).*

*If partners decide to record the net effect of revaluation of assets and liabilities without affecting the old amount of assets and liabilities, a single adjusting entry involving the capital accounts of gaining partners and sacrificing partners is passed.*

*In this regard, we take the following steps*

***Step 1*** *Calculation of the Net Effect of Revaluation*

| | |
|---|---|
| Increase in the value of assets | .... |
| (+) Decrease in amount of liabilities | .... |
| (−) Decrease in value of assets | (....) |
| (−) Increase in amount of liabilities | (....) |
| Net effect of revaluation | .... |

***Step 2*** *To Find Share of Sacrifice/Gain by Partners*

| | |
|---|---|
| (i) Their old share | .... |
| (ii) Their new share | .... |
| Difference (i − ii) | .... |

***Step 3*** *Calculation of Proportional amount of Net Effect of Revaluation*

***For Gaining Partner***

*Proportional Amount of Net Effect of Revaluation = Share Gained × Net Effect of Revaluation*

***For Sacrificing Partner***

*Proportional Amount of Net Effect of Revaluation = Share Sacrificed × Net Effect of Revaluation*

***Step 4*** *Journal Entries*

*For Net Profit on Revaluation*

| | |
|---|---|
| Gaining Partners' Capital/Current A/c | Dr |
| To Sacrificing Partners' Capital/Current A/c | |

*For Net Loss on Revaluation*

| | |
|---|---|
| Sacrificing Partners' Capital/Current A/c | Dr |
| To Gaining Partners' Capital/Current A/c | |

## 8. Treatment of Accumulated Profits, Reserves and Losses

*At the time of change in profit sharing ratio, the past profits, reserves and losses appearing in the balance sheet, shall be treated in following two ways*

***(i) When partners decided to transfer past reserves or losses to their capital/current account***

*(a) For transfer of past reserves or profits*

| | |
|---|---|
| Profit and Loss A/c | Dr |
| General Reserves A/c | Dr |
| Workmen Compensation Reserve A/c | Dr |
| Investment Fluctuation Reserve A/c | Dr |
| To All Partners' Capital/Current A/c | |

*(b) For transfer of past losses*

| | |
|---|---|
| Partners' Capital/Current A/c | Dr |
| To Profit and Loss A/c | |
| To Deferred Revenue Expenditure A/c | |

*(ii)* **When partners decided not to transfer past reserves or losses to their capital/current account**

| | |
|---|---|
| Gaining Partners' Capital/Current A/c | Dr |
| To Sacrificing Partners' Capital/Current A/c | |

**Note** In such a case, we have to find each partners' sacrifice or gain share and then above entry will be made.

## 9. Admission of a Partner

Admission of a partner is one of the modes of reconstituting the firm under which old partnership comes to an end and a new one among all partners (including incoming partner) comes into existence.

## 10. New Profit Sharing Ratio

The ratio in which all the partners (including incoming partner) share the future profits and losses is known as the new profit sharing ratio.

New profit sharing ratio = Old ratio − Sacrificing ratio

## 11. Sacrificing Ratio

The ratio in which old partners agree to sacrifice their share of profit in favour of the new partner is called the sacrificing ratio.

Sacrificing ratio = Old ratio − New ratio

## 12. Various Cases Related to Treatment of Goodwill

**Case I** When premium for goodwill is paid privately by the new partner

In case a new partner pays premium to the old partners privately or directly or outside the business, it will not be recorded because it is an out of business transaction. However, entry for capital brought in by new partner will be recorded.

| | |
|---|---|
| Cash/Bank A/c | Dr |
| To New Partner's Capital A/c | |

**Note** Any goodwill already appearing in the books will also be written-off in old ratio.

**Case II** When premium for goodwill is brought in business by new partner and retained in the business

(i) For bringing premium for goodwill and capital

| | |
|---|---|
| Cash/ Bank A/c | Dr |
| To New Partner's Capital A/c | |
| To Premium for Goodwill A/c | |

(ii) For distributing premium to sacrificing (old) partners

| | |
|---|---|
| Premium for Goodwill A/c | Dr |
| To Sacrificing Partner's Capital/Current A/c (In sacrificing ratio) | |

**Case III** When premium for goodwill brought in business and withdrawn by old (sacrificing) partners

In this case, in addition to the two entries of case II, an entry for drawings will also be passed as follows

For withdrawing of premium by old (sacrificing) partners

| | |
|---|---|
| Old (sacrificing) Partner's Capital/Current A/c (In sacrificing ratio) | Dr |
| To Cash/ Bank A/c | |

**Case IV** When premium for goodwill and capital is brought in kind

| | |
|---|---|
| (a) Assets A/c | Dr |
| To Premium for Goodwill A/c | |
| To New Partner's Capital A/c | |
| (b) Premium for Goodwill A/c | Dr |
| To Sacrificing Partners' Capital/Current A/c | |

**Case V** *When the new partner is unable to bring his share of premium for goodwill in cash*

*New Partner's Current A/c* Dr *(With the share of new partner in goodwill of the firm)*
*To Sacrificing (Old) Partners' Capital/Current A/c* *(In sacrificing ratio)*

**Case VI** *When a new partner brings only a part of premium for goodwill in cash*

*(a) Cash/Bank A/c* Dr
*To Premium for Goodwill A/c (With the amount of goodwill brought in cash)*

*(b) Premium for Goodwill A/c (Goodwill brought in cash)* Dr
*New Partner's Current A/c (Goodwill not brought in cash)* Dr
*To Sacrificing (Old) Partners' Capital/Current A/c (In sacrificing ratio)*

## 13. Writing-off Existing Goodwill

*If goodwill is appearing in the balance sheet at the time of reconstitution, then it will be written-off in old profit sharing ratio because it belonged to the period before admission of a partner (reconstitution).*

*Old Partners' Capital A/c* Dr
*To Goodwill A/c*

## 14. Hidden or Inferred Goodwill

*Hidden or inferred goodwill is the excess of desired total capital of the firm over the actual combined capital of all partners.*

*The following steps will be taken for calculating hidden goodwill*

**Step 1** *Find out the total capital of the new firm on the basis of the capital brought in by the new partner for his share.*

**Step 2** *Ascertain the existing total capital of the new firm by adding the capital of all partners, including new partner's capital after adjustments.*

**Step 3** *Goodwill is assumed to be the excess of the total capital of the new firm on the basis of new partner's capital over the existing total capital of all the partners.*

## 15. Revaluation of Assets and Reassessment of Liabilities

*Revaluation account is a account which is prepared to record changes in the value of assets and liabilities at the time of admission, retirement, death and change in profit sharing ratio.*
*It is a nominal account in nature. It is also known as profit and loss adjustment account. It is prepared in the same manner as in case of change in profit sharing ratio discussed earlier.*

## 16. Accounting Treatment of Reserves, Accumulated Profits/Losses

*The various journal entries to be passed are given below*

*(i)* ***For transfer of reserves and accumulated profits***

| | | |
|---|---|---|
| *Reserves A/c* | Dr | |
| *Profit and Loss A/c* | Dr | |
| *Workmen Compensation Reserve A/c (Excess of reserve over actual liability)* | Dr | |
| *Investment Fluctuation Reserve A/c (Excess of reserve over the difference between the book value and the market value of investments)* | Dr | |
| *To Old Partner's Capital or Current A/c (Individually)* | | *(Old Ratio)* |
| *(Being the reserves and profits transferred to old partners in their old ratio)* | | |

*(ii)* ***For transfer of accumulated losses***

| | | |
|---|---|---|
| *Old Partners' Capital or Current A/c (Individually)* | Dr | *(Old Ratio)* |
| *To Profit and Loss A/c* | | |
| *To Deferred Revenue Expenditure A/c* | | |
| *To Advertisement Suspense A/c* | | |
| *(Being accumulated losses transferred to old partners in their old ratio)* | | |

## 17. Adjustment of Capital

*At the time of admission of a new partner, the partners agree that their capitals should also be adjusted so as to be proportionate to their profit sharing ratio.*

The capital of partners may be adjusted in any of the following ways

(i) Adjusting the capitals of old partners on the basis of the capital of incoming partner (When the total capital of the new firm is not given)

**Step I** Calculate total capital of new firm by using the following formula

$$\text{Total capital} = \frac{\text{New partner's capital}}{\text{New partner's profit share}}$$

**Step II** Calculate new profit sharing ratio (if not given).

**Step III** Distribute total capital of new firm in new profit sharing ratio.

i.e. Step III = Step I × Step II

**Step IV** Find out the adjusted capital through partners' capital account.

**Step V** Calculate the surplus/deficit in the capital account by comparing Step I and Step IV.

(ii) Determining the new partner's capital on the basis of combined capital of old partners

Practical steps involved in the determination of capital of new partner

**Step I** Calculate the adjusted old capitals of old partners (after all adjustments have been made)

**Step II** $$\text{Total capital of new firm} = \frac{\text{Combined adjusted capital of old partners}}{(1 - \text{New partner's profit share})}$$

**Step III** Calculate the total capitals of new partners as follows

Total capital (Step II) × Share of new partner

# Chapter 3 Reconstitution of a Partnership Firm : Retirement/Death of a Partner

### 1. Retirement

Retirement of a partner means retiring from the firm, i.e. ceasing to be a partner of the firm. Retirement of a partner is one of the modes of reconstituting the firm under which an old partnership comes to an end and a new one between the continuing partners (i.e. partners other than the outgoing partner) comes into existence, however, the firm continues its business.

### 2. New Profit Sharing Ratio

After retirement of a partner, the new ratio in which the continuing partners (i.e. partners other than an outgoing partner) decides to share the future profits and losses, is known as new profit sharing ratio.

| New share = Old share + Acquired gaining share |
|---|

### 3. Gaining Ratio

The ratio in which the continuing partners acquire the outgoing (retired or deceased) partners' share is called as gaining ratio.

The ratio is calculated by taking out the difference between new profit ratio and old profit ratio.

| Gaining ratio = New ratio − Old ratio |
|---|

### 4. Treatment of Goodwill

At the time of retirement or death of a partner, his share of profits is taken by the continuing partners. The continuing partners then compensate the retiring or deceased partner in the form of goodwill in their gaining ratio.

Journal entry to be passed is

| | | |
|---|---|---|
| Gaining Partners' Capital A/c | Dr | (Continuing partners in gaining ratio) |
| To Sacrificing Partner's Capital A/c | | (Retiring/Deceased partners) |

### 5. Goodwill Already Appearing in Books

Any goodwill already appearing in the books (balance sheet) will be immediately written-off (debited) to old partners' capital accounts in old profit sharing ratio. Here, the word 'old partners' includes retiring partner also.

*Journal entry to be passed is*

| | | |
|---|---|---|
| *All Partners' Capital/Current A/c* | *Dr* | *(Old partners in old ratio)* |
| *To Goodwill A/c* | | *(Existing value of goodwill)* |

**6. Hidden Goodwill**

*Sometimes, the firm agrees to settle the retiring or deceased partners' account by payment of a lumpsum amount. If such amount is in excess of his capital and share in reserves/revaluation of assets and re-assessment of liabilities etc., the excess will be treated as his share of goodwill.*

**7. Revaluation of Assets and Re-assessment of Liabilities**

*The term 'revaluation' simply means 'to determine the value of assets and liabilities again'.*

*At the time of retirement of a partner, the assets and liabilities are revalued so that the due share of an outgoing partner in the profit/loss, arising from such revaluation may be ascertained and adjusted in capital account.*

***Accounting Treatment*** *For this purpose, revaluation account is prepared. The debit side of this account shows all the reduction/increase in the value of assets/liabilities and the credit side shows the appreciation/decrease in the value of assets/liabilities.*

*Any profit or loss due to revaluation of assets and liabilities is divided among all the partners including the retiring one. (Revaluation account is to be prepared in the same manner as in the case of change in profit sharing ratio of a partner.)*

**8. Adjustment for Reserves and Accumulated Profits/Losses**

*At the time of retirement, net balance (after setting off liability, if any) of specific reserves (e.g. workmen compensation reserve, investment fluctuation reserve, general reserve and accumulated profit or loss, etc.) appearing in the balance sheet is distributed among all the partners in their profit sharing ratio.*

**9. Calculation of Amount Payable to Retiring Partner**

*The amount due to a retiring partner is ascertained by preparing retiring partners' capital account, after taking into account the following*

***Items to be Credited***

*(i) Opening balance of capital and current account of retiring partner.*
*(ii) His share in the profit of revaluation account.*
*(iii) His share of reserves/accumulated profits.*
*(iv) His share of goodwill of the firm.*
*(v) His share of profit till the date of his retirement.*
*(vi) His salary and/or interest on capital due to the retiring partner till the date of his retirement.*

***Items to be Debited***

*(i) Drawings and interest thereon, of the retiring partner.*
*(ii) Share in the accumulated losses of past year/years.*
*(iii) Share in the loss of revaluation account.*
*(iv) Share in goodwill already appearing in the balance sheet on date of retirement.*

**10. Settlement of the Amount Due to the Retiring Partner**

*The amount due to retiring partner is either paid-off immediately or is transferred to his loan account. The retiring partners' loan account will appear in the books of the new firm as a liability until it is paid-off fully.*

***Accounting Treatment***

*(i) If the amount is immediately paid-off*

| | |
|---|---|
| *Retiring Partners' Capital A/c* | *Dr* |
| *To Cash/Bank A/c* | |

*(ii) In case the amount is not immediately paid, then due amount is transferred to retiring partners' loan account by passing following entry*

| | |
|---|---|
| *Retiring Partners' Capital A/c* | *Dr* |
| *To Retiring Partners' Loan A/c* | |

*(iii) If payment is partly paid in cash and the remaining amount is to be treated as loan*

| | |
|---|---|
| *Retiring Partners' Capital A/c* | *Dr* |
| *To Cash/Bank A/c* | |
| *To Retiring Partners' Loan A/c* | |

## 11. Interest on Loan

*The partners may decide that the principal amount of the retiring partner will be paid in instalments. In that case interest will be paid on the outstanding amount of the loan. Accrued interest on loan will also be recorded while preparing loan account. There are two types of accrued interest*

*(i)* ***Interest accrued but not due*** *When interest is recorded in the books of accounts, but its not due for payment, it is called interest accrued but not due. For example, when books are closing on 31st March, 2023 and interest is provided on half-yearly basis, i.e. on 30th June and 31st December, interest from January to March will be recorded on accrual basis in the loan account although the interest will become due for payment on 30th June, 2023.*

*(ii)* ***Interest accrued and due*** *When the interest is recorded in the loan account and its due for payment, is called interest accrued and due. For instance, in the previous example, interest from 1st January to 30th June, 2023 is due for payment and will be called interest accrued and due.*

## 12. Adjustment of Capital

*The capitals of the continuing partners may be required to be adjusted in the following three cases*

***Case I*** *When the total capital of the new firm is given*

*The various steps involved in adjusting the capitals of the partners are given below*

***Step 1*** *Calculate the adjusted old capitals of continuing partners (i.e. after all other adjustment).*

***Step 2*** *Calculate the new capitals of continuing partners.*

*New capital of continuing partners = Total capital of new firm × New profit sharing ratio*

***Step 3*** *Calculate the surplus/deficit capital by comparing Step 2 and 3.*

***Case II*** *When the total capital of the new firm is not given*

*The various steps involved in adjusting the capital of the partners are given below*

***Step 1*** *Calculate the adjusted old capitals of continuing partners after all other adjustments.*

***Step 2*** *Calculate total capital of the new firm by adding the adjusted capitals of the continuing partners.*

***Step 3*** *Calculate the new capitals of the continuing partners on the basis of their new profit sharing ratio.*

***Step 4*** *Calculate the surplus/deficit capital by comparing Step 2 and 3.*

***Case III*** *When the outgoing partner is to be paid through cash brought by the continuing partners in such a way as to make their capitals proportionate to their new profit sharing ratio.*

*The various steps involved in adjusting the capitals of partners are given below*

***Step 1*** *Calculate the adjusted old capital of continuing partners after all other adjustments.*

***Step 2*** *Calculate total capital of the new firm by adding adjusted capitals of continuing partners and amount to be paid to the retiring partner.*

***Step 3*** *Calculate the new capital of continuing partners according to their new profit sharing ratio.*

***Step 4*** *Calculate the amount to be brought in by continuing partners by comparing Step 1 and Step 3.*

## 13. Death of a Partner

*The partnership comes to an end immediately, whenever a partner dies although the firm may continue with the remaining partners. The deceased partner is entitled to get his share in the firm, as per the provision of the partnership agreement. His share in the firm is calculated in the same manner as in the case of a retiring partner.*

### 14. Accounting Treatment of Deceased Partners' Share in Profits

If a partner dies on any date after the date of the balance sheet, then his share of profit is calculated from the beginning of the year to the date of death on the basis of time or sales. When share of profit is calculated on the basis of time, it may be on the basis of previous years' profit or average profit of past years.

**On the Basis of Time**

Profit from the date of last balance sheet to the date of death $= \frac{X}{Y} \times Z$

Where, X = Number of days or months from the date of last balance sheet to the date of death
Y = 365 days or 12 months
Z = Previous year's profits or average profits of a given number of past years

**On the Basis of Sales**

Profit from the date of last balance sheet to the date of death $= \frac{X}{Y} \times Z$

Where, X = Sales from the date of the last balance sheet to the date of death
Y = Previous year's sales or average sales of a given number of past years
Z = Previous year's profits or average profits of a given number of past years

**Accounting Treatment**

(i) If profit sharing ratio of the remaining partners does not change

(a) In case of profit

| | |
|---|---|
| Profit and Loss Suspense A/c | Dr |
| To Deceased Partner's Capital A/c | |

(b) In case of loss

| | |
|---|---|
| Deceased Partner's Capital A/c | Dr |
| To Profit and Loss Suspense A/c | |

(ii) If profit sharing ratio of the remaining partners change

(a) In case of profit

| | |
|---|---|
| Gaining Partner's Capital Ac | Dr |
| To Deceased Partner's Capital A/c | |

(b) In case of loss

| | |
|---|---|
| Deceased Partner's Capital A/c | Dr |
| To Gaining Partner's Capital A/c | |

### 15. Ascertainment of the Amount Due to the Deceased Partner

The deceased partner's share is also calculated in the same manner as in the case of retiring partner. Amount due to a deceased partner shown by his capital account is transferred to his executors' account.

Entry will be

| | |
|---|---|
| Deceased Partner's Capital A/c | Dr |
| To Deceased Partner's Executor's A/c | |

### 16. Settlement of Deceased Partners' Executor Account

(i) If payment is made in full/lumpsum

| | |
|---|---|
| Deceased Partner's Executor's A/c | Dr |
| To Cash/Bank A/c | |

(ii) If payment is made in instalment

| | |
|---|---|
| (a) Deceased Partner's Executor's A/c | Dr |
| To Deceased Partner's Executor's Loan A/c | |
| (b) Deceased Partner's Executor's Loan A/c | Dr |
| To Cash/Bank A/c | |

# Chapter 4 Dissolution of a Partnership Firm

### 1. Dissolution

Dissolution means breaking up or extinction, i.e. discontinuance of existing relationship among the partners. Under the Indian Partnership Act, 1932, the dissolution may be either of partnership or of a firm.

**Dissolution**

Dissolution of Partnership
- Change in relationship (economic) of existing partners
- Firm continues
- At the Admission, Retirement, Change in PSR, etc.

Dissolution of Partnership Firm
- Dissolution of partnership
- Firms also comes to an end

### 2. Modes of Dissolution of Partnership Firm

(i) Dissolution by mutual agreement
(ii) Compulsory dissolution
(iii) Dissolution by notice
(iv) On the happening of an event
(v) Dissolution by court

### 3. Settlement of Accounts in Case of Dissolution of Firm (Section 48)

**Settlement of Accounts**

Treatment of Losses (Including deficiencies)
- First, out of profits ↓
- Then, out of capital ↓
- Lastly, by the partners individually in their PSR [Section 48 (a)]

Payment of Liabilities (Application of assets)
- First, to pay outside debts ↓
- Then, to pay loans and advances from partners ↓
- Then, to pay capitals of partner ↓
- Lastly, surplus to be distributed in their PSR [Section 48 (b)]

### 4. Treatment of Firm's Debts and Private Debts (Section 49)

Where both the debts of the firm and private debts of a partner co-exist, the following rules as stated in Section 49 of the Act, shall apply

(i) Firm's property is applied first in payment of firm's debts and if there is any surplus, then the share of each partner is applied in the payment of his private debts or paid to him.

(ii) Partner's private property is applied first in payment of his private debts and the surplus (if any) in payment of firm's debts, if the firm's liabilities exceed the firm's assets.

### 5. Accounting Treatment on Dissolution

Following accounts are openend in the books of the firm

(i) Realisation account
(ii) Partners' capital account
(iii) Partner's loan account
(iv) Cash/Bank account

### 6. Realisation Account

Realisation account is opened on the dissolution of a firm. It is a nominal account. It is prepared to determine the profit or loss on the realisation of assets and payment of liabilities.

**Accounting Treatment**

| | | | |
|---|---|---|---|
| (i) | Transfer of assets (except cash and bank balance) | Realisation A/c Dr<br>To Sundry Assets A/c | (At book value) |
| (ii) | Transfer of liabilities (except partners' loan, capital and undistributed profits) | Sundry Liabilities A/c Dr<br>To Realisation A/c | (At book value) |
| (iii) | Sale of assets | Cash/Bank A/c Dr<br>To Realisation A/c | (At selling price) |
| (iv) | Assets taken over by partner | Partners' Capital A/c Dr<br>To Realisation A/c | (At agreed value) |
| (v) | Sale of unrecorded assets | Cash/Bank A/c Dr<br>To Realisation A/c | (Amount received on sale) |
| (vi) | Payment of liabilities | Realisation A/c Dr<br>To Cash/Bank A/c | (Amount of payment) |
| (vii) | Any liability taken over by the partner | Realisation A/c Dr<br>To Partners' Capital A/c | (At agreed value) |
| (viii) | Payment of realisation expenses | Realisation A/c Dr<br>To Cash/Bank A/c | (Amount of payment) |
| (ix) | Payment of unrecorded liability (which did not exist in the balance sheet) | Realisation A/c Dr<br>To Cash/Bank A/c | (Amount of payment) |
| (x) | Payment of realisation expenses by any partner | Realisation A/c Dr<br>To Partners' Capital A/c | (Amount of payment) |
| (xi) | Credit balance of realisation account (Profit) | Realisation A/c Dr<br>To Partners' Capital/Current A/c | (In profit sharing ratio) |
| (xii) | Debit balance of realisation account (Loss) | Partners' Capital/Current A/c Dr<br>To Realisation A/c | (In profit sharing ratio) |

**Note**
- Goodwill appearing in the balance sheet is treated as any other asset. In case, question is silent about the realisation of goodwill, it is assumed that goodwill does not have any value and no amount is realised for it.
- When an asset is transferred to realisation account, its corresponding reserve or provision appearing on the liabilities side of balance sheet is also transferred to realisation account.
- In the absence of any information regarding realisation of assets, it should be assumed that tangible assets and investments have been realised at book value itself while intangible assets, accrued income and prepaid expenses have realised nothing.
- In the absence of any information regarding settlement of any outside liabilities, it should be assumed that an amount equal to the book value of such liability has been paid off.
- Bank overdraft is to be taken to the Bank/Cash A/c and not to be transferred to realisation account but bank loan must be transferred to realisation account.

## 7. Format of Realisation Account

Dr **Realisation Account** Cr

| Particulars | Amt (₹) | Particulars | Amt (₹) |
|---|---|---|---|
| To Sundry Assets A/c {Excluding cash, bank, fictitious asset, accumulated losses, debit balance of partners' capital/current A/c, loans to partner(s)} | ... | By Sundry Liabilities A/c {Excluding partners' capital, loan from partner(s), bank overdraft reserve, accumulated profit, etc.} | ... |
| To Bank/Cash A/c (Amount paid for discharging liabilities) | ... | By Provision on any Assets A/c | ... |
| To Bank/Cash A/c (Expenses on realisation) | ... | By Bank/Cash A/c (Amount received on realisation of assets) | ... |
| To Partners' Capital/Current A/c (Liability taken over by a partner or remuneration/ commission paid to him or any expenses beared by him) | ... | By Bank/Cash A/c (Amount received from unrecorded assets) | ... |
| To Partners' Capital/Current A/c (Profit on realisation)* | ... | By Partner's Capital A/c (Assets taken over by a partner recorded or unrecorded) | ... |
| | | By Partners' Capital/Current A/c (Loss on realisation)* | ... |
| | ... | | ... |

*Anyone of two amounts will appear.

*Note* All provisions created against any asset or liabilities, e.g. provision for doubtful debts, provision for depreciation should be transferred to realisation account on credit side or debit side as the case may be and it should be noted that those assets or liabilities should appear in realisation account at gross value.

## 8. Format of Partners' Capital Account

Dr **Partners' Capital Account** Cr

| Particulars | X (₹) | Y (₹) | Particulars | X (₹) | Y (₹) |
|---|---|---|---|---|---|
| To Balance b/d (Debit balance) | ... | ... | By Balance b/d (Credit balance) | ... | ... |
| To Profit and Loss A/c | ... | ... | By General Reserve A/c | ... | ... |
| To Advertisement Expenditure A/c | ... | ... | By Profit and Loss A/c | ... | ... |
| To Realisation A/c (Assets taken over) | ... | ... | By Workmen's Compensation Reserve A/c | ... | ... |
| To Realisation A/c (Loss on realisation) | ... | ... | By Realisation A/c (Liabilities taken over) | ... | ... |
| To Cash/Bank A/c (Excess cash paid) | ... | ... | By Realisation A/c (Profit on realisation) | ... | ... |
| | | | By Cash/Bank A/c (Cash brought in) | ... | ... |
| | ... | ... | | ... | ... |

*Note*
- Loan taken from a partner will be passed through cash or bank account.
- Loan given to a partner will be transferred (debited) to his capital account.

## 9. Partners' Loan Account

Partners' loan will be paid after all outside liabilities are paid.

The following journal entry is passed

| | |
|---|---|
| Partner's Loan A/c | Dr |
| To Cash/Bank A/c | |

## 10. Cash/ Bank Account

It is a real account. On debit side, opening balance, amount realised through sale of assets and any amount paid in by the partners are shown.

On the credit side, all the payments for liabilities, realisation expenses and final settlement made to partners are shown. In case, both cash and bank balances appear in balance sheet, it is always better to open a single account.

## 11. Format of Cash/Bank Account

Dr **Cash/Bank Account** Cr

| Particulars | Amt (₹) | Particulars | Amt (₹) |
|---|---|---|---|
| To Balance b/d (Cash in hand or cash at bank) | ... | By Balance b/d (Bank overdraft) | ... |
| To Realisation A/c (Assets realised) | ... | By Realisation A/c (Liabilities paid) | ... |
| To Partner's Capital A/c (individually) (Cash brought in by a partner) | ... | By Realisation A/c (Realisation expenses paid) | ... |
| | | By Partner's Loan A/c (Partner's loan paid) | ... |
| | | By Partner's Capital A/c (individually) (Excess cash paid to partner) | ... |
| | ... | | ... |

## 12. Preparation of Memorandum Balance Sheet

If a balance sheet, on the date of dissolution, is not given in the question, then it is always advisable to prepare memorandum balance sheet on the date of dissolution to ascertain the amount of balancing figure.

*Note*
- In the absence of any other information, 'sundry assets' should be treated as balancing figure on the assets side of balance sheet.
- If the balance of partners' capital account are not given as on the date of dissolution, first we will find the balance of partners' capital accounts as on the date of dissolution by recasting the capital accounts.
- When 'sundry assets' are given in the question and nothing is specified about the difference on the asset side of balance sheet, the difference should be treated as debit balance of profit and loss account.

# Chapter 5 Issue of Shares

## 1. Share

The share capital of a company is divided into small units. Each of these small units is called a share. Each share has a nominal value or face value which may be ₹ 1 or ₹ 2 or ₹ 5 or ₹ 10 or any amount.

## 2. Classes or Kinds of Shares

Shares are mainly classified into two categories

(i) Preference shares (ii) Equity shares

## 3. Share Capital

It is that part of the capital of a company which is represented by the total nominal value of shares, which it has issued.

## 4. Classification of Share Capital

(i) Authorised share capital (ii) Issued capital

(iii) Subscribed capital

(a) Subscribed and fully paid-up (b) Subscribed but not fully paid-up

(iv) Called-up share capital (v) Paid-up share capital

(vi) Reserve capital

## 5. Capital Reserve

It is the reserve which is not free for distribution as dividend. It is mandatory to create capital reserve in case of capital profits earned by the company. Reserves which are created out of capital profits and are not readily available for distribution as dividend among the shareholders. e.g. Premium on issue of shares or debentures, profits on re-issue of shares, profits prior to incorporation, premium on redemption of debentures, etc.

## 6. Terms of Issue of Shares

(i) **Issue of shares at par** When shares are issued at their face value, the shares are said to have been issued at par, i.e. issue price and face value are same.

(ii) **Issue of shares at premium** When shares are issued at a value that is higher than the face value of the shares, the shares are said to have been issued at premium, i.e. issue price is more than face value.

## 7. Accounting Treatment for Issue of Shares for Cash

(i) On Receipt of Application Money

| | | |
|---|---|---|
| Bank A/c<br>To Share Application A/c | Dr | (With application money received)<br>(Number of shares applied × Application money per share) |

(ii) On Acceptance of Applications

| | | |
|---|---|---|
| Share Application A/c<br>To Share Capital A/c | Dr | (With application money due on shares allotted)<br>(Number of shares allotted × Application money per share) |

(iii) On Making Allotment Money Due

(a) At Par

| | | |
|---|---|---|
| Share Allotment A/c<br>To Share Capital A/c | Dr | (With allotment money due)<br>(Number of shares allotted × Allotment money per share) |

(b) At Premium

| | | |
|---|---|---|
| Share Allotment A/c<br>To Share Capital A/c<br>To Securities Premium A/c | Dr | (With total)<br>(With allotment money due)<br>(With premium money due) |

(iv) On Receipt of Allotment Money

| | | |
|---|---|---|
| Bank A/c<br>  To Share Allotment A/c | Dr | (With allotment money received) |

(v) On Making the First Call

| | | |
|---|---|---|
| Share First Call A/c<br>  To Share Capital A/c | Dr | (With first call money due)<br>(Number of shares allotted × First call money per share) |

(vi) On Receipt of the First Call

| | | |
|---|---|---|
| Bank A/c<br>  To Share First Call A/c | Dr | (With first call money received) |

**8. Issue of Shares for Consideration other than Cash**

Sometimes a company issues shares in payment (consideration) against purchase of assets, business from vendors or to promoters/underwriters for their services, etc. In such cases, the payment is made in the form of fully paid shares of the company.

(i) **Issue of Shares to Vendors** In this regard, the purchase of assets and issue of shares are to be treated as two separate transactions.

(a) When Assets are Purchased

| | |
|---|---|
| Assets A/c (individually)<br>  To Vendor<br>(Being assets purchased from ......) | Dr |

(b) When Business is Purchased

| | |
|---|---|
| Sundry Assets A/c | Dr |
| Goodwill A/c* | Dr |
|   To Sundry Liabilities A/c<br>  To Vendor<br>  To Capital Reserve A/c*<br>(Being business purchased from vendor for purchase consideration of ₹ .......) | |

**Note** 'Vendor' is credited with purchase consideration payable to him.

* Either of the two will appear, to balance out the debit and credit aspect.

Goodwill = Value of net assets taken over − Agreed amount of purchase consideration

Capital reserve = Agreed purchase consideration − Value of net assets taken over

**On Issue of Shares**

- At Par

| | |
|---|---|
| Vendor<br>  To Share Capital A/c | Dr |

- At Premium

| | |
|---|---|
| Vendor<br>  To Share Capital A/c<br>  To Securities Premium A/c | Dr |

(ii) **Issue of Shares to Promoters**

| | |
|---|---|
| Formation Expenses/Incorporation Cost/Goodwill A/c<br>  To Share Capital A/c<br>(Being ... share of ₹ ... each issued to promoters of the company) | Dr |

(iii) **Issue of Shares to Underwriters**

(a) Making Underwriting Expenses Due

| | |
|---|---|
| Underwriting Expenses A/c<br>  To Underwriters A/c<br>(Being underwriting commission due) | Dr |

(b) Issuing Shares to Underwriters

| | |
|---|---|
| Underwriters A/c<br>  To Share Capital A/c<br>(Being...shares issued @ ..... per share to underwriters) | Dr |

### 9. Calls-in-Arrears

When one or more shareholders fail to pay his dues at the time of allotment or call, it is technically called calls-in- arrears. The company is authorised to charge interest on calls-in-arrears at a specified rate mentioned in his articles, from the due date to the date of actual payment, but if the articles are silent, Table-F of Schedule I of the Companies Act, 2013 shall be applicable, according to which interest shall be charged at a rate not exceeding 10% p.a. However, the directors have the right to waive the payment of such interest wholly or in part.

| | |
|---|---|
| Bank A/c | Dr |
| To Interest on Calls-in-Arrears A/c | |
| (Being interest received on calls-in-arrears) | |

### 10. Calls-in-Advance

The part of the whole amount received from the shareholders before the call is made, is called calls-in-advance. According to Section 50 of the Companies Act, 2013, such amount of calls-in-advance can be accepted by the company only when it is so authorised by its Articles of Association.

Calls-in-advance account is shown on the equity and liabilities side of balance sheet under the main head 'curent liabilities' and sub-head 'other current liabilities'.

Generally, the articles of the company specify the rate at which interest is payable. However, if the articles do not contain such rate, Table-F of Schedule I of the Companies Act, 2013 shall be applicable which leaves the matter to the Board of Directors subject to a maximum rate of 12% p.a.

| | |
|---|---|
| Interest on Calls-in-Advance A/c | Dr |
| To Bank A/c | |
| (Being interest on calls-in-advance paid) | |

### 11. Full Subscription of Shares

When the number of shares applied for, is equal to the number of shares offered for subscription, the shares are said to be fully subscribed.

### 12. Over Subscription of Shares

When the number of shares applied for, is more than the number of shares offered for subscription, the shares are said to be oversubscribed. Allotment of shares cannot be made to all the applicants in full.

In case of oversubscription, following three alternatives are available

(i) Rejection of applications
(ii) Partial or pro-rata allotment
(iii) Combination of pro-rata allotment and rejection

### 13. Undersubscription of Shares

When the number of shares applied for, is less than the number of shares offered to the public, the shares are said to be undersubscribed.

### 14. Forfeiture of Shares

It means cancellation of shares and seizure of the amount received from the defaulting shareholders whose shares have been forfeited.

**Accounting Treatment**

(i) At Par

| | | |
|---|---|---|
| Share Capital A/c | Dr | (Called-up value) |
| To Calls-in-arrears A/c | | (Amount not received) |
| To Share Forfeiture A/c | | (Amount received) |

(ii) At Premium

(a) If premium has been received

| | | |
|---|---|---|
| Share Capital A/c | Dr | (Amount called-up less premium) |
| To Calls-in-arrears A/c | | (Amount not received) |
| To Share Forfeiture A/c | | (Amount received, so far excluding securities premium reserve) |

(b) If premium has not been received

| | | |
|---|---|---|
| Share Capital A/c | Dr | (Amount called-up, so far less premium) |
| Securities premium A/c | Dr | (Premium not received) |
| To Calls-in-arrears A/c | | (Amount not received) |
| To Share Forfeiture A/c | | (Amount received) |

## 15. Re-issue of Forfeited Shares

The directors can either cancel or re-issue the forfeited shares. Shares forfeited can be re-issued at par, at premium or at a discount.

### Accounting Treatment for Re-issue of Forfeited Shares

(i) At Par

| | |
|---|---|
| Bank A/c | Dr |
| To Share Capital A/c | |

(ii) At Discount

| | | |
|---|---|---|
| Bank A/c | Dr | (With the amount received on re-issue) |
| Share Forfeiture A/c | Dr | (With the amount of discount allowed on re-issue) |
| To Share Capital A/c | | (With the amount credited as paid-up) |

(iii) At Premium

| | |
|---|---|
| Bank A/c | Dr |
| To Share Capital A/c | |
| To Securities Premium A/c | |

### Transfer of Balance in the Forfeited Shares Account

| | |
|---|---|
| Share Forfeiture A/c | Dr |
| To Capital Reserve A/c | |

## 16. Disclosure of Share Capital in Company's Balance Sheet

As per Schedule III of Companies Act, 2013, share capital is to be disclosed in a company's balance sheet on equity and liabilities part under the head 'shareholders' funds'.

**Balance Sheet**
as at......

| Particulars | Note No. | Current Year (₹) | Previous Year (₹) |
|---|---|---|---|
| I. **EQUITY AND LIABILITIES** | | | |
| **Shareholders' Funds** | | | |
| (a) Share Capital* | 1 | ............. | |

*As per Revised Schedule III, disclosure requirements pertaining to share capital are to be provided in notes to accounts and note number be put against the item in the balance sheet.

### Notes to Accounts

| Particulars | Amt (₹) |
|---|---|
| 1. **Share Capital** | |
| **Authorised Capital** | |
| ............................... Shares of ₹ .............. each | ... |
| **Issued Capital** | |
| ............................... Shares of ₹ ............. each | ... |

| Particulars | Amt (₹) |
|---|---|
| ***Subscribed Capital*** | |
| *Subscribed and Fully Paid-up* | |
| ......... *Shares of ₹ ...........each* | ... |
| *Subscribed but not Fully Paid-up* | |
| ......... *Shares of ₹ ...... each ........ ₹ Called-up* | ... |
| *(−) Calls-in-arrears (if any)* | (...) ... |
| ***Shares Forfeited A/c*** | ... |
| *Total* | ... |

# Chapter 6 Issue and Redemption of Debentures

## 1. Debenture

*It is an instrument acknowledging a debt issued under the common seal of the company. It specifies nominal/par value of debenture, the rate of interest to be paid, periodicity of payment, the tenure of debentures and terms of redemption.*

*Debentures shall be shown in the equity and liabilities part of the balance sheet under the major head 'non-current liabilities' and sub-head 'long-term borrowings'.*

## 2. Issue of Debentures for Cash

*Debentures like shares, whether issued for cash or otherwise may be issued at par, at premium or at discount, as discussed below*

(i) ***Issue of debentures at par*** *Debentures are said to be issued at par when the issue price and face value of the debentures is same.*

(ii) ***Issue of debentures at a premium*** *Debentures are said to be issued at premium when the issue price is more than the face value.*

(iii) ***Issue of debentures at a discount*** *Debentures are said to be issued at discount when they are issued at a price below its nominal or face value.*

## 3. Accounting Treatment

| | | |
|---|---|---|
| (i) On Receipt of Applications | Bank A/c Dr<br>To Debenture Application A/c | [With the application money received] |
| (ii) (a) On Acceptance of Applications | Debenture Application A/c Dr<br>To X% Debentures A/c | [With the amount of application money on the allotted debentures] |
| (b) On Adjustment of Excess Debenture Application Money | Debenture Application A/c Dr<br>To Debenture Allotment A/c | [With the surplus application money on partially accepted applications] |
| (c) On Refund of Excess Debenture Application Money | Debenture Application A/c Dr<br>To Bank A/c | [With the application money on rejected applications] |
| (d) On Making Allotment Money Due | ▪ At Par<br>Debenture Allotment A/c Dr<br>To X% Debentures A/c | [With the amount due on allotment of the debentures] |
| | ▪ At Premium<br>Debenture Allotment A/c Dr<br>To X% Debentures A/c<br>To Securities Premium Reserve A/c | [With the money due on allotment]<br>[With the nominal value of debentures due at the time of allotment]<br>[With the premium money received] |
| | ▪ At Discount<br>Debenture Allotment A/c Dr<br>Discount on Issue of Debentures A/c Dr<br>To X% Debentures A/c | [With the amount due on allotment]<br>[With the amount of discount]<br>[With the face value] |

| | | | |
|---|---|---|---|
| (e) On Receipt of Allotment Money | Bank A/c<br>To Debenture Allotment A/c | Dr | [With the amount actually received on allotment] |
| (iii) (a) On Making Calls | Debenture Call A/c<br>To X% Debentures A/c | Dr | [With the money due on a particular call] |
| (b) On Receipt of Call Money | Bank A/c<br>To Debenture Call A/c | Dr | [With the amount received on a particular call] |

**4. Issue of Debentures as Collateral Security**

When a company takes a loan, it may provide primary security on its assets. However, the lending institution may insist on some more assets as secondary or collateral security.

In such a situation, the company may issue debentures to the lender as secondary or collateral security such an issue of debentures is known as 'debentures issued as collateral security'.

Debentures issued as collateral security can be dealt in two ways, first by passing a journal entry and second, without passing journal entry.

**5. Disclosure of Debenture Issued as Collateral Security in the Balance Sheet**

As debenture issued as collateral security is related to the loan of the company, therefore it is shown in the note in which the loan secured by debenture is shown.

**Balance Sheet**
as at ...

| Particulars | Note No. | Amt (₹) |
|---|---|---|
| I. **EQUITY AND LIABILITIES** | | |
| 1. **Non-current Liabilities** | | |
| Long-term Borrowings | 1 | |

**Notes to Accounts**

| Particulars | | Amt (₹) |
|---|---|---|
| 1. **Long-term Borrowings** | | |
| Term Loan from Bank | | ... |
| X% Debentures of ₹ .... each issued as Collateral Security | ... | |
| (–) Debenture Suspense | (...) | ... |

When the loan is paid back, the following entry is made

| | |
|---|---|
| X% Debentures A/c | Dr |
| To Debentures Suspense A/c | |
| (Being debentures issued as collateral security, now cancelled on payment of loan) | |

**6. Issue of Debentures for Consideration other than Cash**

When debentures are issued to vendors against purchase of assets or against purchase of business, it is termed as issue of debentures for consideration other than cash.

In this case, consideration for issue of debentures is not cash but the assets or business.

**(i) Issue of Debentures to Vendors**

(a) On Purchase of Assets or Business

- When assets are purchased

| | |
|---|---|
| Sundry Assets A/c | Dr |
| To Vendor's A/c | |

- When business is purchased

| | |
|---|---|
| Sundry Assets A/c | Dr |
| Goodwill A/c* | Dr |
| To Sundry Liabilities A/c | |
| To Vendor's A/c | |
| To Capital Reserve A/c* | |

*Either of the two will appear.

(b) On Issue of Debentures

- When debentures are issued at par

| | | |
|---|---|---|
| Vendor's A/c | Dr | |
| To Debentures A/c | | |

- When debentures are issued at premium

| | | |
|---|---|---|
| Vendor's A/c | Dr | |
| To Debentures A/c | | |
| To Securities Premium A/c | | |

- When debentures are issued at discount

| | | |
|---|---|---|
| Vendor's A/c | Dr | |
| Discount on Issue of Debentures A/c | Dr | |
| To Debentures A/c | | |

**(ii) Issue of Debentures to Promoters**

Persons like individuals, firms or companies which promote the company are called promoters. A company may pay its promoters in the form of debentures. Such issue of debentures is put under the category of 'issue of debentures for consideration other than cash'.

| | |
|---|---|
| Formation Expenses/Incorporation Cost/Goodwill A/c | Dr |
| To Debentures A/c | |
| (Being ........ debentures of ₹ ...... each issued to promoters of the company) | |

**(iii) Issue of Debentures to Underwriters**

Sometimes, underwriters are also issued debentures as their fees by the issuing company.

**(a) Making underwriting expenses due**

| | |
|---|---|
| Underwriting Expenses A/c | Dr |
| To Underwriters A/c | |
| (Being underwriting commission due) | |

**(b) Issuing debentures to underwriters**

| | |
|---|---|
| Underwriters A/c | Dr |
| To Debentures A/c | |
| (Being debentures issued @ ...... per debentures to underwriters) | |

**(c) Transferring underwriting expenses to statement of profit and loss**

| | |
|---|---|
| Statement of Profit and Loss | Dr |
| To Underwriting Expenses A/c | |
| (Being underwriting expenses charged to profit and loss) | |

**7. Various Cases from the Point of View of Redemption**

As the issue can be made at par, at premium or at discount, the redemption of debentures can be either at par or at premium. Combining various conditions/terms of issue and redemption of debentures, there may be the following possibilities

(i) When debentures are issued at par and redeemable at par, i.e. redeemable value is equal to the face value

| | | | |
|---|---|---|---|
| (a) | Bank A/c | Dr | |
| | To Debenture Application A/c | | [With the application money] |
| (b) | Debenture Application A/c | Dr | [With the application money] |
| | To X% Debentures A/c | | [With the nominal value] |

(ii) When debentures are issued at par and redeemable at premium, i.e. in excess of nominal value

| | | | |
|---|---|---|---|
| (a) | Bank A/c | Dr | |
| | To Debenture Application A/c | | [With the application money] |
| (b) | Debenture Application A/c | Dr | [With the application money] |
| | Loss on Issue of Debentures A/c | Dr | [For providing premium on redemption] |
| | To X% Debentures A/c | | [With nominal value] |
| | To Premium on Redemption of Debentures A/c | | [With premium payable on redemption] |

*(iii) When debentures are issued at a discount but are redeemable at par*

| | | | |
|---|---|---|---|
| (a) | Bank A/c | Dr | |
| | To Debenture Application A/c | | [With the application money] |
| (b) | Debenture Application A/c | Dr | [With the application money] |
| | Discount on Issue of Debentures A/c | Dr | [With the amount of discount] |
| | To X% Debentures A/c | | [With the nominal value] |

*(iv) When debentures are issued at a discount but are redeemable at premium*

| | | | |
|---|---|---|---|
| (a) | Bank A/c | Dr | |
| | To Debenture Application A/c | | [With the application money] |
| (b) | Debenture Application A/c | Dr | [With the application money] |
| | Discount on Issue of Debentures A/c | Dr | [With discount] |
| | Loss on Issue of Debentures A/c | Dr | [For providing premium on redemption] |
| | To X% Debentures A/c | | [With nominal value] |
| | To Premium on Redemption of Debentures A/c | | [With premium payable on redemption] |

In the above entry, the 'discount on issue of debentures' is also a loss on issue of debentures. This can be further combined into one account under 'loss on issue of debentures account' as follows

| | | |
|---|---|---|
| Debenture Application A/c | Dr | [With the application money] |
| Loss on Issue of Debentures A/c | Dr | [With discount + premium on redemption] |
| To X% Debentures A/c | | [With nominal value] |
| To Premium on Redemption of Debentures A/c | | [With premium payable on redemption] |

*(v) When debentures are issued at a premium and redeemable at par*

| | | | |
|---|---|---|---|
| (a) | Bank A/c | Dr | |
| | To Debenture Application A/c | | [With the application money] |
| (b) | Debenture Application A/c | Dr | [With the application money] |
| | To X% Debentures A/c | | [With nominal value] |
| | To Securities Premium A/c | | [With premium] |

*(vi) When debentures are issued at a premium and are redeemable at premium*

| | | | |
|---|---|---|---|
| (a) | Bank A/c | Dr | [With the application money received] |
| | To Debenture Application A/c | | |
| (b) | Debenture Application A/c | Dr | [With the application money] |
| | Loss on Issue of Debentures A/c | Dr | [With premium on redemption] |
| | To X% Debentures A/c | | [With nominal value] |
| | To Securities Premium A/c | | [With premium on issue] |
| | To Premium on Redemption of Debentures A/c | | [With premium payable on redemption] |

## 8. Interest on Debentures

Interest on debenture is considered as an expense. It is a charge against the profits of the company and is payable irrespective of the fact whether there are profits or not.

Entries for interest on debentures are as follows

*(i) When interest is due*

| | | |
|---|---|---|
| Debentures Interest A/c | Dr | [With gross interest] |
| To Debentureholders A/c | | [With net interest] |
| To Income Tax Payable A/c | | [With income tax deducted] |

*(ii) When interest is paid*

| | | |
|---|---|---|
| Debentureholders A/c | Dr | [With net interest] |
| To Bank or Cash A/c | | |

*(iii) On payment of income tax to government*

| | | |
|---|---|---|
| Income Tax Payable A/c | Dr | [With the amount of income tax deducted at source] |
| To Bank A/c | | |

**Note** Interest is not payable on debentures issued as collateral security.

**9. Disclosure of Debentures in the Company's Balance Sheet**

Debentures being borrowings (liability) of a company are shown in the equity and liabilities part of the balance sheet. Debentures may be either non-current liability or a current liability.

**When non-current liability,** debentures are shown in the balance sheet under the head 'non-current liabilities' and sub-head 'long-term borrowings', when they are due for redemption after 12 months from the date of issue or after the period of operating cycle.

**When current liability,** (a) In case, debentures outstanding in the books of accounts of a company are shown as long-term borrowings under non-current liabilities in the balance sheet and part of it have become due for redemption within 12 months of the date of balance sheet, then, these debentures will be shown under 'current liabilities' as current maturities of long-term debts under 'other current liabilities'.

(b) Debentures issued to be redeemed within 12 months of the date of issue are shown as 'short-term borrowings' under 'current liabilities'.

**10. Writing-off Discount/Loss on Issue of Debentures**

As per ISC Council's instructions, discount or loss on issue of debentures are to be written-off from securities premium (if any) or from general reserve or surplus, i.e. balance in statement of profit and loss under the head 'reserves and surplus' in the year in which they occur.

Following entry is passed for writing-off discount/loss on issue of debentures

| | |
|---|---|
| Securities Premium A/c/ General Reserve/Statement of Profit and Loss | Dr |
| To Discount/Loss on Issue of Debentures A/c | |

**11. Redemption of Debentures**

It refers to extinguishing or discharging the liability on account of debentures in accordance with the terms of issue.

**12. Debenture Redemption Reserve** (DRR)

It is the amount set aside out of surplus, (i.e. balance in statement of profit and loss) for redeeming the debentures. Section 71(4) of the Companies Act, 2013, requires the company to create debenture redemption reserve out of the profits available for payment of dividend.

The amount so credited to DRR shall not be utilised by the company except for the redemption of debentures. DRR is required to be created for Non-Convertible Debentures (NCD) and non-convertible part of Partly Convertible Debentures (PCD).

In view of Section 71(4) of the Companies, Act, 2013 and SEBI guidelines, unlisted companies (other than NBFCs and HFCs) are required to create DRR equivalent to atleast 10% of the nominal (face) value of outstanding debentures.

The following companies are exempted to create DRR (For both public as well as privately placed debentures)

(i) All India Financial Institutions, regulated by Reserve Bank of India (RBI).

(ii) Banking companies.

(iii) Other financial institutions within the meaning of Section 2(72) of the Companies Act, 2013.

(iv) Listed Companies including

  (a) Non-Banking Financing Companies (NBFCs), registered with RBI.

  (b) Housing Finance Companies (HFCs), registered with National Housing Bank (NHB).

  (c) Other listed companies.

(v) Unlisted non-banking financing companies registered with RBI.

(vi) Unlisted housing finance companies registered with national housing bank.

**13. Debenture Redemption Investment** (DRI)

Rule 18 (7)(b) of the Companies (Share capital and debentures) Rules, 2014 (as amended) prescribes that all listed as well as unlisted companies, that are to redeem debentures (except the companies which are exempted from creating DRI), shall on or before 30th April of the each year, invest or deposit in specified securities, a sum at least equal to 15% of the amount of debentures maturing for payment during the year ended 31st March of the next year.

The following companies are not required to make DRI

(i) All India Financial Institutions, regulated by Reserve Bank of India (RBI).

(ii) Banking companies.

(iii) Other financial institutions within the meaning of Section 2 (72) of the Companies Act, 2013.

(iv) Unlisted non-banking financing companies registered with RBI.

(v) Unlisted housing finance companies registered with national housing bank.

Thus, following companies are required to deposit or invest at least 15% of the nominal or face value of its debentures maturing during the year

(i) Listed companies (including NBFCs registered with RBI and HFCs registered with NHB).

(ii) Unlisted companies (other than NBFCs and HFCs mentioned above).

**14. Disclosure of DRR in the Balance Sheet**

Debenture redemption reserve is shown in the equity and liabilities part of the balance sheet under the head 'shareholders' funds' and sub-head 'reserves and surplus'. When all the debentures have been redeemed, debenture redemption reserve account is closed by transferring the amount to general reserve. The entry will be passed

| | |
|---|---|
| Debenture Redemption Reserve A/c | Dr |
| To General Reserve A/c | |

**15. Methods of Redemption of Debentures**

The methods of redemption of debentures are

(i) Redemption of debentures in lumpsum on maturity.

(ii) Redemption of debentures in instalments by draw of lots.

(iii) Redemption of debentures by purchase in open market.

(iv) Redemption of debentures by conversion.

Note Redemption of debentures by purchase in open market and by conversion are not in syllabus, therefore, they have not been discussed.

**16. Redemption of Debentures in Lumpsum on Maturity**

When all the debentures are redeemed by paying in lumpsum at the end of the specified time, it is called redemption in lumpsum. When debentures are redeemed in lumpsum on maturity, a company may adopt any of the following two options for redeeming debentures

(i) **Redemption of debentures out of capital** When adequate profits are not transferred to the DRR from statement of profit and loss for redemption of debentures, it is said to be redemption out of capital.

Note Companies act require every company (except All India Financial Institutions and Banking Companies) to transfer an amount equal to 10% of the value of debentures to DRR before the redemption begins. Therefore, companies act has indirectly placed restriction to redeem debentures out of capital.

(ii) **Redemption of debentures out of profits** When adequate profits are transferred to the DRR from statement of profit and loss for redemption of debentures, it is said to be redemption out of profits.

**JOURNAL**

| Transaction | Entry | | Amt (₹) |
|---|---|---|---|
| **(a) On creation of debenture redemption reserve** | Surplus, i.e. Balance in Statement of Profit and Loss<br>To Debenture Redemption Reserve A/c | Dr | |
| **(b) On investment or deposit being made in specified securities** | Debenture Redemption Investment A/c<br>To Bank A/c | Dr | |
| **(c) On encashing investment** | Bank A/c<br>To Debenture Redemption Investment A/c | Dr | [With the amount paid] |

| Transaction | Entry | | Amt (₹) |
|---|---|---|---|
| **(d) On the amount being due to debentureholders on redemption** | ▪ *If the debentures are to be redeemed at par* | | |
| | X% Debentures A/c | Dr | [With nominal value] |
| | To Debentureholders' A/c | | |
| | ▪ *If the debentures are to be redeemed at a premium* | | |
| | X% Debentures A/c | Dr | [With nominal value] |
| | Premium on Redemption of Debentures A/c | Dr | [With premium payable] |
| | To Debentureholders' A/c | | [With total] |
| **(e) On payment to debentureholders** | Debentureholders' A/c | Dr | [With the amount paid] |
| | To Bank A/c | | |
| **(f) When all debentures are redeemed** | Debenture Redemption Reserve A/c | Dr | [With the amount of DRR] |
| | To General Reserve A/c | | |

*When all the debentures are redeemed, the amount of debenture redemption reserve account is transferred to general reserve account.*

**17. Redemption of Debentures in Instalments by Draw of Lots**

*In this method, the company may redeem its debentures in instalments beginning from a particular year, i.e. by payment of a certain portion in each year. The actual debentures to be redeemed are selected usually by draw of lots. The holders are repaid the amount at par or at a premium as per the terms of issue. The journal entries required to be passed are the same as discussed when debentures are repayable in lumpsum.*

**Note** *DRR must be created and investment in specified securities should be made before commencing redemption of debentures under this method also.*

# Chapter 7 Final Accounts of Companies

**1. Meaning of Financial Statements**

*Financial statements are the final products of an accounting process which begins with the identification of accounting information and recording it in the books of primary entry. Financial statements are prepared following the accounting concepts and principles. Financial statements are historical in nature. A set of financial statements include*

*(i) Balance sheet (ii) Statement of profit and loss (iii) Notes to accounts*

**2. Balance Sheet**

*It may be defined as a statement of assets and liabilities of the company, at a particular date.*
***Format of balance sheet*** *The form of the balance sheet is prescribed in Part I of Schedule III of the Companies Act, 2013. Schedule III for the balance sheet will apply to all companies uniformly for the financial statements to be prepared. The Companies Act, 2013 has prescribed that balance sheet be prepared in vertical form only.*

*The form prescribed under Schedule III, Part I of the Companies Act, 2013 is as follows*

**Balance Sheet**
*as at ..............*

| Particulars | Note No. | Figures as at the End of Current Reporting Period (₹) | Figures as at the End of the Previous Reporting Period (₹) |
|---|---|---|---|
| **I. EQUITY AND LIABILITIES** | | | |
| **1. Shareholders' Funds** | | | |
| (i) Share Capital | | ... | ... |
| (ii) Reserves and Surplus | | ... | ... |
| (iii) Money Received against Share Warrants | | ... | ... |
| **2. Share Application Money Pending Allotment** | | | |

| Particulars | Note No. | Figures as at the End of Current Reporting Period | Figures as at the End of the Previous Reporting Period |
|---|---|---|---|
| 3. Non-current Liabilities | | | |
| (i) Long-term Borrowings | | ... | ... |
| (ii) Deferred Tax Liabilities (Net) | | ... | ... |
| (iii) Other Long-term Liabilities | | ... | ... |
| (iv) Long-term Provisions | | ... | ... |
| 4. Current Liabilities | | | |
| (i) Short-term Borrowings | | ... | ... |
| (ii) Trade Payables | | ... | ... |
| (iii) Other Current Liabilities | | ... | ... |
| (iv) Short-term Provisions | | ... | ... |
| Total | | ... | ... |
| II. ASSETS | | | |
| 1. Non-current Assets | | | |
| (i) Property, Plant and Equipment and Intangible Assets | | | |
| (a) Property, Plant and Equipment | | ... | ... |
| (b) Intangible Assets | | ... | ... |
| (c) Capital Work-in-progress | | ... | ... |
| (d) Intangible Assets under Development | | ... | ... |
| (ii) Non-current Investments | | ... | ... |
| (iii) Deferred Tax Assets (Net) | | ... | ... |
| (iv) Long-term Loans and Advances | | ... | ... |
| (v) Other Non-current Assets | | ... | ... |
| 2. Current Assets | | | |
| (i) Current Investments | | ... | ... |
| (ii) Inventories | | ... | ... |
| (iii) Trade Receivables | | ... | ... |
| (iv) Cash and Cash Equivalents | | ... | ... |
| (v) Short-term Loans and Advances | | ... | ... |
| (vi) Other Current Assets | | ... | ... |
| Total | | ... | ... |

### 3. Statement of Profit and Loss

Statement of profit and loss shows the net result of business operations, i.e. financial performance during an accounting period. A form for preparing statement of profit and loss is prescribed in Part II of Schedule III of the Companies Act, 2013.

### 4. Format of Statement of Profit and Loss

The form for statement of profit and loss as specified in Schedule III is as follows

**Statement of Profit and Loss**
for the year ended.........

| Particulars | Note No. | Figures for the Current Reporting Period (₹) | Figures for the Previous Reporting Period (₹) |
|---|---|---|---|
| I. Revenue from Operations | | ... | ... |
| II. Other Income | | ... | ... |
| III. Total Revenue (I + II) | | ... | ... |
| IV. Expenses | | | |
| Cost of Materials Consumed | | ... | ... |
| Purchases of Stock-in-trade | | ... | ... |
| Changes in Inventories of Finished Goods, | | | |

| Particulars | Note No. | Figures for the Current Reporting Period (₹) | Figures for the Previous Reporting Period (₹) |
|---|---|---|---|
| Work-in-progress and Stock-in-trade | | ... | ... |
| Employees Benefits Expenses | | ... | ... |
| Finance Costs | | ... | ... |
| Depreciation and Amortisation Expenses | | ... | ... |
| Other Expenses | | ... | ... |
| Total Expenses | | ... | ... |
| V. Profit Before Tax (III – IV) | | ... | ... |
| VI. (–) Tax | | (...) | (....) |
| VII. Profit (Loss) for the Period (V – VI) | | ... | ... |

**Note** Schedule III, Part II of Companies Act, 2013 (Statement of Profit and Loss) is excluded for the prupose of preparing final accounts of a company. However, for the preparation of comparative and common size income statements, the extent and format of statement of profit and loss is to be studied.

# Chapter 8 Financial Statement Analysis

### 1. Comparative Statements

Statements used to compare the items of income statement, i.e. statement of profit and loss and position statement, i.e. balance sheet for ascertaining the trend of the performance and profitability of an enterprise are known as comparative statements.

### 2. Significance of Comparative Statements

(i) Data presentation becomes simple and comparable
(ii) Indicates trend
(iii) Indicates strengths and weaknesses
(iv) Facilitates comparison with other firms and industry
(v) Helps in forecasting and planning
(vi) Provides key financial statistics

### 3. Limitations of Comparative Statements

(i) Based on historical records
(ii) Affected by personal judgement
(iii) Ignores qualitative elements
(iv) Ignores price level changes

### 4. Comparative Statement of Profit and Loss or Income Statement

It shows the operating results for a number of accounting periods so that changes in data in terms of absolute amount and percentage from one period to another may be known.

### 5. Format of Comparative Statement of Profit and Loss

**Comparative Statement of Profit and Loss**
for the years ended .........

| Particulars | Previous Year (₹) | Current Year (₹) | Absolute Change (Increase or Decrease) (₹) | Percentage Change (Increase or Decrease) (%) |
|---|---|---|---|---|
| I. Revenue from Operations | ... | ... | ... | ... |
| II. Other Income | ... | ... | ... | ... |
| III. Total Revenue (I + II) | ... | ... | ... | ... |
| IV. Expenses | | | | |
| Cost of Materials Consumed | ... | ... | ... | ... |
| Purchases of Stock-in-trade | ... | ... | ... | ... |

| Particulars | Previous Year (₹) | Current Year (₹) | Absolute Change (Increase or Decrease) (₹) | Percentage Change (Increase or Decrease) (%) |
|---|---|---|---|---|
| Changes in Inventories of Finished Goods, Work-in-progress and Stock-in-trade | ... | ... | ... | ... |
| Employees Benefit Expenses | ... | ... | ... | ... |
| Finance Cost | ... | ... | ... | ... |
| Depreciation and Amortisation | ... | ... | ... | ... |
| Other Expenses | ... | ... | ... | ... |
| Total Expenses | ... | ... | ... | ... |
| V. Profit Before Tax (III – IV) | ... | ... | ... | ... |
| (–) Income Tax | (...) | (...) | (...) | (...) |
| VI. Profit After Tax | ... | ... | ... | ... |

### 6. Comparative Balance Sheet

*Comparative balance sheet analysis is the study of the trend of the same items, group of items and computed items in two or more balance sheets of the same business enterprise on different dates.*

### 7. Format of Comparative Balance Sheet

**Comparative Balance Sheet**
as at ...

| Particulars | Previous Year (₹) | Current Year (₹) | Absolute Change (Increase or Decrease) (₹) | Percentage Change (Increase or Decrease)% |
|---|---|---|---|---|
| **I. EQUITY AND LIABILITIES** | | | | |
| **1. Shareholders' Funds** | | | | |
| (i) Share Capital | | | | |
| (a) Equity Share Capital | ... | ... | ... | ... |
| (b) Preference Share Capital | ... | ... | ... | ... |
| (ii) Reserves and Surplus | ... | ... | ... | ... |
| **2. Non-current Liabilities** | | | | |
| (i) Long-term Borrowings | ... | ... | ... | ... |
| (ii) Long-term Provisions | ... | ... | ... | ... |
| **3. Current Liabilities** | | | | |
| (i) Short-term Borrowings | ... | ... | ... | ... |
| (ii) Trade Payables | ... | ... | ... | ... |
| (iii) Other Current Liabilities | ... | ... | ... | ... |
| (iv) Short-term Provisions | ... | ... | ... | ... |
| **Total** | ... | ... | ... | ... |
| **II. ASSETS** | | | | |
| **1. Non-current Assets** | | | | |
| (i) Property, Plant & Equipment and Intangible Assets | | | | |
| (a) Property, Plant and Equipment | ... | ... | ... | ... |
| (b) Intangible Assets | ... | ... | ... | ... |
| (ii) Non-current Investments | ... | ... | ... | ... |
| (iii) Long-term Loans and Advances | ... | ... | ... | ... |
| **2. Current Assets** | | | | |
| (i) Current Investments | ... | ... | ... | ... |
| (ii) Inventories | ... | ... | ... | ... |
| (iii) Trade Receivables | ... | ... | ... | ... |
| (iv) Cash and Cash Equivalents | ... | ... | ... | ... |
| (v) Short-term Loans and Advances | ... | ... | ... | ... |
| (vi) Other Current Assets | ... | ... | ... | ... |
| **Total** | ... | ... | ... | ... |

**8. Common Size Statements**

*The statement wherein figures reported are converted into percentage to some common base is known as a common size statement. Each percentage shows the relation of the individual item to its respective total.*

**9. Significance of Common Size Statements**

(i) To present the change in various items in relation to revenue from operations, total assets or total liabilities.

(ii) To establish a relationship.

(iii) To provide for a common base for comparison.

**10. Limitations of Common Size Statements**

(i) Under this statement, relative importance of each component of financial statements in whole is exhibited but no comparative study is done between the years.

(ii) In such statement, time value of money is not considered.

(iii) This analysis does not prove to be very useful for important decision-making.

(iv) It does not provide meaningful disclosure while comparing common size statements of two or more years.

**11. Common Size Statement of Profit and Loss**

Statement in which amount of revenue from operations (net sales) is assumed to be equal to 100 and other amounts are expressed as percentage of revenue from operations (net sales) is common size statement of profit and loss.

**12. Format of Common Size Statement of Profit and Loss**

**Common Size Statement of Profit and Loss**
for the years ended................

| Particulars | Absolute Amounts | | Percentage of Revenue from Operations (Net Sales) | |
|---|---|---|---|---|
| | Previous Year (₹) | Current Year (₹) | Previous Year (%) | Current Year (%) |
| I. Revenue from Operations (Net Sales) | ... | ... | ... | ... |
| II. Other Income | ... | ... | ... | ... |
| III. Total Revenue (I + II) | ... | ... | ... | ... |
| IV. Expenses | | | | |
| Cost of Materials Consumed | ... | ... | ... | ... |
| Purchases of Stock-in-trade | ... | ... | ... | ... |
| Changes in Inventories of Finished Goods, Work-in-progress and Stock-in-trade | ... | ... | ... | ... |
| Employess Benefit Expenses | ... | ... | ... | ... |
| Finance Cost | ... | ... | ... | ... |
| Depreciation and Amortisation | ... | ... | ... | ... |
| Other Expenses | ... | ... | ... | ... |
| Total Expenses | ... | ... | ... | ... |
| V. Profit Before Tax (III − IV) | ... | ... | ... | ... |
| VI. (−) Income Tax | (...) | (...) | (...) | (...) |
| VII. Profit After Tax | ... | ... | ... | ... |

**13. Common Size Balance Sheet**

It shows the percentage relations of each asset/liability to total assets/total liabilities including capital. In this, total assets or total equity and liabilities are taken as 100 and all the figures are expressed as percentage of the total.

### 14. Format of Common Size Balance Sheet

**Common Size Balance Sheet**

as at ...

| Particulars | Absolute Amounts | | Percentage of Balance Sheet Total | |
|---|---|---|---|---|
| | Previous Year (₹) | Current Year (₹) | Previous Year (%) | Current Year (%) |
| I. EQUITY AND LIABILITIES | | | | |
| 1. Shareholders' Funds | | | | |
| (i) Share Capital | | | | |
| (a) Equity Share Capital | ... | ... | ... | ... |
| (b) Preference Share Capital | ... | ... | ... | ... |
| (ii) Reserves and Surplus | ... | ... | ... | ... |
| 2. Non-current Liabilities | | | | |
| (i) Long-term Borrowings | ... | ... | ... | ... |
| (ii) Long-term Provisions | ... | ... | ... | ... |
| 3. Current Liabilities | | | | |
| (i) Short-term Borrowings | ... | ... | ... | ... |
| (ii) Trade Payables | ... | ... | ... | ... |
| (iii) Other Current Liabilities | ... | ... | ... | ... |
| (iv) Short-term Provisions | ... | ... | ... | ... |
| Total | ... | ... | 100 | 100 |
| II. ASSETS | | | | |
| 1. Non-current Assets | | | | |
| (i) Property, Plant & Equipment and Intangible Assets | | | | |
| (a) Property, Plant and Equipment | ... | ... | ... | ... |
| (b) Intangible Assets | ... | ... | ... | ... |
| (ii) Non-current Investments | ... | ... | ... | ... |
| (iii) Long-term Loans and Advances | ... | ... | ... | ... |
| 2. Current Assets | | | | |
| (i) Current Investments | ... | ... | ... | ... |
| (ii) Inventories | ... | ... | ... | ... |
| (iii) Trade Receivables | ... | ... | ... | ... |
| (iv) Cash and Cash Equivalents | ... | ... | ... | ... |
| (v) Short-term Loans and Advances | ... | ... | ... | ... |
| (vi) Other Current Assets | ... | ... | ... | ... |
| Total | ... | ... | 100 | 100 |

# Chapter 9 Cash Flow Statement

### 1. Meaning of Cash Flow Statement

*Cash flow statement is a statement showing the changes in financial position of a business concern during different intervals of time in terms of cash and cash equivalents.*

### 2. Cash Flows

*It implies movement of cash in and out of non-cash items. Receipt of cash from a non-cash item is termed as cash inflow while cash payment in respect of such items is termed as cash outflow.*

### 3. Cash and Cash Equivalents

*As per AS-3, 'cash' comprises cash in hand and demand deposits with banks and 'cash equivalents' means short-term highly liquid investments that are readily convertible into known amounts of cash and which are subject to an insignificant risk of changes in value. e.g. Short-term marketable securities which can be readily converted into cash, are treated as cash equivalents.*

### 4. Importance of Cash Flow Statement

*(i) Useful for short-term financial planning*
*(ii) Useful in preparing the cash budget*
*(iii) Comparing with the cash budget*
*(iv) Study of the trend of cash receipts and payments*

(v) Helpful in ascertaining cash flow from various activities separately

(vi) Helpful in making dividend decisions.

**5. Classification of Business Activities**

Accounting Standard-3 (Revised) requires that the changes resulting in inflows and outflows of cash and cash equivalents be classified into following three activities

**Cash Flow Statement**

- Operating Activities
- Financing Activities
- Investing Activities

**6. Cash Flow from Operating Activities**

Operating activities are the principal revenue-producing activities of the enterprise and other activities that are not investing or financing activities.

Cash flow from operating activities is exhibited as follows

**Operating Activities**

**Cash Inflow**

(i) Cash sales
(ii) Cash received from debtors
(iii) Cash received from commission and fees
(iv) Royalty

**Cash Outflow**

(i) Cash purchases
(ii) Payment to creditors
(iii) Cash operating expenses
(iv) Payment of wages
(v) Income tax

**7. Cash Flow from Investing Activities**

As per AS-3, investing activities are the acquisition and disposal of the long-term assets and other investments, not included in cash equivalents.

Cash flow from investing activities are exhibited as follows

**Investing Activities**

**Cash Inflow**

(i) Sale of property, plant and equipment and intangible assets
(ii) Sale of investments
(iii) Interest received
(iv) Dividend received
(v) Repayment of loans and advances given (short-term or long-term)

**Cash Outflow**

(i) Purchase of property, plant and equipment and intangible assets
(ii) Purchase of investments
(iii) Loans and advances given (short-term or long-term)

**8. Cash Flow from Financing Activities**

Financing activities are the activities which result in change in the size and composition of the owner's capital (including preference share capital) and borrowings (including debentures) of the enterprise from other sources. Cash flow arising from financing activities are exhibited as follows

**Financing Activities**

**Cash Inflow**

(i) Issue of shares in cash
(ii) Issue of debentures in cash
(iii) Proceeds from long-term (borrowings and short-term)
(iv) Securities premium received
(v) Interest received on calls-in-arrears
(vi) Increase in balance of bank overdraft or cash credit account

**Cash Outflow**

(i) Payment of loans (long-term and short-term)
(ii) Redemption of preference shares, debentures
(iii) Buy-back of equity shares
(iv) Payment of dividend
(v) Payment of interest
(vi) Premium paid on redemption of preference shares, debentures
(vii) Share issue expenses/underwriting commission paid

## 9. Format of Cash Flow Statement

**Indirect Method** *[As per Accounting Standard-3 (Revised)]*
*for the year ended...*

| Particulars | | Amt (₹) |
|---|---|---|
| I. **Cash Flow from Operating Activities** | | |
| Net Profit before Taxation | | ... |
| Adjustment for Non-cash and Non-operating Items | | ... |
| (+) Items to be Added | | |
| Depreciation | ... | |
| Amortised Expenses (Such as discount in issue of shares, share Issue expenses and loss on issue of debentures, etc) | ... | |
| Goodwill Written-off, Patents and Trademarks Amortised | ... | |
| Interest on Borrowings and Debentures | ... | |
| Loss on Sale of Property, Plant and Equipment and Intangible Assets | ... | ... |
| (−) Items to be Deducted | | |
| Interest Income | (...) | |
| Dividend Income | (...) | |
| Rental Income | (...) | |
| Profit on Sale of Property, Plant and Equipment and Intangible Assets | (...) | (...) |
| Operating Profit before Working Capital Changes | | ... |
| (+) Decrease in Current Assets and Increase in Current Liabilities | | ... |
| (−) Increase in Current Assets and Decrease in Current Liabilities | | (...) |
| Cash Generated from Operations | | ... |
| (−) Income Tax Paid (Net of tax refund received) | | (...) |
| Net Cash from (or used in) Operating Activities | | .../(...) |
| II. **Cash Flow from Investing Activities** | | |
| Proceeds from Sale of Property, Plant and Equipment and Intangible Assets | ... | |
| Proceeds from Sale of Investments | ... | |
| Proceeds from Sale of Intangible Assets | ... | |
| Interest and Dividend Received (For non-financial companies only) | ... | |
| Rental Income | ... | |
| Purchase of Property, Plant and Equipment and Intangible Assets | (...) | |
| Purchase of Investments | (...) | |
| Purchase of Intangible Assets like Goodwill | (...) | |
| Net Cash from (or used in) Investing Activities | | .../(...) |
| III. **Cash Flow from Financing Activities** | | |
| Proceeds from Issue of Shares and Debentures | ... | |
| Proceeds from Other Long-term Borrowings | ... | |
| Final Dividend Paid | (...) | |
| Interim Dividend Paid | (...) | |
| Interest on Debentures and Loans Paid | (...) | |
| Repayment of Loans | (...) | |
| Redemption of Debentures/Preference Shares | (...) | |
| Share Issue Expenses | (...) | |
| Increase/Decrease in Bank Overdraft and Cash Credit | (...) | |
| Net Cash from (or used in) Financing Activities | | .../(...) |
| IV. **Net Increase/Decrease in Cash and Cash Equivalents (I + II + III)** | | .../(...) |
| V. **(+) Cash and Cash Equivalents in the Beginning of the Year** | | |
| Cash in Hand | ... | |
| Cash in Bank | ... | |
| Short-term Investments | ... | |
| Marketable Securities | ... | ... |
| **Cash and Cash Equivalents at the End of the Year** | | |
| Cash in Hand | ... | |
| Cash at Bank | ... | |
| Short-term Investments | ... | |
| Marketable Securities | ... | ... |

# Chapter 10 Ratio Analysis

**1. Ratio Analysis and its Objectives**

*It is a technique which involves regrouping of data by application of arithmetical relationships. It is the most important and powerful tool for measuring performance of a business enterprises.*

**2. Liquidity Ratios** (Short-term solvency)

They show the ability of the enterprise to meet its short-term financial obligations.

The two ratios included in this category are

(i) Current Ratio or Working Capital Ratio

$$\text{Current ratio} = \frac{\text{Current assets}}{\text{Current liabilities}}$$

Current assets = Current investments + Inventories (excluding loose tools and spare parts) + Trade receivables + Cash and cash equivalents + Short-term loans and advances + Other current assets

Current liabilities = Short-term borrowings + Trade payables + Other current liabilities + Short-term provisions

(ii) Liquid Ratio or Quick Ratio or Acid Test Ratio

$$\text{Liquid ratio} = \frac{\text{Quick assets}}{\text{Quick liabilities}}$$

Or

$$= \frac{\text{All current assets} - \text{Inventories (excluding loose tools and spare parts)} - \text{Prepaid expenses}}{\text{Current liabilities}}$$

Or

$$= \frac{\text{Liquid assets}}{\text{Liquid liabilities}}$$

**3. Solvency Ratios** (Long-term solvency)

Solvency ratios are calculated to judge the long-term financial position of the business.

The following ratios are normally computed for evaluating solvency of the business

(i) $$\text{Debt to Equity Ratio} = \frac{\text{Debt (Long - term debt)}}{\text{Equity (Shareholders' funds)}}$$

Debt = Long-term borrowings + Long-term provisions

Equity/Shareholders' funds = Share capital + Reserves and surplus

Or

= Non-current assets + (Current assets − Current liabilities) − Non-current liabilities

Or

= Non-current assets + Working capital − Non-current liabilities

Or

= (Property, plant and equipment + Intangible assets + Non-current investments + Long-term loans and advances) + Working capital − (Long-term borrowings + Long-term provisions)

(ii) $$\text{Proprietary Ratio} = \frac{\text{Proprietors' funds or shareholders' funds}}{\text{Total assets}}$$

Total assets = Non-current assets + Current assets

Or

= Property, plant and equipment + Intangible assets + Non-current investments + Long-term loans and advances + Current investments + Inventories (including loose tools and spare parts) + Trade receivables + Cash and cash equivalents + Short-term loans and advances + Other current assets

(iii) Debt to Total Assets Ratio $= \frac{\text{Debt}}{\text{Total assets}}$

It is to be expressed in pure ratio.

(iv) Interest Coverage Ratio $= \frac{\text{Net profit before interest and tax}}{\text{Fixed interest charges}} = \ldots \text{ times}$

Fixed interest charges includes interest on only long-term borrowings.

**4. Activity/ Performance/ Turnover Ratios**

Activity/Turnover ratios show how efficiently a company is using its assets to generate sales. The important activity/turnover ratios are

(i) Debtors or Trade Receivables Turnover Ratio

$$= \frac{\text{Credit revenue from operations, i.e. net credit sales}}{\text{Average trade receivables}}$$

Credit revenue from operations = Revenue from operations − Cash revenue from operations

$$\text{Average trade receivables} = \frac{\text{Opening trade receivables} + \text{Closing trade receivables}}{2}$$

**Note** Debt Collection Period or Average Collection Period

It is determined as follows

$$\text{Debt collection period} = \frac{365}{\text{Debtors' turnover ratio}} = \text{Number of days}$$

$$\text{Debt collection period} = \frac{12}{\text{Debtors' turnover ratio}} = \text{Number of months}$$

(ii) Creditors or Trade Payables Turnover Ratio $= \frac{\text{Net credit purchases}}{\text{Average trade payables}} = \ldots \text{ times}$

$$\text{Average trade payables} = \frac{\text{Opening trade payables} + \text{Closing trade payables}}{2}$$

**Note** Average payment period $= \frac{\text{Number of days/weeks/months in a year}}{\text{Creditors turnover ratio}}$

(iii) Working Capital Turnover Ratio $= \frac{\text{Revenue from operations}}{\text{Working capital}} = \text{Number of times}$

Working Capital = Current assets − Current liabilities

(iv) Inventory/Stock Turnover Ratio $= \frac{\text{Cost of revenue from operations, i.e. cost of goods sold}}{\text{Average inventory}}$

$= \ldots\ldots$ times

Cost of revenue from operations = Revenue from operations − Gross profit

Or

= Cost of material consumed (Including direct expenses) + Change in inventories of WIP and finished goods

Or

= Opening inventory + Net purchases+ Direct expenses − Closing inventory

$$\text{Average inventory} = \frac{\text{Opening inventory} + \text{Closing inventory}}{2}$$

### 5. Profitability Ratios

*These measure the profitability of a business. Profitability ratios help in assessing the overall efficiency of the business.*

*Various profitability ratios commonly used to analyse the profitability of the business are*

(i) Gross Profit Ratio $= \dfrac{\text{Gross profit}}{\text{Revenue from operations}} \times 100$

Gross profit = Revenue from operations − Cost of revenue from operations or Cost of goods sold Cost of revenue from operations, as per inventory turnover ratio.

(ii) Net Profit Ratio $= \dfrac{\text{Net profit}}{\text{Revenue from operations}} \times 100$

Net profit = Gross profit + Other income − Indirect expenses − Provision for Tax

(iii) Operating Ratio (Operating cost ratio)

$$= \frac{\text{Cost of revenue from operations} + \text{Operating expenses}}{\text{Revenue from operations}} \times 100$$

Or $= \dfrac{\text{Cost of revenue from operations} + \text{operating expenses} - \text{Operating income}}{\text{Revenue from operations}} \times 100$

Operating expenses = Employee benefit expenses + Depreciation and amortisation expenses + Selling and distribution expenses+ Office and administrative expenses

Operating income = Commission received, cash discount received.

(iv) Operating Profit Ratio $= \dfrac{\text{Net operating profit}}{\text{Revenue from operations}} \times 100$

Net operating profit = Net profit after tax+ Provision for tax + Non-operating expenses − Non-operating incomes

Or = Gross profit − Operating expenses + Operating incomes

Non-operating expenses = Finance Cost (Interest on debentures/Long-term loans) + Loss on sale of non-current assets + Amortisation of intangible assets + Writing-off capital losses

Non-operating incomes = Interest and dividend received on investment + Profit on sale of non-current assets

(v) Earning per Share $= \dfrac{\text{Net profit after tax and preference dividend}}{\text{Number of equity shares}}$

(vi) Price Earning Ratio $= \dfrac{\text{Market value of an equity share}}{\text{Earning per share}}$

(vii) Return on Investment $= \dfrac{\text{Net profit before interest and tax}}{\text{Capital employed}} \times 100$

Capital employed = Shareholders' funds + Non-current liabilities − Non-trade investments

Or

= Non-current assets (excluding non-trade investments) + Working capital

Or

= Property, plant & equipment and intangible assets + Trade investments + Working capital